READINGS FOR
SOCIOLOGY

RECENT SOCIOLOGY TITLES
FROM W. W. NORTON

The Contexts Reader, Third Edition, edited by Syed Ali and Philip N. Cohen

Social Problems, Third Edition, by Joel Best

The Art and Science of Social Research by Deborah Carr, Elizabeth Heger Boyle, Benjamin Cornwell, Shelley Correll, Robert Crosnoe, Jeremy Freese, and Mary C. Waters

The Family: Diversity, Inequality, and Social Change, Second Edition, by Philip N. Cohen

You May Ask Yourself: An Introduction to Thinking like a Sociologist, Sixth Edition, by Dalton Conley

Race in America, by Matthew Desmond and Mustafa Emirbayer

The Real World: An Introduction to Sociology, Sixth Edition, by Kerry Ferris and Jill Stein

Introduction to Sociology, Eleventh Edition, by Anthony Giddens, Mitchell Duneier, Richard P. Appelbaum, and Deborah Carr

Essentials of Sociology, Seventh Edition, by Anthony Giddens, Mitchell Duneier, Richard P. Appelbaum, and Deborah Carr

Mix It Up: Popular Culture, Mass Media, and Society, Second Edition, by David Grazian

Doing Race, edited by Hazel Rose Markus and Paula M. L. Moya

Families as They Really Are, Second Edition, edited by Barbara J. Risman and Virginia E. Rutter

The Social Construction of Sexuality, Third Edition, by Steven Seidman

Sex Matters: The Sexuality and Society Reader, Fifth Edition, edited by Mindy Stombler, Dawn M. Baunach, Elisabeth O. Burgess, Wendy Simonds, and Elroi J. Windsor

Gender: Ideas, Interactions, Institutions, Second Edition, by Lisa Wade and Myra Marx Feree

Cultural Sociology: An Introductory Reader, edited by Matt Wray

American Society: How It Really Works, Second Edition, by Erik Olin Wright and Joel Rogers

To learn more about Norton Sociology, please visit wwnorton.com/soc.

NINTH EDITION

READINGS FOR
SOCIOLOGY

EDITED BY

Garth Massey

Timothy L. O'Brien

W. W. Norton & Company ■ New York ■ London

W. W. Norton & Company has been independent since its founding in 1923, when William Warder Norton and Mary D. Herter Norton first published lectures delivered at the People's Institute, the adult education division of New York City's Cooper Union. The firm soon expanded its program beyond the Institute, publishing books by celebrated academics from America and abroad. By midcentury, the two major pillars of Norton's publishing program—trade books and college texts—were firmly established. In the 1950s, the Norton family transferred control of the company to its employees, and today—with a staff of five hundred and hundreds of trade, college, and professional titles published each year—W. W. Norton & Company stands as the largest and oldest publishing house owned wholly by its employees.

Editor: Sasha Levitt
Project Editor: Maura Gaughan
Assistant Editor: Erika Nakagawa
Managing Editor, College: Marian Johnson
Production Manager: Stephen Sajdak
Marketing Manager, Sociology: Julia Hall
Design Director: Juan Paolo Francisco
Director of College Permissions: Megan Schindel
College Permissions Associate: Bethany Salminen
Composition: Westchester Publishing Services
Manufacturing: LSC Crawfordsville

Library of Congress Cataloging-in-Publication Data

Names: Massey, Garth, editor.
Title: Readings for sociology / edited by Garth Massey, Timothy L. O'Brien.
Description: Ninth edition. | New York : W. W. Norton & Company, 2019. |
   Revised edition of Readings for sociology, [2015] | Includes
   bibliographical references.
Identifiers: LCCN 2019013771 | ISBN 9780393674316 (pbk.)
Subjects: LCSH: Sociology.
Classification: LCC HM585 .R427 2019 | DDC 301–dc23 LC record available at
   https://lccn.loc.gov/2019013771

W. W. Norton & Company, Inc., 500 Fifth Avenue, New York, NY 10110
wwnorton.com

W. W. Norton & Company Ltd., 15 Carlisle Street, London W1D 3BS

2 3 4 5 6 7 8 9 0

CONTENTS

PART 4: SOCIAL INTERACTION AND IDENTITY

PART 5: SOCIAL INEQUALITY AND ORGANIZATIONS

PART 6: SOCIAL CONTROL AND ORGANIZATIONAL POWER

PREFACE

Sociology is an exciting, unruly, sometimes offending, and immensely interesting subject. The readings we have retained from the Eighth Edition and the readings we are introducing here are our effort to introduce and excite students to the possibilities of sociology. It is an invitation to know more, to think more clearly, to care, and to be willing to act. For us, sociology is not something you know. It is a way of thinking that opens new vistas while making new demands on our sense of self and what we owe to each other. We hope the promise of sociology becomes a part of the lives of anyone who digs into *Readings for Sociology*.

Readings for Sociology has always emphasized social stratification—of material well-being, status, and power—as the most important structural dimension of society. This focus recognizes that not only fundamental life chances but the values we adhere to, the life of our communities, our interpersonal relations, and the ideas we hold about ourselves are inextricably conditioned by the level and forms of inequality in our society. The inclusion of more than a few readings on the work people do, the way they socialize their children, the space they occupy between security and loss, their efforts to obtain and hold onto their human dignity and personal choice, and the forces impelling societies into an unknown future all capture the centrality of social stratification. Taking direct aim at social inequality are new additions to *Readings for Sociology*, including David A. Snow and Leon Anderson's "Salvaging the Self," Rachel Sherman's "Anxieties of Affluence," Devah Pager's "The Mark of a Criminal Record," and Matthew Stewart's "The Birth of a New American Aristocracy."

New readings usually make up about 20 percent of each new edition. The Ninth Edition includes a little more new material than usual, in part because the editors of *Readings for Sociology* are now two: Garth Massey and Tim O'Brien. Tim's specialties in sociology add to the book's greater attention to women's and racial-ethnic minorities' voices as well as the sociology of law and criminal justice. Among the new essays are Paula England's "The Gender Revolution: Uneven and Stalled," Ta-Nehisi Coates's "The Black Family in the Age of Mass Incarceration," Patricia Hill Collins's "Distinguishing Features of Black Feminist Thought," Eduardo Bonilla-Silva's "The Strange Enigma of Race," Devah Pager's essay and Patrick Sharkey's "The End of Warrior Policing." Look for Tim's interest in the sociology of knowledge to be reflected in the next edition of *Readings for Sociology*.

Approaching the end of the second decade of the new millennium, much seems unsettled. The global alliances created at the end of World War II and the very idea that we are stronger when we cooperate rather than look out only for ourselves are under threat. International migration—spurred by civil conflict, violence, and economic deprivation—and the intensification of globalization that has transformed economic activity and people's lives across the globe have evoked a massive backlash across Europe and in the United States. In the United States, stagnant family income and rising costs for housing, health care, and higher education provide the structural foundation for a cultural and political cleavage that often seems unbridgeable. We have tried to address this unsettling with several new essays, including Arlie Russell Hochschild's "No Country for White Men," Matthew Stewart's essay, Miller McPherson and his colleagues' "The Ties That Bind Are Fraying," and Farah Stockman's "Work Freed Her, Then It Moved to Mexico."

Corporate consolidation to the point of monopoly and monopsony typifies late-stage capitalism, including the academic book market and companies owning the rights to published material. The rapid increase in permissions costs to reprint articles prevented us from adding some wonderful research essays and required the elimination of a few old favorites. Our apologies. But we're very excited about the many new inclusions to *Readings for Sociology*. Two new essays, Lisa Wade's "American Hookup: Deep in the Fog" and Pico Iyer's "The Beauty of the Package," are almost cringe-worthy in their evocation of the power of culture. And Eliza Griswold's "Undermined" reminds us that we are not passive repositories of culture but active citizens who can make the world better and more just if we are willing to put ourselves on the line for what we believe.

More than twenty years has passed since *Readings for Sociology* was first published. It's been a good run, with tens of thousands of students encountering the work of sociology for the first time. Each edition was an improvement, not only because the selection of works included in the book improved but because sociology has continued to get better and better. While highly quantified research dominates the major journals, more qualitative work and inquiries that generate the key concepts and original ideas of the discipline have been published and are available for inclusion here. Contributors have mirrored the growing racial, ethnic, and gender diversity of voices embracing the sociological imagination, indicative of the field of sociology as a whole.

TO THE INSTRUCTOR

Sociological Principles	Corresponding Readings
1. Introduction to Theory	1, 2, 3, 4, 7, 25, 31, 32, 39, 42, 44
2. Methods	1, 5, 6, 8, 45, 46
3. Culture and Society	9, 10, 11, 13, 14, 15, 21, 23, 36, 40, 46
4. Socialization, the Life Course, and Aging	10, 15, 16, 17, 18, 22, 27
5. Social Interaction and Everyday Life	4, 9, 10, 11, 18, 19, 20, 29, 33
6. Groups and Large Organizations	10, 12, 13, 18, 27, 28, 32, 33, 36, 37, 38, 43, 47
7. Deviance and Crime	5, 11, 20, 27, 32, 34, 35, 39
8. Stratification and Inequality	5, 7, 11, 16, 17, 18, 20, 21, 24, 25, 26, 27, 30, 31, 34, 37, 45
9. Globalization and Global Inequality	10, 25, 47, 49
10. Gender and Gender Inequality	7, 9, 15, 18, 37, 45, 47
11. Ethnicity and Race	5, 7, 8, 11, 18, 21, 23, 26, 27, 30, 34, 37, 41
12. Government, Power, and Social Movements	3, 21, 25, 32, 34, 38, 41, 43, 44, 48
13. Work and Political Economy	5, 25, 27, 28, 29, 31, 37, 38, 42, 45, 47
14. Family and Intimate Relationships	9, 15, 16, 17, 24, 26, 34, 40, 41, 46
15. Education and the Mass Media	9, 13, 18, 30, 32, 49
16. Religion	12, 22, 42, 43
17. Health and the Body	8, 13, 22
18. Population and the Environment	3, 21, 38, 48
19. Conflict, War, and Revolution	25, 48

PART ONE

THE STUDY
OF SOCIOLOGY

1

Sociology as an Individual Pastime

FROM *Invitation to Sociology*

PETER L. BERGER

What does it mean to "think sociologically"? In this selection from his book Invitation to Sociology, *Peter Berger explains why sociologists are so annoying to the powers that be, the purveyors of conventional wisdom, advertisers, politicians, and others with a vested interest in your going along with their view of things. Sociologists have a reputation for stirring up the waters and occasionally making trouble. For Berger, this is just part of the way sociologists see the world.*

It is gratifying from certain value positions (including some of this writer's) that sociological insights have served in a number of instances to improve the lot of groups of human beings by uncovering morally shocking conditions or by clearing away collective illusions or by showing that socially desired results could be obtained in more humane fashion. One might point, for example, to some applications of sociological knowledge in the penological practice of Western countries. Or one might cite the use made of sociological studies in the Supreme Court decision of 1954 on racial segregation in the public schools. Or one could look at the applications of other sociological studies to the humane planning of urban redevelopment. Certainly the sociologist who is morally and politically sensitive will derive gratification from such instances. But, once more, it will be well to keep in mind that what is at issue here is not sociological understanding as such but certain applications of this understanding. It is not difficult to see how the same understanding could be applied with opposite intentions. Thus the sociological understanding of the dynamics of racial prejudice can be applied effectively by those promoting intragroup hatred as well as by those wanting to spread tolerance. And the sociological understanding of the nature of human solidarity can be employed in the service of both totalitarian and democratic regimes.

* * *

One [more recent] image [of the sociologist is that of] a gatherer of statistics about human behavior. The sociologist is here seen essentially as an aide-de-camp to an IBM machine. He* goes out with a questionnaire, interviews

---

*Berger wrote this in 1963 using gendered language (preferring *he* to the now-standard *he/she*). Today more than half of all sociology students are women. [*Editors' note*]

people selected at random, then goes home, enters his tabulations onto innumerable punch cards, which are then fed into a machine. In all of this, of course, he is supported by a large staff and a very large budget. Included in this image is the implication that the results of all this effort are picayune, a pedantic restatement of what everybody knows anyway. As one observer remarked pithily, a sociologist is a fellow who spends $100,000 to find his way to a house of ill repute.

This image of the sociologist has been strengthened in the public mind by the activities of many agencies that might well be called parasociological, mainly agencies concerned with public opinion and market trends. The pollster has become a well-known figure in American life, importuning people about their views from foreign policy to toilet paper. Since the methods used in the pollster business bear close resemblance to sociological research, the growth of this image of the sociologist is understandable. The Kinsey studies of American sexual behavior have probably greatly augmented the impact of this image. The fundamental sociological question, whether concerned with premarital petting or with Republican votes or with the incidence of gang knifings, is always presumed to be "how often?" or "how many?"

* * *

Now it must be admitted, albeit regretfully, that this image of the sociologist and his trade is not altogether a product of fantasy. Beginning shortly after World War I, American sociology turned rather resolutely away from theory to an intensive preoccupation with narrowly circumscribed empirical studies. In connection with this turn, sociologists increasingly refined their research techniques. Among these, very naturally, statistical techniques figured prominently. Since about the mid 1940s there has been a revival of interest in sociological theory, and there are good indications that this tendency away from a narrow empiricism is continuing to gather momentum. It remains true, however, that a goodly part of the sociological enterprise in this country continues to consist of little studies of obscure fragments of social life, irrelevant to any broader theoretical concern. One glance at the table of contents of the major sociological journals or at the list of papers read at sociological conventions will confirm this statement.

* * *

Statistical data by themselves do not make sociology. They become sociology only when they are sociologically interpreted, put within a theoretical frame of reference that is sociological. Simple counting, or even correlating different items that one counts, is not sociology. There is almost no sociology in the Kinsey reports. This does not mean that the data in these studies are not true or that they cannot be relevant to sociological understanding. They are, taken by themselves, raw materials that can be used in sociological interpretation. The interpretation, however, must be broader than the data themselves. So the sociologist cannot arrest himself at the frequency tables of premarital petting or extramarital pederasty. These enumerations are meaningful to him only in terms of their much broader implications for an understanding of institutions and values in our society. To arrive at such understanding the sociologist will often have to apply statistical techniques, especially when he is dealing with the mass phenomena of modern social life. But sociology consists of statistics as little as philology consists of conjugating irregular verbs or chemistry of making nasty smells in test tubes.

Sociology has, from its beginnings, understood itself as a science. There has been much controversy about the precise meaning of this self-definition. . . . But the allegiance of sociologists to the scientific ethos has meant everywhere a willingness to be bound by certain scientific canons of procedure. If the sociologist remains faithful to his calling, his statements must be arrived at through the observation of certain rules of evidence that allow others to check on or to repeat or to develop his findings further. It is this scientific discipline that often supplies the motive for reading a sociological work as against, say, a novel on the same topic that might describe matters in much more impressive and convincing language. As sociologists tried to develop their scientific rules of evidence, they were compelled to reflect upon methodological problems. This is why methodology is a necessary and valid part of the sociological enterprise.

At the same time it is quite true that some sociologists, especially in America, have become so preoccupied with methodological questions that they have ceased to be interested in society at all. As a result, they have found out nothing of significance about any aspect of social life, since in science as in love a concentration on technique is quite likely to lead to impotence. Much of this fixation on methodology can be explained in terms of the urge of a relatively new discipline to find acceptance on the academic scene. Since science is an almost sacred entity among Americans in general and American academicians in particular, the desire to emulate the procedures of the older natural sciences is very strong among the newcomers in the marketplace of erudition.

* * *

As they become more secure in their academic status, it may be expected that this methodological inferiority complex will diminish even further.

The charge that many sociologists write in a barbaric dialect must also be admitted with similar reservations. Any scientific discipline must develop a terminology. This is self-evident for a discipline such as, say, nuclear physics that deals with matters unknown to most people and for which no words exist in common speech. However, terminology is possibly even more important for the social sciences, just because their subject matter *is* familiar and just because words *do* exist to denote it. Because we are well acquainted with the social institutions that surround us, our perception of them is imprecise and often erroneous. In very much the same way most of us will have considerable difficulty giving an accurate description of our parents, husbands or wives, children or close friends. Also, our language is often (and perhaps blessedly) vague and confusing in its references to social reality. Take for an example the concept of *class*, a very important one in sociology. There must be dozens of meanings that this term may have in common speech—income brackets, races, ethnic groups, power cliques, intelligence ratings, and many others. It is obvious that the sociologist must have a precise, unambiguous definition of the concept if his work is to proceed with any degree of scientific rigor. In view of these facts, one can understand that some sociologists have been tempted to invent altogether new words to avoid the semantic traps of the vernacular usage.

Finally, we would look at an image of the sociologist not so much in his professional role as in his being, supposedly, a certain kind of person. This is the image of the sociologist as a detached, sardonic observer, and a cold manipulator of men. Where this image prevails, it may represent an ironic triumph of the sociologist's own efforts to be accepted as a genuine scientist. The sociologist here becomes the self-appointed superior man, standing off from the warm vitality of common existence, finding his satisfactions not in living but in coolly appraising the lives of others, filing them away in little categories, and thus presumably missing the real significance of what he is observing. Further, there is the notion that, when he involves himself in social processes at all, the sociologist does so as an uncommitted technician, putting his manipulative skills at the disposal of the powers that be.

This last image is probably not very widely held. . . . As a general portrait of the contemporary sociologist it is certainly a gross distortion. It fits very few individuals that anyone is likely to meet in this country today. The problem of the political role of the social scientist is, nevertheless, a very genuine one. For instance, the employment of sociologists by certain branches of industry and government raises moral questions that ought to be faced more widely than they have been so far. These are, however, moral questions that concern all men in positions of responsibility in modern society. The image of the sociologist as an observer without compassion and a manipulator without conscience need not detain us further here. . . . As for contemporary sociologists, most of them would lack the emotional equipment for such a role, even if they should aspire to it in moments of feverish fantasy.

How then are we to conceive of the sociologist? In discussing the various images of him that abound in the popular mind we have already brought out certain elements that would have to go into our conception.

* * *

The sociologist, then, is someone concerned with understanding society in a disciplined way. The nature of this discipline is scientific. This means that what the sociologist finds and says about the social phenomena he studies occurs within a certain rather strictly defined frame of reference. One of the main characteristics of this scientific frame of reference is that operations are bound by certain rules of evidence. As a scientist, the sociologist tries to be objective, to control his personal preferences and prejudices, to perceive clearly rather than to judge normatively. This restraint, of course, does not embrace the totality of the sociologist's existence as a human being, but is limited to his operations *qua* sociologist. Nor does the sociologist claim that his frame of reference is the only one within which society can be looked at. For that matter, very few scientists in any field would claim today that one should look at the world only scientifically. The botanist looking at a daffodil has no reason to dispute the right of the poet to look at the same object in a very different manner. There are many ways of playing. The point is not that one denies other people's games but that one is clear about the rules of one's own. The game of the sociologist, then, uses scientific rules. As a result, the sociologist must be clear in his own mind as to the meaning of these rules. That is, he must concern himself with methodological questions. Methodology does not constitute his goal. The latter, let us recall once more, is the attempt to understand society. Methodology helps in reaching this goal. In order to understand society, or that segment of it that he is studying at the moment, the sociologist will use a variety of means. Among these are statistical techniques. Statistics can be very useful in answering certain sociological questions. But statistics does not constitute sociology. As a scientist, the sociologist will have to be concerned with the exact significance of the terms he is using. That is, he will have to be careful about terminology. This does not have to mean that he must invent a new language of his own, but it does mean that he cannot naively use the language of everyday discourse. Finally, the interest of the sociologist is primarily theoretical. That is, he is interested in understanding for its own sake. He may be aware of or even concerned with the practical applicability and consequences of his findings, but at that point he leaves the sociological frame of reference as such and moves into realms of values, beliefs and ideas that he shares with other men who are not sociologists.

* * *

[THE MOTIVATION TO DO SOCIOLOGY]

[W]e would like to go a little bit further here and ask a somewhat more personal (and therefore, no doubt, more controversial) question. We would like to ask not only what it is that the sociologist is doing but also what it is that drives him to it. Or, to use the phrase Max Weber used in a similar connection, we want to inquire a little into the nature of the sociologist's demon. In doing so, we shall evoke an image that is not so much ideal-typical in the above sense but more confessional in the sense of personal commitment. Again, we are not interested in excommunicating anyone. The game of sociology goes on in a spacious playground. We are just describing a little more closely those we would like to tempt to join our game.

We would say then that the sociologist (that is, the one we would really like to invite to our game) is a person intensively, endlessly, shamelessly interested in the doings of men. His natural habitat is all the human gathering places of the world, wherever men come together. The sociologist may be interested in many other things. But his consuming interest remains in the world of men, their institutions, their history, their passions. And since he is interested in men, nothing that men do can be altogether tedious for him. He will naturally be interested in the events that engage men's ultimate beliefs, their moments of tragedy and grandeur and ecstasy. But he will also be fascinated by the commonplace, the everyday. He will know reverence, but this reverence will not prevent him from wanting to see and to understand. He may sometimes feel revulsion or contempt. But this also will not deter him from wanting to have his questions answered. The sociologist, in his quest for understanding, moves through the world of men without respect for the usual lines of demarcation. Nobility and degradation, power and obscurity, intelligence and folly—these are equally *interesting* to him, however unequal they may be in his personal values or tastes. Thus his questions may lead him to all possible levels of society, the best and the least-known places, the most respected and the most despised. And, if he is a good sociologist, he will find himself in all these places because his own questions have so taken possession of him that he has little choice but to seek for answers.

It would be possible to say the same things in a lower key. We could say that the sociologist, but for the grace of his academic title, is the man who must listen to gossip despite himself, who is tempted to look through keyholes, to read other peoples mail, to open closed cabinets. Before some otherwise unoccupied psychologist sets out now to construct an aptitude test for sociologists on the basis of sublimated voyeurism, let us quickly say that we are speaking merely by way of analogy. Perhaps some little boys consumed with curiosity to watch their maiden aunts in the bathroom later become inveterate sociologists. This is quite uninteresting. What interests us is the curiosity that grips any sociologist in front of a closed door behind which there are human voices. If he is a good sociologist, he will want to open that door, to understand these voices. Behind each closed door he will anticipate some new facet of human life not yet perceived and understood.

The sociologist will occupy himself with matters that others regard as too sacred or as too distasteful for dispassionate investigation. He will find rewarding the company of priests or of prostitutes, depending not on his personal preferences but on the questions he happens to be asking at the moment. He will also concern himself with matters that others may find much too boring. He will be interested in the human interaction that goes with warfare or with great intellectual discoveries, but also in the relations between people employed in a restaurant or between a group of little girls playing with their dolls. His main focus of attention is not the ultimate significance of what men do, but the action in itself, as another example of the infinite richness of human conduct. So much for the image of our playmate.

In these journeys through the world of men the sociologist will inevitably encounter other professional Peeping Toms. Sometimes these will resent his presence, feeling that he is poaching on their preserves. In some places the sociologist will meet up with the economist, in others with the political scientist, in yet others with the psychologist or the ethnologist. Yet chances are that the questions that have brought him to these same places are different from the ones that propelled his fellow trespassers. The sociologist's questions always remain essentially the same: "What are people doing with each other here?" "What are their relationships to each other?" "How are these relationships organized in institutions?" "What are the collective ideas that move men and institutions?" In trying to answer these questions in specific instances, the sociologist will, of course, have to deal with economic or political matters, but he will do so in a way rather different from that of the economist or the political scientist. The scene that he contemplates is the same human scene that these other scientists concern themselves with. But the sociologist's angle of vision is different. When this is understood, it becomes clear that it makes little sense to try to stake out a special enclave within which the sociologist will carry on business in his own right. . . . There is, however, one traveler whose path the sociologist will cross more often than anyone else's on his journeys. This is the historian. Indeed, as soon as the sociologist turns from the present to the past, his preoccupations are very hard indeed to distinguish from those of the historian. However, we shall leave this relationship to a later part of our considerations. Suffice it to say here that the sociological journey will be much impoverished unless it is punctuated frequently by conversation with that other particular traveler.

Any intellectual activity derives excitement from the moment it becomes a trail of discovery. In some fields of learning this is the discovery of worlds previously unthought and unthinkable. This is the excitement of the astronomer or of the nuclear physicist on the antipodal boundaries of the realities that man is capable of conceiving. But it can also be the excitement of bacteriology or geology. In a different way it can be the excitement of the linguist discovering new realms of human expression or of the anthropologist exploring human customs in faraway countries. In such discovery, when undertaken with passion, a widening of awareness, sometimes a veritable transformation of consciousness, occurs. The universe turns out to be much more wonderful than one had ever dreamed. The excitement of sociology is usually of a different sort. Sometimes, it is true, the sociologist penetrates into worlds that had previously been quite unknown to him—for instance, the world of crime, or the world of some bizarre religious sect, or the world fashioned by the exclusive concerns of some group such as medical specialists or military leaders or advertising executives. However, much of the time the sociologist moves in sectors of experience that are familiar to him and to most people in his society. He investigates communities, institutions and activities that one can read about every day in the newspapers. Yet there is another excitement of discovery beckoning in his investigations. It is not the excitement of coming upon the totally unfamiliar, but rather the excitement of finding the familiar becoming transformed in its meaning. The fascination of sociology lies in the fact that its perspective makes us see in a new light the very world in which we have lived all our lives. This also constitutes a transformation of consciousness. Moreover, this transformation is more relevant existentially than that of many other intellectual disciplines, because it is more difficult to segregate in some special compartment of the mind. The astronomer does not live in the remote galaxies, and the nuclear physicist can, outside his laboratory, eat and laugh and marry and vote without thinking about the insides of the atom. The geologist looks at rocks only at appropriate times, and the linguist speaks English with his wife. The sociologist lives in society, on the job and off it. His own life, inevitably, is part of his subject matter. Men being what they are, sociologists too manage to segregate their professional insights from their everyday affairs. But it is a rather difficult feat to perform in good faith.

The sociologist moves in the common world of men, close to what most of them would call real. The categories he employs in his analyses are only refinements of the categories by which other men live—power, class, status, race, ethnicity. As a result, there is a deceptive simplicity and obviousness about some sociological investigations. One reads them, nods at the familiar scene, remarks that one has heard all this before and don't people have better things to do than to waste their time on truisms—until one is suddenly brought up against an insight that radically questions everything one had previously assumed about this familiar scene. This is the point at which one begins to sense the excitement of sociology.

Let us take a specific example. Imagine a sociology class in a Southern college where almost all the students are white Southerners. Imagine a lecture on the subject of the racial system of the South. The lecturer is talking here of matters that have been familiar to his students from the time of their infancy. Indeed, it may be that they are much more familiar with the minutiae of this system than he is. They are quite bored as a result. It seems to them that he is only using more pretentious words to describe what they already know. Thus he may use the term "caste," one commonly used now by American sociologists to describe the Southern racial system. But in explaining the term he shifts to traditional Hindu society, to make it clearer. He then goes on to analyze the magical beliefs inherent in caste tabus, the social dynamics of commensalism and connubium, the economic interests concealed within the system, the way in which religious beliefs relate to the tabus, the effects of the caste system upon the industrial development of the society and vice versa—all in India. But suddenly India is not very far away at all. The lecture then goes back to its Southern theme. The familiar now seems not quite so familiar any more. Questions are raised that are new, perhaps raised angrily, but raised all the same. And at least some of the students have begun to understand that there are functions involved in this business of race that they have not read about in the newspapers (at least not those in their hometowns) and that their parents have not told them—partly, at least, because neither the newspapers nor the parents knew about them.

It can be said that the first wisdom of sociology is this—things are not what they seem. This too is a deceptively simple statement. It ceases to be simple after a while. Social reality turns out to have many layers of meaning. The discovery of each new layer changes the perception of the whole.

Anthropologists use the term "culture shock" to describe the impact of a totally new culture upon a newcomer. In an extreme instance such shock will be experienced by the Western explorer who is told, halfway through dinner, that he is eating the nice old lady he had been chatting with the previous day—a shock with predictable physiological if not moral consequences. Most explorers no longer encounter cannibalism in their travels today. However, the first encounters with polygamy or with puberty rites or even with the way some nations drive their automobiles can be quite a shock to an American visitor. With the shock may go not only disapproval or disgust but a sense of excitement that things can *really* be that different from what they are at home. To some extent, at least, this is the excitement of any first travel abroad. The experience of sociological discovery could be described as "culture shock" minus geographical displacement. In other words, the sociologist travels at home—with shocking results. He is unlikely to find that he is eating a nice old lady for dinner. But the discovery, for instance, that his own church has considerable money invested in the missile industry or that a few blocks from his home there are people who engage in cultic orgies may not be drastically different in emotional impact. Yet we would not want to imply that sociological discoveries are always or even usually outrageous to moral sentiment. Not at all. What they have in common with exploration in distant lands, however, is the sudden illumination of new and unsuspected facets of human existence in society. This is the excitement and, as we shall try to show later, the humanistic justification of sociology.

People who like to avoid shocking discoveries, who prefer to believe that society is just what they were taught in Sunday School, who like the safety of the rules and the maxims of what Alfred Schuetz has called the "world-taken-for-granted," should stay away from sociology. People who feel no temptation before closed doors, who have no curiosity about human beings, who are content to admire scenery without wondering about the people who live in those houses on the other side of that river, should probably also stay away from sociology. They will find it unpleasant or, at any rate, unrewarding. People who are interested in human beings only if they can change, convert or reform them should also be warned, for they will find sociology much less useful than they hoped. And people whose interest is mainly in their own conceptual constructions will do just as well to turn to the study of little white mice. Sociology will do just as well to turn to the study of little mice. Sociology will be satisfying, in the long run, only to those who can think of nothing more entrancing than to watch men and to understand things human.

* * *

To be sure, sociology is an individual pastime in the sense that it interests some men and bores others. Some like to observe human beings, others to experiment with mice. The world is big enough to hold all kinds and there is no logical priority for one interest as against another. But the word "pastime" is weak in describing what we mean. Sociology is more like a passion. The sociological perspective is more like a demon that possesses one, that drives one compellingly, again and again, to the questions that are its own. An introduction to sociology is, therefore, an invitation to a very special kind of passion.

2

Personal Experiences and Public Issues

FROM *The Sociological Imagination*

C. WRIGHT MILLS

C. Wright Mills wrote of his own work, "I have tried to be objective; I do not claim to be detached." He argues that sociologists' questions come from the same sources as the important questions everyone asks: their own experiences and the things that perplex, confuse, and inspire them. To be effective, sociology must make a connection between the individual and the social. It must allow the individual to see the larger social context in which his or her life is lived, and in this way give both understanding and meaning to personal experiences.

Nowadays men often feel that their private lives are a series of traps. They sense that within their everyday worlds, they cannot overcome their troubles, and in this feeling, they are often quite correct: What ordinary men are directly aware of and what they try to do are bounded by the private orbits in which they live; their visions and their powers are limited to the close-up scenes of job, family, neighborhood; in other milieux, they move vicariously and remain spectators. And the more aware they become, however vaguely, of ambitions and of threats which transcend their immediate locales, the more trapped they seem to feel.

Underlying this sense of being trapped are seemingly impersonal changes in the very structure of continent-wide societies. The facts of contemporary history are also facts about the success and the failure of individual men and women. When a society is industrialized, a peasant becomes a worker; a feudal lord is liquidated or becomes a businessman. When classes rise or fall, a man is employed or unemployed; when the rate of investment goes up or down, a man takes new heart or goes broke. When wars happen, an insurance salesman becomes a rocket launcher; a store clerk, a radar man; a wife lives alone; a child grows up without a father. Neither the life of an individual nor the history of a society can be understood without understanding both.

Yet men do not usually define the troubles they endure in terms of historical change and institutional contradiction. The well-being they enjoy, they do not usually impute to the big ups and downs of the societies in which they live. Seldom aware of the intricate connection between the patterns of their own lives and the course of world history, ordinary men do not usually know what this connection means for the kinds of men they are becoming and for the kinds of history-making in which they might take part. They do not possess the quality of mind essential to grasp the interplay of man and society, of biography and history, of self and world. They cannot cope with their personal troubles in such ways as to control the structural transformations that usually lie behind them.

Surely it is no wonder. In what period have so many men been so totally exposed at so fast a pace to such earthquakes of change? That Americans have not known such catastrophic changes as have the men and women of other societies is due to historical facts that are now quickly becoming 'merely history.' The history that now affects every man is world history. Within this scene and this period, in the course of a single generation, one sixth of mankind is transformed from all that is feudal and backward into all that is modern, advanced, and fearful. Political colonies are freed; new and less visible forms of imperialism installed. Revolutions occur; men feel the intimate grip of new kinds of authority. Totalitarian societies rise, and are smashed to bits—or succeed fabulously. After two centuries of ascendancy, capitalism is shown up as only one way to make society into an industrial apparatus. After two centuries of hope, even formal democracy is restricted to a quite small portion of mankind. Everywhere in the underdeveloped world, ancient ways of life are broken up and vague expectations become urgent demands. Everywhere in the overdeveloped world, the means of authority and of violence become total in scope and bureaucratic in form. Humanity itself now lies before us, the super-nation at either pole concentrating its most coordinated and massive efforts upon the preparation of World War Three.

The very shaping of history now outpaces the ability of men to orient themselves in accordance with cherished values. And which values? Even when they do not panic, men often sense that older ways of feeling and thinking have collapsed and that newer beginnings are ambiguous to the point of moral stasis. Is it any wonder that ordinary men feel they cannot cope with the larger worlds with which they are so suddenly confronted? That they cannot understand the meaning of their epoch for their own lives? That—in defense of selfhood—they become morally insensible, trying to remain altogether private men? Is it any wonder that they come to be possessed by a sense of the trap?

It is not only information that they need—in this Age of Fact, information often dominates their attention and overwhelms their capacities to assimilate it. It is not only the skills of reason that they need—although their struggles to acquire these often exhaust their limited moral energy.

What they need, and what they feel they need, is a quality of mind that will help them to use information and to develop reason in order to achieve lucid summations of what is going on in the world and of what may be happening within themselves. It is this quality, I am going to contend, that journalists and scholars, artists and publics, scientists and editors are coming to expect of what may be called the sociological imagination.

1

The sociological imagination enables its possessor to understand the larger historical scene in terms of its meaning for the inner life and the external career of a variety of individuals. It enables him to take into account how individuals, in the welter of their daily experience, often become falsely conscious of their social positions. Within that welter, the framework of modern society is sought, and within that framework the psychologies of a variety of men and women are formulated. By such means the personal uneasiness of individuals is focused upon explicit troubles and the indifferences of publics is transformed into involvement with public issues.

The first fruit of this imagination—and the first lesson of the social science that embodies it—is the idea that the individual can understand his own experience and gauge his own fate only by locating himself within his period, that he can know his own chances in life only by becoming aware of those of all individuals in his circumstances. In many ways it is a terrible lesson; in many ways a magnificent one. We do not know the limits of man's capacities for supreme effort or willing degradation, for agony or glee, for pleasurable brutality or the sweetness of reason. But in our time we have come to know that the limits of 'human nature' are frighteningly broad. We have come to know that every individual lives, from one generation to the next, in some society; that he lives out a biography, and that he lives it out within some historical sequence. By the fact of his living he contributes, however minutely, to the shaping of this society and to the course of its history, even as he is made by society and by its historical push and shove.

The sociological imagination enables us to grasp history and biography and the relations between the two within society. That is its task and its promise. To recognize this task and this promise is the mark of the classic social analyst. And it is the signal of what is best in contemporary studies of man and society.

No social study that does not come back to the problems of biography, of history and of their intersections within a society has completed its intellectual journey. Whatever the specific problems of the classic social analysts, however limited or however broad the features of social reality they have examined, those who have been imaginatively aware of the promise of their work have consistently asked three sorts of questions:

1. What is the structure of this particular society as a whole? What are its essential components, and how are they related to one another? How does it differ from other varieties of social order? Within it, what is the meaning of any particular feature for its continuance and for its change?
2. Where does this society stand in human history? What are the mechanics by which it is changing? What is its place within and its meaning

for the development of humanity as a whole? How does any particular feature we are examining affect, and how is it affected by, the historical period in which it moves? And this period—what are its essential features? How does it differ from other periods? What are its characteristic ways of history-making?

3. What varieties of men and women now prevail in this society and in this period? And what varieties are coming to prevail? In what ways are they selected and formed, liberated and repressed, made sensitive and blunted? What kinds of 'human nature' are revealed in the conduct and character we observe in this society in this period? And what is the meaning for 'human nature' of each and every feature of the society we are examining?

Whether the point of interest is a great power state or a minor literary mood, a family, a prison, a creed—these are the kinds of questions the best social analysts have asked. They are the intellectual pivots of classic studies of man in society—and they are the questions inevitably raised by any mind possessing the sociological imagination. For that imagination is the capacity to shift from one perspective to another—from the political to the psychological; from examination of a single family to comparative assessment of the national budgets of the world; from the theological school to the military establishment; from considerations of an oil industry to studies of contemporary poetry. It is the capacity to range from the most impersonal and remote transformations to the most intimate features of the human self—and to see the relations between the two. Back of its use there is always the urge to know the social and historical meaning of the individual in the society and in the period in which he has his quality and his being.

That, in brief, is why it is by means of the sociological imagination that men now hope to grasp what is going on in the world, and to understand what is happening in themselves as minute points of the intersections of biography and history within society. In large part, contemporary man's self-conscious view of himself as at least an outsider, if not a permanent stranger, rests upon an absorbed realization of social relativity and of the transformative power of history. The sociological imagination is the most fruitful form of this self-consciousness. By its use men whose mentalities have swept only a series of limited orbits often come to feel as if suddenly awakened in a house with which they had only supposed themselves to be familiar. Correctly or incorrectly, they often come to feel that they can now provide themselves with adequate summations, cohesive assessments, comprehensive orientations. Older decisions that once appeared sound now seem to them products of a mind unaccountably dense. Their capacity for astonishment is made lively again. They acquire a new way of thinking, they experience a transvaluation of values: in a word, by their reflection and by their sensibility, they realize the cultural meaning of the social sciences.

2

Perhaps the most fruitful distinction with which the sociological imagination works is between 'the personal troubles of milieu' and 'the public issues of social structure.' This distinction is an essential tool of the sociological imagination and a feature of all classic work in social science.

Troubles occur within the character of the individual and within the range of his immediate relations with others; they have to do with his self and with those limited areas of social life of which he is directly and personally aware. Accordingly, the statement and the resolution of troubles properly lie within the individual as a biographical entity and within the scope of his immediate milieu—the social setting that is directly open to his personal experience and to some extent his willful activity. A trouble is a private matter: values cherished by an individual are felt by him to be threatened.

Issues have to do with matters that transcend these local environments of the individual and the range of his inner life. They have to do with the organization of many such milieux into the institutions of an historical society as a whole, with the ways in which various milieux overlap and interpenetrate to form the larger structure of social and historical life. An issue is a public matter: some value cherished by publics is felt to be threatened. Often there is a debate about what that value really is and about what it is that really threatens it. This debate is often without focus if only because it is the very nature of an issue, unlike even widespread trouble, that it cannot very well be defined in terms of the immediate and everyday environments of ordinary men.[An issue, in fact, often involves a crisis in institutional arrangements, and often too it involves what Marxists call 'contradictions' or 'antagonisms.']

In these terms, consider unemployment. When, in a city of 100,000, only one man is unemployed, that is his personal trouble, and for its relief we properly look to the character of the man, his skills, and his immediate opportunities. But when in a nation of 50 million employees, 15 million men are unemployed, that is an issue, and we may not hope to find its solution within the range of opportunities open to any one individual. The very structure of opportunities has collapsed. Both the correct statement of the problem and the range of possible solutions require us to consider the economic and political institutions of the society, and not merely the personal situation and character of a scatter of individuals.

Consider war. The personal problem of war, when it occurs, may be how to survive it or how to die in it with honor; how to make money out of it; how to climb into the higher safety of the military apparatus; or how to contribute to the war's termination. In short, according to one's values, to find a set of milieux and within it to survive the war or make one's death in it meaningful. But the structural issues of war have to do with its causes; with what types of men it throws up into command; with its effects upon economic and political, family and religious institutions, with the unorganized irresponsibility of a world of nation-states.

[Consider marriage. Inside a marriage a man and a woman may experience personal troubles, but when the divorce rate during the first four years of marriage is 250 out of every 1,000 attempts, this is an indication of a structural issue having to do with the institutions of marriage and the family and other institutions that bear upon them.]

Or consider the metropolis—the horrible, beautiful, ugly, magnificent sprawl of the great city. For many upper-class people, the personal solution to 'the problem of the city' is to have an apartment with private garage under it in the heart of the city, and forty miles out, a house by Henry Hill, garden by Garrett Eckbo, on a hundred acres of private land. In these two controlled environments— with a small staff at each end and a private helicopter connection—most people could solve many of the problems of personal milieux caused by the facts of the city. But all this, however splendid, does not solve the public issues that the structural fact of the city poses. What should be done with this wonderful monstrosity? Break it all up into scattered units, combining residence and work? Refurbish it as it stands? Or, after evacuation, dynamite it and build new cities according to new plans in new places? What should those plans be? And who is to decide and to accomplish whatever choice is made? These are structural issues; to confront them and to solve them requires us to consider political and economic issues that affect innumerable milieux.

In so far as an economy is so arranged that slumps occur, the problem of unemployment becomes incapable of personal solution. In so far as war is inherent in the nation-state system and in the uneven industrialization of the world, the ordinary individual in his restricted milieu will be powerless—with or without psychiatric aid—to solve the troubles this system or lack of system imposes upon him. In so far as the family as an institution turns women into darling little slaves and men into their chief providers and unweaned dependents, the problem of a satisfactory marriage remains incapable of purely private solution. In so far as the overdeveloped megalopolis and the overdeveloped automobile are built-in features of the overdeveloped society, the issues of urban living will not be solved by personal ingenuity and private wealth.

What we experience in various and specific milieux, I have noted, is often caused by structural changes. Accordingly, to understand the changes of many personal milieux we are required to look beyond them. And the number and variety of such structural changes increase as the institutions within which we live become more embracing and more intricately connected with one another. [To be aware of the idea of social structure and to use it with sensibility is to be capable of tracing such linkages among a great variety of milieux. To be able to do that is to possess the sociological imagination.]

3

The Tragedy of the Commons*

GARRETT HARDIN

This essay, written nearly fifty years ago, has become a classic largely because the issue it poses is perhaps more relevant today than ever. As Émile Durkheim, the great French sociologist, knew, the social world is not simply an accumulation of individual worlds, and what is best for the former is not always determined by what is best for the latter. The author is alarmed by global population growth outstripping Earth's ability to provide enough food. His issue could as easily be global climate change, the depletion of natural resources, or even the pursuit of wealth.

At the end of a thoughtful article on the future of nuclear war, Wiesner and York concluded that: "Both sides in the arms race are . . . confronted by the dilemma of steadily increasing military power and steadily decreasing national security. *It is our considered professional judgment that this dilemma has no technical solution.* If the great powers continue to look for solutions in the area of science and technology only, the result will be to worsen the situation."

I would like to focus your attention not on the subject of the article (national security in a nuclear world) but on the kind of conclusion they reached, namely that there is no technical solution to the problem. An implicit and almost universal assumption of discussions published in professional and semipopular scientific journals is that the problem under discussion has a technical solution. A technical solution may be defined as one that requires a change only in the techniques of the natural sciences, demanding little or nothing in the way of change in human values or ideas of morality.

In our day (though not in earlier times) technical solutions are always welcome. Because of previous failures in prophecy, it takes courage to assert that a desired technical solution is not possible. Wiesner and York exhibited this courage; publishing in a science journal, they insisted that the solution to the problem was not to be found in the natural sciences. They cautiously qualified their statement with the phrase, "It is our considered professional judgment . . ." Whether they were right or not is not the concern of the present article. Rather, the concern here is with the important concept of a class of

---

*References and footnotes can be found in the original article, published in 1968 in *Science*. [*Editors' note*]

human problems which can be called "no technical solution problems," and, more specifically, with the identification and discussion of one of these.

It is easy to show that the class is not a null class. Recall the game of tick-tack-toe. Consider the problem, "How can I win the game of tick-tack-toe?" It is well known that I cannot, if I assume (in keeping with the conventions of game theory) that my opponent understands the game perfectly. Put another way, there is no "technical solution" to the problem. I can win only by giving a radical meaning to the word "win." I can hit my opponent over the head; or I can drug him; or I can falsify the records. Every way in which I "win" involves, in some sense, an abandonment of the game, as we intuitively understand it. (I can also, of course, openly abandon the game—refuse to play it. This is what most adults do.)

The class of "No technical solution problems" has members. My thesis is that the "population problem," as conventionally conceived, is a member of this class. How it is conventionally conceived needs some comment. It is fair to say that most people who anguish over the population problem are trying to find a way to avoid the evils of overpopulation without relinquishing any of the privileges they now enjoy. They think that farming the seas or developing new strains of wheat will solve the problem—technologically. I try to show here that the solution they seek cannot be found. The population problem cannot be solved in a technical way, any more than can the problem of winning the game of tick-tack-toe.

WHAT SHALL WE MAXIMIZE?

Population, as Malthus said, naturally tends to grow "geometrically," or, as we would now say, exponentially. In a finite world this means that the per capita share of the world's goods must steadily decrease. Is ours a finite world?

A fair defense can be put forward for the view that the world is infinite; or that we do not know that it is not. But, in terms of the practical problems that we must face in the next few generations with the foreseeable technology, it is clear that we will greatly increase human misery if we do not, during the immediate future, assume that the world available to the terrestrial human population is finite. "Space" is no escape.

A finite world can support only a finite population; therefore, population growth must eventually equal zero. (The case of perpetual wide fluctuations above and below zero is a trivial variant that need not be discussed.) When this condition is met, what will be the situation of mankind? Specifically, can Bentham's goal of "the greatest good for the greatest number" be realized?

No—for two reasons, each sufficient by itself. The first is a theoretical one. It is not mathematically possible to maximize for two (or more) variables at the same time.

The second reason springs directly from biological facts. To live, any organism must have a source of energy (for example, food). This energy is utilized for two purposes: mere maintenance and work. For man, maintenance of life requires about 1,600 kilocalories a day ("maintenance calories"). Anything that he does over and above merely staying alive will be defined as work, and is supported by "work calories" which he takes in. Work calories are used not only for what we call work in common speech; they are also required for all forms of enjoyment, from swimming and automobile racing to playing music and writing poetry. If our goal is to maximize population it is obvious what we must do: We must make the work calories per person approach as close to zero as possible. No gourmet meals, no vacations, no sports, no music, no literature, no art.... I think that everyone will grant, without argument or proof, that maximizing population does not maximize goods. Bentham's goal is impossible.

In reaching this conclusion I have made the usual assumption that it is the acquisition of energy that is the problem. The appearance of atomic energy has led some to question this assumption. However, given an infinite source of energy, population growth still produces an inescapable problem. The problem of the acquisition of energy is replaced by the problem of its dissipation, as J. H. Fremlin has so wittily shown. The arithmetic signs in the analysis are, as it were, reversed; but Bentham's goal is still unobtainable.

The optimum population is, then, less than the maximum. The difficulty of defining the optimum is enormous; so far as I know, no one has seriously tackled this problem. Reaching an acceptable and stable solution will surely require more than one generation of hard analytical work—and much persuasion.

We want the maximum good per person; but what is good? To one person it is wilderness, to another it is ski lodges for thousands. To one it is estuaries to nourish ducks for hunters to shoot; to another it is factory land. Comparing one good with another is, we usually say, impossible because goods are incommensurable. Incommensurables cannot be compared.

Theoretically this may be true; but in real life incommensurables are commensurable. Only a criterion of judgment and a system of weighting are needed. In nature the criterion is survival. Is it better for a species to be small and hideable, or large and powerful? Natural selection commensurates the incommensurables. The compromise achieved depends on a natural weighting of the values of the variables.

Man must imitate this process. There is no doubt that in fact he already does, but unconsciously. It is when the hidden decisions are made explicit that the arguments begin. The problem for the years ahead is to work out an acceptable theory of weighting. Synergistic effects, nonlinear variation, and difficulties in discounting the future make the intellectual problem difficult, but not (in principle) insoluble.

Has any cultural group solved this practical problem at the present time, even on an intuitive level? One simple fact proves that none has: there is no prosperous population in the world today that has, and has had for some time, a growth rate of zero. Any people that has intuitively identified its optimum point will soon reach it, after which its growth rate becomes and remains zero.

Of course, a positive growth rate might be taken as evidence that a population is below its optimum. However, by any reasonable standards, the most rapidly growing populations on earth today are (in general) the most miserable. This association (which need not be invariable) casts doubt on the optimistic assumption that the positive growth rate of a population is evidence that it has yet to reach its optimum.

We can make little progress in working toward optimum population size until we explicitly exorcize the spirit of Adam Smith in the field of practical demography. In economic affairs, *The Wealth of Nations* (1776) popularized the "invisible hand," the idea that an individual who "intends only his own gain," is, as it were, "led by an invisible hand to promote . . . the public interest." Adam Smith did not assert that this was invariably true, and perhaps neither did any of his followers. But he contributed to a dominant tendency of thought that has ever since interfered with positive action based on rational analysis, namely, the tendency to assume that decisions reached individually will, in fact, be the best decisions for an entire society. If this assumption is correct it justifies the continuance of our present policy of laissez-faire in reproduction. If it is correct we can assume that men will control their individual fecundity so as to produce the optimum population. If the assumption is not correct, we need to reexamine our individual freedoms to see which ones are defensible.

TRAGEDY OF FREEDOM IN A COMMONS

The rebuttal to the invisible hand in population control is to be found in a scenario first sketched in a little-known pamphlet [written] in 1833 by a mathematical amateur named William Forster Lloyd (1794–1852). We may well call it "the tragedy of the commons," using the word "tragedy" as the philosopher Whitehead used it: "The essence of dramatic tragedy is not unhappiness. It resides in the solemnity of the remorseless working of things." He then goes on to say, "This inevitableness of destiny can only be illustrated in terms of human life by incidents which in fact involve unhappiness. For it is only by them that the futility of escape can be made evident in the drama."

The tragedy of the commons develops in this way. Picture a pasture open to all. It is to be expected that each herdsman will try to keep as many cattle as possible on the commons. Such an arrangement may work reasonably satisfactorily for centuries because tribal wars, poaching, and disease keep the numbers of both man and beast well below the carrying capacity of the land. Finally, however, comes the day of reckoning, that is, the day when the long-desired goal of social stability becomes a reality. At this point, the inherent logic of the commons remorselessly generates tragedy.

As a rational being, each herdsman seeks to maximize his gain. Explicitly or implicitly, more or less consciously, he asks, "What is the utility *to me* of adding one more animal to my herd?" This utility has one negative and one positive component.

1. The positive component is a function of the increment of one animal. Since the herdsman receives all the proceeds from the sale of the additional animal, the positive utility is nearly +1.
2. The negative component is a function of the additional overgrazing created by one more animal. Since, however, the effects of overgrazing are shared by all the herdsmen, the negative utility for any particular decision-making herdsman is only a fraction of –1.

Adding together the component partial utilities, the rational herdsman concludes that the only sensible course for him to pursue is to add another animal to his herd. And another; and another. . . . But this is the conclusion reached by each and every rational herdsman sharing a commons. Therein is the tragedy. Each man is locked into a system that compels him to increase his herd without limit—in a world that is limited. Ruin is the destination toward which all men rush, each pursuing his own best interest in a society that believes in the freedom of the commons. Freedom in a commons brings ruin to all.

Some would say that this is a platitude. Would that it were! In a sense, it was learned thousands of years ago, but natural selection favors the forces of psychological denial. The individual benefits as an individual from his ability to deny the truth even though society as a whole, of which he is a part, suffers.

Education can counteract the natural tendency to do the wrong thing, but the inexorable succession of generations requires that the basis for this knowledge be constantly refreshed.

A simple incident that occurred a few years ago in Leominster, Massachusetts, shows how perishable the knowledge is. During the Christmas shopping season the parking meters downtown were covered with plastic bags that bore tags reading: "Do not open until after Christmas. Free parking courtesy of the mayor and city council." In other words, facing the prospect of an increased demand for already scarce space, the city fathers reinstituted the system of the commons. (Cynically, we suspect that they gained more votes than they lost by this retrogressive act.)

In an approximate way, the logic of the commons has been understood for a long time, perhaps since the discovery of agriculture or the invention of private property in real estate. But it is understood mostly only in special cases which are not sufficiently generalized. Even at this late date, cattlemen leasing national land on the western ranges demonstrate no more than an ambivalent understanding, in constantly pressuring federal authorities to increase the head count to the point where overgrazing produces erosion and weed-dominance. Likewise, the oceans of the world continue to suffer from the survival of the philosophy of the commons. Maritime nations still respond automatically to the shibboleth of the "freedom of the seas." Professing to believe in the "inexhaustible resources of the oceans," they bring species after species of fish and whales closer to extinction.

The National Parks present another instance of the working out of the tragedy of the commons. At present, they are open to all, without limit. The parks themselves are limited in extent—there is only one Yosemite Valley—whereas population seems to grow without limit. The values that visitors seek in the parks are steadily eroded. Plainly, we must soon cease to treat the parks as commons or they will be of no value to anyone.

What shall we do? We have several options. We might sell them off as private property. We might keep them as public property, but allocate the right to enter them. The allocation might be on the basis of wealth, by the use of an auction system. It might be on the basis of merit, as defined by some agreed-upon standards. It might be by lottery. Or it might be on a first-come, first-served basis, administered to long queues. These, I think, are all the reasonable possibilities. They are all objectionable. But we must choose—or acquiesce in the destruction of the commons that we call our National Parks.

POLLUTION

In a reverse way, the tragedy of the commons reappears in problems of pollution. Here it is not a question of taking something out of the commons, but of putting something in—sewage, or chemical, radioactive, and heat wastes into water; noxious and dangerous fumes into the air, and distracting and unpleasant advertising signs into the line of sight. The calculations of utility are much the same as before. The rational man finds that his share of the cost of the wastes he discharges into the commons is less than the cost of purifying his wastes before releasing them. Since this is true for everyone, we are locked into a system of "fouling our own nest," so long as we behave only as independent, rational, free-enterprisers.

The tragedy of the commons as a food basket is averted by private property, or something formally like it. But the air and waters surrounding us cannot readily be fenced, and so the tragedy of the commons as a cesspool must be prevented by different means, by coercive laws or taxing devices that make it cheaper for the polluter to treat his pollutants than to discharge them untreated. We have not progressed as far with the solution of this problem as we have with the first. Indeed, our particular concept of private property, which deters us from exhausting the positive resources of the earth, favors pollution. The owner of a factory on the bank of a stream—whose property extends to the middle of the stream, often has difficulty seeing why it is not his natural right to muddy the waters flowing past his door. The law, always behind the times, requires elaborate stitching and fitting to adapt it to this newly perceived aspect of the commons.

The pollution problem is a consequence of population. It did not much matter how a lonely American frontiersman disposed of his waste. "Flowing water purifies itself every 10 miles," my grandfather used to say, and the myth was near enough to the truth when he was a boy, for there were not too many people.

But as population became denser, the natural chemical and biological recycling processes became overloaded, calling for a redefinition of property rights. Analysis of the pollution problem as a function of population density uncovers a not generally recognized principle of morality, namely: *the morality of an act is a function of the state of the system at the time it is performed.*

Using the commons as a cesspool does not harm the general public under frontier conditions, because there is no public, the same behavior in a metropolis is unbearable. A hundred and fifty years ago a plainsman could kill an American bison, cut out only the tongue for his dinner, and discard the rest of the animal. He was not in any important sense being wasteful. Today, with only a few thousand bison left, we would be appalled at such behavior.

* * *

FREEDOM TO BREED IS INTOLERABLE

The tragedy of the commons is involved in population problems in another way. In a world governed solely by the principle of "dog eat dog"—if indeed there ever was such a world—how many children a family had would not be a matter of public concern. Parents who bred too exuberantly would leave fewer descendants, not more, because they would be unable to care adequately for their children. David Lack and others have found that such a negative feedback demonstrably controls the fecundity of birds. But men are not birds, and have not acted like them for millenniums, at least.

If each human family were dependent only on its own resources; if the children of improvident parents starved to death; *if*, thus, overbreeding brought its own "punishment" to the germ line—*then* there would be no public interest in controlling the breeding of families. But our society is deeply committed to the welfare state, and hence is confronted with another aspect of the tragedy of the commons.

In a welfare state, how shall we deal with the family, the religion, the race, or the class (or indeed any distinguishable and cohesive group) that adopts overbreeding as a policy to secure its own aggrandizement?

To couple the concept of freedom to breed with the belief that everyone born has an equal right to the commons is to lock the world into a tragic course of action.

* * *

CONSCIENCE IS SELF-ELIMINATING

It is a mistake to think that we can control the breeding of mankind in the long run by an appeal to conscience. Charles Galton Darwin made this point when he spoke on the centennial of the publication of his grandfather's great book. The argument is straightforward and Darwinian.

People vary. Confronted with appeals to limit breeding, some people will undoubtedly respond to the plea more than others. Those who have more children will produce a larger fraction of the next generation than those with more susceptible consciences. The difference will be accentuated, generation by generation.

* * *

The argument has here been stated in the context of the population problem, but it applies equally well to any instance in which society appeals to an individual exploiting a commons to restrain himself for the general good—by means of his conscience. To make such an appeal is to set up a selective system that works toward the elimination of conscience from the race.

PATHOGENIC EFFECTS OF CONSCIENCE

The long-term disadvantage of an appeal to conscience should be enough to condemn it; but has serious short-term disadvantages as well. If we ask a man who is exploiting a commons to desist "in the name of conscience," what are we saying to him? What does he hear?—not only at the moment but also in the wee small hours of the night when, half asleep, he remembers not merely the words we used but also the nonverbal communication cues we gave him unawares? Sooner or later, consciously or subconsciously, he senses that he has received two communications, and that they are contradictory: (i) (intended communication) "If you don't do as we ask, we will openly condemn you for not acting like a responsible citizen"; (ii) (the unintended communication) "If you do behave as we ask, we will secretly condemn you for a simpleton who can be shamed into standing aside while the rest of us exploit the commons."

* * *

If the word "responsibility" is to be used at all, I suggest that it be in the sense Charles Frankel uses it. "Responsibility," says this philosopher, "is the product of definite social arrangements." Notice that Frankel calls for social arrangements—not propaganda.

MUTUAL COERCION MUTUALLY AGREED UPON

The social arrangements that produce responsibility are arrangements that create coercion, of some sort. Consider bank-robbing. The man who takes money from a bank acts as if the bank were a commons. How do we prevent such action? Certainly not by trying to control his behavior solely by a verbal appeal to his sense of responsibility. Rather than rely on propaganda we follow Frankel's lead and insist that a bank is not a commons; we seek the definite social arrangements that will keep it from becoming a commons. That we thereby infringe on the freedom of would-be robbers we neither deny nor regret.

The morality of bank-robbing is particularly easy to understand because we accept complete prohibition of this activity. We are willing to say, "Thou shalt not rob banks," without providing for exceptions. But temperance also can be created by coercion. Taxing is a good coercive device. To keep downtown shoppers temperate in their use of parking space we introduce parking meters for short periods, and traffic fines for longer ones. We need not actually forbid a citizen to park as long as he wants to; we need merely make it increasingly expensive for him to do so. Not prohibition, but carefully biased options are what we offer him. A Madison Avenue man might call this persuasion; I prefer the greater candor of the word "coercion."

Coercion is a dirty word to most liberals now, but it need not forever be so. As with the four-letter words, its dirtiness can be cleansed away by exposure to the light, by saying it over and over without apology or embarrassment. To many, the word coercion implies arbitrary decisions of distant and irresponsible bureaucrats; but this is not a necessary part of its meaning. The only kind of coercion I recommend is mutual coercion, mutually agreed upon by the majority of the people affected.

To say that we mutually agree to coercion is not to say that we are required to enjoy it, or even to pretend we enjoy it. Who enjoys taxes? We all grumble about them. But we accept compulsory taxes because we recognize that voluntary taxes would favor the conscienceless. We institute and (grumblingly) support taxes and other coercive devices to escape the horror of the commons.

An alternative to the commons need not be perfectly just to be preferable. With real estate and other material goods, the alternative we have chosen is the institution of private property coupled with legal inheritance. Is this system perfectly just? As a genetically trained biologist I deny that it is. It seems to me that, if there are to be differences in individual inheritance, legal possession should be perfectly correlated with biological inheritance—that those who are biologically more fit to be the custodians of property and power should legally inherit more. But genetic recombination continually makes a mockery of the doctrine of "like father, like son" implicit in our laws of legal inheritance. An idiot can inherit millions, and a trust fund can keep his estate intact. We must admit that our legal system of private property plus inheritance is unjust— but we put up with it because we are not convinced, at the moment, that anyone has invented a better system. The alternative of the commons is too horrifying to contemplate. Injustice is preferable to total ruin.

* * *

RECOGNITION OF NECESSITY

Perhaps the simplest summary of this analysis of man's population problems is this: the commons, if justifiable at all, is justifiable only under conditions of low-population density. As the human population has increased, the commons has had to be abandoned in one aspect after another.

First we abandoned the commons in food gathering, enclosing farm land and restricting pastures and hunting and fishing areas. These restrictions are still not complete throughout the world.

Somewhat later we saw that the commons as a place for waste disposal would also have to be abandoned. Restrictions on the disposal of domestic sewage are widely accepted in the Western world; we are still struggling to close the commons to pollution by automobiles, factories, insecticide sprayers, fertilizing operations, and atomic energy installations.

In a still more embryonic state is our recognition of the evils of the commons in matters of pleasure. There is almost no restriction on the propagation of sound waves in the public medium. The shopping public is assaulted with mindless music, without its consent. Our government is paying out billions of dollars to create supersonic transport which will disturb 50,000 people for every one person who is whisked from coast to coast 3 hours faster. Advertisers muddy the airwaves of radio and television and pollute the view of travelers. We are a long way from outlawing the commons in matters of pleasure. Is this because our Puritan inheritance makes us view pleasure as something of a sin, and pain (that is, the pollution of advertising) as the sign of virtue?

Every new enclosure of the commons involves the infringement of somebody's personal liberty. Infringements made in the distant past are accepted because no contemporary complains of a loss. It is the newly proposed infringements that we vigorously oppose; cries of "rights" and "freedom" fill the air. But what does "freedom" mean? When men mutually agreed to pass laws against robbing, mankind became more free, not less so. Individuals locked into the logic of the commons are free only to bring on universal ruin once they see the necessity of mutual coercion, they become free to pursue other goals. I believe it was Hegel who said, "Freedom is the recognition of necessity."

The most important aspect of necessity that we must now recognize, is the necessity of abandoning the commons in breeding. No technical solution can rescue us from the misery of overpopulation. Freedom to breed will bring ruin to all. At the moment, to avoid hard decisions many of us are tempted to propagandize for conscience and responsible parenthood. The temptation must be resisted, because an appeal to independently acting consciences selects for the disappearance of all conscience in the long run, and an increase in anxiety in the short.

The only way we can preserve and nurture other and more precious freedoms is by relinquishing the freedom to breed, and that very soon. "Freedom is the recognition of necessity"—and it is the role of education to reveal to all the necessity of abandoning the freedom to breed. Only so, can we put an end to this aspect of the tragedy of the commons.

4

The Stranger

GEORG SIMMEL

Most students can name the cliques in their high school, but few admit to being in one, at least full time. They were both inside and outside, involved but detached. Why does this seem like a good way to be? Georg Simmel (1858–1918) suggests it allows for intimacies and "confidences," in part because the stranger is not so completely "bound up" with the group itself. In this sketch of the stranger, and in his other sketches of social types (e.g., the poor, the miser, the adventurer), Simmel is presenting sociology as the study of relationships and the possibilities—often contradictory—for different types of interaction. His studies of dyads and triads (two- and three-person groups) have the same playful but insightful examination of bonds, networks, and strategies that make society appear to be almost a dance or a game of chess.

If wandering, considered as a state of detachment from every given point in space, is the conceptual opposite of attachment to any point, then the sociological form of "the stranger" presents the synthesis, as it were, of both of these properties. (This is another indication that spatial relations not only are determining conditions of relationships among men, but are also symbolic of those relationships.) The stranger will thus not be considered here in the usual sense of the term, as the wanderer who comes today and goes tomorrow, but rather as the man who comes today and stays tomorrow—the potential wanderer, so to speak, who, although he has gone no further, has not quite got over the freedom of coming and going. He is fixed within a certain spatial circle—or within a group whose boundaries are analogous to spatial boundaries—but his position within it is fundamentally affected by the fact that he does not belong in it initially and that he brings qualities into it that are not, and cannot be, indigenous to it.

In the case of the stranger, the union of closeness and remoteness involved in every human relationship is patterned in a way that may be succinctly formulated as follows: the distance within this relation indicates that one who is close by is remote, but his strangeness indicates that one who is remote is near. The state of being a stranger is of course a completely positive relation; it is a specific form of interaction. . . .

The following statements about the stranger are intended to suggest how factors of repulsion and distance work to create a form of being together, a form of union based on interaction.

In the whole history of economic activity the stranger makes his appearance everywhere as a trader, and the trader makes his as a stranger. As long as production for one's own needs is the general rule, or products are exchanged within a relatively small circle, there is no need for a middleman within the group. A trader is required only for goods produced outside the group. Unless there are people who wander out into foreign lands to buy these necessities, in which case they are themselves "strange" merchants in this other region, the trader *must* be a stranger; there is no opportunity for anyone else to make a living at it.

This position of the stranger stands out more sharply if, instead of leaving the place of his activity, he settles down there. In innumerable cases even this is possible only if he can live by trade as a middleman. Any closed economic group where land and handicrafts have been apportioned in a way that satisfies local demands will still support a livelihood for the trader. For trade alone makes possible unlimited combinations, and through it intelligence is constantly extended and applied in new areas, something that is much harder for the primary producer with his more limited mobility and his dependence on a circle of customers that can be expanded only very slowly. Trade can always absorb more men than can primary production. It is therefore the most suitable activity for the stranger, who intrudes as a supernumerary, so to speak, into a group in which all the economic positions are already occupied. The classic example of this is the history of European Jews. The stranger is by his very nature no owner of land—land not only in the physical sense but also metaphorically as a vital substance which is fixed, if not in space, then at least in an ideal position within the social environment.

Although in the sphere of intimate personal relations the stranger may be attractive and meaningful in many ways, so long as he is regarded as a stranger he is no "landowner" in the eyes of the other. Restriction to intermediary trade and often (as though sublimated from it) to pure finance gives the stranger the specific character of *mobility*. The appearance of this mobility within a bounded group occasions that synthesis of nearness and remoteness which constitutes the formal position of the stranger. The purely mobile person comes incidentally into contact with *every* single element but is not bound up organically, through established ties of kinship, locality, or occupation, with any single one.

Another expression of this constellation is to be found in the objectivity of the stranger. Because he is not bound by roots to the particular constituents and partisan dispositions of the group, he confronts all of these with a distinctly "objective" attitude, an attitude that does not signify mere detachment and nonparticipation, but is a distinct structure composed of remoteness and nearness, indifference and involvement. I refer to my analysis of the dominating positions gained by aliens, in the discussion of superordination and subordination, typified by the practice in certain Italian cities of recruiting their judges from outside, because no native was free from entanglement in family interests and factionalism.

Connected with the characteristic of objectivity is a phenomenon that is found chiefly, though not exclusively, in the stranger who moves on. This is that he often receives the most surprising revelations and confidences, at times reminiscent of a confessional, about matters which are kept carefully hidden from everybody with whom one is close. Objectivity is by no means nonparticipation, a condition that is altogether outside the distinction between subjective and objective orientations. It is rather a positive and definite kind of participation, in the same way that the objectivity of a theoretical observation clearly does not mean that the mind is a passive tabula rasa on which things inscribe their qualities, but rather signifies the full activity of a mind working according to its own laws, under conditions that exclude accidental distortions and emphases whose individual and subjective differences would produce quite different pictures of the same object.

Objectivity can also be defined as freedom. The objective man is not bound by ties which could prejudice his perception, his understanding, and his assessment of data. This freedom, which permits the stranger to experience and treat even his close relationships as though from a bird's-eye view, contains many dangerous possibilities. From earliest times, in uprisings of all sorts the attacked party has claimed that there has been incitement from the outside, by foreign emissaries and agitators. Insofar as this has happened, it represents an exaggeration of the specific role of the stranger: he is the freer man, practically and theoretically; he examines conditions with less prejudice; he assesses them against standards that are more general and more objective; and his actions are not confined by custom, piety, or precedent.

Finally, the proportion of nearness and remoteness which gives the stranger the character of objectivity also finds practical expression in the more *abstract* nature of the relation to him. That is, with the stranger one has only certain *more general* qualities in common, whereas the relation with organically connected persons is based on the similarity of just those specific traits which differentiate them from the merely universal. In fact, all personal relations whatsoever can be analyzed in terms of this scheme. They are not determined only by the existence of certain common characteristics which the individuals share in addition to their individual differences, which either influence the relationship or remain outside of it. Rather, the kind of effect which that commonality has on the relation essentially depends on whether it exists only among the participants themselves, and thus, although general within the relation, is specific and incomparable with respect to all those on the outside, or whether the participants feel that what they have in common is so only because it is common to a group, a type, or mankind in general. In the latter case, the effect of the common features becomes attenuated in proportion to the size of the group bearing the same characteristics. The commonality provides a basis for unifying the members, to be sure; but it does not specifically direct *these* particular persons to one another. A similarity so widely shared could just as easily unite each person with every possible other. This, too, is evidently a way in which a relationship includes both nearness and remoteness simultaneously. To the extent to which the similarities assume a universal nature, the warmth of the connection based on them will acquire an element of coolness, a sense of the contingent nature of precisely *this* relation—the connecting forces have lost their specific, centripetal character.

In relation to the stranger, it seems to me, this constellation assumes an extraordinary preponderance in principle over the individual elements peculiar to the relation in question. The stranger is close to us insofar as we feel between him and ourselves similarities of nationality or social position, of occupation or of general human nature. He is far from us insofar as these similarities extend beyond him and us, and connect us only because they connect a great many people.

A trace of strangeness in this sense easily enters even the most intimate relationships. In the stage of first passion, erotic relations strongly reject any thought of generalization. A love such as this has never existed before; there is nothing to compare either with the person one loves or with our feelings for that person. An estrangement is wont to set in (whether as cause or effect is hard to decide) at the moment when this feeling of uniqueness disappears from the relationship. A skepticism regarding the intrinsic value of the relationship and its value for us adheres to the very thought that in this relation, after all, one is only fulfilling a general human destiny, that one has had an experience that has occurred a thousand times before, and that, if one had not accidentally met this precise person, someone else would have acquired the same meaning for us.

Something of this feeling is probably not absent in any relation, be it ever so close, because that which is common to two is perhaps never common *only* to them but belongs to a general conception which includes much else besides, many *possibilities* of similarities. No matter how few of these possibilities are realized and how often we may forget about them, here and there, nevertheless, they crowd in like shadows between men, like a mist eluding every designation, which must congeal into solid corporeality for it to be called jealousy. Perhaps this is in many cases a more general, at least more insurmountable, strangeness than that due to differences and obscurities. It is strangeness caused by the fact that similarity, harmony, and closeness are accompanied by the feeling that they are actually not the exclusive property of this particular relation, but stem from a more general one—a relation that potentially includes us and an indeterminate number of others, and therefore prevents that relation which alone was experienced from having an inner and exclusive necessity.

On the other hand, there is a sort of "strangeness" in which this very connection on the basis of a general quality embracing the parties is precluded. The relation of the Greeks to the barbarians is a typical example; so are all the cases in which the general characteristics one takes as peculiarly and merely human are disallowed to the other. But here the expression "the stranger" no longer has any positive meaning. The relation with him is a nonrelation; he is not what we have been discussing here: the stranger as a member of the group itself.

As such, the stranger is near and far *at the same time*, as in any relationship based on merely universal human similarities. Between these two factors of nearness and distance, however, a peculiar tension arises, since the consciousness of having only the absolutely general in common has exactly the effect of putting a special emphasis on that which is not common. For a stranger to the country, the city, the race, and so on, what is stressed is again nothing individual, but alien origin, a quality which he has, or could have, in common with many other strangers. For this reason strangers are not really perceived as individuals, but as strangers of a certain type. Their remoteness is no less general than their nearness.

This form appears, for example, in so special a case as the tax levied on Jews in Frankfurt and elsewhere during the Middle Ages. Whereas the tax paid by Christian citizens varied according to their wealth at any given time, for every single Jew the tax was fixed once and for all. This amount was fixed because the Jew had his social position as a *Jew*, not as the bearer of certain objective contents. With respect to taxes every other citizen was regarded as possessor of a certain amount of wealth, and his tax could follow the fluctuations of his fortune. But the Jew as taxpayer was first of all a Jew, and thus his fiscal position contained an invariable element. This appears most forcefully, of course, once the differing circumstances of individual Jews are no longer considered, limited though this consideration is by fixed assessments, and all strangers pay exactly the same head tax.

Despite his being inorganically appended to it, the stranger is still an organic member of the group. Its unified life includes the specific conditioning of this element. Only we do not know how to designate the characteristic unity of this position otherwise than by saying that it is put together of certain amounts of nearness and of remoteness. Although both these qualities are found to some extent in all relationships, a special proportion and reciprocal tension between them produce the specific form of the relation to the "stranger."

5

The Mark of a Criminal Record

DEVAH PAGER

The prison population in the United States increased dramatically near the turn of the twenty-first century, and African American men are at a far greater risk than others of experiencing incarceration. Although getting a job is one of the best ways to reduce the chances of going back to prison, the stigma of incarceration makes it very difficult for people to find work even after they have paid their debt to society. In this article, sociologist Devah Pager describes a field experiment in which she examines how one's race and criminal record work together to shape the chances of getting a job. By sending real job seekers into the Milwaukee labor market to search for work, Pager's study illustrates the high hurdle a criminal record creates for reintegrating into society. Importantly, her study also shows that African Americans pay a higher toll than whites for the "mark" of a criminal record.

While stratification researchers typically focus on schools, labor markets, and the family as primary institutions affecting inequality, a new institution has emerged as central to the sorting and stratifying of young and disadvantaged men: the criminal justice system. With over 2 million individuals currently incarcerated, and over half a million prisoners released each year, the large and growing numbers of men being processed through the criminal justice system raises important questions about the consequences of this massive institutional intervention.

This article focuses on the consequences of incarceration for the employment outcomes of black and white men. While previous survey research has demonstrated a strong *association* between incarceration and employment, there remains little understanding of the mechanisms by which these outcomes are produced. In the present study, I adopt an experimental audit approach to formally test the degree to which a criminal record affects subsequent employment opportunities. By using matched pairs of individuals to apply for real entry-level jobs, it becomes possible to directly measure the extent to which a criminal record—in the absence of other disqualifying characteristics—serves as a barrier to employment among equally qualified applicants. Further, by varying the race of the tester pairs, we can assess the ways in which the effects of race and criminal record interact to produce new forms of labor market inequalities.

TRENDS IN INCARCERATION

Over the past three decades, the number of prison inmates in the United States has increased by more than 600%, leaving it the country with the highest incarceration rate in the world. During this time, incarceration has changed from a punishment reserved primarily for the most heinous offenders to one extended to a much greater range of crimes and a much larger segment of the population. Recent trends in crime policy have led to the imposition of harsher sentences for a wider range of offenses, thus casting an ever-widening net of penal intervention.

While the recent "tough on crime" policies may be effective in getting criminals off the streets, little provision has been made for when they get back out. Of the nearly 2 million individuals currently incarcerated, roughly 95% will be released, with more than half a million being released each year. According to one estimate, there are currently over 12 million ex-felons in the United States, representing roughly 8% of the working-age population. Of those recently released, nearly two-thirds will be charged with new crimes and over 40% will return to prison within three years. Certainly some of these outcomes are the result of desolate opportunities or deeply ingrained dispositions, grown out of broken families, poor neighborhoods, and little social control. But net of these contributing factors, there is evidence that experience with the criminal justice system in itself has adverse consequences for subsequent opportunities. In particular, incarceration is associated with limited future employment opportunities and earnings potential, which themselves are among the strongest predictors of recidivism.

The expansion of the prison population has been particularly consequential for blacks. The incarceration rate for young black men in the year 2000 was nearly 10%, compared to just over 1% for white men in the same age group. Young black men today have a 28% likelihood of incarceration during their lifetime, a figure that rises above 50% among young black high school dropouts. These vast numbers of inmates translate into a large and increasing population of black ex-offenders returning to communities and searching for work. The barriers these men face in reaching economic self-sufficiency are compounded by the stigma of minority status and criminal record. The consequences of such trends for widening racial disparities are potentially profound.

* * *

RESEARCH QUESTIONS

There are three primary questions I seek to address with the present study. First, in discussing the main effect of a criminal record, we need to ask whether and to what extent employers use information about criminal histories to make hiring decisions. Implicit in the criticism of survey research in this area is the assumption that the signal of a criminal record is not a deter-mining factor. Rather, employers use information about the interactional styles of applicants, or other observed characteristics—which may be corre-lated with criminal records—and this explains the differential outcomes we observe. In this view, a criminal record does not represent a meaningful signal to employers on its own. This study formally tests the degree to which employ-ers use information about criminal histories in the absence of corroborating evidence. It is essential that we conclusively document this effect before mak-ing larger claims about the aggregate consequences of incarceration.

Second, this study investigates the extent to which race continues to serve as a major barrier to employment. While race has undoubtedly played a cen-tral role in shaping the employment opportunities of African Americans over the past century, recent arguments have questioned the continuing signifi-cance of race, arguing instead that other factors—such as spatial location, soft skills, social capital, or cognitive ability—can explain most or all of the contemporary racial differentials we observe. This study provides a compari-son of the experiences of equally qualified black and white applicants, allow-ing us to assess the extent to which direct racial discrimination persists in employment interactions.

The third objective of this study is to assess whether the effect of a crimi-nal record differs for black and white applicants. Most research investigating the differential impact of incarceration on blacks has focused on the differen-tial *rates* of incarceration and how those rates translate into widening racial disparities. In addition to disparities in the rate of incarceration, however, it is also important to consider possible racial differences in the *effects* of incarceration. Almost none of the existing literature to date has explored this issue, and the theoretical arguments remain divided as to what we might expect.

On one hand, there is reason to believe that the signal of a criminal record should be less consequential for blacks. Research on racial stereotypes tells us that Americans hold strong and persistent negative stereotypes about blacks, with one of the most readily invoked contemporary stereotypes relating to perceptions of violent and criminal dispositions. If it is the case that employers view all blacks as potential criminals, they are likely to differentiate less among those with official criminal records and those without. Actual confir-mation of criminal involvement then will provide only redundant information, while evidence against it will be discounted. In this case, the outcomes for all blacks should be worse, with less differentiation between those with criminal records and those without. On the other hand, the effect of a criminal record may be worse for blacks if employers, already wary of black applicants, are more hesitant when it comes to taking risks on blacks with proven criminal tendencies. The literature on racial stereotypes also tells us that stereotypes are most likely to be activated and reinforced when a target matches on more than one dimension of the stereotype. While employers may have learned to keep their racial attributions in check through years of heightened sensitivity around employment discrimination, when combined with knowledge of a criminal history, negative attributions are likely to intensify.

A third possibility, of course, is that a criminal record affects black and white applicants equally. The results of this audit study will help to adjudicate between these competing predictions.

* * *

STUDY DESIGN

The basic design of this study involves the use of four male auditors (also called testers), two blacks and two whites. The testers were paired by race; that is, unlike in the original Urban Institute audit studies, the two black testers formed one team, and the two white testers formed the second team (see fig. [5.1]). The testers were 23-year-old college students from Milwaukee who were matched on the basis of physical appearance and general style of self-presentation. Objective characteristics that were not already identical between pairs—such as educational attainment and work experience—were made similar for the purpose of the applications. Within each team, one auditor was randomly assigned a "criminal record" for the first week; the pair then rotated which member presented himself as the ex-offender for each successive week of employment searches, such that each tester served in the criminal record condition for an equal number of cases. By varying which member of the pair presented himself as having a criminal record, unobserved differences within the pairs of applicants were effectively controlled. No significant differences were found for the outcomes of individual testers or by month of testing.

Job openings for entry-level positions (defined as jobs requiring no previous experience and no education greater than high school) were identified from the Sunday classified advertisement section of the *Milwaukee Journal*

Figure 5.1 Audit Design

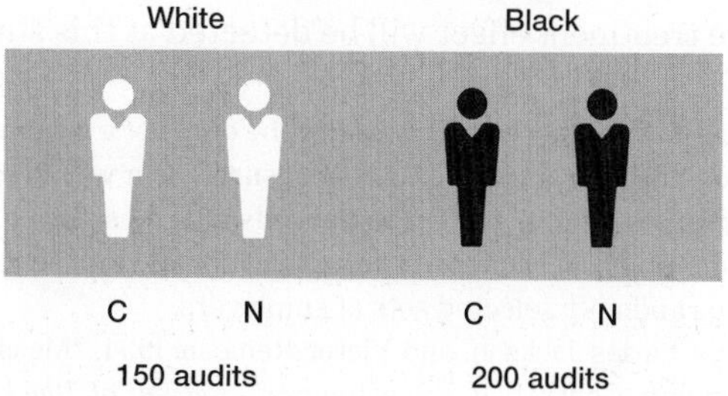

"C" refers to criminal record; "N" refers to no criminal record.

Sentinel.[1] In addition, a supplemental sample was drawn from *Jobnet*, a state-sponsored web site for employment listings, which was developed in connection with the W-2 Welfare-to-Work initiatives. The audit pairs were randomly assigned 15 job openings each week. The white pair and the black pair were assigned separate sets of jobs, with the same-race testers applying to the same jobs. One member of the pair applied first, with the second applying one day later (randomly varying whether the ex-offender was first or second). A total of 350 employers were audited during the course of this study: 150 by the white pair and 200 by the black pair. Additional tests were performed by the black pair because black testers received fewer callbacks on average, and there were thus fewer data points with which to draw comparisons. A larger sample size enables me to calculate more precise estimates of the effects under investigation.

Immediately following the completion of each job application, testers filled out a six-page response form that coded relevant information from the test. Important variables included type of occupation, metropolitan status, wage, size of establishment, and race and sex of employer. Additionally, testers wrote narratives describing the overall interaction and any comments made by employers (or included on applications) specifically related to race or criminal records.

One key feature of this audit study is that it focuses only on the first stage of the employment process. Testers visited employers, filled out applications, and proceeded as far as they could during the course of one visit. If testers were asked to interview on the spot, they did so, but they did not return to the employer for a second visit. The primary dependent variable, then, is the proportion of applications that elicited callbacks from employers. Individual voicemail boxes were set up for each tester to record employer responses. If a tester was offered the job on the spot, this was also coded as a positive response. The reason I chose to focus only on this initial stage of the employment process is because this is the stage likely to be most affected by the barrier of a criminal record. In an audit study of age discrimination, for example, Bendick et al. (1994)* found that 76% of the measured differential treatment occurred at this initial stage of the employment process. Given that a criminal record, like age, is a highly salient characteristic, it is likely that as much, if not more, of the treatment effect will be detected at this stage.

---

1. The primary goal of this study was to measure the effect of a criminal record, and thus it was important for this characteristic to be measured as a within-pair effect. While it would have been ideal for all four testers to have visited the same employers, this likely would have aroused suspicion. The testers were thus divided into separate teams by race and assigned to two randomly selected sets of employers.

*Bendick, Marc, Jr., Charles Jackson, and Victor Reinoso. 1994. "Measuring Employment Discrimination through Controlled Experiments." *Review of Black Political Economy* 23:25–48. Additional references and footnotes can be found in the original article by the same title, in *American Journal of Sociology* 108, no. 5 (March 2003): 937–75. [*Editors' note*]

TESTER PROFILES

In developing the tester profiles, emphasis was placed on adopting character-istics that were both numerically representative and substantively impor-tant. In the present study, the criminal record consisted of a felony drug conviction (possession with intent to distribute, cocaine) and 18 months of (served) prison time. A drug crime (as opposed to a violent or property crime) was chosen because of its prevalence, its policy salience, and its con-nection to racial disparities in incarceration. It is important to acknowledge that the effects reported here may differ depending on the type of offense.

In assigning the educational and work history of testers, I sought a compro-mise between representing the modal group of offenders, while also providing some room for variation in the outcome of the audits. Most audit studies of employment have created tester profiles that include some college experience, so that testers will be highly competitive applicants for entry-level jobs and so that the contrast between treatment and control group is made clear. In the pre-sent study, however, postsecondary schooling experience would detract from the representativeness of the results. More than 70% of federal and nearly 90% of state prisoners have no more than a high school degree (or equivalent). The education level of testers in this study, therefore, was chosen to represent the modal category of offenders (high school diploma).

There is little systematic evidence concerning the work histories of inmates prior to incarceration. Overall, 77.4% of federal and 67.4% of state inmates were employed prior to incarceration. There is, however, a substantial degree of heterogeneity in the quality and consistency of work experience during this time. In the present study, testers were assigned favorable work histories in that they report steady work experience in entry-level jobs and nearly contin-ual employment (until incarceration). In the job prior to incarceration (and, for the control group, prior to the last short-term job), testers report having worked their way from an entry-level position to a supervisory role.

* * *

STUDY CONTEXT AND DESCRIPTIVES

The fieldwork for this project took place in Milwaukee between June and December of 2001. During this time, the economic condition of the metropoli-tan area remained moderately strong, with unemployment rates ranging from a high of 5.2% in June to a low of 4% in September. It is important to note that the results of this study are specific to the economic conditions of this period. It has been well documented in previous research that the level of employment discrimination corresponds closely with the tightness of the labor market. Certainly the economic climate was a salient factor in the minds of these employers. During a pilot interview, for example, an employer reported that a year ago she would have had three applications for an entry-level opening; today she gets 150. Another employer for a janitorial service mentioned that previously their company had been so short of staff that they had to interview virtually everyone who applied. The current conditions, by contrast, allowed them to be far more selective. Since the completion of this study, the unemployment rate has continued to rise. It is likely, therefore, that the effects reported here may understate the impact of race and a criminal record in the context of an economic recession.

* * *

In this sample, roughly 75% of employers asked explicit questions on their application forms about the applicant's criminal history. Generally this was a standard question, "Have you ever been convicted of a crime? If yes, please explain." Even though in most cases employers are not allowed to use criminal background information to make hiring decisions, a vast majority of employers nevertheless request the information.

A much smaller proportion of employers actually perform an official background check. In my sample, 27% of employers indicated that they would perform a background check on all applicants. This figure likely represents a lower-bound estimate, given that employers are not required to disclose their intentions to do background checks.

* * *

THE EFFECT OF A CRIMINAL RECORD FOR WHITES

I begin with an analysis of the effect of a criminal record among whites. White noncriminals can serve as our baseline in the following comparisons, representing the presumptively nonstigmatized group relative to blacks and those with criminal records. Given that all testers presented roughly identical credentials, the differences experienced among groups of testers can be attributed fully to the effects of race or criminal status. . . . [C]riminal records close doors in employment situations. Many employers seem to use the information as a screening mechanism, without attempting to probe deeper into the possible context or complexities of the situation. . . . [I]n 50% of cases, employers were unwilling to consider equally qualified applicants on the basis of their criminal record.

Of course, this trend is not true among all employers, in all situations. There were, in fact, some employers who seemed to prefer workers who had been recently released from prison. One owner told a white tester in the criminal record condition that he "like[d] hiring people who ha[d] just come out of prison because they tend to be more motivated, and are more likely to be hard workers [not wanting to return to prison]." Another employer for a cleaning company attempted to dissuade the white noncriminal tester from applying because the job involved "a great deal of dirty work." The tester with the criminal record, on the other hand, was offered the job on the spot. A criminal record is thus not an obstacle in all cases, but on average, as we see [in Fig. 5.2], it reduces employment opportunities substantially.

THE EFFECT OF RACE

A second major focus of this study concerns the effect of race. African-Americans continue to suffer from lower rates of employment relative to whites, but there is tremendous disagreement over the source of these disparities. The idea that race itself—apart from other correlated characteristics—continues to play a major role in shaping employment opportunities has come under question in recent years. The audit methodology is uniquely suited to address this question. While the present study design does not provide the kind of cross-race matched-pair tests that earlier audit studies of racial discrimination have used, the between-group comparisons (white pair vs. black pair) can nevertheless offer an unbiased estimate of the effect of race on employment opportunities.

Figure [5.2] presents the percentage of callbacks received for both categories of black testers relative to those for whites. The effect of race in these findings is strikingly large. Among blacks without criminal records, only 14% received callbacks, relative to 34% of white noncriminals ($p < .01$). In fact, even whites *with* criminal records received more favorable treatment (17%) than blacks *without* criminal records (14%). The rank ordering of groups in this graph is painfully revealing of employer preferences: race continues to play a dominant role in shaping employment opportunities, equal to or greater than the impact of a criminal record.

The magnitude of the race effect found here corresponds closely to those found in previous audit studies directly measuring racial discrimination.

Figure 5.2 The Effect of a Criminal Record for Black and White Job Applicants

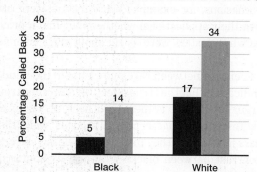

The main effects of race and criminal record are statistically significant ($p < .01$). The interaction between the two is not significant in the full sample. Black bars represent criminal record; [gray] bars represent no criminal record.

Bendick et al. (1994), for example, find that blacks were 24 percentage points less likely to receive a job offer relative to their white counterparts, a finding very close to the 20 percentage point difference (between white and black nonoffenders) found here. Thus in the eight years since the last major employment audit of race was conducted, very little has changed in the reaction of employers to minority applicants. Despite the many rhetorical arguments used to suggest that direct racial discrimination is no longer a major barrier to opportunity, as we can see here, employers, at least in Milwaukee, continue to use race as a major factor in hiring decisions.

RACIAL DIFFERENCES IN THE EFFECTS OF A CRIMINAL RECORD

The final question this study sought to answer was the degree to which the effect of a criminal record differs depending on the race of the applicant. Based on the results presented in figure [5.2], the effect of a criminal record appears more pronounced for blacks than it is for whites. While this interaction term is not statistically significant, the magnitude of the difference is nontrivial. While the ratio of callbacks for nonoffenders relative to ex-offenders for whites is 2:1, this same ratio for blacks is nearly 3:1. The effect of a criminal record is thus 40% larger for blacks than for whites.

This evidence is suggestive of the way in which associations between race and crime affect interpersonal evaluations. Employers, already reluctant to hire blacks, appear even more wary of blacks with proven criminal involvement. Despite the fact that these testers were bright articulate college students with effective styles of self-presentation, the cursory review of entry-level applicants leaves little room for these qualities to be noticed. Instead, the employment barriers of minority status and criminal record are compounded, intensifying the stigma toward this group.

The salience of employers' sensitivity toward criminal involvement among blacks was highlighted in several interactions documented by testers. On three separate occasions, for example, black testers were asked in person (before submitting their applications) whether they had a prior criminal history. None of the white testers were asked about their criminal histories up front.

The strong association between race and crime in the minds of employers provides some indication that the "true effect" of a criminal record for blacks may be even larger than what is measured here. If, for example, the outcomes for black testers *without* criminal records were deflated in part because employers feared that they may nevertheless have criminal tendencies, then the contrast between blacks with and without criminal records would be suppressed.

* * *

DISCUSSION

. . . [T]he persistent effect of race on employment opportunities is painfully clear in these results. Blacks are less than half as likely to receive consideration by employers, relative to their white counterparts, and black nonoffenders fall behind even whites with prior felony convictions. The powerful effects of race thus continue to direct employment decisions in ways that contribute to persisting racial inequality. In light of these findings, current public opinion seems largely misinformed. According to a recent survey of residents in Los Angeles, Boston, Detroit, and Atlanta, researchers found that just over a quarter of whites believe there to be "a lot" of discrimination against blacks, compared to nearly two-thirds of black respondents. Over the past decade, affirmative action has come under attack across the country based on the argument that direct racial discrimination is no longer a major barrier to opportunity. According to this study, however, employers, at least in Milwaukee, continue to use race as a major factor in their hiring decisions. When we combine the effects of race and criminal record, the problem grows more intense. Not only are blacks much more likely to be incarcerated than whites; based on the findings presented here, they may also be more strongly affected by the impact of a criminal record. Previous estimates of the aggregate consequences of incarceration may therefore underestimate the impact on racial disparities.

Finally, in terms of policy implications, this research has troubling conclusions. In our frenzy of locking people up, our "crime control" policies may in fact exacerbate the very conditions that lead to crime in the first place. Research consistently shows that finding quality steady employment is one of the strongest predictors of desistance from crime. The fact that a criminal record severely limits employment opportunities—particularly among blacks—suggests that these individuals are left with few viable alternatives.

As more and more young men enter the labor force from prison, it becomes increasingly important to consider the impact of incarceration on the job prospects of those coming out. No longer a peripheral institution, the criminal justice system has become a dominant presence in the lives of young disadvantaged men, playing a key role in the sorting and stratifying of labor market opportunities.

6

Telling the Truth about Damned Lies and Statistics

JOEL BEST

Many people feel they live in a world of information overload. Statistics are a big part of this feeling, continually thrown about to impress, sell, or convince. In many cases the statistics are not accurate, leading to distrust of all statistics. But as Joel Best explains, we need good statistics, and he shows why. Part of the "sociological imagination" is the capacity to think critically about information, including statistics, in order to answer questions and solve problems. As you read this essay, think of the last time you heard someone misuse a statistic. Better yet, think of the last time you did.

The dissertation prospectus began by quoting a statistic—a "grabber" meant to capture the reader's attention. The graduate student who wrote this prospectus undoubtedly wanted to seem scholarly to the professors who would read it; they would be supervising the proposed research. And what could be more scholarly than a nice, authoritative statistic, quoted from a professional journal in the student's field?

So the prospectus began with this (carefully footnoted) quotation: "Every year since 1950, the number of American children gunned down has doubled." I had been invited to serve on the student's dissertation committee. When I read the quotation, I assumed the student had made an error in copying it. I went to the library and looked up the article the student had cited. There, in the journal's 1995 volume, was exactly the same sentence: "Every year since 1950, the number of American children gunned down has doubled."

This quotation is my nomination for a dubious distinction: I think it may be the worst—that is, the most inaccurate—social statistic ever.

What makes this statistic so bad? Just for the sake of argument, let's assume that "the number of American children gunned down" in 1950 was one. If the number doubled each year, there must have been two children gunned down in 1951, four in 1952, eight in 1953, and so on. By 1960, the number would have been 1,024. By 1965, it would have been 32,768 (in 1965, the F.B.I. identified only 9,960 criminal homicides in the entire country, including adult as well as child victims). By 1970, the number would have passed one million; by 1980, one billion (more than four times the total U.S. population in that year). Only three years later, in 1983, the number of American children gunned down would have been 8.6 billion (nearly twice the earth's population at the time). Another milestone would have been passed in 1987, when the number of gunned-down American children (137 billion) would have surpassed the best estimates for the total human population throughout history (110 billion). By 1995, when the article was published, the annual number of victims would have been over 35 trillion—a really big number, of a magnitude you rarely encounter outside economics or astronomy.

Thus my nomination: estimating the number of American child gunshot victims in 1995 at 35 trillion must be as far off—as hilariously, wildly wrong—as a social statistic can be. (If anyone spots a more inaccurate social statistic, I'd love to hear about it.)

Where did the article's author get this statistic? I wrote the author, who responded that the statistic came from the Children's Defense Fund, a well-known advocacy group for children. The C.D.F.'s *The State of America's Children Yearbook 1994* does state: "The number of American children killed each year by guns has doubled since 1950." Note the difference in the wording—the C.D.F. claimed there were twice as many deaths in 1994 as in 1950; the article's author reworded that claim and created a very different meaning.

It is worth examining the history of this statistic. It began with the C.D.F. noting that child gunshot deaths had doubled from 1950 to 1994. This is not quite as dramatic an increase as it might seem. Remember that the U.S. population also rose throughout this period; in fact, it grew about 73 percent—or nearly double. Therefore, we might expect all sorts of things—including the number of child gunshot deaths—to increase, to nearly double, just because the population grew. Before we can decide whether twice as many deaths indicates that things are getting worse, we'd have to know more. The C.D.F. statistic raises other issues as well: Where did the statistic come from? Who counts child gunshot deaths, and how? What is meant by a "child" (some C.D.F. statistics about violence include everyone under age 25)? What is meant by "killed by guns" (gunshot-death statistics often include suicides and accidents, as well as homicides)? But people rarely ask questions of this sort when they encounter statistics. Most of the time, most people simply accept statistics without question.

Certainly, the article's author didn't ask many probing, critical questions about the C.D.F.'s claim. Impressed by the statistic, the author repeated it—well, meant to repeat it. Instead, by rewording the C.D.F.'s claim, the author created a mutant statistic, one garbled almost beyond recognition.

But people treat mutant statistics just as they do other statistics—that is, they usually accept even the most implausible claims without question. For example, the journal editor who accepted the author's article for publication did not bother to consider the implications of child victims doubling each year. And people repeat bad statistics: The graduate student copied the garbled statistic and inserted it into the dissertation prospectus. Who knows whether still other readers were impressed by the author's statistic and remembered it or repeated it? The article remains on the shelf in hundreds of libraries, available to anyone who needs a dramatic quote. The lesson should be clear: Bad statistics live on; they take on lives of their own.

Some statistics are born bad—they aren't much good from the start, because they are based on nothing more than guesses or dubious data. Other statistics mutate; they become bad after being mangled (as in the case of the author's creative rewording). Either way, bad statistics are potentially important: They can be used to stir up public outrage or fear; they can distort our understanding of our world; and they can lead us to make poor policy choices.

The notion that we need to watch out for bad statistics isn't new. We've all heard people say, "You can prove anything with statistics." The title of my book, *Damned Lies and Statistics*, comes from a famous aphorism (usually attributed to Mark Twain or Benjamin Disraeli): "There are three kinds of lies: lies, damned lies, and statistics." There is even a useful little book, still in print after more than 40 years, called *How to Lie With Statistics*.

Statistics, then, have a bad reputation. We suspect that statistics may be wrong, that people who use statistics may be "lying"—trying to manipulate us by using numbers to somehow distort the truth. Yet, at the same time, we need statistics; we depend upon them to summarize and clarify the nature of our complex society. This is particularly true when we talk about social problems. Debates about social problems routinely raise questions that demand statistical answers: Is the problem widespread? How many people—and which people—does it affect? Is it getting worse? What does it cost society? What will it cost to deal with it? Convincing answers to such questions demand evidence, and that usually means numbers, measurements, statistics.

But can't you prove anything with statistics? It depends on what "prove" means. If we want to know, say, how many children are "gunned down" each year, we can't simply guess—pluck a number from thin air: 100, 1,000, 10,000, 35 trillion, whatever. Obviously, there's no reason to consider an arbitrary guess "proof" of anything. However, it might be possible for someone—using records kept by police departments or hospital emergency rooms or coroners—to keep track of children who have been shot; compiling careful, complete records might give us a fairly accurate idea of the number of gunned-down children. If that number seems accurate enough, we might consider it very strong evidence—or proof.

The solution to the problem of bad statistics is not to ignore all statistics, or to assume that every number is false. Some statistics are bad, but others are pretty good, and we need statistics—good statistics—to talk sensibly about social problems. The solution, then, is not to give up on statistics, but to become better judges of the numbers we encounter. We need to think critically about statistics—at least critically enough to suspect that the number of children gunned down hasn't been doubling each year since 1950.

A few years ago, the mathematician John Allen Paulos wrote *Innumeracy*, a short, readable book about "mathematical illiteracy." Too few people, he argued, are comfortable with basic mathematical principles, and this makes them poor judges of the numbers they encounter. No doubt this is one reason we have so many bad statistics. But there are other reasons, as well.

Social statistics describe society, but they are also products of our social arrangements. The people who bring social statistics to our attention have reasons for doing so; they inevitably want something, just as reporters and the other media figures who repeat and publicize statistics have their own goals. Statistics are tools, used for particular purposes. Thinking critically about statistics requires understanding their place in society.

While we may be more suspicious of statistics presented by people with whom we disagree—people who favor different political parties or have different beliefs—bad statistics are used to promote all sorts of causes. Bad statistics come from conservatives on the political right and liberals on the left, from wealthy corporations and powerful government agencies, and from advocates of the poor and the powerless.

* * *

In order to interpret statistics, we need more than a checklist of common errors. We need a general approach, an orientation, a mind-set that we can use to think about new statistics that we encounter. We ought to approach statistics thoughtfully. This can be hard to do, precisely because so many people in our society treat statistics as fetishes. We might call this the mind-set of the Awestruck—the people who don't think critically, who act as though statistics have magical powers. The awestruck know they don't always understand the statistics they hear, but this doesn't bother them. After all, who can expect to understand magical numbers? The reverential fatalism of the awestruck is not thoughtful—it is a way of avoiding thought. We need a different approach.

* * *

[One] choice is to approach statistics critically. Being critical does not mean being negative or hostile—it is not cynicism. The critical approach statistics thoughtfully; they avoid the extremes of both naive acceptance and cynical rejection of the numbers they encounter. Instead, the critical attempt to evaluate numbers, to distinguish between good statistics and bad statistics.

The critical understand that, while some social statistics may be pretty good, they are never perfect. Every statistic is a way of summarizing complex information into relatively simple numbers. Inevitably, some information, some of the complexity, is lost whenever we use statistics. The critical recognize that this is an inevitable limitation of statistics. Moreover, they realize that every statistic is the product of choices—the choice between defining a category broadly or narrowly, the choice of one measurement over another, the choice of a sample. People choose definitions, measurements, and samples for all sorts of reasons: Perhaps they want to emphasize some aspect of a problem; perhaps it is easier or cheaper to gather data in a particular way—many considerations can come into play. Every statistic is a compromise among choices. This means that every definition—and every measurement and every sample—probably has limitations and can be criticized.

Being critical means more than simply pointing to the flaws in a statistic. Again, every statistic has flaws. The issue is whether a particular statistic's flaws are severe enough to damage its usefulness. . . . Similarly, how do the choices of measurements and samples affect the statistic? What would happen if different measures or samples were chosen? And how is the statistic used? Is it being interpreted appropriately, or has its meaning been mangled to create a mutant statistic? Are the comparisons that are being made appropriate, or are apples being confused with oranges? How do different choices produce the conflicting numbers found in stat wars? These are the sorts of questions the critical ask.

As a practical matter, it is virtually impossible for citizens in contemporary society to avoid statistics about social problems. Statistics arise in all sorts of ways, and in almost every case the people promoting statistics want to persuade us. Activists use statistics to convince us that social problems are serious and deserve our attention and concern. Charities use statistics to encourage donations. Politicians use statistics to persuade us that they understand society's problems and that they deserve our support. The media use statistics to make their reporting more dramatic, more convincing, more compelling. Corporations use statistics to promote and improve their products. Researchers use statistics to document their findings and support their conclusions. Those with whom we agree use statistics to reassure us that we're on the right side, while our opponents use statistics to try and convince us that we are wrong. Statistics are one of the standard types of evidence used by people in our society.

It is not possible simply to ignore statistics, to pretend they don't exist. That sort of head-in-the-sand approach would be too costly. Without statistics, we limit our ability to think thoughtfully about our society; without statistics, we have no accurate ways of judging how big a problem may be, whether it is getting worse, or how well the policies designed to address that problem actually work. And awestruck or naive attitudes toward statistics are no better than ignoring statistics; statistics have no magical properties, and it is foolish to assume that all statistics are equally valid. Nor is a cynical approach the answer; statistics are too widespread and too useful to be automatically discounted.

It would be nice to have a checklist, a set of items we could consider in evaluating any statistic. The list might detail potential problems with definitions, measurements, sampling, mutation, and so on. These are, in fact, common sorts of flaws found in many statistics, but they should not be considered a formal, complete checklist. It is probably impossible to produce a complete list of statistical flaws—no matter how long the list, there will be other possible problems that could affect statistics.

The goal is not to memorize a list, but to develop a thoughtful approach. Becoming critical about statistics requires being prepared to ask questions about numbers. When encountering a new statistic in, say, a news report, the critical try to assess it. What might be the sources for this number? How could one go about producing the figure? Who produced the number, and what interests might they have? What are the different ways key terms might have been defined, and which definitions have been chosen? How might the phenomena be measured, and which measurement choices have been made? What sort of sample was gathered, and how might that sample affect the result? Is the statistic being properly interpreted? Are comparisons being made, and if so, are the comparisons appropriate? Are there competing statistics? If so, what stakes do the opponents have in the issue, and how are those stakes likely to affect their use of statistics? And is it possible to figure out why the statistics seem to disagree, what the differences are in the ways the competing sides are using figures?

At first, this list of questions may seem overwhelming. How can an ordinary person—someone who reads a statistic in a magazine article or hears it on a news broadcast—determine the answers to such questions? Certainly news reports rarely give detailed information on the process by which statistics are created. And few of us have time to drop everything and investigate the background of some new number we encounter. Being critical, it seems, involves an impossible amount of work.

In practice, however, the critical need not investigate the origin of every statistic. Rather, being critical means appreciating the inevitable limitations that affect all statistics, rather than being awestruck in the presence of numbers. It means not being too credulous, not accepting every statistic at face value. But it also means appreciating that statistics, while always imperfect, can be useful. Instead of automatically discounting every statistic, the critical reserve judgment. When confronted with an interesting number, they may try to learn more, to evaluate, to weigh the figure's strengths and weaknesses.

Of course, this critical approach need not—and should not—be limited to statistics. It ought to apply to all the evidence we encounter when we scan a news report, or listen to a speech—whenever we learn about social problems. Claims about social problems often feature dramatic, compelling examples; the critical might ask whether an example is likely to be a typical case or an extreme, exceptional instance. Claims about social problems often include quotations from different sources, and the critical might wonder why those sources have spoken and why they have been quoted: Do they have particular expertise? Do they stand to benefit if they influence others? Claims about social problems usually involve arguments about the problem's causes and potential solutions. The critical might ask whether these arguments are convincing. Are they logical? Does the proposed solution seem feasible and appropriate? And so on. Being critical—adopting a skeptical, analytical stance when confronted with claims—is an approach that goes far beyond simply dealing with statistics.

Statistics are not magical. Nor are they always true—or always false. Nor need they be incomprehensible. Adopting a critical approach offers an effective way of responding to the numbers we are sure to encounter. Being critical requires more thought, but failing to adopt a critical mind-set makes us powerless to evaluate what others tell us. When we fail to think critically, the statistics we hear might just as well be magical.

7

Distinguishing Features of Black Feminist Thought*

FROM *Black Feminist Thought: Knowledge, Conciousness, and the Politics of Empowerment*

PATRICIA HILL COLLINS

Critical theories are part of a sociological tradition stretching back to at least the ideas of Karl Marx in the mid-nineteenth century. They are distinguished by their emphasis on social justice and social change. Black feminist thought is one of these critical theories, and as its name suggests, it focuses specifically on the ideas and experiences of women of color. However, as Patricia Hill Collins explains in this reading, black feminist thought is more than just a framework for rectifying racial and gender inequities. It provides a lens for understanding many other inequalities, including those related to social class, sexuality, and ethnicity. As you read, pay special attention to the concept of intersectionality—that is, the recognition that our lives are shaped simultaneously by our race, gender, and other social identities. Also observe the importance Collins places on the relationship between social thought and social action, as this is at the heart of critical theories in sociology.

I am a product of an intellectual tradition which until twenty-five years ago did not exist within the academy. Like patchwork in a quilt, it is a tradition gathered from meaningful bits and pieces. My tradition has no name, because it embraces more than womanism, Blackness, or African studies, although those terms will do for now.

—Barbara Omolade 1994, ix

It seems I am running out of words these days. I feel as if I am on a linguistic treadmill that has gradually but unmistakably increased its speed, so that no word I use to positively describe myself or my scholarly projects lasts for more than five seconds. I can no longer justify my presence in academia, for example, with words that exist in the English language. The moment I find some symbol of my presence in the rarefied halls of elite institutions, it gets stolen, co-opted, filled with negative meaning.

—Patricia Williams 1995, 27

---

*References and footnotes can be found in Chapter 2 of the author's *Black Feminist Thought* (Routledge, 2000). [*Editors' note*]

U.S. Black women's struggles on this "linguistic treadmill" to name this tradition with "no name" reveal the difficulties of making do with "terms [that] will do for now." Widely used yet increasingly difficult to define, U.S. Black feminist thought encompasses diverse and often contradictory meanings. Despite the fact that U.S. Black women, in particular, have expended considerable energy on naming Black women's knowledge, definitional tensions not only persist but encounter changing political climates riddled with new obstacles. When the very vocabulary used to describe Black feminist thought comes under attack, Black women's self-definitions become even more difficult to achieve. For example, despite continued acceptance among many African-Americans of Afrocentrism as a term referencing traditions of Black consciousness and racial solidarity, academics and media pundits maligned the term in the 1980s and 1990s. Similarly, the pejorative meanings increasingly attached to the term feminist seem designed to discredit a movement dedicated to women's empowerment. Even the term *Black* fell victim to the deconstructive moment, with a growing number of "Black" intellectuals who do "race" scholarship questioning the very terms used to describe both themselves and their political struggles. Collectively, these developments produced a greatly changed political and intellectual context for defining Black feminist thought.

Despite these difficulties, finding some sort of common ground for thinking through the boundaries of Black feminist thought remains important because, as U.S. Black feminist activist Pearl Cleage reminds us, "we have to see clearly that we are a unique group, set undeniably apart because of race and sex with a unique set of challenges." Rather than developing definitions and arguing over naming practices—for example, whether this thought should be called Black feminism, womanism, Afrocentric feminism, Africana womanism, and the like—a more useful approach lies in revisiting the reasons why Black feminist thought exists at all. Exploring six distinguishing features that characterize Black feminist thought may provide the common ground that is so sorely needed both among African-American women, and between African-American women and all others whose collective knowledge or thought has a similar purpose. Black feminist thought's distinguishing features need not be unique and may share much with other bodies of knowledge. Rather, it is the *convergence* of these distinguishing features that gives U.S. Black feminist thought its distinctive contours.

WHY U.S. BLACK FEMINIST THOUGHT?

Black feminism remains important because U.S. Black women constitute an oppressed group. As a collectivity, U.S. Black women participate in a *dialectical* relationship linking African-American women's oppression and activism. Dialectical relationships of this sort mean that two parties are opposed and opposite. As long as Black women's subordination within intersecting oppressions of race, class, gender, sexuality, and nation persists, Black feminism as an activist response to that oppression will remain needed.

In a similar fashion, the overarching purpose of U.S. Black feminist thought is also to resist oppression, both its practices and the ideas that justify it. If intersecting oppressions did not exist, Black feminist thought and similar oppositional knowledges would be unnecessary. As a critical social theory, Black feminist thought aims to empower African-American women within the context of social injustice sustained by intersecting oppressions. Since Black women cannot be fully empowered unless intersecting oppressions themselves are eliminated, Black feminist thought supports broad principles of social justice that transcend U.S. Black women's particular needs.

Because so much of U.S. Black feminism has been filtered through the prism of the U.S. context, its contours have been greatly affected by the specificity of American multiculturalism. In particular, U.S. Black feminist thought and practice respond to a fundamental contradiction of U.S. society. On the one hand, democratic promises of individual freedom, equality under the law, and social justice are made to all American citizens. Yet on the other hand, the reality of differential group treatment based on race, class, gender, sexuality, and citizenship status persists. Groups organized around race, class, and gender in and of themselves are not inherently a problem. However, when African-Americans, poor people, women, and other groups discriminated against see little hope for group-based advancement, this situation constitutes social injustice.

Within this overarching contradiction, U.S. Black women encounter a distinctive set of social practices that accompany our particular history within a unique matrix of domination characterized by intersecting oppressions. Race is far from being the only significant marker of group difference—class, gender, sexuality, religion, and citizenship status all matter greatly in the United States. Yet for African-American women, the effects of institutionalized racism remain visible and palpable. Moreover, the institutionalized racism that African-American women encounter relies heavily on racial segregation and accompanying discriminatory practices designed to deny U.S. Blacks equitable treatment. Despite important strides to desegregate U.S. society since 1970, racial segregation remains deeply entrenched in housing, schooling, and employment. For many African-American women, racism is not something that exists in the distance. We encounter racism in everyday situations in workplaces, stores, schools, housing, and daily social interaction. Most Black women do not have the opportunity to befriend White women and men as neighbors, nor do their children attend school with White children. Racial segregation remains a fundamental feature of the U.S. social landscape, leaving many African-Americans with the belief that "the more things change, the more they stay the same." Overlaying these persisting inequalities is a rhetoric of color blindness designed to render these social inequalities invisible. In a context where many believe that to talk of race fosters racism, equality allegedly lies in treating everyone the same. Yet as Kimberle Crenshaw (1997) points out, "it is fairly obvious that treating different things the same can generate as much inequality as treating the same things differently" (p. 285).

* * *

Historically, Black women's group location in intersecting oppressions produced commonalities among individual African-American women. At the same time, while common experiences may predispose Black women to develop a distinctive group consciousness, they guarantee neither that such a consciousness will develop among all women nor that it will be articulated as such by the group. As historical conditions change, so do the links among the types of experiences Black women will have and any ensuing group consciousness concerning those experiences. Because group standpoints are situated in, reflect, and help shape unjust power relations, standpoints are not static. Thus, common challenges may foster similar angles of vision leading to a group knowledge or standpoint among African-American women. Or they may not.

DIVERSE RESPONSES TO COMMON CHALLENGES WITHIN BLACK FEMINISM

A second distinguishing feature of U.S. Black feminist thought emerges from a tension linking experiences and ideas. On the one hand, all African-American women face similar challenges that result from living in a society that historically and routinely derogates women of African descent. Despite the fact that U.S. Black women face common challenges, this neither means that individual African-American women have all had the same experiences nor that we agree on the significance of our varying experiences. Thus, on the other hand, despite the common challenges confronting U.S. Black women as a group, diverse responses to these core themes characterize U.S. Black women's group knowledge or standpoint.

Despite differences of age, sexual orientation, social class, region, and religion, U.S. Black women encounter societal practices that restrict us to inferior housing, neighborhoods, schools, jobs, and public treatment and hide this differential consideration behind an array of common beliefs about Black women's intelligence, work habits, and sexuality. These common challenges in turn result in recurring patterns of experiences for individual group members. For example, African-American women from quite diverse backgrounds report similar treatment in stores. Not every *individual* Black woman consumer need experience being followed in a store as a potential shoplifter, ignored while others are waited on first, or seated near restaurant kitchens and rest rooms, for African-American women as a collectivity to recognize that differential *group* treatment is operating.

Since standpoints refer to group knowledge, recurring patterns of differential treatment such as these suggest that certain themes will characterize U.S. Black women's group knowledge or standpoint. For example, one core theme concerns multifaceted legacies of struggle, especially in response to forms of violence that accompany intersecting oppressions. Katie Cannon observes, "[T]hroughout the history of the United States, the interrelationship of white supremacy and male superiority has characterized the Black woman's reality as a situation of struggle—a struggle to survive in two contradictory worlds simultaneously, one white, privileged, and oppressive, the other black, exploited, and oppressed" (1985, 30). Black women's vulnerability to assaults in the workplace, on the street, at home, and in media representations has been one factor fostering this legacy of struggle.

* * *

Despite the common challenges confronting African-American women as a group, individual Black women neither have identical experiences nor interpret experiences in a similar fashion. The existence of core themes does not mean that African-American women respond to these themes in the same way. Differences among individual Black women produce different patterns of experiential knowledge that in turn shape individual reactions to the core themes. For example, when faced with controlling images of Black women as being ugly and unfeminine, some women—such as Sojourner Truth—demand, "Ain't I a woman?" By deconstructing the conceptual apparatus of the dominant group, they challenge notions of Barbie-doll femininity premised on middle-class White women's experiences. In contrast, other women internalize the controlling images and come to believe that they are the stereotypes. Still others aim to transgress the boundaries that frame the images themselves. Jaminica, a 14-year-old Black girl, describes her strategies: "Unless you want to get into a big activist battle, you accept the stereotypes given to you and just try and reshape them along the way. So in a way, this gives me a lot of freedom. I can't be looked at any worse in society than I already am—black and female is pretty high on the list of things not to be".

Many factors explain these diverse responses. For example, although all African-American women encounter institutionalized racism, social class differences among African-American women influence patterns of racism in housing, education, and employment. Middle-class Blacks are more likely to encounter a pernicious form of racism that has left many angry and disappointed. A young manager who graduated with honors from the University of Maryland describes the specific form racism can take for middle-class Blacks. Before she flew to Cleveland to explain a marketing plan for her company, her manager made her go over it three or four times in front of him so that she would not forget *her* marketing plan. Then he explained how to check luggage at an airport and how to reclaim it. "I just sat at lunch listening to this man talking to me like I was a monkey who could remember but couldn't think," she recalled. When she had had enough, "I asked him if he wanted to tie my money up in a handkerchief and put a note on me saying that I was an employee of this company. In case I got lost I would be picked up by Traveler's Aid, and Traveler's Aid would send me back" (Davis and Watson 1985, 86). Most middle-class Black women do not encounter such blatant incidents, but many working-class Blacks do. Historically, working-class Blacks have struggled with forms of institutionalized racism directly organized by White institutions and by forms mediated by some segments of the Black middle class. Thus, while it shares much with middle-class Black women, the legacy of struggle by working-class Blacks and by working-class Black women in particular will express a distinctive character.

Sexuality signals another important factor that influences African-American women's varying responses to common challenges. Black lesbians have identified heterosexism as a form of oppression and the issues they face living in homophobic communities as shaping their interpretations of everyday events. Beverly Smith describes how being a lesbian affected her perceptions of the wedding of one of her closest friends: "God, I wish I had one friend here. Someone who knew me and would understand how I feel. I am masquerading as a nice, straight, middle-class Black 'girl'" (1983, 172). While the majority of those attending the wedding saw only a festive event, Beverly Smith felt that her friend was being sent into a form of bondage. In a similar fashion, varying ethnic and citizenship statuses within the U.S. nation-state as well also shape differences among Black women in the United States. For example, Black Puerto Ricans constitute a group that combines categories of race, nationality, and ethnicity in distinctive ways. Black Puerto Rican women thus must negotiate a distinctive set of experiences that accrue to being racially Black, holding a special form of American citizenship, and being ethnically Latino.

Given how these factors influence diverse responses to common challenges, it is important to stress that no homogeneous Black *woman's* standpoint exists. There is no essential or archetypal Black woman whose experiences stand as normal, normative, and thereby authentic. An essentialist understanding of a Black woman's standpoint suppresses differences among Black women in search of an elusive group unity. Instead, it may be more accurate to say that a Black *women's* collective standpoint does exist, one characterized by the tensions that accrue to different responses to common challenges. Because it both recognizes and aims to incorporate heterogeneity in crafting Black women's oppositional knowledge, this Black *women's* standpoint eschews essentialism in favor of democracy. Since Black feminist thought both arises within and aims to articulate a Black *women's* group standpoint regarding experiences associated with intersecting oppressions, stressing this group standpoint's heterogeneous composition is significant.

* * *

BLACK FEMINIST PRACTICE AND BLACK FEMINIST THOUGHT

A third distinguishing feature of Black feminist thought concerns the connections between U.S. Black women's experiences as a heterogeneous collectivity and any ensuing group knowledge or standpoint. One key reason that standpoints of oppressed groups are suppressed is that self-defined standpoints can stimulate resistance. Annie Adams, a Southern Black woman, describes how she became involved in civil rights activities:

> When I first went into the mill we had segregated water fountains. . . . Same thing about the toilets. I had to clean the toilets for the inspection room and then, when I got ready to go to the bathroom, I had to go all the way to the bottom of the stairs to the cellar. So I asked my boss man, "what's the difference? If I can go in there and clean them toilets, why can't I use them?" Finally, I started to use that toilet, I decided I wasn't going to walk a mile to go to the bathroom. (Byerly 1986, 134)

In this case Ms. Adams found the "boss man's" point of view inadequate, developed one of her own, and acted on it. On the individual level, her actions illustrate the connections among lived experiences with oppression, developing one's own point of view concerning those experiences, and the acts of resistance that can follow. A similar relationship characterizes African-American women's group knowledge. U.S. Black women's collective historical experiences with oppression may stimulate a self-defined Black women's standpoint that in turn can foster Black women's activism.

As members of an oppressed group, U.S. Black women have generated alternative practices and knowledges that have been designed to foster U.S. Black women's group empowerment. In contrast to the dialectical relationship linking oppression and activism, a *dialogical* relationship characterizes Black women's collective experiences and group knowledge. On both the individual and the group level, a dialogical relationship suggests that changes in thinking may be accompanied by changed actions and that altered experiences may in turn stimulate a changed consciousness. For U.S. Black women as a collectivity, the struggle for a self-defined Black feminism occurs through an ongoing dialogue whereby action and thought inform one another.

U.S. Black feminism itself illustrates this dialogical relationship. On the one hand, there is U.S. Black feminist practice that emerges in the context of lived experience. When organized and visible, such practice has taken the form of overtly Black feminist social movements dedicated to the empowerment of U.S. Black women. Two especially prominent moments characterize Black feminism's visibility. Providing many of the guiding ideas for today, the first occurred at the turn of the century via the Black women's club movement. The second or modern Black feminist movement was stimulated by the antiracist and women's social justice movements of the 1960s and 1970s and continues to the present. However, these periods of overt political activism where African-American women lobbied in our own behalf remain unusual. They appear to be unusual when juxtaposed to more typical patterns of quiescence regarding Black women's advocacy.

*　*　*

When it comes to the dialogical relationship within U.S. Black feminism, on the other hand, there is U.S. Black feminist thought as a critical social theory. Critical social theory constitutes theorizing about the social in defense of economic and social justice. As critical social theory, Black feminist thought encompasses bodies of knowledge and sets of institutional practices that actively grapple with the central questions facing U.S. Black women as a group. Such theory recognizes that U.S. Black women constitute one group among many that are differently placed within situations of injustice. What makes critical social theory "critical" is its commitment to justice, for one's own group and for other groups.

Within these parameters, knowledge for knowledge's sake is not enough—Black feminist thought must both be tied to Black women's lived experiences and aim to better those experiences in some fashion. When such thought is sufficiently grounded in Black feminist practice, it reflects this dialogical relationship. Black feminist thought encompasses general knowledge that helps U.S. Black women survive in, cope with, and resist our differential treatment. It also includes more specialized knowledge that investigates the specific themes and challenges of any given period of time. Conversely, when U.S. Black women cannot see the connections among themes that permeate Black feminist thought and those that influence Black women's everyday lives, it is appropriate to question the strength of this dialogical relationship. Moreover, it is also reasonable to question the validity of that particular expression of Black feminist thought. For example, during slavery, a special theme within Black feminist thought was how the institutionalized rape of enslaved Black women operated as a mechanism of social control. During the period when Black women worked primarily in agriculture and service, countering the sexual harassment of live-in domestic workers gained special importance. Clear connections could be drawn between the content and purpose of Black feminist thought and important issues in Black women's lives.

*　*　*

DIALOGICAL PRACTICES AND BLACK WOMEN INTELLECTUALS

A fourth distinguishing feature of Black feminist thought concerns the essential contributions of African-American women intellectuals. The existence of a Black women's standpoint does not mean that African-American women, academic or otherwise, appreciate its content, see its significance, or recognize its potential as a catalyst for social change. One key task for Black women intellectuals of diverse ages, social classes, educational backgrounds, and occupations consists of asking the right questions and investigating all dimensions of a Black women's standpoint with and for African-American women. Historically, Black women intellectuals stood in a special relationship to the larger community of African-American women, a relationship that framed Black feminist thought's contours as critical social theory. Whether this relationship will persist depends, ironically, on Black women intellectuals' ability to analyze their own social locations.

Very different kinds of "thought" and "theories" emerge when abstract thought is joined with pragmatic action. Denied positions as scholars and writers which allow us to emphasize purely theoretical concerns, the work of most Black women intellectuals has been influenced by the merger of action and theory. The activities of nineteenth-century educated Black women intellectuals such as Anna J. Cooper, Frances Ellen Watkins Harper, Ida B. Wells-Barnett, and Mary Church Terrell exemplify this tradition of merging intellectual work and activism. These women both analyzed the intersecting oppressions that circumscribed Black women's lives and worked for social justice. The Black women's club movement they created was both an activist and an intellectual endeavor. Working-class Black women also engaged in a parallel joining of ideas and activism. But because they were denied formal educations, the form of their activism as well as the content of the ideas they developed differed from those of middle-class Black women. The live performances of classic Black women blues singers in the 1920s can be seen as one important arena where working-class women gathered and shared ideas especially germane to them.

Many contemporary Black women intellectuals continue to draw on this tradition of using everyday actions and experiences in our theoretical work. Black feminist historian Elsa Barkley Brown describes the importance her mother's ideas played in the scholarship she eventually produced on African-American washerwomen. Initially Brown used the lens provided by her training as a historian and saw her sample group as devalued service workers. But over time she came to understand washerwomen as entrepreneurs. By taking the laundry to whoever had the largest kitchen, they created a community and a culture among themselves. In explaining the shift of vision that enabled her to reassess this portion of Black women's history, Brown notes, "It was my mother who taught me how to ask the right questions—and all of us who try to do this thing called scholarship on a regular basis are fully aware that asking the right questions is the most important part of the process" (1986, 14).

This special relationship of Black women intellectuals to the community of African-American women parallels the existence of two interrelated levels of knowledge. The commonplace, taken-for-granted knowledge shared by

African-American women growing from our everyday thoughts and actions constitutes a first and most fundamental level of knowledge. The ideas that Black women share with one another on an informal, daily basis about topics such as how to style our hair, characteristics of "good" Black men, strategies for dealing with White folks, and skills of how to "get over" provide the foundations for this taken-for-granted knowledge.

Experts or specialists who participate in and emerge from a group produce a second, more specialized type of knowledge. Whether working-class or middle-class, educated or not, famous or everyday, the range of Black women intellectuals are examples of these specialists. Their theories that facilitate the expression of a Black women's standpoint form the specialized knowledge of Black feminist thought. The two types of knowledge are interdependent. While Black feminist thought articulates the often taken-for-granted knowledge shared by African-American women as a group, the consciousness of Black women may be transformed by such thought. Many Black women blues singers have long sung about taken-for-granted situations that affect U.S. Black women. Through their music, they not only depict Black women's realities, they aim to shape them.

* * *

By advocating, refining, and disseminating Black feminist thought, individuals from other groups who are engaged in similar social justice projects— Black men, African women, White men, Latinas, White women, and members of other U.S. racial/ethnic groups, for example—can identify points of connection that further social justice projects. Very often, however, engaging in the type of coalition envisioned here requires that individuals become "traitors" to the privileges that their race, class, gender, sexuality, or citizenship status provide them. For example, in *Memoir of a Race Traitor*, Mab Segrest (1994) writes of how coming to terms with her lesbian identity spurred her recognition of how her Whiteness gave her unearned privileges. Unlike most U.S. White women, Segrest turned her back on this privilege, embraced her new identity as a "race traitor," and came to see her role as confronting social injustice. Similarly, sociologist Joe Feagin's antiracist scholarship exemplifies a similar rejection of the unearned privileges of Whiteness. Feagin chooses to use benefits that may accrue to him as a White male to engage in collaborative scholarship with Black men and with Black women. While many might see Segrest and Feagin as "race traitors," their intellectual work illustrates how coalition building that advances Black feminist thought might operate.

Just as African-American women who aim to advance Black feminism as a social justice project can support other social justice projects—U.S. Black women who are respectful of the importance of Latina autonomy to Latina social justice projects can study, learn from, research, and teach about Latinas if they do so in non-exploitative ways—so can others approach Black feminist thought in a similar fashion. Thus, U.S. Black feminist thought fully actualized is a collaborative enterprise. It must be open to coalition building with individuals engaged in similar social justice projects.

* * *

BLACK FEMINISM AS DYNAMIC AND CHANGING

A fifth distinguishing feature of U.S. Black feminist thought concerns the significance of change. In order for Black feminist thought to operate effectively within Black feminism as a social justice project, both must remain dynamic. Neither Black feminist thought as a critical social theory nor Black feminist practice can be static; as social conditions change, so must the knowledge and practices designed to resist them. For example, stressing the importance of Black women's centrality to Black feminist thought does not mean that all African-American women desire, are positioned, or are qualified to exert this type of intellectual leadership. Under current conditions, some Black women thinkers have lost contact with Black feminist practice. Conversely, the changed social conditions under which U.S. Black women now come to womanhood—class-segregated neighborhoods, some integrated, far more not—place Black women of different social classes in entirely new relationships with one another.

* * *

The changing social conditions that confront African-American women stimulate the need for new Black feminist analyses of the common differences that characterize U.S. Black womanhood. Some Black women thinkers are already engaged in this process. Take, for example, Barbara Omolade's (1994) insightful analysis of Black women's historical and contemporary participation in mammy work. Most can understand mammy work's historical context, one where Black women were confined to domestic service, with Aunt Jemima created as a controlling image designed to hide Black women's exploitation. Understanding the limitations of domestic service, much of Black women's progress in the labor market has been measured by the move out of domestic service. Currently, few U.S. Black women work in domestic service in private homes. Instead, a good deal of this work in private homes is now done by undocumented immigrant women of color who lack U.S. citizenship; their exploitation resembles that long visited upon African-American women. But, as Omolade points out, these changes do not mean that U.S. Black women have escaped mammy work. Even though few Aunt Jemimas exist today, and those that do have been cosmetically altered, leading to the impression that mammy work has disappeared, Omolade reminds us that mammy work has assumed new forms. Within each segment of the labor market—the low-paid jobs at fast-food establishments, nursing homes, day-care centers, and dry cleaners that characterize the secondary sector, the secretaries and clerical workers of the primary lower tier sector, or the teachers, social workers, nurses, and administrators of the primary upper tier sector—U.S. Black women still do a remarkable share of the emotional nurturing and cleaning up after other people, often for lower pay. In this context, the task for contemporary Black feminist thought lies in explicating these changing relationships and developing analyses of how these commonalities are experienced differently.

The changing conditions of Black women's work overall has important implications for Black women's intellectual work. Historically, the suppression of Black feminist thought has meant that Black women intellectuals have traditionally relied on alternative institutional locations to produce specialized knowledge about a Black women's standpoint. Many Black women scholars, writers, and artists have worked either alone, as was the case with Maria W. Stewart, or within African-American community organizations, the case for Black women in the club movement and in Black churches. The grudging incorporation of work on Black women into curricular offerings of historically White colleges and universities, coupled with the creation of a critical mass of African-American women writers such as Toni Morrison, Alice Walker, and Gloria Naylor within these institutional locations, means that Black women intellectuals can now find employment within academia. Black women's history and Black feminist literary criticism constitute two focal points of this renaissance in Black women's intellectual work. Moreover, U.S. Black women's access to the media remains unprecedented, as talk show hostess Oprah Winfrey's long-running television show and forays into film production suggest.

The visibility provided U.S. Black women and our ideas via these new institutional locations has been immense. However, one danger facing African-American women intellectuals working in these new locations concerns the potential isolation of individual thinkers from Black women's collective experiences—lack of access to other U.S. Black women and to Black women's communities. Another is the pressure to separate thought from action—particularly political activism—that typically accompanies training in standard academic disciplines or participating in allegedly neutral spheres like the "free" press. Yet another involves the inability of some Black women "superstars" to critique the terms of their own participation in these new relations. Blinded by their self-proclaimed Black feminist diva aspirations, they feel that they owe no one, especially other Black women. Instead, they become trapped within their own impoverished Black feminist universes. Despite these dangers, these new institutional locations provide a multitude of opportunities for enhancing Black feminist thought's visibility. In this new context, the challenge lies in remaining dynamic, all the while keeping in mind that a moving target is more difficult to hit.

U.S. BLACK FEMINISM AND OTHER SOCIAL JUSTICE PROJECTS

A final distinguishing feature of Black feminist thought concerns its relationship to other projects for social justice. A broad range of African-American women intellectuals have advanced the view that Black women's struggles are part of a wider struggle for human dignity, empowerment, and social justice. In an 1893 speech to women, Anna Julia Cooper cogently expressed this worldview:

> We take our stand on the solidarity of humanity, the oneness of life, and the unnaturalness and injustice of all special favoritisms, whether of sex, race, country, or condition.... The colored woman feels that woman's cause is one and universal; and that ... not till race, color, sex, and condition are seen as accidents, and not the substance of life; not till the universal title of humanity to life, liberty, and the pursuit of happiness is conceded to be inalienable to all; not till then is woman's lesson taught and woman's cause won—not the white woman's nor the black woman's, not the red woman's but the cause of every man and of every woman who has writhed silently under a mighty wrong. (Loewenberg and Bogin 1976, 330–31)

Like Cooper, many African-American women intellectuals embrace this perspective regardless of particular political solutions we propose, our educational backgrounds, our fields of study, or our historical periods. Whether we advocate working through autonomous Black women's organizations, becoming part of women's organizations, running for political office, or supporting Black community institutions. African-American women intellectuals repeatedly identify political actions such as these as a *means* for human empowerment rather than ends in and of themselves. Thus one important guiding principle of Black feminism is a recurring humanist vision.

* * *

This humanist orientation within U.S. Black feminism also resembles similar stances taken with Black diasporic feminisms. Ama Ata Aidoo, a former minister of education in Ghana and author of novels, poetry, and short stories, describes the inclusive nature of her political philosophy:

> When people ask me rather bluntly every now and then whether I am a feminist, I not only answer yes, but I go on to insist that every woman and every man should be a feminist—especially if they believe that Africans should take charge of African land, African wealth, African lives, and the burden of African development. It is not possible to advocate independence for the African continent without also believing that African women must have the best that the environment can offer. For some of us, this is the crucial element in our feminism.

Aidoo recognizes that neither African nor U.S. Black women nor any other group will ever be empowered in situations of social injustice. Social justice projects are not either/or endeavors where one can say, "We have our movement and you have yours—our movements have nothing to do with one another." Instead, such projects counsel, "We have our movement, and we support yours." In a context of intersecting oppressions. Black feminism requires searching for justice not only for U.S. Black women, but for everyone.

REFERENCES

Aidoo, Ama Ata. 1991. *Changes: A Love Story.* New York: Feminist Press.

Brown, Cynthia Stokes, ed. 1986. *Ready from Within: Septima Clark and the Civil Rights Movement.* Navarro, CA: Wild Trees Press.

Byerly, Victoria. 1986. *Hard Times Cotton Mills Girls.* Ithaca, NY: Cornell University Press.

Cannon, Katie G. 1985. "The Emergence of a Black Feminist Consciousness." In *Feminist Interpretations of the Bible*, ed. Letty M. Russell, 30–40. Philadelphia: Westminster Press.

Crenshaw, Kimberle Williams. 1997. "Color Blindness, History, and the Law." In *The House That Race Built*, ed. Wahneema Lubiano, 280–88. New York: Pantheon.

Davis, George, and Glegg Watson. 1985. *Black Life in Corporate America.* New York: Anchor.

Loewenberg, Bert J., and Ruth Bogin, eds. 1976. *Black Women in Nineteenth-Century American Life.* University Park: Pennsylvania State University Press.

Omolade, Barbara. 1994. *The Rising Song of African American Women.* New York: Routledge.

Segrest, Mab. 1994. *Memoir of a Race Traitor.* Boston: South End Press.

Smith, Beverly. 1983. "The Wedding." In *Home Girls: A Black Feminist Anthology*, ed. Barbara Smith, 171–76. New York: Kitchen Table Press.

Williams, Patricia J. 1995. *The Rooster's Egg: On the Persistence of Prejudice.* Cambridge, MA: Harvard University Press.

8

Racism and Research:
The Case of the Tuskegee Syphilis Study

ALLAN M. BRANDT

Was it scientific zeal and the search for medical knowledge? Or was it a callous disregard for the lives and suffering of persons thought to be inferior in a racist society? Probably both, and the lessons remain important for everyone. This tragic study has become a classic example of how to do unethical research. Perhaps the lessons to be learned from it can somehow begin to make amends for the harm it did.

In 1932 the U.S. Public Health Service (USPHS) initiated an experiment in Macon County, Alabama, to determine the natural course of untreated, latent syphilis in black males. The test comprised 400 syphilitic men, as well as 200 uninfected men who served as controls. The first published report of the study appeared in 1936 with subsequent papers issued every four to six years, through the 1960s. When penicillin became widely available by the early 1950s as the preferred treatment for syphilis, the men did not receive therapy. In fact on several occasions, the USPHS actually sought to prevent treatment. Moreover, a committee at the federally operated Center for Disease Control decided in 1969 that the study should be continued. Only in 1972, when accounts of the study first appeared in the national press, did the Department of Health, Education, and Welfare halt the experiment. At that time seventy-four of the test subjects were still alive; at least twenty-eight, but perhaps more than 100, had died directly from advanced syphilitic lesions. In August 1972, HEW appointed an investigatory panel, which issued a report the following year. The panel found the study to have been "ethically unjustified," and argued that penicillin should have been provided to the men.

This article attempts to place the Tuskegee Study in a historical context and to assess its ethical implications. Despite the media attention which the study received, the HEW *Final Report*, and the criticism expressed by several professional organizations, the experiment has been largely misunderstood. The most basic questions of *how* the study was undertaken in the first place and *why* it continued for forty years were never addressed by the HEW investigation. Moreover, the panel misconstrued the nature of the experiment, failing to consult important documents available at the National Archives which bear significantly on its ethical assessment. Only by examining the specific ways in which values are engaged in scientific research can the study be understood.

RACISM AND MEDICAL OPINION

A brief review of the prevailing scientific thought regarding race and heredity in the early twentieth century is fundamental for an understanding of the Tuskegee Study. By the turn of the century, Darwinism had provided a new rationale for American racism. Essentially primitive peoples, it was argued, could not be assimilated into a complex, white civilization. Scientists speculated that in the struggle for survival the Negro in America was doomed. Particularly prone to disease, vice, and crime, black Americans could not be helped by education or philanthropy. Social Darwinists analyzed census data to predict the virtual extinction of the Negro in the twentieth century, for they believed the Negro race in America was in the throes of a degenerative evolutionary process.⌋

The medical profession supported these findings of late nineteenth- and early twentieth-century anthropologists, ethnologists, and biologists. Physicians studying the effects of emancipation on health concluded almost universally that freedom had caused the mental, moral, and physical deterioration of the black population. They substantiated this argument by citing examples in the comparative anatomy of the black and white races. As Dr. W. T. English wrote: "A careful inspection reveals the body of the negro a mass of minor defects and imperfections from the crown of the head to the soles of the feet. . . ." Cranial structures, wide nasal apertures, receding chins, projecting jaws, all typed the Negro as the lowest species in the Darwinian hierarchy.

Interest in racial differences centered on the sexual nature of blacks. The Negro, doctors explained, possessed an excessive sexual desire, which threatened the very foundations of white society. As one physician noted in the *Journal of the American Medical Association*, "The negro springs from a southern race, and as such his sexual appetite is strong; all of his environments stimulate this appetite, and as a general rule his emotional type of religion certainly does not decrease it." Doctors reported a complete lack of morality on the part of blacks:

> Virtue in the negro race is like angels' visits—few and far between. In a practice of sixteen years I have never examined a virgin negro over fourteen years of age.

A particularly ominous feature of this overzealous sexuality, doctors argued, was the black males' desire for white women. "A perversion from which most races are exempt," wrote Dr. English, "prompts the negro's inclination towards white women, whereas other races incline towards females of their own." Though English estimated the "gray matter of the negro brain" to be at least a thousand years behind that of the white races, his genital organs were overdeveloped. As Dr. William Lee Howard noted:

> The attacks on defenseless white women are evidences of racial instincts that are about as amenable to ethical culture as is the inherent odor of the race. . . .

When education will reduce the size of the negro's penis as well as bring about the sensitiveness of the terminal fibers which exist in the Caucasian, then will it also be able to prevent the African's birth-right to sexual madness and excess.

One southern medical journal proposed "Castration Instead of Lynching," as retribution for black sexual crimes. "An impressive trial by a ghost-like kuklux klan [sic] and a 'ghost' physician or surgeon to perform the operation would make it an event the 'patient' would never forget," noted the editorial.

According to these physicians, lust and immorality, unstable families, and reversion to barbaric tendencies made blacks especially prone to venereal diseases. One doctor estimated that over 50 percent of all Negroes over the age of twenty-five were syphilitic. Virtually free of disease as slaves, they were now overwhelmed by it, according to informed medical opinion. Moreover, doctors believed that treatment for venereal disease among blacks was impossible, particularly because in its latent stage the symptoms of syphilis become quiescent. As Dr. Thomas W. Murrell wrote:

> They come for treatment at the beginning and at the end. When there are visible manifestations or when harried by pain, they readily come, for as a race they are not averse to physic; but tell them not, though they look well and feel well, that they are still diseased. Here ignorance rates science a fool . . .

Even the best-educated black, according to Murrell, could not be convinced to seek treatment for syphilis. Venereal disease, according to some doctors, threatened the future of the race. The medical profession attributed the low birth rate among blacks to the high prevalence of venereal disease, which caused stillbirths and miscarriages. Moreover, the high rates of syphilis were thought to lead to increased insanity and crime. One doctor writing at the turn of the century estimated that the number of insane Negroes had increased thirteenfold since the end of the Civil War. Dr. Murrell's conclusion echoed the most informed anthropological and ethnological data:

> So the scourge sweeps among them. Those that are treated are only half cured, and the effort to assimilate a complex civilization driving their diseased minds until the results are criminal records. Perhaps here, in conjunction with tuberculosis, will be the end of the negro problem. Disease will accomplish what man cannot do.

This particular configuration of ideas formed the core of medical opinion concerning blacks, sex, and disease in the early twentieth century. Doctors generally discounted socioeconomic explanations of the state of black health, arguing that better medical care could not alter the evolutionary scheme. These assumptions provide the backdrop for examining the Tuskegee Syphilis Study.

THE ORIGINS OF THE EXPERIMENT

In 1929, under a grant from the Julius Rosenwald Fund, the USPHS conducted studies in the rural South to determine the prevalence of syphilis among blacks and explore possibilities for mass treatment. The USPHS found Macon County, Alabama, in which the town of Tuskegee is located, to have the highest syphilis rate of the six counties surveyed. The Rosenwald Study concluded that mass treatment could be successfully implemented among rural blacks. Although it is doubtful that the necessary funds would have been allocated even in the best economic conditions, after the economy collapsed in 1929, the findings were ignored. It is, however, ironic that the Tuskegee Study came to be based on findings of the Rosenwald Study that demonstrated the possibilities of mass treatment.

Three years later, in 1932, Dr. Taliaferro Clark, Chief of the USPHS Venereal Disease Division and author of the Rosenwald Study report, decided that conditions in Macon County merited renewed attention. Clark believed the high prevalence of syphilis offered an "unusual opportunity" for observation. From its inception, the USPHS regarded the Tuskegee Study as a classic "study in nature,"[1] rather than an experiment. As long as syphilis was so prevalent in Macon and most of the blacks went untreated throughout life, it seemed only natural to Clark that it would be valuable to observe the consequences. He described it as a "ready-made situation." Surgeon General H. S. Cumming wrote to R. R. Moton, Director of the Tuskegee Institute:

> The recent syphilis control demonstration carried out in Macon County, with the financial assistance of the Julius Rosenwald Fund, revealed the presence of an unusually high rate in this county and, what is more remarkable, the fact that 99 percent of this group was entirely without previous treatment. This combination, together with the expected cooperation of your hospital, offers an unparalleled opportunity for carrying on this piece of scientific research which probably cannot be duplicated anywhere else in the world.

Although no formal protocol appears to have been written, several letters of Clark and Cumming suggest what the USPHS hoped to find. Clark indicated that it would be important to see how disease affected the daily lives of the men:

---

1. In 1865, Claude Bernard, the famous French physiologist, outlined the distinction between a "study in nature" and experimentation. A study in nature required simple observation, an essentially passive act, while experimentation demanded intervention which altered the original condition. The Tuskegee Study was thus clearly not a study in nature. The very act of diagnosis altered the original conditions. "It is on this very possibility of acting or not acting on a body," wrote Bernard, "that the distinction will exclusively rest between sciences called sciences of observation and sciences called experimental."

The results of these studies of case records suggest the desirability of making a further study of the effect of untreated syphilis on the human economy among people now living and engaged in their daily pursuits.

It also seems that the USPHS believed the experiment might demonstrate that antisyphilitic treatment was unnecessary. As Cumming noted: "It is expected the results of this study may have a marked bearing on the treatment, or conversely the non-necessity of treatment, of cases of latent syphilis. . . ."

SELECTING THE SUBJECTS

Clark sent Dr. Raymond Vonderlehr to Tuskegee in September 1932 to assemble a sample of men with latent syphilis for the experiment. The basic design of the study called for the selection of syphilitic black males between the ages of twenty-five and sixty, a thorough physical examination including x-rays, and finally, a spinal tap to determine the incidence of neuro-syphilis. They had no intention of providing any treatment for the infected men. The USPHS originally scheduled the whole experiment to last six months; it seemed to be both a simple and inexpensive project.

The task of collecting the sample, however, proved to be more difficult than the USPHS had supposed. Vonderlehr canvassed the largely illiterate, poverty-stricken population of sharecroppers and tenant farmers in search of test subjects. If his circulars requested only men over twenty-five to attend his clinics, none would appear, suspecting he was conducting draft physicals. Therefore, he was forced to test large numbers of women and men who did not fit the experiments specifications. This involved considerable expense since the USPHS had promised the Macon County Board of Health that it would treat those who were infected, but not included in the study. Clark wrote to Vonderlehr about the situation: "It never once occured to me that we would be called upon to treat a large part of the county as return for the privilege of making this study. . . . I am anxious to keep the expenditures for treatment down to the lowest possible point because it is the one item of expenditure in connection with the study most difficult to defend despite our knowledge of the need therefor." Vonderlehr responded: "If we could find from 100 to 200 cases . . . we would not have to do another Wassermann on useless individuals. . . ."

Significantly, the attempt to develop the sample contradicted the prediction the USPHS had made initially regarding the prevalence of the disease in Macon County. Overall rates of syphilis fell well below expectations; as opposed to the USPHS projection of 35 percent, 20 percent of those tested were actually diseased. Moreover, those who had sought and received previous treatment far exceeded the expectations of the USPHS. Clark noted in a letter to Vonderlehr:

I find your report of March 6th quite interesting but regret the necessity for Wassermanning [sic] . . . such a large number of individuals in order to uncover this relatively limited number of untreated cases.

Further difficulties arose in enlisting the subjects to participate in the experiment, to be "Wassermanned," and to return for a subsequent series of examinations. Vonderlehr found that only the offer of treatment elicited the cooperation of the men. They were told they were ill and were promised free care. Offered therapy, they became willing subjects. [The USPHS did not tell the men that they were participants in an experiment; on the contrary, the subjects believed they were being treated for "bad blood"—the rural South's colloquialism for syphilis.] They thought they were participating in a public health demonstration similar to the one that had been conducted by the Julius Rosenwald Fund in Tuskegee several years earlier. In the end, the men were so eager for medical care that the number of defaulters in the experiment proved to be insignificant.

To preserve the subjects' interest, Vonderlehr gave most of the men mercurial ointment, a noneffective drug, while some of the younger men apparently received inadequate dosages of neoarsphenamine. This required Vonderlehr to write frequently to Clark requesting supplies. [He feared the experiment would fail if the men were not offered treatment.]

* * *

The readiness of the test subjects to participate of course contradicted the notion that blacks would not seek or continue therapy.

The final procedure of the experiment was to be a spinal tap to test for evidence of neuro-syphilis. The USPHS presented this purely diagnostic exam, which often entails considerable pain and complications, to the men as a "special treatment." Clark explained to Moore:

> We have not yet commenced the spinal punctures. This operation will be deferred to the last in order not to unduly disturb our field work by any adverse reports by the patients subjected to spinal puncture because of some disagreeable sensations following this procedure [These negroes are very ignorant and easily influenced by things that would be of minor significance in a more intelligent group.]

[The letter to the subjects announcing the spinal tap read:

> Some time ago you were given a thorough examination and since that time we hope you have gotten a great deal of treatment for bad blood. You will now be given your last chance to get a second examination. This examination is a very special one and after it is finished you will be given a special treatment if it is believed you are in a condition to stand it. . . .
> REMEMBER THIS IS YOUR LAST CHANCE FOR SPECIAL FREE TREATMENT. BE SURE TO MEET THE NURSE.]

[The HEW investigation did not uncover this crucial fact: the men participated in the study under the guise of treatment.]

Despite the fact that their assumption regarding prevalence and black attitudes toward treatment had proved wrong, the USPHS decided in the summer of 1933 to continue the study. Once again, it seemed only "natural" to pursue
the research since the sample already existed, and with a depressed economy,
the cost of treatment appeared prohibitive—although there is no indication it
was ever considered. Vonderlehr first suggested extending the study in letters
to Clark and Wenger:

> At the end of this project we shall have a considerable number of cases present-
> ing various complications of syphilis, who have received only mercury and may
> still be considered untreated in the modern sense of therapy. Should these cases
> be followed over a period of from five to ten years many interesting facts could
> be learned regarding the course and complications of untreated syphilis.

"As I see it," responded Wenger, "we have no further interest in these
patients *until they die*." Apparently, the physicians engaged in the experiment
believed that only autopsies could scientifically confirm the findings of the
study.

Bringing the men to autopsy required the USPHS to devise a further series
of deceptions and inducements. Wenger warned Vonderlehr that the men must
not realize that they would be autopsied:

> [There is one danger in the latter plan and that is if the colored population become
> aware that accepting free hospital care means a postmortem; every darkey will
> leave Macon County and it will hurt [Dr. Eugene] Dibble's hospital.]

The USPHS offered several inducements to maintain contact and to procure the continued cooperation of the men. Eunice Rivers, a black nurse, was
hired to follow their health and to secure approval for autopsies. She gave the
men non-effective medicines—"spring tonic" and aspirin—as well as transportation and hot meals on the days of their examinations. More important, Nurse
Rivers provided continuity to the project over the entire forty-year period. By
supplying "medicinals," the USPHS was able to continue to deceive the participants, who believed that they were receiving therapy from the government
doctors. Deceit was integral to the study. When the test subjects complained
about spinal taps one doctor wrote:

> They simply do not like spinal punctures. A few of those who were tapped are
> enthusiastic over the results but to most, the suggestion causes violent shaking
> of the head; others claim they were robbed of their procreative powers (regard-
> less of the fact that I claim it stimulates them).

Letters to the subjects announcing an impending USPHS visit to Tuskegee
explained: "[The doctor] wants to make a special examination to find out how

you have been feeling and whether the treatment has improved your health." In fact, after the first six months of the study, the USPHS had furnished no treatment whatsoever.

Finally, because it proved difficult to persuade the men to come to the hospital when they became severely ill, the USPHS promised to cover their burial expenses. The Milbank Memorial Fund provided approximately $50 per man for this purpose beginning in 1935. This was a particularly strong inducement as funeral rites constituted an important component of the cultural life of rural blacks. One report of the study concluded. "Without this suasion it would, we believe, have been impossible to secure the cooperation of the group and their families."

Reports of the study's findings, which appeared regularly in the medical press beginning in 1936, consistently cited the ravages of untreated syphilis. The first paper, read at the 1936 American Medical Association annual meeting, found "that syphilis in this period [latency] tends to greatly increase the frequency of manifestations of cardiovascular disease." Only 16 percent of the subjects gave no sign of morbidity as opposed to 61 percent of the controls. Ten years later, a report noted coldly, "The fact that nearly twice as large a proportion of the syphilitic individuals as of the control group has died is a very striking one." Life expectancy, concluded the doctors, is reduced by about 20 percent.

A 1955 article found that slightly more than 30 percent of the test group autopsied had died *directly* from advanced syphilitic lesions of either the cardiovascular or the central nervous system. Another published account stated, "Review of those still living reveals that an appreciable number have late complications of syphilis which probably will result, for some at least, in contributing materially to the ultimate cause of death." In 1950, Dr. Wenger had concluded, "We now know, where we could only surmise before, that we have contributed to their ailments and shortened their lives." As black physician Vernal Cave, a member of the HEW panel, later wrote, "They proved a point, then proved a point, then proved a point."

During the forty years of the experiment the USPHS had sought on several occasions to ensure that the subjects did not receive treatment from other sources. To this end, Vonderlehr met with groups of local black doctors in 1934, to ask their cooperation in not treating the men. Lists of subjects were distributed to Macon County physicians along with letters requesting them to refer these men back to the USPHS if they sought care. The USPHS warned the Alabama Health Department not to treat the test subjects when they took a mobile VD unit into Tuskegee in the early 1940s. In 1941, the Army drafted several subjects and told them to begin antisyphilitic treatment immediately. The USPHS supplied the draft board with a list of 256 names they desired to have excluded from treatment, and the board complied.

In spite of these efforts, by the early 1950s many of the men had secured some treatment on their own. By 1952, almost 30 percent of the test subjects had received some penicillin, although only 7.5 percent had received what could be considered adequate doses. Vonderlehr wrote to one of the participating physicians, "I hope that the availability of antibiotics has not interfered too much with this project." A report published in 1955 considered whether the treatment that some of the men had obtained had "defeated" the study. The article attempted to explain the relatively low exposure to penicillin in an age of antibiotics, suggesting as a reason "the stoicism of these men as a group; they still regard hospitals and medicines with suspicion and prefer an occasional dose of time-honored herbs or tonics to modern drugs." The authors failed to note that the men believed they already were under the care of the government doctors and thus saw no need to seek treatment elsewhere. Any treatment which the men might have received, concluded the report, had been insufficient to compromise the experiment.

When the USPHS evaluated the status of the study in the 1960s they continued to rationalize the racial aspects of the experiment. For example, the minutes of a 1965 meeting at the Center for Disease Control recorded:

> Racial issue was mentioned briefly. Will not affect the study. Any questions can be handled by saying these people were at the point that therapy would no longer help them. They are getting better medical care than they would under any other circumstances.

A group of physicians met again at the CDC in 1969 to decide whether or not to terminate the study. Although one doctor argued that the study should be stopped and the men treated, the consensus was to continue. Dr. J. Lawton Smith remarked, "You will never have another study like this; take advantage of it." A memo prepared by Dr. James B. Lucas, Assistant Chief of the Venereal Disease Branch, stated: "Nothing learned will prevent, find, or cure a single case of infectious syphilis or bring us closer to our basic mission of controlling veneral disease in the United States." He concluded, however, that the study should be continued "along its present lines." When the first accounts of the experiment appeared in the national press in July 1972, data were still being collected and autopsies performed.

THE NEW FINAL REPORT

HEW finally formed the Tuskegee Syphilis Study Ad Hoc Advisory Panel on August 28, 1972, in response to criticism that the press descriptions of the experiment had triggered The panel, composed of nine members, five of them black, concentrated on two issues. First, was the study justified in 1932 and had the men given their informed consent? Second, should penicillin have been provided when it became available in the early 1950s? The panel was also charged with determining if the study should be terminated and assessing current policies regarding experimentation with human subjects. The group issued their report in June 1973.

By focusing on the issues of penicillin therapy and informed consent, the *Final Report* and the investigation betrayed a basic misunderstanding of the experiment's purposes and design. The HEW report implied that the failure to provide penicillin constituted the study's major ethical misjudgment; implicit was the assumption that no adequate therapy existed prior to penicillin. Nonetheless medical authorities firmly believed in the efficacy of arsenotherapy for treating syphilis at the time of the experiment's inception in 1932. The panel further failed to recognize that the entire study had been predicated on nontreatment. Provision of effective medication would have violated the rationale of the experiment—to study the natural course of the disease until death. On several occasions, in fact, the USPHS had prevented the men from receiving proper treatment. Indeed, there is no evidence that the USPHS ever considered providing penicillin.

The other focus of the *Final Report*—informed consent—also served to obscure the historical facts of the experiment. In light of the deceptions and exploitations which the experiment perpetrated, it is an understatement to declare, as the *Report* did, that the experiment was "ethically unjustified," because it failed to obtain informed consent from the subjects. The *Final Report's* statement, "Submitting voluntarily is not informed consent," indicated that the panel believed that the men had volunteered *for the experiment.* The records in the National Archives make clear that the men did not submit voluntarily to an experiment; they were told and they believed that they were getting free treatment from expert government doctors for a serious disease. The failure of the HEW *Final Report* to expose this critical fact—that the USPHS lied to the subjects—calls into question the thoroughness and credibility of their investigation.

Failure to place the study in a historical context also made it impossible for the investigation to deal with the essentially racist nature of the experiment. The panel treated the study as an aberration, well-intentioned but misguided. Moreover, concern that the *Final Report* might be viewed as a critique of human experimentation in general seems to have severely limited the scope of the inquiry. The *Final Report* is quick to remind the reader on two occasions: "The position of the Panel must not be construed to be a general repudiation of scientific research with human subjects." The *Report* assures us that a better-designed experiment could have been justified:

> It is possible that a scientific study in 1932 of untreated syphilis, properly conceived with a clear protocol and conducted with suitable subjects who fully understood the implications of their involvement, might have been justified in the pre-penicillin era. This is especially true when one considers the uncertain nature of the results of treatment of late latent syphilis and the highly toxic nature of therapeutic agents then available.

This statement is questionable in view of the proven dangers of untreated syphilis known in 1932.

Since the publication of the HEW *Final Report,* a defense of the Tuskegee Study has emerged. These arguments, most clearly articulated by Dr. R. H. Kampmeier in the *Southern Medical Journal,* center on the limited knowledge of effective therapy for latent syphilis when the experiment began. Kampmeier argues that by 1950, penicillin would have been of no value for these men. Others have suggested that the men were fortunate to have been spared the highly toxic treatments of the earlier period. Moreover, even these contemporary defenses assume that the men never would have been treated anyway. As Dr. Charles Barnett of Stanford University wrote in 1974, "The lack of treatment was not contrived by the USPHS but was an established fact of which they proposed to take advantage." Several doctors who participated in the study continued to justify the experiment. Dr. J. R. Heller, who on one occasion had referred to the test subjects as the "Ethiopian population," told reporters in 1972:

> I don't see why they should be shocked or horrified. There was no racial side to this. It just happened to be in a black community. I feel this was a perfectly straightforward study, perfectly ethical, with controls. Part of our mission as physicians is to find out what happens to individuals with disease and without disease.

These apologies, as well as the HEW *Final Report,* ignore many of the essential ethical issues which the study poses. The Tuskegee Study reveals the persistence of beliefs within the medical profession about the nature of blacks, sex, and disease—beliefs that had tragic repercussions long after their alleged "scientific" bases were known to be incorrect. Most strikingly, the entire health of a community was jeopardized by leaving a communicable disease untreated. There can be little doubt that the Tuskegee researchers regarded their subjects as less than human. As a result, the ethical canons of experimenting on human subjects were completely disregarded.

The study also raises significant questions about professional self-regulation and scientific bureaucracy. Once the USPHS decided to extend the experiment in the summer of 1933, it was unlikely that the test would be halted short of the men's deaths. The experiment was widely reported for forty years without evoking any significant protest within the medical community. Nor did any bureaucratic mechanism exist within the government for the periodic reassessment of the Tuskegee experiment's ethics and scientific value. The USPHS sent physicians to Tuskegee every several years to check on the study's progress, but never subjected the morality or usefulness of the experiment to serious scrutiny. Only the press accounts of 1972 finally punctured the continued rationalizations of the USPHS and brought the study to an end. Even the HEW investigation was compromised by fear that it would be considered a threat to future human experimentation.

In retrospect the Tuskegee Study revealed more about the pathology of racism than it did about the pathology of syphilis; more about the nature of scientific inquiry than the nature of the disease process. The injustice committed by the experiment went well beyond the facts outlined in the press and the HEW *Final Report*. The degree of deception and damages have been seriously underestimated. As this history of the study suggests, the notion that science is a value-free discipline must be rejected. The need for greater vigilance in assessing the specific ways in which social values and attitudes affect professional behavior is clearly indicated.*

---

*In the summer of 2010 Susan Reverby, history professor at Wellesley College, revealed that from 1946 to 1948 doctors from the United States deliberately infected Guatemalans with venereal diseases, ostensibly to study the use of penicillin as a preventative as well as a curative for syphilis. Dr. John C. Cutler, involved in the Tuskegee experiments, led the experiment in Guatemala. It is unclear if the Guatemalan subjects were effectively treated once they were infected with venereal diseases. See Donald G. McNeil's article, "U.S. Infected Guatemalans with Syphilis in '40s," *New York Times*, October 1, 2010, pages A1 and A6. [*Editors' note*]

PART TWO

CULTURE AND SOCIETY

9

American Hookup: Deep in the Fog

FROM *American Hookup: The New Culture of Sex on Campus*

LISA WADE

Many groups establish subcultural practices and attitudes that accommodate and make sense in their setting (e.g., prison subculture or soldiers living and fighting in a foreign land) or that establish themselves as outside the mainstream (e.g., jazz musicians, religious cults, extreme-sports enthusiasts). These subcultures are not radically different from the larger culture familiar to their practitioners but are distinct enough to be identifiable and imitable and are strong enough to impel conformity for those within their sphere. A university is in many ways what Erving Goffman called a "total institution," where "inmates" eat, sleep, recreate, and work in a semi-confined environment and create their own subcultural practices. In this excerpt from her book American Hookup, *sociologist Lisa Wade explores how partying and its attendant sexual activity—especially for students new to the total institution—follow a script of seemingly wild abandon. In studying this she found much more going on in the way of identity, image, and belonging. This piece, too, can be read as a chapter in the book of the #MeToo movement.*

* * *

On campuses across America, students are sounding an alarm. They are telling us that they are depressed, anxious, and overwhelmed. Half of first-year students express concern that they are not emotionally healthy, and one in ten say that they frequently feel depressed. The transition from teenager to young adult is rarely easy, but this is more than just youthful angst. Students are less happy and healthy than in previous generations, less so even than just ten or twenty years ago. . . .

* * *

One in three students say that their intimate relationships have been "traumatic" or "very difficult to handle," and 10 percent say that they've been sexually coerced or assaulted in the past year. In addition, there is a persistent malaise: a deep, indefinable disappointment. Students find that their sexual experiences are distressing or boring. They worry that they're feeling too much or too little. They are frustrated and feel regret, but they're not sure why. They consider the possibility that they're inadequate, unsexy, and unlovable. And it goes far beyond the usual suspects. . . .

Thus far, the culprit seems to be the hookup. Sociologist Kathleen Bogle sparked the conversation in 2008 with *Hooking Up: Sex, Dating, and Relationships on Campus*. She described a new norm on campus that favored casual sexual contact and argued that this was especially harmful to women. Michael Kimmel, the well-known sociologist of masculinity, agreed. Hooking up is "guys' sex," he explained in *Guyland* that year; "guys run the scene." More recently, journalist Jon Birger added math, concluding that a shortage of men in college gives them the power to dictate sexual terms, making campuses a "sexual nirvana for heterosexual men." These thinkers, and many more, argue that hooking up is just a new way for men to get what they want from women.

Journalists Hanna Rosin and Kate Taylor have countered the idea that hooking up only benefits men. At the *Atlantic* and in the *New York Times*, they've suggested that casual sex allows women to put their careers and education before men. In their view, it's a way of giving the middle finger to the "Mrs. Degree," that now outdated but once quite real reason why women sought higher education. Rosin goes so far as to say that future feminist progress "depends on" hooking up, with serious relationships a "danger to be avoided at all costs." Their anecdotal evidence is backed up by social scientists like Elizabeth Armstrong and Laura Hamilton, who show in *Paying for the Party* that women with economically stable families and ambitious career plans are more likely than other women to be successful at hookup-heavy party schools.

Meanwhile, at *Rolling Stone* and *New York* magazine, the whole scene is portrayed as a poly, queer, bacchanalian utopia with lots of skin and a little light BDSM. Not only is it not sexist, it's non-binary. Maybe this is what the future looks like. At *Elle*, columnist Karley Sciortino seems to think so. She defends hooking up, but only because she thinks that worrying about it amounts to little more than old-fashioned fuddy-duddery. All this talk about young people and their sexual choices, she insists, is just "moral panic" and "reactionary hysteria." What's really harmful, she argues, is suggesting that women might not enjoy casual sex. She's not alone in expressing annoyance at the "kids these days" fretting. It can seem like a lot of hand-wringing to students, many of whom wish everyone would just mind their own business.

Hookups have been damned, praised, and dismissed in the popular and academic presses, feeding a debate about whether we should applaud or condemn the "hookup generation," and drawing out prescriptions for students' sex lives from both the right and the left. But, as is so often the case, the very premise of the debate is wrong.

The idea that college students are having a lot of sex is certainly an enthralling myth. Even students believe it. In Bogle's landmark study, students guessed that their peers were doing it fifty times a year. That's twenty-five times what the numbers actually show. In Kimmel's *Guyland*, young men figured that 80 percent of college guys were having sex any given weekend; they would have been closer to the truth if they were guessing the percent of men who had *ever* had sex. Students overestimate how much sex their peers are having, and by quite a lot.

In fact, today's students boast no more sexual partners than their parents did at their age. Scholars using the University of Chicago's General Social Survey have shown that they actually report slightly fewer sexual partners than Gen-Xers did. Millennials look more similar to the baby boomer generation than they do to the wild sexual cohort that they are frequently imagined to be.

There are students on campus with active sex lives, of course, but there are plenty with none at all and some with sexual escapades that are, at best, only "slightly less nonexistent" than they were in high school. The average graduating senior reports hooking up just eight times in four years. That amounts to one hookup per semester. Studies looking specifically at the sexual cultures at Duke, Yale, and East Carolina universities, the universities of Georgia and Tennessee, the State University of New York at Geneseo, and UC Berkeley report similar numbers. Not all students are hooking up, and those that do aren't necessarily doing so very often. Neither are students always hopping out of one bed and into another; half of those eight hookups are with someone the student has hooked up with before. Almost a third of students will graduate without hooking up a single time.

Despite the rumors, then, there is no epidemic of casual sexual encounters on college campuses. So, hookups can't be blamed. There just aren't enough of them to account for the malaise. Neither does two sexual encounters every twelve months, possibly with the same person, look like either female empowerment or male domination; if so, it's quite a tepid expression of power. There certainly is no bacchanalian utopia, poly, queer, or otherwise. Students are too busy not having sex to be enacting the next revolution. The cause of students' unhappiness, then, can't be the hookup. But it *is* about hooking up. It's hookup *culture*.

* * *

Hookup culture is an occupying force, coercive and omnipresent. For those who love it, it's all sunshine, but it isn't for everyone else. Deep in the fog, students often feel dreary, confused, helpless. Many behave in ways they don't like, hurt other people unwillingly, and consent to sexual activity they don't desire.

Campuses of all kinds are in this fog. No matter the size of the college, how heavy a Greek or athletic presence it boasts, its exclusivity, its religious affiliation, or whether it's public or private, hookup culture is there. We find it in all regions of the country, from the Sunshine State of Florida to the sunny state of California. Students all over say so. Hookups are "part of our collegiate culture," writes a representative of the American South in the University of Florida's *Alligator*. If you don't hook up, warns a woman at the University of Georgia, then you're "failing at the college experience." A woman at Tulane puts it succinctly: "Hookup culture," she says, "it's college."

Up north, a student at Cornell confirms: "We go to parties. And then after we're good and drunk, we hook up. Everyone just hooks up." "At the end of the day," boasts a student at Yale, "you can get laid." Nearby, at Connecticut College, a female student describes it as the "be-all and end-all" of social life. "Oh, sure," says a guy 2,500 miles away at Arizona State, "you go to parties on the prowl." "A one-night stand," admits a student a few hundred miles north at Chico State, "is a constant possibility." Further up, at Whitman in Walla Walla, a female student calls hookup culture "an established norm."

Students like these almost certainly overestimate how much hooking up is going on, but they're not wrong to feel that hookup culture is everywhere. And while the exhilaration and delight in their voices is real, so is the disappointment and trauma. In response, many students opt out of hooking up, but they can't opt out of hookup culture. It's more than just a behavior; it's the climate. It can't be wished away any more than we can wish away a foggy day.

I learned this from first-year students themselves. In the first year, the fog is thickest. Most incoming students think that casual sex in college is expected, encounter impressive amounts of (often free) alcohol, and are away from their parents for the first time. The average student reports hooking up more in the first year than any subsequent year. It is in this year, as well, that they are at highest risk of sexual assault.

The students whose firsthand accounts fill this book were enrolled in either an "Introduction to Sociology" or a sexuality-themed writing intensive course taught between 2010 and 2015 at one of two liberal arts colleges, a secular school in the American Southwest and a religious one in the South. Somewhere between introductions and the overview of the syllabus, I stood in front of their loosely arranged desks and announced that each student would collect data about sex and romance on campus, writing as much or as little as they liked about their own experiences or those of the people around them. The project would last through the semester, with their data or "journals" to be submitted each Tuesday. I also explained that I hoped, with their consent, to include facts and quotes from their accounts in my own research that I expected eventually to publish, although I would not know whether any student had consented until all grades had been safely recorded. All but nine of the 110 students gave consent. I promised to keep their identities confidential, so while I stay true to the stories their lives tell us, their names, some identifying information, and other details have been changed and sometimes dramatized.

Some students were thrilled by the opportunity to tell the world about their experiences, but I'll admit that some were skeptical. More than a few worried that they'd have no sexual activity worth writing about. Others weren't sure they wanted to tell their professor the details of their sex lives. I encouraged them to disclose only what they felt comfortable sharing. They didn't always lead with their most harrowing memories but, with time, many chose to disclose their deeper secrets.

The documents they submitted—varyingly rants, whispered gossip, critical analyses, protracted tales, or simple streams of consciousness—came to over 1,500 single-spaced pages and exceeded a million words. As the semester progressed, we talked about their insights and experiences, interpreting them together, testing theories, and reading what other scholars had found. In their journals, they described their hopes and dreams, exposed their insecurities, lamented their disappointments, and celebrated their victories. As the semesters progressed, their insights became keen. They were able to see their environment increasingly clearly and explain it with sometimes gut-wrenching clarity.

Consistent with existing research, I found little difference in the hookup cultures of the two institutions where I collected data. With the exception of evangelical and Mormon campuses (and my second school was neither of those), the sexual attitudes and behavior on secular and religiously affiliated schools look remarkably alike. In any case, only a handful of students at either school emphasized that their faith was an important part of why they made the choices they did.

All of my students were very recently out of high school and all but five lived on campus. Twenty-two came from a working-class or poor background, and fifteen were the first in their families to go to college. Sixteen identified as a sexual minority and another three hadn't quite decided how to identify. Reflecting gender disparities in college enrollment and those who opt to take social science classes, twenty-six of my students were male and seventy-five were female. None identified as trans or non-gender binary. Fifty-six students were white; thirteen were Asian or East Indian, ten were African American, fourteen were Latino or Latina, and seven identified primarily as mixed race. No students were Native American.

* * *

Drawn in by their stories, I took my research on tour. I've traveled to speak about hookup culture at twenty-four colleges and universities of all types in eighteen states. I visited Ivy League schools such as Harvard, Yale, and Dartmouth; religiously affiliated schools such as Loyola in New Orleans and Pacific Lutheran University in Tacoma; private universities such as Tulane; liberal arts schools such as Carlton in Minnesota and Westminster in Utah; as well as large public universities in California, Idaho, Illinois, Indiana, Kansas, Louisiana, Missouri, Ohio, West Virginia, and Wisconsin.

At all of these schools, I presented my research, interacted with students, probed them with questions, and got their responses. I met them over lunch, dropped in on clubs, or hosted discussions in classrooms. I brainstormed with graduate students interested in embarking on sexuality research and had the pleasure, too, of talking to college employees: residence life advisors, counselors, faith leaders, Title IX officers, other faculty, and more. Together, these informal interviews and focus groups added up to hundreds more little bits of data, an opportunity to learn something new or confirm a theory. At only two of the schools—both commuter campuses with fewer than 10 percent of students living in residence halls—did students question whether they were in the fog of hookup culture. . . .

I bring my students' stories into dialogue with the hundreds of well-crafted scholarly and news articles that have been published in the last ten years. Hookup culture has been surveyed, observed, queried, experimented on, and more. I also take advantage of publicly available data from the Online College Social Life Survey. Designed and generously shared by sociologist Paula England, the OCSLS is a survey about college students' sexual behaviors, experiences, and attitudes. Between 2005 and 2011, over 24,000 students at twenty-one four-year colleges and universities submitted responses. Finally, I scoured hundreds of firsthand accounts of sex on campus written for student newspapers and other media outlets. I include quotes and the occasional story from these students as well, revealing the influence of hookup culture across many types of institutions in all regions of the country.

* * *

STEP 1: PREGAME.

"You don't walk out of the house without your shoes on and you don't walk into a party without a couple of shots of vodka," insisted one of my students. "It's real." The first step in hooking up is to get, as Miranda put it, "shitfaced."

Party-oriented students believe that drinking enhances their experience. Destiny, for example, gushed about how it felt to be a bit drunk at a college-sponsored concert:

> I honestly think I would not have had as much fun as I did if I wasn't intoxicated. . . . I couldn't care less about what people thought about me and felt free enough just to do whatever I wanted and to be bubbly and carefree. That night I didn't have a care in the world and it felt absolutely fantastic.

Students also tend to think that alcohol improves their personality. Getting drunk, they argue, brings out their "intoxicated self," one that is freer, more relaxed, less anxious, and generally more fun to be around. Destiny emphasized how alcohol made her feel carefree three times in as many sentences. Others believe that it gives them confidence. "I rely on mixed drinks and shots," wrote another female student. "They are not lying when they call it 'liquid courage.'"

When everyone is being their intoxicated self, students collectively bring into existence a thing called "drunkworld." This is the word that the Ohio University sociologist Thomas Vander Ven uses to describe a typical college night out in his book *Getting Wasted: Why College Students Drink Too Much and Party So Hard*. Drunkworld is an alternative reality in which it's normal for people to "fall down, slur their words, break things, laugh uncontrollably, act crazy, flirt, hook up, get sick, pass out, fight, dance, sing, and get overly emotional," where "taken-for-granted human abilities (e.g., motor skills) are challenged and everyday interactions take on a dramatic air."

Because drunkworld is a group accomplishment, everyone needs to be on board. Hence, the pregame: a get-together immediately before attending a party where students get ready and get sloshed. All parties on and off campus involve pregaming, especially the dry ones. "When the school hosts a dance with no alcohol," wrote one observer, *"of course* all of the students arrive drunk out of their minds."

* * *

STEP 2: GRIND.

"If you can't dirty dance," insisted one of my female students, "then you can't dance at all." Grinding is the main activity at most college parties. Women who are willing press their backs and backsides against men's bodies and dance rhythmically. "It is a bestial rubbing of genitals reminiscent of mating zebras," Laura wrote scornfully after attending a party. "Guys were coming up behind women on the dance floor and placing their hands on their hips like two wayward lobster claws, clamping on and pulling them close."

* * *

Reflecting twentieth-century gender roles, women can be overtly receptive, but the men choose whom they approach. "There's girls dancing in the middle, and there's guys lurking on the sides and then coming and basically pressing their genitals up against you," wrote one University of Pennsylvania student. "They rarely *ask* a girl to dance," a student of mine clarified, though sometimes they'll make eye contact before approaching. A verbal inquiry is so off-script that one male student reported that his female friends reacted with "incredulity" when he inquired as to whether they wanted to be asked to dance: "They said you should just walk up, say hi, grab her, and start grinding without any discussion of intentions." One of my students called it the "sneak attack."

* * *

It is essential that he be "cute" because the ultimate goal in hookup culture isn't just to hook up, it's to hook up with the right person. Or, more specifically, a *hot* person. Hotness, says one female student, "is the only qualification one needs to be considered for a hookup." "Average guys just don't cut it," another wrote:

> Sure, it's not a social tragedy to hook up with an average-looking guy. But hooking up with someone attractive is a social asset for sure. It raises your standing in the hierarchy of potential partners. It makes you more attractive.

About a guy she actually quite disliked, one of my female students said plainly, "I want to hook up with him for the social status." Hooking up with students who are widely considered hot was a way to get some of their status to rub off on you. "In our room," one of my male students wrote, "sex is a commodity, which, like gold, increases a man's social status, especially if he 'scores' or 'pounds' an especially blonde girl." Blonde is hot.

Bragging about sexual exploits is traditionally the purview of men, and such conversations continue to be a central way in which they bond with one another. As one University of Wisconsin student quoted in *Guyland* put it:

> When I've just got laid, the first thing I think about—really, I shouldn't be telling you this, but really it's the very first thing, before I've even like "finished"—is that I can't wait to tell my crew who I just did. Like, I say to myself, "Ohmigod, they're not going to believe that I just did Kristy!"

At the University of Northern Iowa, another student explained it this way:

> It's like the girl you hook up with, they're like a way of showing off to other guys. I mean, you tell your friends you hooked up with Melissa, and they're like, "Whoa, dude, you are one stud." So, I'm into Melissa because my guy friends think she is so hot, and now they think more of me because of it.

"It's totally a guy thing," he added, but I'm not so sure. Many of my female students were also quick to brag. "The whole point of hookups," wrote one, "is get some and then be able to point the person out to your friends and be like, 'Yeah, that guy. That's right. The hot one over there. I got that.'" "It's almost bragging rights," revealed another, "if you hook up with a guy with a higher social status."

* * *

STEP 3: INITIATE A HOOKUP.

"The classic move to establish that you want to hook up with someone," Miranda's friend Ruby wrote from a woman's perspective, "is to turn around to face him, rather than dance with your back pressed against his front." Initiation can come from behind, too. He may tug on her arm or pull one hip back gently to suggest she spin. Or, he might put his face next to hers, closing the distance between them such that, with the turn of her head, there might be a kiss.

If she spins around, Miranda explained, it "seals the deal." Turning around isn't just turning around; it's an advance, an invitation to escalate. Once students are face to face, it's *on*. This is why women look to their friends when a guy approaches them from behind instead of taking a look for themselves.

Turning around is tantamount to agreeing to a "difmo"—a DFMO, or "dance-floor make-out."

* * *

STEP 4: DO . . . SOMETHING.

According to the Online College Social Life Survey, in 40 percent of hookups, Ruby's "it" means intercourse. Another 12 percent include only what we might call foreplay: nudity and some touching of genitals, while 13 percent proceed to oral sex, mostly performed by women on men, but don't include intercourse. A full 35 percent of hookups don't go any further than open-mouth kissing and groping.

* * *

"It's ambiguous," admitted a student at Tufts University. "When someone says they 'hooked up' last night, you would be wise to ask them to clarify." Such ambiguity is the case across the U.S. Students at Radford, Tulane, and Southern Methodist are on the record that it could be "everything and anything from kissing to consummating." "Out on the dance floor, either for like five seconds or like, all night long," specified a student at the University of Southern California. "Or you leave in the morning in his clothes!" countered her friend. It "could mean anything," says a Bowdoin student. *Guyland*'s Michael Kimmel calls the word "hookup" the "yada yada yada of sex."

This can be confusing. "I sometimes have a hard time distinguishing what a particular person means when mentioning a hookup," reported one of my students. Currier argues that the ambiguity is strategic, allowing students to exaggerate or downplay their encounters depending on what they want others to think. Specifically, she found that it allowed women to "protect their status as 'good girls' (sexual but not promiscuous)" and men to "protect their social status as 'real men' (heterosexual, highly sexually active)." It also has to do with how they feel about the person they hooked up with the next morning. Hookups with high-status people may be exaggerated and those with lower-status people minimized.

* * *

STEP 5: ESTABLISH MEANINGLESSNESS.

[D]espite the language we have for dismissing the significance of sex in practice, establishing that a hookup was meaningless is a challenging personal and interpersonal task.

It's difficult logistically, too, because hooking up always involves actual people. In theory, as one female student maintained, "It doesn't really matter who you hook up with in hookup culture. The point is just to get some." Or, as a University of Michigan guy explained, "It's not really about the actual like person per se." It's just "sexual." In practice, however, people have to *choose*. When two students hook up, it means that they picked each other when they could have picked someone else. If the hookup is going to be understood as meaningless, all of these implications have to be nullified.

This is how they do it.

Truly, step 5 is the trickiest. How do two people establish that an intimate moment between them wasn't meaningful?

Step 5a: Be (or claim to be) plastered.

When students talk about meaningless sex on college campuses, they are almost always referring to drunk sex. According to the Online College Social Life Survey, most casual sex occurring on college campuses involves alcohol; men have drunk an average of six drinks and women an average of four. "People who hook up casually are almost always drunk or have at least been drinking," a female student observed. "Thank god for vodka?" Levi asked rhetorically. "I blame it on the Cuervo," countered a student at Marist College. One University of Florida, Gainesville student half-joked, "If you don't remember the sex, it didn't count."

* * *

Being drunk, then, is useful to students, and not only because alcohol is liquid courage; it also frames the sexual activity, boxing it into the realm of meaninglessness. It's how students show that they are being careless in both senses of the word: they aren't being careful and they don't care. If students are being careless, they can't be held responsible for *what* they did, but neither can they be held accountable for *who* they did.

Step 5b: Cap your hookups.

"We've only hooked up once," explained a male student, "so . . . it automatically is not a big deal." A second trick for dismissing the significance of hookups is to limit how many times two students hook up together. One hookup, students argue, isn't anything to get serious about. "One and done," is what they say. A female student snorted when asked if she would hook up with a guy a second time. "No way," she said gruffly.

* * *

Step 5c: Create emotional distance.

After it's all over, students confirm that a hookup meant nothing by giving their relationship—whatever it was—a demotion. The rule is to be less close after a hookup than before, at least for a time. If students were good friends, they should act like acquaintances. If they were acquaintances, they should act like strangers. And if they were strangers, they shouldn't acknowledge each other's existence at all. "Unless at the beginning you've made it clear that you want more than a hookup," wrote a male student at Bowdoin, "then the expectation is . . . just to pretend it didn't happen."

The logic gets wacky, but it goes something like this: an unrequited crush will probably be more damaging to a friendship than being temporarily unfriendly. After a hookup, then, when the possibility of romance is a specter that must be eliminated, acting aloof is the best way to ensure that students remain friends. "People act very strangely," one student commented, "to make sure, almost to prove, they're keeping things casual."

Plenty of students feel uncomfortable with this proposition, but hookup culture has a way of enforcing compliance. If the rule is to be unfriendly, then even the slightest kindness—essentially, any effort to connect or reach out—can be interpreted as romantic interest. So, if students are nice after a hookup, they risk making an impression that they don't want to make.

* * *

That's the hookup: a drunken sexual encounter with ambiguous content that is supposed to mean nothing and happen just once. It's a scrappy little sex act, a wayward Cupid. Armed with dark of night and blur of intoxication, its aim is a fun, harmless romp, a supposedly free expression of one's sexuality, but within oddly strict parameters. It's spontaneous, but scripted; order out of disorder; an unruly routine. It is, in short, a feat of social engineering.

The hookup is not in itself new. It's been around for a very long time, at least as long as college has been around. It was around in the 1970s when students started experimenting with free love and psychedelics. It was around in the 1950s when coeds, in blatant violation of school rules, snuck past the house mother and out the windows of their dormitories to consort with boys. It was around in the 1920s when a quarter of college women engaged in homosexual activity. And it was around in the 1880s when certain men in fraternities discovered a carnal brotherhood.

In none of these decades, though, did students think they were *supposed* to be having casual sex. The imperative is the critical difference. "Casual sex was happening before in college," says Indiana University psychologist Debby Herbenick, "but there wasn't the sense that it's what you should be doing. It is now." It's the elevation of the hookup over all other ways of engaging sexually that has transformed campuses from places where there is hooking up to places with a hookup culture.

* * *

Sociologist Emily Kane sat across the table from the father of two preschool boys and asked him how he felt about them playing with girl toys. "If they asked for a Barbie doll," he replied, bringing to mind the most iconic girl toy of all, "I would probably say no, you don't want [that] . . . boys play with trucks." Another father, when asked about his five-year-old, expressed concern about his tendency to cry. "Stop crying like a girl," he would say to his son when he wept out of desire for a toy or a later bedtime. "If you decide you want [some] thing, you are going to fight for it." "If he was acting feminine," said a mother who was posed the same question, "I would try to get involved and make sure he's not gay."

At about the same time that today's traditional-age college students were children, between 1999 and 2002, Kane interviewed almost four dozen parents about their children's gender performance. She found that they were generally apprehensive about boys who were a bit girlish. Some parents didn't approve of boys who strayed too far from stereotypical masculinity; other parents were just well aware of what comes to boys who do. As one mother explained, "He's not the rough-and-tumble kid, and I do worry about him being an easy target."

This is a reasonable fear. As boys become men, being seen as appropriately manly translates into social opportunities: getting invited to parties, making cool friends, and attracting the attention of desirable women. It's also how they avoid being a victim of emotional and physical abuse. In many fields, manliness will be vital for pulling off a job interview and standing out for promotion. For men to deliberately wave off the imperative to prove their masculinity is akin to deliberately sacrificing social and occupational success.

It's not particularly surprising, then, that parents recognized the value of masculinity for boys; what's really interesting is that they saw it as best for their girls, too. When Emily Kane asked a father about his hopes for his young daughter's personality, his answer was clear: "I never wanted a girl who was a little princess, who was so fragile," he said. "I want her to take on more masculine characteristics." Another day, across another table, a mother said about her daughter, "I don't want her to just color and play with dolls, I want her to be athletic." The parents of girls interviewed by Kane didn't express the same concern regarding cross-gender behavior that parents of boys did. They were more than tolerant of their girls' boylike behavior; they were *tickled*.

We tell our girls, from the time they're in diapers, that being "girly" is okay, but being a little bit "boyish" is pretty great. A girl might be encouraged when she discovers a fascination with backyard bugs or engineering toys. Getting ready for elementary school, she may be signed up for a youth sport. Her coach may praise her once in a while for not throwing "like a girl," an obvious jab at femininity. In middle school, she might join her teammates in cracking jokes about the girls in cheerleading. Even if she's somewhat jealous about the attention they get from boys, she's sure that what she's doing is more badass precisely because it's less girly.

In high school history class, the women her teachers talk about are all ones who broke out of traditional gender roles: Joan of Arc, warrior; Sojourner

Truth, activist; Marie Curie, scientist; Amelia Earhart, adventurer. Likewise, our contemporary feminist icons are overwhelmingly women who are admired for succeeding in male arenas of life: Hillary Clinton, politician; Oprah Winfrey, media mogul; Sonia Sotomayor, Supreme Court justice; Pussy Riot, rebels; Danica Patrick, race car driver. As the famous saying goes, "Well-behaved women rarely make history." This is a lesson easily learned by any child paying a modicum of attention.

Most girls in America today grow up being told that they can do anything, and they know when this is emphasized that what it really means is that they can do anything *boys* do. So, today's young women are quick to incorporate masculinity into their personalities and lifestyles. They do this in a myriad of ways, picking and choosing the mix that works best for them. Some girls major in computer science, some aim to ascend the hierarchy at a Fortune 500 company, some brag about a taste for hard liquor, and some have sex for fun. We shouldn't be the slightest bit surprised. It's exactly the kind of choice they have been rewarded for every day in essentially all realms of life.

Feminists wanted this for women. They wanted them to have the right to put themselves first, to build impressive careers, and to have sex freely. And they got that. But they also wanted men to embrace having sex for love. They wanted to share with men the beauty of a life driven by empathy, care, and tenderness. That's not what happened. Instead, the average woman became more masculine, and so did the average man.

In the midst of the sexual revolution, a Stanford psychologist named Sandra Lipsitz Bem developed what would later be called the Bem Sex Role Inventory. It was a survey that asked respondents to evaluate themselves on sixty traits, many of which were gendered ones, such as aggression, warmth, self-reliance, competitiveness, and sincerity. The result was a quantitative measure of the extent to which a person's personality was stereotypically masculine, feminine, or balanced between both. The Bem Inventory was first used in 1971 and, as is typical in the field, used repeatedly in studies done all around the U.S.

Decades later, in the mid-1990s, another psychologist decided to use it to look back through time. Jean Twenge, then at the University of Michigan, amassed and compared all of the studies that had used the Bem Sex Role Inventory to see if men and women had changed. They had. Both were increasingly likely to claim masculine traits as their own. Women's scores, especially, had shifted, and their personalities were measuring as masculine as men's.

Women came to embrace the same self-concept that men had once claimed for themselves because American society has continued to value the masculine over the feminine. It's why women flock to male-dominated occupations, break into male-identified sports and adopt masculine fashions, but men generally aren't doing the inverse. Because of this asymmetry, when women adopt masculine ways of life, they're doing more than just breaking out of their gender role; they're breaking into a better one. They're liberating themselves.

Many women apply this logic to sex, too, adopting a stereotypically masculine approach that puts sex before love.

"I railed against the idea that women were needy, dependent, easily heartsick, easily made hysterical by men, attention-obsessed, and primarily fixated on finding romance," one of my female students explained insistently. "I did this by proving how very like a boy I could behave." She engaged in what she called "sexual tomboyery":

> I figured the best way for a girl to reject oppressive sexism would be to act in exact opposition of what our sexist society expects of a decent woman; to get exactly what she wants from men, whenever she wants it. In essence, objectify them back.

She wanted to prove that she could do so just for fun. "I had an aversion to the idea that all girls were left in mushy little puddles of attachment," she wrote. She was going to show the world otherwise.

Many of my female students feel the same. They argue that hooking up is a way to "reject oppressive sexism," "pursue sexual liberation," and challenge the idea "that women are supposed to be passive." They're not alone. The hookup is "the road to sexual emancipation," asserted a woman at the University of Florida.

* * *

"I know it sounds hyperbolic," wrote a female senior at Northwestern:

> but I mean it when I say that getting married right now would ruin my life. I want the chance to pick up and move to a new city for a new job or for adventure, without having to worry about a spouse or a family. I need to be able to stay at the office until three in the morning if I have to and not care about putting dinner on the table.

This is Hanna Rosin's argument in *The End of Men*. In her estimation, hooking up is liberating women from reliance on men in both the short and long terms. "Feminist progress is largely dependent on hook-up culture," she writes, arguing that a "serious suitor" is as dangerous to a woman's future today as an unintended pregnancy was to an unmarried girl in the nineteenth century.

I'm not so sure that hookup culture is unequivocally good for women, but Rosin is certainly not wrong to notice that they make this argument. Many young women today think that hitching themselves to a man, even a successful one, is a bad idea and backward to boot.

* * *

A Duke student described college partying as a "whirlwind of drunkenness and horniness." Those are the two main ingredients. In fact, students from Bowdoin, the University of Pennsylvania, and the University of Illinois at Chicago have all used the phrase "hand-in-hand" to describe the relationship between partying and hooking up. "That's the culture," wrote one of my students. "You go to a party together, everyone gets wasted, and the goal of the night is to get some." It's "more than just a norm," insisted another, "it is near an obligation!" Sex and alcohol, she continues, are the two essential ingredients for any college party that is deemed "fun," and the potential for sexual contact is quite often "the only reason students socialize." It's "what *all* the parties are about," wrote a third with finality.

Of course, some students absolutely love this. At the University of Pennsylvania, an enthusiastic female student wrote, "Sometimes, we just want to have sex for sex's sake. What's wrong with that?" At Princeton; a woman found hookups to be "rewarding, mutually fulfilling and memorable." "From a single guy's point of view," explained a student at Yale, "I find few things more fun than going out at night and seeing what I can come home with." One of my female students put it like this: "Practically unlimited and uninterrupted sex whenever I feel like it? I don't think I could pass that offer up." She was delighted by hookup culture.

Students who are on the fence about whether to hook up, though, can find that doing so can feel, as four of my students separately intoned, "inevitable." It certainly felt that way for Mara. She described five hookups in her first year, but only a couple of times were they intentional. The rest were "happenstance." One night, for example, she found herself stranded at a house party at a college across town. Her two girlfriends had disappeared and she watched as the first floor of the house slowly emptied out.

She found herself alone with an acquaintance who lived there. When she told him that she wasn't sure how to get home, he gestured hospitably to a threadbare tan couch that she remembered seeing someone spill beer on earlier in the night. "At this point it was very late and I was very tired," she recalled, "so I figured I just had to take my chances."

She accepted his hospitality, but she didn't take the couch. Not because it was less than inviting, which it was, but because she felt obligated to hook up with her host. In her mind, she owed him a hookup because he was "providing shelter." Sleeping on the couch was akin to having bad manners. They hooked up but it was "low-key," she reported, and they went to sleep pretty quickly. "I was VERY lucky that this guy ended up not being creepy," she wrote in retrospect.

Mara may have been lucky, and sexual coercion by peers is a serious problem on college campuses, but her story reveals a different kind of coercive pressure. In fact, she specified that she generally didn't feel pressured by men. She knew that she could say no, and felt capable of doing so, but hookups were so powerfully built into the party script that it seemed wrong not to go along. Saying no to a hookup at that stage of the night was like going for a jog in a tuxedo or taking your cat to the park. It was just *weird*. She wasn't always motivated enough to make things weird. "It was only worth making a scene if

I really didn't want to [do it]," she explained. "If I didn't really care, it would just continue." So, there were several instances in which she hooked up with a guy because it felt like it was just the thing to do.

* * *

In some ways, residential colleges today aren't that different from the colonial colleges of the 1700s. They still coordinate groups of young people, organizing their lives in sometimes rigid ways. Many colleges are, in other words, still "total institutions," planned entities that collect large numbers of like individuals, cut them off from the wider society, and provide for all their needs. Prisons, mental hospitals, army barracks, and nursing homes are total institutions. So are cruise ships, cults, convents, and summer camps. Behemoths of order, these organizations swallow up their constituents and structure their lives.

Each year, millions of young people are swallowed by thousands of college campuses. They are sequestered in dormitories. Their food, rest, and work is bureaucratically regimented. Rooms and roommates are assigned. Classes are scheduled. Minimum units are specified. Work study is doled out. The gym doors are opened. Cafeteria hours are posted. Food is prepared. And activities are organized.

When students move into dorms, they are truly *in* the institution. To live on campus is to be a part of something wholly, which is part of the appeal. Students are free to leave, but there is no need to do so. Most everything essential is provided for them and, barring that, there is a campus store with clothes, school supplies, electronics, hygiene products, and any other essentials they could possibly want.

In both large and small ways, though never completely, students become one with the institution. Its rules, scripts, languages, logics, technologies, timetables, and architectures become their own. Like the nun who recites traditional prayers, the soldier who reports for breakfast at 0500 hours, and the cult member who tends the garden, students' lives play out within a structure that they don't control, but largely accept and even embrace.

Because many colleges are total institutions and hookup culture is totally institutionalized, colleges don't just control what students learn, when they eat, where they sleep, and how they exercise; they also have an influence on whether and how they have sex. Thanks to the last few hundred years, most colleges now offer a very specific kind of nightlife, a drunkworld that is also the site for sex.

Drunkworld incites sexual activity. The delighted, the willing, and many of the reluctant go along. And while students can always break the rules or rewrite the scripts, in general hookups follow the logic of the institution: they occur at predetermined places and on particular days of the week, allowing students to fit sex into their schedule in a way that is compatible with the college's needs. Sex is now a part of how students do higher education. That's why it can feel inevitable.

Of course, one way to avoid the inevitability of hooking up is to refuse to get off the boat, to stay buttoned up tight in one's cabin and in bed by nine. And people do. Many do, in fact. They opt out. Like the reluctant cruise vacationer, they're on board but not on board. They've paid for their ticket and they're along for the ride, whether they want to be or not. As one student wrote forebodingly, "Even if you aren't hooking up, there is no escaping hookup culture."

* * *

Since the Victorian idea that women are motivated by love persists even alongside the more modern idea that they want to have sex for fun, women's efforts to stay cool are less credible than men's. So, no matter how good women are at pretending to be uninterested—indeed, no matter how uninterested they actually are—many men simply *assume* that the women they hook up with want a monogamous relationship.

It was Deanna's story that brought this point home for me. One day her regular hookup partner met her at a picnic bench nestled into an alcove outside of her building. It was a sunny day but Reid looked glum and it quickly became clear why he had dropped by: he had fallen for someone else. "So I think we need to stop sleeping together," he said, his voice soft and serious-sounding.

Deanna let the news wash over her and watched Reid's face contort gently as he told his story: how they hadn't been exclusive (she knew), how the hookup had just happened (as they do), and that he hadn't meant to like this new girl (but he did). For a moment, she felt a tight sensation in her chest that was familiar—she hadn't been chosen—but she didn't feel that way about Reid anyway. She wasn't heartbroken. Instead, she was "genuinely happy for him." She said so and told him that she was flattered that he hadn't ended their hookups sooner.

But Reid's face didn't relax. He continued, still looking concerned, stressing what a lovely person she was and how he hoped she wasn't too upset. "You too will find love someday," he said reassuringly. Deanna started to get annoyed. "He more and more drastically emphasized asking if I was okay," she recounted, "as if he had somehow damaged me, seeming to expect a flood of tears." She reiterated that she wasn't hurt and failed to collapse into a blubbery mess, but he wouldn't let it go. "Although this started out subtly," she recalled, "by the end of our talk it was awkwardly apparent that there would be no way that he would believe me when I said that I was fine."

This experience was a wakeup call. Deanna had thought that their hookups had been about exploring sexual attraction as equals, but this incident revealed that he didn't and hadn't ever thought of them that way. Reflecting on their encounters, she wrote:

> The stigma attached to women being the emotional creatures in the relationship and the men being the physical ones had never been so apparent to me. . . .
> He clearly thought that he was the one with the power to hurt and I was the one that was expected to cry with anguish.

It was ironic, she commented, because Reid's concern for her feelings was "a far more womanly trait" than any feelings she had for him, but there was no convincing him otherwise. "The hardest part of the whole affair," she wrote, was "seeing in an equal's eyes their opinion that I was inferior."

* * *

The irony is that most college students actually want to be in a caring relationship. Of the students who filled out the Online College Social Life Survey, 71 percent of men and 67 percent of women said that they wished they had more opportunities to find a long-term partner. Despite their claims to be too busy and focused on their careers, students overwhelmingly find the idea of a committed partnership appealing and, in fact, many of them get what they want. Over two-thirds of college seniors report having been in at least one relationship lasting six months or more.

Most of these relationships start as hookups. Rachel Kalish, a sociologist who studied student dating for her dissertation, found that dates do occur between college students, but the dates almost always come after they have been hooking up together for a while. Dates aren't how today's college students get to know each other; they're how the transition from casual sex to a potential monogamous relationship is signified. . . .

When . . . Kalish asked students if they thought hookup culture was good or bad for relationships, the majority said that it was bad. They felt that it made investing in other people feel unimportant, made sex seem less special, and interfered with learning how to be a caring partner. The skills needed for managing hookup culture, they noted, are in direct contradiction to the skills needed to propose, build, and sustain committed relationships. Perhaps most of all, students recognized that seeing "feelings as negative" could make it hard to experience them as positive. "It's just a relationship killer, I think," said one of her male interviewees in his first year, noting that the women he knew seemed "numb."

* * *

Trust may, indeed, be having a lull. Young people today are significantly more likely than the two generations before them to agree that "people are just looking out for themselves." A full 60 percent of millennials and 62 percent of college students say so, compared to less than half of generation X and just over a third of the boomer generation. There is "an inherent lack of trust in everyone and everything," wrote a female student. "Like most girls I want to hook up with," explained a male student about a prospect, "I don't trust her." Hookups lead to "trust issues," said three students separately. Young people today are more cynical, in general, and they're more cynical about love in particular.

In *The End of Men*, Hanna Rosin calls freedom from love relationships "feminist progress," and lots of students are inclined to agree, but my students would have liked a little compassion alongside their liberation. They want fun and freedom, and women don't want to go back to a world where being sexually active marks them as disreputable by definition, but they also want to be treated with basic courtesy and to have kind and generous sexual exchanges with others. "What I really want right now," one sighed, "is for someone to be nice to me and just want me in that way." Men wanted this, too. Students wanted to hook up with someone who they knew felt goodwill toward them and would be courteous to them, treating them at least as well as they treat total strangers. It didn't often happen.

* * *

The little we do know about post-college experiences suggests that most grads do transition to something that looks at least a little more like dating. For *Hooking Up*, which was published in 2008, sociologist Kathleen Bogle interviewed people about how their lives had changed since leaving college; "across the board," she said, they described a different life-style. They started full-time jobs, moved to new cities where they didn't know anyone, and found that apartment buildings weren't anything like residence halls. They spent more time alone. They got up early and went to bed on time. Women were surprised to find that they were asked out to dinner.

For Bogle's interviewees, dating had almost entirely replaced hooking up. They were no longer surrounded by peers in whom they placed an implicit (if unadvisable) trust. If they did meet someone they were interested in hooking up with, they probably weren't neighbors. Women, especially, but some men, too, were reluctant to get into a car and drive to someone else's turf. There were also fewer Saturday and Sunday morning recaps, and casual sex was an inappropriate topic around the water cooler at work.

Bogle's interviewees also suggested that the time for hooking up had passed. College was for going wild, but after graduation, Bogle explained, "a new 'definition of the situation' [took] hold." Even fraternity men, she noted, were leaving their hard-partying, womanizing ways behind. Everyone seemed to be looking for something a little more subdued. One of her male interviewees described the change in himself this way:

> I don't know, you are looking for more [of a] relationship. I know this person, I can trust them, I can share things. If I have a bad day, they will listen to me, those kinds of concepts. Meeting someone in a bar, buying them drinks, getting them drunk and hooking up in your car, there is not quality there at all. You don't even know if that is their real name they gave you . . . As you get older, you . . . want something more solid.

So, Bogle's grads dated, quite traditionally in fact, with men proposing outings, paying, opening car doors, and the like. "Men seemed to interact with the opposite sex as one might expect their grandfathers would have done,"

Bogle said, seeming surprised. Though they may have hooked up with abandon in their college years, everyone seemed to transition quite seamlessly to dating once college was over.

* * *

It may be that dating culture isn't as strong as it was almost a decade ago. Things may really be changing quickly. We know they sometimes do. At the colleges where I've lectured, seniors sometimes pull me aside anxiously and ask how they are supposed to behave once they graduate. For quite some time, I thought they were exaggerating their confusion, but I've come to think that they mean it seriously. Some seem to find dating as mysterious as they would a VHS tape or a rotary phone. When the subject of dating came up, they would frequently inquire, "Like, dinner and a movie?" The phrase "dinner and a movie" came to stand in for this thing they had heard of called a "date," but they didn't really have any idea what it was or how to do it.

At Boston College, a philosophy professor named Kerry Cronin similarly discovered that her students didn't seem to know what dating involved. She decided to make asking someone on a date a required activity in one of her classes, but her students were so stumped as to how to do it that she had to develop an elaborate set of instructions: A date must involve only two people; there has to be genuine romantic interest; . . . the date has to be an activity that allows for a conversation (no dance clubs and no dark movie theaters); it has to be over before 10 p.m.; and it can end in a kiss, but that's it. Cronin specified, too, how a person initiates a second date if they want one or communicates that they do not. I think some of my grads would be grateful for such clear instructions.

Open communication in general seemed strange and new to some of my students. Dating felt weird to them in part because it required that they be at least a little honest about their intentions.

"[Because] you have to arrange a meet-up," Mara explained, it was impossible to make it seem careless and meaningless. When a guy she went on a couple of dates with was "earnest" and "transparent" with her, she said it was "almost comical" compared to what she was used to. Some grads are stumped, too, by how to express interest in nonsexual ways. If they don't try to have sex with you, one asked, how can you tell if they're attracted to you?

Some of my students were still learning how to be nice to one another. Sydney learned by example. She was the student who hooked up with men she distinctly disliked, only to go through that terrible night when Brad called her a "bitch" for not wanting to have sex without a condom. Eventually, she met a man who showed her that it didn't have to be that way.

"The best description of Wes that I can give," she said affectionately,

> is that he's the kind of guy you already know would be a great father. He's really smart, sincerely friendly, patient, and almost always has a smile on his face.

He's not exactly the type of guy you scope out at a party—I mean he's sort of a nerd—but he's just *Wes*.

Sydney met him in college at a typical hookup-inducing party. Normally, she explained, she wouldn't have "given Wes a second thought," but it was 3 a.m. and she was "plastered." It was one of those "inevitable" hookups, the kind that just happen because it's late and everyone's drunk and hooking up is what people do. She shrugged and they went back to his place. They kissed, but he surprised her by deciding that she was too drunk to go further.

The next morning, he "shattered" everything she thought she knew about men. At first her intention was to flee—"I remember waking up next to him in the morning," she said, "wondering why I was even there"—but there was something in his voice. He acted nonchalant about whether she stayed or went, as the rules of hookup culture required, but Sydney heard a "hint of pleading." So, she decided to take a chance. Reflecting, she said:

> I knew that I felt safe with him—drunk, sober, as a friend, and in bed. I wanted to let him know he was safe with me too. So I got back in bed, and I told him that I would stay as long as I was welcome to.

They stayed together for quite some time.

* * *

The inevitable churn of history has brought us a brave new world. College students are at its brink, but all of the problems with hookup culture are problems off campus, too. The fog, in other words, isn't just on college campuses; it's everywhere. It has infiltrated our lives, obscuring our ability to envision better alternatives: sexualities that are more authentic, kinder, safer, more pleasurable, and less warped by prejudice, consumerism, status, and superficiality. We need to understand what's happening on college campuses because what's happening there is happening everywhere.

10

McDonald's in Hong Kong: Consumerism, Dietary Change, and the Rise of a Children's Culture

FROM *Golden Arches East*

JAMES L. WATSON

McDonald's has not only become the symbol of globalization. It is emblematic of the influence of the West, and particularly the United States, on the rest of the world. Many people question the value of this bequest, seeing fast food as a corrosive and crude intrusion on traditional practices, to say nothing of its questionable nutritional value. James Watson takes exception, not because he necessarily loves fast food and wants to speed up the erosion of local practices, but because he finds in those who are encouraged to take up Western practices—in this case the McDonald's "experience"—more selectivity and creativity. Although South Koreans openly oppose and reject McDonald's, many in Hong Kong have redefined McDonald's in ways that reveal the human capacity to shape culture and find compatibility between the old and the new.

TRANSNATIONALISM AND THE FAST FOOD INDUSTRY

Does the roaring success of McDonald's and its rivals in the fast food industry mean that Hong Kong's local culture is under siege? Are food chains helping to create a homogeneous, "global" culture better suited to the demands of a capitalist world order? Hong Kong would seem to be an excellent place to test the globalization hypothesis, given the central role that cuisine plays in the production and maintenance of a distinctive local identity. Man Tso-chuen's great-grandchildren are today avid consumers of Big Macs, pizza, and Coca-Cola; does this somehow make them less "Chinese" than their grandfather?

It is my contention that the cultural arena in places like Hong Kong is changing with such breathtaking speed that the fundamental assumptions underlining such questions are themselves questionable. Economic and social realities make it necessary to construct an entirely new approach to global issues, one that takes the consumers' own views into account. Analyses based on neomarxian and dependency (center/periphery) models that were popular in the 1960s and 1970s do not begin to capture the complexity of emerging transnational systems.

This chapter represents a conscious attempt to bring the discussion of globalism down to earth, focusing on one local culture. The people of Hong Kong have embraced American-style fast foods, and by so doing they might appear to be in the vanguard of a worldwide culinary revolution. But they have not been stripped of their cultural traditions, nor have they become "Americanized" in any but the most superficial of ways. Hong Kong in the late 1990s constitutes one of the world's most heterogeneous cultural environments. Younger people, in particular, are fully conversant in transnational idioms, which include language, music, sports, clothing, satellite television, cyber-communications, global travel, and—of course—cuisine. It is no longer possible to distinguish what is local and what is not. In Hong Kong, as I hope to show in this chapter, the transnational *is* the local.

EATING OUT: A SOCIAL HISTORY OF CONSUMPTION

By the time McDonald's opened its first Hong Kong restaurant in 1975, the idea of fast food was already well established among local consumers. Office workers, shop assistants, teachers, and transport workers had enjoyed various forms of take-out cuisine for well over a century; an entire industry had emerged to deliver mid-day meals direct to workplaces. In the 1960s and 1970s thousands of street vendors produced snacks and simple meals on demand, day or night. Time has always been money in Hong Kong; hence, the dual keys to success in the catering trade were speed and convenience. Another essential characteristic was that the food, based primarily on rice or noodles, had to be hot. Even the most cosmopolitan or local consumers did not (and many still do not) consider cold foods, such as sandwiches and salads, to be acceptable meals. Older people in South China associate cold food with offerings to the dead and are understandably hesitant to eat it.

The fast food industry in Hong Kong had to deliver hot items that could compete with traditional purveyors of convenience foods (noodle shops, dumpling stalls, soup carts, portable grills). The first modern chain to enter the fray was Café de Coral, a local corporation that began operation in 1969 and is still a dominant player in the Hong Kong fast food market (with 109 outlets and a 25 percent market share, compared to McDonald's 20 percent market share in 1994).[1] Café de Coral's strategy was simple: It moved Hong Kong's street foods indoors, to a clean, well-lighted cafeteria that offered instant service and moderate prices; popular Cantonese items were then combined with (sinicized) "Western" foods that had been popular in Hong Kong for decades. Café de Coral's menu reads like the *locus classicus* of Pacific Rim cuisine: deep-fried chicken wings, curry on rice, hot dogs, roast pork in soup noodles, spaghetti

---

1. When Watson wrote this, seven of the world's ten busiest McDonald's restaurants were located in Hong Kong. When McDonald's first opened in 1975, few thought it would survive more than a few months. By January 1, 1997, Hong Kong had 125 outlets, which means that there was one McDonald's for every 51,200 residents, compared to one for every 30,000 people in the United States.

with meat balls, barbecued ribs, red bean sundaes, Oval-tine, Chinese tea, and Coca-Cola (with lemon, hot or cold). The formula was so successful it spawned dozens of imitators, including three full-scale chains.

* * *

McDonald's mid-1970s entry also corresponded to an economic boom associated with Hong Kong's conversion from a low-wage, light-industrial outpost to a regional center for financial services and high-technology industries. McDonald's' takeoff thus paralleled the rise of a new class of highly educated, affluent consumers who thrive in Hong Kong's ever-changing urban environment—one of the most stressful in the world. These new consumers eat out more often than their parents and have created a huge demand for fast, convenient foods of all types. In order to compete in this market, McDonald's had to offer something different. That critical difference, at least during the company's first decade of operation, was American culture packaged as all-American, middle-class food.

* * *

MENTAL CATEGORIES: SNACK VERSUS MEAL

As in other parts of East Asia, McDonald's faced a serious problem when it began operation in Hong Kong: Hamburgers, fries, and sandwiches were perceived as snacks (Cantonese *siu sihk*, literally "small eats"); in the local view these items did not constitute the elements of a proper meal. This perception is still prevalent among older, more conservative consumers who believe that hamburgers, hot dogs, and pizza can never be "filling." Many students stop at fast food outlets on their way home from school; they may share hamburgers and fries with their classmates and then eat a full meal with their families at home. This is not considered a problem by parents, who themselves are likely to have stopped for tea and snacks after work. Snacking with friends and colleagues provides a major opportunity for socializing (and transacting business) among southern Chinese. Teahouses, coffee shops, bakeries, and ice cream parlors are popular precisely because they provide a structured yet informal setting for social encounters. Furthermore, unlike Chinese restaurants and banquet halls, snack centers do not command a great deal of time or money from customers.

Contrary to corporate goals, therefore, McDonald's entered the Hong Kong market as a purveyor of snacks. Only since the late 1980s has its fare been treated as the foundation of "meals" by a generation of younger consumers who regularly eat non-Chinese food. Thanks largely to McDonald's, hamburgers and fries are now a recognized feature of Hong Kong's lunch scene. The evening hours remain, however, the weak link in McDonald's marketing plan; the real surprise was breakfast, which became a peak traffic period.

The mental universe of Hong Kong consumers is partially revealed in the everyday use of language. Hamburgers are referred to, in colloquial Cantonese, as *han bou bao*—*han* being a homophone for "ham" and *bao* the common term for stuffed buns or bread rolls. *Bao* are quintessential snacks, and however excellent or nutritious they might be, they do not constitute the basis of a satisfying (i.e., filling) meal. In South China that honor is reserved for culinary arrangements that rest, literally, on a bed of rice (*fan*). Foods that accompany rice are referred to as *sung*, probably best translated as "toppings" (including meat, fish, and vegetables). It is significant that hamburgers are rarely categorized as meat (*yuk*); Hong Kong consumers tend to perceive anything that is served between slices of bread (Big Macs, fish sandwiches, hot dogs) as *bao*. In American culture the hamburger is categorized first and foremost as a meat item (with all the attendant worries about fat and cholesterol content), whereas in Hong Kong the same item is thought of primarily as bread.

FROM EXOTIC TO ORDINARY: MCDONALD'S BECOMES LOCAL

Following precedents in other international markets, the Hong Kong franchise promoted McDonald's basic menu and did not introduce items that would be more recognizable to Chinese consumers (such as rice dishes, tropical fruit, soup noodles). Until recently the food has been indistinguishable from that served in Mobile, Alabama, or Moline, Illinois. There are, however, local preferences: the best-selling items in many outlets are fish sandwiches and plain hamburgers; Big Macs tend to be the favorites of children and teenagers. Hot tea and hot chocolate outsell coffee, but Coca-Cola remains the most popular drink.

McDonald's conservative approach also applied to the breakfast menu. When morning service was introduced in the 1980s, American-style items such as eggs, muffins, pancakes, and hash brown potatoes were not featured. Instead, the local outlets served the standard fare of hamburgers and fries for breakfast. McDonald's initial venture into the early morning food market was so successful that Mr. Ng hesitated to introduce American-style breakfast items, fearing that an abrupt shift in menu might alienate consumers who were beginning to accept hamburgers and fries as a regular feature of their diet. The transition to eggs, muffins, and hash browns was a gradual one, and today most Hong Kong customers order breakfasts that are similar to those offered in American outlets. But once established, dietary preferences change slowly: McDonald's continues to feature plain hamburgers (but not the Big Mac) on its breakfast menu in most Hong Kong outlets.

Management decisions of the type outlined above helped establish McDonald's as an icon of popular culture in Hong Kong. From 1975 to approximately 1985, McDonald's became the "in" place for young people wishing to associate themselves with the laid-back, nonhierarchical dynamism they perceived American society to embody. The first generation of consumers patronized McDonald's precisely because it was *not* Chinese and was *not* associated with Hong Kong's past as a backward-looking colonial outpost where (in their view) nothing of consequence ever happened. Hong Kong was changing and, as noted earlier, a new consumer culture was beginning to take shape. McDonald's caught the wave of this cultural movement and has been riding it ever since.

* * *

Today, McDonald's restaurants in Hong Kong are packed—wall-to-wall—with people of all ages, few of whom are seeking an American cultural experience. Twenty years after Mr. Ng opened his first restaurant, eating at McDonald's has become an ordinary, everyday experience for hundreds of thousands of Hong Kong residents. The chain has become a local institution in the sense that it has blended into the urban landscape; McDonald's outlets now serve as rendezvous points for young and old alike.

* * *

WHAT'S IN A SMILE? FRIENDLINESS AND PUBLIC SERVICE

American consumers expect to be served "with a smile" when they order fast food, but this is not true in all societies. In Hong Kong people are suspicious of anyone who displays what is perceived to be an excess of congeniality, solicitude, or familiarity. The human smile is not, therefore, a universal symbol of openness and honesty. "If you buy an apple from a hawker and he smiles at you," my Cantonese tutor once told me, "you know you're being cheated."

Given these cultural expectations, it was difficult for Hong Kong management to import a key element of the McDonald's formula—service with a smile—and make it work. Crew members were trained to treat customers in a manner that approximates the American notion of "friendliness." Prior to the 1970s, there was not even an indigenous Cantonese term to describe this form of behavior. The traditional notion of friendship is based on loyalty to close associates, which by definition cannot be extended to strangers. Today the concept of *public* friendliness is recognized—and verbalized—by younger people in Hong Kong, but the term many of them use to express this quality is "friendly," borrowed directly from English. McDonald's, through its television advertising, may be partly responsible for this innovation, but to date it has had little effect on workers in the catering industry.

During my interviews it became clear that the majority of Hong Kong consumers were uninterested in public displays of congeniality from service personnel. When shopping for fast food, most people cited convenience, cleanliness, and table space as primary considerations; few even mentioned service except to note that the food should be delivered promptly. Counter staff in Hong Kong's fast food outlets (including McDonald's) rarely make great efforts to smile or to behave in a manner Americans would interpret as friendly. Instead, they project qualities that are admired in the local culture: competence, directness, and unflappability. In a North American setting the facial expression that Hong Kong employees use to convey these qualities would likely be interpreted as a deliberate attempt to be rude or indifferent. Workers who smile on the job are assumed to be enjoying themselves at the consumer's (and management's) expense: In the words of one diner I overheard while standing in a queue, "They must be playing around back there. What are they laughing about?"

CONSUMER DISCIPLINE?

[A] hallmark of the American fast food business is the displacement of labor costs from the corporation to the consumers. For the system to work, consumers must be educated—or "disciplined"—so that they voluntarily fulfill their side of an implicit bargain: We (the corporation) will provide cheap, fast service, if you (the customer) carry your own tray, seat yourself, and help clean up afterward. Time and space are also critical factors in the equation: Fast service is offered in exchange for speedy consumption and a prompt departure, thereby making room for others. This system has revolutionized the American food industry and has helped to shape consumer expectations in other sectors of the economy. How has it fared in Hong Kong? Are Chinese customers conforming to disciplinary models devised in Oak Brook, Illinois?

The answer is both yes and no. In general Hong Kong consumers have accepted the basic elements of the fast food formula, but with "localizing" adaptations. For instance, customers generally do not bus their own trays, nor do they depart immediately upon finishing. Clearing one's own table has never been an accepted part of local culinary culture, owing in part to the low esteem attaching to this type of labor. During McDonald's' first decade in Hong Kong, the cost of hiring extra cleaners was offset by low wages. A pattern was thus established, and customers grew accustomed to leaving without attending to their own rubbish. Later, as wages escalated in the late 1980s and early 1990s McDonald's tried to introduce self-busing by posting announcements in restaurants and featuring the practice in its television advertisements. As of February 1997, however, little had changed. Hong Kong consumers . . . have ignored this aspect of consumer discipline.

What about the critical issues of time and space? Local managers with whom I spoke estimated that the average eating time for most Hong Kong customers was between 20 and 25 minutes, compared to 11 minutes in the United States fast food industry. This estimate confirms my own observations of McDonald's consumers in Hong Kong's central business district (Victoria and Tsimshatsui).

A survey conducted in the New Territories city of Yuen Long—an old market town that has grown into a modern urban center—revealed that local McDonald's consumers took just under 26 minutes to eat.

Perhaps the most striking feature of the American-inspired model of consumer discipline is the queue. Researchers in many parts of the world have reported that customers refuse, despite "education" campaigns by the chains involved, to form neat lines in front of cashiers. Instead, customers pack themselves into disorderly scrums and jostle for a chance to place their orders. Scrums of this nature were common in Hong Kong when McDonald's opened in 1975. Local managers discouraged this practice by stationing queue monitors near the registers during busy hours and, by the 1980s, orderly lines were the norm at McDonald's. The disappearance of the scrum corresponds to a general change in Hong Kong's public culture as a new generation of residents, the children of refugees, began to treat the territory as their home. Courtesy toward strangers was largely unknown in the 1960s: Boarding a bus during rush hour could be a nightmare and transacting business at a bank teller's window required brute strength. Many people credit McDonald's with being the first public institution in Hong Kong to enforce queuing, and thereby helping to create a more "civilized" social order. McDonald's did not, in fact, introduce the queue to Hong Kong, but this belief is firmly lodged in the public imagination.

HOVERING AND THE NAPKIN WARS

Purchasing one's food is no longer a physical challenge in Hong Kong's McDonald's but finding a place to sit is quite another matter. The traditional practice of "hovering" is one solution: Choose a group of diners who appear to be on the verge of leaving and stake a claim to their table by hovering nearby, sometimes only inches away. Seated customers routinely ignore the intrusion; it would, in fact, entail a loss of face to notice. Hovering was the norm in Hong Kong's lower- to middle-range restaurants during the 1960s and 1970s, but the practice has disappeared in recent years. Restaurants now take names or hand out tickets at the entrance; warning signs, in Chinese and English, are posted: "Please wait to be seated." Customers are no longer allowed into the dining area until a table is ready.

Fast food outlets are the only dining establishments in Hong Kong where hovering is still tolerated, largely because it would be nearly impossible to regulate. Customer traffic in McDonald's is so heavy that the standard restaurant design has failed to reproduce American-style dining routines: Rather than ordering first and finding a place to sit afterward, Hong Kong consumers usually arrive in groups and delegate one or two people to claim a table while someone else joins the counter queues. Children make ideal hoverers and learn to scoot through packed restaurants, zeroing in on diners who are about to finish. It is one of the wonders of comparative ethnography to witness the speed with which Hong Kong children perform this reconnaissance duty. Foreign visitors are sometimes unnerved by hovering, but residents accept it as part of everyday life in one of the worlds most densely populated cities. It is not surprising, therefore, that Hong Kong's fast food chains have made few efforts to curtail the practice.

Management is less tolerant of behavior that affects profit margins. In the United States fast food companies save money by allowing (or requiring) customers to collect their own napkins, straws, plastic flatware, and condiments. Self-provisioning is an essential feature of consumer discipline, but it only works if the system is not abused. In Hong Kong napkins are dispensed, one at a time, by McDonald's crew members who work behind the counter; customers who do not ask for napkins do not receive any. This is a deviation from the corporation's standard operating procedure and adds a few seconds to each transaction, which in turn slows down the queues. Why alter a well-tested routine? The reason is simple: napkins placed in public dispensers disappear faster than they can be replaced.

* * *

Buffets, like fast food outlets, depend upon consumers to perform much of their own labor in return for reduced prices. Abuse of the system—wasting food or taking it home—is taken for granted and is factored into the price of buffet meals. Fast food chains, by contrast, operate at lower price thresholds where consumer abuse can seriously affect profits.

Many university students of my acquaintance reported that they had frequently observed older people pocketing wads of paper napkins, three to four inches thick, in restaurants that permit self-provisioning. Management efforts to stop this behavior are referred to, in the Cantonese-English slang of Hong Kong youth, as the "Napkin Wars." Younger people were appalled by what they saw as the waste of natural resources by a handful of customers. As they talked about the issue, however, it became obvious that the Napkin Wars represented more—in their eyes—than a campaign to conserve paper. The sight of diners abusing public facilities reminded these young people of the bad old days of their parents and grandparents, when Hong Kong's social life was dominated by refugees who had little stake in the local community. During the 1960s and 1970s, economic insecurities were heightened by the very real prospect that Red Guards might take over the colony at any moment. The game plan was simple during those decades: Make money as quickly as possible and move on. In the 1980s a new generation of local-born youth began treating Hong Kong as home and proceeded to build a public culture better suited to their vision of life in a cosmopolitan city. In this new Hong Kong, consumers are expected to be sophisticated and financially secure, which means that it would be beneath their dignity to abuse public facilities. Still, McDonald's retains control of its napkins.

CHILDREN AS CONSUMERS

During the summer of 1994, while attending a business lunch in one of Hong Kong's fanciest hotels, I watched a waiter lean down to consult with a customer at an adjoining table. The object of his attention was a six-year-old child who studied the menu with practiced skill. His parents beamed as their prodigy performed; meanwhile, sitting across the table, a pair of grandparents sat bolt upright, scowling in obvious disapproval. Twenty years ago the sight of a child commanding such attention would have shocked the entire restaurant into silence. No one, save the immediate party (and this observer), even noticed in 1994.

Hong Kong children rarely ate outside their home until the late 1970s, and when they did, they were expected to eat what was put in front of them. The idea that children might actually order their own food or speak to a waiter would have outraged most adults; only foreign youngsters (notably the off-spring of British and American expatriates) were permitted to make their preferences known in public. Today, Hong Kong children as young as two or three participate in the local economy as full-fledged consumers, with their own tastes and brand loyalties. Children now have money in their pockets and they spend it on personal consumption, which usually means snacks. In response, new industries and a specialized service sector has emerged to "feed" these discerning consumers. McDonald's was one of the first corporations to recognize the potential of the children's market; in effect, the company started a revolution by making it possible for even the youngest consumers to *choose* their own food.

* * *

Many Hong Kong children of my acquaintance are so fond of McDonald's that they refuse to eat with their parents or grandparents in Chinese-style restaurants or *dim sam* teahouses. This has caused intergenerational distress in some of Hong Kong's more conservative communities. In 1994, a nine-year-old boy, the descendant of illustrious ancestors who settled in the New Territories eight centuries ago, talked about his concerns as we consumed Big Macs, fries, and shakes at McDonald's: "A-bak [uncle], I like it here better than any place in the world. I want to come here every day." His father takes him to McDonald's at least twice a week, but his grandfather, who accompanied them a few times in the late 1980s, will no longer do so. "I prefer to eat *dim sam*," the older man told me later. "That place [McDonald's] is for kids." Many grandparents have resigned themselves to the new consumer trends and take their preschool grandchildren to McDonald's for midmorning snacks—precisely the time of day that local teahouses were once packed with retired people. Cantonese grandparents have always played a prominent role in child minding, but until recently the children had to accommodate to the proclivities of their elders. By the 1990s grandchildren were more assertive and the mid-morning *dim sam* snack was giving way to hamburgers and Cokes.

* * *

RONALD MCDONALD AND THE INVENTION OF BIRTHDAY PARTIES

Until recently most people in Hong Kong did not even know, let alone celebrate, their birthdates in the Western calendrical sense; dates of birth according to the lunar calendar were recorded for divinatory purposes but were not noted in annual rites. By the late 1980s, however, birthday parties, complete with cakes and candles, were the rage in Hong Kong. Any child who was anyone had to have a party, and the most popular venue was a fast food restaurant, with McDonald's ranked above all competitors. The majority of Hong Kong people live in overcrowded flats, which means that parties are rarely held in private homes.

Except for the outlets in central business districts, McDonald's restaurants are packed every Saturday and Sunday with birthday parties, cycled through at the rate of one every hour. A party hostess, provided by the restaurant, leads the children in games while the parents sit on the sidelines, talking quietly among themselves. For a small fee celebrants receive printed invitation cards, photographs, a gift box containing toys and a discount coupon for future trips to McDonald's. Parties are held in a special enclosure, called the Ronald Room, which is equipped with low tables and tiny stools—suitable only for children. Television commercials portray Ronald McDonald leading birthday celebrants on exciting safaris and expeditions. The clown's Cantonese name, Mak Dong Lou Suk-Suk ("Uncle McDonald"), plays on the intimacy of kinship and has helped transform him into one of Hong Kong's most familiar cartoon figures.

* * *

MCDONALD'S AS A YOUTH CENTER

Weekends may be devoted to family dining and birthday parties for younger children, but on weekday afternoons, from 3:00 to 6:00 P.M., McDonald's restaurants are packed with teenagers stopping for a snack on their way home from school. In many outlets 80 percent of the late afternoon clientele appear in school uniforms, turning the restaurants into a sea of white frocks, light blue shirts, and dark trousers. The students, aged between 10 and 17, stake out tables and buy snacks that are shared in groups. The noise level at this time of day is deafening; students shout to friends and dart from table to table. Few adults, other than restaurant staff, are in evidence. It is obvious that McDonald's is treated as an informal youth center, a recreational extension of school where students can unwind after long hours of study.

* * *

In contrast to their counterparts in the United States, where fast food chains have devised ways to discourage lingering, McDonald's in Hong Kong does not set a limit on table time. When I asked the managers of several Hong Kong outlets how they coped with so many young people chatting at tables that might otherwise be occupied by paying customers, they all replied that the students were "welcome." The obvious strategy is to turn a potential liability into an asset: "Students create a good atmosphere which is good for our business," said one manager as he watched an army of teenagers—dressed in identical school uniforms—surge into his restaurant. Large numbers of students also use McDonald's as a place to do homework and prepare for exams, often in groups. Study space of any kind, public or private, is hard to find in overcrowded Hong Kong. . . .

CONCLUSIONS: WHOSE CULTURE IS IT?

In concluding this chapter, I would like to return to the questions raised in my opening remarks: In what sense, if any, is McDonald's involved in these cultural transformations (the creation of a child-centered consumer culture, for instance)? Has the company helped to create these trends, or merely followed the market? Is this an example of American-inspired, transnational culture crowding out indigenous cultures?

* * *

The deeper I dig into the lives of consumers themselves, in Hong Kong and elsewhere, the more complex the picture becomes. Having watched the processes of culture change unfold for nearly thirty years, it is apparent to me that the ordinary people of Hong Kong have most assuredly *not* been stripped of their cultural heritage, nor have they become the uncomprehending dupes of transnational corporations. Younger people—including many of the grandchildren of my former neighbors in the New Territories—are avid consumers of transnational culture in all of its most obvious manifestations: music, fashion, television, and cuisine. At the same time, however, Hong Kong has itself become a major center for the *production* of transnational culture, not just a sinkhole for its *consumption*. Witness, for example, the expansion of Hong Kong popular culture into China, Southeast Asia, and beyond: "Cantopop" music is heard on radio stations in North China, Vietnam, and Japan; the Hong Kong fashion industry influences clothing styles in Los Angeles, Bangkok, and Kuala Lumpur; and, perhaps most significant of all, Hong Kong is emerging as a center for the production and dissemination of satellite television programs throughout East, Southeast, and South Asia.

A lifestyle is emerging in Hong Kong that can best be described as post-modern, postnationalist, and flamboyantly transnational. The wholesale acceptance and appropriation of Big Macs, Ronald McDonald and birthday parties are small but significant aspects of this redefinition of Chinese cultural identity. In closing, therefore, it seems appropriate to pose an entirely new set of questions: Where does the transnational end and the local begin? Whose culture is it, anyway? In places like Hong Kong the postcolonial periphery is fast becoming the metropolitan center, where local people are consuming and simultaneously producing new cultural systems.

* * *

11

The Code of the Streets

ELIJAH ANDERSON

The capacity of sociology to look beyond the headlines is captured in this ethnographic account of a culture of respect, violence, and control on urban streets. Anderson describes this as "a cultural adaptation" to poverty, discrimination in public services, and social marginality. The "presentation of self" examined in this essay is a fascinating social construction and one with deadly serious consequences for everyone, not only for those who embrace the code of the street. The rich complexity of social life is revealed in Anderson's account, as is the difficulty in altering cultural practices without changing the circumstances of those who live the code.

Of all the problems besetting the poor inner-city black community, none is more pressing than that of interpersonal violence and aggression. It wreaks havoc daily with the lives of community residents and increasingly spills over into downtown and residential middle-class areas. Muggings, burglaries, carjackings, and drug-related shootings, all of which may leave their victims or innocent bystanders dead, are now common enough to concern all urban and many suburban residents. The inclination to violence springs from the circumstances of life among the ghetto poor—the lack of jobs that pay a living wage, the stigma of race, the fallout from rampant drug use and drug trafficking, and the resulting alienation and lack of hope for the future.

Simply living in such an environment places young people at special risk of falling victim to aggressive behavior. Although there are often forces in the community which can counteract the negative influences, by far the most powerful being a strong, loving, "decent" (as inner-city residents put it) family committed to middle-class values, the despair is pervasive enough to have spawned an oppositional culture, that of "the streets," whose norms are often consciously opposed to those of mainstream society. These two orientations—decent and street—socially organize the community, and their coexistence has important consequences for residents, particularly children growing up in the inner city. Above all, this environment means that even youngsters whose home lives reflect mainstream values—and the majority of homes in the community do—must be able to handle themselves in a street-oriented environment.

This is because the street culture has evolved what may be called a code of the streets, which amounts to a set of informal rules governing interpersonal public behavior, including violence. The rules prescribe both a proper comportment and a proper way to respond if challenged. They regulate the use of violence and so allow those who are inclined to aggression to precipitate violent encounters in an approved way. The rules have been established and are enforced mainly by the street-oriented, but on the streets the distinction between street and decent is often irrelevant; everybody knows that if the rules are violated, there are penalties. Knowledge of the code is thus largely defensive; it is literally necessary for operating in public. Therefore, even though families with a decency orientation are usually opposed to the values of the code, they often reluctantly encourage their children's familiarity with it to enable them to negotiate the inner-city environment.

At the heart of the code is the issue of respect—loosely defined as being treated "right," or granted the deference one deserves. However, in the troublesome public environment of the inner city, as people increasingly feel buffeted by forces beyond their control, what one deserves in the way of respect becomes more and more problematic and uncertain. This in turn further opens the issue of respect to sometimes intense interpersonal negotiation. In the street culture, especially among young people, respect is viewed as almost an external entity that is hard-won but easily lost, and so must constantly be guarded. The rules of the code in fact provide a framework for negotiating respect. The person whose very appearance—including his clothing, demeanor, and way of moving—deters transgressions feels that he possesses, and may be considered by others to possess, a measure of respect. With the right amount of respect, for instance, he can avoid "being bothered" in public. If he is bothered, not only may he be in physical danger but he has been disgraced or "dissed" (disrespected). Many of the forms that dissing can take might seem petty to middle-class people (maintaining eye contact for too long, for example), but to those invested in the street code, these actions become serious indications of the other person's intentions. Consequently, such people become very sensitive to advances and slights, which could well serve as warnings of imminent physical confrontation.

This hard reality can be traced to the profound sense of alienation from mainstream society and its institutions felt by many poor inner-city black people, particularly the young. The code of the streets is actually a cultural adaptation to a profound lack of faith in the police and the judicial system. The police are most often seen as representing the dominant white society and not caring to protect inner-city residents. When called, they may not respond, which is one reason many residents feel they must be prepared to take extraordinary measures to defend themselves and their loved ones against those who are inclined to aggression. Lack of police accountability has in fact been incorporated into the status system: the person who is believed capable of "taking care of himself" is accorded a certain deference, which translates into a sense of physical and psychological control. Thus the street code emerges where the influence of the police ends and personal responsibility for one's safety is felt to begin. Exacerbated by the proliferation of drugs and easy access to guns, this volatile situation results in the ability of the street-oriented minority (or those who effectively "go for bad") to dominate the public spaces.

DECENT AND STREET FAMILIES

Although almost everyone in poor inner-city neighborhoods is struggling financially and therefore feels a certain distance from the rest of America, the decent and the street family in a real sense represent two poles of value orientation, two contrasting conceptual categories. The labels "decent" and "street," which the residents themselves use, amount to evaluative judgments that confer status on local residents. The labeling is often the result of a social contest among individuals and families of the neighborhood. Individuals of the two orientations often coexist in the same extended family. Decent residents judge themselves to be so while judging others to be of the street, and street individuals often present themselves as decent, drawing distinctions between themselves and other people. In addition, there is quite a bit of circumstantial behavior—that is, one person may at different times exhibit both decent and street orientations, depending on the circumstances. Although these designations result from so much social jockeying, there do exist concrete features that define each conceptual category.

Generally, so-called decent families tend to accept mainstream values more fully and attempt to instill them in their children. Whether married couples with children or single-parent (usually female) households, they are generally "working poor" and so tend to be better off financially than their street-oriented neighbors. They value hard work and self-reliance and are willing to sacrifice for their children. Because they have a certain amount of faith in mainstream society, they harbor hopes for a better future for their children, if not for themselves. Many of them go to church and take a strong interest in their children's schooling. Rather than dwelling on the real hardships and inequities facing them, many such decent people, particularly the increasing number of grandmothers raising grandchildren, see their difficult situation as a test from God and derive great support from their faith and from the church community.

Extremely aware of the problematic and often dangerous environment in which they reside, decent parents tend to be strict in their child-rearing practices, encouraging children to respect authority and walk a straight moral line. They have an almost obsessive concern about trouble of any kind and remind their children to be on the lookout for people and situations that might lead to it. At the same time, they are themselves polite and considerate of others, and teach their children to be the same way. At home, at work, and in church, they strive hard to maintain a positive mental attitude and a spirit of cooperation.

So-called street parents, in contrast, often show a lack of consideration for other people and have a rather superficial sense of family and community. Though they may love their children, many of them are unable to cope with the physical and emotional demands of parenthood, and find it difficult to reconcile their needs with those of their children. These families, who are more fully invested in the code of the streets than the decent people are, may aggressively socialize their children into it in a normative way. They believe in the code and judge themselves and others according to its values.

In fact the overwhelming majority of families in the inner-city community try to approximate the decent-family model, but there are many others who clearly represent the worst fears of the decent family. Not only are their financial resources extremely limited, but what little they have may easily be misused. The lives of the street-oriented are often marked by disorganization. In the most desperate circumstances people frequently have a limited understanding of priorities and consequences, and so frustrations mount over bills, food, and, at times, drink, cigarettes, and drugs. Some tend toward self-destructive behavior; many street-oriented women are crack-addicted ("on the pipe"), alcoholic, or involved in complicated relationships with men who abuse them. In addition, the seeming intractability of their situation, caused in large part by the lack of well-paying jobs and the persistence of racial discrimination, has engendered deep-seated bitterness and anger in many of the most desperate and poorest blacks, especially young people. The need both to exercise a measure of control and to lash out at somebody is often reflected in the adults' relations with their children. At the least, the frustrations of persistent poverty shorten the fuse in such people—contributing to a lack of patience with anyone, child or adult, who irritates them.

In these circumstances a woman—or a man, although men are less consistently present in children's lives—can be quite aggressive with children, yelling at and striking them for the least little infraction of the rules she has set down. Often little if any serious explanation follows the verbal and physical punishment. This response teaches children a particular lesson. They learn that to solve any kind of interpersonal problem one must quickly resort to hitting or other violent behavior. Actual peace and quiet, and also the appearance of calm, respectful children conveyed to her neighbors and friends, are often what the young mother most desires, but at times she will be very aggressive in trying to get them. Thus she may be quick to beat her children, especially if they defy her law, not because she hates them but because this is the way she knows to control them. In fact, many street-oriented women love their children dearly. Many mothers in the community subscribe to the notion that there is a "devil in the boy" that must be beaten out of him or that socially "fast girls need to be whupped." Thus much of what borders on child abuse in the view of social authorities is acceptable parental punishment in the view of these mothers.

Many street-oriented women are sporadic mothers whose children learn to fend for themselves when necessary, foraging for food and money any way they can get it. The children are sometimes employed by drug dealers or become addicted themselves. These children of the street, growing up with little supervision, are said to "come up hard." They often learn to fight at an early age, sometimes using short-tempered adults around them as role models. The street-oriented home may be fraught with anger, verbal disputes, physical aggression, and even mayhem. The children observe these goings-on, learning the lesson that might makes right. They quickly learn to hit those who cross them, and the dog-eat-dog mentality prevails. In order to survive, to protect oneself, it is necessary to marshal inner resources and be ready to deal with adversity in a hands-on way. In these circumstances physical prowess takes on great significance. * * *

CAMPAIGNING FOR RESPECT

These realities of inner-city life are largely absorbed on the streets. At an early age, often even before they start school, children from street-oriented homes gravitate to the streets, where they "hang"—socialize with their peers. Children from these generally permissive homes have a great deal of latitude and are allowed to "rip and run" up and down the street. They often come home from school, put their books down, and go right back out the door. On school nights eight- and nine-year-olds remain out until nine or ten o'clock (and teenagers typically come in whenever they want to). On the streets they play in groups that often become the source of their primary social bonds. Children from decent homes tend to be more carefully supervised and are thus likely to have curfews and to be taught how to stay out of trouble.

When decent and street kids come together, a kind of social shuffle occurs in which children have a chance to go either way. Tension builds as a child comes to realize that he must choose an orientation. The kind of home he comes from influences but does not determine the way he will ultimately turn out—although it is unlikely that a child from a thoroughly street-oriented family will easily absorb decent values on the streets. Youths who emerge from street-oriented families but develop a decency orientation almost always learn those values in another setting—in school, in a youth group, in church. Often it is the result of their involvement with a caring "old head" (adult role model).

In the street, through their play, children pour their individual life experiences into a common knowledge pool, affirming, confirming, and elaborating on what they have observed in the home and matching their skills against those of others. And they learn to fight. Even small children test one another, pushing and shoving, and are ready to hit other children over circumstances not to their liking. In turn, they are readily hit by other children, and the child who is toughest prevails. Thus the violent resolution of disputes, the hitting and cursing, gains social reinforcement. The child in effect is initiated into a system that is really a way of campaigning for respect.

In addition, younger children witness the disputes of older children, which are often resolved through cursing and abusive talk, if not aggression or outright violence. They see that one child succumbs to the greater physical and mental abilities of the other. They are also alert and attentive witnesses to the verbal and physical fights of adults, after which they compare notes and share their interpretations of the event. In almost every case the victor is the person who physically won the altercation, and this person often enjoys the esteem and respect of onlookers. These experiences reinforce the lessons the children have learned at home: might makes right, and toughness is a virtue, while humility is not. In effect they learn the social meaning of fighting. When it is left virtually unchallenged, this understanding becomes an ever more important part of the child's working conception of the world. Over time the code of the streets becomes refined.

Those street-oriented adults with whom children come in contact—including mothers, fathers, brothers, sisters, boyfriends, cousins, neighbors, and friends—help them along in forming this understanding by verbalizing the messages they are getting through experience: "Watch your back." "Protect yourself." "Don't punk out." "If somebody messes with you, you got to pay them back." "If someone disses you, you got to straighten them out." Many parents actually impose sanctions if a child is not sufficiently aggressive. For example, if a child loses a fight and comes home upset, the parent might respond, "Don't you come in here crying that somebody beat you up; you better get back out there and whup his ass. I didn't raise no punks! Get back out there and whup his ass. If you don't whup his ass, I'll whup your ass when you come home." Thus the child obtains reinforcement for being tough and showing nerve.

* * *

SELF-IMAGE BASED ON "JUICE"

By the time they are teenagers, most youths have either internalized the code of the streets or at least learned the need to comport themselves in accordance with its rules, which chiefly have to do with interpersonal communication. The code revolves around the presentation of self. Its basic requirement is the display of a certain predisposition to violence. Accordingly, one's bearing must send the unmistakable if sometimes subtle message to "the next person" in public that one is capable of violence and mayhem when the situation requires it, that one can take care of oneself. The nature of this communication is largely determined by the demands of the circumstances but can include facial expressions, gait, and verbal expressions—all of which are geared mainly to deterring aggression. Physical appearance, including clothes, jewelry, and grooming, also plays an important part in how a person is viewed; to be respected, it is important to have the right look.

Even so, there are no guarantees against challenges, because there are always people around looking for a fight to increase their share of respect—or "juice," as it is sometimes called on the street. Moreover, if a person is assaulted, it is important, not only in the eyes of his opponent but also in the eyes of his "running buddies," for him to avenge himself. Otherwise he risks being "tried" (challenged) or "moved on" by any number of others. To maintain his honor he must show he is not someone to be "messed with" or "dissed." In general, the person must "keep himself straight" by managing his position of respect among others; this involves in part his self-image, which is shaped by what he thinks others are thinking of him in relation to his peers.

Objects play an important and complicated role in establishing self-image. Jackets, sneakers, gold jewelry, reflect not just a person's taste, which tends to be tightly regulated among adolescents of all social classes, but also a willingness to possess things that may require defending. A boy wearing a fashionable, expensive jacket, for example, is vulnerable to attack by another who covets the jacket and either cannot afford to buy one or wants the added satisfaction of depriving someone else of his. However, if the boy forgoes the desirable jacket and wears one that isn't "hip," he runs the risk of being teased and possibly even assaulted as an unworthy person. To be allowed to hang with certain prestigious crowds, a boy must wear a different set of expensive clothes—sneakers and athletic suit—every day. Not to be able to do so might make him appear socially deficient. The youth comes to covet such items—especially when he sees easy prey wearing them.

In acquiring valued things, therefore, a person shores up his identity—but since it is an identity based on having things, it is highly precarious. This very precariousness gives a heightened sense of urgency to staying even with peers, with whom the person is actually competing. Young men and women who are able to command respect through their presentation of self—by allowing their possessions and their body language to speak for them—may not have to campaign for regard but may, rather, gain it by the force of their manner. Those who are unable to command respect in this way must actively campaign for it—and are thus particularly alive to slights.

One way of campaigning for status is by taking the possessions of others. In this context, seemingly ordinary objects can become trophies imbued with symbolic value that far exceeds their monetary worth. Possession of the trophy can symbolize the ability to violate somebody—to "get in his face," to take something of value from him, to "dis" him, and thus to enhance one's own worth by stealing someone else's. The trophy does not have to be something material. It can be another person's sense of honor, snatched away with a derogatory remark. It can be the outcome of a fight. It can be the imposition of a certain standard, such as a girl's getting herself recognized as the most beautiful. Material things, however, fit easily into the pattern. Sneakers, a pistol, even somebody else's girlfriend, can become a trophy. When a person can take something from another and then flaunt it, he gains a certain regard by being the owner, or the controller, of that thing. But this display of ownership can then provoke other people to challenge him. This game of who controls what is thus constantly being played out on inner-city streets, and the trophy—extrinsic or intrinsic, tangible or intangible—identifies the current winner.

An important aspect of this often violent give-and-take is its zero-sum quality. That is, the extent to which one person can raise himself up depends on his ability to put another person down. This underscores the alienation that permeates the inner-city ghetto community. There is a generalized sense that very little respect is to be had, and therefore everyone competes to get what affirmation he can of the little that is available. The craving for respect that results gives people thin skins. Shows of deference by others can be highly soothing, contributing to a sense of security, comfort, self-confidence, and self-respect. Transgressions by others which go unanswered diminish these feelings and are believed to encourage further transgressions. Hence one must be ever vigilant against the transgressions of others or even *appearing* as if transgressions will be tolerated. Among young people, whose sense of self-esteem is particularly vulnerable, there is an especially heightened concern with being disrespected. Many inner-city young men in particular crave respect to such a degree that they will risk their lives to attain and maintain it.

The issue of respect is thus closely tied to whether a person has an inclination to be violent, even as a victim. In the wider society people may not feel required to retaliate physically after an attack, even though they are aware that they have been degraded or taken advantage of. They may feel a great need to defend themselves *during* an attack, or to behave in such a way as to deter aggression (middle-class people certainly can and do become victims of street-oriented youths), but they are much more likely than street-oriented people to feel that they can walk away from a possible altercation with their self-esteem intact. Some people may even have the strength of character to flee, without any thought that their self-respect or esteem will be diminished.

In impoverished inner-city black communities, however, particularly among young males and perhaps increasingly among females, such flight would be extremely difficult. To run away would likely leave one's self-esteem in tatters. Hence people often feel constrained not only to stand up and at least attempt to resist during an assault but also to "pay back"—to seek revenge—after a successful assault on their person. This may include going to get a weapon or even getting relatives involved. Their very identity and self-respect, their honor, is often intricately tied up with the way they perform on the streets during and after such encounters. This outlook reflects the circumscribed opportunities of the inner-city poor. Generally people outside the ghetto have other ways of gaining status and regard, and thus do not feel so dependent on such physical displays.

BY TRIAL OF MANHOOD

On the street, among males these concerns about things and identity have come to be expressed in the concept of "manhood." Manhood in the inner city means taking the prerogatives of men with respect to strangers, other men, and women—being distinguished as a man. It implies physicality and a certain ruthlessness. Regard and respect are associated with this concept in large part because of its practical application: if others have little or no regard for a person's manhood, his very life and those of his loved ones could be in jeopardy. But there is a chicken-and-egg aspect to this situation: one's physical safety is more likely to be jeopardized in public *because* manhood is associated with respect. In other words, an existential link has been created between the idea of manhood and one's self-esteem, so that it has become hard to say which is primary. For many inner-city youths, manhood and respect are flip sides of the same coin; physical and psychological well-being are inseparable, and both require a sense of control, of being in charge.

The operating assumption is that a man, especially a real man, knows what other men know—the code of the streets. And if one is not a real man, one is somehow diminished as a person, and there are certain valued things one simply does not deserve. There is thus believed to be a certain justice to the code, since it is considered that everyone has the opportunity to know it. Implicit in this is that everybody is held responsible for being familiar with the code. If the victim of a mugging, for example, does not know the code and so responds "wrong," the perpetrator may feel justified even in killing him and may feel no remorse. He may think, "Too bad, but it's his fault. He should have known better."

So when a person ventures outside, he must adopt the code—a kind of shield, really—to prevent others from "messing with" him. In these circumstances it is easy for people to think they are being tried or tested by others even when this is not the case. For it is sensed that something extremely valuable is at stake in every interaction, and people are encouraged to rise to the occasion, particularly with strangers. For people who are unfamiliar with the code—generally people who live outside the inner city—the concern with respect in the most ordinary interactions can be frightening and incomprehensible. But for those who are invested in the code, the clear object of their demeanor is to discourage strangers from even thinking about testing their manhood. And the sense of power that attends the ability to deter others can be alluring even to those who know the code without being heavily invested in it—the decent inner-city youths. Thus a boy who has been leading a basically decent life can, in trying circumstances, suddenly resort to deadly force.

Central to the issue of manhood is the widespread belief that one of the most effective ways of gaining respect is to manifest "nerve." Nerve is shown when one takes another person's possessions (the more valuable the better), "messes with" someone's woman, throws the first punch, "gets in someone's face," or pulls a trigger. Its proper display helps on the spot to check others who would violate one's person and also helps to build a reputation that works to prevent future challenges. But since such a show of nerve is a forceful expression of disrespect toward the person on the receiving end, the victim may be greatly offended and seek to retaliate with equal or greater force. A display of nerve, therefore, can easily provoke a life-threatening response, and the background knowledge of that possibility has often been incorporated into the concept of nerve.

True nerve exposes a lack of fear of dying. Many feel that it is acceptable to risk dying over the principle of respect. In fact, among the hard-core street-oriented, the clear risk of violent death may be preferable to being "dissed" by another. The youths who have internalized this attitude and convincingly display it in their public bearing are among the most threatening people of all, for it is commonly assumed that they fear no man. As the people of the community say, "They are the baddest dudes on the street." They often lead an existential life that may acquire meaning only when they are faced with the possibility of imminent death. Not to be afraid to die is by implication to have few compunctions about taking another's life. Not to be afraid to die is the quid pro quo of being able to take somebody else's life—for the right reasons, if the situation demands it. When others believe this is one's position, it gives one a real sense of power on the streets. Such credibility is what many inner-city youths strive to achieve, whether they are decent or street-oriented, both because of its practical defensive value and because of the positive way it makes them feel about themselves. The difference between the decent and the street-oriented youth is often that the decent youth makes a conscious decision to appear tough and manly; in another setting—with teachers, say, or at his part-time job—he can be polite and deferential. The street-oriented youth, on the other hand, has made the concept of manhood a part of his very identity; he has difficulty manipulating it—it often controls him.

GIRLS AND BOYS

Increasingly, teenage girls are mimicking the boys and trying to have their own version of "manhood." Their goal is the same—to get respect, to be recognized as capable of setting or maintaining a certain standard. They try to achieve this end in the ways that have been established by the boys, including posturing, abusive language, and the use of violence to resolve disputes, but the issues for the girls are different. Although conflicts over turf and status exist among the girls, the majority of disputes seem rooted in assessments of beauty (which girl in a group is "the cutest"), competition over boyfriends, and attempts to regulate other people's knowledge of and opinions about a girl's behavior or that of someone close to her, especially her mother.

A major cause of conflicts among girls is "he say, she say." This practice begins in the early school years and continues through high school. It occurs when "people," particularly girls, talk about others, thus putting their "business in the streets." Usually one girl will say something negative about another in the group, most often behind the person's back. The remark will then get back to the person talked about. She may retaliate or her friends may feel required to "take up for" her. In essence this is a form of group gossiping in which individuals are negatively assessed and evaluated. As with much gossip, the things said may or may not be true, but the point is that such imputations can cast aspersions on a person's good name. The accused is required to defend herself against the slander, which can result in arguments and fights, often over little of real substance. Here again is the problem of low self-esteem, which encourages youngsters to be highly sensitive to slights and to be vulnerable to feeling easily "dissed." To avenge the dissing, a fight is usually necessary.

Because boys are believed to control violence, girls tend to defer to them in situations of conflict. Often if a girl is attacked or feels slighted, she will get a brother, uncle, or cousin to do her fighting for her. Increasingly, however, girls are doing their own fighting and are even asking their male relatives to teach them how to fight. Some girls form groups that attack other girls or take things from them. A hard-core segment of inner-city girls inclined toward violence seems to be developing. As one thirteen-year-old girl in a detention center for youths who have committed violent acts told me, "To get people to leave you alone, you gotta fight. Talking don't always get you out of stuff." One major difference between girls and boys: girls rarely use guns. Their fights are therefore not life-or-death struggles. Girls are not often willing to put their lives on the line for "manhood." The ultimate form of respect on the male-dominated inner-city street is thus reserved for men.

"GOING FOR BAD"

In the most fearsome youths such a cavalier attitude toward death grows out of a very limited view of life. Many are uncertain about how long they are going to live and believe they could die violently at any time. They accept this fate; they live on the edge. Their manner conveys the message that nothing intimidates them; whatever turn the encounter takes, they maintain their attack—rather like a pit bull, whose spirit many such boys admire. The demonstration of such tenacity "shows heart" and earns their respect.

This fearlessness has implications for law enforcement. Many street-oriented boys are much more concerned about the threat of "justice" at the hands of a peer than at the hands of the police. Moreover, many feel not only that they have little to lose by going to prison but that they have something to gain. The toughening-up one experiences in prison can actually enhance one's reputation on the streets. Hence the system loses influence over the hard core who are without jobs, with little perceptible stake in the system. If mainstream society has done nothing *for* them, they counter by making sure it can do nothing *to* them.

At the same time, however, a competing view maintains that true nerve consists in backing down, walking away from a fight, and going on with one's business. One fights only in self-defense. This view emerges from the decent philosophy that life is precious, and it is an important part of the socialization process common in decent homes. It discourages violence as the primary means of resolving disputes and encourages youngsters to accept nonviolence and talk as confrontational strategies. But "if the deal goes down," self-defense is greatly encouraged. When there is enough positive support for this orientation, either in the home or among one's peers, then nonviolence has a chance to prevail. But it prevails at the cost of relinquishing a claim to being bad and tough, and therefore sets a young person up as at the very least alienated from street-oriented peers and quite possibly a target of derision or even violence.

Although the nonviolent orientation rarely overcomes the impulse to strike back in an encounter, it does introduce a certain confusion and so can prompt a measure of soul-searching, or even profound ambivalence. Did the person back down with his respect intact or did he back down only to be judged a "punk"—a person lacking manhood? Should he or she have acted? Should he or she have hit the other person in the mouth? These questions beset many young men and women during public confrontations. What is the "right" thing to do? In the quest for honor, respect, and local status—which few young people are uninterested in—common sense most often prevails, which leads many to opt for the tough approach, enacting their own particular versions of the display of nerve. The presentation of oneself as rough and tough is very often quite acceptable until one is tested. And then that presentation may help the person pass the test, because it will cause fewer questions to be asked about what he did and why. It is hard for a person to explain why he lost the fight or why he backed down. Hence many will strive to appear to "go for bad," while hoping they will never be tested. But when they are tested, the outcome of the situation may quickly be out of their hands, as they become wrapped up in the circumstances of the moment.

AN OPPOSITIONAL CULTURE

The attitudes of the wider society are deeply implicated in the code of the streets. Most people in inner-city communities are not totally invested in the code, but the significant minority of hard-core street youths who are have to maintain the code in order to establish reputations, because they have—or feel they have—few other ways to assert themselves. For these young people the standards of the street code are the only game in town. The extent to which some children—particularly those who through upbringing have become most alienated and those lacking in strong and conventional social support—experience, feel, and internalize racist rejection and contempt from mainstream society may strongly encourage them to express contempt for the more conventional society in turn. In dealing with this contempt and rejection, some youngsters will consciously invest themselves and their considerable mental resources in what amounts to an oppositional culture to preserve themselves and their self-respect. Once they do, any respect they might be able to garner in the wider system pales in comparison with the respect available in the local system; thus they often lose interest in even attempting to negotiate the mainstream system.

At the same time, many less alienated young blacks have assumed a street-oriented demeanor as a way of expressing their blackness while really embracing a much more moderate way of life; they, too, want a nonviolent setting in which to live and raise a family. These decent people are trying hard to be part of the mainstream culture, but the racism, real and perceived, that they encounter helps to legitimate the oppositional culture. And so on occasion they adopt street behavior. In fact, depending on the demands of the situation, many people in the community slip back and forth between decent and street behavior.

A vicious cycle has thus been formed. The hopelessness and alienation many young inner-city black men and women feel, largely as a result of endemic joblessness and persistent racism, fuels the violence they engage in. This violence serves to confirm the negative feelings many whites and some middle-class blacks harbor toward the ghetto poor, further legitimating the oppositional culture and the code of the streets in the eyes of many poor young blacks. Unless this cycle is broken, attitudes on both sides will become increasingly entrenched, and the violence, which claims victims black and white, poor and affluent, will only escalate.

12

From *Amish Society*

JOHN A. HOSTETLER

One of the most basic sociological truths is that people seek to organize their lives, families, and communities in order to become the kind of people they most admire. This is especially true for the Amish, who see their own beliefs as tied to the mainte- nance of their communities. In this study you can see how beliefs dictate a way of living, while at the same time a pattern of social structure upholds and reinforces the beliefs that dominate the society.

Small communities, with their distinctive character—where life is stable and intensely human—are disappearing. Some have vanished from the face of the earth, others are dying slowly, but all have undergone change as they have come into contact with an expanding machine civilization. The merging of diverse peoples into a common mass has produced tension among members of the minorities and the majority alike.

The Old Order Amish, who arrived on American shores in colonial times, have survived in the modern world in distinctive, viable, small communities. They have resisted the homogenization process more successfully than others. In planting and harvest time one can see their bearded men working the fields with horses and their women hanging out the laundry in neat rows to dry. Many American people have seen Amish families, with the men wearing broad-brimmed black hats and the women in bonnets and long dresses, in rail- way depots or bus terminals. Although the Amish have lived with industrial- ized America for over two and a half centuries, they have moderated its influence on their personal lives, their families, communities, and their values.

The Amish are often perceived by other Americans to be relics of the past who live an austere, inflexible life dedicated to inconvenient and archaic cus- toms. They are seen as renouncing both modern conveniences and the Amer- ican dream of success and progress. But most people have no quarrel with the Amish for doing things the old-fashioned way. Their conscientious objection was tolerated in wartime, for after all, they are meticulous farmers who prac- tice the virtues of work and thrift.

In recent years the status of the Amish in the minds of most Americans has shifted toward a more favorable position. This change can scarcely be attrib- uted to anything the Amish have done; rather, it is the result of changes in the way Americans perceive their minority groups. A century ago, hardly anyone knew the Amish existed. A half-century ago they were viewed as an obscure sect living by ridiculous customs, as stubborn people who resisted education and exploited the labor of their children. Today the Amish are the unwilling objects of a thriving tourist industry on the eastern seaboard. They are revered as hard-working, thrifty people with enormous agrarian stamina, and by some, as islands of sanity in a culture gripped by commercialism and technology run wild.

In the academic community several models have been advanced for understanding Amish society. Social scientists, like other Americans, have been influenced by the upward push of an advancing civilization and changes in the social discourse between the dominant society and its minorities. University teachers have traditionally taught their students to think of the Amish people as one of many old-world cultural islands left over in the modern world.

* * *

The Amish are a church, a community, a spiritual union, a conservative branch of Christianity, a religion, a community whose members practice simple and austere living, a familistic entrepreneuring system, and an adaptive human community. In this chapter several models will be discussed in terms of their usefulness and limitations as avenues for understanding Amish society as a whole. By models I mean structured concepts currently used by anthropologists to characterize whole societies. The serious reader will want to transcend the scientific orientation and ask, What is the meaning of the Amish system? What, if anything, is it trying to say to us?

A COMMONWEALTH

The Amish are in some ways a little commonwealth, for their members claim to be ruled by the law of love and redemption. The bonds that unite them are many. Their beliefs, however, do not permit them solely to occupy and defend a particular territory. They are highly sensitive in caring for their own. They will move to other lands when circumstances force them to do so.

Commonwealth implies a place, a province, which means any part of a national domain that geographically and socially is sufficiently unified to have a true consciousness of its unity. Its inhabitants feel comfortable with their own ideas and customs, and the "place" possesses a sense of distinction from other parts of the country. Members of a commonwealth are not footloose. They have a sense of productivity and accountability in a province where "the general welfare" is accepted as a day-to-day reality. Commonwealth has come to have an archaic meaning in today's world, because when groups and institutions become too large, the sense of commonwealth or the common good is lost. Thus it is little wonder that the most recent dictionaries of the American English language render the meaning of commonwealth as "obsolescent." In reality, the Amish are in part a commonwealth. There is, however, no provision for outcasts.

It may be argued that the Amish have retained elements of wholesome provincialism, a saving power to which the world in the future will need more and more to appeal. Provincialism need not turn to ancient narrowness and ignorance, confines from which many have sought to escape. A sense of province or commonwealth, with its cherished love of people and self-conscious dignity, is a necessary basis for relating to the wider world community. Respect for locality, place, custom, and local idealism can go a long way toward checking the monstrous growth of consolidation in the nation and thus help to save human freedom and individual dignity.

A SECTARIAN SOCIETY

Sociologists tend to classify the Amish as a sectarian society. Several European scholars have compared the social structure of "sect" and "church" types of religious institutions. The established church was viewed as hierarchic and conservative. It appealed to the ruling classes, administered grace to all people in a territorial domain, and served as an agency of social control. The sect was egalitarian. Essentially a voluntary religious protest movement, its members separated themselves from others on the basis of beliefs, practices, and institutions. The sects rejected the authority of the established religious organizations and their leaders. The strains between sect and church were viewed as a dialectic principle at work within Christianity. The use of an ideal type helped to clarify particular characteristics of the sectarian groups. The Anabaptists, for example, were described as small, voluntary groupings attempting to model their lives after the spirit of the Sermon on the Mount (Matt. 5, 6, 7) while also exercising the power to exclude and discipline members. Absolute separation from all other religious loyalties was required. All members were considered equal, and none were to take oaths, participate in war, or take part in worldly government.

Sects have employed various techniques of isolation for maintaining separateness. Today the extreme mobility of modern life brings people together in multiple contexts. The spatial metaphors of separation (i.e., valley, region, sector, etc.) are fast becoming obsolete. Nevertheless, modern sectarians turn to psychic insularity and contexts that protect them from mainstream values and competing systems. Members of the sect remain segregated in various degrees, chiefly by finding a group whose philosophy of history contradicts the existing values so drastically that the group sustains itself for a generation or more. To the onlooker, sectarianism, like monasticism, may appear to serve as a shelter from the complications of an overly complex society. For its participants, it provides authentic ways of realizing new forms of service and humility as well as protection from mainstream culture.

Sectarians, it is claimed, put their faith first by ordering their lives in keeping with it. The established churches compromise their faith with other interests and with the demands of the surrounding environment. Sectarians are pervasively religious in that they practice their beliefs in everyday life. Sects are often considered marginal or odd groups of alienated people with fanatic ideas. Yet the sects have had an immense influence in shaping the course of history. The British sociologist Bryan Wilson has observed that sects are "self-conscious attempts by men to construct their own societies, not merely as political entities with constitutions, but as groups with a firm set of values and mores, of which they are conscious." The growth of religious toleration in America has resulted in the development of religious pluralism in a manner that has not been realized in Europe. Wilson, who has characterized modern Christian sects into several types, classes the Amish as *introversionist* rather than *conversionist* or *reformist*. "Salvation is to be found in the community of those who withdraw from involvement in the affairs of mankind." The Amish recognize the evil circumstance of man, attempt to moderate its influence upon them, and retreat into a community to experience, cultivate, and preserve the attributes of God in ethical relationships.

The sectarian model lends itself to a historical, religious context. As a model, it offers some insight into the proliferation of groups with a negative orientation during a specific time period. Today there are many types of movements that did not exist in the early stages of industrialization. Sects may lose their spontaneity in a variety of ways. While the model may teach us something of how sects originate and grow from a protest movement to a separate religious entity, it does not provide us with a knowledge of the dynamics of the group. The Amish, for example, are not sectarians in the sense that they demand that others conform to their practices. Nor do they claim to base all actions on holy writ. They are not in conflict with the dominant culture in the same way, or with the same intensity, as are a number of sects such as the "apocalyptic" or "manipulationist" types.

Many sectarian societies, including the Amish, make little or no attempt to communicate their message. They recognize instinctively that authentic communication would mean greater literacy, education, and sophistication, and this would mean the beginning of the end. "The contribution of the sect to the larger society is," according to Martin Marty, "made best through the sympathetic observer who carries with him a picture of the advantages or particularity and assertiveness back to the world of dialogical complexity." In the Amish case, the message of the sectarian society is exemplary. A way of living is more important than communicating it in words. The ultimate message is the life. An Amish person will have no doubt about his basic convictions, his view of the meaning and purpose of life, but he cannot explain it except through the conduct of his life.

A FOLK SOCIETY

Anthropologists, who have compared societies all over the world, have tended to call semi-isolated peoples "folk societies," "primitives," or merely "simple societies." These societies constitute an altogether different type in contrast to the industrialized, or so-called civilized, societies. The "folk society," as conceptualized by Robert Redfield, is a small, isolated, traditional, simple, homogeneous society in which oral communication and conventionalized ways are important factors in integrating the whole of life. In such an ideal-type society, shared practical knowledge is more important than science, custom is valued more than critical knowledge, and associations are personal and emotional rather than abstract and categoric.

Folk societies are uncomfortable with the idea of change. Young people do what the old people did when they were young. Members communicate intimately with one another, not only by word of mouth but also through custom and symbols that reflect a strong sense of belonging to one another. A folk society is *Gemeinschaft*-like,[1] there is a strong sense of "we-ness." Leadership is personal rather than institutionalized. There are no gross economic inequalities. Mutual aid is characteristic of the society's members. The goals of life are never stated as matters of doctrine, but neither are they questioned. They are implied by the acts that constitute living in a small society. Custom tends to become sacred. Behavior is strongly patterned, and acts as well as cultural objects are given symbolic meaning that is often pervasively religious. Religion is diffuse and all-pervasive. In the typical folk society, planting and harvesting are as sacred in their own ways as singing and praying.

The significance of the Amish as an intimate, face-to-face primary group has long been recognized. Charles P. Loomis was the first to conceptualize the character of the Amish. In his construction of a scale he contrasted the Amish as a familistic *Gemeinschaf*-type system with highly rational social systems of the *Gesellschaft*-type in contemporary civilization.

The folk model lends itself well to understanding the tradition-directed character of Amish society. The heavy weight of tradition can scarcely be explained in any other way. The Amish, for example, have retained many of the customs and small-scale technologies that were common in rural society in the nineteenth century. Through a process of syncretism, Amish religious values have been fused with an earlier period of simple country living when everyone farmed with horses and on a scale where family members could work together. The Amish exist as a folk or "little" community in a rural subculture within the modern state, as distinguished from the primitive or peasant types described in anthropological literature. Several aspects of Redfield's folk-society model and features of the Töennies-Loomis *Gemeinscliaft* aid us in understanding the parameters of Amish society. They are *distinctiveness, smallness of scale, homogeneous culture patterns*, and the *strain toward self-sufficiency*.

Distinctiveness. The Amish people are highly visible. The outsider who drives through an Amish settlement cannot help but recognize them by their clothing, farm homes, furnishings, fields, and other material traits of culture. Although

---

1. The German term *Gemeinschaft* is often translated as "community." Ferdinand Tönnies's classic work *Gemeinschaft und Gesellschaft* provided sociology with this concept, which is contrasted to urban, modern, and industrialized society (*Gesellschaft*). [*Editors' note*]

they speak perfect English with outsiders, they speak a dialect of German among themselves.

Amish life is distinctive in that religion and custom blend into a way of life. The two are inseparable. The core values of the community are religious beliefs. Not only do the members worship a deity they understand through the revelation of Jesus Christ and the Bible, but their patterned behavior has a religious dimension. A distinctive way of life permeates daily life, agriculture, and the application of energy to economic ends. Their beliefs determine their conceptions of the self, the universe, and man's place in it. The Amish world view recognizes a certain spiritual worth and dignity in the universe in its natural form. Religious considerations determine hours of work and the daily, weekly, seasonal, and yearly rituals associated with life experience. Occupation, the means and destinations of travel, and choice of friends and mate are determined by religious considerations. Religious and work attitudes are not far distant from each other. The universe includes the divine, and Amish society itself is considered divine insofar as the Amish recognize themselves as "a chosen people of God." The Amish do not seek to master nature or to work against the elements, but try to work with them. The affinity between Amish society and nature in the form of land, terrain, and vegetation is expressed in various degrees of intensity.

Religion is highly patterned, so one may properly speak of the Amish as a tradition-directed group. Though allusions to the Bible play an important role in determining their outlook on the world, and on life after death, these beliefs have been fused with several centuries of struggling to survive in community. Out of intense religious experience, societal conflict, and intimate agrarian experience, a mentality has developed that prefers the old rather than the new. While the principle seems to apply especially to religion, it has also become a charter for social behavior. "The old is the best, and the new is of the devil," has become a prevalent mode of thought. By living in closed communities where custom and a strong sense of togetherness prevail, the Amish have formed an integrated way of life and a folklike culture. Continuity of conformity and custom is assured and the needs of the individual from birth to death are met within an integrated and shared system of meanings. Oral tradition, custom, and conventionality play an important part in maintaining the group as a functioning whole. To the participant, religion and custom are inseparable. Commitment and culture are combined to produce a stable human existence.

These are some of the qualities of the little Amish community that make it distinctive. "Where the community begins and where it ends is apparent. The distinctiveness is apparent to the outside observer and is expressed in the group consciousness of the people of the community." The Amish community is in some aspects a functional part of modern society but is a distinctive subculture within it.

13

America's National Eating Disorder

FROM *The Omnivore's Dilemma: A Natural History of Four Meals*

MICHAEL POLLAN

One of the most popular and talked-about books of recent years, The Omnivore's Dilemma, *includes this essay, which asks, What should I eat? In an affluent society where grocery items come from all over the world, everything is available. Or, I can skip the grocery store and just eat out. But in either case, I may not know what I'm eating. Michael Pollan has tapped the root of food insecurity and come up with a critique of both American culture and corporate capitalism. It is certainly food for thought.*

All the customs and rules culture has devised to mediate the clash of human appetite and society probably bring greater comfort to us as eaters than as sexual beings. Freud and others lay the blame for many of our sexual neuroses at the door of an overly repressive culture, but that doesn't appear to be the principal culprit in our neurotic eating. To the contrary, it seems as though our eating tends to grow more tortured as our culture's power to manage our relationship to food weakens.

This seems to me precisely the predicament we find ourselves in today as eaters, particularly in America. America has never had a stable national cuisine; each immigrant population has brought its own foodways to the American table, but none has ever been powerful enough to hold the national diet very steady. We seem bent on reinventing the American way of eating every generation, in great paroxysms of neophilia and neophobia. That might explain why Americans have been such easy marks for food fads and diets of every description.

This is the country, after all, where at the turn of the last century Dr. John Harvey Kellogg persuaded great numbers of the country's most affluent and best educated to pay good money to sign themselves into his legendarily nutty sanitarium at Battle Creek, Michigan, where they submitted to a regime that included all-grape diets and almost hourly enemas. Around the same time millions of Americans succumbed to the vogue for "Fletcherizing"—chewing each bite of food as many as one hundred times—introduced by Horace Fletcher, also known as the Great Masticator.

This period marked the first golden age of American food faddism, though of course its exponents spoke not in terms of fashion but of "scientific eating," much as we do now. Back then the best nutritional science maintained that carnivory promoted the growth of toxic bacteria in the colon; to battle these evildoers Kellogg vilified meat and mounted a two-fronted assault on his patients' alimentary canals, introducing quantities of Bulgarian yogurt at both ends. It's easy to make fun of people who would succumb to such fads, but it's not at all clear that we're any less gullible. It remains to be seen whether the current Atkins school theory of ketosis—the process by which the body resorts to burning its own fat when starved of carbohydrates—will someday seem as quaintly quackish as Kellogg's theory of colonic autointoxication.

What is striking is just how little it takes to set off one of these applecart-toppling nutritional swings in America; a scientific study, a new government guideline, a lone crackpot with a medical degree can alter this nation's diet overnight. One article in the *New York Times Magazine* in 2002 almost single-handedly set off the recent spasm of carbophobia in America. But the basic pattern was fixed decades earlier, and suggests just how vulnerable the lack of stable culinary traditions leaves us to the omnivore's anxiety, and the companies and quacks who would prey on it. So every few decades some new scientific research comes along to challenge the prevailing nutritional orthodoxy; some nutrient that Americans have been happily chomping for decades is suddenly found to be lethal; another nutrient is elevated to the status of health food; the industry throws its weight behind it; and the American way of dietary life undergoes yet another revolution.

Harvey Levenstein, a Canadian historian who has written two fascinating social histories of American foodways, neatly sums up the beliefs that have guided the American way of eating since the heyday of John Harvey Kellogg: "that taste is not a true guide to what should be eaten; that one should not simply eat what one enjoys; that the important components of food cannot be seen or tasted, but are discernible only in scientific laboratories; and that experimental science has produced rules of nutrition that will prevent illness and encourage longevity." The power of any orthodoxy resides in its ability not to seem like one and, at least to a 1906 or 2006 genus American, these beliefs don't seem in the least bit strange or controversial.

It's easy, especially for Americans, to forget just how novel this nutritional orthodoxy is, or that there are still cultures that have been eating more or less the same way for generations, relying on such archaic criteria as taste and tradition to guide them in their food selection. We Americans are amazed to learn that some of the cultures that set their culinary course by the lights of habit and pleasure rather than nutritional science and marketing are actually healthier than we are—that is, suffer a lower incidence of diet-related health troubles.

The French paradox is the most famous such case, though as Paul Rozin points out, the French don't regard the matter as paradoxical at all. We Americans resort to that term because the French experience—a population of wine-swilling cheese eaters with lower rates of heart disease and obesity—confounds our orthodoxy about food. That orthodoxy regards certain tasty foods as poisons (carbs now, fats then), failing to appreciate that how we eat, and even how we feel about eating, may in the end be just as important as what we eat. The French eat all sorts of supposedly unhealthy foods, but they do it according to a strict and stable set of rules: They eat small portions and don't go back for seconds; they don't snack; they seldom eat alone; and communal meals are long, leisurely affairs. In other words, the French culture of food successfully negotiates the omnivore's dilemma, allowing the French to enjoy their meals without ruining their health.

Perhaps because we have no such culture of food in America almost every question about eating is up for grabs. Fats or carbs? Three squares or continuous grazing? Raw or cooked? Organic or industrial? Veg or vegan? Meat or mock meat? Foods of astounding novelty fill the shelves of our supermarket, and the line between a food and a "nutritional supplement" has fogged to the point where people make meals of protein bars and shakes. Consuming these neo-pseudo-foods alone in our cars, we have become a nation of antinomian eaters, each of us struggling to work out our dietary salvation on our own. Is it any wonder Americans suffer from so many eating disorders? In the absence of any lasting consensus about what and how and where and when to eat, the omnivore's dilemma has returned to America with an almost atavistic force.

This situation suits the food industry just fine, of course. The more anxious we are about eating, the more vulnerable we are to the seductions of the marketer and the expert's advice. Food marketing in particular thrives on dietary instability and so tends to exacerbate it. Since it's difficult to sell more food to such a well-fed population (though not, as we're discovering, impossible), food companies put their efforts into grabbing market share by introducing new kinds of highly processed foods, which have the virtue of being both highly profitable and infinitely adaptable. Sold under the banner of "convenience," these processed foods are frequently designed to create whole new eating occasions, such as in the bus on the way to school (the protein bar or Pop-Tart) or in the car on the way to work (Campbell's recently introduced a one-handed microwaveable microchunked soup in a container designed to fit a car's cup holder).

The success of food marketers in exploiting shifting eating patterns and nutritional fashions has a steep cost. Getting us to change how we eat over and over again tends to undermine the various social structures that surround and steady our eating, institutions like the family dinner, for example, or taboos on snacking between meals and eating alone. In their relentless pursuit of new markets, food companies (with some crucial help from the microwave oven, which made "cooking" something even small children could do) have broken Mom's hold over the American menu by marketing to every conceivable demographic—and especially to children.

A vice president of marketing at General Mills once painted for me a picture of the state of the American family dinner, courtesy of video cameras that the company's consulting anthropologists paid families to let them install in the ceiling above the kitchen and dining room tables. Mom, perhaps feeling sentimental about the dinners of her childhood, still prepares a dish and a salad that she usually winds up eating by herself. Meanwhile, the kids, and Dad, too, if he's around, each fix something different for themselves, because Dad's on a low-carb diet, the teenager's become a vegetarian, and the eight-year-old is on a strict ration of pizza that the shrink says it's best to indulge (lest she develop eating disorders later on in life). So over the course of a half hour or so each family member roams into the kitchen, removes a single-portion entree from the freezer, and zaps it in the microwave. (Many of these entrees have been helpfully designed to be safely "cooked" by an eight-year-old.) After the sound of the beep each diner brings his microwaveable dish to the dining room table, where he or she may or may not cross paths with another family member at the table for a few minutes. Families who eat this way are among the 47 percent of Americans who report to pollsters that they still sit down to a family meal every night.

Several years ago, in a book called *The Cultural Contradictions of Capitalism*, sociologist Daniel Bell called attention to the tendency of capitalism, in its single-minded pursuit of profit, to erode the various cultural underpinnings that steady a society but often impede the march of commercialization. The family dinner, and more generally a cultural consensus on the subject of eating, appears to be the latest such casualty of capitalism. These rules and rituals stood in the way of the food industry's need to sell a well-fed population more food through ingenious new ways of processing, packaging, and marketing it. Whether a stronger set of traditions would have stood up better to this relentless economic imperative is hard to say; today America's fast-food habits are increasingly gaining traction even in places like France.

So we find ourselves as a species almost back where we started: anxious omnivores struggling once again to figure out what it is wise to eat. Instead of relying on the accumulated wisdom of a cuisine, or even on the wisdom of our senses, we rely on expert opinion, advertising, government food pyramids, and diet books, and we place our faith in science to sort out for us what culture once did with rather more success. Such has been the genius of capitalism, to re-create something akin to a state of nature in the modern supermarket or fast-food outlet, throwing us back on a perplexing, nutritionally perilous landscape deeply shadowed again by the omnivore's dilemma.

14

The Beauty of the Package

PICO IYER

The California-born author of this essay has resided in Japan for many years. His wife and children are Japanese. Yet, he struggles to understand the culture in which he lives. Living abroad is an exhilarating experience, full of wonder and surprises. It can also be opaque, perplexing, and frustrating. Even an observant and thoughtful long-term émigré may conclude that the culture just doesn't make sense. Of course, culture does make sense, but not necessarily to someone who grew up elsewhere and is not a native speaker. This essay invites a discussion about experiences in a "new culture" and should be led by those of you for whom the United States is more or less strange.

"It's My Life," by Bon Jovi, is thumping at high volume through the banquet room in the five-star hotel and people are rising from their chairs to shout, "Hiroko, Hiroko!" This is a summons to my wife, the fifty-three-year-old mother of the groom, celebrated for her love of both Metallica and the Dalai Lama, to get up from her seat and join her son, a frequent companion at Marilyn Manson concerts, in dancing through the room, hands linked together as they punch the air. The music is deafening in this great space in the Tokyo suburbs and the spirit is freer, wilder than at any wedding I've known. A local girl is clapping her hands as furiously as her Cuban-American husband back in Florida might. The boys in Armani—products of the country's finest universities—are roaring their approval, as if everything is quite normal. It looks to ignorant me as if the whole, immaculately programmed ceremony is coming apart. But what allows everyone to be so uninhibited is that each one has a keen sense of what's coming next. As soon as the song subsides, we'll be back on a fast-moving bullet train that will carry us through moments of tears and quiet laughter, scenes of reminiscence and silent community, aching ballads and rousing photographs, before ending up at a place called Guaranteed Satisfaction.

I look at my wife, the glamorous soon-to-be grandma still pumping her fist, and wonder how one begins to negotiate a society that somehow meets expectation and confounds it in every gesture, sets up a platonic model and then encourages individuals to flood it with surprises. Her parents, not long after the war, went through more or less arranged marriages, as many Japanese couples did then; her children are stepping into a world in which one in every three Japanese under the age of thirty has never dated and almost two-thirds of unmarried men between the ages of eighteen and thirty-four are in no romantic relationship at all.

Not long after we met—my third week in the country, twenty-six years ago—Hiroko said to me, "You're a little difficult, so I'm going to have to change."

"Change me, you mean?"

"No!" she said. "I can't change you! I'll have to change myself to make my peace with what's not easy in you."

I was so moved by that spirit of selfless adaptability—in Japan, I saw, you try to fit yourself to the situation rather than expecting it to adapt itself to you—that I aspired to change myself to live up to her example. Yet even as this dance of harmony-making was unfolding, the larger whole around us was rewriting its script with every hour: when Hiroko got divorced, in 1989, it was such an unheard-of transgression that her parents cut her off for three months, and her brother, though long resident in the West, refuses to speak to her to this day. Nowadays, one in three Japanese marriages ends in divorce. Bon Jovi, meanwhile, is shouting, "I ain't gonna be just a face in the crowd / You gonna hear my voice / When I shout it loud," and I recall the neighbour of mine, a single mom with two kids in suburban Nara, who has painted I ♥ JON across her wall, next to the health club with the Easter Island statue outside it that we walk past on the way to the supermarket. She once packed her two kids into a taxi, flew them to JFK, rented a car so that all three could be taken to Bon Jovi's mansion in New Jersey, stood in silent homage outside his gates—"My heart is like an open highway," he's now wailing—then headed back to JFK to fly home.

You can throw yourself into any fantasy, she (and her country) might have been saying, so long as you don't mistake it for real life. That part hasn't changed much since Hiroko's day—or, maybe, Genji's.

Soon after breakfast this bright October morning, the bride's family was led into a special waiting room in the many-storeyed Brighton Hotel, separated from our clan by a small, low barrier, as if the two were on opposite sides, negotiating terms. Perhaps they should be: the girl's family is dressed impeccably, according to the classical model—the patriarch's hands squarely on the thighs of his spotless black trousers, his wife in a kimono that chimes with the early-autumn day, nobody in their group daring to efface the dream with the smudge of personality. On our side is a Spanish boyfriend, a daughter who lives in Valladolid and a mother who's done up her hair in the hotel beauty salon to go with a grey dress that suggests she's off to lunch in the 6th arrondissement.

I watch the mothers introduce their family members to one another, one by one, as if in matching kimonos. Everyone sips from little cups of cherry-blossom tea, lightly salted—the taste of spring in early autumn—and the bride looks like a picture-book model of a girl in white. For months, I'm guessing, she's kept herself on an unforgiving diet, while growing her hair long, so it will tumble down as in a heart-shaped frame the minute the special day arrives: now, in her tiara and pearls, her gossamer arms catching the light as she rearranges a curl, she might be Audrey Hepburn in *Roman Holiday*, though even fresher and more delicate.

At 9:45 on the dot, an unsmiling man in a stern black suit comes in to lead the families to the hotel photo studio, accompanied by a friendly lady in a kimono, the sweet, smart wedding planner (in self-effacing black) and the man with the camera. The room they enter might be in Versailles—so long as you ignore the puppets and toy monkeys on hand to distract restless babies. Three experts, male and female, slip forward, kneeling discreetly, to position features just right, to tweak shoulders to the ideal angle, to advise how best to put clenched fists on thighs (thumbs out). A chic girl in a loose black jacket works to apply make-up between shots as if on a set of an even more professional kind.

There are two photographers working from a huge camera on a dolly, which rolls back and forth across the polished floor. The pictures will be framed and ready for collection before the day is over. And then the couple, ready for a thousand close-ups, heads out into the radiant sunshine, and walks towards an entire church set up on a middle floor of the hotel, as thin and elegant as a huge communion wafer in concrete.

It takes a while, I think, to learn how to appreciate the packaging, which is the pageantry, of Japan. In California, growing up in the sixties, I'd been taught that the most important thing is to "be yourself"; in Japan this, like most Californian pieties, is reversed. The great thing is not to be yourself: to conform to some archetype that the world knows how to deal with, to subordinate your private agenda to a larger whole. What someone wants when she goes to a wedding may not be Pico or Hiroshi or Yuki-chan; it's the model of a bridal couple, going through the rites that have been deemed most pleasing, delivering the scripted words with unwavering sincerity.

It's not just that surface and depth are different here, but that you can't begin to infer one from the other. That college-age girl in the microskirt, flaunting her bare flesh as a streetwalker might, will, if you talk to her, sweetly tell you she's a virgin; romance has little to do with fashion when it comes to choosing a role. And the prim matron in the twinset beside her on the train—Hiroko, who works with her, will tell me—is off to see her young lover tonight.

I've never lived in a society where parts are so perfectly choreographed; my wife calls her boss "Department Head," which ensures that as little as possible is personal, on either side. I've also never lived somewhere so open with its feelings when the moment allows. I step into a locker room after an American football game in Kyoto, and the 280-pound linebackers are sobbing, too full of emotion to speak, whether they've just won or been trounced. When Daniel Day-Lewis acts, I often reflect in Japan, he moves us not because he's so good at simulating emotions, but, rather, because he can so powerfully access true emotions, with such depth, as soon as his director shouts, "Rolling!"

Now, as we take our places in the chapel, we're greeted by a girl at an organ playing Bach. Three women in elegant black dresses walk to the front—one with a flute, another with a violin and a third who begins to sing as if her heart might break. The minute she hits her highest note, the bride comes stepping up what's known in Japanese as the Virgin Road, in perfectly synchronized paces, with her father beside her, before being taken over by her groom a few feet in front of the altar just as "Here Comes the Bride" subsides.

Neither of the two is Christian; I'm not sure they've ever been to a place of Christian worship before (though their honeymoon will take them through the churches of Vienna, Prague and Budapest). But this is how it's done in movies, in dreams, and this is what they've been rehearsing for months to make meaningful and true.

The couple stands in front of a tiny sliver of light that casts October sunshine down on them. A priest appears—a hotel employee, perhaps, though maybe truly connected to some church—and leads us in a Christian prayer in Japanese, having told the audience when to recite "amen." The young ones kneel, they close their eyes in prayer, exchange oaths. The groom gently parts the bride's veil, the priest raises his voice above them, translating "God" as "kami-sama," the word originally meant for a Shinto deity. The two share their first kiss as a married couple.

There are to be six weddings in the hotel this holiday Monday, and there were nine here the day before; for all I know, this man is leading amens in every one. But his voice quivers with intensity as he recites his words and when I look at his eyes, tightly clenched, I wonder whether he will burst into tears as well. The nature of what's authentic and what's not confounds me daily in Japan. I've read that older couples hire actresses to visit them on Sundays at lunchtime and say, "Hi, Mom! Hi, Dad! How are you doing?" if their own daughters are disinclined to do so.

When the couple walks out into the light again, we shower them with the confetti we've been given for the purpose, and there are more elaborate photo ops in the sun. I think of the time, twenty-one years before, when Hiroko wrote me a card that moved me. I told her how much I liked one phrase, and she began to reproduce it, in every letter she sent me for years thereafter, regardless of the context. If you've given happiness with a sentence—or a gesture—why not repeat it again and again?

In a stylish antechamber, we're brought tingling sorbets in transparent, light-blue goblets, and drinks, and then, after a suitable pause, led into the banquet room, where a gorgeous announcer in a floating, thin black dress starts putting us at ease with bright chatter. In truth, this professional-seeming emcee turns out to be a friend of the bride's, moonlighting as a favour, and I appear to be the only one worried that she might upstage the bride. The announcer's job, after all, is to look gorgeous, while the bride only has to be Audrey Hepburn: in a role-correct society, there's less room for competition.

And here a whole different movement in the carefully arranged symphony begins. Arcade Fire comes onto the soundtrack, and new husband and wife walk in, spotlit, so we can admire the bride's dress again. The two sit alone onstage, and the groom apologizes for the simplicity, the modesty of the occasion (for which he has paid, out of his own pocket, $30,000).

Then, over a seven-course meal, a wedding ceremony is turned into a wedding party. A speech from the groom's boss, very long, and a toast from the guy who'd been their chaperone on early dates. A giggle from the announcer. A friend of the bride comes up and, through tears, expresses her congratulations, before escorting her friend out of the room for another change of costume.

Bags of money are handed out, following a pattern I can't begin to discern. Envelopes of cash are slipped into certain hands. Members of the staff steal in and out, whispering directions. More sorbets arrive, a beautifully cut steak. An onstage "interview" is held with the cupid who first introduced the couple, though now he's a Buddhist priest, munching on steak beside his wife.

I think of what a leap of faith this occasion entails. One Japanese man in four nowadays says that he has "no interest" in sex, even "despises" it; more and more Japanese women are marrying out of Japan, so as to escape their traditional roles and constraints. Not so many years ago, there were two thousand "Narita Divorces" in the space of twelve months (young Japanese man and woman enjoy a wedding; they go to Honolulu or Surfers Paradise for their honeymoon—and the girl is so at ease with [being abroad] and English, her husband so ill at ease, that by the time they return to Narita Airport six days later, roles unhappily reversed, they decide they have to get a divorce).

Three former band mates of the bride now come to the front and deliver a stirring, *American Idol*-worthy version of "Seasons of Love" from *Rent*. The words appear on a screen that fills one wall, and one of the young beauties takes a solo, belting her words out as if she were Diana Ross, while the others trade quieter turns. Then all three dance in perfect sync, the Supremes translated to a *Mikado* world.

I could go on, describing every last detail matched to each passing moment, and refined over decades: the bride's re-entry and the bridal couple's visit to every table; the cake wheeled out in advance of the meal so that everyone can crowd forward and take photos of the bride stuffing pieces of it into her proud husband's grinning mouth. (Once the photo op is complete, the cake is wheeled out, never to be seen again.) The champagne, and the beautiful moment when the couple goes out and returns with a candle, with which the two of them set off a flicker of light on every last table. The films made up of slides of them both through the years, as if a segment of the old TV programme *This Is Your Life* were set now to the wistful chimes of U2 and A-ha.

Yet the point, really, is not in the details but in the idea. When foreign friends visit me in Kyoto, they often marvel at the perfection of Japanese packaging, the way every candy will be individually wrapped, and a popsicle will be placed inside a bag with a sachet of ice to keep it cool, the way a three-dollar stick of incense will be sold in a cool, cylindrical box and then placed within a gossamer bag and then draped in elegant paper, with a little business card placed under the bow, reminding you that Lisn, the elegant shop, sells "sophisticated incense for listeners."*

But if those friends stay longer, they start to complain about the individual wrapping of the self, the packaging of rituals and the heart. As if something dishevelled is automatically more authentic; as if personal feelings can't be set within impersonal frames, the way the wedding photos from this day will be, and the memories of what was felt when Bono and The Edge sang "One" on the sound system.

Now the parents of the happy couple are standing, backs straight, against the main doors to the room, and the bride is reading a letter of thanks to her mother and father, moving her groom to tears. He does the same and then his mother, my wife, delivers a speech apologizing for all the ways she made life difficult for him when she got a divorce, and his sister, at a nearby table, collapses into sobs. There are hankies in every young woman's hand at this point, and the sound of sniffled tears; by candlelight, the scene is as affecting as the climax of any rapturously photographed, impeccably storyboarded movie.

Then the groom's friends gather round him in a circle and toss him up into the air five times, shouting, "Banzai!" The same thing is done after every season with every single winning baseball coach. But it's always stirring, always the perfect gesture of warmth and celebration. Does the fact we all say "I love you" make it mean less every time?

The guests now start to disperse; they know what formalities to expect, perhaps, but still they have tears in their eyes, and voices crack as they say goodbye, the way I can listen to the song that wiped me out at seventeen and still be fairly confident it will do the same now (if only because it brings back the memory of being seventeen, wide open). I think of the priest—he looked like an aging Elvis, but he carried himself like a solemn man of Rome—and the place-mats, on every one of which the groom has written a description of each of the eighty or so guests. I think of the Bach—it's always Bach, I suspect—and yet "Jesu, Joy of Man's Desiring" always stirs and uplifts.

Upstairs, in the third-floor fitting room, there are so many sobbing brides and kimonoed old women that people start welcoming the wrong grandmother, or thanking a bewildered-looking man who belongs to another wedding party. In the hallway, everyone is wiping off tears and mascara as the party from the next wedding streams out, in a similar state of emotional disarray. Our newlyweds are now in their room—part of the wedding package (though it's not, I gather, the Moonlight Forest room, the Lovers' Suite or any of the other love-hotel options, such as the View Bath Luna Suite).

A young boy from our group slips me a perfectly folded scrap of paper with a hand-drawn map on it. "We're having a second party," he explains, in English. "Not far from here. In the park. Very relaxed. Lots of frisbees; kind of like a picnic. Please come."

---

*See Hideyuki Oka's *How to Wrap Five Eggs*. [*Editors' note*]

Outside, the bright autumnal sunshine catches flocks of kids heading back from a radiant day at Tokyo Disneyland nearby. I remember hearing that the wartime emperor, Hirohito, was buried with his Mickey Mouse wristwatch, the smallest thing changing value as it moves between cultures so that it becomes folly to laugh at any prop or to see it as out of context.

I've been to plenty of weddings in English churches where the women in broad hats whisper about the young Thai wife Charlie has brought back from his stint out East with Swire's, or say, "Surely that woman couldn't be a member of the bridal party?" I've been to my share of New Age weddings in California where groom and bride stand barefoot above the ocean, a friend of theirs having acquired a certificate from the Universal Life Church to marry them, and recite Rumi before playing Van Morrison singing, "Have I told you lately that I love you . . . ."

I've even officiated at weddings in Californian gardens where the groom declaims from Shakespeare and the bride takes pains to prevent me from seeing how many previous husbands are listed on the certificate I'm obliged to sign.

But none has so affected or filled me up as this one. Somehow this seems more authentic, precisely because it's planned so seamlessly, more full of feeling exactly because every moment is choreographed. Is that the Japanese secret? That the emotions we find when rehearsed may be at least as powerful—as real—as the ones we so cherish for their spontaneity and distinctness? That somebody else's model, honed and perfected over centuries, may be better and wiser than the one we've come up with ourselves last month? Might that even be the secret of a happy marriage? Play your part to perfection, and before long, the feelings that belong to it may be yours. Hit your mark and, before you know it, those marks will disappear and you will be the wife and husband of the picture books.

I don't have time to think of any of this; the new married couple is heading out into the autumn sun, as the next couple steps into the bridal salon.

PART THREE

GROWING UP SOCIAL

15

Boyhood, Organized Sports, and the Construction of Masculinities

MICHAEL A. MESSNER

Though young women are now participating in sports in unprecedented numbers, the influence of sports activity on boys' identity and socialization experience remains a major interest in gender studies. Michael Messner, one of the pioneers and most prominent researchers of this topic, examines the way sports focus and define what it is to be masculine, the variations in sports' influence across social classes, and some unsuspected lessons sports participation imparts for relationships beyond the gym, pool, and fields of play. In reading this article, you might want to ask yourself: What would this article be saying if the subject was young women?

In this study I explore and interpret the meanings that males themselves attribute to their boyhood participation in organized sport. In what ways do males construct masculine identities within the institution of organized sports? In what ways do class and racial differences mediate this relationship and perhaps lead to the construction of different meanings, and perhaps different masculinities? And what are some of the problems and contradictions within these constructions of masculinity?

DESCRIPTION OF RESEARCH

Between 1983 and 1985, I conducted interviews with 30 male former athletes. Most of the men I interviewed had played the (U.S.) "major sports"—football, basketball, baseball, track. At the time of the interview, each had been retired from playing organized sports for at least five years. Their ages ranged from 21 to 48, with the median, 33; 14 were black, 14 were white, and two were Hispanic; 15 of the 16 black and Hispanic men had come from poor or working-class families, while the majority (9 of 14) of the white men had come from middle-class or professional families. All had at some time in their lives based their identities largely on their roles as athletes and could therefore be said to have had "athletic careers." Twelve had played organized sports through high school, 11 through college, and seven had been professional athletes. Though the sample was not randomly selected, an effort was made to see that the sample had a range of difference in terms of race and social class backgrounds, and that there was some variety in terms of age, types of sports played and levels of success in athletic careers. Without exception each man contacted agreed to be interviewed.

The tape-recorded interviews were semi-structured and took from one and one-half to six hours, with most taking about three hours. I asked each man to talk about four broad eras in his life: (1) his earliest experiences with sports in boyhood, (2) his athletic career, (3) retirement or disengagement from the athletic career, and (4) life after the athletic career. In each era, I focused the interview on the meanings of "success and failure," and on the boy's/man's relationships with family, with other males, with women, and with his own body.

In collecting what amounted to life histories of these men, my overarching purpose was to use feminist theories of masculine gender identity to explore how masculinity develops and changes as boys and men interact within the socially constructed world of organized sports. In addition to using the data to move toward some generalizations about the relationship between "masculinity and sport," I was also concerned with sorting out some of the variations among boys, based on class and racial inequalities, that led them to relate differently to athletic careers. I divided my sample into two comparison groups. The first group was made up of 10 men from higher-status backgrounds, primarily white, middle-class, and professional families. The second group was made up of 20 men from lower status backgrounds, primarily minority, poor, and working-class families.

BOYHOOD AND THE PROMISE OF SPORTS

Zane Grey once said, "All boys love baseball. If they don't they're not real boys" (as cited in Kimmel 1990). This is, of course, an ideological statement; in fact, some boys do *not* love baseball, or any other sports, for that matter. There are millions of males who at an early age are rejected by, become alienated from, or lose interest in organized sports. Yet all boys are, to a greater or lesser extent, judged according to their ability, or lack of ability, in competitive sports (Eitzen 1975; Sabo 1985). In this study I focus on those males who did become athletes—males who eventually poured thousands of hours into the development of specific physical skills. It is in boyhood that we can discover the roots of their commitment to athletic careers.

How did organized sports come to play such a central role in these boys' lives? When asked to recall how and why they initially got into playing sports, many of the men interviewed for this study seemed a bit puzzled: after all, playing sports was "just the thing to do." A 42-year-old black man who had played college basketball put it this way:

> It was just what you did. It's kind of like, you went to school, you played athletics, and if you didn't, there was something wrong with you. It was just like brushing your teeth: it's just what you did. It's part of your existence.

Spending one's time playing sports with other boys seemed as natural as the cycle of the seasons: baseball in the spring and summer, football in the fall, basketball in the winter—and then it was time to get out the old baseball glove and begin again. As a black 35-year-old former professional football star said:

> I'd say when I wasn't in school, 95% of the time was spent in the park playing. It was the only thing to do. It just came as natural.

And a black, 34-year-old professional basketball player explained his early experiences in sports:

> My principal and teacher said, "Now if you work at this you might be pretty damned good." So it was more or less a community thing—everybody in the community said, "Boy, if you work hard and keep your nose clean, you gonna be good." 'Cause it was natural instinct.

"It was natural instinct." "I was a natural." Several athletes used words such as these to explain their early attraction to sports. But certainly there is nothing "natural" about throwing a ball through a hoop, hitting a ball with a bat, or jumping over hurdles. A boy, for instance, may have amazingly dexterous inborn hand-eye coordination, but this does not predispose him to a career of hitting baseballs any more than it predisposes him to a life as a brain surgeon. When one listens closely to what these men said about their early experiences in sports, it becomes clear that their adoption of the self-definition of "natural athlete" was the result of what Connell (1990) has called "a collective practice" that constructs masculinities. The boyhood development of masculine identity and status—truly problematic in a society that offers no official rite of passage into adulthood—results from a process of interaction with people and social institutions. Thus, in discussing early motivations in sports, men commonly talk of the importance of relationships with family members, peers, and the broader community.

FAMILY INFLUENCES

Though most of the men in this study spoke of their mothers with love, respect, even reverence, their descriptions of their earliest experiences in sports are stories of an exclusively male world. The existence of older brothers or uncles who served as teachers and athletic role models—as well as sources of competition for attention and status within the family—was very common. An older brother, uncle, or even close friend of the family who was a successful athlete appears to have acted as a sort of standard of achievement against whom to measure oneself. A 34-year-old black man who had been a three-sport star in high school said:

> My uncles—my Uncle Harold went to the Detroit Tigers, played pro ball—all of 'em, everybody played sports, so I wanted to be better than anybody else. I knew

that everybody in this town knew them—their names were something. I wanted my name to be just like theirs.

Similarly, a black 41-year-old former professional football player recalled:

I was the younger of three brothers and everybody played sports, so consequently I was more or less forced into it. 'Cause one brother was always better than the next brother and then I came along and had to show them that I was just as good as them. My oldest brother was an all-city ballplayer, then my other brother comes along he's all-city and all-state, and then I have to come along.

For some, attempting to emulate or surpass the athletic accomplishments of older male family members created pressures that were difficult to deal with. A 33-year-old white man explained that he was a good athlete during boyhood, but the constant awareness that his two older brothers had been better made it difficult for him to feel good about himself, or to have fun in sports:

I had this sort of reputation that I followed from the playgrounds through grade school, and through high school. I followed these guys who were all-conference and all-state.

Most of these men, however, saw their relationships with their athletic older brothers and uncles in a positive light; it was within these relationships that they gained experience and developed motivations that gave them a competitive "edge" within their same-aged peer group. As a 33-year-old black man describes his earliest athletic experiences:

My brothers were role models. I wanted to prove—especially to my brothers— that I had heart, you know, that I was a man.

When asked, "What did it mean to you to be 'a man' at that age?" he replied:

Well, it meant that I didn't want to be a so-called scaredy-cat. You want to hit a guy even though he's bigger than you to show that, you know, you've got this macho image. I remember that at that young an age, that feeling was exciting to me. And that carried over, and as I got older, I got better and I began to look around me and see, well hey! I'm competitive with these guys, even though I'm younger, you know? And then of course all the compliments come—and I began to notice a change, even in my parents—especially in my father—he was proud of that, and that was very important to me. He was extremely important . . . he showed me more affection, now that I think of it.

As this man's words suggest, if men talk of their older brothers and uncles mostly as role models, teachers, and "names" to emulate, their talk of their relationships with their fathers is more deeply layered and complex. Athletic skills and competition for status may often be learned from older brothers, but it is in boys' relationships with fathers that we find many of the keys to the emotional salience of sports in the development of masculine identity.

RELATIONSHIPS WITH FATHERS

The fact that boys' introductions to organized sports are often made by fathers who might otherwise be absent or emotionally distant adds a powerful emotional charge to these early experiences (Osherson 1986). Although playing organized sports eventually came to feel "natural" for all of the men interviewed in this study, many needed to be "exposed" to sports, or even gently "pushed" by their fathers to become involved in activities like Little League baseball. A white, 33-year-old-man explained:

> I still remember it like it was yesterday—Dad and I driving up in his truck, and I had my glove and my hat and all that—and I said, "Dad, I don't want to do it." He says, "What?" I says, "I don't want to do it." I was nervous. That I might fail. And he says, "Don't be silly. Lookit: There's Joey and Petey and all your friends out there." And so Dad says, "You're gonna do it, come on." And in my memory he's never said that about anything else; he just knew I needed a little kick in the pants and I'd do it. And once you're out there and you see all the other kids making errors and stuff, and you know you're better than those guys, you know: Maybe I *do* belong here. As it turned out, Little League was a good experience.

Some who were similarly "pushed" by their fathers were not so successful as the aforementioned man had been in Little League baseball, and thus the experience was not altogether a joyous affair. One 34-year-old white man, for instance, said he "inherited" his interest in sports from his father, who started playing catch with him at the age of four. Once he got into Little League, he felt pressured by his father, one of the coaches, who expected him to be the star of the team:

> I'd go zero-for-four sometimes, strike out three times in a Little League game, and I'd dread the ride home. I'd come home and he'd say, "Go in the bathroom and swing the bat in the mirror for an hour," to get my swing level . . . It didn't help much, though, I'd go out and strike out three or four times again the next game too [laughs ironically].

When asked if he had been concerned with having his father's approval, he responded:

Failure in his eyes? Yeah, I always thought that he wanted me to get some kind of [athletic] scholarship. I guess I was afraid of him when I was a kid. He didn't hit that much, but he had a rage about him—he'd rage, and that voice would just rattle you.

Similarly, a 24-year-old black man described his awe of his father's physical power and presence, and his sense of inadequacy in attempting to emulate him:

My father had a voice that sounded like rolling thunder. Whether it was intentional on his part or not, I don't know, but my father gave me a sense, an image of him being the most powerful being on earth, and that no matter what I ever did I would never come close to him . . . There were definite feelings of physical inadequacy that I couldn't work around.

It is interesting to note how these feelings of physical inadequacy relative to the father lived on as part of this young man's permanent internalized image. He eventually became a "feared" high school football player and broke school records in weight-lifting, yet,

As I grew older, my mother and friends told me that I had actually grown to be a larger man than my father. Even though in time I required larger clothes than he, which should have been a very concrete indication, neither my brother nor I could ever bring ourselves to say that I was bigger. We simply couldn't conceive of it.

Using sports activities as a means of identifying with and "living up to" the power and status of one's father was not always such a painful and difficult task for the men I interviewed. Most did not describe fathers who "pushed" them to become sports stars. The relationship between their athletic strivings and their identification with their fathers was more subtle. A 48-year-old black man, for instance, explained that he was not pushed into sports by his father, but was aware from an early age of the community status his father had gained through sports. He saw his own athletic accomplishments as a way to connect with and emulate his father:

I wanted to play baseball because my father had been quite a good baseball player in the Negro leagues before baseball was integrated, and so he was kind of a model for me. I remember, quite young, going to a baseball game he was in— this was before the war and all—I remember being in the stands with my mother and seeing him on first base, and being aware of the crowd . . . I was aware of people's confidence in him as a serious baseball player. I don't think my father ever said anything to me like "play sports" . . . [But] I knew he would like it if I did well. His admiration was important . . . he mattered.

Similarly, a 24-year-old white man described his father as a somewhat distant "role model" whose approval mattered:

> My father was more of an example . . . he definitely was very much in touch with and still had very fond memories of being an athlete and talked about it, bragged about it. . . . But he really didn't do that much to teach me skills, and he didn't always go to every game I played like some parents. But he approved and that was important, you know. That was important to get his approval. I always knew that playing sports was important to him, so I knew implicitly that it was good and there was definitely a value on it.

First experiences in sports might often come through relationships with brothers or older male relatives, and the early emotional salience of sports was often directly related to a boy's relationship with his father. The sense of commitment that these young boys eventually made to the development of athletic careers is best explained as a process of development of masculine gender identity and status in relation to same-sex peers.

MASCULINE IDENTITY AND EARLY COMMITMENT TO SPORTS

When many of the men in this study said that during childhood they played sports because "it's just what everybody did," they of course meant that it was just what *boys* did. They were introduced to organized sports by older brothers and fathers, and once involved, found themselves playing within an exclusively male world. Though the separate (and unequal) gendered worlds of boys and girls came to appear as "natural," they were in fact socially constructed. Thorne's observations of children's activities in schools indicated that rather than "naturally" constituting "separate gendered cultures," there is considerable interaction between boys and girls in classrooms and on playgrounds. When adults set up legitimate contact between boys and girls, Thorne observed, this usually results in "relaxed interactions." But when activities in the classroom or on the playground are presented to children as sex-segregated activities and gender is marked by teachers and other adults ("boys line up here, girls over there"), "gender boundaries are heightened, and mixed-sex interaction becomes an explicit arena of risk" (Thorne 1986; 70). Thus sex-segregated activities such as organized sports as structured by adults, provide the context in which gendered identities and separate "gendered cultures" develop and come to appear natural. For the boys in this study, it became "natural" to equate masculinity with competition, physical strength, and skills. Girls simply did not (could not, it was believed) participate in these activities.

Yet it is not simply the separation of children, by adults, into separate activities that explains why many boys came to feel such a strong connection with sports activities, while so few girls did. As I listened to men recall their earliest experiences in organized sports, I heard them talk of insecurity, loneliness, and especially a need to connect with other people as a primary motivation in their early sports strivings. As a 42-year-old white man stated, "The most important thing was just being out there with the rest of the guys—being friends." Another 32-year-old interviewee was born in Mexico and moved to the United States at a fairly young age. He never knew his father, and his mother died when he was only nine years old. Suddenly he felt rootless, and threw himself into sports. His initial motivations, however, do not appear to be based on a need to compete and win:

> Actually, what I think sports did for me is it brought me into kind of an instant family. By being on a Little League team, or even just playing with all kinds of different kids in the neighborhood, it brought what I really wanted, which was some kind of closeness. It was just being there, and being friends.

Clearly, what these boys needed and craved was that which was most problematic for them: connection and unity with other people. But why do these young males find *organized sports* such an attractive context in which to establish "a kind of closeness" with others? Comparative observations of young boys' and girls' game-playing behaviors yield important insights into this question. Piaget (1965) and Lever (1976) both observed that girls tend to have more "pragmatic" and "flexible" orientations to the rules of games; they are more prone to make exceptions and innovations in the middle of a game in order to make the game more "fair." Boys, on the other hand, tend to have a more firm, even inflexible orientation to the rules of a game; to them, the rules are what protects any fairness. This difference, according to Gilligan (1982), is based on the fact that early developmental experiences have yielded deeply rooted differences between males' and females' developmental tasks, needs, and moral reasoning. Girls, who tend to define themselves primarily through connection with others, experience highly competitive situations (whether in organized sports or in other hierarchical institutions) as threats to relationships, and thus to their identities. For boys, the development of gender identity involves the construction of positional identities, where a sense of self is solidified through separation from others (Chodorow 1978). Yet feminist psychoanalytic theory has tended to oversimplify the internal lives of men (Lichterman 1986). Males do appear to develop positional identities, yet despite their fears of intimacy, they also retain a human need for closeness and unity with others. This ambivalence toward intimate relationships is a major thread running through masculine development throughout the life course. Here we can conceptualize what Craib (1987) calls the "elective affinity" between personality and social structure: For the boy who both seeks and fears attachment with others, the rule-bound structure of organized sports can promise to be a safe place in which to seek nonintimate attachment with others within a context that maintains clear boundaries, distance, and separation.

COMPETITIVE STRUCTURES AND CONDITIONAL SELF-WORTH

Young boys may initially find that sports gives them the opportunity to experience "some kind of closeness" with others, but the structure of sports and athletic careers often undermines the possibility of boys learning to transcend their fears of intimacy, thus becoming able to develop truly close and intimate relationships with others (Kidd 1990; Messner 1987). The sports world is extremely hierarchical, and an incredible amount of importance is placed on winning, on "being number one." For instance, a few years ago I observed a basketball camp put on for boys by a professional basketball coach and his staff. The youngest boys, about eight years old (who could barely reach the basket with their shots) played a brief scrimmage. Afterwards, the coaches lined them up in a row in front of the older boys who were sitting in the grandstands. One by one, the coach would stand behind each boy, put his hand on the boy's head (much in the manner of a priestly benediction), and the older boys in the stands would applaud and cheer, louder or softer, depending on how well or poorly the young boy was judged to have performed. The two or three boys who were clearly the exceptional players looked confident that they would receive the praise they were due. Most of the boys, though, had expressions ranging from puzzlement to thinly disguised terror on their faces as they awaited the judgments of the older boys.

This kind of experience teaches boys that it is not "just being out there with the guys—being friends," that ensures the kind of attention and connection that they crave; it is being *better* than the other guys—*beating* them—that is the key to acceptance. Most of the boys in this study did have some early successes in sports, and thus their ambivalent need for connection with others was met, at least for a time. But the institution of sport tends to encourage the development of what Schafer (1975) has called "conditional self-worth" in boys. As boys become aware that acceptance by others is contingent upon being good—a "winner"—narrow definitions of success, based upon performance and winning become increasingly important to them. A 33-year-old black man said that by the time he was in his early teens:

> It was expected of me to do well in all my contests—I mean by my coaches, my peers, and my family. So I in turn expected to do well, and if I didn't do well, then I'd be very disappointed.

The man from Mexico, discussed [earlier], who said that he had sought "some kind of closeness" in his early sports experiences began to notice in his early teens that if he played well, was a *winner*, he would get attention from others:

It got to the point where I started realizing, noticing that people were always there for me, backing me all the time—sports got to be really fun because I always had some people there backing me. Finally my oldest brother started going to all my games, even though I had never really seen who he was [laughs]—after the game, you know, we never really saw each other, but he was at all my baseball games, and it seemed like we shared a kind of closeness there, but only in those situations. Off the field, when I wasn't in uniform, he was never around.

By high school, he said, he felt "up against the wall." Sports hadn't delivered what he had hoped it would, but he thought if he just tried harder, won one more championship trophy, he would get the attention he truly craved. Despite his efforts, this attention was not forthcoming. And, sadly, the pressures he had put on himself to excel in sports had taken most of the fun out of playing.

For many of the men in this study, throughout boyhood and into adolescence, this conscious striving for successful achievement became the primary means through which they sought connection with other people (Messner 1987). But it is important to recognize that young males' internalized ambivalences about intimacy do not fully determine the contours and directions of their lives. Masculinity continues to develop through interaction with the social world—and because boys from different backgrounds are interacting with substantially different familial, educational, and other institutions, these differences will lead them to make different choices and define situations in different ways. Next, I examine the differences in the ways that boys from higher- and lower-status families and communities related to organized sports.

STATUS DIFFERENCES AND COMMITMENTS TO SPORTS

In discussing early attractions to sports, the experiences of boys from higher- and lower-status backgrounds are quite similar. Both groups indicate the importance of fathers and older brothers in introducing them to sports. Both groups speak of the joys of receiving attention and acceptance among family and peers for early successes in sports. Note the similarities, for instance, in the following descriptions of boyhood athletic experiences of two men. First, a man born in a white, middle-class family:

> I loved playing sports so much from a very early age because of early exposure. A lot of the sports came easy at an early age, and because they did, and because you were successful at something, I think that you're inclined to strive for that gratification. It's like, if you're good, you like it, because it's instant gratification. I'm doing something that I'm good at and I'm gonna keep doing it.

Second, a black man from a poor family:

Fortunately I had some athletic ability, and, quite naturally, once you start doing good in whatever it is—I don't care if it's jacks—you show off what you do. That's your ability, that's your blessing, so you show it off as much as you can.

For boys from both groups, early exposure to sports, the discovery that they had some "ability," shortly followed by some sort of family, peer, and community recognition, all eventually led to the commitment of hundreds and thousands of hours of playing, practicing, and dreaming of future stardom. Despite these similarities, there are also some identifiable differences that begin to explain the tendency of males from lower-status backgrounds to develop higher levels of commitment to sports careers. The most clear-cut differences was that while men from higher-status backgrounds are likely to describe their earliest athletic experiences and motivations almost exclusively in terms of immediate family, men from lower-status backgrounds more commonly describe the importance of a broader community context. For instance, a 46-year-old man who grew up in a "poor working class" black family in a small town in Arkansas explained:

> In that community, at the age of third or fourth grade, if you're a male, they expect you to show some kind of inclination, some kind of skill in football or basketball. It was an expected thing, you know? My mom and my dad, they didn't push at all. It was the general environment.

A 48-year-old man describes sports activities as a survival strategy in his poor black community:

> Sports protected me from having to compete in gang stuff, or having to be good with my fists. If you were an athlete and got into the fist world, that was your business, and that was okay—but you didn't have to if you didn't want to. People would generally defer to you, give you your space away from trouble.

A 35-year-old man who grew up in "a poor black ghetto" described his boyhood relationship to sports similarly:

> Where I came from, either you were one of two things: you were in sports or you were out on the streets being a drug addict, or breaking into places. The guys who were in sports, we had it a little easier, because we were accepted by both groups. . . . So it worked out to my advantage, cause I didn't get into a lot of trouble—some trouble, but not a lot.

The fact that boys in lower-status communities faced these kinds of realities gave salience to their developing athletic identities. In contrast, sports were important to boys from higher-status backgrounds, yet the middle-class environment seemed more secure, less threatening, and offered far more options. By the time most of these boys got into junior high or high school, many had made conscious decisions to shift their attentions away from athletic careers to educational and (nonathletic) career goals. A 32-year-old white college athletic director told me that he had seen his chance to pursue a pro baseball career as "pissing in the wind," and instead, focused on education. Similarly, a 33-year-old white dentist who was a three-sport star in high school, decided not to play sports in college, so he could focus on getting into dental school. As he put it,

> I think I kind of downgraded the stardom thing. I thought it was small potatoes. And sure, that's nice in high school and all that, but on a broad scale, I didn't think it amounted to all that much.

This statement offers an important key to understanding the construction of masculine identity within a middle-class context. The status that this boy got through sports had been *very* important to him, yet he could see that "on a broad scale," this sort of status was "small potatoes." This sort of early recognition is more than a result of the oft-noted middle-class tendency to raise "future-oriented" children (Rubin 1976; Sennett and Cobb 1973). Perhaps more important, it is that the *kinds* of future orientations developed by boys from higher-status backgrounds are consistent with the middle-class context. These men's descriptions of their boyhoods reveal that they grew up immersed in a wide range of institutional frameworks, of which organized sports was just one. And—importantly—they could see that the status of adult males around them was clearly linked to their positions within various professions, public institutions, and bureaucratic organizations. It was clear that access to this sort of institutional status came through educational achievement, not athletic prowess. A 32-year-old black man who grew up in a professional-class family recalled that he had idolized Wilt Chamberlain and dreamed of being a pro basketball player, yet his father discouraged his athletic strivings:

> He knew I liked the game. I *loved* the game. But basketball was not recommended; my dad would say, "That's a stereotyped image for black youth. . . . When your basketball is gone and finished, what are you gonna do? One day, you might get injured. What are you gonna look forward to?" He stressed education.

Similarly, a 32-year-old man who was raised in a white, middle-class family, had found in sports a key means of gaining acceptance and connection in his peer group. Yet he was simultaneously developing an image of himself as a "smart student," and becoming aware of a wide range of nonsport life options:

> My mother was constantly telling me how smart I was, how good I was, what a nice person I was, and giving me all sorts of positive strokes, and those positive

strokes became a self-motivating kind of thing. I had this image of myself as smart, and I lived up to that image.

It is not that parents of boys in lower-status families did not also encourage their boys to work hard in school. Several reported that their parents "stressed books first, sports second." It's just that the broader social context—education, economy, and community—was more likely to *narrow* lower-status boys' perceptions of real-life options, while boys from higher-status backgrounds faced an expanding world of options. For instance, with a different socioeconomic background, one 35-year-old black man might have become a great musician instead of a star professional football running back. But he did not. When he was a child, he said, he was most interested in music:

> I wanted to be a drummer. But we couldn't afford drums. My dad couldn't go out and buy me a drum set or a guitar even—it was just one of those things; he was just trying to make ends meet.

But he *could* afford, as could so many in his socioeconomic condition, to spend countless hours at the local park, where he was told by the park supervisor

> that I was a natural—not only in gymnastics or baseball—whatever I did, I was a natural. He told me I shouldn't waste this talent, and so I immediately started watching the big guys then.

In retrospect, this man had potential to be a musician or any number of things, but his environment limited his options to sports, and he made the best of it. Even within sports, he, like most boys in the ghetto, was limited:

> We didn't have any tennis courts in the ghetto—we used to have a lot of tennis balls, but no racquets. I wonder today how good I might be in tennis if I had gotten a racquet in my hands at an early age.

It is within this limited structure of opportunity that many lower-status young boys found sports to be *the* place, rather than *a* place, within which to construct masculine identity, status, the relationships. A 36-year-old white man explained that his father left the family when he was very young and his mother faced a very difficult struggle to make ends meet. As his words suggest, the more limited a boy's options, and the more insecure his family situation, the more likely he is to make an early commitment to an athletic career.

> I used to ride my bicycle to Little League practice—if I'd waited for someone to pick me up and take me to the ball park I'd have never played. I'd get to the ball park and all the other kids would have their dad bring them to practice or games. But I'd park my bike to the side and when it was over I'd get on it and go home.

Sports was the way for me to move everything to the side—family problems, just all the embarrassments—and think about one thing, and that was sports . . . In the third grade, when the teacher went around the classroom and asked every-body, "What do you want to be when you grow up?," I said, "I want to be a major league baseball player," and everybody laughed their heads off.

This man eventually did enjoy a major league baseball career. Most boys from lower-status backgrounds who make similar early commitments to ath-letic careers are not so successful. As stated earlier, the career structure of organized sports is highly competitive and hierarchical. In fact, the chances of attaining professional status in sports are approximately 4:100,000 for a white man, 2:100,000 for a black man, and 3:1 million for a Hispanic man in the United States (Leonard and Reyman 1988). Nevertheless, the immediate rewards (fun, status, attention), along with the constricted (nonsports) struc-ture of opportunity, attract disproportionately large numbers of boys from lower-status backgrounds to athletic careers as their major means of construct-ing a masculine identity. These are the boys who later, as young men, had to struggle with "conditional self-worth," and, more often than not, occupational dead ends. Boys from higher-status backgrounds, on the other hand, bolstered their boyhood, adolescent, and early adult status through their athletic accom-plishments. Their wider range of experiences and life chances led to an early shift away from sports careers as the major basis of identity (Messner 1989).

CONCLUSION

The conception of the masculinity-sports relationship developed here begins to illustrate the idea of an "elective affinity" between social structure and per-sonality. Organized sports is a "gendered institution"—an institution con-structed by gender relations. As such, its structure and values (rules, formal organization, sex composition, etc.), reflect dominant conceptions of mascu-linity and femininity. Organized sports is also a "gendering institution"—an institution that helps to construct the current gender order. Part of this con-struction of gender is accomplished through the "masculinizing" of male bod-ies and minds.

Yet boys do not come to their first experiences in organized sports as "blank slates," but arrive with already "gendering" identities due to early developmen-tal experiences and previous socialization. I have suggested here that an impor-tant thread running through the development of masculine identity is males' ambivalence toward intimate unity with others. Those boys who experience early athletic successes find in the structure of organized sport an affinity with this masculine ambivalence toward intimacy: The rule-bound, competitive, hierarchical world of sport offers boys an attractive means of establishing an emotionally distant (and thus "safe") connection with others. Yet as boys begin to define themselves as "athletes," they learn that in order to be accepted (to have connection) through sports, they must be winners. And in order to be winners, they must construct relationships with others (and with themselves) that are consistent with the competitive and hierarchical values and structure of the sports world. As a result, they often develop a "conditional self-worth" that leads them to construct more instrumental relationships with themselves and others. This ultimately exacerbates their difficulties in constructing intimate relationships with others. In effect, the interaction between the young male's preexisting internalized ambivalence toward intimacy with the competitive hierarchical institution of sport has resulted in the construction of a masculine personality that is characterized by instrumental rationality, goal-orientation, and difficulties with intimate connection and expression (Messner 1987).

This theoretical line of inquiry invites us not simply to examine how social institutions "socialize" boys, but also to explore the ways that boys' already-gendering identities interact with social institutions (which, like organized sport, are themselves the product of gender relations). This study has also suggested that it is not some singular "masculinity" that is being constructed through athletic careers. It may be correct, from a psychoanalytic perspective, to suggest that all males bring ambivalences toward intimacy to their interactions with the world, but "the world" is a very different place for males from different racial and socioeconomic backgrounds. Because males have substantially different interactions with the world, based on class, race, and other differences and inequalities, we might expect the construction of masculinity to take on different meanings for boys and men from differing backgrounds (Messner 1989). Indeed, this study has suggested that boys from higher-status backgrounds face a much broader range of options than do their lower-status counterparts. As a result, athletic careers take on different meanings for these boys. Lower-status boys are likely to see athletic careers as *the* institutional context for the construction of their masculine status and identities, while higher-status males make an early shift away from athletic careers toward other institutions (usually education and nonsports careers). A key line of inquiry for future studies might begin by exploring this irony of sports careers: Despite the fact that "the athlete" is currently an example of an exemplary form of masculinity in public ideology, the vast majority of boys who become most committed to athletic careers are never well-rewarded for their efforts. The fact that class and racial dynamics lead boys from higher-status backgrounds, unlike their lower status counterparts to move into non-sports careers illustrates how the construction of different kinds of masculinities is a key component of the overall construction of the gender order.

REFERENCES

Chodorow, N. 1978. *The Reproduction of Mothering.* Berkeley: Univ. of California Press.
Connell, R. W. 1987. *Gender and Power.* Stanford, CA: Stanford Univ. Press.

Connell, R. W. 1990. "An iron man: the body and some contradictions of hegemonic masculinity." In M. A. Messner and D. F. Sabo (eds.) *Sport, Men and the Gender Order: Critical Feminist Perspectives.* Champaign, IL: Human Kinetics.

Craib, I. 1987. "Masculinity and male dominance." *Soc. Rev.* 38: 721–743.

Eitzen, D. S. 1975. "Athletics in the status system of male adolescents: a replication of Coleman's *The Adolescent Society." Adolescence* 10: 268–276.

Gilligan, C. 1982. *In a Different Voice: Psychological Theory and Women's Development.* Cambridge, MA: Harvard Univ. Press.

Kidd, B. 1990. "The men's cultural center: sports and the dynamic of women's oppression/men's repression," In M. A. Messner and D. F. Sabo (eds.) *Sport, Men and the Gender Order: Critical Feminist Perspectives.* Champaign, IL: Human Kinetics.

Kimmel, M. S. 1990. "Baseball and the reconstitution of American masculinity: 1880–1920." In M. A. Messner and D. F. Sabo (eds.) *Sport, Men and the Gender Order: Critical Feminist Perspectives.* Champaign, IL: Human Kinetics.

Leonard, W. M. II and J. M. Reyman 1988. "The odds of attaining professional athlete status: refining the computations." *Sociology of Sport J.* 5: 162–169.

Lever, J. 1976. "Sex differences in the games children play." *Social Problems* 23: 478–487.

Lichterman, P. 1986. "Chodorow's psychoanalytic sociology: a project half-completed." *California Sociologist* 9: 147–166.

Messner, M. 1987. "The meaning of success: the athletic experience and the development of male identity," pp. 193–210 in H. Brod (ed.) *The Making of Masculinities: The New Men's Studies.* Boston: Allen and Unwin.

Messner, M. 1989. "Masculinities and athletic careers." *Gender and Society* 3: 71–88.

Osherson, S. 1986. *Finding Our Fathers: How a Man's Life Is Shaped by His Relationship with His Father.* New York: Fawcett Columbine.

Piaget, J. H. 1965. *The Moral Judgment of the Child.* New York: Free Press.

Rubin, L. B. 1976. *Worlds of Pain: Life in the Working Class Family.* New York: Basic Books.

Sabo, D. 1985. "Sport, patriarchy and male identity: new questions about men and sport." *Arena Rev.* 9: 2.

Schafer, W. E. 1975. "Sport and male sex role socialization." *Sport Sociology Bull* 47–54.

Sennett, R. and J. Cobb 1973. *The Hidden Injuries of Class.* New York: Random House.

Thorne, B. 1986. "Girls and boys together . . . but mostly apart: gender arrangement in elementary schools," pp. 167–184 in W. W. Hartup and Z. Rubin (eds.) *Relationships and Development.* Hillsdale, NJ: Lawrence Erlbaum.

16

Concerted Cultivation and the Accomplishment of Natural Growth

FROM *Unequal Childhoods: Class, Race, and Family Life*

ANNETTE LAREAU

For many years sociologists have studied socialization (child-rearing) practices. These studies often negatively contrast working-class practices against middle-class ones, especially in terms of preparation for success in a rapidly changing society and world. Annette Lareau implicitly challenges this bias, suggesting that the "concerted cultivation" practices of more affluent middle-class families may have their drawbacks. She and her students observed the lives of children across a range of social classes for several years and determined not only fairly distinct class differences but the benefits of a "accomplishment of natural growth" practices among the nonaffluent.

Laughing and yelling, a white fourth-grader named Garrett Tallinger splashes around in the swimming pool in the backyard of his four-bedroom home in the suburbs on a late spring afternoon. As on most evenings, after a quick dinner his father drives him to soccer practice. This is only one of Garrett's many activities. His brother has a baseball game at a different location. There are evenings when the boys' parents relax, sipping a glass of wine. Tonight is not one of them. As they rush to change out of their work clothes and get the children ready for practice, Mr. and Mrs. Tallinger are harried.

Only ten minutes away, a Black fourth-grader, Alexander Williams, is riding home from a school open house. His mother is driving their beige, leather-upholstered Lexus. It is 9:00 P.M. on a Wednesday evening. Ms. Williams is tired from work and has a long Thursday ahead of her. She will get up at 4:45 A.M. to go out of town on business and will not return before 9:00 P.M. On Saturday morning, she will chauffeur Alexander to a private piano lesson at 8:15 A.M., which will be followed by a choir rehearsal and then a soccer game. As they ride in the dark, Alexander's mother, in a quiet voice, talks with her son, asking him questions and eliciting his opinions.

Discussions between parents and children are a hallmark of middle-class child rearing. Like many middle-class parents, Ms. Williams and her husband see themselves as "developing" Alexander to cultivate his talents in a concerted fashion. Organized activities, established and controlled by mothers and fathers, dominate the lives of middle-class children such as Garrett and Alexander. By making certain their children have these and other experiences, middle-class parents engage in a process of *concerted cultivation*. From this, a robust sense of entitlement takes root in the children. This sense of entitlement plays an especially important role in institutional settings, where middle-class children learn to question adults and address them as relative equals.

Only twenty minutes away, in blue-collar neighborhoods, and slightly farther away, in public housing projects, childhood looks different. Mr. Yanelli, a white working-class father, picks up his son Little Billy, a fourth-grader, from an after-school program. They come home and Mr. Yanelli drinks a beer while Little Billy first watches television, then rides his bike and plays in the street. Other nights, he and his Dad sit on the sidewalk outside their house and play cards. At about 5:30 P.M. Billys mother gets home from her job as a house cleaner. She fixes dinner and the entire family sits down to eat together. Extended family are a prominent part of their lives. Ms. Yanelli touches base with her "entire family every day" by phone. Many nights Little Billy's uncle stops by, sometimes bringing Little Billy's youngest cousin. In the spring, Little Billy plays baseball on a local team. Unlike for Garrett and Alexander, who have at least four activities a week, for Little Billy, baseball is his only organized activity outside of school during the entire year. Down the road, a white working-class girl, Wendy Driver, also spends the evening with her girl cousins, as they watch a video and eat popcorn, crowded together on the living room floor.

Farther away, a Black fourth-grade boy, Harold McAllister, plays outside on a summer evening in the public housing project in which he lives. His two male cousins are there that night, as they often are. After an afternoon spent unsuccessfully searching for a ball so they could play basketball, the boys had resorted to watching sports on television. Now they head outdoors for a twilight water balloon fight. Harold tries to get his neighbor, Miss Latifa, wet. People sit in white plastic lawn chairs outside the row of apartments. Music and television sounds waft through the open windows and doors.

The adults in the lives of Billy, Wendy, and Harold want the best for them. Formidable economic constraints make it a major life task for these parents to put food on the table, arrange for housing, negotiate unsafe neighborhoods, take children to the doctor (often waiting for city buses that do not come), clean children's clothes, and get children to bed and have them ready for school the next morning. But unlike middle-class parents, these adults do not consider the concerted development of children, particularly through organized leisure activities, an essential aspect of good parenting. Unlike the Tallingers and Williamses, these mothers and fathers do not focus on concerned cultivation. For them, the crucial responsibilities of parenthood do not lie in eliciting their children's feelings, opinions, and thoughts. Rather, they see a clear boundary between adults and children. Parents tend to use directives: they tell their children what to do rather than persuading them with reasoning. Unlike their middle-class counterparts, who have a steady diet of adult organized activities, the working-class and poor children have more control over the character of their leisure activities. Most children are free to go out and play with friends and relatives who typically live close by. Their parents and guardians facilitate the *accomplishment of natural growth*. Yet these children and their parents interact with central institutions in the society, such as schools, which firmly and decisively promote strategies of concerted cultivation in child rearing. For working-class and poor families, the cultural logic of child rearing at home is out of synch with the standards of institutions. As a result, while children whose parents adopt strategies of concerted cultivation appear to gain a sense of entitlement, children such as Billy Yanelli, Wendy Driver, and Harold McAllister appear to gain an emerging sense of distance, distrust, and constraint in their institutional experiences.

CULTURAL REPERTOIRES

Professionals who work with children, such as teachers, doctors, and counselors, generally agree about how children should be raised. Of course, from time to time they may disagree on the ways standards should be enacted for an individual child or family. For example, teachers may disagree about whether or not parents should stop and correct a child who mispronounces a word while reading. Counselors may disagree over whether a mother is being too protective of her child. Still, there is little dispute among professionals on the broad principles for promoting educational development in children through proper parenting. These standards include the importance of talking with children, developing their educational interests, and playing an active role in their schooling. Similarly, parenting guidelines typically stress the importance of reasoning with children and teaching them to solve problems through negotiation rather than with physical force. Because these guidelines are so generally accepted, and because they focus on a set of practices concerning how parents should raise children, they form a *dominant set of cultural repertoires* about how children should be raised. This widespread agreement among professionals about the broad principles for child rearing permeates our society. A small number of experts thus potentially shape the behavior of a large number of parents.

Professionals' advice regarding the best way to raise children has changed regularly over the last two centuries. From strong opinions about the merits of bottle feeding, being stern with children, and utilizing physical punishment (with dire warnings of problematic outcomes should parents indulge children), there have been shifts to equally strongly worded recommendations about the benefits of breast feeding, displaying emotional warmth toward children, and using reasoning and negotiation as mechanisms of parental control. Middle-class parents appear to shift their behaviors in a variety of spheres more rapidly and more thoroughly than do working-class or poor parents. As professionals have shifted their recommendations from bottlefeeding to breast feeding, from stern approaches to warmth and empathy, and from spanking to time-outs, it is middle-class parents who have responded most promptly. Moreover, in recent decades, middle-class children in the United States have had to face the prospect of "declining fortunes." Worried about how their children will get ahead, middle-class parents are increasingly determined to make sure that their children are not excluded from any opportunity that might eventually contribute to their advancement.

Middle-class parents who comply with current professional standards and engage in a pattern of concerted cultivation deliberately try to stimulate their children's development and foster their cognitive and social skills. The commitment among working-class and poor families to provide comfort, food, shelter, and other basic support requires ongoing effort, given economic challenges and the formidable demands of child rearing. But it stops short of the deliberate cultivation of children and their leisure activities that occurs in middle-class families. For working-class and poor families, sustaining children's natural growth is viewed as an accomplishment.

What is the outcome of these different philosophies and approaches to child rearing? Quite simply, they appear to lead to the *transmission of differential advantages* to children. In this study, there was quite a bit more talking in middle-class homes than in working-class and poor homes, leading to the development of greater verbal agility, larger vocabularies, more comfort with authority figures, and more familiarity with abstract concepts. Importantly, children also developed skill differences in interacting with authority figures in institutions and at home. Middle-class children such as Garrett Tallinger and Alexander Williams learn, as young boys, to shake the hands of adults and look them in the eye. In studies of job interviews, investigators have found that potential employees have less than one minute to make a good impression. Researchers stress the importance of eye contact, firm handshakes, and displaying comfort with bosses during the interview. In poor families like Harold McAllister's, however, family members usually do not look each other in the eye when conversing. In addition, as Elijah Anderson points out, they live in neighborhoods where it can be dangerous to look people in the eye too long. The types of social competence transmitted in the McAllister family are valuable, but they are potentially less valuable (in employment interviews, for example) than those learned by Garrett Tallinger and Alexander Williams.

The white and Black middle-class children in this study also exhibited an emergent version of the *sense of entitlement* characteristic of the middle class. They acted as though they had a right to pursue their own individual preferences and to actively manage interactions in institutional settings. They appeared comfortable in these settings; they were open to sharing information and asking for attention. Although some children were more outgoing than others, it was common practice among middle-class children to shift interactions to suit *their* preferences. Alexander Williams knew how to get the doctor to listen to his concerns (about the bumps under his arm from his new deodorant). His mother explicitly trained and encouraged him to speak up with the doctor. Similarly, a Black middle-class girl, Stacey Marshall, was taught by her mother to expect the gymnastics teacher to accommodate her individual learning style. Thus, middle-class children were trained in "the rules of the game" that govern interactions with institutional representatives. They were not conversant in other important social skills, however, such as organizing their time for hours on end during weekends and summers, spending long periods of time away from adults, or hanging out with adults in a nonobtrusive, subordinate fashion. Middle-class children also learned (by imitation and by direct training) how to make the rules work in their favor. Here, the enormous stress on reasoning and negotiation in the home also has a potential advantage for future institutional negotiations. Additionally, those in authority responded positively to such interactions. Even in fourth grade, middle-class children appeared to be acting on their own behalf to gain advantages. They made special requests of teachers and doctors to adjust procedures to accommodate their desires.

The working-class and poor children, by contrast, showed an emerging *sense of constraint* in their interactions in institutional settings. They were less likely to try to customize interactions to suit their own preferences. Like their parents, the children accepted the actions of persons in authority (although at times they also covertly resisted them). Working-class and poor parents sometimes were not as aware of their children's school situation (as when their children were not doing homework). Other times, they dismissed the school rules as unreasonable. For example, Wendy Driver's mother told her to "punch" a boy who was pestering her in class; Billy Yanelli's parents were proud of him when he "beat up" another boy on the playground, even though Billy was then suspended from school. Parents also had trouble getting "the school" to respond to their concerns. When Ms. Yanelli complained that she "hates" the school, she gave her son a lesson in powerlessness and frustration in the face of an important institution. Middle-class children such as Stacey Marshall learned to make demands on professionals, and when they succeeded in making the rules work in their favor they augmented their "cultural capital" (i.e., skills individuals inherit that can then be translated into different forms of value as they move through various institutions) for the future. When working-class and poor children confronted institutions, however, they generally were unable to make the rules work in their favor nor did they obtain capital for adulthood. Because of these patterns of legitimization, children raised according to the logic of concerted cultivation can gain advantages, in the form of an emerging sense of entitlement, while children raised according to the logic of natural growth tend to develop an emerging sense of constraint.

* * *

In this study, the research assistants and I followed a small number of families around in an intensive fashion to get a sense of the rhythms of their everyday lives. On the basis of the data collected, I develop the claim that common economic position in the society, defined in terms of social class membership, is closely tied to differences in the cultural logic of child-rearing. Following a well-established Western European tradition, I provide a categorical analysis,

Table 1 Typology of Differences in Child Rearing

	Child-Rearing Approach	
	Concerted Cultivation	Accomplishment of Natural Growth
Key Elements	Parent actively fosters and assesses child's talents, opinions, and skills	Parent cares for child and allows child to grow
Organization of Daily Life	Multiple child leisure activities orchestrated by adults	"Hanging out," particularly with kin, by child
Language Use	Reasoning/directives Child contestation of adult statements Extended negotiations between parents and child	Directives Rare questioning or challenging of adults by child General acceptance by child of directives
Interventions in Institutions	Criticisms and interventions on behalf of child Training of child to take on this role	Dependence on institutions Sense of powerlessness and frustration Conflict between child-rearing practices at home and at school
Consequences	Emerging sense of entitlement on the part of the child	Emerging sense of constraint on the part of the child

grouping families into the social categories of middle class, working class, and poor. . . . I see this approach as more valuable than the gradational analysis often adopted by American scholars. In addition, I demonstrate that class differences in family life cut across a number of different and distinct spheres, which are usually not analyzed together by social scientists.

In particular, I delineate a pattern of concerted cultivation in middle-class families and a pattern of the accomplishment of natural growth in working-class and poor families. Table I provides an overview of the main points of the book. It indicates that concerted cultivation entails an emphasis on children's structured activities, language development and reasoning in the home, and active intervention in schooling. By contrast, the accomplishment of natural growth describes a form of child rearing in which children "hang out" and play, often with relatives, are given clear directives from parents with limited negotiation, and are granted more autonomy to manage their own affairs in institutions outside of the home. These patterns help us unpack the mechanisms through which social class conveys an advantage in daily life.

* * *

Social class differences in children's life experiences can be seen in the details of life. In our study, the pace of life was different for middle-class families compared to working-class and poor families. In the middle class, life was hectic. Parents were racing from activity to activity. In families with more than one child, parents often juggled conflicts between children's activities. In these families, economic resources for food, clothing, shelter, transportation, children's activities, and other routine expenses were in ample supply. Of course, some parents often *felt* short of money. At times they were not able to enjoy the vacations that they would have liked. But, as I show, families routinely spent hundreds and even thousands of dollars per year promoting children's activities.

Because there were so many children's activities, and because they were accorded so much importance, children's activities determined the schedule for the entire family. Siblings tagged along, sometimes willingly and sometimes not. Adults' leisure time was absorbed by children's activities. Children also spent much of their time in the company of adults or being directed by adults. They also had informal free time, but generally it was sandwiched between structured activities. In the organization of daily life, children's interests and activities were treated as matters of consequence.

In working-class and poor families, the organization of daily life differed from that of middle-class families. Here, there was economic strain not felt by many middle-class families. Particularly in poor families, it took enormous labor to get family members through the day, as mothers scrimped to make food last until they were able to buy more, waited for buses that didn't come, carried children's laundry out to public washers, got young children up, fed, dressed, and ready for school and oversaw children's daily lives. Children were aware of the economic strain. Money matters were frequently discussed.

Although money was in short supply, children's lives were more relaxed and, more importantly, the pace of life was slower. Children played with other children outside of the house. They frequently played with their cousins. Some children had organized activities, but they were far fewer than in middle-class families. Other times, children wanted to be in organized activities, but economic constraints, compounded by lack of transportation, made participation prohibitive. When children sought to display their budding talents and pursue activities more informally around the house, adults often treated children's interests as inconsequential. In addition, since they were not riding around in cars with parents going to organized activities or being directed by adults in structured activities, children in working-class and poor families had more autonomy from adults. Working-class and poor children had long stretches of free time during which they watched television and played with relatives and friends in the neighborhood, creating ways to occupy themselves. In these activities, there was more of a separation between adults' worlds and children's worlds.

In sum, there were social class differences in the number of organized activities, pace of family life, economic strain of family life, time spent in informal play, interest on the part of adults in children's activities, domination by children's activities of adult lives, and the amount of autonomy children had from adults. To be sure, other things also mattered in addition to social class. Gender differences were particularly striking. Girls and boys enjoyed different types of activities. Girls had more sedentary lives compared to boys. They also played closer to home. Race also played a role, particularly as racial segregation of residential neighborhoods divided children into racially segregated informal play groups (although race did not influence the number of activities children had).

* * *

THE POWER OF SOCIAL CLASS

In the United States, people disagree about the importance of social class in daily life. Many Americans believe that this country is fundamentally *open*. They assume the society is best understood as a collection of individuals. They believe that people who demonstrate hard work, effort, and talent are likely to achieve upward mobility. Put differently, many Americans believe in the American Dream. In this view, children should have roughly equal life chances. The extent to which life chances vary can be traced to differences in aspirations, talent, and hard work on the part of individuals. This perspective rejects the notion that parents' social location systematically shapes children's life experiences and outcomes. Instead, outcomes are seen as resting more in the hands of individuals.

In a distinctly different but still related vein, some social scientists acknowledge that there are systemic forms of inequality, including, for example, differences in parents' educational levels, occupational prestige, and income, as well as in their child-rearing practices. These scholars, however, see such differences within society as a matter of *graduation*. To explain unequal life outcomes, they see it as helpful to look at, for example, differences in mothers' years of education or the range of incomes by households in a particular city. These different threads are interwoven in an intricate and often baffling pattern. Scholars who take this perspective on inequality typically focus on the ways specific patterns are related (e.g., the number of years of mothers' schooling and the size of children's vocabularies, or the number of years of mothers' education and parental involvement in schooling). Implicitly and explicitly, social scientists who share this perspective do not accept the position that there are identifiable, categorical differences in groups. They do not believe that the differences that do exist across society cohere into patterns recognizable as social classes.

. . . I have challenged both views. Rather than seeing society as a collection of individuals, I stressed the importance of individuals' social structural location in shaping their daily lives. Following a well-established European tradition, I rejected analyses that see differences in American families as best interpreted as a matter of fine gradations. Instead, I see as more valuable a *categorical* analysis, wherein families are grouped into social categories such as poor, working class, and middle class. I argued that these categories are helpful in understanding the behavior of family members, not simply in one particular aspect but across a number of spheres. Family practices cohere by social class. Social scientists who accept this perspective may disagree about the number and type of categories and whether there should be, for example, an upper-middle-class category as well as a lower-middle-class one. Still, they agree that the observed differences in how people act can be meaningfully and fruitfully grouped into categories, without violating the complexity of daily life. My own view is that seeing selected aspects of family life as differentiated by social class is simply a better way to understand the reality of American family life. I also believe that social location at birth can be very important in shaping the routines of daily life, even when family members are not particularly conscious of the existence of social classes.

Thus, I have stressed how social class dynamics are woven into the texture and rhythm of children and parents' daily lives. Class position influences critical aspects of family life: time use, language use, and kin ties. Working-class and middle-class mothers may express beliefs that reflect a similar notion of "intensive mothering," but their behavior is quite different.

When children and parents move outside the home into the world of social institutions, they find that these cultural practices are not given equal value. There are signs that middle-class children benefit, in ways that are invisible to them and to their parents, from the degree of similarity between the cultural repertoires in the home and those standards adopted by institutions.

* * *

CONCERTED CULTIVATION AND THE ACCOMPLISHMENT OF NATURAL GROWTH

... [S]ocial class made a significant difference in the routines of children's daily lives. The white and Black middle-class parents engaged in practices of *concerted cultivation*. In these families, parents actively fostered and assessed their children's talents, opinions, and skills. They scheduled their children for activities. They reasoned with them. They hovered over them and outside the home they did not hesitate to intervene on the children's behalf. They made a deliberate and sustained effort to stimulate children's development and to cultivate their cognitive and social skills. The working-class and poor parents viewed children's development as unfolding spontaneously, as long as they were provided with comfort, food, shelter, and other basic support. I have called this cultural logic of child rearing the *accomplishment of natural growth*. As with concerted cultivation, this commitment, too, required ongoing effort; sustaining children's natural growth despite formidable life challenges is properly viewed as accomplishment. Parents who relied on natural growth generally organized their children's lives so they spent time in and around home, in informal play with peers, siblings, and cousins. As a result, the children had more autonomy regarding leisure time and more opportunities for child-initiated play. They also were more responsible for their lives outside the home. Unlike in middle-class families, adult-organized activities were uncommon. Instead of the relentless focus on reasoning and negotiation that took place in middle-class families, there was less speech (including less whining and badgering) in working-class and poor homes. Boundaries between adults and children were clearly marked; parents generally used language not as an aim in itself but more as a conduit for social life. Directives were common. In their institutional encounters, working-class and poor parents turned over responsibility to professionals; when parents did try to intervene, they felt that they were less capable and less efficacious than they would have liked. While working-class and poor children differed in important ways, particularly in the stability of their lives, surprisingly there was not a major difference between them in their cultural logic of child rearing. Instead, in this study the cultural divide appeared to be between the middle class and everyone else.

17

The Anxieties of Affluence

FROM *Uneasy Street: The Anxieties of Affluence*

RACHEL SHERMAN

Anyone in the United States today may find it difficult to reconcile the fantastic wealth of a few in a highly unequal society with the ideals of human equality and equal opportunity. Parents who are wealthy must find a way to do this with their children, both in attitude and behavior. Historically, this has not been a dilemma for hereditary royalty or self-made tyrants who rapaciously siphon off the wealth of a nation for their personal use, but it can be problematic for today's most wealthy families living in a democracy. Sociologist Rachel Sherman explores "how people who were benefiting from rising economic inequality experience their own social advantages." In this reading, she describes a self-imposed moral dilemma in wealthy parents' efforts to guide their children away from a sense of entitlement. It's difficult, however, to instill middle-class values when you live so far removed from the day-to-day travails and challenges of the middle class.

The wealthy women Susan Ostrander* studied around 1980, who had been born mainly from 1900 to 1940, appeared comfortable with their class privilege. For the most part raised in a homogenous wealthy community, they saw themselves as pillars of that community, publicly carrying out charitable works and preparing their children to follow in their upper-class footsteps by organizing their prep school educations and debutante parties. Ostrander sees this community participation as an attempt to justify their privilege, but she does not describe any significant conflict about their class advantages (although some felt constrained by their gender roles). In fact, these women saw themselves as "being better than other people," expressing "a sense of moral, as well as social, superiority." They seem never to have mentioned any desire for diversity in their communities. Indeed, some were doubtful about or openly hostile to admitting nonwhite, non-Protestant people to their clubs.

The New Yorkers I spoke with, in contrast, were much less complacent about their social advantages. I was surprised at how many conflicts they expressed about spending. Over time, I came to see that these were often moral conflicts about *having* privilege in general. Some, like Scott and Olivia, talked about these struggles quite openly with me, while others were more indirect.

---

*Footnotes and references can be found in Rachel Sherman's *Uneasy Street: The Anxieties of Affluence.* Princeton, NJ: Princeton University Press, 2017. [*Editors' note*]

... Some of those I interviewed tended not even to think of themselves as socially advantaged because they were focused on others around them who had the same resources or more than they did. I call these people "upward-oriented," while "downward-oriented" people, including Scott and Olivia, were more likely to see themselves as privileged. Downward-oriented people tended to have more economically diverse social networks and thus to compare their own lifestyles to a broader range of other possibilities. Either way, the vast majority implicitly or explicitly indicated that they had some kind of moral concern about having wealth.

* * *

At the same time, however, my interviewees did recognize that they were privileged. So, although they were silent with others, they struggled with themselves over the question of how *to be worthy* of this privilege in a moral sense. In order to feel that they deserved their advantages, they tried to interpret themselves as "good people." My reading of these efforts constitutes the core of this book.

* * *

I chose to start my study by seeking participants with annual household incomes of $250,000, which is in the top 5 percent in New York City.[1] I also decided to look for people in their thirties and forties who had children, as I believed that such people would be especially likely to be making important lifestyle decisions such as buying homes and choosing schools. I wanted to talk with both inheritors and earners of wealth. And I wanted to make sure to include people of color as well as gays and lesbians to investigate their underrepresented perspectives on these questions. In general, I was seeking a range of perspectives rather than a representative sample.

I found participants primarily through my own social networks, using snowball sampling; I located a few through nonprofit organizations oriented toward progressives with wealth. After interviewing ten or fifteen participants recruited on the basis of different lifestyle decisions, I narrowed the focus to those engaged in home renovation, which combined aesthetic, familial, and financial elements and seemed like a clear place to start.

I ultimately interviewed fifty parents in forty-two households (including both members of eight couples). Most families had two or three children, usually under 10 years old. Annual incomes across the group ranged from $250,000 to over $10 million; the range of assets was $80,000 to over $50 million. Most households (thirty-six, or 86 percent) had incomes of over

---

1. New York is an ideal place to explore these issues. It is a "global city" in which finance and related industries are concentrated. Indeed, astronomical compensation in these industries, the low-wage service jobs they generate, and city development strategies favoring the rich have made New York the most unequal large city in the United States.

$500,000 per year, assets of over $3 million, or both. About half earned over $1 million annually and/or had assets of over $8 million. The median household income of the sample was about $625,000, which is twelve times the New York City median of about $52,000. The estimated median net worth was $3.25 million compared to $77,000 in the United States as a whole in 2010 and $126,000 in 2007. About half had earned their primary assets; 25 percent had inherited the majority of their wealth (from $3 million to over $50 million); the remaining 25 percent both earned income of at least $400,000 per year and had inherited significant assets. Most were what Shamus Khan calls "new elite" in that they believe in diversity, openness, and meritocracy rather than status based on birth.

* * *

For my respondents to be a "good person" was *not* to be "entitled." Betsy, for example, was a management consultant turned stay-at-home mother with a household income of about $1 million. She said of her lifestyle, "I don't think we feel entitled to it." When I asked what she meant by "entitlement," she said, "Feeling that you deserve it because you were born into it or had the right education, and [that] it *should* be this way." Monica, who worked with people much wealthier than she, said she would not want to "have the money they have, and be the ass that they are. . . . They're just not nice people. And part of it is that they feel that they're owed things because they either have money or they're famous."

Notably, being morally worthy and avoiding entitlement involve both *behaving* and *feeling* in particular ways. *Practices* of working hard, consuming prudently, and giving back are matched by *affects* of independence, modest desire, and appreciation rather than a feeling of being "owed things," in Monica's words.

* * *

Finally, the parents I talked with want to pass these behaviors, feelings, and values on to their children.

. . . [A]nxieties about children's entitlement were especially prominent throughout my interviews. Parents want to raise nonmaterialistic, hardworking, nice people rather than, in Scott's words, "lazy jerks." Of course this desire is widespread among parents regardless of class. But for these affluent people the concern about entitlement harbors a deep contradiction. They want their children to see themselves as "normal" (and therefore just like everyone else) but also to appreciate their advantages (which make them different from others). In the end, they instill and reproduce ideas about how to occupy privilege legitimately without giving it up—how to be a "good person" with wealth.

As a result, it becomes hard to articulate a distributional critique rather than a behavioral one: that some people should not have so much while others have so little, regardless of how nice or hard-working or charitable they are.

Furthermore, the focus on individual behavior and affect also draws attention away from social processes that foster the unequal distribution of resources, including the decline of public education and social welfare programs, employers' assault on trade unions, and tax policy that favors the rich.

. . . [M]any parents' narratives were brightly threaded with anxieties about the kind of people their children would turn out to be. Also like Lucy's, their anxieties turned particularly on the threat of "entitlement," a concept they brought up frequently, usually unprompted. In general, as we have seen, to be "entitled" is to believe (or behave as if one believes) that one should receive certain benefits simply by virtue of who one is. Implicitly, these parents grouped a number of different fears under the umbrella of entitlement. They worried that their children would lack a work ethic and would expect others to do everything for them, that they would think they could have everything they wanted, that they would be covetous and materialistic, that they would not be aware of their advantages relative to others, and that they would treat other people disrespectfully. Instead, these parents wanted their kids to grow up to be "good people": hard workers, with prudent consumption desires and practices who respected others, were aware and appreciative of their advantages, and gave back. Although such ideals are common to parents across social classes, these privileged parents are specifically concerned with how their children can be best prepared to occupy their social position, as we will see.

In order to cultivate these characteristics, these parents used two strategies: *constraint* and *exposure*. First, they talked about limiting children's behavior and their consumption of material goods, experiences, and labor. Placing boundaries on kids' entitlement to consume would, parents hoped, also constrain their sense of entitlement more broadly. And requiring labor of them would instill a strong work ethic and a sense of self-sufficiency. Second, these parents tried to *expose* their children to class difference, in both imaginary and concrete ways, in order to help them understand their advantaged social location and get a sense of what a "normal" life is. These ideals had instrumental aspects—that is, parents imagined that having a solid work ethic and being comfortable with people different from themselves would help their children succeed in a risky world. But they also cared about the moral integrity of their children, both for its own sake and because it reflected on the parents themselves as moral actors. As Eliana put it, "Another moral warrant" for her was that "I'm raising people with good values."

However, creating limits stood in tension with a more conventional form of cultivation: giving children more. As previous research would predict, elite parents wanted their kids to have access to a vast array of experiences and opportunities, receive all the attention they might need, and be able to develop any interests and skills they might desire. So they struggled with the idea of limiting these and thus the children's "boundless potential." Furthermore, as we have seen, the parents themselves were conflicted about how much is enough—for their children as well as for themselves. It was also a challenge to define exactly what was "normal," and for whom. They wanted their kids to *be* "normal," meaning similar to others with less; but they also wanted them to be aware that they were *not* normal and appreciate their advantages.

I came to see that the kind of entitlement parents wanted to avoid was behavioral and emotional, not material. As long as they don't *act* or *feel* entitled, children remain legitimately entitled to resources. Their advantages remain essentially the same. Ultimately, the parents are not challenging their children's advantage but, instead, teaching them how to occupy their advantaged position appropriately. They inculcate an identity, or a *habitus*, as Pierre Bourdieu called it, of legitimate privilege. This legitimately entitled self faces the contradiction we have seen before: between *erasing* class difference through treating everyone the same and *recognizing* this difference through "awareness" of privilege.

DISCIPLINING THE SELF: BEHAVIOR AND CONSUMPTION

One central parental concern had to do with how their children acted vis-à-vis others. They wanted to teach their kids to take other people into account and to be generous in the world more broadly.

Paul told me, "I think one thing [his wife] and I are, very, very, very—it's very important for us, is that our kids are, at a minimum, respectful to people. They're nice. That's number one." Nadine said, "I don't want my kids to be entitled or snobby or spoiled in any way. I come down pretty hard on them about—I mean, the main thing is, like, 'You're going to be, like, a good fucking person, you know? Like, you're going to say please and thank you, and you're going to be, like, kind towards other people. And you're going to be responsible for yourself and make good choices.'"

* * *

My respondents saw consumption decisions and the constraints discussed earlier as important for how kids would locate themselves in relation to the rest of the world. They tried to model appropriate consumption for their children, often using the word "normal." Gary and his family were invited to a wedding in India that he and his wife "would have loved to go to." But they did not attend, in part because the wedding fell just a few weeks after another international family trip but also because it felt "over the top." Gary said, "it was this feeling that, what's the message we're imparting to our kids?" Parents struggled frequently over these decisions, which, like Gary's dilemma, often clustered around leisure travel.

One very wealthy mother said her biggest disagreements with her husband were about spending money. When I asked for an example, she first reiterated how confidential our conversation was. She then recounted:

Like, he would fly privately all the time. And I want our kids to not get too used to that. Every once in a while. But, I don't know. I value that I went to public school, and I slept in many motels, and I drove long distances in cars. And the way I grew up is still much more affluent than the way most—but I feel like I have somewhat of an understanding. I think it's important to understand the way everyone else lives. That doesn't sound right, but . . . but . . . so, I just don't want our kids to go to college and never have cleaned a toilet. And never have slept in a motel instead of a hotel. And then to appreciate that there are some kids that don't even ever sleep in a motel. I mean, so I just want our kids to have—you know, a reality check every once in a while.

This mother resists her husband's desire to live lavishly in order to instill an understanding of how "everyone else lives" in her kids. In talking about his clients' conflicts around money, Robert, a real estate broker, spoke approvingly of this kind of modeling. He said, "I have some healthy clients. I have one client— very rich people. She said, like, when they fly with the kids . . . they fly coach. When the husband flies by himself, he flies first class. They're constantly struggling to set an example for their children that, 'just because we have, not everybody else has.' They're trying not to turn their kids into assholes."

Many parents encouraged their children to interpret such experiences as "special." Olivia said her family flew business class "a lot." She told her kids, "'It's a privilege that you get to do this. And it's great that we can do this as a family. But I expect behavior and good manners.' And they [behave]. There's no wild acting out. And it's a big treat." Olivia asks her children to experience this travel as both a "privilege" and a "treat"—typically defined by being exceptional—even though it is something they do often. Furthermore, she is teaching them that high-end consumption is acceptable as long as it is inhabited appropriately in a behavioral sense.

* * *

These practices and discourses illuminate two meanings of *normal*. The explicit meaning, which parents invoked to try to help their kids situate themselves in relation to others, is what most people have—that is, people who are less advantaged than they are. But the normal that kids actually experience, in the reality of their daily lives, is the more advantaged form. Rather than acknowledge this tension, parents represented certain goods or experiences that were actually normal for their children as a "treat" and hoped the children would experience them as such. This kind of consumption is *not* special for their children. But these parents want them to see that it *is* special relative to the rest of the world.

Not surprisingly, then, these parents sometimes got tangled up in discourse around this question of "normal" consumption. For example, Allison, the stay-at-home mother with a household income of $3 million, gave a somewhat disjointed account of how she wanted her middle-school-aged kids to understand the two vacations her family takes each year. She said, "Some way or another, we have to instill in the kids that we're doing this, but it's not extravagant. So you try to not make it too extravagant."

* * *

Allison's reasoning illuminates her ambivalence about her own privilege as well as that of her children. She jumbles multiple discourses, first suggesting that the legitimacy of entitlement rests on hard work, then indicating that legitimate entitlement is impossible ("nobody deserves it"), and then alluding to appreciation as the legitimate mode of experience. Allison and her husband addressed this problem *practically* by flying in first class while the children sat in coach as a way of controlling the kids' access to privileges they had not yet "earned." But they *were* entitled to the vacation itself.

Environments and Social Others

In thinking about their children's self-location, parents were also concerned about the social others to whom their kids were exposed. They therefore thought carefully about the environments their children spent time in. Many parents worried about their children's exposure to those with *more*, fearing a kind of contamination from other kids and families about what con- stitutes reasonable consumption. . . . Sara was at a transitional moment with her husband, trying to decide whether they would stay in the city. In speaking of the challenges of raising wealthy children, she said:

> I mean, that is a huge reason why we're like, "Maybe we want to leave New York." Because we're still kind of like, even if we could afford the fancy apartment, we don't want our kid to think that that's—you know, to be surrounded by every- one else with fancy apartments. I don't know. A colleague of [her husband's] went on vacation with his family. You know, like, a nice vacation. They went ski- ing for a week, stayed somewhere super nice. He asked the son, who was, like, eight at the time, "What'd you think?" And the son was like, "It was great, but next time we fly private like everyone else." . . . He spent, like, you know, ten grand on this vacation, with, like, ski lodge—you know, a ton of money. What do you do? He's like, how do you insulate kids, you know? I don't know what you do.

Speaking of her children's summer camp, one stay-at-home mother said,

> I worry because my kids are at camp, sleep-away camp in Maine. And the whole idea to send them is for them to learn independence and a little bit of social acceptance and, you know, how to fend for themselves and the whole thing. And my daughter's going to a place where there's no electricity, and we're sitting here in the air conditioning, and she has really hot days and really cold days and learns to live with it. Which I think is all a good thing. But then you have the kids that show up in their private plane . . . It's just warped.

This mother is trying to engineer a sense of deprivation for her daughter to promote her learning how to be independent, but because she is doing this in an environment of wealthy people, the child is still exposed to people with more. As I discuss later, this concern permeated decisions about schooling as well.

Although parents did *not* usually want their children to be exposed to those with more, they *did* want them to be exposed to those with less. Using an especially compelling phrase, progressive inheritor Eliana said she wanted her children to have "fluency outside the bubble," by which she meant an exposure to and understanding of the lives of people with less. Yet it was not always clear to me which social others Eliana and my other respondents were invoking and what kind of contact they desired. Some parents wanted to instill a sense of awareness of and obligation to *poor* people, often in a relatively abstract sense, in a way that was reminiscent of noblesse oblige. Others seemed more interested in their kids' having ongoing relationships with people who were "normal"—that is, not poor, but not as privileged as they were.

Some parents recounted trying to have conversations with their kids about poor people, such as impoverished kids in Haiti or the residents of the homeless shelter around the corner. A few parents told me they required their kids to give away one or two birthday gifts or to participate in charitable enterprises such as a swim-a-thon. Paul said, of his kids, "Always for their birthday we ask them to pick one present and donate it to kids who are less fortunate, because they understand not everyone gets what they get."

* * *

Monica said she felt a responsibility to those with less: "We help out. We go to public schools around the city that are—you know, there's this thing where you go and you help them paint it, so it looks better and it doesn't look like a dungeon. My kids should know what the other places look like, down in the outer boroughs, where other kids have to go to school. Be thankful for what they have. Sure. We do that kind of stuff. Not to prove that we're better, but just to take part in a community. And my son does community service."

Monica's remarks highlight a tension present throughout these parents' accounts: that between "being part of a community" and making clear that these poorer children are completely other ("my kids should know what the other places look like") and exist primarily to help her kids in order to "be thankful for what they have." Indeed, these accounts demonstrate that, as Rubén Gaztambide-Fernández and Adam Howard put it, a "conception of the wealthy as moral and deserving . . . requires suffering others (i.e., 'the people') as a way to enact 'good citizenship.'" Furthermore, there is a class assumption here that these parents' children should have access to the lives of others even when they would not want those others to have access to their own lives.

* * *

A final kind of exposure, which overlaps but is not congruent with exposures to class and racial-ethnic others, is experience of cultural difference more broadly. My interviewees often talked about travel, especially outside the United States, as providing this type of exposure. Julia, a stay-at-home mother, said of her children:

> I want them to see the world as a big place that everybody, we all share in. [As opposed to] being kind of small-minded and just seeing your thing as the only important thing that's going on, whatever that may be. I want to travel with them a lot so that they see that people live in different ways. That you don't have to have a big house and have TVs and all that stuff to be happy. You can be just as happy living in a little grass hut in the Serengeti or whatever. You know? I don't know. I just feel like we're just surrounded by so much stuff. Which I love. I love all this stuff that we have. But sometimes that's not what's important.

Julia's statement represents exposure to class difference as a *subset* of exposure to cultural difference more broadly. It fits into the project of self-location, an awareness that "your thing" is not the only thing that matters. But travel also provides the lesson that material goods are not always "what's important." Julia expresses a dilemma common to most parents I interviewed: the desire to keep the "stuff" but without kids' thinking it is "what's important." Again, the fantasy here is that kids can have material and experiential comforts and at the same time understand that it is possible (for other people, at least) to live without them.

These parents hope exposure to those with less will discipline the affective selves of their children into appreciation and awareness. At the same time, exposure connotes an expansion of a child's experience in ways that might be valuable in reproducing advantage later.

* * *

School Choice

These questions of exposure and advantage came to the forefront in talking about children's central social environment: school. In New York, as in many other cities, public schools are much more likely than private ones to provide the exposure to difference that many parents said they wanted. But, as noted earlier, most parents I talked with ultimately enrolled their children in private schools. Yet they struggled over these decisions, in two ways: choosing public versus private, and, once they had chosen private, deciding which private school was the best fit for their children.

Parents who chose or seriously considered public school expressed concern that private school would, in Betsy's words, "warp their sense of what's normal." They worried that their children would be exposed to too much "entitlement" in private school, and they liked the idea of the diverse groups of people that their kids would be exposed to in public school. Some of them had political commitments to public school. Yet they were drawn to the private schools because of smaller class sizes and more individualized attention, the possibility of a better education, including classes in the arts, and the perceived link to college admission.

It is not private school for its own sake but rather the brilliance or restlessness or some other personality trait of a child that *forces* these parents to choose private school. This process, which Allison Pugh calls "the luxury of difference," "perform[s] a certain magic for upper-income parents by producing urgent needs." The close-to-home need of the child takes priority over the more abstract goal of supporting the public school system, though many of these parents still struggled over the decision—and sometimes, as I have argued, saw struggle itself as morally worthy. Eliana called herself "a public-school believer" and thought it was "selfish" that "my child should have all the advantages. . . . What's special about my kid?" She felt bad about "using all my privilege to the advantage of my one [child]." But her daughter was not being challenged in her public school. Though Eliana spent a year soul-searching about it, she ultimately placed her daughter in a private school.

. . . Most often this is a fear that the children will be bored in public school. Linda told me, of her decision to send her son to private school, that it "seemed really like the right place for him." When I asked why, she responded, "Just because he's like this kind of weird dude. I mean, he taught himself how to read when he was really young, and he loves learning and he wanted to learn. . . . [In the public school] he would just be in the corner bored out of his mind, I think." Beatrice described her son as "a super-duper high-energy kid who teaches himself a lot of stuff. He doesn't actually need a teacher to teach him very much. And when he's not learning stuff he's running all over the place and jumping on things, and I can just see the situation where he's bored and he's, like, crawling the walls. It's that combination of being very smart and very active that I think is going to be real trouble in a situation of 28 to 1 [the student-teacher ratio in the local public school]."

* * *

Several parents of older children similarly said they saw homework as their children's "job." This is not surprising because, as children get older, these issues become less hypothetical and parents become more concerned with conventional forms of advancement, such as college admission, in a competitive environment. Indeed, only parents with children under 10 said their kids would work for money, and to my knowledge none of the children in the six households with high-school-age children actually had jobs. Miriam, whose children were quite young, said, "I would like for them to have to have summer jobs starting at a certain age, but I don't even know if that's realistic anymore. It seems crazy to say, but, you know what I mean, everyone's like spending all summer enriching their kids. And I'm like, 'Well, I think you should go scoop ice cream and earn some money, because if you want to buy some clothes for the fall . . . ,' you know what I'm saying? But, like, am I really going to do that? I don't know."

In articulating these concerns, parents sometimes invoked future risk, arguing that their children needed to know how to work hard because they could not necessarily depend on family money. For example, Marie said, speaking of herself and her husband,

> We had this conversation with our older daughter, who seems to think we're millionaires—billionaires. And so [her husband] said, you know, "The reality of it is, we could probably give you everything you want. We're not going to." . . . So we can give you everything you want now. But when you become an adult, we can't afford for you to be a screw-up. We don't have the kind of generational wealth that can support that. So at some point, you've got to stand on your own and figure it out. So why you don't get everything is because we can't support that, later down the road. You've got to be able to figure out strategies and ways to deal with it.

(Notably, Marie changes the word "millionaires" to "billionaires," perhaps because she realizes that she and her husband are millionaires.) Other parents also emphasized that it is especially important for their kids to have skills in order to navigate the unpredictable future.

Often, however, this risk was almost entirely hypothetical. Olivia told me, "I don't want my kids, actually, to be in a position where their whole self-worth, and their whole identity, and their capacity to function, is connected to what they have. 'Cause it can go away. You know? I mean, it can—things happen. And you want capacities that aren't attached to that." She described an imaginary scenario in which the family lost all its money, saying "I could go out there and work hard." She said she could work again as a social worker, or "go work at Starbucks. I have worked at Starbucks before. I can do it again." For this reason, she said she would be "much more comfortable with" her children's having real marketable skills rather than being, for example, conceptual artists. Yet in the end she said that this possibility was remote. I asked if she cared about these skills "because of this issue of risk? I mean, if it all went away? Or because there's something you think is morally better about that?" She responded, "I think it's a moral issue. Yeah, I do think it is a moral—because I think the risk is fairly minor."

So having a strong work ethic and marketable abilities is not only a hedge against risk; it also helps make children better people. Indeed, passing down this discourse of risk helps constitute children's legitimate dispositions in three ways. First, as Olivia's account shows, it teaches children that having a work ethic is part of being a morally worthy person. Second, it teaches children to *feel* at risk, which is another way not to feel entitled. . . .

And third, it helps parents and children feel that they don't really *need* their privilege, that they could survive without it, which also distances them from being "entitled."

* * *

In these families, constraint and exposure also stand in tension with *expansion*, or, to pick up Kate and Nadine's word, "enrichment": the imperative to amplify children's experience and develop their potential. In the end, of course, expansion mostly wins. In terms of consumption, what is taken away from these children is at the margins, and what is required of them is relatively minimal. They live in spacious homes, usually with their own rooms (and often bathrooms). They play music and sports and travel internationally. They receive significant customized attention from paid workers including tutors, teachers, and therapists of many varieties. And their parents spend significantly on the "pathway consumption" that ensures their advantaged futures. In terms of exposure, parents try to help their children situate themselves in relation to others with less, but only inasmuch as such exposure does not interfere with their getting a wide range of life experiences and the best schooling for their individual needs. They are *told* how "normal" others live and encouraged to appreciate their own advantages, but those advantages are very rarely curtailed.

Instead of limiting material entitlements, these parents are giving their children a "sense of their place." In showing their children what is "normal" for others, these parents implicitly delineate another kind of normal for themselves. And, as they help their kids locate themselves in the world, these practices and discourses cultivate their children to be capable of inhabiting that space appropriately, in a behavioral and emotional sense. Having a good work ethic, being a nice person, and knowing how to navigate difference are useful skills, so fostering these traits is a form of giving children the tools to survive in an uncertain world. But, I have argued, this cultivation also produces a particular set of dispositions, a *habitus* that helps them occupy their social advantages with moderation, appreciation, effort, and reciprocity. As Donovan said, about his children's education around money, "I do think that I've done the most important things. Which is modeling behavior for them, again about appropriateness, about being grateful for what you have, about recognizing that it can in fact disappear fairly easily if it's not handled prudently." Affluent parents want their kids to see that they have more than others but not to feel that they are better than others. They try to pass down the sense of obligation they feel to make themselves worthy of their privilege. And, as they produce good people, parents also become good people.

18

Women without Class: *Chicas*, *Cholas*, Trash, and the Presence/Absence of Class Identity

JULIE BETTIE

This essay predates the author's award-winning book by the same title. It tells the complex story of high school females finding and presenting (performing) identities that express different versions of femininity. The author's participant observation study seeks to make these young women, and their gender, more visible objects of study, with a steady eye on social class as being critical to who they are and wish to become. Add to this the dimension of ethnicity, and you have a quintessential analysis of the major dimensions of social inequality as they play out in contemporary youth culture.

A cover story in the San Francisco *Examiner Magazine* (Wagner 1996) on the topic of "wiggas" (which, the article explains, is shorthand for "white niggas") reads, "suburban kidz hip-hop across the color line." The story is about white youth who appropriate hip-hop culture and perform "black" identity. The cover picture is a collage of magazine cutouts showing white kids with blue eyes and blond hair (functioning as a code for racial purity) wearing hip-hop fashion and standing in front of a white picket fence behind which sits a charming two-story house and an apple tree. Although there is a girl pictured on the front cover, girls are absent from the story itself.

In a 1993 episode of the TV talk show *Oprah* on the same topic, several groups of boys, white and black, sat on the stage. The audience was confounded by the white boys in hip-hop style who "grew up in 'the 'hood'" and by the young black man who, as one guest explained, "looks like he walked out of Eddie Bauer," as participants debated what it meant to dress black or dress white. During the course of the hour-long program all parties failed to note that, race and ethnicity aside, these were different versions of *masculinity* and that girls were missing again from this story about "youth." The "urban romanticism" and "masculinist overtones" (McRobbie 1991, 20) of subculture studies, where the supposedly gender-neutral term *youth* actually stands for male, are equally often present in popular culture and news media portrayals of youth. In order to envision themselves as class or racial/ethnic subjects in either site, girls must read themselves as boys.

But beyond the invisibility of gender, there is also a failure to "think class" with much clarity. On the *Oprah* show, as with the magazine cover, the same sets of binaries surface repeatedly: white is middle class is suburban; black is lower class is urban. But a slippage occurs where the class references are dropped out and white stands in for middle, where black stands in for lower, or where suburban stands in for white and urban for black. Class and race signifiers are melded together in such a way that "authentic" black, and sometimes brown, identity is imagined as lower class, urban, and often violent and male as well. These are the overly simplified identity categories offered, but they do not reflect the complexity of life. Middle-class youth of color are missing, for example, as are multiracial/multiethnic identity and small-town or rural poverty. The racial/ethnic and class subject positions offered by the "identity formation material" (McRobbie 1994, 192) of popular culture often do not allow for more nuanced social locations.

The observations I make in this article are based on my ethnographic study of working-class white and Mexican-American girls in their senior year of high school in a small town in California's central valley.

* * *

These were girls who knew from experience in their own families of origin that male wages cannot support families alone and that men cannot be counted on to meet their ideals of intimacy and egalitarianism in relationships. These were girls who saw that the men in their working-class community were often unemployed or underemployed and too often dealt with this hardship by abandoning their obligation and responsibilities to the women in their lives and to the children they helped create. These girls were not holding out for princes.

My title, "Women without Class," has multiple meanings. Most simply, it reflects my interest in young women from families of modest means and low educational attainment who therefore have little "cultural capital" (Bourdieu 1984) to enable class mobility. The other meanings of the title speak to the theory debates I engage and to which I already have alluded: a second meaning refers to the fact that class analysis and social theory have, until recently perhaps, remained insufficiently transformed by feminist theory, unable to conceptualize women as class subjects. Ignoring women's experience of class results in a profound androcentric bias such that women are routinely invisible as class subjects. In much leftist analysis women are assumed to be without class, as these theorists often seem unable to see the category "working class" unless it is marked white and male. Such biases promote the invisibility of both white women and women of color as class subjects.

Ironically, some versions of feminism have been complicit in constructing women as without either class or racial/ethnic subjectivity. On a third level, then, my title considers debates *within* feminist theory and refers to feminist accounts that, while working as correctives to androcentric biases and class reduction, tend toward gender reductionism, focusing primarily on the differences between boys and girls or women and men and failing to account for gender differences *within* sex categories. Historically such studies have focused on white middle-class girls or women but have failed to define them as such. Thus, they too were perceived and presented not as class or racial/ethnic subjects but only as gendered.

It was with these theory debates and empirical gaps in mind that I set off to explore if and how young women understand class difference. I intended to foreground, while not privileging, class as I examined how gender, color, and ethnicity intersect with and shape class as a lived culture and a subjective identity. The context of the lives of these young women includes a deindustrializing economy, the growth of service-sector occupations held largely by women and men of color and by white women, the related family revolutions of the twentieth century, the elimination of affirmative action, a rise in anti-immigrant sentiment, and changing cultural representations and iconographies of class, race, and gender meanings. These are social forces that render the term *working class* anachronistic even as many of these girls move toward low-wage, low-prestige jobs in their community.

NOTES TOWARD CLASS AS "PERFORMANCE" AND "PERFORMATIVE"

My study was done in a small town of approximately forty thousand people. The high school reflects the town demographically, being about 60 percent white and 40 percent Mexican-American, with other people of color composing less than 2 percent each of the population. Located in California's central valley, the town was built on agriculture and the industries that support it. Approximately 16 percent of the Mexican-American students were Mexican-born, while the remainder were second and third generation. The majority of students at the school, both white and Mexican American, were from working-class families, but the children of middle-class professionals were a present minority. Most of the latter were white, but a handful were Mexican American. Working-class students ranged from "hard-living" to "settled-living" (Howell 1973) in experience. The former term describes lives that are chaotic and unpredictable, characterized by low-paying, unstable occupations, lack of health care benefits, and no home ownership. The latter describes lives that are orderly and predictable, characterized by relatively secure, higher-paying jobs, sometimes health benefits, and sometimes ownership of a modest home.

I "hung out" with girls in classrooms and hallways, during lunch hours, at school dances, sports events, Future Homemakers of America meetings, at a Future Farmers of America hay-bucking contest and similar events, at MEChA meetings (Movimiento Estudiantil Chicano de Aztlán; the Chicano student movement organization), in coffee shops, restaurants, the shopping mall, and the school parking lot, near the bleachers behind the school, at birthday parties, and sometimes sitting cross-legged on the floor of a girl's bedroom, "just talkin'." I spent almost every day at the school during the school year, often returning in the evening to attend an extracurricular event and sometimes on weekends to meet and "kick it" with the girls. I came to know more than sixty girls well (approximately half were white and half Mexican American) and many more as acquaintances. I talked with them about such details of their lives as friendships, dating, partying, clothes, makeup, popular culture, school, family, work, and their hopes and expectations for the future.

Over the course of the school year, I came to know the clique structure, or informal peer hierarchy, at the school, as it was the primary way students understood class and racial/ethnic differences among themselves. Labels and descriptions of each group varied, of course, depending on the social location of the student providing the description. Nonetheless, there was a general mapping that almost all students agreed on and provided easily when asked. Although there were exceptions, the groups were largely race/ethnic and class segregated. Among whites they included "preps" (middle class), "skaters/alternatives" (settled-living), "hicks" (settled- and hard-living), and "smokers/rockers /trash" (hard-living); among Mexican-American students there were "Mexican preps" (middle class and settled- and hard-living), "*las chicas*" (settled-living), and "*cholas/os*" or "hard cores" (hard-living).[1]

Group membership was linked to social roles, including curriculum choices (college prep or vocational track) and extracurricular activities (whether a student was involved in what are considered either college-prep or nonprep activities). These courses and activities combined to shape class futures leading some girls to four-year colleges, some to vocational programs at junior colleges, and some to low-wage jobs directly out of high school. While there is a strong correlation between a girl's class of "origin" (by which I mean her parents' socioeconomic status) and her class performance at school (which includes academic achievement, prep or nonprep activities, and membership in friendship groups and their corresponding style), it is an imperfect one, and there are exceptions in which middle-class girls perform working-class identity and vice versa. In other words, some students were engaged in class "passing" as they chose to perform class identities that were not their "own."

Although clique membership was not entirely determined by class, there was certainly "a polarization of attitudes toward class characteristics," and group categories (such as preps, smokers, *cholas*, etc.) were "embodiment[s] of the middle and working-class[es]" (Eckert 1989, 4–5). On the one hand, embracing and publicly performing a particular class culture mattered more than origins in terms of a student's aspirations, her treatment by teachers and other students, and her class future. On the other hand, class origins did matter significantly, of course, as girls' life chances were shaped by the economic and

---

1. *Chola/o* describes a Mexican-American street style that sometimes marks identification with gangs, but it also can mark merely racial/ethnic belonging. Moreover, the degree of commitment to a gang exists on a continuum. Nonetheless, *cholas/os*, like *pachucas/os* before them, are often wrongly assumed to engage in criminal behavior (Vigil 1988).

cultural resources provided at home. Because of the imperfect correlation, I came to define students not only as working or middle class in origin but also as working- or middle-class *performers* (and, synonymously, as prep and non-prep students). Girls who were passing, or metaphorically cross-dressing, had to negotiate their "inherited" identity from home with their "chosen" public identity at school. There was a disparity for them between how their and their friends' families looked and talked at home and their own class performances at school. As I came to understand these negotiations of class as cultural (not political) identities, it became useful to conceptualize class as not only a material location but also a performance.

Consequently, I ask: What are the cultural gestures involved in the performance of class? How is class "authenticity" accomplished? And how is it imbued with racial/ethnic and gender meaning? Little attention has been paid to the ways class subjectivity, as a cultural identity, is experienced in relation to the cultural meanings of race/ethnicity, gender, and sexuality.

DISSIDENT FEMININITIES

Because I spent my first few days at the school in a college-preparatory class (one that fulfills a requirement for admission to state universities), the first girls I met were college bound. Later I came to know these girls through the eyes of non-college-prep students as "the preps." They were mostly white but included a handful of Mexican-American girls. Some of the white girls were also known as "the 90210s" after the television show *Beverly Hills 90210* about wealthy high schoolers in Beverly Hills. The preps related easily to what they saw as my "school project." They eagerly volunteered to help me out and were ready and willing to talk at length about themselves and others. Displaying both social and academic skills, they were, in short, "teacher's pets" (Luttrell 1993) or "the rich and populars" (Lesko 1988).

The first day I attended Ms. Parker's business skills class was characteristic of my future visits to nonprep classes. On this particular day, there was a substitute teacher taking her place. These girls appeared different from the girls in the college-prep class: they wore more makeup, tight-fitting clothing, and seemed to have little interest in the classroom curriculum. In fact, the class was out of the teacher's hands. The girls, mostly Mexican American, were happy to have me as a distraction, and one, whom I later came to know as Lorena, said loudly (Lorena was always loud), "Oh, we heard you might be coming. What do you want to know? I'll tell you." Completely ignoring the substitute, who had clearly given up on having any control over the class, they invited me to play cards. I hesitated: "What if Mr. D. (the vice principal) comes by?"

LORENA: Oh he never does, besides (flirtatiously) he *likes* me.
  BECKY: He doesn't like me. He's always callin' me into his office for something.
LORENA: He'll just ask me where's the other half of my shirt?

Lorena was referring to her short crop top, fashionable at the moment and against school dress codes because it reveals the midriff. Lorena went on, "That's Mr. H. He's our sub. Don't you think he's attractive? He's from the university too." She called him over to ask a question, and when he arrived, Lorena opened her book and pointed entirely randomly at a paragraph on the page and said coyly, "I don't understand *this*." He tried to respond appropriately by explaining the course material.

* * *

The expression of self through one's relationship to and creative use of commodities (both artifacts and the discourses of popular culture) is a central practice in capitalist society. The girls' alternative versions of gender performance were shaped by a nascent knowledge of race and class hierarchies. They were very able to communicate a sense of unfairness, a "structure of feeling" (Williams 1965), where inequalities were felt but not politically articulated. Their struggles were often waged less over explicit political ideologies than over modes of identity expression. In short, among students there existed a symbolic economy of style that was the ground on which class and race relations were played out. A whole array of gender-specific commodities were used as markers of distinction among different groups of girls who performed race/ethnic- and class-specific versions of femininity. Hairstyles, clothes, shoes, and the colors of lip liner, lipstick, and nail polish were key markers used to express group membership as the body became a resource and a site on which difference was inscribed. For example, Lorena and her friends preferred darker colors for lips and nails, in comparison to the preps who either went without or wore clear lip gloss, pastel lip and nail color, or French manicures (the natural look). Each group knew the other's stylistic preferences and was aware that their own style was in opposition. Girls created and maintained symbolic oppositions in which, as Penelope Eckert puts it, "elements of behavior that come to represent one category [are] rejected by the other, and . . . may be exploited by the other category through the development of a clearly opposed element" (1989, 50).

The importance of colors as a tool of distinction became evident when *las chicas* explained that the darker lip color they chose and the lighter colors the preps wore were not simply related to skin color. Lorena explained, "it's not that, 'cause some Mexican girls who look kinda white, they wear real dark lip color" so that no one will mistake them as white. When I mentioned that I rarely saw white girls in dark lipstick, Lisa, a white prep, explained, scoffing and rolling her eyes, "oh there are some, but they're girls who are trying to be hard-core," which meant they were white girls who were performing *chola* identity.

Where middle-class performers experienced an extended adolescence by going to college, working-class performers across race began their adult lives earlier. And where middle-class performing girls (both white and Mexican American) chose academic performance and the praise of teachers and parents as signs of achieving adult status, nonprep girls wore different "badges of dignity" (Sennett and Cobb 1972; MacLeod 1995). For them, expressions of sexuality operated as a sign of adult status and served to reject teachers' and parents' methods of keeping them childlike.

It is too simple to treat the meaning of the expression of what appears as a sexualized version of femininity for working-class girls, and girls of color in particular, as a consequence of competitive heterosexuality and gender-subordinate learning. This fails to explain why girls made the choices they did from a variety of gender performances available to them. Rather, girls were negotiating meanings in a race- and class-stratified society, using commodities targeted at them as girls. They performed different versions of femininity that were integrally linked and inseparable from their class and race performances.

Las chicas, having "chosen" and/or been tracked into non-college-prep courses, were bored with their vocational schooling and often brought heterosexual romance and girl culture into the classroom as a favorite form of distraction, demonstrated in their repeated attempts to "set me up" with subs (which became almost a hazing ritual). But their gender performance and girl culture were not necessarily designed to culminate in a heterosexual relationship. Despite what appeared to be an obsession with heterosexual romance, a "men are dogs" theme was prevalent among them. Some said they didn't want to marry until their thirties if at all, and they resented their boyfriends' infidelities and attempts to police their sexuality by telling them what they should and should not wear. They knew that men should not be counted on to support them and any children they might have, and they desired economic independence. Their girl culture was less about boys than about sharing rituals of traditional femininity as a kind of friendship bonding among girls. Although the overt concern in girl culture may be with boys and romance, girls often set themselves physically apart from boys (McRobbie 1991). Lorena made this clear one day:

> LORENA: Well, when we go out, to the clubs or someplace. We all get a bunch of clothes and makeup and stuff and go to one person's house to get ready. We do each other's hair and makeup and try on each other's clothes. It takes a long time. It's more fun that way. [Thoughtfully, as if it just occurred to her,] sometimes, I think we have more fun getting ready to go out than we do going out. 'Cause when we go out we just *sit* there.
>
> JULIE BETTIE: So then the clothes and makeup and all aren't for the men, or about getting their attention?
>
> LORENA: Well, we like to see how many we can *meet*. But, well *you* know I don't fall for their lines. We talk to them, but when they start buggin' then we just go.

In short, *las chicas* had no more or less interest in heterosexual romance than did girls who performed prep or school-sanctioned femininity. Nonetheless, teachers and preps often confused the expression of class and race differences in style and activities among working-class girls as evidence of heterosexual interest. They often failed to perceive girls' class and race performances and unknowingly reproduced the commonsense belief that what is most important about girls, working-class performers in particular, is their girlness. *Las chicas'* style was not taken as a marker of race/ethnic and class distinction but was reduced to gender and sexuality.

In spite of the meanings that working-class girls themselves gave to their gender-specific cultural markers, their performances were always overdetermined by broader cultural meanings that code women in heavy makeup and tight clothes as oversexed—in short, cheap. In other words, class differences are often understood as sexual differences, where "the working class is cast as the bearer of an exaggerated sexuality, against which middle-class respectability is defined" (Ortner 1991, 177). Among women, "clothing and cosmetic differences are taken to be indexes of the differences in sexual morals" between classes (178). Indeed, this is what I observed: middle-class performing prep girls (both white and Mexican American) perceived *las chicas*, as well as working-class performing white girls, as overly sexually active.

But Mexican-American nonprep girls were perceived as even more sexually active than their white counterparts because, although there was no evidence that they were more sexually active, they were more likely to keep their babies if they became pregnant, so there was more often a visible indicator of their sexual activity. And while school personnel at times explained working-class Mexican-American girls' gender performances as a consequence of "their" culture—an assumed real ethnic cultural difference in which women are expected to fulfill traditional roles and/or are victims of machismo and a patriarchal culture—the girls' generational status (according to two meanings) was not taken into account. On the one hand, *las chicas* were a generation of girls located in a historical context of dual-wage families, and they did not describe parents who had traditional roles in mind for their daughters. Moreover, they were second-generation Mexican-Americans, young women with no intention of submitting to traditional gender ideologies.

Class was thus a present social force in the versions of femininity that the girls performed, but it was unarticulated and rendered invisible because it was interpreted (by school personnel, by preps, and at times by working-class girls themselves) as primarily about gender and a difference of sexual morality between good girls and bad girls.

"ACTING WHITE"

Many of the Mexican-American students did have a way to both recognize and displace class simultaneously, at times explaining differences among themselves solely in racial/ethnic terms, such as "acting white" versus acting "the Mexican role." The class coding of these descriptions is revealed when they are pushed only slightly. When I asked Lorena what she meant by "acting white," she gave an animated imitation of a white girl she had met at a Future Business Leaders of America meeting, affecting a stereotypical "valley girl" demeanor and speech pattern: "Ohmigod, like I can't believe I left my cell phone in my car. It was so nice to meet you girls, do keep in touch." Lorena perceived this sentiment as quite disingenuous, since they had just met. Part of working-class girls' interpretation of preps was that they were "fake" and their friendships phony and insincere, always in the interest of social ambition. Lorena went on, "I'm going to play volleyball for Harvard next year." Clearly, "Harvard" was an exaggeration on Lorena's part. But to Lorena any university may as well have been Harvard as it was just as distant a possibility. Erica, a Filipina-American girl who had befriended and been accepted as one of *las chicas*, confided to me, "There's a lot of trashing of white girls really, and Mexican girls who act white." When I asked her what she meant by "acting white," her answer was straightforward: "The preps." "Not the smokers or the hicks?" I asked. "Oh no, never smokers, basically preps."

At some level, the girls knew that they didn't mean white generally but preps specifically (that is, a particular middle-class version of white), but "class" as a way of making distinctions among whites was not easily articulated. The whites most visible to them were those who inflicted the most class injuries, the preps. In fact, working-class whites were often invisible in their talk, unless I asked specifically about them. The most marginalized ones, known as the "smokers," were either unknown to the Mexican-American students or perplexing. As Mariana, a Mexican-American middle-class performer said, almost exasperated, "I mean they're white. They've had the opportunity. What's wrong with them?" Students found it useful or necessary to describe class performances in racial terms such as "acting white" because of the difficulty of coming up with a more apt way to describe class differences in a society in which class discourse as such is absent and because the correlation of race and class (the overrepresentation of people of color among the poor) was a highly visible reality to Mexican-American students.

MIDDLE-CLASS *CHOLAS*

A handful of the girls were third-generation Mexican Americans from professional middle-class families. They had struggled to find their place in this race-class system. They had grown up in white neighborhoods and gone to elementary school with primarily white kids, where, as Rosa explained, "I knew I was different, because I was brown." In junior high, which was less segregated, some of them became *cholas* and were "jumped in" to a gang. When I asked why, Ana explained that she hated her family:

ANA: My mom wanted this picture-perfect family, you know. And I just hated it.
JULIE: What do you mean by a perfect family?

ANA: You know, we had dinner at night together, and everything was just, okay. She was so *happy*. And I hated that. My life was sad, my friends' lives were sad.

JULIE: Why were they sad?

ANA: One friend's mom was on welfare, the other didn't know who her dad was. Everything was wrong in their families.

As she described class differences between herself and her friends, she struggled for the right words to describe it. And as Lorena sought to describe the difference between herself and her friend Ana, she too searched for words: "Well, in junior high she was way down kinda low, she got in with the bad crowd. But in high school she is higher up kinda. I mean not as high as Patricia is (another middle-class performer) but she's not as low as she used to be." Lorena's perception of Ana as high but low was shaped by Ana's crossover style and the sense that she had "earned" her "low" status by performing *chola* identity and gang-banging. In Ana's attempt to understand her place in a social order where color and poverty correlate more often than not, the salience of color was integral to her identity formation. She felt compelled to perform working-class identity at school as a marker of racial/ethnic belonging. As she explained, "the Mexican Mexicans, they aren't worried about whether they're Mexican or not."

Although Ana, Rosa, and Patricia eventually had accepted the cultural capital their parents had to give them and were now college prep and headed to four-year colleges, they were friendly with *las chicas* and still dressed and performed the kind of race-class femininity that *las chicas* did. In this way, they distanced themselves from preps and countered potential accusations of "acting white." In short, their style confounded the race-class equation and was an intentional strategy. By design, they had middle-class aspirations without assimilation to prep, which for them meant white, style. It went beyond image to a set of race politics as they tried to recruit *las chicas* to be a part of MEChA. In fact, when I went along on a bus ride to tour a nearby business school with *las chicas*, I was surprised to find that Ana, Rosa, and Patricia came along. I asked why they had come along since they had already been accepted to four-year schools. Rosa responded, "Because we're with the girls, you know, we have to be supportive, do these things together."

Mexican-American girls' friendships crossed class performance boundaries more often than white girls' did because of a sense of racial alliance that drew them together in relation to white students at school and because the Mexican-American community brought them together in activities outside school. They were also far more pained about divisions among themselves than white girls ever were (an aspect of whiteness that can seem invisible). They felt the need to present a united front, and this was particularly acute among girls who were politicized about their racial/ethnic identity and participated in MEChA. For white girls, competition among them did not threaten them as a racial/ethnic minority community.

WHITE TRASH *CHOLA*

Not surprisingly, white students generally did not explain class differences among themselves in racial terms. Rather, class difference was articulated as individual difference (she's "popular" or she's a "loser") and as differences in group membership and corresponding style (hicks, smokers, preps, etc.). But class meaning was at times bound to racial signifiers in the logic of white students, as it was among Mexican-American students. This was apparent in the way the most marginalized white working-class students, who were at times described by other white students as "white trash," worked hard interactionally to clarify that they were not Mexican.[2] In our very first conversation, Tara explained, without any solicitation, "I'm kinda dark, but I'm not Mexican." In our conversation about her boyfriend's middle-class parents, she explained that his mom had "accused me of being Mexican." She explained to me that she was Italian-American, and her color and features did match this self-description.

Similarly, Starr, a white girl who grew up in a Mexican-American neighborhood and went to the largely Mexican-American elementary school in town, also had the sense that some whites, those at the bottom of the heap like herself, were almost brown. We were talking in the lunchroom one day about girls and fights when she told me this story:

STARR: Well the worst one was back in junior high. All of my friends were Mexican, 'cause I went to London. So I was too.

JULIE: You were what?

STARR: Mexican. Well I acted like it, and they thought I was. I wore my hair up high in front you know. And I had an accent. Was in a gang. I banged [gang-banged] red [gang color affiliation].

JULIE: Were you the only white girl?

STARR: Yeah.

JULIE: What happened? Why aren't you friends with them now?

STARR: We got into a fight. I was in the bowling alley one day with my boyfriend. They came in and called him a piece of white trash. That made me mad and I smacked her. Lucky for her someone called the cops. They came pretty fast.

JULIE: What did she mean by white trash?

STARR: Welfare people. He was a rocker. Had long hair, smoked.

---

2. See Bettie 1995 and Wray and Newitz 1997 for explorations of the race and class meanings of the designation "poor white trash."

This episode ended her *chola* performance, and she was part of the white smoker crowd when I met her. Like most other girls, Starr had told me that girls fight primarily about "guys." But her actual story reveals something different. A boy was central to the story, but the girls were not fighting *over* him. Rather, Starr's *chola* friends were bothered by her association with him, which pointed to her violation of the race-class identity she had been performing as a *chola*. Her friends forced her to make a choice.

Starr's race-class performance was a consequence of the neighborhood in which she grew up, and, like Tara, she had absorbed the commonsense notions that white is middle, that brown is low, and, most interesting, that low may become brown in certain contexts. Not unlike the experience of middle-class *cholas* for whom being middle-class Mexican-American felt too close to being white, Starr's working-class version of whiteness felt too close to being Mexican-American in this geographic context. Girls reported that cross-race friendships were more common in grade school, but in junior high a clear sorting out along racial lines emerged (and along class lines too, although with less awareness). Starr's story is about junior-high girls working to sort out class and color and ethnicity, about the social policing of racial boundaries, and about her move from a brown to a white racial performance (where both remained working class). Not insignificantly, her white performance included a racist discourse by which she distanced herself from Mexican-Americans via derogatory statements about them.

(MIS)USES OF "CLASS": A CAUTION

Class difference was salient, although not articulated as such, *within* these racial/ethnic groups. But in relationships *across* racial/ethnic groups, race often "trumps" class. One way racial/ethnic alliances across class were manifested was in attitudes toward California's Proposition 209 (misleadingly called the California Civil Rights Initiative), passed in 1996, which eliminated state affirmative-action programs, including admissions policies for the state's university systems. To the pleasure of white conservatives, University of California regent Ward Connerly, a black man, became the leading spokesperson and argued for income instead of race as a fairer admission criterion. In this conservative community, all of the white students I spoke to, without exception, supported Proposition 209. Both working- and middle-class white students were easily swayed by the "class instead of race" logic, which both groups interpreted as white instead of brown, where "class" stands in for white, and "race" stands in for brown (and black).

Working-class performers were less concerned with college admission than with job competition, since the decisive moment of whether a student is going on to college had occurred two to three years earlier, when they began the vocational track. Consequently, by their senior year they lacked the coursework for admission to state universities. Although white working-class students experienced a feeling of unfairness in relation to preps regarding educational achievement and college, they lacked a discourse of class that could explain their own and their parents' "failure" and that would allow them to articulate the class antagonism they felt toward middle-class students. In its absence, a discourse of individualism and meritocracy helped render institutionalized class inequality invisible and consequently left white working-class students feeling like individually flawed "losers." . . . Unfortunately, working-class students were less likely to see themselves as victims of class inequality than as victims of "reverse discrimination."

Somewhat curiously, white middle-class students were also swayed by the color-blind class logic of Proposition 209. Preps' sense of racial competition regarded who was and who was not getting into which college. The students of color most visible to them were the handful who sat next to them in college-prep classes. Preps' own class privilege was unapparent to them, so much so that the mass of working-class whites and working-class Mexican Americans were so "othered" as to be invisible. The only Mexican-American students whom preps could imagine going to college seemed to be very much like them in that they were middle-class performers. At times, these college-prep Mexican-American students were resented as "box checkers" who were perceived to be unfairly benefiting from their "minority" status, as middle-class white students constructed themselves as victims of reverse discrimination. These college-prep Mexican-American students were highly visible, to the disadvantage of their vocational-track peers. Since the large body of working-class vocational students were not in the running for college admission anyway, among college-prep students discussing college admissions, *class* was taken as a code for *white*.

And perhaps rightly so. Class inequality is not adequately addressed by eliminating race as an admission criterion since the vast majority of working-class students of all colors had been tracked out two to three years earlier. When liberal education policy attempts to deal with social inequality by trying to get everyone into college, it fails to address the fundamental fact that the global economy needs uneducated, unskilled workers, and workers need living wages.

CONCLUSION

Thinking through class as a performance enables us to acknowledge exceptions to the rule that class origin equals class future and to understand that economic and cultural resources often, but not inevitably, determine class futures. It allows us to explore the experience of negotiating inherited and chosen identities, as, for example, when middle-class students of color felt compelled to perform working-class identities as a marker of racial/ethnic belonging. It helps demonstrate, too, how other axes of identity intersect with and inform class identity and consequently shape class futures. Thinking through class as a performance is useful for understanding exceptions, those who are consciously "passing" (whether it be up or down).

But it is also useful to think of class as performative in the sense that class as cultural identity is an *effect* of social structure. Social actors largely perform the cultural capital that is a consequence of the material and cultural resources to which they have had access. Cultural performances most often reflect one's habitus or unconscious learned dispositions, which are not natural or inherent or prior to the social organization of class inequality but are in fact produced by it. Considering class as performative is consistent with regarding it more as a cultural than a political identity and more as a "sense of place" than as class consciousness in a political, marxist sense. It helps explain why class struggle is often waged more over modes of identity expression than over explicit political ideologies.

REFERENCES

Bettie, Julie. 1995. "Class Dismissed? *Roseanne* and the Changing Face of Working-Class Iconography." *Social Text* 45, vol. 14, no. 4:125–49.

Bourdieu, Pierre. 1984. *Distinction: A Social Critique of the Judgment of Taste*. Cambridge, Mass.: Harvard University Press.

Eckert, Penelope. 1989. *Jocks and Burnouts: Social Categories and Identity in the High School*. New York: Teachers College Press.

Howell, Joseph. 1973. *Hard Living on Clay Street: Portraits of Blue-Collar Families*. Garden City, N.Y.: Anchor.

Lesko, Nancy. 1988. "The Curriculum of the Body: Lessons from a Catholic High School." In *Becoming Feminine: The Politics of Popular Culture*, ed. Leslie G. Roman, Linda K. Christian-Smith, and Elizabeth Ellsworth, 123–42. London: Falmer.

Luttrell, Wendy. 1993. "The Teachers, They All Had Their Pets: Concepts of Gender, Knowledge, and Power." *Signs* 18(3):505–46.

MacLeod, Jay. 1995. *Ain't No Makin' It: Aspirations and Attainment in a Low-Income Neighborhood*. Boulder, Colo.: Westview.

McRobbie, Angela. 1991. *Feminism and Youth Culture*. London: Macmillan.

———. 1994. *Postmodernism and Popular Culture*. London: Routledge.

Ortner, Sherry. 1991. "Preliminary Notes on Class and Culture." In *Recapturing Anthropology: Working in the Present*, ed. Richard G. Fox. Santa Fe, N.M.: School of American Research Press.

Sennett, Richard, and Jonathan Cobb. 1972. *The Hidden Injuries of Class*. New York: Vintage.

Vigil, James Diego. 1988. *Barrio Gangs: Street Life and Identity in Southern California*. Austin: University of Texas Press.

Wagner, Venise. 1996. "Crossover." *San Francisco Examiner Magazine*, November 10, 8–32.

Williams, Raymond. 1965. *Marxism and Literature*. New York: Oxford University Press.

Wray, Matt, and Annalee Newitz, eds. 1997. *White Trash: Race and Class in America*. New York: Routledge.

PART FOUR

SOCIAL INTERACTION AND IDENTITY

19

On Face-Work

ERVING GOFFMAN

Many students find the idea of a "self-presentation" to be manipulative, insincere, and inauthentic. What Goffman's work shows is that we cannot avoid the work of presenting a "face" or identity in social interaction. We can deny that this activity goes on and we can be unaware of what we are doing, but all of us must do this work in order to carry on social interaction. Goffman takes sociology into the deepest realm of social life: our most intimate relations and our most private ideas about who we are.

Every person lives in a world of social encounters, involving him either in face-to-face or mediated contact with other participants. In each of these contacts, he tends to act out what is sometimes called a *line*—that is, a pattern of verbal and nonverbal acts by which he expresses his view of the situation and through this his evaluation of the participants, especially himself. Regardless of whether a person intends to take a line, he will find that he has done so in effect. The other participants will assume that he has more or less willfully taken a stand, so that if he is to deal with their response to him he must take into consideration the impression they have possibly formed of him.

The term *face* may be defined as the positive social value a person effectively claims for himself by the line others assume he has taken during a particular contact. Face is an image of self-delineation in terms of approved social attributes—albeit an image that others may share, as when a person makes a good showing for his profession or religion by making a good showing for himself.

A person tends to experience an immediate emotional response to the face which a contact with others allows him; he cathects his face; his "feelings" become attached to it. If the encounter sustains an image of him that he has long taken for granted, he probably will have few feelings about the matter. If events establish a face for him that is better than he might have expected, he is likely to "feel good"; if his ordinary expectations are not fulfilled, one expects that he will "feel bad" or "feel hurt." In general, a person's attachment to a particular face, coupled with the ease with which disconfirming information can be conveyed by himself and others, provides one reason why he finds that participation in any contact with others is a commitment. A person will also have feelings about the face sustained for the other participants, and while these feelings may differ in quantity and direction from those he has for his own face, they constitute an involvement in the face of others that is as immediate and spontaneous as the involvement he has in his own face. One's own face and the face of others are constructs of the same order; it is the rules of the group and the definition of the situation which determine how much feeling one is to have for face and how this feeling is to be distributed among the faces involved.

A person may be said to *have*, or *be in*, or *maintain* face when the line he effectively takes presents an image of him that is internally consistent, that is supported by judgments and evidence conveyed by other participants, and that is confirmed by evidence conveyed through impersonal agencies in the situation. At such times the person's face clearly is something that is not lodged in or on his body, but rather something that is diffusely located in the flow of events in the encounter and becomes manifest only when these events are read and interpreted for the appraisals expressed in them.

The line maintained by and for a person during contact with others tends to be of a legitimate institutionalized kind. During a contact of a particular type, an interactant of known or visible attributes can expect to be sustained in a particular face and can feel that it is morally proper that this should be so. Given his attributes and the conventionalized nature of the encounter, he will find a small choice of lines will be open to him and a small choice of faces will be waiting for him. Further, on the basis of a few known attributes, he is given the responsibility of possessing a vast number of others. His coparticipants are not likely to be conscious of the character of many of these attributes until he acts perceptibly in such a way as to discredit his possession of them; then everyone becomes conscious of these attributes and assumes that he willfully gave a false impression of possessing them.

* * *

A person may be said to *be in wrong face* when information is brought forth in some way about his social worth which cannot be integrated, even with effort, into the line that is being sustained for him. A person may be said to *be out of face* when he participates in a contact with others without having ready a line of the kind participants in such situations are expected to take. The intent of many pranks is to lead a person into showing a wrong face or no face, but there will also be serious occasions, of course, when he will find himself expressively out of touch with the situation.

When a person senses that he is in face, he typically responds with feelings of confidence and assurance. Firm in the line he is taking, he feels that he can hold his head up and openly present himself to others. He feels some security and some relief—as he also can when the others feel he is in wrong face but successfully hide these feelings from him.

When a person is in wrong face or out of face, expressive events are being contributed to the encounter which cannot be readily woven into the expressive fabric of the occasion. Should he sense that he is in wrong face or out of face, he is likely to feel ashamed and inferior because of what has happened to the activity on his account and because of what may happen to his reputation as a participant. Further, he may feel bad because he had relied upon the encounter to support an image of self to which he has become emotionally attached and which he now finds threatened. Felt lack of judgmental support from the encounter may take him aback, confuse him, and momentarily incapacitate him as an interactant. His manner and bearing may falter, collapse and crumble. He may become embarassed and chagrined; he may become shamefaced. The feeling, whether warranted or not, that he is perceived in flustered state by others, and that he is presenting no usable line, may add further injuries to his feelings, just as his change from being in wrong face or out of face to being shamefaced can add further disorder to the expressive organization of the situation. Following common usage, I shall employ the term *poise* to refer to the capacity to suppress and conceal any tendency to become shamefaced during encounters with others.

In our Anglo-American society, as in some others, the phrase "to lose face" seems to mean to be in wrong face, to be out of face, or to be shamefaced. The phrase "to save one's face" appears to refer to the process by which the person sustains an impression for others that he has not lost face. Following Chinese usage, one can say that "to give face" is to arrange for another to take a better line than he might otherwise have been able to take, the other thereby gets face given him, this being one way in which he can gain face.

* * *

Just as the member of any group is expected to have self-respect, so also he is expected to sustain a standard of considerateness; he is expected to go to certain lengths to save the feelings and the face of others present, and he is expected to do this willingly and spontaneously because of emotional identification with the others and with their feelings. In consequence, he is disinclined to witness the defacement of others. The person who can witness another's humiliation and unfeelingly retain a cool countenance himself is said in our society to be "heartless," just as he who can unfeelingly participate in his own defacement is thought to be "shameless."

The combined effect of the rule of self-respect and the rule of considerateness is that the person tends to conduct himself during an encounter so as to maintain both his own face and the face of the other participants. This means that the line taken by each participant is usually allowed to prevail, and each participant is allowed to carry off the role he appears to have chosen for himself. A state where everyone temporarily accepts everyone else's line is established. This kind of mutual acceptance seems to be a basic structural feature of interaction, especially the interaction of face-to-face talk. It is typically a "working" acceptance, not a "real" one, since it tends to be based not on agreement of candidly expressed heart-felt evaluations, but upon a willingness to give temporary lip service to judgments with which the participants do not really agree.

The mutual acceptance of lines has an important conservative effect upon encounters. Once the person initially presents a line, he and the others tend to build their later responses upon it, and in a sense become stuck with it. Should the person radically alter his line, or should it become discredited, then confusion results, for the participants will have prepared and committed themselves for actions that are now unsuitable.

Ordinarily, maintenance of face is a condition of interaction, not its objective. Usual objectives, such as gaining face for oneself, giving free expression to one's true beliefs, introducing depreciating information about the others, or solving problems and performing tasks, are typically pursued in such a way as to be consistent with the maintenance of face. To study face-saving is to study the traffic rules of social interaction; one learns about the code the person adheres to in his movement across the paths and designs of others, but not where he is going, or why he wants to get there. One does not even learn why he is ready to follow the code, for a large number of different motives can equally lead him to do so. He may want to save his own face because of his emotional attachment to the image of self which it expresses, because of his pride or honor, because of the power his presumed status allows him to exert over the other participants, and so on. He may want to save the others' face because of his emotional attachment to an image of them, or because he feels that his coparticipants have a moral right to this protection, or because he wants to avoid the hostility that may be directed toward him if they lose their face. He may feel that an assumption has been made that he is the sort of person who shows compassion and sympathy toward others, so that to retain his own face, he may feel obliged to be considerate of the line taken by the other participants.

* * *

THE BASIC KINDS OF FACE-WORK

The Avoidance Process. The surest way for a person to prevent threats to his face is to avoid contacts in which these threats are likely to occur. In all societies one can observe this in the avoidance relationship and in the tendency for certain delicate transactions to be conducted by go-betweens. Similarly, in many societies, members know the value of voluntarily making a gracious withdrawal before an anticipated threat to face has had a chance to occur.

Once the person does chance an encounter, other kinds of avoidance practices come into play. As defensive measures, he keeps off topics and away from activities that would lead to the expression of information that is inconsistent with the line he is maintaining. At opportune moments he will change the topic of conversation or the direction of activity. He will often present initially a front of diffidence and composure, suppressing any show of feeling until he has found out what kind of line the others will be ready to support for him. Any claims regarding self may be made with belittling modesty, with strong qualifications, or with a note of unseriousness; by hedging in these ways he will have prepared a self for himself that will not be discredited by exposure, personal failure, or the unanticipated acts of others. And if he does not hedge his claims about self, he will at least attempt to be realistic about them, knowing that otherwise events may discredit him and make him lose face.

Certain protective maneuvers are as common as these defensive ones. The person shows respect and politeness, making sure to extend to others any ceremonial treatment that might be their due. He employs discretion; he leaves unstated facts that might implicitly or explicitly contradict and embarrass the positive claims made by others. He employs circumlocutions and deceptions, phrasing his replies with careful ambiguity so that the others' face is preserved even if their welfare is not. He employs courtesies, making slight modifications of his demands on or appraisals of the others so that they will be able to define the situation as one in which their self-respect is not threatened. In making a belittling demand upon the others, or in imputing uncomplimentary attributes to them, he may employ a joking manner, allowing them to take the line that they are good sports, able to relax from their ordinary standards of pride and honor. And before engaging in a potentially offensive act, he may provide explanations as to why the others ought not to be affronted by it. For example, if he knows that it will be necessary to withdraw from the encounter before it has terminated, he may tell the others in advance that it is necessary for him to leave, so that they will have faces that are prepared for it. But neutralizing the potentially offensive act need not be done verbally; he may wait for a propitious moment or natural break—for example, in conversation, a momentary lull when no one speaker can be affronted—and then leave, in this way using the context instead of his words as a guarantee of inoffensiveness.

When a person fails to prevent an incident, he can still attempt to maintain the fiction that no threat to face has occurred. The most blatant example of this is found where the person acts as if an event that contains a threatening expression has not occurred at all. He may apply this studied nonobservance to his own acts—as when he does not by any outward sign admit that his stomach is rumbling—or to the acts of others, as when he does not "see" that another has stumbled. Social life in mental hospitals owes much to this process; patients employ it in regard to their own peculiarities, and visitors employ it, often with tenuous desperation, in regard to patients. In general, tactful blindness of this kind is applied only to events that, if perceived at all, could be perceived and interpreted only as threats to face.

* * *

Another kind of avoidance occurs when a person loses control of his expressions during an encounter. At such times he may try not so much to overlook the incident as to hide or conceal his activity in some way, thus making it possible for the others to avoid some of the difficulties created by a participant who has not maintained face. Correspondingly, when a person is caught out of face because he had not expected to be thrust into interaction, or because strong feelings have disrupted his expressive mask, the others may protectively turn away from him or his activity for a moment, to give him time to assemble himself.

The Corrective Process. When the participants in an undertaking or encounter fail to prevent the occurrence of an event that is expressively incompatible with the judgments of social worth that are being maintained, and when the event is of the kind that is difficult to overlook, then the participants are likely to give it accredited status as an incident—to ratify it as a threat that deserves direct official attention—and to proceed to try to correct for its effects. At this point one or more participants find themselves in an established state of ritual disequilibrium or disgrace, and an attempt must be made to reestablish a satisfactory ritual state for them. I use the term *ritual* because I am dealing with acts through whose symbolic component the actor shows how worthy he is of respect or how worthy he feels others are of it. The imagery of equilibrium is apt here because the length and intensity of the corrective effort is nicely adapted to the persistence and intensity of the threat. One's face, then, is a sacred thing, and the expressive order required to sustain it is therefore a ritual one.

The sequence of acts set in motion by an acknowledged threat to face, and terminating in the re-establishment of ritual equilibrium, I shall call an *interchange.* Defining a message or move as everything conveyed by an actor during a turn at taking action, one can say that an interchange will involve two or more moves and two or more participants. Obvious examples in our society may be found in the sequence of "Excuse me" and "Certainly," and in the exchange of presents or visits. The interchange seems to be a basic concrete unit of social activity and provides one natural empirical way to study interaction of all kinds. Face-saving practices can be usefully classified according to their position in the natural sequence of moves that comprise this unit. Aside from the event which introduces the need for a corrective interchange, four classic moves seem to be involved.

There is, first, the challenge, by which participants take on the responsibility of calling attention to the misconduct; by implication they suggest that the threatened claims are to stand firm and that the threatening event itself will have to be brought back into line.

The second move consists of the offering, whereby a participant, typically the offender, is given a chance to correct for the offense and reestablish the expressive order. Some classic ways of making this move are available. On the one hand, an attempt can be made to show that what admittedly appeared to be a threatening expression is really a meaningless event, or an unintentional act, or a joke not meant to be taken seriously, or an unavoidable, "understandable" product of extenuating circumstances. On the other hand, the meaning of the event may be granted and effort concentrated on the creator of it. Information may be provided to show that the creator was under the influence of something and not himself, or that he was under the command of somebody else and not acting for himself. When a person claims that an act was meant in jest, he may go on and claim that the self that seemed to lie behind the act was also projected as a joke. When a person suddenly finds that he has demonstrably failed in capacities that the others assumed him to have and to claim for himself—such as the capacity to spell, to perform minor tasks, to talk without malapropisms, and so on—he may quickly add, in a serious or unserious way, that he claims these incapacities as part of his self. The meaning of the threatening incident thus stands, but it can now be incorporated smoothly into the flow of expressive events.

As a supplement to or substitute for the strategy of redefining the offensive act or himself, the offender can follow two other procedures: he can provide compensations to the injured—when it is not his own face that he has threatened; or he can provide punishment, penance, and expiation for himself. These are important moves or phases in the ritual interchange. Even though the offender may fail to prove his innocence, he can suggest through these means that he *is* now a renewed person, a person who has paid for his sin against the expressive order and is once more to be trusted in the judgmental scene. Further, he can show that he does not treat the feelings of the others lightly, and that if their feelings have been injured by him, however innocently he is prepared to pay a price for his action. Thus he assures the others that they can accept his explanations without this acceptance constituting a sign of weakness and a lack of pride on their part. Also, by his treatment of himself, by his self-castigation, he shows that he is clearly aware of the kind of crime he would have committed had the incident been what it first appeared to be, and that he knows the kind of punishment that ought to be accorded to one who would commit such a crime. The suspected person thus shows that he is thoroughly capable of taking the role of the others toward his own activity, that he can still be used as a responsible participant in the ritual process, and that the rules of conduct which he appears to have broken are still sacred, real, and unweakened. An offensive act may arouse anxiety about the ritual code; the offender allays this anxiety by showing that both the code and he as an upholder of it are still in working order.

After the challenge and the offering have been made, the third move can occur: the persons to whom the offering is made can accept it as a satisfactory means of reestablishing the expressive order and the faces supported by this order. Only then can the offender cease the major part of his ritual offering.

In the terminal move of the interchange, the forgiven person conveys a sign of gratitude to those who have given him the indulgence of forgiveness.

The phases of the corrective process—challenge, offering, acceptance, and thanks—provide a model for interpersonal ritual behavior, but a model that may be departed from in significant ways. For example, the offended parties may give the offender a chance to initiate the offering on his own before a challenge is made and before they ratify the offense as an incident. This is a common courtesy, extended on the assumption that the recipient will introduce a self-challenge. Further, when the offended persons accept the corrective offering, the offender may suspect that this has been grudgingly done from tact, and so he may volunteer additional corrective offerings, not allowing the matter to rest until he has received a second or third acceptance of his repeated apology. Or the offended persons may tactfully take over the role of the offender and volunteer excuses for him that will, perforce, be acceptable to the offended persons.

An important departure from the standard corrective cycle occurs when a challenged offender patently refuses to heed the warning and continues with his offending behavior, instead of setting the activity to rights. This move shifts the play back to the challengers. If they countenance the refusal to meet their demands, then it will be plain that their challenge was a bluff and that the bluff has been called. This is an untenable position; a face for themselves cannnot be derived from it, and they are left to bluster. To avoid this fate, some classic moves are open to them. For instance, they can resort to tactless, violent retaliation, destroying either themselves or the person who had refused to heed their warning. Or they can withdraw from the undertaking in a visible huff—righteously indignant, outraged, but confident of ultimate vindication. Both tacks provide a way of denying the offender his status as an interactant, and hence denying the reality of the offensive judgment he has made. Both strategies are ways of salvaging face, but for all concerned the costs are usually high. It is partly to forestall such scenes that an offender is usually quick to offer apologies; he does not want the affronted persons to trap themselves into the obligation to resort to desperate measures.

It is plain that emotions play a part in these cycles of response, as when anguish is expressed because of what one has done to another's face, or anger because of what has been done to one's own. I want to stress that these emotions function as moves, and fit so precisely into the logic of the ritual game that it would seem difficult to understand them without it.[1] In fact, spontaneously expressed feelings are likely to fit into the formal pattern of the ritual interchange more elegantly than consciously designed ones.

---

1. Even when a child demands something and is refused, he is likely to cry and sulk not as an irrational expression of frustration but as a ritual move, conveying that he already has a face to lose and that its loss is not to be permitted lightly. Sympathetic parents may even allow for such display, seeing in these crude strategies the beginnings of a social self.

COOPERATION IN FACE-WORK

When a face has been threatened, face-work must be done, but whether this is initiated and primarily carried through by the person whose face is threatened, or by the offender, or by a mere witness, is often of secondary importance. Lack of effort on the part of one person induces compensative effort from others; a contribution by one person relieves the others of the task. In fact, there are many minor incidents in which the offender and the offended simultaneously attempt to initiate an apology. Resolution of the situation to everyone's apparent satisfaction is the first requirement; correct apportionment of blame is typically a secondary consideration.

Since each participant in an undertaking is concerned, albeit for differing reasons, with saving his own face and the face of the others, then tacit cooperation will naturally arise so that the participants together can attain their shared but differently motivated objectives.

One common type of tacit cooperation in face-saving is the tact exerted in regard to face-work itself. The person not only defends his own face and protects the face of the others, but also acts so as to make it possible and even easy for the others to employ face-work for themselves and him. He helps them to help themselves and him. Social etiquette, for example, warns men against asking for New Year's Eve dates too early in the season, lest the girl find it difficult to provide a gentle excuse for refusing. This second-order tact can be further illustrated by the widespread practice of negative-attribute etiquette. The person who has an unapparent negatively valued attribute often finds it expedient to begin an encounter with an unobtrusive admission of his failing, especially with persons who are uninformed about him. The others are thus warned in advance against making disparaging remarks about his kind of person and are saved from the contradiction of acting in a friendly fashion to a person toward whom they are unwittingly being hostile. This strategy also prevents the others from automatically making assumptions about him which place him in a false position and saves him from painful forbearance or embarrassing remonstrances.

* * *

Another form of tacit cooperation, and one that seems to be much used in many societies, is reciprocal self-denial. Often the person does not have a clear idea of what would be a just or acceptable apportionment of judgments during the occasion, and so he voluntarily deprives or depreciates himself while indulging and complimenting the others, in both cases carrying the judgments safely past what is likely to be just. The favorable judgments about himself he allows to come from the others; the unfavorable judgments of himself are his own contributions. This "after you, Alphonse" technique works, of course, because in depriving himself he can reliably anticipate that the others will compliment or indulge him. Whatever allocation of favors is eventually established, all participants are first given a chance to show that they are not bound or constrained by their own desires and expectations, that they have a properly modest view of themselves, and that they can be counted upon to support the ritual code. Negative bargaining, through which each participant tries to make the terms of trade more favorable to the other side, is another instance; as a form of exchange perhaps it is more widespread than the economist's kind.

A person's performance of face-work, extended by his tacit agreement to help others perform theirs, represents his willingness to abide by the ground rules of social interaction. Here is the hallmark of his socialization as an interactant. If he and the others were not socialized in this way, interaction in most societies and most situations would be a much more hazardous thing for feelings and faces. The person would find it impractical to be oriented to symbolically conveyed appraisals of social worth, or to be possessed of feelings—that is, it would be impractical for him to be a ritually delicate object. And as I shall suggest, if the person were not a ritually delicate object, occasions of talk could not be organized in the way they usually are. It is no wonder that trouble is caused by a person who cannot be relied upon to play the face-saving game.

THE RITUAL ROLES OF THE SELF

So far I have implicitly been using a double definition of self: the self as an image pieced together from the expressive implications of the full flow of events in an undertaking; and the self as a kind of player in a ritual game who copes honorably or dishonorably, diplomatically or undiplomatically, with the judgmental contingencies of the situation. A double mandate is involved. As sacred objects, men are subject to slights and profanation; hence as players of the ritual game they have had to lead themselves into duels, and wait for a round of shots to go wide of the mark before embracing their opponents.

* * *

Further, within limits the person has a right to forgive other participants for affronts to his sacred image. He can forbearantly overlook minor slurs upon his face, and in regard to somewhat greater injuries he is the one person who is in a position to accept apologies on behalf of his sacred self. This is a relatively safe prerogative for the person to have in regard to himself, for it is one that is exercised in the interests of the others or of the undertaking. Interestingly enough, when the person commits a *gaffe* against himself, it is not he who has the license to forgive the event; only the others have that prerogative, and it is a safe prerogative for them to have because they can exercise it only in his interests or in the interests of the undertaking. One finds, then, a system of checks and balances by which each participant tends to be given the right to handle only those matters which he will have little motivation for mishandling. In short, the rights and obligations of an interactant are designed to prevent him from abusing his role as an object of sacred value.

When a person begins a mediated or immediate encounter, he already stands in some kind of social relationship to the others concerned, and expects to stand in a given relationship to them after the particular encounter ends. This, of course, is one of the ways in which social contacts are geared into the wider society. Much of the activity occurring during an encounter can be understood as an effort on everyone's part to get through the occasion and all the unanticipated and unintentional events that can cast participants in an undesirable light, without disrupting the relationships of the participants. And if relationships are in the process of change, the object will be to bring the encounter to a satisfactory close without altering the expected course of development. This perspective nicely accounts, for example, for the little ceremonies of greeting and farewell which occur when people begin a conversational encounter or depart from one. Greetings provide a way of showing that a relationship is still what it was at the termination of the previous coparticipation and, typically, that this relationship involves sufficient suppression of hostility for the participants temporarily to drop their guards and talk. Farewells sum up the effect of the encounter upon the relationship and show what the participants may expect of one another when they next meet. The enthusiasm of greetings compensates for the weakening of the relationship caused by the absence just terminated, while the enthusiasm of farewells compensates the relationship for the harm that is about to be done to it by separation.

20

Salvaging the Self

from *Down on Their Luck: A Study of Homeless Street People*

DAVID A. SNOW and LEON ANDERSON

In the United States, the homeless reside in "the lowest reaches of the social system." Avoided, pitied, reviled, controlled, and dismissed as personal failures, the growing ranks of the homeless—individuals and families—has become one of the most intractable and inscrutable problems in urban America. For their book Down on Their Luck, *sociologists David Snow and Leon Anderson conducted two years of fieldwork among those without a home in Austin, Texas, studying the lives of people who live on the street. In contrast to people who have a place to live ("the domiciled"), the homeless struggle not only for subsistence and a dry place to sleep but also to establish and maintain a sense of who they are and their worth as human beings. Sociology's promise is to show us something familiar in a new way. The authors, by using concepts such as stigma and role distance from Erving Goffman (reading 19) and symbolic interaction theory, seek to humanize those who are literally society's outcasts.*

To be homeless in America is not only to have fallen to the bottom of the status system; it is also to be confronted with gnawing doubts about self-worth and the meaning of existence. Such vexing concerns are not just the psychic fallout of having descended onto the streets, but are also stoked by encounters with the domiciled that constantly remind the homeless of where they stand in relation to others.

One such encounter occurred early in the course of our fieldwork. It was late afternoon, and the homeless were congregating in front of the Sally* for dinner. A school bus approached that was packed with Anglo junior high school students being bused from an eastside barrio school to their upper-middle- and upper-class homes in the city's northwest neighborhoods. As the bus rolled by, a fusillade of coins came flying out the windows, as the students made obscene gestures and shouted, "Get a job." Some of the homeless gestured back, some scrambled for the scattered coins—mostly pennies, others angrily threw the coins at the bus, and a few seemed oblivious to the encounter. For the passing junior high schoolers, the exchange was harmless fun, a way to work off the restless energy built up in school; but for the homeless it

---

*Sally is slang for the Salvation Army. Additional references and footnotes can be found in the authors' *Down on Their Luck: A Study of Homeless Street People* (University of California Press, 1993). [*Editors' Note*]

was a stark reminder of their stigmatized status and of the extent to which they are the objects of negative attention.

Initially, we did not give much thought to this encounter. We were more interested in other issues and were neither fully aware of the frequency of such occurrences nor appreciative of their psychological consequences. We quickly came to learn, however, that this was hardly an isolated incident. The buses passed by the Sally every weekday afternoon during the school year; other domiciled citizens occasionally found pleasure in driving by and similarly hurling insults at the homeless and pennies at their feet; and, as we have seen, the hippie tramps and other homeless in the university area were derisively called "Drag worms," the police often harassed the homeless, and a number of neighborhoods took turns vilifying and derogating them.

Not all encounters with the domiciled are so stridently and intentionally demeaning, of course, but they are no less piercingly stigmatizing. One Saturday morning, for instance, as we walked with Willie Hastings and Ron Whitaker along a downtown street, a woman with a station wagon full of children drove by. As they passed, several of the children pointed at us and shouted, "Hey, Mama, look at the street people!" Ron responded angrily:

> "Mama, look at the street people!" You know, it pisses me off the way fucking thieves steal shit and they can still hold their heads high 'cause they got money. Sure, they have to go to prison sometimes, but when they're out, nobody looks down on them. But I wouldn't steal from nobody, and look how those kids stare at us!

The pain of being objects of curiosity and negative attention are experienced fairly regularly by the homeless, but they suffer just as frequently from what has been called "attention deprivation." In *The Pursuit of Attention*, Charles Derber commented that "members of the subordinate classes are regarded as less worthy of attention in relations with members of dominant classes and so are subjected to subtle yet systematic face-to-face deprivation." For no one is Derber's observation more true than for the homeless, who are routinely ignored or avoided by the domiciled. As previously noted, pedestrians frequently avert their eyes when passing the homeless on the sidewalk, and they often hasten their pace and increase the distance between themselves and the homeless when they sense they may be targeted by a panhandler. Pedestrians sometimes go so far as to cross the street in order to avoid anticipated interaction with the homeless. Because of the fear and anxiety presumably engendered in the domiciled by actual or threatened contact with the homeless, efforts are often made at the community level, as we saw earlier, to regulate and segregate the homeless both spatially and institutionally. Although these avoidance rituals and segregative measures are not as overtly demeaning as the more active and immediate kinds of negative attention the homeless receive, they can be equally stigmatizing, for they also cast the homeless as objects of contamination. This, too, constitutes an assault upon the self, albeit a more subtle and perhaps more insidious one.

Occurring alongside the negative attention and attention deprivation the homeless experience are an array of gestures and acts that are frequently altruistic and clearly indicative of goodwill. People do on occasion give to panhandlers and beggars out of sincere concern rather than merely to get them off their backs. Domiciled citizens sometimes even provide assistance without being asked. One evening, for instance, we found Pat Manchester sitting on a bench near the university eating pizza. "Man, I was just sitting here," he told us, "and this dude walked up and gave me half a pizza and two dollar bills." Several of the students who worked at restaurants in the university area occasionally brought leftovers to Rhyming Mike and other hippie tramps. Other community members occasionally took street people to their home for a shower, dinner, and a good night's sleep. Even Jorge Herrera, who was nearly incoherent, appeared never to wash or bathe, and was covered with rashes and open sores, was the recipient of such assistance. Twice during our field research he appeared on the streets after a brief absence in clean clothes, shaved, and with a new haircut. When we asked about the changes in his appearance, he told us that someone had taken him home, cleaned him up, and let him spend the night. These kinds of unorganized, sporadic gestures of goodwill clearly facilitate the survival of some of the homeless, but the numbers they touch in comparison to those in need are minuscule. Nor do they occur in sufficient quantity or consistently enough to neutralize the stigmatizing and demeaning consequences of not only being on the streets but being objects of negative attention or little attention at all.

In addition to those who make sporadic gestures of goodwill, thousands of domiciled citizens devote occasional time and energy to serving the homeless in an organized fashion in churches, soup kitchens, and shelters. Angels House kitchen was staffed in part by such volunteers, and their support was essential to the operation of the kitchen. Yet the relationship between these well-meaning volunteers and the homeless is highly structured and sanitized. The volunteers typically prepare sandwiches and other foods in a separate area from the homeless or encounter them only across the divide of a serving counter that underscores the distance between the servers and the served. Thus, however sincere and helpful the efforts of domiciled volunteers, the structure of their encounters with the homeless often underscores the immense status differences and thereby reminds the homeless again of where they stand in relation to others.

* * *

The task the homeless face of salvaging the self is not easy, especially since wherever they turn they are reminded that they are at the very bottom of the status system. As Sonny McCallister lamented shortly after he became homeless, "The hardest thing's been getting used to the way people look down on street people. It's real hard to feel good about yourself when almost everyone you see is looking down on you." Tom Fisk, who had been on the streets longer, agreed. But he said that he had become more calloused over time:

> I used to let it bother me when people stared at me while I was trying to sleep on the roof of my car or change clothes out of my trunk, but I don't let it get to me anymore. I mean, they don't know who I am, so what gives them the right to judge me? I know I'm okay.

But there was equivocation and uncertainty in his voice. Moreover, even if he no longer felt the stares and comments of others, he still had to make sense of the distance between himself and them.

How, then, do the homeless deal with the negative attention they receive or the indifference they encounter as they struggle to survive materially? How do they salvage their selves? And to what extent do the webs of meaning they spin and the personal identities they construct vary with patterns of adaptation? We address these questions in the remainder of the chapter by considering two kinds of meaning: existential and identity-oriented. The former term refers to the kinds of accounts the homeless invoke in order to make sense of their plight; the latter refers to the kinds of meaning they attach to self in interactions with others.

MAKING SENSE OF THE PLIGHT OF HOMELESSNESS

The plight of human beings brought face-to-face with the meaning of their existence by suffocating social structures, unanticipated turns of events, dehumanizing living conditions, or the specter of death has been a long and persistent theme in both literature and philosophy. Underlying this strand of writing, generally discussed under the rubric of existentialism, are two consistent themes: that the quest for meaning, while an ongoing challenge in everyday life, is particularly pressing for those individuals whose routines and expectations have been disrupted; and that the burden of finding meaning in such disruptive moments rests on the shoulders of the individual. From this perspective, meaning is not an essence that inheres in a particular object or situation, but a construction or imputation; and the primary architects of such constructions are human actors. The burden of infusing problematic situations with meaning is heavier for some actors than for others, however. Certainly this is true of the homeless, with their pariah-like status, limited resources, and the often demeaning treatment they receive.

How do the homeless carve out a sense of meaning in the seemingly insane and meaningless situation in which they find themselves? Are they able to make sense of their plight in a fashion that helps to salvage the self?

Some are able to do so and others are not. Many of the homeless invoke causal accounts of their situation that infuse it with meaning and rescue the self; others abandon both concerns by drifting into the world of alcoholism or into an alternative reality that is in this world but not of it and that is often treated as symptomatic of insanity by those not privy to it. Of the two lines of response, the first is clearly the most pronounced.

INVOKING CAUSAL ACCOUNTS

By causal accounts we refer to the reasons people give to render understandable their behavior or the situations in which they find themselves. Such accounts are essentially commonsense attributions that are invoked in order to explain some problematic action or situation. Whether such accounts seem reasonable to an observer is irrelevant; what is at issue is their meaningfulness to the actor.

These explanatory accounts are seldom new constructions. Rather, they are likely to be variants of folk understandings or aphorisms that are invoked from time to time by many citizens and thus constitute part of a larger cultural vocabulary. This view of causal accounts accords with the contention that culture can best be thought of as a repertoire or "'tool kit' of symbols, stories, rituals, and world views which people use in varying configurations to solve different kinds of problems." These stories, symbols, or accounts are not pulled out of that cultural tool kit at random, however. Instead, the appropriation and articulation process is driven by some pressing problem or imperative. In the case of the homeless, that predicament is the existential need to infuse their situation with a sense of meaning that helps to salvage the self. In the service of that imperative, three folk adages or accounts surfaced rather widely and frequently among the homeless in Austin in their conversations with us and each other. One says, "I'm down on my luck." Another reminds us, "What goes around, comes around." And the third says, "I've paid my dues."

* * *

"I'm down on my luck"

The term *luck*, which most citizens invoke from time to time to account for unanticipated happenings in their lives, is generally reserved for events that influence the individual's life but are thought to be beyond his or her control. To assert that "I'm down on my luck," then, is to attribute my plight to misfortune, to chance. For the homeless, such an attribution not only helps to make sense of their situation, but it does so in a manner that is psychologically functional in two ways: it exempts the homeless from responsibility for their plight, and it leaves open the possibility of a better future.

* * *

"What goes around, comes around"

... [I]nsofar as there is a moral code affecting interpersonal relations on the streets, it is manifested in the phrase, "What goes around, comes around." But the relevance of this phrase is not confined solely to the interpersonal domain. It is also brought into service with respect to the issue of meaning in general and the luck factor in particular.

Regarding the former, the contention that "what goes around, comes around" suggests a cyclical rather than linear conception of the process by which events unfold. This circularity implies, among other things, a transposition of opposites at some point in the life course. Biblical examples of such transpositions abound, as in the New Testament declarations that "The last shall be first and the first last" and "The meek shall inherit the earth." Although few homeless harbor realistic thoughts of such dramatic transpositions, many do assume that things will get better because "what goes around, comes around."

This logic also holds for luck. Thus, if a person has been down on his or her luck, it follows that the person's luck is subject to change. Hoyt, among others, talked as though he believed this proposition. "Look," he told us one evening over dinner and a few beers at a local steak house:

> I've been down on my luck for so damn long, it's got to change.... Like I said before, I believe what goes around, comes around, so I'm due a run of good luck, don't you think?

We nodded in agreement, but not without wondering how strongly Hoyt and others actually believed in the presumed link between luck and the cyclical principle of "what goes around, comes around." Whatever the answer, there is certainly good reason for harboring such a belief, for it introduces a ray of hope into a dismal situation and thereby infuses it with meaning of the kind that helps keep the self afloat.

"I've paid my dues"

This linkage is buttressed further by the third frequently articulated causal account: "I've paid my dues." To invoke this saying is to assert, as Marilyn Fisch often did in her more sober moments, that "I deserve better" after "what I've been through" or "what I've done." The phrase implies that if there are preconditions for a run of good luck, then those conditions have been met. Thus, Gypsy Bill told us one afternoon that he felt his luck was about to change as he was fantasizing about coming into some money. "You may think I'm crazy," he said, "but it's this feeling I've got. Besides, I deserve it 'cause I've paid my dues."

* * *

AVENUES OF ESCAPE: ALCOHOL AND ALTERNATIVE REALITIES

Not all homeless attend to the existential business of making sense of their situation by invoking conventional folk understandings. Some individuals may have been on the streets too long or have endured too many hardships, experienced too many frustrations, and suffered too many insults to the self to bother any longer with the accounting process. Instead, they gradually drift down alternative avenues for dealing with the oppressive realities of street life and the resultant brutalization of the self. These avenues, while stigmatized by the larger culture, are often consonant with the subculture of street life itself. One such avenue is alcoholism; the other involves the creation or adoption of alternative realities frequently associated with mental illness.

The suggestion that some of the homeless drift into alcoholism and mental illness as a consequence of the hopeless and demeaning situation in which they find themselves runs counter to the tendency to treat these conditions as precipitants of homelessness or at least as disabilities that increase vulnerability to becoming homeless. That this presumed causal connection holds for some of the homeless is no doubt true, but it is also true that alcoholism and mental illness sometimes function as means of coping psychologically with the traumas of street life. Clearly, they do not guarantee literal escape from the streets, but they can serve as insulation from further psychic assaults and thereby create illusions of personal autonomy and well-being. How often this process occurs is unclear, but that it is not an infrequent occurrence we are certain.

* * *

Marilyn's experience with alcohol is similar. As she explained one morning over coffee:

> I didn't have much of a drinking problem before I landed on the streets. But I found it all so depressing. And everybody else was drinking and asking me to drink. So I said, "Why not?" I mean, what did I have to lose? Everything was so depressing. Drinking sure couldn't make it any worse!

Her claim of gradually increasing levels of drinking was substantiated by our frequent contacts with her for over two years. When we first met her Marilyn, like many of the homeless, was a spree or binge drinker, but as time passed the period between the sprees became shorter and her drinking became more chronic, all of which was manifested in her increasingly emaciated, weathered, and scarred physical appearance. The experiences of Shotgun, Gypsy, Nona George, and JJ and Indio, as well as other outsiders we met, are all quite similar: increasing use of alcohol with the passage of time, resulting eventually in apparent physiological and psychological dependence.

* * *

Like much of the drinking that occurs on the streets, some of the behaviors and verbalizations customarily read as symptomatic of mental illness can be construed as forms of adaptive behavior. Undoubtedly, some of the homeless who might be diagnosed as mentally ill were that way prior to their descent onto the streets, but others evince symptoms of such illness as a result of the trauma of living on the streets. The symptoms we refer to are not those of depression and demoralization, which are understandably widespread on the streets, but more "bizarre" patterns of thought and behavior that are less prevalent but more conspicuous. These include auditory and visual hallucinations, that is, hearing or seeing things to which others are not privy; conspiratorial delusions, such as the belief that others are talking about you or are out to get you; grandiose delusions, like the belief that you have extraordinary powers, insights, or contacts; and the public verbalization of these hallucinations and delusions as well as audible conversations with others not present. Such beliefs and behaviors suggest an alternative inner reality that is neither publicly shared nor fully accessible to others and is therefore "out of this world." Although such alternative realities frequently invite both folk labels of "nuts" and "crazy" and clinical labels of schizophrenia and paranoia, they may often be quite functional for some individuals who find themselves in a demeaning and inhumane context in which they are the frequent objects of negative attention or attention deprivation. After all, if you are rarely the recipient of any positive attention or are ignored altogether, creating and retreating into a private reality that grants you privileged insights and special status may be more adaptive than it appears at first glance.

Certainly this appeared to be the case with Tanner Sutton, the badly burned and disfigured Sally street employee who was preoccupied with the occult and higher forms of consciousness and who claimed to be a "spiritually gifted person" with "special mystical powers" that enabled him "to read people," live in "many different dimensions of space," and "look into the future when humans will be transformed into another life form." Taken at face value, such claims appear to be outlandish and perhaps even symptomatic of psychosis. Even some of Tanner's street associates regarded him as "far out." . . . Yet Tanner was able to function quite resourcefully on the streets, as was evidenced by his ability to discharge his duties at the Sally. Moreover, however weird or bizarre Tanner's claims, to evaluate him in terms of their veracity misses the point. Tanner's biography and the context in which he found himself make the issue one not of verisimilitude but of psychological functionality. For Tanner, as for others who appear to have lodged their self in some alternative reality, that reality provides a psychological alternative to the material world in which they find themselves, thus insulating them from further psychic assaults emanating from that world and providing an alternative source of self-regard.

* * *

CONSTRUCTING IDENTITY-ORIENTED MEANING

However the homeless deal with the issue of existential meaning, whether by stringing together causal accounts borrowed from conventional cultural vocabularies or by seeking refuge in alcohol, drugs, or alternative realities, they are still confronted with establishing who they are in the course of interaction with others, for interaction between two or more individuals minimally requires that they be situated or placed as social objects. In other words, situationally specific identities must be established. Such identities can be established in two ways: they can be attributed or imputed by others, or they can be claimed or asserted by the actor. The former can be thought of as social or role identities in that they are imputations based primarily on information gleaned from the appearance or behavior of others and from the time and location of their action, as when children in a passing car look out the window and yell, "Hey, Mama, look at the street people!" or when junior high school students yell out the windows of their school bus to the homeless lining up for dinner in front of the Sally, "Get a job, you bums!" In each case, the homeless in question have been situated as social objects and thus assigned social identities.

When individuals claim or assert an identity, by contrast, they attribute meaning to themselves. Such self-attributions can be thought of as personal identities rather than social identities, in that they are self-designations brought into play or avowed during the course of actual or anticipated interaction with others. Personal identities may be consistent with imputed social identities, as when Shotgun claims to be "a tramp," or inconsistent, as when Tony Jones yells back to the passing junior high schoolers, "Fuck you, I ain't no lazy bum!" The presented personal identities of individuals who are frequent objects of negative attention or attention deprivation, as are the homeless, can be especially revealing, because they offer a glimpse of how those people deal interactionally with their pariah-like status and the demeaning social identities into which they are frequently cast. Personal identities thus provide further insight into the ways the homeless attempt to salvage the self.

What, then, are the personal identities that the homeless construct and negotiate when in interaction with others? Are they merely a reflection of the highly stereotypic and stigmatized identities attributed to them, or do they reflect a more positive sense of self or at least an attempt to carve out and sustain a less demeaning self-conception?

The construction of personal identity typically involves a number of complementary activities: (a) procurement and arrangement of physical settings and props; (b) cosmetic face work or the arrangement of personal appearance; (c) selective association with other individuals and groups; and (d) verbal construction and assertion of personal identity. Although some of the homeless engage in conscious manipulation of props and appearance—for example, Pushcart, with his fully loaded shopping cart, and Shotgun, who fancies himself a con artist—most do not resort to such measures. Instead, the primary means by which the homeless announce their personal identities is verbal. They engage, in other words, in a good bit of identity talk. This is understandable, since the homeless seldom have the financial or social resources to pursue the other identity construction activities. Additionally, since the structure of their daily routines ensures that they spend a great deal of time waiting here and there, they have ample opportunity to converse with each other.

Sprinkled throughout these conversations with each other, as well as those with agency personnel and, occasionally, with the domiciled, are numerous examples of identity talk. Inspection of the instances of the identity talk to which we were privy yielded three generic patterns: (1) distancing; (2) embracement; and (3) fictive storytelling. Each pattern was found to contain several subtypes that tend to vary in use according to whether the speaker is recently dislocated, a straddle, or an outsider. We elaborate in turn each of the generic patterns, their varieties, and how they vary in use among the different types of homeless.

DISTANCING

When individuals have to enact roles, associate with others, or utilize institutions that imply social identities inconsistent with their actual or desired self-conceptions, they often attempt to distance themselves from those roles, associations, or institutions. A substantial proportion of the identity talk we recorded was consciously focused on distancing from other homeless individuals, from street and occupational roles, and from the caretaker agencies servicing the homeless. Nearly a third of the identity statements were of this variety.

Associational Distancing

Since a claim to a particular self is partly contingent on the imputed social identities of the person's associates, one way people can substantiate that claim when their associates are negatively evaluated is to distance themselves from those associates. This distancing technique manifested itself in two ways among the homeless: disassociation from the homeless as a general social category, and disassociation from specific groupings of homeless individuals.

Categoric associational distancing was particularly evident among the recently dislocated. Illustrative is Tony Jones's comment in response to our initial query about life on the streets:

I'm not like the other guys who hang out down at the Sally. If you want to know about street people, I can tell you about them; but you can't really learn about street people from studying me, because I'm different.

Role Distancing

Role distancing, the second form of distancing employed by the homeless, involves a self-conscious attempt to foster the impression of a lack of commitment or attachment to a particular role in order to deny the self implied. Thus, when individuals find themselves cast into roles in which the social identities implied are inconsistent with desired or actual self-conceptions, role distancing is likely to occur. Since the homeless routinely find themselves being cast into or enacting low-status, negatively evaluated roles, it should not be surprising that many of them attempt to disassociate themselves from those roles.

As did associational distancing, role distancing manifested itself in two ways: distancing from the general role of street person, and distancing from specific occupational roles. The former, which is also a type of categorical distancing, was particularly evident among the recently dislocated. It was not uncommon for these individuals to state explicitly that they should "not be mistaken as a typical street person." Role distancing of the less categoric and more situationally specific type was most evident among those who performed day labor, such as painters' helpers, hod carriers, warehouse and van unloaders, and those in unskilled service occupations such as dishwashing and janitorial work. As we saw earlier, the majority of the homeless we encountered would avail themselves of such job opportunities, but they seldom did so enthusiastically, since the jobs offered low status and low wages. This was especially true of the straddlers and some of the outsiders, who frequently reminded others of their disdain for such jobs and of the belief that they deserved better.

* * *

EMBRACEMENT

Embracement connotes a person's verbal and expressive confirmation of acceptance of and attachment to the social identity associated with a general or specific role, a set of social relationships, or a particular ideology. So defined, embracement implies that social identity is congruent with personal identity. Thus, embracement involves the avowal of implied social identities rather than their disavowal, as in the case of distancing. Thirty-four percent of the identity statements were of this variety.

Role Embracement

The most conspicuous kind of embracement encountered was categoric role embracement, which typically manifested itself by the avowal and acceptance of street-role identities such as tramp and bum. Occasionally we would encounter an individual who would immediately announce that he or she was a tramp or a bum. A case in point is provided by our initial encounter with Shotgun, when he proudly told us that he was "the tramp who was on the front page of yesterday's newspaper." In that and subsequent conversations his talk was peppered with references to himself as a tramp. He said, for example, that he had appeared on a television show in St. Louis as a tramp and that he "tramped" his way across the country, and he revealed several "cons" that "tramps use to survive on the road."

Shotgun and others like him identified themselves as traditional "brethren of the road" tramps. A number of other individuals identified themselves as "hippie tramps." When confronted by a passing group of young punk-rockers, for instance, Gimpy Dan and several other hippie tramps voiced agreement with the remark one made that "these kids will change but we'll stay the same." As if to buttress this claim, they went on to talk about "Rainbow," the . . . annual gathering of old hippies which functions in part as a kind of identity-reaffirmation ritual. For these street people, there was little doubt about who they were; they not only saw themselves as hippie tramps, but they embraced that identity both verbally and expressively.

* * *

FICTIVE STORYTELLING

A third form of identity talk engaged in by the homeless is fictive storytelling about past, present, or future experiences and accomplishments. We characterize as fictive stories that range from minor exaggerations of experience to full-fledged fabrications. We observed two types of fictive storytelling: embellishment of the past and present, and fantasizing about the future. Slightly more than a third of the identity statements we recorded fell into one of these two categories.

Embellishment

By *embellishment* we refer to the exaggeration of past *or* present experiences with fanciful and fictitious particulars so as to assert a positive personal identity. Embellishment involves enlargement of the truth, an overstatement of what transpired or is unfolding. Embellished stories, then, are only partly fictional.

Examples of embellishment for identity construction abound among the homeless. Although a wide array of events and experiences, ranging from the accomplishments of offspring to sexual and drinking exploits and predatory activities, were embellished, such storytelling was most commonly associated with past and current occupational and financial themes. The typical story of financial embellishment entailed an exaggerated claim regarding past or current wages. A case in point is provided by a forty-year-old homeless man who spent much of his time hanging around a bar boasting about having been offered a job as a Harley-Davidson mechanic for $18.50 per hour, although at the same time he constantly begged for cigarettes and spare change for beer.

* * *

Fantasizing

The second type of fictive storytelling among the homeless is verbal fantasizing, which involves the articulation of fabrications about the speaker's future. Such fabrications place the narrator in positively framed situations that seem far removed from, if at all connected to, his or her past and present. These fabrications are almost always benign, usually have a Walter Mitty/pipe dream quality to them, and vary from fanciful reveries involving little self-deception to fantastic stories in which the narrator appears to be taken in by his or her constructions.

Regardless of the degree of self-deception, the verbal fantasies we heard were generally organized around one or more of four themes: self-employment, money, material possessions, and women. Fanciful constructions concerning self-employment usually involved business schemes. On several occasions, for example, Tony Jones told us and others about his plans to set up a little shop near the university to sell leather hats and silver work imported from New York. In an even more expansive vein, two straddlers who had befriended each other seemed to be scheming constantly about how they were going to start one lucrative business after another. Once we overheard them talking about "going into business" for themselves, "either roofing houses or rebuilding classic cars and selling them." A few days later, they were observed trying to find a third party to bankroll one of these business ventures, and they even asked us if we "could come up with some cash."

* * *

Fanciful identity assertions were also constructed around material possessions and sexual encounters with women. These two identity pegs were clearly illustrated one evening among several homeless men along the city's major nightlife strip. During the course of making numerous overtures to passing women, two of the fellows jointly fantasized about how they would attract these women in the future. "Man, these chicks are going to be all over us when we come back into town with our new suits and Corvettes," one exclaimed. The other added, "We'll have to get some cocaine too. Cocaine will get you women every time." This episode and fantasy occurred early in the second month of our fieldwork, and we quickly came to learn that such fantasizing was fairly commonplace and that it was typically occasioned by "woman-watching," which exemplifies one of the ways in which homeless men are both deprived of attention and respond to that deprivation.

* * *

Starved for female attention, the homeless men are quick to fantasize, attributing great significance to the slightest response. One Saturday afternoon, for example, as we were sitting by the jogging trail drinking beer with Pat Manchester and Ron Whitaker, we noticed several groups of young women who had laid out blankets on the grassy strip that borders the trail. Pat and Ron were especially interested in the women who were wearing shorts and halter tops. Pat called out for them to take their tops off. It was not clear that they heard him, but he insisted, "They really want it. I can tell they do." He suggested we go over with him to "see what we can get," but he was unwilling to go by himself. Instead, he constructed a fantasy in which the young women were very interested in him. Occasionally the women glanced toward us with apprehension, and Pat always acted as though it was a sign of interest. "If I go over there and they want to wrap me up in that blanket and fuck me," he said, "man, I'm going for it." Nonetheless, he continued to sit and fantasize, unwilling to acknowledge openly the obdurate reality staring him in the face.

Although respectable work, financial wealth, material possessions, and women are intimately interconnected in actuality, only one or two of the themes were typically highlighted in the stories we heard. Occasionally, however, we encountered a particularly accomplished storyteller who wove together all four themes in a grand scenario. Such was the case with the straddle from Pittsburgh who told the following tale over a meal of bean stew and stale bread at the Sally, and repeated it after lights-outs as he lay on the concrete floor of the winter warehouse: "Tomorrow morning I'm going to get my money and say, 'Fuck this shit.' I'm going to catch a plane to Pittsburgh and tomorrow night I'll take a hot bath, have a dinner of linguine and red wine in my own restaurant, and have a woman hanging on my arm." When encountered on the street the next evening, he attempted to explain his continued presence on the streets by saying, "I've been informed that all my money is tied up in a legal battle back in Pittsburgh," an apparently fanciful amplification of the original fabrication.

* * *

SUMMARY

All animals are confronted with the challenge of material subsistence, but only humans are saddled with the vexing question of its meaning. We must not only sustain ourselves physically to survive, but we are also impelled to make sense of our mode of subsistence, to place it in some meaningful context, to develop an account of our situation that does not destroy our sense of self-worth. Otherwise, the will to persist falters and interest in tomorrow wanes. The biblical prophets understood this well when they told us that "man does not live by bread alone." The homeless appear to understand this existential dilemma, too, at least experientially; for while they struggle to subsist materially, they confront the meaning of their predicament and its implications for the self. These concerns weigh particularly heavily on the recently dislocated, but they gnaw at the other homeless as well—sometimes when they drift off at night, sometimes when they are jarred from sleep by their own dreams or the cries of others, and often throughout the day when their encounters with other homeless and with the domiciled remind them in myriad subtle and not-so-subtle ways of their descent into the lowest reaches of the social system and of their resultant stigmatized status.

21

No Country for White Men

ARLIE RUSSELL HOCHSCHILD

The economist John Lanchester wrote of the Great Recession, "Sociology would have been a better social science than economics for understanding the last ten years. Three dominos fell. The initial event was economic. The meaning of it was experienced in ways best interpreted by sociology. The consequences were acted out through politics. From a sociological point of view, the crisis exacerbated faultlines running through contemporary societies."[1] In this essay, one of sociology's best and most widely read ethnographers grapples with the cultural faultline that permeates politics today. Often described as "tribal," two camps have laid claim to issues and lifestyle choices that appear as conflicting values but have their basis in the shifting social fabric and political economy of late-stage capitalism. Highly sympathetic to people who are dramatically different from her, Arlie Hochschild finds in their concerns and anxiety a "deep story" that resonates with them and goes some way toward explaining their allegiance to politicians and policies that seem antithetical to everything in their lives.

In a framed photo of herself taken in 2007, Sharon Galicia stands, fresh-faced and beaming, beside first lady Laura Bush at a Washington, DC, luncheon, thrilled to be honored as an outstanding GOP volunteer. We are in her office in the Aflac insurance company in Lake Charles, Louisiana, and Sharon is heading out to pitch medical and life insurance to workers in a bleak corridor of industrial plants servicing the rigs in the Gulf of Mexico and petrochemical plants that make the plastic feedstock for everything from car seats to bubble gum.

After a 20-minute drive along flat terrain, we pull into a dirt parking lot beside a red truck with a decal of the Statue of Liberty, her raised arm holding an M-16. A man waves from the entrance to an enormous warehouse. Warm, attractive, well-spoken, Sharon has sold a lot of insurance policies around here and made friends along the way.

A policy with a weekly premium of $5.52 covers accidents that aren't covered by a worker's other insurance—if he has any. "How many of you can go a week without your paycheck?" is part of Sharon's pitch. "Usually no hands go

---

1. The Great Recession was 2008–2010. John Lanchester, "After the Fall," *London Review of Books*, July 5, 2018: 8.

up," she tells me. Her clients repair oil platforms, cut sheet metal, fix refrigerators, process chicken, lay asphalt, and dig ditches. She sells to entry-level floor sweepers who make $8 an hour and can't afford to get sick. She sells to flaggers in highway repair crews who earn $12 an hour, and to welders and operators who, with overtime, make up to $100,000 a year. For most, education stopped after high school. "Pipe fitters. Ditch diggers. Asphalt layers," Sharon says. "I can't find one that's not for Donald Trump."

I first met Sharon at a gathering of tea party enthusiasts in Lake Charles in 2011. I told them I was a sociologist writing a book about America's ever-widening political divide. In their 2008 book, *The Big Sort*, Bill Bishop and Robert Cushing showed that while Americans used to move mainly for individual reasons like higher-paid jobs, nicer weather, and better homes, today they also prioritize living near people who think like they do. Left and Right have become subnations, as George Saunders recently wrote in *The New Yorker*, living like housemates "no longer on speaking terms" in a house set afire by Trump, gaping at one another "through the smoke."

I wanted to leave my subnation of Berkeley, California, and enter another as far right as Berkeley is to the left. White Louisiana looked like it. In the 2012 election, 39 percent of white voters nationwide cast a ballot for President Barack Obama. That figure was 28 percent in the South, but about 11 percent in Louisiana.

To try to understand the tea party supporters I came to know—I interviewed 60 people in all—over the next five years I did a lot of "visiting," as they call it. I asked people to show me where they'd grown up, been baptized, and attended school, and the cemetery where their parents had been buried. I perused high school yearbooks and photograph albums, played cards, and went fishing. I attended meetings of Republican Women of Southwest Louisiana and followed the campaign trails of two right-wing candidates running for Congress.

When I asked people what politics meant to them, they often answered by telling me what they believed ("I believe in freedom") or who they'd vote for ("I was for Ted Cruz, but now I'm voting Trump"). But running beneath such beliefs like an underwater spring was what I've come to think of as a *deep story*. The deep story was a feels-as-if-it's-true story, stripped of facts and judgments, that reflected the feelings underpinning opinions and votes. It was a story of unfairness and anxiety, stagnation and slippage—a story in which shame was the companion to need. Except Trump had opened a divide in how tea partiers felt this story should end.

"Hey Miss Sharon, how ya' doin'?" A fiftysomething man I'll call Albert led us through the warehouse, where sheet metal had been laid out on large tables. "Want to come over Saturday, help us make sausage?" he called over the *eeeeech* of an unseen electrical saw. "I'm seasoning it different this year." The year before, Sharon had taken her 11-year-old daughter along to help stuff the spicy smoked-pork-and-rice sausage, to which Albert added ground deer meat. "I'll bring Alyson," Sharon said, referring to her daughter. Some days they'd have 400 pounds of deer meat and offer her some. "They're really good to me. And I'm there for them too when they need something."

These men had little shelter from bad news. "If you die, who's going to bury you?" Sharon would ask on such calls. "Do you have $10,000 sitting around? Will your parents have to borrow money to bury you or your wife or girl-friend? For $1.44 a week, you get $20,000 of life insurance."

Louisiana is the country's third-poorest state; 1 in 5 residents live in poverty. It ranks third in the proportion of residents who go hungry each year, and dead last in overall health. A quarter of the state's students drop out from high school or don't graduate on time. Partly as a result, Louisiana leads the nation in its proportion of "disconnected youth"—20 percent of 16- to 24-year-olds in 2013 were neither in school nor at work. (Nationally, the figure is 14 percent.) Only 6 percent of Louisiana workers are members of labor unions, about half the rate nationwide.

Louisiana is also home to vast pollution, especially along Cancer Alley, the 85-mile strip along the lower Mississippi between Baton Rouge and New Orleans, with some 150 industrial plants where once there were sugar and cotton plantations. According to the American Cancer Society, Louisiana had the nation's second-highest incidence of cancer for men and the fifth-highest rate of male deaths from cancer. "When I make a presentation, if I say, 'How many of you know someone that has had cancer?' every hand is going to go up. Just the other day I was in Lafayette doing my enrollments for the insurance, and I was talking to this one guy. And he said, 'My brother-in-law just died. He was 29 or 30.' He's the third person working for his company that's been in their early 30s that's died of cancer in the last three years. I file tons and tons of cancer claims."

Sharon also faced economic uncertainty. A divorced mother of two, she supported herself and two children on an ample but erratic income, all from commission on her Aflac sales. "If you're starting out, you might get 99 'noes' for every one 'yes.' After 16 years on the job, I get 50 percent 'yeses.'" This put her at the top among Aflac salespeople; still, she added, "If it's a slow month, we eat peanut butter."

Until a few years ago, Sharon had also collected rent from 80 tenants in a trailer court. Her ex-husband earned $40,000 as a sales manager at Pacific Sunwear, she explained, and helped with child support; altogether it allowed her to pay her children's tuition at a parochial school and stay current on the mortgage of a tastefully furnished, spacious ranch house in suburban Moss Bluff. She lived in the anxious middle.

And from this vantage point, the lives of renters in her trailer park, called Crestwood Community, had both appalled and unnerved her. Some of her tenants, 80 percent of whom were white, had matter-of-factly admitted to lying to get Medicaid and food stamps. When she'd asked a boy her son's age about his plans for the future, he answered, "I'm just going to get a [disability] check, like my mama." Many renters had been, she told me, able-bodied, idle, and on disability. One young man had claimed to have seizures. "If you have seizures, that's almost a surefire way to get disability without proving an ailment," she said. A lot of Crestwood Community residents supposedly had seizures, she added. "Seizures? Really?"

As we drove through the vacated lot, we passed abandoned trailers with doors flung open, tall grass pockmarked with holes where mailboxes once stood. Unable to pay an astronomical water bill, Sharon had been forced to close the trailer park, giving residents a month's notice and provoking their resentment.

In truth, Sharon felt relief. Her renters, she said, had been a hard-living lot. A jealous boyfriend had murdered his girlfriend. Some men drank and beat their wives. One man had married his son's ex-wife. Beyond that, Sharon had felt unfairly envied by them. "I've been called a rich bitch. They think Miss Sharon lives the life of Riley." And while her home was a 25-minute drive away, the life of her renters had felt entirely too close for comfort. "You couldn't talk to anyone at Crestwood whose teeth weren't falling out, gums black, missing teeth," adding that she gave out toothbrushes and toothpaste one Christmas. "My kids make fun of me because I brush my teeth so much."

To her, the trailer park both did and did not feel worlds away. For one thing, a person's standard of living, their worldview and basic identity, seemed already set on a floor of Jell-O. Who could know for sure how you would fare in the era of an expanding bottom, spiking top, and receding middle class?

Sharon's maternal grandfather had established a successful line of local furniture stores and shown how far up a man with gumption could rise. Sharon herself had graduated magna cum laude from McNeese State University in Lake Charles and been elected president of Republican Women of Southwest Louisiana. But her youngest brother had dropped out of high school and, while very bright and able-bodied, had not found his way. Her father, a plant worker who'd left her mom when Sharon was a teen, had remarried and moved to a trailer in Sulphur with his new wife, a mother of four. Looking around her, Sharon saw family and friends who struggled with bad relationships and joblessness. Some collected food stamps. "I don't get it," she said, "and it drives me nuts."

For Sharon, being on the dole raised basic issues of duty, honor, and shame. It had been hard to collect rent that she knew derived from disability checks, paid, in the end, by hardworking taxpayers like her. "I pay $9,000 in taxes every year and we get nothing for it," she said. Like others I interviewed, she felt that the federal government—especially under President Obama—was bringing down the hardworking rich and struggling middle while lifting the idle poor. She'd seen it firsthand and it felt unfair.

As we drove from the trailer park to her home, Sharon reflected on human ambition: "You can just see it in some guys' eyes; they're aiming higher. They don't want a handout." This was the central point of one of Sharon's favorite books, *Barefoot to Billionaire*, by oil magnate Jon Huntsman Sr. (whose son ran in the 2012 Republican presidential primary). Ambition was good. Earning money was good. The more money you earned, the more you could give to others. Giving was good. So ambition was the key to goodness, which was the basis for pride.

If you *could* work, even for pennies, receiving government benefits was a source of shame. It was okay if you were one of the few who really needed it, but not otherwise. Indignation at the overuse of welfare spread, in the minds of tea party supporters I got to know, to the federal government itself, and to state and local agencies. A retired assistant fire chief in Lake Charles told me, "I got told we don't *need* an assistant fire chief. A lot of people around here don't like *any* public employees, apart from the police." His wife said, "We were making such low pay that we could have been on food stamps every month and other welfare stuff. And [an official] told our departments that if we went and got food stamps or welfare it would look bad for Lake Charles so that he would fire us." A public school teacher complained, "I've had people tell me, 'It's the teachers who need to pass the kids' tests.' They have no idea what I know." A social worker who worked with drug addicts said, "I've been told the church should take care of addicts, not the government." Both receivers and givers of public services were tainted—in the eyes of nearly all I came to know—by the very touch of government.

Sharon especially admired Albert, a middle-aged sheet metal worker who could have used help but was too proud to ask for it. "He's had open-heart surgery. He's had stomach surgery. He's had like eight surgeries. He's still working, though. He wants to work. He's got a daughter in jail—her third DUI, so he's raising her son—and this and that. But he doesn't want anything from the government. He's *such* a *neat* guy." There was no mention of the need for a good alcoholism rehab program for his daughter or after-school programs for his grandson. Until a few days before his death Albert continued working, head high, shame-free.

Sharon's politics were partly rooted, it seemed, in the class slippage of her childhood. As the oldest of three, the "little mama" to two younger brothers, she said, "I got them up in the morning, made their beds for them, so my mama wouldn't come down hard on them." Sharon's mother, the daughter of that prosperous furniture store owner, had grown up with a black maid who'd made her bed for her. She'd married a highly intelligent but high-school-educated plant worker, a Vietnam vet who never spoke of the war and seemed in search of peace and quiet. Privileges came and went in deeply unsettling ways and made a person want to hold on to a reassuring past. "One time when I had to travel to Florida on work, I left the kids with my mom, and Bailey called me for help: 'Grandma's forcing me to make her bed!'" Sharon answered, "I'm really sorry, Bailey; make her bed."

With the proud memory of an affluent Southern white girlhood, her mother took a dim view of the federal government. She'd trained as a social worker, volunteered in a women's prison, and remembered its inmates in her daily prayer. A devoted Christian, Sharon's mother believed in a generous church. But government benefits were a very different story. Taking them meant you'd fallen and weren't proudly trying to rise back up.

As we pulled up to her home, Sharon reflected on various theories her mother had. "Have you heard of the Illuminati? The New World Order?" Sharon asked so as to prepare me. "I'm tea party," Sharon said, "but I don't go along with a lot that my mom does." Whether they clung to such dark notions or laughed them off, tea party enthusiasts lived in a roaring rumor-sphere that offered answers to deep, abiding anxieties. Why did President Obama take off his wristwatch during Ramadan? Why did Walmart run out of ammunition on the third Tuesday in March? Did you know drones can detect how much money you have? Many described these as suspicions other people held. Many seemed to float in a zone of half-belief.

The most widespread of these suspicions, of course—shared by 66 percent of Trump supporters—is that Obama is Muslim.

What the people I interviewed were drawn to was not necessarily the particulars of these theories. It was the deep story underlying them—an account of life *as it feels* to them. Some such account underlies all beliefs, right or left, I think. The deep story of the right goes like this:

> *You are patiently standing in the middle of a long line stretching toward the horizon, where the American Dream awaits. But as you wait, you see people cutting in line ahead of you. Many of these line-cutters are black—beneficiaries of affirmative action or welfare. Some are career-driven women pushing into jobs they never had before. Then you see immigrants, Mexicans, Somalis, the Syrian refugees yet to come. As you wait in this unmoving line, you're being asked to feel sorry for them all. You have a good heart. But who is deciding who you should feel compassion for? Then you see President Barack Hussein Obama waving the line-cutters forward. He's on their side. In fact, isn't he a line-cutter too? How did this fatherless black guy pay for Harvard? As you wait your turn, Obama is using the money in your pocket to help the line-cutters. He and his liberal backers have removed the shame from taking. The government has become an instrument for redistributing your money to the undeserving. It's not your government anymore; it's theirs.*

I checked this distillation with those I interviewed to see if this version of the deep story rang true. Some altered it a bit ("the line-waiters form a new line") or emphasized a particular point (those in back are *paying* for the line-cutters). But all of them agreed it was their story. One man said, "I live your analogy." Another said, "You read my mind."

The deep story reflects pain; you've done everything right and you're still slipping back. It focuses blame on an ill-intentioned government. And it points to rescue: The tea party for some, and Donald Trump for others. But what had happened to make this deep story ring true?

Most of the people I interviewed were middle class—and nationally more than half of all tea party supporters earn at least $50,000, while almost a third earn more than $75,000 a year. Many, however, had been poor as children and felt their rise to have been an uncertain one. As one wife of a well-to-do contractor told me, gesturing around the buck heads hanging above the large stone fireplace in the spacious living room of her Lake Charles home, "We have our American Dream, but we could *lose it all* tomorrow."

Being middle class didn't mean you felt secure, because that class was thinning out as a tiny elite shot up to great wealth and more people fell into a life of broken teeth, unpaid rent, and shame.

Growing up, Sharon had felt the struggle it took for her family to "stand in line" in a tumultuous world. Three years after her father wordlessly left home when she was 17, Sharon married, soon embracing a covenant marriage—one that requires premarital counseling and sets stricter grounds for divorce. But then they did divorce, and Sharon, once the little mother to her own siblings, now found herself a single mother of two—a mom and dad both. She was doing her level best but wondered why the travails of others so often took precedence over families such as her own. Affirmative-action blacks, immigrants, refugees seemed to so routinely receive sympathy and government help. She, too, had sympathy for many, but, as she saw it, a liberal sympathy machine had been set on automatic, disregarding the giving capacity of families like hers.

Or as one tea partier wrote to me: "We're so broke. Where does this food & welfare money come from? How can free stuff (including college, which my 4.2 student needs) even be on the table when the US owes $19,343,541,768,824.00 as of July 1? Is it just me or does it seem like the only thing ANYONE cares about is themselves and their immediate circumstances?"

Pervasive among the people I talked to was a sense of detachment from a distant elite with whom they had ever less contact and less in common. And, as older white Christians, they were acutely aware of their demographic decline. "You can't say 'merry Christmas,' you have to say 'happy holidays,'" one person said. "People aren't clean living anymore. You're considered ignorant if you're for that." An accountant told me, "Other people say, 'You're too hard-nosed about [morals].' Better to be hard-nosed than to be like it is now, so permissive about everything." They also felt disrespected for holding their values: "You're a weak woman if you don't believe that women should, you know, just elbow your way through society. You're not in the 'in' crowd if you're not a liberal. You're an old-fashioned old fogey, small thinking, small town, gun loving, religious," said a minister's wife. "The media tries to make the tea party look like bigots, homophobic; it's not." They resented all labels "the liberals" had for them, especially "backward" or "ignorant Southerners" or, worse, "rednecks."

Liberal television pundits and bloggers took easy potshots at them, they felt, which hardened their defenses. Their Facebook pages then filled with news coverage of liberals beating up fans at Trump rallies and Fox News coverage of white policemen shot by black men.

For some, age had also become a source of humiliation. One white evangelical tea party supporter in his early 60s had lost a good job as a sales manager with a telecommunications company when it merged with another. He took the shock bravely. But when he tried to get rehired, it was terrible. "I called, emailed, called, emailed. I didn't hear a thing. That was totally an age discrimination thing." At last he found a job at $10 an hour, the same wage he had earned at a summer factory union job as a college student 40 years ago. Age brought no dignity. Nor had the privilege linked to being white and male trickled down to him. Like Sharon's clients in the petrochemical plants, he felt like a stranger in his own land.

But among those walking in this wilderness, Trump had opened up a divide. Those more in the middle class, such as Sharon, wanted to halt the "line-cutters" by slashing government giveaways. Those in the working class, such as her Aflac clients, were drawn to the idea of hanging onto government services but limiting access to them.

Sharon was a giving person, but she wanted to roll back government help. It was hard supporting her kids and being a good mom too. Managing the trailer park had called on her grit, determination, even hardness—which she regretted. She mused, "Having to cope, run the trailer court, even threaten to shoot a dog"—her tenant's pet had endangered children—"it's hardened me, made me act like a man. I hate that. It's not really *me*." There was a price for doing the right and necessary thing, invisible, she felt, to many liberals.

And with all the changes, the one thing America needed, she felt, was a steady set of values that rewarded the good and punished the bad. Sharon honored the act of giving when it came from the private sector. "A businessperson gives other people *jobs*," she explained. She was proud to have employed two people at the trailer park, and sad she'd had to let them go. "I promised, 'The whole month of October you're going to get paid because you're out looking for another job.' That's a whole month. I feel an obligation." If you rose up in business, you took others with you, and this would be a point of pride. There was nothing wrong with *having*; if you had, you gave. But if you took—if you took from the government—you should be ashamed.

It was the same principle evident across the conservative movement, the one Mitt Romney had hewed to when he disparaged 47 percent of Americans as people who "pay no income tax" and "believe that they are victims," or when Romney's running mate, Paul Ryan, spoke of "makers and takers." The rich deserve honor as makers and givers and should be rewarded with the proud fruits of their earnings, on which taxes should be drastically cut. Such cuts would require an end to many government benefits that were supporting the likes of Sharon's trailer park renters. For her, the deep story ended there, with welfare cuts.

But for the blue-collar workers in the plants she visited, the guys who *loved Donald Trump*, it did not. When Sharon and I last had dinner in March, shortly after Trump's 757 jet swooped into New Orleans for his boisterous rally ahead of his big win in the Louisiana primary, Sharon told me about conversations with her Aflac clients that had shocked her. "They were talking about getting benefits from the government as if it were a *good* thing—*even the white guys.*"

Sharon was leery of Trump and tried to puzzle out his appeal for them. "For the first few weeks I was very intrigued. I was like, 'What is this guy talking about? He's a jerk, but I like some of what he says.' But when you really start listening, no!" What troubled her most was that Trump was not a real conservative, that he was for big government. "Is he going to be a dictator? My gut tells me yes, he's an egomaniac. I don't care if you're Ronald Reagan, I don't want a dictator. That's not America." So, I asked, what did her clients see in Trump? "They see him as very strong. A blue-collar billionaire. Honest and refreshing, not having to be politically correct. They want someone that's macho, that can chew tobacco and shoot the guns—that type of manly man."

But something else seemed at play. Many blue-collar white men now face the same grim economic fate long endured by blacks. With jobs lost to automation or offshored to China, they have less security, lower wages, reduced benefits, more erratic work, and fewer jobs with full-time hours than before. Having been recruited to cheer on the contraction of government benefits and services—a trend that is particularly pronounced in Louisiana—many are unable to make ends meet without them. In *Coming Apart: The State of White America*, conservative political scientist Charles Murray traces the fate of working-age whites between 1960 and 2010. He compares the top 20 percent of them—those who have at least a bachelor's degree and are employed as managers or professionals—with the bottom 30 percent, those who never graduated from college and are employed in blue-collar or low-level white-collar jobs. In 1960, the personal lives of the two groups were quite similar. Most were married and stayed married, went to church, worked full time (if they were men), joined community groups, and lived with their children.

A half-century later, the 2010 top looked much like their counterparts in 1960. But for the bottom 30 percent, family life had drastically changed. While more than 90 percent of children of blue-collar families lived with both parents in 1960, by 2010, 22 percent did not. Lower-class whites were also less likely to attend church, trust their neighbors, or say they were happy. White men worked shorter hours, and those who were unemployed tended to pass up the low-wage jobs available to them. Another study found that in 2005, men with low levels of education did two things substantially more than both their counterparts in 1985 and their better-educated contemporaries: They slept longer and watched more television.

How can we understand this growing gap between male lives at the top and bottom? For Murray, the answer is a loss of moral values. But is sleeping longer and watching television a loss of morals, or a loss of morale? A recent study shows a steep rise in deaths of middle-aged working-class whites— much of it due to drug and alcohol abuse and suicide. These are not signs of abandoned values, but of lost hope. Many are in mourning and see rescue in the phrase "Great Again."

Trump's pronouncements have been vague and shifting, but it is striking that he has not called for cuts to Medicaid, or food stamps, or school lunch programs, and that his daughter Ivanka nods to the plight of working moms. He plans to replace Obamacare, he says, with a hazy new program that will be "terrific" and that some pundits playfully dub "Trumpcare." For the blue-collar white male Republicans Sharon spoke to, and some whom I met, this change was welcome.

Still, it was a difficult thing to reconcile. How wary should a little-bit-higher-up-the-ladder white person now feel about applying for the same benefits that the little-bit-lower-down-the-ladder people had? Shaming the "takers" below had been a precious mark of higher status. What if, as a vulnerable blue-collar white worker, one were now to become a "taker" oneself?

Trump, the King of Shame, has covertly come to the rescue. He has shamed virtually every line-cutting group in the Deep Story—women, people of color, the disabled, immigrants, refugees. But he's hardly uttered a single bad word about unemployment insurance, food stamps, or Medicaid, or what the tea party calls "big government handouts," for anyone—including blue-collar white men.

In this feint, Trump solves a white male problem of pride. Benefits? If you need them, okay. He masculinizes it. You can be "high energy" macho—and yet may need to apply for a government benefit. As one auto mechanic told me, "Why not? Trump's for that. If you use food stamps because you're working a low-wage job, you don't want someone looking down their nose at you." A lady at an after-church lunch said, "If you have a young dad who's working full time but can't make it, if you're an American-born worker, can't make it, and not having a slew of kids, okay. For any conservative, that is fine."

But in another stroke, Trump adds a key proviso: restrict government help to real Americans. White men are counted in, but undocumented Mexicans and Muslims and Syrian refugees are out. Thus, Trump offers the blue-collar white men relief from a taker's shame: If you make America great again, how can you not be proud? Trump has put on his blue-collar cap, pumped his fist in the air, and left mainstream Republicans helpless. Not only does he speak to the white working class' grievances; as they see it, he has finally stopped their story from being politically suppressed. We may never know if Trump has done this intentionally or instinctively, but in any case he's created a movement much like the anti-immigrant but pro-welfare-state right-wing populism on the rise in Europe. For these are all based on variations of the same Deep Story of personal protectionism.

During my last dinner with Sharon, over gumbo at the Pujo Street Café in Lake Charles, our talk turned to motherhood. Sharon wanted to give Bailey and Alyson the childhood she never had. She wanted to expose them to the wider world, and to other ways of thinking. "When I was a kid, the only place I'd ever been, outside of Louisiana, was Dallas," she mused. "I want my kids to see the whole world." She'd taken them on an American-history tour through Boston, Philadelphia, New York, and Washington, DC, where nine years ago she'd lunched with Laura Bush. She'd taken them to Iceland, which "they loved," and she'd just scored three round-trip tickets for a surprise tour of Finland, Sweden, and Russia.

But Sharon's gift to her children of a wider world carried risks. Her thoughtful 17-year-old, Bailey, had been watching Bernie Sanders decry the growing gap between rich and poor, push for responsive government, and propose free college tuition for all. "Bailey likes Sanders!" Sharon whispered across the table, eyebrows raised. Sanders had different ideas about good government and about shame, pride, and goodness. Bailey was rethinking these values himself. "He can't stand Trump," Sharon mused, "but we've found common ground. We both agree we should stop criminalizing marijuana and stop being the world's policeman, though we completely disagree on men using women's bathrooms." The great political divide in America had come to Sharon's kitchen table. She and Bailey were earnestly, bravely, searchingly hashing it out, with young Alyson eagerly listening in. Meanwhile, this tea party mom of a Sanders-loving son was reluctantly gearing up to vote for Donald Trump.

22

The Body and Bathing: Help with Personal Care at Home

JULIA TWIGG

The sociology of the body is a fascinating area of inquiry, whether focused on notions of beauty, fitness, health, or infirmity. The body is a significant object of social meaning and personal identity. In this essay, set in England where bathing is more often preferred to showering, the challenges of being an elderly adult in need of assistance in the bath is explored with considerable sociological imagination. Young, healthy medical professionals can project a sense of superiority when looking upon the infirm elderly. How can an older person, then, maintain a dignified sense of self in such a situation?

To write about the body is to write about the mundane and the everyday, for that is what the body is: something that is with us always and everywhere—both our constant companion and our essence. Nothing could be more mundane or day to day than the processes of body care. These actions punctuate our daily lives in the forms of dressing, shaving, showering, combing, washing, eating, drinking, excreting, and sleeping, providing us with a rhythm and pattern to the day. The bodily rhythms provide a basic experiential security in daily life. We are, however, mostly acculturated to ignore these patterns, at least at the level of polite speech. The processes of body care are assumed to be both too private and too trivial for comment, certainly too trivial for traditional academic analysis. They belong with those other aspects of bodily life that we are socialized to pass over in silence. Though such bodily processes form the bedrock of daily life, they are bedrocks assumed, rather than reflected on. So long as they are there, functioning correctly, we have no need to comment.

But for many older people this easeful state of bodily ignorance and transcendence is no longer available. Their bodies force themselves into the front of their thoughts, posing a mass of practical problems. The body assumes new prominence by virtue of its inability to do things. Among those things can be the tasks of body care such as washing, showering, and bathing. This chapter explores what happens when older people can no longer cope with these aspects of life but need assistance in doing them. In particular, it focuses on the situation of older people living at home receiving help with personal care, typically washing and bathing.

While a discussion of the everyday activities of washing and bathing is, by definition, concerned with micro-processes, these actions are not outside wider discursive concerns. Bathing is located in a wider set of discourses than the simple discussion of hygiene that tends to permeate accounts in the area. In this chapter, I will explore how far the provision of help does indeed draw on these wider discourses and how far it remains located in a narrower set of pre-occupations. Help with bathing also entails negotiating the management of the body; it involves touch and nakedness and at times verges on the taboo. I will explore how older people feel about this, and who they prefer to help them in these areas. Before doing so, however, I will discuss briefly the paradoxical neglect of the subject of the body in relation to the support of older people.

THE NEGLECTED BODY OF SOCIAL CARE

Though body care lies at the heart of service provision, this has not been empha-sized in accounts of the sector. There are three primary reasons for this: The first derives from a concern within gerontology to resist the dominant dis-courses of medicine and popular accounts of aging that present it in terms of inevitable bodily decline. The excessive focus on the body is seen as damaging—endorsing ageist stereotypes in which older people are reduced to their aging and sick bodies, which visibly mark them as old. Progressive gerontology by contrast aims to present a more rounded account of age: one that gives due weight to social rather than just bodily elements in the structuring of its expe-riences. The "political economy" approach, in particular, that has dominated social gerontology in Britain and North America since the 1980s, emphasizes the degree to which old age is the product of social structural factors such as retirement age, pension provision, and ageist assumptions (Phillipson and Walker 1986; Estes and Binney 1989; Arber and Ginn 1991). From this perspec-tive, factors like the differential access to resources or social exclusion primar-ily determine the social experience of old age not bodily decline. Close, analytic attention to the body from this perspective is thus regarded as a step backwards.

The second reason for the neglect of the body derives from the way in which the field of community care has traditionally been conceptualized within the debate on aging. "Community care" is the term commonly used in Britain and elsewhere for the support of older and disabled people enabling them to live in the community, typically in their own homes, and it is the principal policy objective in most advanced industrial societies.

Community care is not, however, predominantly conceptualized in terms of the body. Partly this is because the dominant professional group in the field is social work, which concentrates on questions of interpersonal and social func-tioning and whose remit tends to stop short of the body. This territory is tra-ditionally handed over to the care of medicine. As a result, though community care is inherently about the body and its day-to-day problems, this fact is not emphasized in accounts of the sector. The evasion is further compounded by the increasing influence of managerialism in the sector. Managerial discourse, constructed as it is out of the disciplines of economics, business studies, organization, and methods, embodies an abstract and distancing form of theorizing that is far from the messy, dirty realities of bodily life. When community care is discussed, it is done so in a manner that largely dismisses the body, rendering it invisible as a site of concern.

The third reason for neglect comes from work on the body itself. Since the 1980s there has been an explosion of writing in this area (Williams and Bendelow 1998), but its focus has been on younger, sexier, more transgressive bodies. The roots of much of this literature in feminism, queer theory, and cultural studies have not encouraged it to venture into the territory of old age. Indeed, these approaches have displayed a significant degree of ageism in their assumptions about what is interesting and important. More recently, however, new work has begun to address bodily issues in relation to later years (Öberg 1996; Tulle-Winton 2000; Gilleard and Higgs 2000). Some of the best of this work has—belatedly—come out of feminism (Woodward 1991, 1999; Andrews 1999; Furman 1997, 1999). It has been marked by a sense of agency and a desire to emphasize the subjective, meaning-making experiences of people as they engage in the aging process. Often these ideas are linked to concepts of the Third Age.

The Third Age represents a postretirement period of extended middle age in which people who are no longer confined by the labor market and are free from direct responsibility for children can pursue leisure interests, develop aspects of their personalities, and enjoy the fruits of later life. The emergence of this new social space is often linked to theories about identity and selfhood in postmodernity, particularly ones that emphasize self-fashioning. It is open, however, to the familiar critique that such optimistic accounts of the Third Age are only possible by virtue of projecting the negative aspects of aging into a dark Fourth Age, a period of declining health and social loss, sometimes also termed "deep" old age. As Gilliard and Higgs (2000) note, accounts of the Third Age emphasize agency and subjectivity and are described from the perspective of the optimistic self. But accounts of the Fourth Age focus on dependency and are written from the outside. A macro-level perspective dominates this literature. In such accounts, older persons are rarely seen as agents at all but are often presented as the "other."

Physical decline is frequently presented as marking the point of transition between the Third and Fourth ages, and receiving personal care of a close and intimate kind is a key marker in this transition. In this chapter we focus on just such a personal care situation. In doing so I am thus attempting to extend the analysis in terms of the body to a group who until recently has been excluded from such a perspective. The literature on the body and aging that has emerged of late has tended to focus on the earlier optimistic stage of the Third Age, exploring the ways in which people negotiate issues of bodily aging as they make the transitions from middle to later life. . . .

PERSONAL CARE AS A SOCIAL MARKER

Why is personal care such a marker of social states? The reason lies in the profound social symbolism that relates to the body and its management. This means that receiving help in these areas erodes the personhood and adult status of the subject. Personal care means being helped with precisely those tasks that as adults we do for ourselves: getting washed and dressed, moving, eating, and excreting. However rich we are, these are things that—at least in the modern West—we do for ourselves, typically alone or in the company of intimates. Body care of this type thus marks the boundary of the truly personal and individual in modern life. Having to be helped in these areas transgresses this boundary and undermines adulthood. Only babies and children are helped in this way, and this underwrites the profoundly infantalizing tendencies of "care."

* * *

Personal care also involves nakedness. Nakedness is not, largely, part of ordinary social interaction. It is a special state reserved for certain situations and relationships, and it is a marker of close, typically sexual, intimacy. To be naked in a social situation, as recipients of personal care are, is therefore to be put in a disjunctive context. It is made all the more so by the fact that the nakedness is asymmetrical: the recipient is naked, while the helper is fully clothed. To be naked in this way is to be exposed and vulnerable, and it inevitably creates a power dynamic in which the helper, usually younger and stronger, is clearly the dominant party.

Personal Care and Bathing

Personal care has become an increasingly significant issue for social care agencies across the Western world as a result of widespread social and political policies aimed at supporting frail elders living at home. Home care in Britain and elsewhere is no longer primarily a matter of housework and shopping, but of personal care, in which washing and bathing form an important aspect. Historically, in Britain such help was primarily provided by the community nursing service but is now largely provided within a home care system. This same shift in home care can be detected in other Western welfare systems.

The principal driver behind it has been cost reduction, with the desire to move the provision of home care away from the relatively expensive health care sector where staff are trained and where the provision of personal care is often free to the recipient, into the less expensive social care sector where staff are typically untrained and where recipients are often required to fund their care. The shift has, however, also arisen from concerns about the over-medicalization of older people's lives. Home care services are seen as embodying a potentially more sympathetic and caring approach than that of medically directed ones.

This chapter draws on a study of help with washing and bathing provided to older and disabled people living at home in Britain (Twigg 2000a). The study was based on interviews with recipients, caregivers, and managers. In the research, elders received help with bathing from a variety of sources: the local authority home care service; voluntary sector or for profit agencies; or a specialist voluntary sector bathing service (the last is unusual in Britain). Depending on their income, users either received such help free or were expected to meet some or all of the costs.

The Meanings of Bathing

Within public welfare services, washing and bathing tend to be presented narrowly in terms of a discourse of hygiene and cleanliness. The broader meanings of bathing in terms of luxury, pleasure, and well-being are not emphasized. There are a number of reasons for this: Partly it arises from a narrow concern with health and physical functioning, which is regarded as a particularly legitimate aim for such interventions. Bathing in this context is presented as a concern for hygiene; though in reality, dirtiness has to be extreme before health is genuinely threatened. Partly it comes from long-established political pressures to ensure that the remit of public welfare remains limited in scope and extent; and this is linked to a related puritanism that regards ideas of bodily pleasure in connection with public provision as—at the very least—discordant. . . .

But bathing has much broader meanings. While there is certainly not space here to explore the history of washing and bathing and of the various practices and discourses that have led to its construction (see Twigg 2000a for such a discussion), I will, however, refer briefly here to four recurring strands in that history to suggest some of the ways in which bathing is located in a wider set of discourses than just those of hygiene.

Historically, bathing has long been connected with luxury, pleasure, and to some degree, eroticism. For the Romans, bathing was a social activity associated with relaxation, exercise, conviviality, and pleasure (Yegül 1992). During the Middle Ages it was recurringly presented in connection with images of feasting and courtship (Vigarello 1988). These meanings narrowed by the nineteenth century, when bathing lost its social dimension and became a more private affair, more closely connected with the tasks of getting clean, though the sense of luxury and pleasure that derived from abundant hot water remains (Wilkie 1986; Bushman and Bushman 1988). During the twentieth century, luxurious bathrooms, whether presented in the celebratory imagery of Hollywood or the dreams of real estate promoters, continued to draw on this discourse of pleasure and luxury and only barely suppressed eroticism (Kira 1967).

Bathing is also located in a wider discourse of well-being. Again, this has been so since Roman times, when baths were seen as part of a general regimen of health and well-being. Baths have also been prominent in the alternative medical tradition from hydrotherapy to nature cure, and they remain a central element in the recent revival of spa culture, often in association with diffuse concepts of "Eastern" medicine, which has become a feature of modern Western lifestyles or at least aspirations. Spa treatments are presented as an antidote to stress and other ills of modern living. Through all of this, well-being is the key concept; and the focus is on the experiential body, not the medical body.

The third theme concerns the frequent use of baths and water as markers of social transitions. This is clearest in relation to classic rites of passage, such as Christian baptism, but it also operates in secular contexts like prisons, schools, and hospitals, where people are commonly compelled to have a bath as part of the initiation into the institution, marking their transition from the status of a citizen outside to that of an inmate inside. Individuals also draw on such symbolism in their daily lives, clearly marking out the transitions of the day or week through bodily practices such as bathing and showering. The bedrock of body care punctuates the day, providing a framework of time and of social states in terms of eating and drinking, washing and dressing, and sleeping and rising. No small part of our sense of ontological security is derived from these practices.

Last, bathing also contains darker themes. Baths have been widely used as part of coercive cultures, particularly within institutions. For example, cold plunges, sudden showers, and shockingly cold water have all been used as part of the history of the treatment of the insane. Though the justification for such techniques has often been in terms of shocking the patient back into reason, a clearly coercive, even sadistic, element is also often intensified by the use of machinery or the enforcement of humiliating bodily postures. . . .

THE ADAPTABILITY OF THE OLD

Before exploring what people feel about receiving help, it is worth reflecting briefly on the adaptability of the old. Accounts of older people often present them as inflexible and unable to cope with change. In fact, the changes imposed on people in their later lives are enormous. No amount of jet travel, adaptation to new information technology systems, or learning to appreciate new music can remotely compare with the changes that older people have to learn to become accustomed to on a day-to-day basis. The aged may lose their lifetime companion; may have to move to a new home, town, or region; and may have to learn to live in an institution among random strangers in a collective way that is wholly at odds with their earlier lives and under the auspices of a staff whose background and worldview may be completely alien to them.

In all of this, bodily experiences can be among the most significant: not being able to move freely, to speak clearly, or to manage your bodily functions present major changes in life. Having to receive help with personal care, in particular, breaches some of the most profound of social expectations, requiring people to cope with new situations and new relationships. As we shall see, some of the respondents expressed dismay at what they had to face, but it is testimony to their adaptability that they did indeed manage to cope. The majority approached old age with stoicism, concentrating on the day and trying to make the best of it. Some developed ingenious and innovative ways to circumvent their physical difficulties.

WHAT DOES BATHING MEAN IN THIS CONTEXT?

Within the British tradition, the predominant ways of getting clean have been baths, in the sense of bathtubs, and washing at a basin. This is in contrast to Continental and American traditions where showering established itself much earlier as the main alternative to strip washing at a basin. Showering is now common among younger people in Britain, but is still largely unfamiliar or disliked among this older age group. Few people in the study had showers in their homes. In the context of drafty houses and feeble flows of hot water, showers do not warm the body in the way that hot baths do. One or two respondents of Continental origin did prefer showers, sharing the mainland European view that baths are not an adequate way to clean oneself.

People varied in how important baths were to them. Some respondents had never been great bathers and relied instead on a strip wash. For others, a daily bath was a long-established habit and one that they greatly missed. As Mrs. Fitzgerald (all respondents' names have been changed) explained, she loved bathing and continues to see it as a vital part of the day: "All my life, up in a morning, throw open the bed, into the bathroom—that's the way I lived. . . . It's always been terribly important to me. And that's when I got panic-stricken when I thought I wasn't going to be able to have any baths."

The care people actually received from the bathing service was not always in line with their hopes. Some individuals did indeed have a "proper bath," in the sense of being placed directly under the water, with all the warmth and buoyancy that this could bring. But for many, "bathing" really meant sitting on a board over the bath while the caregiver helped them to wash and poured warm water over their bodies. This was enjoyable, but it was not a proper bath, and many regretted this. Mrs. Kennelly, whose severe Parkinson's meant that she could no longer have a bath, remembered the experience with a sense of nostalgia, "I'd love to be able to get in the bath. Just lay there and splash it over . . . wallow in it. Lovely." Mrs. Bridgeman tells of how wonderful it would be to just once receive a proper bath, "I *long* to get my bum in the water. It would be bliss you know."

The problem was that many recipients did not have sufficient flexibility to get down into the tub or the strength to get up, and very few homes had the kind of expensive equipment that would allow for this. Workers were forbidden by Health and Safety legislation from lifting the clients out of the bath (though sometimes they still performed the task). This meant that many had more in the way of an assisted wash than a bath. By and large, recipients were resigned to these limitations and grateful for what assistance they received, but problems did occasionally arise, particularly if clients rebelled and attempted to preempt the situation by sitting down fully in the bath. In these cases, the caregivers were instructed to tell the person that they would not help them up, but would instead ring for an ambulance. The potential humiliation of this was sufficient to keep most clients in line.

The Experience of Bathing

For some individuals, bathing did remain a pleasurable, even luxurious, experience. Mrs. Fitzgerald, who had most feared the loss, now saw the coming of the bathing service as "the rose of [her] week." Mrs. Napier also relished the experience as something that brings back pleasurable memories of the past, explaining how "we have nice foamy shower gel. . . . It's lovely, like being a baby again." Baths were also a source of pleasure because of the number of aches and pains that many older people suffer from. The warmth and buoyancy of the water restored lightness to limbs that had become heavy, giving back something of the easy, youthful, bodily experience of the past.

Baths also retained their capacity to wash away more than just dirt. For some, they had always been both a source of renewal and a marker of social transitions. As Miss Garfield explained, baths are "part of, sort of washing the day away and all the bothers and troubles, and you're there and it's all very comfortable and nice." But the experience of bathing was inevitably strongly affected by the presence of the caregiver in the room. For most people, bathing is a private affair, a time apart, when individuals can attend to themselves and not worry about others. But the presence of the worker changes that to some degree, disturbing the ease. Their presence in the room inevitably refocuses the event on tasks to be accomplished, rather than a state to be experienced; recipients were no longer free to control the timing of the event as they had been in the past. Workers needed to get the job done, and this sometimes meant that time was now of the essence, not pleasure. This acted to limit the nature of the experience, removing luxury, and centering it instead on cleaning of the client.

Having a worker in the room also removed much of the spontaneity of bathing; it was no longer possible to draw a bath when you simply felt like it. With this also went much of the capacity of baths to act as personal rites of passage or markers of social transitions. Body care still marked out the rhythm of people's days, in the sense of dressing, washing, and eating, but baths now had to be taken at the times they were scheduled; this could mean otherwise "meaningless" times, such as eleven-thirty in the morning, that disrupted rather than underwrote social patterns. For some people this was less disruptive than expected. This was because those who received such bathing assistance were often among the most frail and dependent, people who rarely if ever left the house. For them, the world of conventional timings had become less significant. To quite an extent, they had reordered the pattern of their lives *around* the provision of care. Care-giving had come to operate as a social structure in itself.

The Gaze of Youth

Much of the recent work in gerontology has emphasized the ways in which we are aged by culture—by the meanings that are ascribed to bodily aging, rather than the aging process itself. Gullette (1997) has described the subtle and omnipresent means by which such meanings are conveyed. We inhale this atmosphere daily, imbuing doses of its toxicity wafting from cartoons, billboards, birthday cards, coffee mugs, newspaper articles, fiction, and poetry: "The system is busy at whatever level of literacy or orality or visual impressionability the acculturated subject is comfortable with." Consumer culture, with its emphasis on youth, is particularly saturated with such messages (Featherstone 1991; Gilleard and Higgs 2000).

The dominant theme in all of this work is that old age is constructed as a negative entity and the bodily process of aging is seen in the same light. Aging represents a form of Otherness, on to which culture projects its fear and denial. As Woodward (1991) argues, our cultural categories here are essentially reducible to two, youth and age, set in a hierarchical arrangement. We are not judged by how old we are, but by how young we are not. Aging is a falling away, a failure to be young. Like disabled people, the old are evaluated as "less than." The bodily realities of aging thus create a version of Erving Goffman's spoilt identity, something that people are, at some level, ashamed of and marked in terms of.

We are accustomed to the idea of the medical gaze in the context of professional power, or the phallic gaze in the context of gender relations, but there is also a gaze of youth. It, too, is an exercise of power in which the "other"—in this case older people—are constituted under its searching eye. Nowhere is the gaze of youth more evident than in relation to bathing care. Here the bodies of older people are directly subject to the gaze of younger workers. From the workers' perspective, this sometimes presents them with a shock. Modern culture, though saturated with visual images of young perfect bodies, rarely permits old imperfect ones to be on display. As a result, the way in which the body looks in old age was something that the younger workers were unprepared for. As one worker explained, seeing old people naked was "weird, and I just had to stop myself staring at people, because I hadn't really seen . . . because you don't really see people naked."

At times this element of gaze was itself part of the professional task. Nurses who do bathing work often comment how the activity is useful in assessing the general state of the older person, in terms not only of illness and physical condition but also in a more extensive way. To be bathed is indeed to be made subject to—very directly subject to—the professional gaze. It is indeed a kind of developed, intimate surveillance.

So how did older people feel about this? It was certainly the case that many respondents appeared to have internalized the wider cultural denigration of the bodies of the old. They constituted their own bodies under the gaze of youth, presenting them as something that it might be unattractive, even distasteful, for people to see or handle. As Mrs. Fitzgerald once remarked of the caregiver, "They're so young and beautiful, it must be awful for them to have to handle old, awkward bodies." At the same time, she added that "they're wonderful people. . . . I must say, I mean they must have something inside them because—it's not the sort of thing—I don't know when I was young whether I would have wanted to have looked after old people." For some, the contrast between their aging bodies and the youthful flesh of the workers was painful to see and experience:

> MRS. KENNELLY: I say to them, "I feel sorry for you, getting up in the morning and this is the kind of job you've got to do." You know, not very nice. . . . This young girl, Amanda it was, came in—twenty-eight, beautiful girl. She's very pretty. And there's the ugly lump. Oh dear!

To be caught within the youthful gaze was disturbing, and many of the elders had turned its corrosive force back on themselves, in turn disciplining their own bodies in the course of assistive practice.

* * *

Parts of the Body

The body is a landscape onto which meanings are inscribed. These are not, however, evenly distributed over the body, and certain parts come to be more heavily freighted with significance than other bodily parts. In general, there is a familiar privacy gradient whereby certain parts of the body are deemed more personal and private. Access to them by sight or touch is socially circumscribed and varies according to relationship and situation. . . . Areas of the body such as the upper arms and back are relatively neutral and can be touched by a range of people. Knees and thighs are less so. Breasts and genitals are in general off-limits in all but erotic relations. Touch is also a vector of status and authority with the powerful accorded more leeway to touch than the less powerful. There is a gender dimension, with women more likely to receive touch than men. Within a service provision context, women are more likely to interpret touch from a service provider in a positive way, while men are more inclined to see it negatively, interpreting it as a marker of inferiority and dependency. In addition, men are also more likely to see touch as sexual.

These sensitivities affect the experience of bathing. Receiving hands-on help with soaping, rinsing, and washing is more tolerable in relation to some parts of the body than to others. Arms, legs, feet, and hair are all fine. Matters become more sensitive, however, in relation to what is often termed "down below": the genital and anal areas. In practice nearly everyone in the study could manage to wash these parts themselves, at least with some indirect assistance, and a number of respondents expressed relief that they were able to do so. Having to be washed in these areas was seen as humiliating and embarrassing, yet another twist in the spiral of dependency. Maintaining one's independence in relation to these intimate areas was an important part of self-esteem. Caregivers were also reluctant to involve themselves with these parts of the body, which they, too, regarded with a certain amount of ambivalence. In general, bathing was practically managed in such a way as to limit direct contact in relation to more sensitive bodily parts.

* * *

There was one part of the body that was recurringly mentioned in the interviews by both recipients and workers: this was the back. In the context of bathing and the ambivalent intimacies it creates, the back has a special meaning, coming to stand for the body in general, or at least for an acceptable version of the body, one that has a certain neutrality about it. In the interviews, the back was the only part of the body that was spontaneously named by recipients, and they sometimes talked about the process of bathing as if it were confined to the process of washing the back. The back was also the one part of the body where pleasure in touch was openly acknowledged.

A number of recipients described how much they enjoyed having their backs scrubbed. Expressing pleasure in this form of touching was acceptable. Caregivers agreed with this account. One in particular commented that "they do enjoy it, that you know, a lot of people really, 'Oooh,' you know, 'give my back a good rub.'" In general, expressing pleasure in touch was something that recipients were reluctant to do. It seemed to suggest in their eyes something that was not quite right, an ambivalent element that did not belong in this context of relative strangers and of public provision. Presenting bathing in terms of scrubbing the back was one means of deflecting an otherwise disturbing intimacy onto a relatively neutral and public part of the body.

The back is also significant in the bath encounter in that it is the part of the body that is both offered to the gaze of the worker and also used to shelter more private and sensitive parts. It stands in for the public presentation of the body in the context of an otherwise discordant intimacy. The back also offers a safe setting for the expression of affection and closeness. Putting an arm across the back while giving the recipient a hug fits in easily with the way bathing disposes the body, while at the same time providing a relatively neutral form of physical contact. Touch could thus be used to express closeness, but in a manner that does not transgress social codes.

Bounded Relationships and Access to the Body

Bathing makes for a strange relationship: in one sense intimate and close, involving physical contact, nakedness, and access to the private dimensions of life; yet in another, it is a meeting of strangers in which the worker is paid to do a job and may never have met the recipient before. The intimacy, moreover, occurs in a context that is forced. It arises from disability, not choice. The closeness is imposed, not sought. As a result there is an inherent discordance in the relationship. It is transgressive of normal social codes, and effort is needed on both sides to define the character of the relationship and to put limits on the nature of its intimacy.

How the relationship was experienced was clearly affected by who the helper was. What were people's preferences in this regard? Did they, for example, prefer to be helped by close relatives? An assumption of this sort is often made, resting on the idea that kinship closeness renders the negotiation of bodily closeness easier. While this can certainly sometimes be so, often it is not. We have evidence from other studies (Parker 1993; Daatland 1990) that suggests that while people may like to receive more neutral forms of help from relatives, personal care is different. In these cases many people prefer the formal service system. The reason is that bodily care threatens the nature of a relationship. In particular it erodes the status of the recipient and with that their identity in the relationship.

What older people fear is that the person that they once were—and in their own eyes still are—will be lost, and that person, by and large, is someone with their clothes on, managing their own bodily functions and relating to their families in a sociable way. We should not thus make any easy assumptions about kinship closeness translating unproblematically into bodily closeness.

Even less do people want friends to perform this activity. It is in the nature of friendship that it rests on equality and reciprocity, and few friendships survive marked change in circumstances when these occur on only one side of a valued relationship. Intimate care represents just such a change. Lawler (1991) notes how nurses experience similar unease if cared for by a friend and colleague. Though recipients wanted the care worker to be "friendly," they were quite clear that this was a different and defined sort of relationship. These were not friends in the full sense of the word. As Mrs. Ostrovski said to me, "Friend is a very big word."

Bath work involves a kind of intimacy, though it is of a different nature from that of kinship or friendship. What recipients want is a bounded intimacy, something that is close, but in a specialized and limited way. For these reasons they preferred someone whom they had got to know in these particular circumstances and where the relationship was defined by them. This is not to say that it was not close, friendly, or based on a kind of trust. In most cases it was all of these, but the relationship was of a special kind, in which bodily closeness played a part but was defined and limited.

At the same time, recipients disliked the experience of having to deal with strangers. Bathing involves both a literal and a psychic unwrapping of the self. Having to participate in this process repeatedly with strangers was exposing and dispiriting. Recipients wanted the ease that comes with familiarity; they did not want constantly to have to readjust to a new person. But agencies could not always be relied on to send the same person, and indeed the constant staff turnover that is characteristic of low-wage sectors in cities like London meant that it was quite difficult for them to do so. Some recipients subverted the problem by refusing to have a bath if an unfamiliar worker was sent, diverting them into other household tasks rather than facing the unwelcome process of self-disclosure. What recipients wanted, therefore, was someone they knew, who was friendly and sensitive and who would offer emotional support, but who understood the limits of the relationship.

* * *

The recipients also made assumptions about gender. This invariably focuses on who was appropriate to do the care work. Responses varied according to whether the person was a man or woman. In general, women-to-women care was regarded as "natural" and unproblematic. Issues arose, however, in relation to cross-gender tending and, to some extent, in relation to same-sex male tending.

What underpinned this asymmetrical pattern were wider assumptions about the meaning and management of the body. Within Western culture, men's and women's bodies have traditionally been treated differently. Women's bodies tend to be regarded with greater circumspection. Access to them, both physical and visual, is more guarded. They are seen as more private, something that is secluded and hidden. Women's bodies are also often presented as more sexual, indeed often coming to represent the principle of sexuality more widely within culture. Women's bodies are also subject to greater control. There is more constraint over what they may do and express. Men's bodies are, by contrast, presented as more public and neutral in character. They tend to embody active principles rather than the passive ones circumscribed on the female body. They desire, rather than are constituted by the desire of others.

These cultural patterns underwrite responses to bathing help. In general women preferred not to have a male worker, and some expressed their feelings very strongly in this regard, "Oh, no. I wouldn't have a man. No thank you!" This was not universal, and some said that they would not mind. But in practice this situation only rarely arose. The majority of workers are female, as are the clients, and this "naturally" delivers a pattern in accord with dominant values. Most agencies also have a policy against men giving personal care to women in their own homes, partly out of respect for client's assumed preferences and partly to avoid accusations of abuse. Running through attitudes toward male care workers was a set of assumptions about the nature of male sexuality as something that is active and potentially predatory. This is in contrast to the assumptions that are made about women. They are presented as passive or asexual in this context, dominated by the values of maternity, not sexuality.

For men, the experience of receiving cross-gender tending was, by its very nature, different. Men are accustomed to being helped by women from childhood onwards, and many saw such assistance in old age as a natural extension of that. Such care contained no sense of threat. Indeed, for many men the idea of being helped by a woman was pleasant. As one manager remarked: "A lot of the men quite enjoy having a woman. And honestly I think, you know, specially a nice young girl come to help them have a bath, they like it. You know, not in any sort of perverted way, just, just in a you know, they like the attention."

As Mr. Lambert said, provided the women were married—that is where women were accustomed to seeing men naked—there was no difficulty in cross-gender tending. Mr. Wagstaff concurred with this sentiment:

> INTERVIEWER: Did you find it embarrassing at first or . . . ?
>
> MR. WAGSTAFFE: Well not really. I thought it might be more embarrassing for *them* than for me, but they don't seem to mind a bit.
>
> INTERVIEWER: Why did you think it would be more embarrassing for them?
>
> MR. WAGSTAFFE: Well, the first girl I had she was only about eighteen I think. She was a sort of punk, she'd got bright red hair and earrings in her eyebrows. Sort of girl that a person of my age looks at and thinks Gawd Almighty. But she was absolutely sweet, she was a lovely girl. It turns out that they nearly all live with their boyfriends or something, so I don't bother about it now. . . . And young ladies in their early twenties these days are rather different from when I was the same age.

For men, therefore, cross-gender tending contains no sense of threat. The issue is one of managing the encounter in such a way as to avoid embarrassment, in which they had some remaining sense of responsibility for not disturbing the innocence of the young. Even in old age, men experience a residual sense of the power of the phallus.

For men being cared for by men, the assumptions were slightly different. In many cases this occurred without comment or problems. But for some men the idea was unwelcome. Men construct other men as sexually predatory in relation to themselves (Connell 1995). Intimate care by a man raises the possibility of a homosexual encounter, a concern reinforced by ideas that caregiver was not proper work for a man at all.

* * *

CONCLUSION

Throughout this chapter, I have argued that bathing and washing exemplify day-to-day and mundane activities of the old. As a result they have received little in the way of academic attention, often considered too practical and too banal to be of interest. But it is in these ordinary and banal patterns that much of the texture and meaning of life exists. The life of the body is the bedrock on which our existence rests. Tending, caring for, managing our bodies, and using and presenting them in a social life are central to our day-to-day experience, though it is not often brought to the front of our consciousness. Until, that is, some disruption in these taken-for-granted activities forces them and the existential life of the body into conscious consideration. Old age is one such source of disruption. Though we are indeed aged by culture as some theorists suggest, we are also aged by our bodies. The body can impose its own constraints, as we have seen concerning the practical difficulties some people experience in relation to personal care. The ways in which personal care is managed, the meanings it contains, and the discourses that encode it significantly affect how these bodily constraints are experienced.

Among the discourses within which personal care is encoded are those relating to bathing. As we have seen, the official account of service provision presents the activity in a narrow, utilitarian way—as the achievement of adequate standards of hygiene. The discourse of social welfare is a constrained one in which the scope of interventions are limited and in which health and hygiene have a privileged status. But as we have seen, baths and bathing are about more than this. They touch on other matters; their meanings are wider and more diffuse, and the experiences they offer more various. Bathing is part of the experiential life of the body and as such is drawn into a variety of discourses and sets of meanings around pleasure, luxury, eroticism, renewal, initiation, and power. Echoes of these wider meanings reverberate through the experience of bathing in the community. Hearing them enables us to set community care in a broader social and cultural context and thus to rescue it from too narrow a policy context. It also allows us to hear something of the voices of some of the most disabled older people, people whose bodily experiences have received little analytic attention in our overarching focus on the body.

REFERENCES

Andrews, M. 1999. The Seductiveness of Agelessness. *Ageing and Society* 19: 301–18.
Arber, S., and J. Ginn. 1991. *Gender and Later Life: A Sociological Analysis of Resources and Constraints.* London: Sage Publications.
Bushman, R. L., and C. L. Bushman. 1988. The Early History of Cleanliness in America. *Journal of American History* 74: 1213–38.
Connell, R. W. 1995. *Masculinities.* Cambridge, U.K.: Polity.
Daatland, S. 1990. What are Families For: On Family Solidarity and Preference for Help. *Ageing and Society* 10: 1–15.
Estes, C. L., and E. A Binney. 1989. Biomedicalization of Aging: Dangers and Dilemmas. *The Gerontologist* 29(5): 587–596.
Featherstone, M. 1991. The Body in Consumer Culture. In *The Body: Social Process and Cultural Theory.* Edited by M. Featherstone, M. Hepworth, and B. S. Turner, 170–96. London: Sage.

Furman, F. K. 1997. *Facing the Mirror: Older Women and Beauty Shop Culture.* New York: Routledge.

———. 1999. There Are No Old Venuses: Older Women's Responses to Their Aging Bodies. In *Mother Time: Women, Aging and Ethics.* Edited by M. U. Walker, 7–22. Boulder, Colo.: Rowman & Littlefield.

Gilleard, C, and P. Higgs. 2000. *Culture of Ageing: Self, Citizen and the Body.* London: Prentice Hall.

Gullette, M. M. 1997. *Declining to Decline: Cultural Combat and the Politics of Midlife.* Charlottesville: University Press of Virginia.

Kira, A. 1967. *The Bathroom: Criteria for Design.* New York: Bantam.

Lawler, J. 1991. *Behind the Screens: Nursing, Somology, and the Problems of the Body.* London: Churchill Livingstone.

Lawler, J. (ed.) 1997. Knowing the Body and Embodiment: Methodologies, Discourses and Nursing. In *The Body in Nursing.* Melbourne, Australia: Churchill Livingstone.

Öberg, P. 1996. The Absent Body: A Social Gerontological Paradox. *Ageing and Society* 16: 701–19.

Parker, G. 1993. *With This Body: Caring and Disability in Marriage.* Buckingham, U.K.: Open University Press.

Phillipson, C, and A. Walker. 1986. *Ageing and Social Policy: A Critical Assessment.* Aldershot, U.K.: Gower.

Tulle-Winton, E. 2000. Old Bodies. In *The Body, Culture and Society.* Edited by P. Hancock, B. Hughes, E. Jagger, K. Patterson, R. Russell, E. Tulle-Winton, and M. Tyler. Buckingham, U.K.: Open University Press.

Twigg, J. 2000a. *Bathing: The Body and Community Care.* London: Routledge.

———. 2000b. Carework as a Form of Bodywork. *Ageing and Society* 20: 389–411.

Vigarello, G. 1988. *Concepts of Cleanliness: Changing Attitudes in France Since the Middle Ages.* Cambridge, U.K.: CUP.

Williams, S. J., and G. Bendelow. 1998. *The Lived Body: Sociological Themes, Embodied Issues.* London: Routledge.

Wilkie, J. S. 1986. Submerged Sensuality: Technology and Perceptions of Bathing. *Journal of Social History* 19: 649–54.

Woodward, K. 1991. *Aging and Its Discontents: Freud and Other Fictions.* Bloomington: Indiana University Press.

Woodward, K. (ed.) 1999. *Figuring Age: Women, Bodies, Generations.* Bloomington: Indiana University Press.

Yegül, F. 1992. *Baths and Bathing in Classical Antiquity.* Cambridge: MIT Press.

23

Optional Ethnicities: For Whites Only?

MARY C. WATERS

Social status—both positive and negative—is often a matter of choice or accomplishment, what sociologists call achieved status. In other cases status is ascribed, based on features associated with the group with which we are identified or associated, like it or not. Sex, age, visible disabilities, and skin color are important ascribed characteristics in American society. Less visible are national origin and ethnicity. Some people choose to be ethnically identified, usually to benefit from a positive personal identity or the celebration of a proud tradition. Others do not choose an ethnic identity, nor does it always confer benefits. For them, ethnicity is not optional. This essay may help some students understand a little better what others are saying about the meaning of being Black or Chicano or Asian or American Indian or another non-optional ethnicity.

ETHNIC IDENTITY FOR WHITES IN THE 1990s

What does it mean to talk about ethnicity as an option for an individual? To argue that an individual has some degree of choice in their ethnic identity flies in the face of the commonsense notion of ethnicity many of us believe in—that one's ethnic identity is a fixed characteristic, reflective of blood ties and given at birth. However, social scientists who study ethnicity have long concluded that while ethnicity is based in a *belief* in a common ancestry, ethnicity is primarily a *social* phenomenon, not a biological one. The belief that members of an ethnic group have that they share a common ancestry may not be a fact. There is a great deal of change in ethnic identities across generations through intermarriage, changing allegiances, and changing social categories. There is also a much larger amount of change in the identities of individuals over their life than is commonly believed. While most people are aware of the phenomenon known as "passing"—people raised as one race who change at some point and claim a different race as their identity—there are similar life course changes in ethnicity that happen all the time and are not given the same degree of attention as "racial passing."

White Americans of European ancestry can be described as having a great deal of choice in terms of their ethnic identities. The two major types of options White Americans can exercise are (1) the option of whether to claim any specific ancestry, or to just be "White" or American, and (2) the choice of which of their European ancestries to choose to include in their description of their own identities. In both cases, the option of choosing how to present yourself on surveys and in everyday social interactions exists for Whites because of social changes and societal conditions that have created a great deal of social mobility, immigrant assimilation, and political and economic power for Whites in the United States. Specifically, the option of being able to not claim any ethnic identity exists for Whites of European background in the United States because they are the majority group—in terms of holding political and social power, as well as being a numerical majority. The option of choosing among different ethnicities in their family backgrounds exists because the degree of discrimination and social distance attached to specific European backgrounds has diminished over time.

The Ethnic Miracle

When European immigration to the United States was sharply curtailed in the late 1920s, a process was set in motion whereby the European ethnic groups already in the United States were for all intents and purposes cut off from any new arrivals. As a result, the composition of the ethnic groups began to age generationally. The proportion of each ethnic group made up of immigrants or the first generation began to gradually decline, and the proportion made up of the children, grandchildren, and eventually greatgrandchildren began to increase. Consequently, by 1990 most European-origin ethnic groups in the United States were composed of a very small number of immigrants, and a very large proportion of people whose link to their ethnic origins in Europe was increasingly remote.

This generational change was accompanied by unprecedented social and economic changes. The very success of the assimilation process these groups experienced makes it difficult to imagine how much the question of the immigrants' eventual assimilation was an open one at the turn of the century. At the peak of immigration from southern and central Europe there was widespread discrimination and hostility against the newcomers by established Americans. Italians, Poles, Greeks, and Jews were called derogatory names, attacked by nativist mobs, and derided in the press. Intermarriage across ethnic lines was very uncommon—castelike in the words of some sociologists (Pagnini and Morgan 1990). The immigrants and their children were residentially segregated, occupationally specialized, and generally poor.

After several generations in the United States, the situation has changed a great deal. The success and social mobility of the grandchildren and greatgrandchildren of that massive wave of immigrants from Europe has been called "The Ethnic Miracle" (Greeley 1976). These Whites have moved away from the inner-city ethnic ghettos to White middle-class suburban homes. They are doctors, lawyers, entertainers, academics, governors, and Supreme Court justices. But contrary to what some social science theorists and some politicians predicted or hoped for, these middle-class Americans have not completely given up ethnic identity. Instead, they have maintained some connection with their immigrant ancestors' identities—becoming Irish American doctors, Italian American Supreme Court justices, and Greek American presidential candidates. In the tradition of cultural pluralism, successful middle-class Americans in the late twentieth century maintain some degree of identity with their ethnic backgrounds. They have remained "hyphenated Americans." So while social mobility and declining discrimination have created the option of not identifying with any European ancestry, most White Americans continue to report some ethnic background.

* * *

Symbolic Ethnicities for White Americans

What do these ethnic identities mean to people and why do they cling to them rather than just abandoning the tie and calling themselves American? My own field research with suburban Whites in California and Pennsylvania found that later-generation descendants of European origin maintain what are called "symbolic ethnicities." Symbolic ethnicity is a term coined by Herbert Gans (1979) to refer to ethnicity that is individualistic in nature and without real social cost for the individual. These symbolic identifications are essentially leisure time activities, rooted in nuclear family traditions and reinforced by the voluntary enjoyable aspects of being ethnic (Waters 1990). Richard Alba (1990) also found later-generation Whites in Albany, New York, who chose to keep a tie with an ethnic identity because of the enjoyable and voluntary aspects to those identities, along with the feelings of specialness they entailed. An example of symbolic ethnicity is individuals who identify as Irish, for example, on occasions such as Saint Patrick's Day, on family holidays, or for vacations. They do not usually belong to Irish American organizations, live in Irish neighborhoods, work in Irish jobs, or marry other Irish people. The symbolic meaning of being Irish American can be constructed by individuals from mass media images, family traditions, or other intermittent social activities. In other words, for later-generation White ethnics, ethnicity is not something that influences their lives unless they want it to. In the world of work and school and neighborhood, individuals do not have to admit to being ethnic unless they choose to. And for an increasing number of European-origin individuals whose parents and grandparents have intermarried, the ethnicity they claim is largely a matter of personal choice as they sort through all of the possible combinations of groups in their genealogies.

* * *

In responding to the ancestry question, the comparative latitude that White respondents have does not mean that Whites pick and choose ethnicities out of thin air. For the most part people choose an identity that corresponds with some element of their family tree. However, there are many anecdotal instances of people adopting ethnicities when they marry or move to a strongly identified neighborhood or community. For instance Micaela di Leonardo (1984) reported instances of non-Italian women who married into Italian American families and "became Italian." Karen Leonard (1992) describes a community of Mexican American women who married Punjabi immigrants in California. Some of the Punjabi immigrants and their descendants were said to have "become Mexican" when they joined their wives' kin group and social worlds. Alternatively she describes the community acknowledging that Mexican women made the best curry, as they adapted to life with Indian-origin men.

But what do these identities mean to individuals? Surely an identity that is optional in a number of ways—not legally defined on a passport or birth certificate, not socially consequential in terms of societal discrimination in terms of housing or job access, and not economically limiting in terms of blocking opportunities for social mobility—cannot be the same as an identity that results from and is nurtured by societal exclusion and rejection. The choice to have a symbolic ethnicity is an attractive and widespread one despite its lack of demonstrable content, because having a symbolic ethnicity combines individuality with feelings of community. People reported to me that they liked having an ethnic identity because it gave them a uniqueness and a feeling of being special. They often contrasted their own specialness by virtue of their ethnic identities with "bland" American-ness. Being ethnic makes people feel unique and special and not just "vanilla," as one of my respondents put it. . . .

* * *

Symbolic ethnicity is the best of all worlds for these respondents. These White ethnics can claim to be unique and special, while simultaneously finding the community and conformity with others that they also crave. But that "community" is of a type that will not interfere with a person's individuality. It is not as if these people belong to ethnic voluntary organizations or gather as a group in churches or neighborhoods or union halls. They work and reside within the mainstream of American middle-class life, yet they retain the interesting benefits—the "specialness"—of ethnic allegiance, without any of its drawbacks.

* * *

RACE RELATIONS AND SYMBOLIC ETHNICITY

However much symbolic ethnicity is without cost for the individual, there is a cost associated with symbolic ethnicity for the society. That is because symbolic ethnicities of the type described here are confined to White Americans of European origin. Black Americans, Hispanic Americans, Asian Americans, and American Indians do not have the option of a symbolic ethnicity at present in the United States. For all of the ways in which ethnicity does not matter for White Americans, it does matter for non-Whites. Who your ancestors are does affect your choice of spouse, where you live, what job you have, who your friends are, and what your chances are for success in American society, if those ancestors happen not to be from Europe. The reality is that White ethnics have a lot more choice and room for maneuver than they themselves think they do. The situation is very different for members of racial minorities, whose lives are strongly influenced by their race or national origin regardless of how much they may choose not to identify themselves in terms of their ancestries.

When White Americans learn the stories of how their grandparents and great-grandparents triumphed in the United States over adversity, they are usually told in terms of their individual efforts and triumphs. The important role of labor unions and other organized political and economic actors in their social and economic successes are left out of the story in favor of a generational story of individual Americans rising up against communitarian, Old World intolerance and New World resistance. As a result, the "individualized" voluntary, cultural view of ethnicity for Whites is what is remembered.

One important implication of these identities is that they tend to be very individualistic. There is a tendency to view valuing diversity in a pluralist environment as equating all groups. The symbolic ethnic tends to think that all groups are equal; everyone has a background that is their right to celebrate and pass on to their children. This leads to the conclusion that all identities are equal and all identities in some sense are interchangeable—"I'm Italian American, you're Polish American. I'm Irish American, you're African American." The important thing is to treat people as individuals and all equally. However, this assumption ignores the very big difference between an individualistic symbolic ethnic identity and a socially enforced and imposed racial identity.

* * *

When White Americans equate their own symbolic ethnicities with the socially enforced identities of non-White Americans, they obscure the fact that the experiences of Whites and non-Whites have been qualitatively different in the United States and that the current identities of individuals partly reflect that unequal history.

In the next section I describe how relations between Black and White students on college campuses reflect some of these asymmetries in the understanding of what a racial or ethnic identity means. While I focus on Black and White students in the following discussion, you should be aware that the myriad other groups in the United States—Mexican Americans, American Indians, Japanese Americans—all have some degree of social and individual influences on their identities, which reflect the group's social and economic history and present circumstance.

Relations on College Campuses

Both Black and White students face the task of developing their race and ethnic identities. Sociologists and psychologists note that at the time people leave home and begin to live independently from their parents, often ages eighteen to twenty-two, they report a heightened sense of racial and ethnic identity as they sort through how much of their beliefs and behaviors are idiosyncratic to their families and how much are shared with other people. It is not until one comes in close contact with many people who are different from oneself that individuals realize the ways in which their backgrounds may influence their individual personality. This involves coming into contact with people who are different in terms of their ethnicity, class, religion, region, and race. For White students, the ethnicity they claim is more often than not a symbolic one—with all of the voluntary, enjoyable, and intermittent characteristics I have described above.

Black students at the university are also developing identities through interactions with others who are different from them. Their identity development is more complicated than that of Whites because of the added element of racial discrimination and racism, along with the "ethnic" developments of finding others who share their background. Thus Black students have the positive attraction of being around other Black students who share some cultural elements, as well as the need to band together with other students in a reactive and oppositional way in the face of racist incidents on campus.

Colleges and universities across the country have been increasing diversity among their student bodies in the last few decades. This has led in many cases to strained relations among students from different racial and ethnic backgrounds. The 1980s and 1990s produced a great number of racial incidents and high racial tensions on campuses. While there were a number of racial incidents that were due to bigotry, unlawful behavior, and violent or vicious attacks, much of what happens among students on campuses involves a low level of tension and awkwardness in social interactions.

Many Black students experience racism personally for the first time on campus. The upper-middle-class students from White suburbs were often isolated enough that their presence was not threatening to racists in their high schools. Also, their class background was known by their residence and this may have prevented attacks being directed at them. Often Black students at the university who begin talking with other students and recognizing racial slights will remember incidents that happened to them earlier that they might not have thought were related to race.

* * *

Black students do experience a tension and a feeling of being singled out. It is unfair that this is part of their college experience and not that of White students. Dealing with incidents like this, or the ever-present threat of such incidents, is an ongoing developmental task for Black students that takes energy, attention, and strength of character. It should be clearly understood that this is an asymmetry in the "college experience" for Black and White students. It is one of the unfair aspects of life that results from living in a society with ongoing racial prejudice and discrimination. It is also very understandable that it makes some students angry at the unfairness of it all, even if there is no one to blame specifically. . . .

In some sense then, as Blauner (1992) has argued, you can see Black students coming together on campus as both an "ethnic" pull of wanting to be together to share common experiences and community, and a "racial" push of banding together defensively because of perceived rejection and tension from Whites. In this way the ethnic identities of Black students are in some sense similar to, say, Korean students wanting to be together to share experiences. And it is an ethnicity that is generally much stronger than, say, Italian Americans. But for Koreans who come together there is generally a definition of themselves as "different from" Whites. For Blacks reacting to exclusion, there is a tendency for the coming together to involve both being "different from" but also "opposed to" Whites.

The anthropologist John Ogbu (1990) has documented the tendency of minorities in a variety of societies around the world, who have experienced severe blocked mobility for long periods of time, to develop such oppositional identities. An important component of having such an identity is to describe others of your group who do not join in the group solidarity as devaluing and denying their very core identity. This is why it is not common for successful Asians to be accused by others of "acting White" in the United States, but it is quite common for such a term to be used by Blacks and Latinos. The oppositional component of a Black identity also explains how Black people can question whether others are acting "Black enough." On campus, it explains some of the intense pressures felt by Black students who do not make their racial identity central and who choose to hang out primarily with non-Blacks. This pressure from the group, which is partly defining itself by not being White, is exacerbated by the fact that race is a physical marker in American society. No one immediately notices the Jewish students sitting together in the dining hall, or the one Jewish student sitting surrounded by non-Jews, or the Texan sitting with the Californians, but everyone notices the Black student who is or is not at the "Black table" in the cafeteria.

An example of the kinds of misunderstandings that can arise because of different understandings of the meanings and implications of symbolic versus oppositional identities concerns questions students ask one another in the dorms about personal appearances and customs. A very common type of interaction in the dorm concerns questions Whites ask Blacks about their hair. Because Whites tend to know little about Blacks, and Blacks know a lot about Whites, there is a general asymmetry in the level of curiosity people have about one another. Whites, as the numerical majority, have had little contact with Black culture; Blacks, especially those who are in college, have had to develop bicultural skills—knowledge about the social worlds of both Whites and Blacks. Miscommunication and hurt feelings about White students' questions about Black students' hair illustrate this point. One of the things that happens freshman year is that White students are around Black students as they fix their hair. White students are generally quite curious about Black students' hair—they have basic questions such as how often Blacks wash their hair, how they get it straightened or curled, what products they use on their hair, how they comb it, etc. Whites often wonder to themselves whether they should ask these questions. One thought experiment Whites perform is to ask themselves whether a particular question would upset them. Adopting the "do unto others" rule, they ask themselves, "If a Black person was curious about my hair would I get upset?" The answer usually is "No, I would be happy to tell them." Another example is an Italian American student wondering to herself, "Would I be upset if someone asked me about calamari?" The answer is no, so she asks her Black roommate about collard greens, and the roommate explodes with an angry response such as, "Do you think all Black people eat watermelon too?" Note that if this Italian American knew her friend was Trinidadian American and asked about peas and rice the situation would be more similar and would not necessarily ignite underlying tensions.

. . . Because Blacks tend to have more knowledge about Whites than vice versa, there is not an even exchange going on, the Black freshman is likely to have fewer basic questions about his White roommate than his White roommate has about him. Because of the differences historically in the group experiences of Blacks and Whites there are some connotations to Black hair that don't exist about White hair. (For instance, is straightening your hair a form of assimilation, do some people distinguish between women having "good hair" and "bad hair" in terms of beauty and how is that related to looking "White"?). Finally, even a Black freshman who cheerfully disregards or is unaware that there are these asymmetries will soon slam into another asymmetry if she willingly answers every innocent question asked of her. In a situation where Blacks make up only 10 percent of the student body, if every non-Black needs to be educated about hair, she will have to explain it to nine other students. As one Black student explained to me, after you've been asked a couple of times about something so personal you begin to feel like you are an attraction in a zoo, that you are at the university for the education of the White students.

Institutional Responses

Our society asks a lot of young people. We ask young people to do something that no one else does as successfully on such a wide scale—that is to live together with people from very different backgrounds, to respect one another, to appreciate one another, and to enjoy and learn from one another. The successes that occur every day in this endeavor are many, and they are too often overlooked. However, the problems and tensions are also real, and they will not vanish on their own. We tend to see pluralism working in the United States in much the same way some people expect capitalism to work. If you put together people with various interests and abilities and resources, the "invisible hand" of capitalism is supposed to make all the parts work together in an economy for the common good.

There is much to be said for such a model—the invisible hand of the market can solve complicated problems of production and distribution better than any "visible hand" of a state plan. However, we have learned that unequal power relations among the actors in the capitalist marketplace, as well as "externalities" that the market cannot account for, such as long-term pollution, or collusion between corporations, or the exploitation of child labor, means that state regulation is often needed. Pluralism and the relations between groups are very similar. There is a lot to be said for the idea that bringing people who belong to different ethnic or racial groups together in institutions with no interference will have good consequences. Students from different backgrounds will make friends if they share a dorm room or corridor, and there is no need for the institution to do any more than provide the locale. But like capitalism, the invisible hand of pluralism does not do well when power relations and externalities are ignored. When you bring together individuals from groups that are differentially valued in the wider society and provide no guidance, there will be problems. In these cases the "invisible hand" of pluralist relations does not work, and tensions and disagreements can arise without any particular individual or group of individuals being "to blame." On college campuses in the 1990s some of the tensions between students are of this sort. They arise from honest misunderstandings, lack of a common background, and very different experiences of what race and ethnicity mean to the individual.

The implications of symbolic ethnicities for thinking about race relations are subtle but consequential. If your understanding of your own ethnicity and its relationship to society and politics is one of individual choice, it becomes harder to understand the need for programs like affirmative action, which recognize the ongoing need for group struggle and group recognition, in order to bring about social change.* It also is hard for a White college student to understand the need that minority students feel to band together against discrimination. It also is easy, on the individual level, to expect everyone else to be able to turn their ethnicity on and off at will, the way you are able to, without understanding that ongoing discrimination and societal attention to minority status makes that impossible for individuals from minority groups to do. The paradox of symbolic ethnicity is that it depends upon the ultimate goal of a pluralist society, and at the same time makes it more difficult to achieve that ultimate goal. It is dependent upon the concept that all ethnicities mean the same thing, that enjoying the traditions of one's heritage is an option available to a

---

*This point is explored further in "Thinking About Affirmative Action" (Massey 2004). [*Editors' note*]

group or an individual, but that such a heritage should not have any social costs associated with it.

... [T]here are many societal issues and involuntary ascriptions associated with non-White identities. The developments necessary for this to change are not individual but societal in nature. Social mobility and declining racial and ethnic sensitivity are closely associated. The legacy and the present reality of discrimination on the basis of race or ethnicity must be overcome before the ideal of a pluralist society, where all heritages are treated equally and are equally available for individuals to choose or discard at will, is realized.

REFERENCES

Alba, Richard D. 1990. *Ethnic Identity: The Transformation of White America.* New Haven: Yale University Press.

Blauner, Robert 1992. "Talking Past Each Other: Black and White Languages of Race." *American Prospect* (summer): 55–64.

di Leonardo, Micaela 1984. *The Varieties of Ethnic Experience: Kinship, Class and Gender Among Italian Americans.* Ithaca, NY: Cornell University Press.

Gans, Herbert 1979. "Symbolic Ethnicity: The Future of Ethnic Groups and Cultures in America." *Ethnic and Racial Studies* 2: 1–20.

Greeley, Andrew H. 1976. "The Ethnic Miracle." *Public Interest* 45 (fall): 20–36.

Leonard, Karen 1992. *Making Ethnic Choices: Califonia's Punjabi Mexican Americans.* Philadelphia: Temple University Press.

Massey, Garth 2004. "Thinking about Affirmative Action: Arguments Supporting Preferential Policies." *Review of Policy Research*, 21 (6): 783–797.

Ogbu, John 1990. "Minority Status and Literacy in Comparative Perspective." *Daedalus* 119: 141–169.

Pagnini, Deanna L., and S. Philip Morgan 1990. "Intermarriage and Social Distance among U.S. Immigrants at the Turn of the Century." *American Journal of Sociology* 96(2): 405–432.

Waters, Mary C. 1990. *Ethnic Options: Choosing Identities in America.* Berkeley and Los Angeles: University of California Press.

PART FIVE

SOCIAL INEQUALITY AND ORGANIZATIONS

24

The Birth of a New American Aristocracy*

MATTHEW STEWART

In the past four decades in the United States, the unequal distributions of income and wealth have increased greatly, making the gap between rich and poor wider than in any other industrialized nation. At the same time, the middle class has experienced stagnant wage growth and soaring costs for health care, housing, and education, while the pathway to a life better than their parents' has diminished. Written in a self-effacing and occasionally sarcastic tone, this essay shows how a small group of Americans—what the author calls the "9.9 percent," or the upper 10 percent minus the upper-upper 0.1 percent—has not only captured much of the largess of late-stage capitalism but done so while embracing the illusion of meritocracy.

For about a week every year in my childhood, I was a member of one of America's fading aristocracies. Sometimes around Christmas, more often on the Fourth of July, my family would take up residence at one of my grandparents' country clubs in Chicago, Palm Beach, or Asheville, North Carolina. The breakfast buffets were magnificent, and Grandfather was a jovial host, always ready with a familiar story, rarely missing an opportunity for gentle instruction on proper club etiquette. At the age of 11 or 12, I gathered from him, between his puffs of cigar smoke, that we owed our weeks of plenty to Great-Grandfather, Colonel Robert W. Stewart, a Rough Rider with Teddy Roosevelt who made his fortune as the chairman of Standard Oil of Indiana in the 1920s. I was also given to understand that, for reasons traceable to some ancient and incomprehensible dispute, the Rockefellers were the mortal enemies of our clan. Only much later in life did I learn that the stories about the Colonel and his tangles with titans fell far short of the truth.

At the end of each week, we would return to our place. My reality was the aggressively middle-class world of 1960s and '70s U.S. military bases and the communities around them. Life was good there, too, but the pizza came from a box, and it was Lucky Charms for breakfast. Our glory peaked on the day my parents came home with a new Volkswagen camper bus. As I got older, the holiday pomp of patriotic luncheons and bridge-playing rituals came to seem faintly ridiculous and even offensive, like an endless birthday party for people

---

*References and footnotes can be found in the author's original publication, "The 9.9 Percent Is the New American Aristocracy" (*The Atlantic*, June 2018). [*Editors' note*]

whose chief accomplishment in life was just showing up. I belonged to a new generation that believed in getting ahead through merit, and we defined merit in a straightforward way: test scores, grades, competitive résumé-stuffing, supremacy in board games and pickup basketball, and, of course, working for our keep. For me that meant taking on chores for the neighbors, punching the clock at a local fast-food restaurant, and collecting scholarships to get through college and graduate school. I came into many advantages by birth, but money was not among them.

I've joined a new aristocracy now, even if we still call ourselves meritocratic winners. If you are a typical reader of *The Atlantic,* you may well be a member too. (And if you're not a member, my hope is that you will find the story of this new class even more interesting—if also more alarming.) To be sure, there is a lot to admire about my new group, which I'll call—for reasons you'll soon see—the 9.9 percent. We've dropped the old dress codes, put our faith in facts, and are (somewhat) more varied in skin tone and ethnicity. People like me, who have waning memories of life in an earlier ruling caste, are the exception, not the rule.

By any sociological or financial measure, it's good to be us. It's even better to be our kids. In our health, family life, friendship networks, and level of education, not to mention money, we are crushing the competition below. But we do have a blind spot, and it is located right in the center of the mirror: We seem to be the last to notice just how rapidly we've morphed, or what we've morphed into.

The meritocratic class has mastered the old trick of consolidating wealth and passing privilege along at the expense of other people's children. We are not innocent bystanders to the growing concentration of wealth in our time. We are the principal accomplices in a process that is slowly strangling the economy, destabilizing American politics, and eroding democracy. Our delusions of merit now prevent us from recognizing the nature of the problem that our emergence as a class represents. We tend to think that the victims of our success are just the people excluded from the club. But history shows quite clearly that, in the kind of game we're playing, everybody loses badly in the end.

THE DISCREET CHARM OF THE 9.9 PERCENT

Let's talk first about money—even if money is only one part of what makes the new aristocrats special. There is a familiar story about rising inequality in the United States, and its stock characters are well known. The villains are the fossil-fueled plutocrat, the Wall Street fat cat, the callow tech bro, and the rest of the so-called top 1 percent. The good guys are the 99 percent, otherwise known as "the people" or "the middle class." The arc of the narrative is simple: Once we were equal, but now we are divided. The story has a grain of truth to it. But it gets the characters and the plot wrong in basic ways.

It is in fact the top 0.1 percent who have been the big winners in the growing concentration of wealth over the past half century. According to the UC

Figure 24.1 A Tale of Three Classes

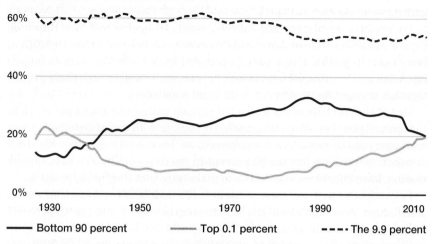

The 9.9 percent hold most of the wealth in the United States.

Berkeley economists Emmanuel Saez and Gabriel Zucman, the 160,000 or so households in that group held 22 percent of America's wealth in 2012, up from 10 percent in 1963. If you're looking for the kind of money that can buy elections, you'll find it inside the top 0.1 percent alone.

Every piece of the pie picked up by the 0.1 percent, in relative terms, had to come from the people below. But not everyone in the 99.9 percent gave up a slice. Only those in the bottom 90 percent did. At their peak, in the mid-1980s, people in this group held 35 percent of the nation's wealth. Three decades later that had fallen 12 points—exactly as much as the wealth of the 0.1 percent rose.

In between the top 0.1 percent [1 of 1000 households] and the bottom 90 percent is a group that has been doing just fine. It has held on to its share of a growing pie decade after decade. And as a group, it owns substantially more wealth than do the other two combined. In the tale of three classes (see Figure [24.1]), it is represented by the . . . line [of dashes] floating high and steady while the other two duke it out. You'll find the new aristocracy there. We are the 9.9 percent.

So what kind of characters are we, the 9.9 percent? We are mostly not like those flamboyant political manipulators from the 0.1 percent. We're a well-behaved, flannel-suited crowd of lawyers, doctors, dentists, mid-level investment bankers, MBAs with opaque job titles, and assorted other professionals—the kind of people you might invite to dinner. In fact, we're so self-effacing, we deny our own existence. We keep insisting that we're "middle class."

As of 2016, it took $1.2 million in net worth to make it into the 9.9 percent; $2.4 million to reach the group's median; and $10 million to get into the top 0.9 percent. "We are the 99 percent" sounds righteous, but it's a slogan, not an analysis.[1] The families at our end of the spectrum wouldn't know what to do with a pitchfork.

We are also mostly, but not entirely, white. According to a Pew Research Center analysis, African Americans represent 1.9 percent of the top 10th of households in wealth; Hispanics, 2.4 percent; and all other minorities, including Asian and multiracial individuals, 8.8 percent—even though those groups together account for 35 percent of the total population.

One of the hazards of life in the 9.9 percent is that our necks get stuck in the upward position. We gaze upon the 0.1 percent with a mixture of awe, envy, and eagerness to obey. As a consequence, we are missing the other big story of our time. We have left the 90 percent in the dust—and we've been quietly tossing down roadblocks behind us to make sure that they never catch up.

Let's suppose that you start off right in the middle of the American wealth distribution. How high would you have to jump to make it into the 9.9 percent? In financial terms, the measurement is easy and the trend is unmistakable. In 1963, you would have needed to multiply your wealth six times. By 2016, you would have needed to leap twice as high—increasing your wealth 12-fold—to scrape into our group. If you boldly aspired to reach the middle of our group rather than its lower edge, you'd have needed to multiply your wealth by a factor of 25. On this measure, the 2010s look much like the 1920s.

If you are starting at the median for people of color, you'll want to practice your financial pole-vaulting. The Institute for Policy Studies calculated that, setting aside money invested in "durable goods" such as furniture and a family car, the median black family had net wealth of $1,700 in 2013, and the median Latino family had $2,000, compared with $116,800 for the median white family. A 2015 study in Boston found that the wealth of the median white family there was $247,500, while the wealth of the median African American family was $8. That is not a typo. That's two grande cappuccinos. That and another 300,000 cups of coffee will get you into the 9.9 percent.

None of this matters, you will often hear, because in the United States everyone has an opportunity to make the leap: Mobility justifies inequality. As a matter of principle, this isn't true. In the United States, it also turns out not to be true as a factual matter. Contrary to popular myth, economic mobility in the land of opportunity is not high, and it's going down.

Imagine yourself on the socioeconomic ladder with one end of a rubber band around your ankle and the other around your parents' rung. The strength of the rubber determines how hard it is for you to escape the rung on which you were born. If your parents are high on the ladder, the band will pull you up should you fall; if they are low, it will drag you down when you start to rise. Economists represent this concept with a number they call "intergenerational earnings elasticity," or IGE, which measures how much of a child's deviation from average income can be accounted for by the parents' income. An IGE of

---

1. This was the rallying cry of the short-lived Occupy Wall Street Movement of 2011.

zero means that there's no relationship at all between parents' income and that of their offspring. An IGE of one says that the destiny of a child is to end up right where she came into the world.

According to Miles Corak, an economics professor at the City University of New York, half a century ago IGE in America was less than 0.3. Today, it is about 0.5. In America, the game is half over once you've selected your parents. IGE is now higher here than in almost every other developed economy. On this measure of economic mobility, the United States is more like Chile or Argentina than Japan or Germany.

The story becomes even more disconcerting when you see just where on the ladder the tightest rubber bands are located. Canada, for example, has an IGE of about half that of the U.S. Yet from the middle rungs of the two countries' income ladders, offspring move up or down through the nearby deciles at the same respectable pace. The difference is in what happens at the extremes. In the United States, it's the children of the bottom decile and, above all, the top decile—the 9.9 percent—who settle down nearest to their starting point. Here in the land of opportunity, the taller the tree, the closer the apple falls.

* * *

A few years ago, Alan Krueger, an economist and a former chairman of the Obama administration's Council of Economic Advisers, was reviewing the international mobility data when he caught a glimpse of the fundamental process underlying our present moment. Rising immobility and rising inequality aren't like two pieces of driftwood that happen to have shown up on the beach at the same time, he noted. They wash up together on every shore. Across countries, the higher the inequality, the higher the IGE (see Figure [24.2]). It's as if human societies have a natural tendency to separate, and then, once the classes are far enough apart, to crystallize.

Economists are prudent creatures, and they'll look up from a graph like that and remind you that it shows only correlation, not causation. That's a convenient hedge for those of us at the top because it keeps alive one of the founding myths of America's meritocracy: that *our* success has nothing to do with *other people's* failure. It's a pleasant idea. But around the world and throughout history, the wealthy have advanced the crystallization process in a straightforward way. They have taken their money out of productive activities and put it into walls. Throughout history, moreover, one social group above all others has assumed responsibility for maintaining and defending these walls. Its members used to be called aristocrats. Now we're the 9.9 percent. The main difference is that we have figured out how to use the pretense of being part of the middle as one of our strategies for remaining on top.

Krueger liked the graph shown in Figure [24.2] so much that he decided to give it a name: the Great Gatsby Curve. It's a good choice, and it resonates strongly with me. F. Scott Fitzgerald's novel about the breakdown of the American dream is set in 1922, or right around the time that my great-grandfather

Figure 24.2 The Great Gatsby Curve

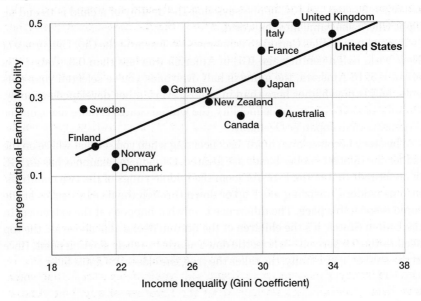

Inequality and class immobility go together.

was secretly siphoning money from Standard Oil and putting it into a shell company in Canada. It was published in 1925, just as special counsel was turning up evidence that bonds from that company had found their way into the hands of the secretary of the interior. Its author was drinking his way through the cafés of Paris just as Colonel Robert W. Stewart was running away from subpoenas to testify before the United States Senate about his role in the Teapot Dome scandal. We are only now closing in on the peak of inequality that his generation achieved, in 1928. I'm sure they thought it would go on forever, too.

THE ORIGIN OF A SPECIES

Money can't buy you class, or so my grandmother used to say. But it can buy a private detective. Grandmother was a Kentucky debutante and sometime fashion model (kind of like Daisy Buchanan in *The Great Gatsby*, weirdly enough), so she knew what to do when her eldest son announced his intention to marry a woman from Spain. A gumshoe promptly reported back that the prospective bride's family made a living selling newspapers on the streets of Barcelona. Grandmother instituted an immediate and total communications embargo. In fact, my mother's family owned and operated a large paper-goods factory. When children came, Grandmother at last relented. Determined to do the right thing, she arranged for the new family, then on military assignment in Hawaii, to be inscribed in the New York *Social Register*.

Sociologists would say, in their dry language, that my grandmother was a zealous manager of the family's social capital—and she wasn't about to let some Spanish street urchin run away with it. She did have a point, even if her facts were wrong. Money may be the measure of wealth, but it is far from the only form of it. Family, friends, social networks, personal health, culture, education, and even location are all ways of being rich, too. These nonfinancial forms of wealth, as it turns out, aren't simply perks of membership in our aristocracy. They define us.

We are the people of good family, good health, good schools, good neighborhoods, and good jobs. We may want to call ourselves the "5Gs" rather than the 9.9 percent. We are so far from the not-so-good people on all of these dimensions, we are beginning to resemble a new species. And, just as in Grandmother's day, the process of speciation begins with a love story—or, if you prefer, sexual selection.

The polite term for the process is *assortative mating*. The phrase is sometimes used to suggest that this is another of the wonders of the internet age, where popcorn at last meets butter and Yankees fan finds Yankees fan. In fact, the frenzy of assortative mating today results from a truth that would have been generally acknowledged by the heroines of any Jane Austen novel: Rising inequality decreases the number of suitably wealthy mates even as it increases the reward for finding one and the penalty for failing to do so. According to one study, the last time marriage partners sorted themselves by educational status as much as they do now was in the 1920s.

. . . Ivy Leaguers looking to mate with their equals can apply to join a dating service called the League. It's selective, naturally: Only 20 to 30 percent of New York applicants get in. It's sometimes called "Tinder for the elites."

It is misleading to think that assortative mating is symmetrical, as in city mouse marries city mouse and country mouse marries country mouse. A better summary of the data would be: Rich mouse finds love, and poor mouse gets screwed. It turns out—who knew?—that people who are struggling to keep it all together have a harder time hanging onto their partner. According to the Harvard political scientist Robert Putnam, 60 years ago just 20 percent of children born to parents with a high-school education or less lived in a single-parent household; now that figure is nearly 70 percent. Among college-educated households, by contrast, the single-parent rate remains less than 10 percent. Since the 1970s, the divorce rate has declined significantly among college-educated couples, while it has risen dramatically among couples with only a high-school education—even as marriage itself has become less common. The rate of single parenting is in turn the single most significant predictor of social immobility across countries, according to a study led by the Stanford economist Raj Chetty.

None of which is to suggest that individuals are wrong to seek a suitable partner and make a beautiful family. People should—and presumably always will—pursue happiness in this way. It's one of the delusions of our meritocratic class, however, to assume that if our actions are individually blameless, then the sum of our actions will be good for society. We may have studied Shakespeare on the way to law school, but we have little sense for the tragic possibilities of life. The fact of the matter is that we have silently and collectively opted for inequality, and this is what inequality does. It turns marriage into a luxury good, and a stable family life into a privilege that the moneyed elite can pass along to their children. How do we think that's going to work out?

This divergence of families by class is just one part of a process that is creating two distinct forms of life in our society. Stop in at your local yoga studio or SoulCycle class, and you'll notice that the same process is now inscribing itself in our own bodies. In 19th-century England, the rich really were different. They didn't just have more money; they were taller—a lot taller. According to a study colorfully titled "On English Pygmies and Giants," 16-year-old boys from the upper classes towered a remarkable 8.6 inches, on average, over their undernourished, lower-class countrymen. We are reproducing the same kind of division via a different set of dimensions.

Obesity, diabetes, heart disease, kidney disease, and liver disease are all two to three times more common in individuals who have a family income of less than $35,000 than in those who have a family income greater than $100,000. Among low-educated, middle-aged whites, the death rate in the United States—alone in the developed world—increased in the first decade and a half of the 21st century. Driving the trend is the rapid growth in what the Princeton economists Anne Case and Angus Deaton call "deaths of despair"—suicides and alcohol- and drug-related deaths.

The sociological data are not remotely ambiguous on any aspect of this growing divide. We 9.9 percenters live in safer neighborhoods, go to better schools, have shorter commutes, receive higher-quality health care, and, when circumstances require, serve time in better prisons. We also have more friends—the kind of friends who will introduce us to new clients or line up great internships for our kids.

* * *

Most important of all, we have learned how to pass all of these advantages down to our children. In America today, the single best predictor of whether an individual will get married, stay married, pursue advanced education, live in a good neighborhood, have an extensive social network, and experience good health is the performance of his or her parents on those same metrics.

We're leaving the 90 percent and their offspring far behind in a cloud of debts and bad life choices that they somehow can't stop themselves from making. We tend to overlook the fact that parenting is more expensive and motherhood more hazardous in the United States than in any other developed country, that campaigns against family planning and reproductive rights are an assault on the families of the bottom 90 percent, and that law-

and-order politics serves to keep even more of them down. We prefer to interpret their relative poverty as vice: *Why can't they get their act together?*

New forms of life necessarily give rise to new and distinct forms of consciousness. If you doubt this, you clearly haven't been reading the "personal and household services" ads on Monster.com. At the time of this writing, the section for my town of Brookline, Massachusetts, featured one placed by a "busy professional couple" seeking a "Part Time Nanny." The nanny (or manny—the ad scrupulously avoids committing to gender) is to be "bright, loving, and energetic"; "friendly, intelligent, and professional"; and "a very good communicator, both written and verbal." She (on balance of probability) will "assist with the care and development" of two children and will be "responsible for all aspects of the children's needs," including bathing, dressing, feeding, and taking the young things to and from school and activities. That's why a "college degree in early childhood education" is "a plus."

In short, Nanny is to have every attribute one would want in a terrific, professional, college-educated parent. Except, of course, the part about being an actual professional, college-educated parent. There is no chance that Nanny will trade places with our busy 5G couple. She "must know the proper etiquette in a professionally run household" and be prepared to "accommodate changing circumstances." She is required to have "5+ years experience as a Nanny," which makes it unlikely that she'll have had time to get the law degree that would put her on the other side of the bargain. All of Nanny's skills, education, experience, and professionalism will land her a job that is "Part Time."

The ad is written in flawless, 21st-century business-speak, but what it is really seeking is a governess—that exquisitely contradictory figure in Victorian literature who is both indistinguishable in all outward respects from the upper class and yet emphatically not a member of it. Nanny's best bet for moving up in the world is probably to follow the example of Jane Eyre and run off with the lord (or lady) of the manor.

If you look beyond the characters in this unwritten novel about Nanny and her 5G masters, you'll see a familiar shape looming on the horizon. The Gatsby Curve has managed to reproduce itself in social, physiological, and cultural capital. Put more accurately: There is only one curve, but it operates through a multiplicity of forms of wealth.

Rising inequality does not follow from a hidden law of economics, as the otherwise insightful Thomas Piketty suggested when he claimed that the historical rate of return on capital exceeds the historical rate of growth in the economy. Inequality necessarily entrenches itself through other, nonfinancial, intrinsically invidious forms of wealth and power. We use these other forms of capital to project our advantages into life itself. We look down from our higher virtues in the same way the English upper class looked down from its taller bodies, as if the distinction between superior and inferior were an artifact of nature. That's what aristocrats do.

THE PRIVILEGE OF AN EDUCATION

* * *

In the United States, the premium that college graduates earn over their non-college-educated peers in young adulthood exceeds 70 percent. The return on education is 50 percent higher than what it was in 1950, and is significantly higher than the rate in every other developed country. In Norway and Denmark, the college premium is less than 20 percent; in Japan, it is less than 30 percent; in France and Germany, it's about 40 percent.

All of this comes before considering the all-consuming difference between "good" schools and the rest. Ten years after starting college, according to data from the Department of Education, the top decile of earners from all schools had a median salary of $68,000. But the top decile from the 10 highest-earning colleges raked in $220,000—make that $250,000 for No. 1, Harvard—and the top decile at the next 30 colleges took home $157,000. (Not surprisingly, the top 10 had an average acceptance rate of 9 percent, and the next 30 were at 19 percent.)

It is entirely possible to get a good education at the many schools that don't count as "good" in our brand-obsessed system. But the "bad" ones really are bad for you. For those who made the mistake of being born to the wrong parents, our society offers a kind of virtual education system. It has places that look like colleges—but aren't really. It has debt—and that, unfortunately, is real. The people who enter into this class hologram do not collect a college premium; they wind up in something more like indentured servitude.

* * *

Behind both of these stories lies one of the founding myths of our meritocracy. One way or the other, we tell ourselves, the rising education premium is a direct function of the rising value of meritorious people in a modern economy. That is, not only do the meritorious get ahead, but the rewards we receive are in direct proportion to our merit.

But the fact is that degree holders earn so much more than the rest not primarily because they are better at their job, but because they mostly take different categories of jobs. Well over half of Ivy League graduates, for instance, typically go straight into one of four career tracks that are generally reserved for the well educated: finance, management consulting, medicine, or law. To keep it simple, let's just say that there are two types of occupations in the world: those whose members have collective influence in setting their own pay, and those whose members must face the music on their own. It's better to be a member of the first group. Not surprisingly, that is where you will find the college crowd.

Why do America's doctors make twice as much as those of other wealthy countries? Given that the United States has placed dead last five times running in the Commonwealth Fund's ranking of health-care systems in high-income countries, it's hard to argue that they are twice as gifted at saving lives. Dean Baker, a senior economist with the Center for Economic and Policy Research, has a more plausible suggestion: "When economists like me look at medicine in America—whether we lean left or right politically—we see something that looks an awful lot like a cartel." Through their influence on the number of slots at medical schools, the availability of residencies, the licensing of foreign-trained doctors, and the role of nurse practitioners, physicians' organizations can effectively limit the competition their own members face—and that is exactly what they do.

Lawyers (or at least a certain elite subset of them) have apparently learned to play the same game. Even after the collapse of the so-called law-school bubble, America's lawyers are No. 1 in international salary rankings and earn more than twice as much, on average, as their wig-toting British colleagues. The University of Chicago law professor Todd Henderson, writing for *Forbes* in 2016, offered a blunt assessment: "The American Bar Association operates a state-approved cartel."

Similar occupational licensing schemes provide shelter for the meritorious in a variety of other sectors. The policy researchers Brink Lindsey and Steven Teles detail the mechanisms in *The Captured Economy*. Dentists' offices, for example, have a glass ceiling that limits what dental hygienists can do without supervision, keeping their bosses in the 9.9 percent. Copyright and patent laws prop up profits and salaries in the education-heavy pharmaceutical, software, and entertainment sectors. These arrangements are trifles, however, compared with what's on offer in tech and finance, two of the most powerful sectors of the economy.

By now we're thankfully done with the tech-sector fairy tales in which whip-smart cowboys innovate the heck out of a stodgy status quo. The reality is that five monster companies—you know the names—are worth about $3.5 trillion combined, and represent more than 40 percent of the market capital on the NASDAQ stock exchange. Much of the rest of the technology sector consists of virtual entities waiting patiently to feed themselves to these beasts.

Let's face it: This is Monopoly money with a smiley emoji. Our society figured out some time ago how to deal with companies that attempt to corner the market on viscous substances like oil. We don't yet know what to do with the monopolies that arise out of networks and scale effects in the information marketplace. Until we do, the excess profits will stick to those who manage to get closest to the information honeypot. You can be sure that these people will have a great deal of merit.

The candy-hurling godfather of today's meritocratic class, of course, is the financial-services industry. Americans now turn over $1 of every $12 in GDP to the financial sector; in the 1950s, the bankers were content to keep only $1 out of $40. The game is more sophisticated than a two-fisted money grab, but its essence was made obvious during the 2008 financial crisis. The public underwrites the risks; the financial gurus take a seat at the casino; and it's heads they win, tails we lose. The financial system we now have is not a product of nature. It has been engineered, over decades, by powerful bankers, for their own benefit and for that of their posterity.

Who is not in on the game? Auto workers, for example. Caregivers. Retail workers. Furniture makers. Food workers. The wages of American manufacturing and service workers consistently hover in the middle of international rankings. The exceptionalism of American compensation rates comes to an end in the kinds of work that do not require a college degree.

You see, when educated people with excellent credentials band together to advance their collective interest, it's all part of serving the public good by ensuring a high quality of service, establishing fair working conditions, and giving merit its due. That's why we do it through "associations," and with the assistance of fellow professionals wearing white shoes. When working-class people do it—through unions—it's a violation of the sacred principles of the free market. It's thuggish and anti-modern. Imagine if workers hired consultants and "compensation committees," consisting of their peers at other companies, to recommend how much they should be paid. The result would be—well, we know what it would be, because that's what CEOs do.

It isn't a coincidence that the education premium surged during the same years that membership in trade unions collapsed. In 1954, 28 percent of all workers were members of trade unions, but by 2017 that figure was down to 11 percent.

* * *

OUR BLIND SPOT

In my family, Aunt Sarah was the true believer. According to her version of reality, the family name was handed down straight from the ancient kings of Scotland. Great-great-something-grandfather William Stewart, a soldier in the Continental Army, was seated at the right hand of George Washington. And Sarah herself was somehow descended from "Pocahontas's sister." The stories never made much sense. But that didn't stop Sarah from believing in them. My family had to be special for a reason.

The 9.9 percent are different. We don't delude ourselves about the ancient sources of our privilege. That's because, unlike Aunt Sarah and her imaginary princesses, we've convinced ourselves that we don't have any privilege at all.

Consider the reception that at least some members of our tribe have offered to those who have foolishly dared to draw attention to our advantages. Last year, when the Brookings Institution researcher Richard V. Reeves, following up on his book *Dream Hoarders*, told the readers of *The New York Times* to "Stop Pretending You're Not Rich," many of those readers accused him of engaging in "class warfare," of writing "a meaningless article," and of being "rife with guilt."

In her incisive portrait of my people, *Uneasy Street*, the sociologist Rachel Sherman documents the syndrome.[†] A number among us, when reminded of our privilege, respond with a counternarrative that generally goes like this: *I was born in the street. I earned everything all by myself. I barely get by on my $250,000 salary. You should see the other parents at our kids' private school.*

* * *

We feel in our bones that class works only for itself; that every individual is dispensable; that some of us will be discarded and replaced with fresh blood. This insecurity of privilege only grows as the chasm beneath the privileged class expands. It is the restless engine that drives us to invest still more time and energy in the walls that will keep us safe by keeping others out.

Here's another fact of life in West Egg: Someone is always above you. In Gatsby's case, it was the old-money people of East Egg. In the Colonel's case, it was John D. Rockefeller Jr. You're always trying to please them, and they're always ready to pull the plug.

The source of the trouble, considered more deeply, is that we have traded rights for privileges. We're willing to strip everyone, including ourselves, of the universal right to a good education, adequate health care, adequate representation in the workplace, genuinely equal opportunities, because we think we can win the game. But who, really, in the end, is going to win this slippery game of escalating privileges?

[†]See "The Anxieties of Affluence," essay 17 in this reader. [*Editors' note*]

25

Manifesto of the Communist Party

KARL MARX and FRIEDRICH ENGELS

Europe in the eighteenth and nineteenth centuries changed dramatically with the onset of industrialization and the phenomenal growth of cities. While some writers saw great promise of abundance and freedom in these changes, the reality for millions of people was increased labor and grinding poverty. Karl Marx (1818–1883) was one of the nineteenth century's most articulate critics of the disparity between possibility and reality. Here he and his collaborator, Friedrich Engels, explain the reasons for this in their pamphlet written for workers.

I. BOURGEOIS AND PROLETARIANS[1]

The history of all hitherto existing society[2] is the history of class struggles.

Freeman and slave, patrician and plebeian, lord and serf, guild-master[3] and journeyman, in a word, oppressor and oppressed, stood in constant opposition to one another, carried on an uninterrupted, now hidden, now open fight, a fight that each time ended, either in a revolutionary re-constitution of society at large, or in the common ruin of the contending classes.

In the earlier epochs of history, we find almost everywhere a complicated arrangement of society into various orders, a manifold gradation of social rank.

---

1. By bourgeoisie is meant the class of modern Capitalists, owners of the means of social production and employers of wage-labour. By proletariat, the class of modern wage-labourers who, having no means of production of their own, are reduced to selling their labour-power in order to live. [*Engels, English edition of 1888*]

2. That is, all *written* history. In 1847, the pre-history of society, the social organisation existing previous to recorded history, was all but unknown. Since then, Haxthausen discovered common ownership of land in Russia, Maurer proved it to be the social foundation from which all Teutonic races started in history, and by and by village communities were found to be, or to have been the primitive form of society everywhere from India to Ireland. The inner organisation of this primitive Communistic society was laid bare, in its typical form, by Morgan's crowning discovery of the true nature of the *gens* and its relation to the *tribe*. With the dissolution of these primaeval communities society begins to be differentiated into separate and finally antagonistic classes. I have attempted to retrace this process of dissolution in: "Der Ursprung der Familie, des Privateigenthums und des Staats" [*The Origin of the Family, Private Property and the State*], 2nd edition, Stuttgart 1886. [*Engels, English edition of 1888*]

3. Guild-master, that is, a full member of a guild, a master within, not a head of a guild. [*Engels, English edition of 1888*]

In ancient Rome we have patricians, knights, plebeians, slaves; in the Middle Ages, feudal lords, vassals, guild-masters, journey-men, apprentices, serfs; in almost all of these classes, again, subordinate gradations.

The modern bourgeois society that has sprouted from the ruins of feudal society has not done away with class antagonisms. It has but established new classes, new conditions of oppression, new forms of struggle in place of the old ones.

Our epoch, the epoch of the bourgeoisie, possesses, however, this distinctive feature: it has simplified the class antagonisms: Society as a whole is more and more splitting up into two great hostile camps, into two great classes directly facing each other: Bourgeoisie and Proletariat.

From the serfs of the Middle Ages sprang the chartered burghers of the earliest towns. From these burgesses the first elements of the bourgeoisie were developed.

The discovery of America, the rounding of the Cape, opened up fresh ground for the rising bourgeoisie. The East-Indian and Chinese markets, the colonisation of America, trade with the colonies, the increase in the means of exchange and in commodities generally, gave to commerce, to navigation, to industry, an impulse never before known, and thereby, to the revolutionary element in the tottering feudal society, a rapid development.

The feudal system of industry, under which industrial production was monopolised by closed guilds, now no longer sufficed for the growing wants of the new markets. The manufacturing system took its place. The guild-masters were pushed on one side by the manufacturing middle class; division of labour between the different corporate guilds vanished in the face of division of labour in each single workshop.

Meantime the markets kept ever growing, the demand ever rising. Even manufacture no longer sufficed. Thereupon, steam and machinery revolutionised industrial production. The place of manufacture was taken by the giant, Modern Industry, the place of the industrial middle class, by industrial millionaires, the leaders of whole industrial armies, the modern bourgeois.

Modern industry has established the world-market, for which the discovery of America paved the way. This market has given an immense development to commerce, to navigation, to communication by land. This development has, in its turn, reacted on the extension of industry; and in proportion as industry, commerce, navigation, railways extended, in the same proportion the bourgeoisie developed, increased its capital, and pushed into the background every class handed down from the Middle Ages.

We see, therefore, how the modern bourgeoisie is itself the product of a long course of development, of a series of revolutions in the modes of production and of exchange.

Each step in the development of the bourgeoisie was accompanied by a corresponding political advance of that class. An oppressed class under the sway of the feudal nobility, an armed and self-governing association in the mediaeval commune;[4] here independent urban republic (as in Italy and Germany), there taxable "third estate" of the monarchy (as in France), afterwards, in the period of manufacture proper, serving either the semi-feudal or the absolute monarchy as a counterpoise against the nobility, and, in fact, corner-stone of the great monarchies in general, the bourgeoisie has at last, since the establishment of Modern Industry and of the world-market, conquered for itself, in the modern representative State, exclusive political sway. The executive of the modem State is but a committee for managing the common affairs of the whole bourgeoisie.

The bourgeoisie, historically, has played a most revolutionary part.

The bourgeoisie, wherever it has got the upper hand, has put an end to all feudal, patriarchal, idyllic relations. It has pitilessly torn asunder the motley feudal ties that bound man to his "natural superiors," and has left remaining no other nexus between man and man than naked self-interest, than callous "cash payment." It has drowned the most heavenly ecstasies of religious fervour, of chivalrous enthusiasm, of philistine sentimentalism, in the icy water of egotistical calculation. It has resolved personal worth into exchange value, and in place of the numberless indefeasible chartered freedoms, has set up that single, unconscionable freedom—Free Trade. In one word, for exploitation, veiled by religious and political illusions, it has substituted naked, shameless, direct, brutal exploitation.

The bourgeoisie has stripped of its halo every occupation hitherto honoured and looked up to with reverent awe. It has converted the physician, the lawyer, the priest, the poet, the man of science, into its paid wage-labourers.

The bourgeoisie has torn away from the family its sentimental veil, and has reduced the family relation to a mere money relation.

The bourgeoisie has disclosed how it came to pass that the brutal display of vigour in the Middle Ages, which Reactionists so much admire, found its fitting complement in the most slothful indolence. It has been the first to show what man's activity can bring about. It has accomplished wonders far surpassing Egyptian pyramids, Roman aqueducts, and Gothic cathedrals; it has conducted expeditions that put in the shade all former Exoduses of nations and crusades.

The bourgeoisie cannot exist without constantly revolutionising the instruments of production, and thereby the relations of production, and with them

---

4. "Commune" was the name taken, in France, by the nascent towns even before they had conquered from their feudal lords and masters local self-government and political rights as the "Third Estate." Generally speaking, for the economical development of the bourgeoisie, England is here taken as the typical country; for its political development, France. [*Engels, English edition of 1888*]

This was the name given their urban communities by the townsmen of Italy and France, after they had purchased or wrested their initial rights of self-government from their feudal lords. [*Engels, Gentian edition of 1890*] the whole relations of society. Conservation of the old modes of production in unaltered form, was, on the contrary, the first condition of existence for all earlier industrial classes. Constant revolutionising of production, uninterrupted disturbance of all social conditions, everlasting uncertainty and agitation distinguish the bourgeois epoch from all earlier ones. All fixed, fast-frozen relations, with their train of ancient and venerable prejudices and opinions, are swept away, all new-formed ones become antiquated before they can ossify. All that is solid melts into air, all that is holy is profaned, and man is at last compelled to face with sober senses, his real conditions of life, and his relations with his kind.

The need of a constantly expanding market for its products chases the bourgeoisie over the whole surface of the globe. It must nestle everywhere, settle everywhere, establish connexions everywhere.

The bourgeoisie has through its exploitation of the world-market given a cosmopolitan character to production and consumption in every country. To the great chagrin of Reactionists, it has drawn from under the feet of industry the national ground on which it stood. All old-established national industries have been destroyed or are daily being destroyed. They are dislodged by new industries, whose introduction becomes a life and death question for all civilised nations, by industries that no longer work up indigenous raw material, but raw material drawn from the remotest zones; industries whose products are consumed, not only at home, but in every quarter of the globe. In place of the old wants, satisfied by the productions of the country, we find new wants, requiring for their satisfaction the products of distant lands and climes. In place of the old local and national seclusion and self-sufficiency, we have intercourse in every direction, universal inter-dependence of nations. And as in material, so also in intellectual production. The intellectual creations of individual nations become common property. National one-sidedness and narrow-mindedness become more and more impossible, and from the numerous national and local literatures, there arises a world literature.

The bourgeoisie, by the rapid improvement of all instruments of production, by the immensely facilitated means of communication, draws all, even the most barbarian, nations into civilisation. The cheap prices of its commodities are the heavy artillery with which it batters down all Chinese walls, with which it forces the barbarians' intensely obstinate hatred of foreigners to capitulate. It compels all nations, on pain of extinction, to adopt the bourgeois mode of production; it compels them to introduce what it calls civilisation into their midst, *i.e.*, to become bourgeois themselves. In one word, it creates a world after its own image.

The bourgeoisie has subjected the country to the rule of the towns. It has created enormous cities, has greatly increased the urban population as compared with the rural, and has thus rescued a considerable part of the population from the idiocy of rural life. Just as it has made the country dependent on the towns, so it has made barbarian and semi-barbarian countries dependent on the civilised ones, nations of peasants on nations of bourgeois, the East on the West.

The bourgeoisie keeps more and more doing away with the scattered state of the population, of the means of production, and of property. It has agglomerated population, centralised means of production, and has concentrated property in a few hands. The necessary consequence of this was political centralisation. Independent, or but loosely connected provinces, with separate interests, laws, governments and systems of taxation, became lumped together into one nation, with one government, one code of laws, one national class-interest, one frontier and one customs-tariff.

The bourgeoisie, during its rule of scarce one hundred years, has created more massive and more colossal productive forces than have all preceding generations together. Subjection of Nature's forces to man, machinery, application of chemistry to industry and agriculture, steam-navigation, railways, electric telegraphs, clearing of whole continents for cultivation, canalisation of rivers, whole populations conjured out of the ground—what earlier century had even a presentiment that such productive forces slumbered in the lap of social labour?

We see then: the means of production and of exchange, on whose foundation the bourgeoisie built itself up, were generated in feudal society. At a certain stage in the development of these means of production and of exchange, the conditions under which feudal society produced and exchanged, the feudal organisation of agriculture and manufacturing industry, in one word, the feudal relations of property became no longer compatible with the already developed productive forces; they became so many fetters. They had to be burst asunder; they were burst asunder.

Into their place stepped free competition, accompanied by a social and political constitution adapted to it, and by the economical and political sway of the bourgeois class.

A similar movement is going on before our own eyes. Modern bourgeois society with its relations of production, of exchange and of property, a society that has conjured up such gigantic means of production and of exchange, is like the sorcerer, who is no longer able to control the powers of the nether world whom he has called up by his spells. For many a decade past the history of industry and commerce is but the history of the revolt of modern productive forces against modern conditions of production, against the property relations that are the conditions for the existence of the bourgeoisie and of its rule. It is enough to mention the commercial crises that by their periodical return put on its trial, each time more threateningly, the existence of the entire bourgeois society. In these crises a great part not only of the existing products, but also of the previously created productive forces, are periodically destroyed. In these crises there breaks out an epidemic that, in all earlier epochs, would have seemed an absurdity—the epidemic of over-production. Society suddenly finds itself put back into a state of momentary barbarism; it appears as if a famine, a universal war of devastation had cut off the supply of every means of subsistence; industry and commerce seem to be destroyed; and why? Because there is too much civilisation, too much means of subsistence, too much industry, too much commerce. The productive forces at the disposal of society no longer tend to further the development of the conditions of bourgeois property; on the contrary, they have become too powerful for these conditions, by which they are fettered, and so soon as they overcome these fetters, they bring disorder into the whole of bourgeois society, endanger the existence of bourgeois property. The conditions of bourgeois society are too narrow to comprise the wealth created by them. And how does the bourgeoisie get over these crises? On the one hand by enforced destruction of a mass of productive forces; on the other, by the conquest of new markets, and by the more thorough exploitation of the old ones. That is to say, by paving the way for more extensive and more destructive crises, and by diminishing the means whereby crises are prevented.

The weapons with which the bourgeoisie felled feudalism to the ground are now turned against the bourgeoisie itself.

But not only has the bourgeoisie forged the weapons that bring death to itself; it has also called into existence the men who are to wield those weapons the modern working class—the proletarians.

In proportion as the bourgeoisie, *i.e.*, capital, is developed, in the same proportion is the proletariat, the modern working class, developed—a class of labourers, who live only so long as they find work, and who find work only so long as their labour increases capital. These labourers, who must sell themselves piece-meal, are a commodity, like every other article of commerce, and are consequently exposed to all the vicissitudes of competition, to all the fluctuations of the market.

Owing to the extensive use of machinery and to division of labour, the work of the proletarians has lost all individual character, and consequently, all charm for the workman. He becomes an appendage of the machine, and it is only the most simple, most monotonous, and most easily acquired knack, that is required of him. Hence, the cost of production of a workman is restricted, almost entirely, to the means of subsistence that he requires for his maintenance, and for the propagation of his race. But the price of a commodity, and therefore also of labour,[5] is equal to its cost of production. In proportion, therefore, as the repulsiveness of the work increases, the wage decreases. Nay more, in proportion as the use of machinery and division of labour increases, in the same proportion the burden of toil also increases, whether by prolongation of the working hours, by increase of the work exacted in a given time or by increased speed of the machinery, etc.

Modern industry has converted the little workshop of the patriarchal master into the great factory of the industrial capitalist. Masses of labourers,

---

5. Subsequently Marx pointed out that the worker sells not his labour but his labour power.

crowded into the factory, are organised like soldiers. As privates of the industrial army they are placed under the command of a perfect hierarchy of officers and sergeants. Not only are they slaves of the bourgeois class, and of the bourgeois State; they are daily and hourly enslaved by the machine, by the overlooker, and, above all, by the individual bourgeois manufacturer himself. The more openly this despotism proclaims gain to be its end and aim, the more petty, the more hateful and the more embittering it is.

The less the skill and exertion of strength implied in manual labour, in other words, the more modern industry becomes developed, the more is the labour of men superseded by that of women. Differences of age and sex have no longer any distinctive social validity for the working class. All are instruments of labour, more or less expensive to use, according to their age and sex.

No sooner is the exploitation of the labourer by the manufacturer, so far, at an end, that he receives his wages in cash, than he is set upon by the other portions of the bourgeoisie, the landlord, the shopkeeper, the pawnbroker, etc.

The lower strata of the middle class—the small tradespeople, shopkeepers, and retired tradesmen generally, the handicraftsmen and peasants—all these sink gradually into the proletariat, partly because their diminutive capital does not suffice for the scale on which Modern Industry is carried on, and is swamped in the competition with the large capitalists, partly because their specialised skill is rendered worthless by new methods of production. Thus the proletariat is recruited from all classes of the population.

The proletariat goes through various stages of development. With its birth begins its struggle with the bourgeoisie. At first the contest is carried on by individual labourers, then by the workpeople of a factory, then by the operatives of one trade, in one locality, against the individual bourgeois who directly exploits them. They direct their attacks not against the bourgeois conditions of production, but against the instruments of production themselves; they destroy imported wares that compete with their labour, they smash to pieces machinery, they set factories ablaze, they seek to restore by force the vanished status of the workman of the Middle Ages.

At this stage the labourers still form an incoherent mass scattered over the whole country, and broken up by their mutual competition. If anywhere they unite to form more compact bodies, this is not yet the consequence of their own active union, but of the union of the bourgeoisie, which class, in order to attain its own political ends, is compelled to set the whole proletariat in motion, and is moreover yet, for a time, able to do so. At this stage, therefore, the proletarians do not fight their enemies, but the enemies of their enemies, the remnants of absolute monarchy, the landowners, the non-industrial bourgeois, the petty bourgeoisie. Thus the whole historical movement is concentrated in the hands of the bourgeoisie; every victory so obtained is a victory for the bourgeoisie.

But with the development of industry the proletariat not only increases in number; it becomes concentrated in greater masses, its strength grows, and it feels that strength more. The various interests and conditions of life within the ranks of the proletariat are more and more equalised, in proportion as machinery obliterates all distinctions of labour, and nearly everywhere reduces wages to the same low level. The growing competition among the bourgeois, and the resulting commercial crises, make the wages of the workers ever more fluctuating. The unceasing improvement of machinery, ever more rapidly developing, makes their livelihood more and more precarious; the collisions between individual workmen and individual bourgeois take more and more the character of collisions between two classes. Thereupon the workers begin to form combinations (Trades Unions) against the bourgeois; they club together in order to keep up the rate of wages; they found permanent associations in order to make provision beforehand for these occasional revolts. Here and there the contest breaks out into riots.

Now and then the workers are victorious, but only for a time. The real fruit of their battles lies, not in the immediate result, but in the ever-expanding union of the workers. This union is helped on by the improved means of communication that are created by modern industry and that place the workers of different localities in contact with one another. It was just this contact that was needed to centralise the numerous local struggles, all of the same character, into one national struggle between classes. But every class struggle is a political struggle. And that union, to attain which the burghers of the Middle Ages, with their miserable highways, required centuries, the modern proletarians, thanks to railways, achieve in a few years.

This organisation of the proletarians into a class, and consequently into a political party, is continually being upset again by the competition between the workers themselves. But it ever rises up again, stronger, firmer, mightier. It compels legislative recognition of particular interests of the workers, by taking advantage of the divisions among the bourgeoisie itself. Thus the ten-hours' bill in England was carried.

Altogether collisions between the classes of the old society further, in many ways, the course of development of the proletariat. The bourgeoisie finds itself involved in a constant battle. At first with the aristocracy; later on, with those portions of the bourgeoisie itself, whose interests have become antagonistic to the progress of industry; at all times, with the bourgeoisie of foreign countries. In all these battles it sees itself compelled to appeal to the proletariat, to ask for its help, and thus, to drag it into the political arena. The bourgeoisie itself, therefore, supplies the proletariat with its own elements of political and general education, in other words, it furnishes the proletariat with weapons for fighting the bourgeoisie.

Further, as we have already seen, entire sections of the ruling classes are, by the advance of industry, precipitated into the proletariat, or are at least threatened in their conditions of existence. These also supply the proletariat with fresh elements of enlightenment and progress.

Finally, in times when the class struggle nears the decisive hour, the process of dissolution going on within the ruling class, in fact within the whole range of society, assumes such a violent, glaring character, that a small section of the ruling class cuts itself adrift, and joins the revolutionary class, the class that holds the future in its hands. Just as, therefore, at an earlier period, a section of the nobility went over to the bourgeoisie, so now a portion of the bourgeoisie goes over to the proletariat, and in particular, a portion of the bourgeois ideologists, who have raised themselves to the level of comprehending theoretically the historical movement as a whole.

Of all the classes that stand face to face with the bourgeoisie today, the proletariat alone is a really revolutionary class. The other classes decay and finally disappear in the face of Modern Industry; the proletariat is its special and essential product.

The lower middle class, the small manufacturer, the shopkeeper, the artisan, the peasant, all these fight against the bourgeoisie, to save from extinction their existence as fractions of the middle class. They are therefore not revolutionary, but conservative. Nay more, they are reactionary, for they try to roll back the wheel of history. If by chance they are revolutionary, they are so only in view of their impending transfer into the proletariat, they thus defend not their present, but their future interests, they desert their own standpoint to place themselves at that of the proletariat.

The "dangerous class," the social scum, that passively rotting mass thrown off by the lowest layers of old society, may, here and there, be swept into the movement by a proletarian revolution; its conditions of life, however, prepare it far more for the part of a bribed tool of reactionary intrigue.

In the conditions of the proletariat, those of old society at large are already virtually swamped. The proletarian is without property; his relation to his wife and children has no longer anything in common with the bourgeois family-relations; modern industrial labour, modern subjection to capital, the same in England as in France, in America as in Germany, has stripped him of every trace of national character. Law, morality, religion, are to him so many bourgeois prejudices, behind which lurk in ambush just as many bourgeois interests.

All the preceding classes that got the upper hand, sought to fortify their already acquired status by subjecting society at large to their conditions of appropriation. The proletarians cannot become masters of the productive forces of society, except by abolishing their own previous mode of appropriation, and thereby also every other previous mode of appropriation. They have nothing of their own to secure and to fortify; their mission is to destroy all previous securities for, and insurances of, individual property.

All previous historical movements were movements of minorities, or in the interests of minorities. The proletarian movement is the self-conscious, independent movement of the immense majority, in the interests of the immense majority. The proletariat, the lowest stratum of our present society, cannot stir, cannot raise itself up, without the whole superincumbent strata of official society being sprung into the air.

Though not in substance, yet in form, the struggle of the proletariat with the bourgeoisie is at first a national struggle. The proletariat of each country must, of course, first of all settle matters with its own bourgeoisie.

In depicting the most general phases of the development of the proletariat, we traced the more or less veiled civil war, raging within existing society, up to the point where that war breaks out into open revolution, and where the violent overthrow of the bourgeoisie lays the foundation for the sway of the proletariat.

Hitherto, every form of society has been based, as we have already seen, on the antagonism of oppressing and oppressed classes. But in order to oppress a class, certain conditions must be assured to it under which it can, at least, continue its slavish existence. The serf, in the period of serfdom, raised himself to membership in the commune, just as the petty bourgeois, under the yoke of feudal absolutism, managed to develop into a bourgeois. The modern labourer, on the contrary, instead of rising with the progress of industry, sinks deeper and deeper below the conditions of existence of his own class. He becomes a pauper, and pauperism develops more rapidly than population and wealth. And here it becomes evident, that the bourgeoisie is unfit any longer to be the ruling class in society, and to impose its conditions of existence upon society as an over-riding law. It is unfit to rule because it is incompetent to assure an existence to its slave within his slavery, because it cannot help letting him sink into such a state, that it has to feed him, instead of being fed by him. Society can no longer live under this bourgeoisie, in other words, its existence is no longer compatible with society.

The essential condition for the existence, and for the sway of the bourgeois class, is the formation and augmentation of capital; the condition for capital is wage-labour. Wage-labour rests exclusively on competition between the labourers. The advance of industry, whose involuntary promoter is the bourgeoisie, replaces the isolation of the labourers, due to competition, by their revolutionary combination, due to association. The development of Modern Industry, therefore, cuts from under its feet the very foundation on which the bourgeoisie produces the appropriates products. What the bourgeoisie, therefore, produces, above all, is its own grave-diggers. Its fall and the victory of the proletariat are equally inevitable.

26

The Strange Enigma of Race in Contemporary America*

FROM *Racism without Racists: Color-Blind Racism and the Persistence of Racial Inequality in America*

EDUARDO BONILLA-SILVA

In the United States, racial inequalities persist in almost every measurable life out-come, from where one lives, the education one receives, the work one does, to how long one is likely to live. How do these inequities endure when so many whites insist that race doesn't matter? In this piece, sociologist Eduardo Bonilla-Silva describes the changing face of racism in the United States following the civil rights movement. Contemporary racism, what Bonilla-Silva calls "color-blind racism," is more subtle than traditional Jim Crow racism, though its effects on individuals and communi-ties are often just as pernicious. Moreover, beliefs about biological superiority have been replaced by beliefs about cultural superiority, paving the way for the maintenance of a racial hierarchy through seemingly race-neutral policies and practices. Pay special attention to the distinction between institutional racism and individual racism. As Bonilla-Silva describes, once racism is woven into the fabric of a society's institutions, racial inequalities are likely to endure even if individual acts and expressions of racism decline or disappear.

> There is a strange kind of enigma associated with the problem of racism. No one, or almost no one, wishes to see themselves as racist; still, racism persists, real and tenacious.
>
> —Albert Memmi, *Racism*

RACISM WITHOUT "RACISTS"

Nowadays, except for members of white supremacist organizations, few whites in the United States claim to be "racist." Most whites assert they "don't see any color, just people"; that although the ugly face of discrimination is still with us, it is no longer the central factor determining minorities' life chances; and, finally, that like Dr. Martin Luther King Jr., they aspire to live in a society where "people are judged by the content of their character, not by the color of their skin." More poignantly, most whites insist that minorities (especially blacks) are the ones responsible for whatever "race problem" we have in this

---

*References and footnotes can be found in Chapter 1 of the author's *Racism without Racists: Color-Blind Racism and the Persistence of Racial Inequality in America* (Rowman & Littlefield, 2006). [*Editors' note*]

country. They publicly denounce blacks for "playing the race card," for demanding the maintenance of unnecessary and divisive race-based programs, such as affirmative action, and for crying "racism" whenever they are criticized by whites. Most whites believe that if blacks and other minorities would just stop thinking about the past, work hard, and complain less (particularly about racial discrimination), then Americans of all hues could "all get along."

But regardless of whites' "sincere fictions," racial considerations shade almost everything in America. Blacks and dark-skinned racial minorities lag well behind whites in virtually every area of social life; they are about three times more likely to be poor than whites, earn about 40 percent less than whites, and have about an eighth of the net worth that whites have. They also receive an inferior education compared to whites, even when they attend integrated institutions. In terms of housing, black-owned units comparable to white-owned ones are valued at 35 percent less. Blacks and Latinos also have less access to the entire housing market because whites, through a variety of exclusionary practices by white realtors and homeowners, have been successful in effectively limiting their entrance into many neighborhoods. Blacks receive impolite treatment in stores, in restaurants, and in a host of other commercial transactions. Researchers have also documented that blacks pay more for goods such as cars and houses than do whites. Finally, blacks and dark-skinned Latinos are the targets of racial profiling by the police that, combined with the highly racialized criminal court system, guarantees their overrepresentation among those arrested, prosecuted, incarcerated, and if charged for a capital crime, executed. Racial profiling on the highways has become such a prevalent phenomenon that a term has emerged to describe it: driving while black. In short, blacks and most minorities are, "at the bottom of the well."

How is it possible to have this tremendous degree of racial inequality in a country where most whites claim that race is no longer relevant? More important, how do whites explain the apparent contradiction between their professed color blindness and the United States' color-coded inequality? . . . I contend that whites have developed powerful explanations—which have ultimately become justifications—for contemporary racial inequality that exculpate them from any responsibility for the status of people of color. These explanations emanate from a new racial ideology that I label *color-blind racism*. This ideology, which acquired cohesiveness and dominance in the late 1960s, explains contemporary racial inequality as the outcome of nonracial dynamics. Whereas Jim Crow racism explained blacks' social standing as the result of their biological and moral inferiority, color-blind racism avoids such facile arguments. Instead, whites rationalize minorities' contemporary status as the product of market dynamics, naturally occurring phenomena, and blacks' imputed cultural limitations. For instance, whites can attribute Latinos' high poverty rate to a relaxed work ethic ("the Hispanics are mañana, mañana, mañana—tomorrow, tomorrow, tomorrow") or residential segregation as the result of natural tendencies among groups ("Does a cat and a dog mix? I can't see it. You can't drink milk and scotch. Certain mixes don't mix").

Color-blind racism became the dominant racial ideology as the mechanisms and practices for keeping blacks and other racial minorities "at the bottom of the well" changed. I have argued elsewhere that contemporary racial inequality is reproduced through "New Racism" practices that are subtle, institutional, and apparently nonracial. In contrast to the Jim Crow era, where racial inequality was enforced through overt means (e.g., signs saying "No Niggers Welcomed Here" or shotgun diplomacy at the voting booth), today racial practices operate in "now you see it, now you don't" fashion. For example, residential segregation, which is almost as high today as it was in the past, is no longer accomplished through overtly discriminatory practices. Instead, covert behaviors such as not showing all the available units, steering minorities and whites into certain neighborhoods, quoting higher rents or prices to minority applicants, or not advertising units at all are the weapons of choice to maintain separate communities. In the economic field, "smiling face" discrimination ("We don't have jobs now, but please check later"), advertising job openings in mostly white networks and ethnic newspapers, and steering highly educated people of color into poorly remunerated jobs or jobs with limited opportunities for mobility are the new ways of keeping minorities in a secondary position. Politically, although the Civil Rights struggles have helped remove many of the obstacles for the electoral participation of people of color, "racial gerrymandering, multimember legislative districts, election runoffs, annexation of predominantly white areas, at-large district elections, and anti–single-shot devices (disallowing concentrating votes in one or two candidates in cities using at-large elections) have become standard practices to disenfranchise" people of color. Whether in banks, restaurants, school admissions, or housing transactions, the maintenance of white privilege is done in a way that defies facile racial readings. Hence, the contours of color-blind racism fit America's new racism quite well.

Compared to Jim Crow racism, the ideology of color blindness seems like "racism lite." Instead of relying on name calling (niggers, Spics, Chinks), color-blind racism otherizes softly ("these people are human, too"); instead of proclaiming God placed minorities in the world in a servile position, it suggests they are behind because they do not work hard enough; instead of viewing interracial marriage as wrong on a straight racial basis, it regards it as "problematic" because of concerns over the children, location, or the extra burden it places on couples. Yet this new ideology has become a formidable political tool for the maintenance of the racial order. Much as Jim Crow racism served as the glue for defending a brutal and overt system of racial oppression in the pre–Civil Rights era, color-blind racism serves today as the ideological armor for a covert and institutionalized system in the post–Civil Rights era.

And the beauty of this new ideology is that it aids in the maintenance of white privilege without fanfare, without naming those who it subjects and those who it rewards. It allows a president to state things such as, "I strongly support diversity of all kinds, including racial diversity in higher education," yet, at the same time, to characterize the University of Michigan's affirmation action program as "flawed" and "discriminatory" against whites. Thus whites enunciate positions that safeguard their racial interests without sounding "racist." Shielded by color blindness, whites can express resentment toward minorities; criticize their morality, values, and work ethic; and even claim to be the victims of "reverse racism.". . .

WHITES' RACIAL ATTITUDES IN THE POST–CIVIL RIGHTS ERA

Since the late 1950s surveys on racial attitudes have consistently found that fewer whites subscribe to the views associated with Jim Crow. For example, whereas the majority of whites supported segregated neighborhoods, schools, transportation, jobs, and public accommodations in the 1940s, less than a quarter indicated they did in the 1970s. Similarly, fewer whites than ever now seem to subscribe to stereotypical views of blacks. Although the number is still high (ranging from 20 percent to 50 percent, depending on the stereotype), the proportion of whites who state in surveys that blacks are lazy, stupid, irresponsible, and violent has declined since the 1940s.

These changes in whites' racial attitudes have been explained by the survey community and commentators in four ways. First, are the *racial optimists*. This group of analysts agrees with whites' common sense on racial matters and believes the changes symbolize a profound transition in the United States. Early representatives of this view were Herbert Hyman and Paul B. Sheatsley, who wrote widely influential articles on the subject in *Scientific American*. In a reprint of their earlier work in the influential collection edited by Talcott Parsons and Kenneth Clark, *The Negro American*, Sheatsley rated the changes in white attitudes as "revolutionary" and concluded,

> The mass of white Americans have shown in many ways that they will not follow a racist government and that they will not follow racist leaders. Rather, they are engaged in the painful task of adjusting to an integrated society. It will not be easy for most, but one cannot at this late date doubt the basic commitment. In their hearts they know that the American Negro is right.

In recent times, Glenn Firebaugh and Kenneth Davis, Seymour Lipset, and Paul Sniderman and his coauthors, in particular, have carried the torch for racial optimists. Firebaugh and Davis, for example, based on their analysis of survey results from 1972 to 1984, concluded that the trend toward less antiblack prejudice was across the board. Sniderman and his coauthors, as well as Lipset, go a step further than Firebaugh and Davis because they have openly advocated color-blind politics as *the* way to settle the United States' racial dilemmas. For instance, Sniderman and Edward Carmines made this explicit appeal in their recent book, *Reaching beyond Race,*

> To say that a commitment to a color-blind politics is worth undertaking is to call for a politics centered on the needs of those most in need. It is not to argue for a politics in which race is irrelevant, but in favor of one in which race is relevant so far as it is a gauge of need. Above all, it is a call for a politics which, because it is organized around moral principles that apply regardless of race, can be brought to bear with special force on the issue of race.

The problems with this optimistic interpretation are twofold. First, as I have argued elsewhere, relying on questions that were framed in the Jim Crow era to assess whites' racial views today produces an artificial image of progress. Since the central racial debates and the language used to debate those matters have changed, our analytical focus ought to be dedicated to the analysis of the new racial issues. Insisting on the need to rely on old questions to keep longitudinal (trend) data as the basis for analysis will, by default, produce a rosy picture of race relations that misses what is going on on the ground. Second, and more important, because of the change in the normative climate in the post–Civil Rights era, analysts must exert extreme caution when interpreting attitudinal data, particularly when it comes from single-method research designs. The research strategy that seems more appropriate for our times is mixed research designs (surveys used in combination with interviews, ethnosurveys, etc.), because it allows researchers to cross-examine their results.

A second, more numerous group of analysts exhibit what I have labeled elsewhere as the *racial pesoptimist* position. Racial pesoptimists attempt to strike a "balanced" view and suggest that whites' racial attitudes reflect progress and resistance. The classical example of this stance is Howard Schuman. Schuman has argued for more than thirty years that whites' racial attitudes involve a mixture of tolerance and intolerance, of acceptance of the principles of racial liberalism (equal opportunity for all, end of segregation, etc.) and a rejection of the policies that would make those principles a reality (from affirmative action to busing).

Despite the obvious appeal of this view in the research community (the appearance of neutrality, the pondering of "two sides," and this view's "balanced" component), racial pesoptimists are just closet optimists. Schuman, for example, has pointed out that, although "White responses to questions of principle are . . . more complex than is often portrayed . . . they nevertheless do show in almost every instance a positive movement over time." Furthermore, it is his belief that the normative change in the United States is real and that the issue is that whites are having a hard time translating those norms into personal preferences.

A third group of analysts argues that the changes in whites' attitudes represent the emergence of a *symbolic racism*. This tradition is associated with the work of David Sears and his associate, Donald Kinder. They have defined symbolic racism as "a blend of anti-black affect and the kind of traditional American moral values embodied in the Protestant Ethic." According to these authors, symbolic racism has replaced biological racism as the primary way whites express their racial resentment toward minorities. In Kinder and Sanders's words:

> A new form of prejudice has come to prominence, one that is preoccupied with matters of moral character, informed by the virtues associated with the traditions of individualism. At its center are the contentions that blacks do not try hard enough to overcome the difficulties they face and that they take what they have not earned. Today, we say, prejudice is expressed in the language of American individualism.

Authors in this tradition have been criticized for the slipperiness of the concept "symbolic racism," for claiming that the blend of antiblack affect and individualism is new, and for not explaining why symbolic racism came about. The first critique, developed by Howard Schuman, is that the concept has been "defined and operationalized in complex and varying ways." Despite this conceptual slipperiness, indexes of symbolic racism have been found to be in fact different from those of old-fashioned racism and to be strong predictors of whites' opposition to affirmative action. The two other critiques, made forcefully by Lawrence Bobo, have been partially addressed by Kinder and Sanders in their recent book, *Divided by Color*. First, Kinder and Sanders, as well as Sears, have made clear that their contention is not that this is the first time in history that antiblack affect and elements of the American Creed have combined. Instead, their claim is that this combination has become *central* to the new face of racism. Regarding the third critique, Kinder and Sanders go at length to explain the transition from old-fashioned to symbolic racism. Nevertheless, their explanation hinges on arguing that changes in blacks' tactics (from civil disobedience to urban violence) led to an onslaught of a new form of racial resentment that later found more fuel in controversies over welfare, crime, drugs, family, and affirmative action. What is missing in this explanation is a materially based explanation for why these changes occurred. Instead, their theory of prejudice is rooted in the "process of socialization and the operation of routine cognitive and emotional psychological processes."

Yet, despite its limitations, the symbolic racism tradition has brought attention to key elements of how whites explain racial inequality today.

Whether this is "symbolic" of antiblack affect or not is beside the point and hard to assess, since as a former student of mine queried, "How does one test for the unconscious?"

The fourth explanation of whites' contemporary racial attitudes is associated with those who claim that whites' racial views represent a *sense of group position.* This position, forcefully advocated by Lawrence Bobo and James Kluegel, is similar to Jim Sidanius's "social dominance" and Mary Jackman's "group interests" arguments. In essence, the claim of all these authors is that white prejudice is an ideology to defend white privilege. Bobo and his associates have specifically suggested that because of socio-economic changes that transpired in the 1950s and 1960s, a *laissez-faire racism* emerged that was fitting of the United States' "modern, nationwide, postindustrial free labor economy and polity." Laissez-faire racism "encompasses an ideology that blames blacks themselves for their poorer relative economic standing, seeing it as the function of perceived cultural inferiority."

Some of the basic arguments of authors in the symbolic and modern racism traditions and, particularly, of the laissez-faire racism view are fully compatible with my color-blind racism interpretation. As these authors, I argue that color-blind racism has rearticulated elements of traditional liberalism (work ethic, rewards by merit, equal opportunity, individualism, etc.) for racially illiberal goals. I also argue like them that whites today rely more on cultural rather than biological tropes to explain blacks' position in this country. Finally, I concur with most analysts of post–Civil Rights' matters in arguing that whites do not perceive discrimination to be a central factor shaping blacks' life chances.

Although most of my differences with authors in the symbolic racism and laissez-faire traditions are methodological . . . , I have one central theoretical disagreement with them. Theoretically, most of these authors are still snarled in the prejudice problematic and thus interpret actors' racial views as *individual psychological* dispositions. Although Bobo and his associates have a conceptualization that is closer to mine, they still retain the notion of prejudice and its psychological baggage rooted in interracial hostility. In contrast, my model is not anchored in actors' affective dispositions (although affective dispositions may be manifest or latent in the way many express their racial views). Instead, it is based on a materialist interpretation of racial matters and thus sees the views of actors as corresponding to their systemic location. Those at the bottom of the racial barrel tend to hold oppositional views and those who receive the manifold wages of whiteness tend to hold views in support of the racial status quo. Whether actors express "resentment" or "hostility" toward minorities is largely irrelevant for the maintenance of white privilege. As David Wellman points out in his *Portraits of White Racism,* "[p]rejudiced people are not the only racists in America."

KEY TERMS: RACE, RACIAL STRUCTURE, AND RACIAL IDEOLOGY

One reason why, in general terms, whites and people of color cannot agree on racial matters is because they conceive terms such as "racism" very differently. Whereas for most whites racism is prejudice, for most people of color racism is systemic or institutionalized. Although this is not a theory book, my examination of color-blind racism has etched in it the indelible ink of a "regime of truth" about how the world is organized. Thus, rather than hiding my theoretical assumptions, I state them openly for the benefit of readers and potential critics.

The first key term is the notion of *race*. There is very little formal disagreement among social scientists in accepting the idea that race is a socially constructed category. This means that notions of racial difference are human creations rather than eternal, essential categories. As such, racial categories have a history and are subject to change. And here ends the agreement among social scientists on this matter. There are at least three distinct variations on how social scientists approach this constructionist perspective on race. The first approach, which is gaining popularity among white social scientists, is the idea that because race is socially constructed, it is not a fundamental category of analysis and praxis. Some analysts go as far as to suggest that because race is a constructed category, then it is not real and social scientists who use the category are the ones who make it real.

The second approach, typical of most sociological writing on race, gives lip service to the social constructionist view—usually a line in the beginning of the article or book. Writers in this group then proceed to discuss "racial" differences in academic achievement, crime, and SAT scores as if they were truly racial. This is the central way in which contemporary scholars contribute to the propagation of racist interpretations of racial inequality. By failing to highlight the social dynamics that produce these racial differences, these scholars help reinforce the racial order.

The third approach, and the one I use in this book, acknowledges that race, as other social categories such as class and gender, is constructed but insists that it has a *social* reality. This means that after race—or class or gender—is created, it produces real effects on the actors racialized as "black" or "white." Although race, as other social constructions, is unstable, it has a "changing same" quality at its core.

In order to explain how a socially constructed category produces real race effects, I need to introduce a second key term: the notion of *racial structure*. When race emerged in human history, it formed a social structure (a racialized social system) that awarded systemic privileges to Europeans (the peoples who became "white") over non-Europeans (the peoples who became "nonwhite"). Racialized social systems, or white supremacy for short, became global and affected all societies where Europeans extended their reach. I therefore conceive a society's racial structure as *the totality of the social relations and practices that reinforce white privilege.* Accordingly, the task of analysts interested in studying racial structures is to uncover the particular social, economic, political, social control, and ideological mechanisms responsible for the reproduction of racial privilege in a society.

But why are racial structures reproduced in the first place? Would not humans, after discovering the folly of racial thinking, work to abolish race as a category as well as a practice? Racial structures remain in place for the same reasons that other structures do. Since actors racialized as "white"—or as members of the dominant race—receive material benefits from the racial order, they struggle (or passively receive the manifold wages of whiteness) to maintain their privileges. In contrast, those defined as belonging to the subordinate race or races struggle to change the status quo (or become resigned to their position). Therein lies the secret of racial structures and racial inequality the world over. They exist because they benefit members of the dominant race.

If the ultimate goal of the dominant race is to defend its collective interests (i.e., the perpetuation of systemic white privilege), it should surprise no one that this group develops rationalizations to account for the status of the various races. And here I introduce my third key term, the notion of *racial ideology.* By this I mean *the racially based frameworks used by actors to explain and justify* (dominant race) or *challenge* (subordinate race or races) *the racial status quo.* Although all the races in a racialized social system have the *capacity* of developing these frameworks, the frameworks of the dominant race tend to become the master frameworks upon which *all* racial actors ground (for or against) their ideological positions. Why? Because as Marx pointed out in *The German Ideology,* "the ruling *material* force of society, is at the same time its ruling *intellectual* force." This does not mean that ideology is almighty. In fact, . . . ideological rule is always partial. Even in periods of hegemonic rule, such as the current one, subordinate racial groups develop oppositional views. However, it would be foolish to believe that those who rule a society do not have the power to at least color (pun intended) the views of the ruled.

Racial ideology can be conceived for analytical purposes as comprising the following elements: common frames, style, and racial stories. . . . The frames that bond together a particular racial ideology are rooted in the group-based conditions and experiences of the races and are, at the symbolic level, the representations developed by these groups to explain how the world is or ought to be. And because the group life of the various racially defined groups is based on hierarchy and domination, the ruling ideology expresses as "common sense" the interests of the dominant race, while oppositional ideologies attempt to challenge that common sense by providing alternative frames, ideas, and stories based on the experiences of subordinated races.

Individual actors employ these elements as "building blocks . . . for manufacturing versions on actions, self, and social structures" in communicative situations. The looseness of the elements allows users to maneuver within various contexts (e.g., responding to a race-related survey, discussing racial issues with family, or arguing about affirmative action in a college classroom) and produce various accounts and presentations of self (e.g., appearing ambivalent, tolerant, or strong minded). This loose character enhances the legitimating role of racial ideology because it allows for accommodation of contradictions, exceptions, and new information. As Jackman points out about ideology in general: "Indeed, the strength of an ideology lies in its loose-jointed, flexible application. *An ideology is a political instrument, not an exercise in personal logic:* consistency is rigidity, the only pragmatic effect of which is to box oneself in."

. . . [T]wo important caveats should be offered. First, although whites, because of their privileged position in the racial order, form a social group (the dominant race), they are fractured along class, gender, sexual orientation, and other forms of "social cleavage." Hence, they have multiple and often contradictory interests that are not easy to disentangle and that predict a priori their mobilizing capacity (Do white workers have more in common with white capitalists than with black workers?). However, because all actors awarded the dominant racial position, regardless of their multiple structural locations (men or women, gay or straight, working class or bourgeois) benefit from what Mills calls the "racial contract," *most* have historically endorsed the ideas that justify the racial status quo.

Second, although not every single member of the dominant race defends the racial status quo or spouts color-blind racism, *most* do. To explain this point by analogy, although not every capitalist defends capitalism (e.g., Frederick Engels, the coauthor of *The Communist Manifesto,* was a capitalist) and not every man defends patriarchy (e.g., *Achilles Heel* is an English magazine published by feminist men), *most* do in some fashion. In the same vein, although some whites fight white supremacy and do not endorse white common sense, *most* subscribe to substantial portions of it in a casual, uncritical fashion that helps sustain the prevailing racial order.

27

The Economic Plight of Inner-City Black Males*

FROM *More than Just Race: Being Black and Poor in the Inner City*

WILLIAM JULIUS WILSON

Reading this essay, you are stepping into a minefield. Fortunately, William Julius Wilson, one of our preeminent sociologists for the past thirty years, skillfully leads the way. As a newcomer to sociology you don't know that academic battles have raged, unkind words and accusations have been hurled, character has been impugned, and friends have become enemies over the question Wilson is addressing: Why are so many black males overrepresented among school dropouts, the unemployed, the incarcerated, and the unwed fathers in this country? Fortunately, we no longer have to rely on an explanation that "blames the victim" by castigating their "culture of poverty" and lack of personal responsibility. Nor do we have to blame "the system" and treat those in distress as if they are puppets or robots on a downward-sloping treadmill. Wilson knows what he is talking about when he looks closely at the structural barriers to success and the many ways opportunity is denied millions of black males, including many young black men today. He also knows about the beliefs and attitudes fostered in the inner city and the accepted practices that keep many men from pursuing possibilities that could change their lives. For too long the odds have been against them.

The economic predicament of low-skilled black men in the inner city has reached catastrophic proportions. Americans may not fully understand the dreadful social and economic circumstances that have moved these black males further and further behind the rest of society, but they often fear black males and perceive that they pose a problem for those who live in the city. Elliot Liebow helped expand our understanding of low-skilled black males when he wrote *Tally's Corner: A Study of Street Corner Men* in the mid-1960s. Since then, researchers have paid more attention to this group.

Although many of Liebow's arguments concerning the work experiences and family lives of black men in a Washington DC ghetto are still applicable to contemporary urban communities, the social and economic predicament of low-skilled black males today, especially their rate of joblessness, has become even more severe. Liebow was perhaps the first scholar to demonstrate that an ongoing lack of success in the labor market (ranging from outright unemployment

---

*Footnotes and references can be found in the original publication of William Julius Wilson's *More than Just Race: Being Black and Poor in the Inner City* (New York: W. W. Norton & Company, 2009). [*Editors' note*]

to being trapped in menial jobs) leads to a lessening of self-confidence and, eventually, to feelings of resignation that frequently result in temporary, or even permanent, abandonment of looking for work.

Even when Liebow's men were successful in finding work, the jobs they occupied paid little and were dirty, physically demanding, and uninteresting. This work did not foster respect, build status, or offer opportunity for advancement. "The most important fact [in becoming discouraged from looking for or keeping a job] is that a man who is able and willing to work cannot earn enough to support himself, his wife, and one or more children," declared Liebow. "A man's chances for working regularly are good only if he is willing to work for less than he can live on, sometimes not even then." Because they held the same ideas about work and reward as other Americans, the street-corner men viewed such jobs disdainfully. "He cannot do otherwise," stated Liebow. "He cannot draw from a job those values which other people do not put into it." Unlike today, menial employment was readily available to these men during the 1960s, and they drifted from one undesirable job to the next.

When I analyzed the data collected from the mid-1980s to the mid-1990s by our research team on poverty and joblessness among black males in inner-city Chicago neighborhoods, I was repeatedly reminded of Liebow's book. Although the job prospects for low-skilled black men were bleak when Liebow conducted his field research in the early 1960s, they were even worse in the last quarter of the twentieth century, when even menial jobs in the service sector were difficult for low-skilled black males to find. That situation persists today.

THE ROLE OF STRUCTURAL FACTORS

Although African American men continue to confront racial barriers in the labor market, many inner-city black males have also been victimized by other structural factors, such as the decreased relative demand for low-skilled labor. The propagation of new technologies is displacing untrained workers and rewarding those with specialized, technical training, while globalization of the economy is increasingly pitting low-skilled workers in the United States against their counterparts around the world, including laborers in countries such as China, India, and Bangladesh who can be employed for substantially lower wages. This decreasing relative demand in the United States for low-skilled labor means that untrained workers face the growing threat of eroding wages and job displacement.

Over the past several decades, African Americans have experienced sharp job losses in the manufacturing sector. Indeed, as John Schmitt and Ben Zipperer point out, "the share of black workers in manufacturing has actually been falling more rapidly than the overall share of manufacturing employment. From the end of the 1970s through the early 1990s, African Americans were just as likely as workers from other racial and ethnic groups to have manufacturing jobs. Since the early 1990s, however, black workers have lost considerable ground in manufacturing. By 2007, blacks were about 15 percent less likely than other workers to have a job in manufacturing." The dwindling proportion of African American workers in manufacturing is important because manufacturing jobs, especially those in the auto industry, have been a significant source of better-paid employment for black Americans since World War II.

The relative decline of black workers in manufacturing parallels their decreasing involvement in unions. From 1983 to 2007 the proportion of all African American workers who were either in unions or represented by a union at their employment site dropped considerably, from 31.7 to 15.7 percent. In 2007, African American workers were still more likely to be unionized (15.7 percent) than whites (13.5) and Hispanics (10.8). Nonetheless, this reduction (down 16 percentage points) over that time span was greater than that for whites (down 8.9 percentage points) and Hispanics (down 13.4). The lack of union representation renders workers more vulnerable in the workplace, especially to cuts in wages and benefits.

Because they tend to be educated in poorly performing public schools, low-skilled black males often enter the job market lacking some of the basic tools that would help them confront changes in their employment prospects. Such schools have rigid district bureaucracies, poor morale among teachers and school principals, low expectations for students, and negative ideologies that justify poor student performance. Inner-city schools fall well below more advantaged suburban schools in science and math resources, and they lack teachers with appropriate preparation in these subjects. As a result, students from these schools tend to have poor reading and math skills, important tools for competing in the globalized labor market. Few thoughtful observers of public education would disagree with the view that the poor employment prospects of low-skilled black males are in no small measure related to their public-education experiences.

Their lack of education, which contributes to joblessness, is certainly related to their risk of incarceration. As Bruce Western so brilliantly revealed in his important book *Punishment and Inequality in America*, following the collapse of the low-skilled urban labor markets and the creation of jobless ghettos in our nation's inner cities, incarceration grew among those with the highest rates of joblessness. "By the early 2000s," states Western, "the chances of imprisonment were more closely linked to race and school failure than at any time in the previous twenty years." Between 1979 and 1999, the risk of imprisonment for less educated men nearly doubled. Indeed, a significant proportion of black men who have been in prison are high school dropouts. "Among [black] male high school dropouts the risk of imprisonment [has] increased to 60 percent, establishing incarceration as a normal stopping point on the route to midlife."

However, Western's research also revealed that national cultural shifts in values and attitudes contributed to a political context associated with a resurgent Republican Party that focused on punitive "solutions" and worsened the plight of low-skilled black men. This more penal approach to crime was reinforced during Bill Clinton's administration. Indeed, rates of incarceration soared even during periods when the overall crime rate had declined. "The growth in violence among the ghetto poor through the 1960s and 1970s stoked fears of white voters and lurked in the rhetoric of law and order," states Western. "Crime, however, did not drive the rise in imprisonment directly, but formed the background for a new style of politics and punishment. As joblessness and low wages became enduring features of the less skilled inner-city economy, the effects of a punitive criminal justice system concentrated on the most disadvantaged." Western estimates that as many as 30 percent of all civilian young adult black males ages sixteen to thirty-four are ex-offenders. In short, cultural shifts in attitudes toward crime and punishment created structural circumstances—a more punitive criminal justice system—that have had a powerful impact on low-skilled black males.

* * *

For inner-city black male workers, the problems created by these structural factors have been aggravated by employers' negative attitudes toward black men as workers. A representative sample of Chicago-area employers by my research team in the late 1980s clearly reveals employer bias against black males. A substantial majority of employers considered inner-city black males to be uneducated, uncooperative, unstable, or dishonest. For example, a suburban drug store manager made the following comment:

> It's unfortunate but, in my business I think overall [black men] tend to be known to be dishonest. I think that's too bad but that's the image they have. (*Interviewer*: So you think it's an image problem?) *Respondent*: An image problem of being dishonest men and lazy. They're known to be lazy. They are [laughs]. I hate to tell you, but. It's all an image though. Whether they are or not. I don't know, but, it's an image that is perceived. (*Interviewer*: I see. How do you think that image was developed?) *Respondent*: Go look in the jails [laughs].

The president of an inner-city manufacturing firm expressed a different reservation about employing black males from certain ghetto neighborhoods:

> If somebody gave me their address, uh, Cabrini Green I might unavoidably have some concerns. (*Interviewer*: What would your concerns be?) *Respondent*: That the poor guy probably would be frequently unable to get to work and . . . I probably would watch him more carefully even if it wasn't fair, than I would with somebody else. I know what I should do though is recognize that here's a guy that is trying to get out of his situation and probably will work harder than somebody else who's already out of there and he might be the best one around here. But I think I would have to struggle accepting that premise at the beginning.

The prevalence of such attitudes, combined with the physical and social isolation of minorities living in inner-city areas of concentrated poverty, severely limits the access that poor black men have to informal job networks (the casual networks of people or acquaintances who can pass along information about employment prospects). This is a notable problem for black males, especially considering that many low-skilled employees first learn about their jobs through an acquaintance or were recommended by someone associated with the company. Research suggests that only a small percentage of low-skilled employees are hired through advertised job openings or cold calls. The importance of knowing someone who knows the boss can be seen by another employer's comments to our interviewer:

> All of a sudden, they take a look at a guy, and unless he's got an in, the reason why I hired this black kid the last time is cause my neighbor said to me, yeah I used him for a few [days], he's good, and I said, you know what, I'm going to take a chance. But it was a recommendation. But other than that, I've got a walk-in, and, who knows? And I think that for the most part, a guy sees a black man, he's a bit hesitant.

These attitudes are classic examples of what social scientists call statistical discrimination: employers make generalizations about inner-city, black male workers and reach decisions based on those assumptions without reviewing the qualifications of an individual applicant. The net effect is that many inner-city, black male applicants are never given the opportunity to prove themselves. Although some of these men scorn entry-level jobs because of the poor working conditions and low wages, many others would readily accept such employment. And although statistical discrimination contains some elements of class bias against poor, inner-city workers, it is clearly a racially motivated practice. It is a frustrating and disturbing fact that inner-city black males are effectively screened out of employment far more often than their Hispanic or white peers who apply for the same jobs. A number of other studies have documented employer bias against black males. For example, research by Devah Pager revealed that a white applicant with a felony conviction was more likely to receive a callback or job offer than was a black applicant with a clean record.†

* * *

Forced to turn to the low-wage service sector for employment, inner-city black males—including a significant number of ex-offenders—have to compete, often unsuccessfully, with a growing number of female and immigrant workers. If these men complain or otherwise manifest their dissatisfaction, they seem even more unattractive to employers and therefore encounter even greater discrimination when they search for employment. Because the feelings that

---

†See "The Mark of a Criminal Record," essay 5 in this reader. [*Editors' note*]

many inner-city black males express about their jobs and job prospects reflect their plummeting position in a changing economy, it is important to link these attitudes and other cultural traits with the opportunity structure—that is, the spectrum of life chances available to them in society at large.

Many people would agree that both the structural factors and the national cultural factors discussed earlier have had a very large impact on the experiences of low-skilled black males. But no such consensus exists with respect to the role of cultural factors that have emerged in inner-city ghetto neighborhoods in shaping and directing the lives of young black men.

THE ROLE OF CULTURAL FACTORS

Throughout this discussion I have suggested that cultural factors must be brought to bear if we are to explain economic and social outcomes for racial groups. The exploration of the cultural dimension must do three things: (1) provide a compelling reason for including cultural factors in a comprehensive discussion of race and poverty, (2) show the relationship between cultural analysis and structural analysis, and (3) determine the extent to which cultural factors operate independently to contribute to or reinforce poverty and racial inequality. However, the evidence for the influence of cultural factors on the social and economic circumstances of low-skilled black males is far less compelling than structural arguments, in part because of a dearth of research in this area.

According to Orlando Patterson of Harvard University, since the mid-1960s a strong bias against cultural explanations for human behavior has led social scientists and policy analysts to ignore different groups' distinctive cultural attributes in favor of an emphasis on structural factors to account for the behavior and social outcomes of its members. So instead of looking at attitudes, norms, values, habits, and worldviews (all indications of cultural orientations), we focus on joblessness, low socioeconomic status, and under-performing public schools—in short, structural factors.

Patterson revisited the role of culture and raised several questions that might be better addressed when cultural elements are considered in conjunction with structural and historical explanations. Patterson asks, "Why do so many young unemployed black men have children—several of them—which they have no resources or intention to support? And why . . . do they murder each other at nine times the rate of white youths?" And, he adds, why do young black males turn their backs on low-wage jobs that immigrants are happy to fill? Referring to research conducted by UCLA sociologist Roger Waldinger, Patterson states that such jobs enable the chronically unemployed to enter the labor market and obtain basic work skills that they can later use in securing better jobs. But he also notes that those who accepted the low-paying jobs in Waldinger's study were mostly immigrants.

To help answer his own questions about the behavior of young black men in the ghetto, Patterson refers to anecdotal evidence collected several years ago by one of his former students. He states that the student visited her former high school to discover why "almost all the black girls graduated and went to college whereas nearly all the black boys either failed to graduate or did not go on to college." Her distressing finding was that all of the black boys were fully aware of the consequences of failing to graduate from high school and go on to college. (They indignantly exclaimed, "We're not stupid!") So, Patterson wonders, why were they flunking out? The candid answer that these young men gave to his former student was their preference for what some call the "cool-pose culture" of young black men, which they found too fulfilling to give up. "For these young men, it was almost like a drug, hanging out on the street after school, shopping and dressing sharply, sexual conquests, party drugs, hip-hop music and culture."

Patterson maintains that cool-pose culture blatantly promotes the most anomalous models of behavior in urban, lower-class neighborhoods, featuring gangsta rap, predatory sexuality, and irresponsible fathering. "It is reasonable to conclude," he states, "that among a large number of urban, Afro-American lower-class young men, these models are now fully normative and that men act in accordance with them whenever they can." For example, Patterson argues that black male pride has become increasingly defined in terms of the impregnation of women. However, this trend is not unique to the current generation of young black males, he notes. Several decades ago the sociologist Lee Rainwater uncovered a similar pattern. Not only did a majority of the inner-city, young black male respondents he interviewed state that they were indifferent to the fact that their girlfriends were pregnant, but some even expressed the proud belief that getting a girl pregnant proves you're a man. The fact that Elijah Anderson and others discovered identical models decades later suggests the possibility of a pattern of cultural transmission—that is, the attitudes and behaviors valorizing a kind of "footloose fatherhood" have been passed down to younger generations. A counterargument—one that does not assume cultural transmission—could also be posed: young black men in roughly similar structural positions in different generations developed similar cultural responses.

Patterson argues that a thoughtful cultural explanation of the self-defeating behavior of poor, young black men could not only speak to the immediate relationship of their attitudes, behavior, and undesirable outcomes, but also examine their brutalized past, perhaps over generations, to investigate the origins and changing nature of these views and practices. Patterson maintains that we cannot understand the behavior of young black men without deeply examining their collective past.

I believe that Patterson tends to downplay the importance of immediate socioeconomic factors: if there is indeed a cool-pose culture, it is reasonable to assume that it is partly related to employment failures and disillusionment with the poorly performing public schools and possibly has its roots in the special social circumstances fostered by pre-1960s legal segregation. But I fully concur with Patterson's view that cultural explanations that include historical context should be part of our attempt to fully account for behavior that is so contradictory to mainstream ideas of how work and family should fit into a man's life.

In her ethnographic research—that is, work using evidence gathered through field observation and through extended, often repeated, interviews—Katherine Newman reveals that young, low-wage workers in New York City's Harlem neighborhood not only adhere to mainstream values regarding work, but also tend to accept low-skilled, low-wage, often dead-end jobs. In his impressive study of how young, inner-city black men perceive opportunity and mobility in the United States, Alford Young found that although some men associated social mobility with the economic opportunity structure, including race- and class-based discrimination, all of his respondents shared the view that individuals are largely accountable for their failure to advance in society.

The research conducted by my team in Chicago provides only mixed evidence for a subculture of defeatism. Consistent with Liebow's findings in *Tally's Corner*, the ethnographic research in our study revealed that many young black males had experienced repeated failures in their job search, had given up hope, and therefore no longer bothered to look for work. . . . [O]ur research pointed to negative employer attitudes and actions toward low-skilled black males as powerful influences in this cycle. Our ethnographic research suggested that repeated failure results in resignation and the development of cultural attitudes that discourage the pursuit of steady employment in the formal labor market.

On the other hand, data from our large, random survey of black residents in the inner city revealed that despite the overwhelming joblessness and poverty around them, black residents in ghetto neighborhoods, consistent with the findings of Alford Young, spoke unambiguously in support of basic American values concerning individual initiative. For example, nearly all of the black people we questioned felt that plain hard work is either very important or somewhat important for getting ahead. In addition, in a series of open-ended interviews conducted by members of our research team, participants overwhelmingly endorsed the dominant American belief system concerning poverty. The views of some of these individuals—who lived in some of the most destitute neighborhoods in America—were particularly revealing. A substantial majority agreed that America is a land of opportunity where anybody can get ahead, and that individuals get pretty much what they deserve.

The response of a thirty-four-year-old black male, a resident in a ghetto area of the South Side of Chicago where 29 percent of the population was destitute (i.e., with incomes 75 percent below the poverty line) was typical: "Everybody get pretty much what they deserve because if everybody wants to do better they got to go out there and try. If they don't try, they won't make it." Another black male who was residing in an equally impoverished South Side neighborhood stated, "For some it's a land of opportunity, but you can't just let opportunity come knock on your door, you just got to go ahead and work for it. You got to go out and get it for yourself." Although their support of this abstract American ideal was not always consistent with their perceptions and descriptions of the social barriers that impeded the social progress of their neighbors and friends, these endorsements stand in strong contrast to the subculture of defeatism. Nonetheless, I should note that there is frequently a gap between what people state in the abstract and what they perceive to be possible for themselves given their own situations. In other words, it should not be surprising if some residents support the abstract American ideal of individual initiative and still feel that they cannot get ahead, because of factors beyond their control.

The inconsistency between what people say in the abstract and what they believe applies to them maybe seen in other ways. Jennifer Hochschild's analysis of national survey data reveals that poor blacks tend to acknowledge the importance of discrimination when they respond to national surveys, but they are not likely to feel that it affects them personally. Often, discrimination is the least mentioned factor among other important forces that black people select when asked what determines their chances in life. Thus, among poor blacks, structural factors such as discrimination and declining job opportunities "do not register as major impediments to achieving their goals. Deficient motivation and individual effort do." The emphasis that poor blacks place on the importance of personal attributes over structural factors for success in America should not come as a surprise. As Hochschild astutely points out, "poor African Americans are usually badly educated and not widely traveled, so they are unlikely to see structural patterns underlying individual actions and situations. Thus even if (or because) the American dream fails as a description of American society, it is a highly seductive prescription for succeeding in that society to those who cannot see the underlying flaw." To repeat, the evidence for a subculture of defeatism is mixed. Nonetheless, until more compelling studies are produced, it remains an important hypothesis for research.

* * *

Sandra Smith provides a compelling and nuanced cultural analysis of other factors that contribute to the complex and often difficult world of work inhabited by low-skilled blacks. Smith conducted in-depth interviews with 105 black men and women in Michigan between the ages of twenty and forty who had no more than a high school education so that she could examine the informal personal networks of low-skilled black job holders and job seekers.

Smith's data provide new information to help explain why informal job networks among blacks were less useful in helping job seekers find employment in the formal economy. She found that distrust on the part of black job holders and the defensive individualism typical of black job seekers profoundly affected the use of job referrals in the search for employment. She points out that the neighborhoods of the black poor are "characterized by chronic poverty and a history of exploitation" and tend to feed the inclination to distrust, "inhibiting the development of mutually beneficial cooperative relationships such as those that facilitate the job-matching process." The cooperation between job seekers and job holders is thwarted by a lack of mutual trust. Thus, low-skilled black job seekers are frequently unable to use their friendships, acquaintances, and family ties—their informal network—to gain employment. Black job holders were reluctant to refer their relatives and friends for jobs because they feared that their own reputations with employers could be jeopardized if the work of the people they recommended was substandard.

* * *

CONCLUSION

The disproportionate number of low-skilled black males in this country is one of the legacies of historical segregation and discrimination. However, aside from the effects of current segregation and discrimination, including those caused by employer bias, I highlighted a number of impersonal economic forces that have contributed to the incredibly high jobless rate of low-skilled black males and their correspondingly low incomes. These forces include the decreased relative demand for low-skilled labor caused by the computer revolution, the globalization of economic activity, the declining manufacturing sector, and the growth of service industries in which most of the new jobs for workers with limited skills and education are concentrated.

I noted that the shift to service industries has created a new set of problems for low-skilled black males because those industries feature jobs that require workers to serve and relate to consumers. Why are such requirements a problem for black men? Simply because employers believe that women and recent immigrants of both genders are better suited than black males, especially those with prison records, for such jobs. This image has been created partly by cultural shifts in national attitudes that reflected concerns about the growth of violence in the ghettos through the 1960s and '70s. In the eyes of many Americans, black males symbolized this violence. Cries for "law and order" resulted in a more punitive criminal justice system and a dramatic increase in black male incarceration.

Cultural arguments have been advanced to explain the social and economic woes of low-skilled black males, but the evidence is mixed. For example, a number of studies have associated black joblessness with high reservation wages, the lowest wages that a worker is willing to accept. Nonetheless, one of the more compelling studies found no significant relationship between the reservation wages of black men and the duration of joblessness. The findings in an important recent study, however, clearly suggest that chronic poverty and exploitation in poor black neighborhoods tend to feed inclinations to distrust. These cultural traits undermine the development of cooperative relationships that are so vital in informal job networks. Black workers in the inner city tend to be less willing to recommend friends and relatives for jobs that become available. Thus, the structural problem of employer job discrimination and the cultural inclination to distrust combine to severely handicap low-skilled, black male workers, especially those with prison records.

28

Employing Parents Who Can't Make a Living*

FROM *The Moral Underground: How Ordinary Americans Subvert an Unfair Economy*

LISA DODSON

The author's years of ethnographic fieldwork inform her examination of one of the dilemmas of the low-wage economy. It reveals the "human agency" we all have in broaching the rules and practices of large organizations in order to be true to our moral values. Worker resistance is one way to see what is happening here, as the ranks of the working poor grow and the wealth of the 1 percent swells. What does this mean for managers who feel pressure from above but an obligation to those below them? More broadly, how do we hold a society together—with the moral fabric early sociologists like Émile Durkheim thought was essential—in the face of such problematic rents in the social fabric?

Do we have any responsibility for what happens to them?
—Ellen, a manager in a company that employed many low-wage workers, 2002

Ellen raised this question during a community conversation with other employers from a variety of businesses in the Milwaukee area. They had been talking about common problems they faced with "entry-level" employees. Together they came up with a list of inconveniences and disruptions that come with people "who are disorganized" and bring that disarray to the workplace. They are absent too much, come to work late, get calls that distract them, or leave early, and they are often just "not focused on the job." They said that there always seems to be some problem going on that complicates getting work done; their lives "just aren't organized" or "they don't have that work ethic."

Most of the employers at this meeting supervised workers who were mothers, and they spoke at length about "family problems." Eventually, their description of these troubles turned into a discussion about how inconvenient it was that these workers *had families at all*, because raising children is so time demanding. With some honesty, members of this group acknowledged that if you make $18,000—even $30,000—a year and have kids, "family life is going to create a problem" for those who employ you. Frequently, employers who discussed such issues were raising families themselves and had intimate knowledge of

---

*References and footnotes can be found in the original publication of Lisa Dodson's *The Moral Underground: How Ordinary Americans Subvert an Unfair Economy* (New York: The New Press, 2009). [*Editors' note*]

how much time—or in lieu of time, money—it takes to keep kids on a schedule; manage all their schooling, extracurricular, and emotional needs; and just keep a stable family routine. If you can't be home to make sure all this is taken care of and you can't buy substitute care, well, "it's just a mess," said one young manager, herself a mother of two.

On this day, the five men and two women started examining an idea that reemerged in employer conversations over the years that followed. They raised the notion that if you pay people wages that guarantee they can't really "keep things organized at home" and then, because of that, the flow of work is disrupted, well, is that only the employee's problem? Or is it just built into this labor market? And if it is wired into America's jobs, as Ellen, a middle-aged white woman, asked the others, "do we have any responsibility for what happens to them?" Over the course of hundreds of interviews and discussions this question was often at the center.

INEQUALITY AT WORK

During the 1990s and into the first part of the first decade of the millennium, the United States saw a surge in wealth among the richest Americans. But that decade of economic gain was largely limited to those at the very top. Today, one in four U.S. workers earns less than $9 an hour—about $19,000 per year; 39 percent of the nation's children live in low-income households. The Economic Policy Institute reported that in 2005, minimum-wage workers earned only 32 percent of the average hourly wage. And African American and Latino families are much more likely to be poor or low-income and are less likely to have assets or home equity to offset low wages. Furthermore, the living standards for households in the middle relative to the previous decade have seen a decline, particularly "working-age households," those headed by at least one adult of working age. Thus the nation increasingly became divided into acutely different ways of life: millions of working families—the economic bottom third—that cannot make a living, millions in the middle clinging to their standard of living, and the very top economic tier of ever-greater wealth.

This America is not lost on ordinary people. As a Midwestern father of two who drives a "big rig" across states for a living said, "*That* money [gained by the richest people] came from somewhere, didn't it? It came out of my pocket and my kids' mouths." While most busy working people don't sit down to study the macro economy, many understand the rippling effects that shake their world.

At the university where I teach about poverty issues, I always ask students if they think that it *matters* if wealth increases for a few while others lose ground. For example, does it matter if that dad, driving his truck eighteen hours a day and seldom seeing his family, is able to buy less now than he could five years ago, when his days were shorter? Yes, of course it matters to him, his spouse, and his children. But does it matter beyond their private world? And always students point out that "maybe he's not driving as well" after eighteen hours. Thus, certainly with many jobs, there is a danger effect of low wages and overwork, causing damage that can spread. But a fair number of other students ponder harm beyond self-interest and even our public interest in avoiding a forty-ton truck slamming down the highway with a sleepy driver. Do losses to a family, probably an extended family, maybe even a community eroded by mounting poverty-induced problems—does all that matter in a larger way? Even assuming that we can avoid all those trucks, is *America* harmed when our workers and their families are ground down by an economy that has been funneling wealth to only a few?

There is always a range of responses to this challenge to the way the economy distributes its resources. Many young people particularly believe that we can do better, and they are ready to get on board. In every class that I have ever taught some students speak of wanting the chance to devote real time—years, not just term breaks—to working for another kind of democracy. They are part of a deep, still untapped well of commitment to an economically just society—not the only source by any means, but a very valuable one. As young people have pointed out, this is the world they will take on and they should make it a more equitable one.

Alongside that sentiment, some young people point out that there is also a sound business management argument that doing better by our lower-wage workers means that we all gain, because both the society *and* businesses do better. This "high road" argument counsels investing in better wages, decent schedules, and benefits for low-wage workers because, ultimately, this pays off for companies and the nation. Others also point out that investing in lower-income families will mean that millions of children are better prepared for school, are healthier, and have more stable families, all of which build the nation. Essentially, this is the argument that other nations use to invest public funding in families raising children and guarantee a minimum family income. So there is a defensible set of arguments—albeit not a winning one in the United States, but a compelling one—that we ought to pay people a decent income because it takes care of our people, serves productivity, and upholds the nation as a whole.

Yet, talking with employers, students, and many others, I found another public impulse largely left outside most economic debate. Sometimes middle-class people talked about a sense of obligation—a social obligation—at the core of their individual identity and their understanding of being part of this country. And many talked about their jobs—the work they do each day—as key to fulfilling the sense of being part of something bigger.

This idea of work was almost always explained to me personally, not as a philosophical stand. Middle-income people would describe relationships with others at work whose earnings were so low that *if* you decided to think about it, you knew there was no way they could support a family. Managers, business owners, and other professionals told me about getting to know certain people who seemed to be doing everything they possibly could, but that wasn't enough. And so all kinds of personal and family troubles would mount up, spill over, and eventually turn up at work. I heard about how when you hire, supervise, or even just work next to working-poor people—and, like it or not, get close to them—the harms they live with can start leaking into your world too.

A question would be raised: do we have some responsibility for people to whom we are connected through our jobs and economic role in their daily lives, and indirectly, the families that count on them? Do we have some obligation to others—not just our family, but those who are co-workers, neighbors, part of our society, and who are being diminished? I found nothing near a consensus. But a wide array of people diverse in background, religion, profession, race, ethnicity, and geography spoke of this reflection as part of their workaday lives, where they are connected to those who are working hard but living poor.

As a young mother who was a sales clerk in Denver in 2001 put it, "This took everything . . . just to keep this job. You know, you're a single mother, you're not born with a silver spoon in your mouth. . . . My child keeps calling me [while the child is home alone] and begging me to quit. . . . This is my responsibility."

"I COULDN'T HELP FEELING LIKE I WAS ALMOST TO BLAME"

Bea was a fortyish white woman in a flowery blouse and pink slacks; she wore a square plastic badge that read BEA, FLOOR MANAGER. In 2004 she agreed to talk to me over a cup of coffee near the store where she was a manager of "about thirty-five" employees. It was a well-known low-end retail chain, a "big box." She had worked there for five years. She described the workforce as largely local people, and that meant "almost all white, mostly women, and with maybe high school diplomas, for the most part." Bea herself had lived in that general area of Maine all her life.

After many interviews, my questions had been honed for gathering information about how it is to manage a workforce and what if any conflicts arise. Bea quickly focused on the dilemma of "knowing too much" about the personal lives of the people who worked for her and how that contrasted poorly with what she understood as the model of how a professional manager behaves.

"Some of what they teach you in this business is to learn to think of them as part of the job . . . the way to try to get the job done. That means being friendly [to the workers], learning everybody's name; that's very important. But you keep people . . . it's important to keep a distance. You do that to keep it professional. But I think . . . it is also how to keep it clean."

"What does that mean?"

"It can get messy quickly if you start encouraging people to tell you what is going on, because they all have these problems. They have child care problems, problems with someone is sick . . . there's domestic abuse. They have a lot of crises. It's better not to ask because it opens the door to all that and then you have to tell them they have to stay late or you have to cut hours or someone wants a raise . . . all of that other comes up in your mind."

"And that makes it hard to . . . ?"

"That makes it hard to flip back into the business mode. I have to keep in mind my job is to serve the business, which is serving the public. We serve the public." This phrase, often repeated among the managers I met, seemed like a mooring, something to grab on to when human matters started to rock the boat.

"And . . . these people . . . aren't really . . . the public?"

"No, in business the public is the people who pay. . . . It isn't the public, really, it is the customer, the paying public."

"So . . . how does this work, for you?"

Bea's capitulation was immediate.

"Not very well really. I actually break my rules all the time. I know a lot more about a lot of people than I should. I get involved more than I should. I am that kind of person; my husband is always telling me that. Not that he really blames me; he does the same thing at [a local lumber business]. But, like before . . . when we were talking about what they pay . . . ?" Bea and I had discussed the company wages of $6–8 an hour. "I know that when someone asks for a raise, *they really need it*." At that point Bea started reciting the needs of many of these workers. Clearly she had annihilated her dictate to "keep it clean."

Here is just one of the stories that she told.

" 'Nancy' has two kids, her husband's on disability, and she couldn't buy her daughter a prom dress. This kid has worked very, very hard to graduate." Apparently Nancy's daughter had been employed throughout most of her high school years to help the family. "I'm like, 'How is it fair that this family can't buy her a prom dress?' "

Bea looked away, out the window. She disconnected from me for a few seconds as though recalling and applying manager rules. But it didn't work. When she looked back at me, she was teary. And she seemed a little angry too.

"I remember how much my prom meant to me. I don't know about where you live, but around here, it's a big deal. The girls . . . we all hope for a big wedding someday but your high school graduation, that's something you have earned. You want to look glamorous—not just good, but runway good. No way was Edy going to have the dress, the hair, the manicure. And I couldn't help but feeling that I was almost to blame, or partly. Nancy doesn't make what she deserves. . . . I am not saying they all work that hard, but . . . really, many do."

Bea was quiet for a while, and I began to think that was the end of the story. I tried to think of how to draw out what was being said, to hear more about this balance of roles and rules and Bea's conflict. She had started with her manager badge. But then she moved along a spectrum of moral thinking that I was to hear about many times. Bea put it simply. "Actually we sell prom dresses in this store. . . . Did you see them?" I had not.

Again Bea was silent and she looked at my tape recorder. I asked, "You want me to turn it off?"

Bea said, "No, that's okay . . . Well, let's just say . . . we made some mistakes with our prom dress orders last year. Too many were ordered, some went back. It got pretty confusing."

When Bea looked me in the eye this time, there were no tears and no apology.

I thought I knew my line. "So . . . Edy looked good at her prom?" Bea laughed, with a touch of gratitude I thought. "She knocked them dead," she said.

Over this and another conversation, Bea talked about how she could not make up for even a small part of what the workforce was lacking, because their wages meant they could not make their bills, never mind buy prom dresses, a fan for hot days, a child's plastic pool. So she found small ways to help out, to subsidize poor wages and try to make jobs move workers an inch closer to a decent life.

I thought a lot about Bea's story as I reread other employer interviews over the years that followed. In the short time I spent with her, she had quickly traveled the length of a moral domain I was trying to map out. I sat down with a woman who struck me as cautious and proud of her success as a manager, and who would offer me the straight and narrow supervisor line. She set it out and then trespassed all over it, trampled on the idea of "keeping her distance."

But more came out. She had been engaging in subtle acts of resistance from inside her small corner of the economy by subsidizing its extremely low wages. Bea told me that she wouldn't pass along cash to augment low wages. But she took advantage of everyday moments of abundant commerce—mixed-up orders, unsold goods, end-of-season returns, layaways that sometimes lay away forever. Bea was making her own little market adjustments to keep from feeling complicit with what she saw as unfair compensation. Sometimes, as she said, "you just have to level the playing field a little."

But what does that make Bea?

I didn't ask her if she was a thief. I would have loved to hear her words on that question, but it didn't feel right to ask. I knew that other people would say that her actions made her one. And they have when I have presented Bea's story in public talks. But I am glad to say others in the audiences have countered that idea, calling that pretense of moral simplicity "a sham." In community discussions, people have argued that all taking is not equal. It's one thing to steal for yourself when you don't need it; *that* most people view as morally illegitimate and corrupt. But most say it's something else to steal when your children are in real need, for example. Just about everyone I've ever talked with over the years—working- or middle-class—says that when it comes to a hungry child, there is no such thing as stealing.

Yet breaking the rules as Bea did, for someone who has a hungry child or hungers for a moment of triumph after years of work, like a prom dress for their daughter—this is a morally complicated place. Rule breaking in these cases was not seen merely as an act of survival. Rather, these transgressions were discussed as acts of conscience and finally acts of solidarity. And they mark what is usually kept invisible, how people will step out of a culture of utter self-interest, the market culture, and then intentionally turn against it.

RESIGNING CONSCIENCE TO THOSE IN POWER

The tension between obedience to the rule of law and obedience to deeply held beliefs about justice and fairness is as old as America. Long before tea was dumped in Boston Harbor, people were weighing the necessity of disobedience in the face of tyranny. Long before an active underground railroad gave passage out of hell, Americans were reflecting on their moral identity in a nation in which slavery was legal, whether or not they were slave owners. In 1849, in his essay on civil disobedience, Henry David Thoreau asks, "Must the citizen ever for a moment, or in the least degree, resign his conscience to the legislator? Why has every man a conscience then?"

Why do we possess our own moral response to circumstances if we should remain unquestionably bound by the current rules and rulers? I heard Bea answer Thoreau's challenge. But Bea wasn't focused on the local or even larger legislative bodies; rather, Bea's act of conscience was directed at the center of power in American society today, corporate power.

The massive shift of the nation's wealth and power to an inestimably wealthy few *is* the American social landscape. But Bea thinks it's ugly. She sees the economy down in the small cracks of social life amid long hours and tiny paychecks and children left to languish, in the sense that they are not worth a dress or a chance. And she has rejected the idea that business should be free to treat workers as disposable and their families as collateral damage. More, she refused to resign her conscience to others' rules no matter how powerful they are. Rule by market interest, others like Bea have told me, requires that matters of conscience are supposed to be "left at the door" of the company, of the market system, regardless of the human harm you see. But I have heard it said, "I need to be able to sleep at night" or "I have to look at myself in the mirror." When the apparatus of business and voices of institutions are silent, sometimes looking into the face of a rule breaker lets you sleep at night.

Bea was one of the first of a wide spectrum of middle-income people who explained to me that being asked to collude with rules that are immoral and treat people unfairly eventually will lead to acts of disobedience.

Others agreed.

Andrew, the manager of the Midwestern fast food restaurant quoted in the introduction, had given more detail: "I don't think [the workers] are paid enough. They don't make enough to live. Yeah, so I do try to do what I can."

With a little nudging he continued. "Okay, I'll tell you that I add to their paychecks. I actually put them in for more hours, or what I can do more easily is put them in as working overtime and they get paid a higher rate. And sometimes I just pad them; that's all there is to it. I pad their paychecks because you can't live on what they make. I punch them out after they have left for a doctor's appointment or to take care [of a family member]. And I give them food to take home . . . I actually order extra and send some home with them." Andy referred to himself as a "Robin Hood" with a chuckle, but he meant it.

Margaret, a business owner in the Midwest, said, "I would like to share a story, where I decided it was a turning point in my life, being involved in management with single parents. . . . You can't go on about this being business as usual. I have changed how I supervise people."

Margaret described being geared up to confront a young mother who was absent from work, again, as she had been several times in recent weeks. But when she looked at the young woman who came into the store carrying two sick children despite the bitter cold, Margaret suddenly imagined what that young mother had to do each day just to come to work. She called it a turning point in her life.

Joaquin, a food company manager in the West, confessed, "I basically try to feed them most of the time. I let them make meals for after their shifts. And the truth is that some of the women, some of them are single moms, and when their kids come in after school, I feed them . . . pretty regularly, really. I don't think they can feed their families on what they make here. . . . I think part of my issue is that, how would I feel if my kids weren't getting enough to eat? I can't imagine that idea that I can't afford to feed them, so you know, here are these people and they don't make enough money to really feed their kids."

Joaquin seemed a little embarrassed because his voice got tight when he spoke of the idea of being unable to feed children. To Joaquin, watching parents working hard and going home without enough money to buy food for their kids is far worse than breaking the rules, funneling some food their way, and risking the consequences.

Judy, a health care business manager in the East, said quietly, "I have to say that most of these parents are doing everything . . . to be there [for their children] and at the same time do this job. They are doing everything, but, honestly, I don't see how they are supposed to. . . . I couldn't. So sometimes I just look the other way . . . when, you know, there's an issue about . . . something." She did not want to elaborate but repeated, "Sometimes you just look the other way."

If these four people found themselves sitting in a room together, they might have assumed that they had little in common. While they were all middle-class, their earnings ranged widely from the median to a high income. They were racially, culturally, and geographically diverse; one was in his early twenties while another was in her late fifties. I didn't ask about their religious or political views but heard opinions that suggested a wide range. They would seem truly different by any ordinary opinion poll measures. But I found that they have something profound in common. They all think that working people should earn a livelihood and be able to keep their families safe. That's the kind of society they want to live in. While they did not go into an elaborate discussion about fairness, each acted upon the idea of economic justice, even at some personal risk. And though these gestures are small, they are also disruptive; they send tiny shivers through a market system that relies on obedience to the rule of self-interest regardless of harm to others.

29

"Getting" and "Making" a Tip

FROM *Dishing It Out: Power and Resistance among Waitresses in a New Jersey Restaurant*

GRETA FOFF PAULES

Waitresses, like many people who provide a service, are highly vulnerable to the whims of the customers who, by their tips, decide their daily earnings. Waitresses structure their encounters with more care than most of us realize. The reason for this is the need to have some power over their work and their livelihood. For those of you who have never been a waiter or waitress, this participant observation study may forever change the way you think about being served and treat those who serve you.

> The waitress can't help feeling a sense of personal failure and public censure when she is "stiffed."
>
> —*William F. Whyte*, "When Workers and Customers Meet"

> They're rude, they're ignorant, they're obnoxious, they're inconsiderate.... Half these people don't deserve to come out and eat, let alone try and tip a waitress.
>
> —*Route [Restaurant] waitress*

The financial and emotional hazards inherent in the tipping system have drawn attention from sociologists, and more recently anthropologists, concerned with the study of work. In general these researchers have concluded that workers who receive gratuities exercise little control over the material outcome of tipping and less over its symbolic implications.

* * *

MAKING A TIP AT ROUTE [RESTAURANT]

A common feature of past research is that the worker's control over the tipping system is evaluated in terms of her efforts to con, coerce, compel, or otherwise manipulate a customer into relinquishing a bigger tip. Because these efforts have for the most part proven futile, the worker has been seen as having little defense against the financial vicissitudes of the tipping system. What these studies have overlooked is that an employee can increase her tip income by controlling the number as well as the size of tips she receives. This oversight has arisen from the tendency of researchers to concentrate narrowly on the relationship between server and served, while failing to take into account the broader organizational context in which this relationship takes place.

Like service workers observed in earlier studies, waitresses at Route strive to boost the amount of individual gratuities by rendering special services and being especially friendly. As one waitress put it, "I'll sell you the world if you're in my station." In general though, waitresses at Route Restaurant seek to boost their tip income, not by increasing the amount of individual gratuities, but by increasing the number of customers they serve. They accomplish this (a) by securing the largest or busiest stations and working the most lucrative shifts; (b) by "turning" their tables quickly; and (c) by controlling the flow of customers within the restaurant.

Technically, stations at Route are assigned on a rotating basis so that all waitresses, including rookies, work fast and slow stations equally. Station assignments are listed on the work schedule that is posted in the office window where it can be examined by all workers on all shifts, precluding the possibility of blatant favoritism or discrimination. Yet a number of methods exist whereby experienced waitresses are able to circumvent the formal rotation system and secure the more lucrative stations for themselves. A waitress can trade assignments with a rookie who is uncertain of her ability to handle a fast station; she can volunteer to take over a large station when a *call-out* necessitates reorganization of station assignments; or she can establish herself as the only waitress capable of handling a particularly large or chaotic station. Changes in station assignments tend not to be formally recorded, so inconsistencies in the rotation system often do not show up on the schedule. Waitresses on the same shift may notice of course that a co-worker has managed to avoid an especially slow station for many days, or has somehow ended up in the busiest station two weekends in a row, but the waitresses' code of noninterference . . . inhibits them from openly objecting to such irregularities.

A waitress can also increase her tip income by working the more lucrative shifts. Because day is the busiest and therefore most profitable shift at Route, it attracts experienced, professional waitresses who are most concerned and best able to maximize their tip earnings. There are exceptions; some competent, senior-ranking waitresses are unable to work during the day due to time constraints of family or second jobs. Others choose not to work during the day despite the potential monetary rewards, because they are unwilling to endure the intensely competitive atmosphere for which day shift is infamous.

The acutely competitive environment that characterizes day shift arises from the aggregate striving of each waitress to maximize her tip income by serving the greatest possible number of customers. Two strategies are enlisted to this end. First, each waitress attempts to *turn* her tables as quickly as possible. Briefly stated, this means she takes the order, delivers the food, clears and resets a table, and begins serving the next party as rapidly as customer lingering and the speed of the kitchen allow. A seven-year veteran of Route describes the strategy and its rewards:

> What I do is I prebus my tables. When the people get up and go all I got is glasses and cups, pull off, wipe, set, and I do the table turnover. But see that's from day shift. See the girls on graveyard . . . don't understand the more times you turn that table the more money you make. You could have three tables and still make a hundred dollars. If you turn them tables.

As the waitress indicates, a large part of turning tables involves getting the table cleared and set for the next customer. During a rush, swing and grave waitresses tend to leave dirty tables standing, partly because they are less experienced and therefore less efficient, partly to avoid being given parties, or *sat*, when they are already behind. In contrast, day waitresses assign high priority to keeping their tables cleared and ready for customers. The difference in method reflects increased skill and growing awareness of and concern with money-making strategies.

A waitress can further increase her customer count by controlling the flow of customers within the restaurant. Ideally the hostess or manager running the front house rotates customers among stations, just as stations are rotated among waitresses. Each waitress is given, or *sat*, one party at a time in turn so that all waitresses have comparable customer counts at the close of a shift. When no hostess is on duty, or both she and the manager are detained and customers are waiting to be seated, waitresses will typically seat incoming parties.

Whether or not a formal hostess is on duty, day waitresses are notorious for bypassing the rotation system by racing to the door and directing incoming customers to their own tables. A sense of the urgency with which this strategy is pursued is conveyed in the comment of one five-year veteran, "They'll run you down to get that person at the door, to seat them in their station." The competition for customers is so intense during the day that some waitresses claim they cannot afford to leave the floor (even to use the restroom) lest they return to find a co-worker's station filled at their expense. "In the daytime, honey," remarks an eight-year Route waitress, "in the daytime it's like pulling teeth. You got to stay on the floor to survive. To survive." It is in part because they do not want to lose customers and tips to their co-workers that waitresses do not take formal breaks. Instead, they rest and eat between waiting tables or during lulls in business, returning to the floor intermittently to check on parties in progress and seat customers in their stations.

The fast pace and chaotic nature of restaurant work provide a cover for the waitress's aggressive pursuit of customers, since it is difficult for other servers to monitor closely the allocation of parties in the bustle and confusion of a rush. Still, it is not uncommon for waitresses to grumble to management and co-workers if they notice an obvious imbalance in customer distribution. Here again, the waitress refrains from directly criticizing her fellow servers, voicing her displeasure by commenting on the paucity of customers in her own station, rather than the overabundance of customers in the stations of certain co-waitresses. In response to these grumblings, other waitresses may moderate somewhat their efforts to appropriate new parties, and management may make a special effort to seat the disgruntled server favorably.

A waitress can also exert pressure on the manager or hostess to keep her station filled. She may, for instance, threaten to leave if she is not seated enough customers.

> I said, "Innes [a manager], I'm in [station] one and two. If one and two is not filled at all times from now until three, I'm getting my coat, my pocketbook, and I'm leaving." And one and two was filled, and I made ninety-five dollars.

Alternatively, she can make it more convenient for the manager or hostess to seat her rather than her co-workers, either by keeping her tables open (as described), or by taking extra tables. If customers are waiting to be seated, a waitress may offer to pick up parties in a station that is closed or, occasionally, to pick up parties in another waitress's station. In attempting either strategy, but especially the latter, the waitress must be adept not only at waiting tables, but in interpersonal restaurant politics. Autonomy and possession are of central concern to waitresses, and a waitress who offers to pick up tables outside her station must select her words carefully if she is to avoid being accused of invading her co-workers' territory. Accordingly, she may choose to present her bid for extra parties as an offer to help—the manager, another waitress, the restaurant, customers—rather than as a request.

The waitress who seeks to increase her tip income by maximizing the number of customers she serves may endeavor to cut her losses by refusing to serve parties that have stiffed her in the past. If she is a low-ranking waitress, her refusal is likely to be overturned by the manager. If she is an experienced and valuable waitress, the manager may ask someone else to take the party, assure the waitress he will take care of her (that is, pad the bill and give her the difference), or even pick up the party himself. Though the practice is far from common, a waitress may go so far as to demand a tip from a customer who has been known to stiff in the past.

> This party of two guys come in and they order thirty to forty dollars worth of food . . . and they stiff us. Every time. So Kaddie told them, "If you don't tip us, we're not going to wait on you." They said, "We'll tip you." So Kaddie waited on them, and they tipped her. The next night they came in, I waited on them and they didn't tip me. The third time they came in [the manager] put them in my station and I told [the manager] straight up, "I'm not waiting on them . . ." So he made Hailey pick them up. And they stiffed Hailey. So when they came in the next night . . . [they] said, "Are you going to give us a table?" I said, "You going to tip me? I'm not going to wait on you. You got all that money, you sell all that crack on the streets and you come here and you can't even leave me a couple bucks?" . . . So they left me a dollar. So when they come in Tuesday night, I'm telling them a dollar ain't enough.

The tactics employed by waitresses, and particularly day-shift waitresses, to increase their customer count and thereby boost their tip earnings have earned them a resounding notoriety among their less competitive co-workers. Day (and some swing) waitresses are described as "money hungry," "sneaky little bitches," "self-centered," "aggressive," "backstabbing bitches," and "cut-throats over tables." The following remarks of two Route waitresses, however, indicate that those who employ these tactics see them as defensive, not aggressive measures. A sense of the waitress's preoccupation with autonomy and with protecting what is hers also emerges from these comments.

> You have to be like that. Because if you don't be like that, people step on you. You know, like as far as getting customers. I mean, you know, I'm sorry everybody says I'm greedy. I guess that's why I've survived this long at Route. Cause I am greedy. . . . *I want what's mine,* and if it comes down to me cleaning your table or my table, I'm going to clean my table. Because see I went through all that stage where I would do your table. To be fair. And you would walk home with seventy dollars, and I'd have twenty-five, cause I was being fair all night. (emphasis added)
>
> If the customer comes in the door and I'm there getting that door, don't expect me to cover your backside while you in the back smoking a cigarette and I'm here working for myself. You not out there working for me. . . . When I go to the door and get the customers, when I keep my tables clean and your tables are dirty, and you wonder why you only got one person . . . then that's just tough shit. . . . You're damn right my station is filled. *I'm not here for you.* (emphasis added)

Whether the waitress who keeps her station filled with customers is acting aggressively or defensively, her tactics are effective. It is commonly accepted that determined day waitresses make better money than less competitive co-workers even when working swing or grave. Moreover Nera, the waitress most infamous for her relentless use of "money-hungry" tactics, is at the same time most famous for her consistently high daily takes. While other waitresses jingle change in their aprons, Nera is forced to store wads of bills in her shoes and in paper bags to prevent tips from overflowing her pockets. She claims to make a minimum of five hundred dollars a week in tip earnings; her record for one day's work exceeds two hundred dollars and is undoubtedly the record for the restaurant.

INVERTING THE SYMBOLISM OF TIPPING

It may already be apparent that the waitress views the customer—not as a master to pamper and appease—but as substance to be processed as quickly and in as large a quantity as possible. The difference in perspective is expressed in the objectifying terminology of waitresses: a customer or party is referred to as a *table,* or by table number, as *table five* or simply *five;* serving successive parties at a table is referred to as *turning the table;* taking an order is also known as *picking up a table;* and to serve water, coffee, or other beverages is to *water, coffee,* or *beverage* a table, number, or customer. Even personal acquaintances assume the status of inanimate matter, or tip-bearing plants, in the language of the server:

> I got my fifth-grade teacher [as a customer] one time. . . . I kept her coffeed. I kept her boyfriend coked all night. Sodaed. . . . And I kept them filled up.

If the customer is perceived as material that is processed, the goal of this processing is the production or extraction of a finished product: the tip. This image too is conveyed in the language of the floor. A waitress may comment that she "got a good tip" or "gets good tips," but she is more likely to say that she "made" or "makes good tips." She may also say that she "got five bucks out of" a customer, or complain that some customers "don't want to give up on" their money. She may accuse a waitress who stays over into her shift of "tapping on" her money, or warn an aspiring waitress against family restaurants on the grounds that "there's no money in there." In all these comments (and all are actual), the waitress might as easily be talking about mining for coal or drilling for oil as serving customers.

Predictably, the waitress's view of the customer as substance to be processed influences her perception of the meaning of tips, and especially substandard tips. At Route, low tips and stiffs are not interpreted as a negative reflection on the waitress's personal qualities or social status. Rather, they are felt to reveal the refractory nature or poor quality of the raw material from which the tip is extracted, produced, or fashioned. In less metaphorical terms, a low tip or stiff is thought to reflect the negative qualities and low status of the customer who is too cheap, too poor, too ignorant, or too coarse to leave an appropriate gratuity. In this context, it is interesting to note that *stiff,* the term used in restaurants to refer to incidents of nontipping or to someone who does not tip, has also been used to refer to a wastrel or penniless man, . . . a hobo, tramp, vagabond, deadbeat, and a moocher.

* * *

Evidence that waitresses assign blame for poor tips to the tipper is found in their reaction to being undertipped or stiffed. Rather than breaking down in tears and lamenting her "personal failure," the Route waitress responds to a stiff by announcing the event to her co-workers and managers in a tone of angry disbelief. Co-workers and managers echo the waitress's indignation and typically ask her to identify the party (by table number and physical description), or if she has already done so, to be more specific. This identification is crucial for it allows sympathizers to join the waitress in analyzing the cause of the stiff, which is assumed a priori to arise from some shortcoming of the party, not the waitress. The waitress and her co-workers may conclude that the customers in question were rude, troublemakers, or bums, or they may explain their behavior by identifying them as members of a particular category of customers. It might be revealed for instance, that the offending party was a church group: church groups are invariably tightfisted. It might be resolved that the offenders were senior citizens, Southerners, or business people: all well-known cheapskates. If the customers were European, the stiff will be attributed to ignorance of the American tipping system; if they were young, to immaturity; if they had children, to lack of funds.

These classifications and their attendant explanations are neither fixed nor trustworthy. New categories are invented to explain otherwise puzzling incidents, and all categories are subject to exception. Though undependable as predictive devices, customer typologies serve a crucial function: they divert blame for stiffs and low tips from the waitress to the characteristics of the customer. It is for this reason that it is "important" for workers to distinguish between different categories of customers, despite the fact that such distinctions are based on "unreliable verbal and appearance clues." In fact, it is precisely the unreliability, or more appropriately the flexibility, of customer typologies that makes them valuable to waitresses. When categories can be constructed and dissolved on demand, there is no danger that an incident will fall outside the existing system of classification and hence be inexplicable.

While waitresses view the customer as something to be processed and the tip as the product of this processing, they are aware that the public does not share their understanding of the waitress-diner-tip relationship. Waitresses at Route recognize that many customers perceive them as needy creatures willing to commit great feats of service and absorb high doses of abuse in their anxiety to secure a favorable gratuity or protect their jobs. They are also aware that some customers leave small tips with the intent to insult the server and that others undertip on the assumption that for a Route waitress even fifty cents will be appreciated. One waitress indicated that prior to being employed in a restaurant, she herself subscribed to the stereotype of the down-and-out waitress "because you see stuff on television, you see these wives or single ladies who waitress and they live in slummy apartments or slummy houses and they dress in rags." It is these images of neediness and desperation, which run so strongly against the waitress's perception of herself and her position, that she attacks when strained relations erupt into open conflict.

> Five rowdy black guys walked in the door and they went to seat themselves at table seven. I said, "Excuse me. You all got to wait to be seated." "We ain't got to do *shit*. We here to eat. . . ." So they went and sat down. And I turned around and just looked at them. And they said, "Well, I hope you ain't our waitress, cause you blew your tip. Cause you ain't getting nothing from us." And I turned around and I said, "You need it more than I do, baby."

This waitress's desire to confront the customer's assumption of her destitution is widely shared among service workers whose status as tipped employees marks them as needy in the eyes of their customers. [One study] reports that among cabdrivers "a forever repeated story is of the annoyed driver, who, after a grueling trip with a Lady Shopper, hands the coin back, telling her, 'Lady, keep your lousy dime. You need it more than I do.'" [Another study reports] a hotel waitress's claim that "if she had served a large family with children for one or two weeks, and then was given a 10p[ence] piece, she would give the money back, saying, 'It's all right, thank you, I've got enough change for my bus fare home.'" In an incident I observed (not at Route), a waitress followed two male customers out of a restaurant calling, "Excuse me! You forgot this!" and holding up the coins they had left as a tip. The customers appeared embarrassed, motioned for her to keep the money, and continued down the sidewalk. The waitress, now standing in the outdoor seating area of the restaurant and observed by curious diners, threw the money after the retreating men and returned to her work. Episodes such as these allow the worker to repudiate openly the evaluation of her financial status that is implied in an offensively small gratuity, and permit her to articulate her own understanding of what a small tip says and about whom. If customers can only afford to leave a dime, or feel a 10p piece is adequate compensation for two weeks' service, they must be very hard up or very ignorant indeed.

In the following incident the waitress interjects a denial of her neediness into an altercation that is not related to tipping, demonstrating that the customer's perception of her financial status is a prominent and persistent concern for her.

> She [a customer] wanted a California Burger with mayonnaise. And when I got the mayonnaise, the mayonnaise had a little brown on it. . . . So this girl said to me, she said, "What the fuck is this you giving me?" And I turned around, I thought, "Maybe she's talking to somebody else in the booth with her." And I turned around and I said, "Excuse me?" She said, "You hear what I said, I said, 'What the fuck are you giving me?'" And I turned around, I said, "I don't know if you're referring your information to *me*," I said, "but if you're referring your information to *me*," I said, "I don't *need* your bullshit." I said, "I'm not going to even take it. . . . Furthermore, I could care less if you eat or *don't* eat. . . . And you see this?" And I took her check and I ripped it apart. . . . And I took the California Burger and I says, "You don't have a problem anymore now, right?" She went up to the manager. And she says, "That black waitress"—I says, "Oh. By the way, what is my name? I don't have a name, [using the words] 'that black waitress.' . . . My name happens to be Nera. . . . That's N-E-R-A. . . . And I don't need your bullshit, sweetheart. . . . People like you I can walk on, because you don't know how to talk to human beings." And I said, "I don't need you. I don't need your quarters. I don't need your nickels. I don't need your dimes. So if you want service, be my guest. Don't you *ever* sit in my station, cause I won't wait on you." The manager said, "Nera, please. Would you wait in the back?" I said, "No. I don't take back seats no more for nobody."

In each of these cases, the waitress challenges the customer's definition of the relationship in which tipping occurs. By speaking out, by confronting the customer, she demonstrates that she is not subservient or in fear of losing her job; that she is not compelled by financial need or a sense of social hierarchy to accept abuse from customers; that she does not, in Nera's words, "take back seats no more for nobody." At the same time, she reverses the symbolic force of the low tip, converting a statement on her social status or work skills into a statement on the tipper's cheapness or lack of savoir faire.

30

Upward Mobility through Sport?

D. STANLEY EITZEN

You can trace the history of twentieth-century immigration in the United States by reading the list of boxers who held the title of Champion of the World. The names of Irish, Jewish, Italian, African American, and Latino boxers record the stirrings of upward mobility for those who shared the boxers' ethnicity or nationality. But the lives of the boxers themselves were often far less successful than a championship title would indicate. And what of sports more generally? In true sociological fashion, Stanley Eitzen shows us that sports may do far less in advancing the life chances of young people than is often assumed.

Typically, Americans believe that sport is a path to upward social mobility. This belief is based on the obvious examples we see as poor boys and men (rarely girls and women) from rural and urban areas, whether white or black, sometimes skyrocket to fame and fortune through success in sports. Sometimes the financial reward has been astounding, such as the high pay that some African American athletes received in recent years. In 1997 Tracy McGrady, an NBA-bound high school star, bypassed college, signed a $12 million deal over 6 years with Adidas. Golfer Tiger Woods in his first year as a professional made $6.82 million in winnings (U.S. and worldwide) and appearance fees plus signed a series of five-year deals with Nike, Titleist, American Express, and Rolex worth $95.2 million. In 1998 Wood's earnings from endorsements totaled $28 million. Boxer Mike Tyson made $75 million in 1996. It is estimated that Michael Jordan made over $100 million in 1998, including salary, endorsements, and income from merchandise and videos. The recent deals for baseball stars, some exceeding $15 million a year for multiyear contracts, further underscores the incredible money given to some individuals for their athletic talents.

But while the possibility of staggering wealth and status through sport is possible, the reality is that dramatic upward mobility through sport is highly improbable. A number of myths, however, combine to lead us to believe that sport is a social mobility escalator.

MYTH: SPORT PROVIDES A FREE EDUCATION

Good high school athletes get college scholarships. These athletic scholarships are especially helpful to poor youth who otherwise would not be able to attend college because of the high costs. The problem with this assumption is that while true for some, very few high school athletes actually receive full scholarships. Football provides the easiest route to a college scholarship because Division I-A colleges have 85 football scholarships, but even this avenue is exceedingly narrow. In Colorado there were 3,481 male high school seniors who played football during the 1994 season. Of these, 31 received full scholarships at Division I-A schools (0.0089 percent).

Second, of all the male varsity athletes at all college levels only about 15 percent to 20 percent have full scholarships. Another 15 percent to 25 percent have partial scholarships, leaving 55 percent to 70 percent of all intercollegiate athletes without any sport related financial assistance. Third, as low as the chances are for men, women athletes have even less chance to receive an athletic scholarship. While women comprise about 52 percent of all college students, they make up only 35 percent of intercollegiate athletes with a similar disproportionate distribution of scholarships. Another reality is that if you are a male athlete in a so-called minor sport (swimming, tennis, golf, gymnastics, cross-country, wrestling), the chances of a full scholarship are virtually nil. The best hope is a partial scholarship, if that, since these sports are underfunded and in danger of elimination at many schools.

MYTH: SPORT LEADS TO A COLLEGE DEGREE

College graduates exceed high school graduates by hundreds of thousands of dollars in lifetime earnings. Since most high school and college athletes will never play at the professional level, the attainment of a college degree is a crucial determinant of upward mobility through sport. The problem is that relatively few male athletes in the big time revenue producing sports, compared to their non-athletic peers, actually receive college degrees. This is especially the case for African American men who are over represented in the revenue producing sports. In 1996, for example, looking at the athletes who entered Division I schools in 1990, only 45 percent of African American football players and 39 percent of African American basketball players had graduated (compared to 56 percent of the general student body).

There are a number of barriers to graduation for male athletes. The demands on their time and energy are enormous even in the off-season. Many athletes, because of these pressures, take easy courses to maintain eligibility but do not lead to graduation. The result is either to delay graduation or to make graduation an unrealistic goal.

Another barrier is that they are recruited for athletic prowess rather than academic ability. Recent data show that football players in big time programs are, on average, more than 200 points behind their non-athletic classmates on SAT test scores. Poorly prepared students are the most likely to take easy courses, cheat on exams, hire surrogate test takers, and otherwise do the minimum.

A third barrier to graduation for male college athletes is themselves, as they may not take advantage of their scholarships to obtain a quality education. This is especially the case for those who perceive their college experience only as preparation for their professional careers in sport. Study for them is necessary only to maintain their eligibility. The goal of a professional career is unrealistic for all but the superstars. The superstars who do make it at the professional level, more likely than not, will have not graduated from college; nor will they go back to finish their degrees when their professional careers are over. This is also because even a successful professional athletic career is limited to a few years, and not many professional athletes are able to translate their success in the pros to success in their post-athletic careers. Such a problem is especially true for African Americans, who often face employment discrimination in the wider society.

MYTH: A SPORTS CAREER IS PROBABLE

A recent survey by the Center for the Study of Sport in Society found that two-thirds of African American males between the ages of 13 and 18 believe that they can earn a living playing professional sports (more than double the proportion of young white males who hold such beliefs). Moreover, African American parents were four times more likely than white parents to believe that their sons are destined for careers as professional athletes.

If these young athletes could play as professionals, the economic rewards are excellent, especially in basketball and baseball. In 1998 the average annual salary for professional basketball was $2.24 million. In baseball the average salary was $1.37 million with 280 of the 774 players on opening day rosters making $1 million or more (of them, 197 exceeded $2 million or more, while 32 of them made $6 million or more). The average salaries for the National Hockey League and National Football League were $892,000 and $795,000, respectively. In football, for example, 19 percent of the players (333 of 1,765) exceeded $1 million in salary. These numbers are inflated by the use of averages, which are skewed by the salaries of the superstars. Use of the median (in which half the players make more and half make less), reveals that the median salary in basketball was $1.4 million; baseball—$500,000; football—$400,000; and hockey—$500,000. Regardless of the measure, the financial allure of a professional sports career is great.

A career in professional sports is nearly impossible to attain because of the fierce competition for so few openings. In an average year there are approximately 1,900,000 American boys playing high school football, basketball, and baseball. Another 68,000 men are playing those sports in college, and 2,490 are participating at the major professional level. In short, one in 27 high school players in these sports will play at the college level, and only one in 736 high school players will play at the major professional level (0.14 percent). In baseball, each year about 120,000 players are eligible for the draft (high school seniors, college seniors, collegians over 21, junior college players, and foreign players). Only about 1,200 (1 percent) are actually drafted, and most of them will never make it to the major leagues. Indeed, only one in ten of those players who sign a professional baseball contract ever play in the major leagues for at least one day.

The same rigorous condensation process occurs in football. About 15,000 players are eligible for the NFL draft each year. Three hundred thirty-six are drafted and about 160 actually make the final roster. Similarly, in basketball and hockey, only about 40 new players are added to the rosters in the NBA and 60 rookies make the NHL each year. In tennis only about 100 men and 100 women make enough money to cover expenses. In golf, of the 165 men eligible for the PGA tour in 1997, their official winnings ranged from $2,066,833 (Tiger Woods) to $10,653 (Chip Beck). The competition among these golfers is fierce. On average, the top 100 golfers on the tour play within 2 strokes of each other for every 18 holes, yet Tiger Woods, the tops in winnings won over $2 million, and the 100th finisher won only $250,000. Below the PGA tour is the Nike Tour where the next best 125 golfers compete. Their winnings were a top of $225,201 to a low of $9,944.

MYTH: SPORT IS A WAY OUT OF POVERTY

Sport appears to be a major way for African Americans to escape the ghetto. African Americans dominate the major professional sports numerically. While only 12 percent of the population, African Americans comprise about 80 percent of the players in professional basketball, about 67 percent of professional football players, and 18 percent of professional baseball players (Latinos also comprise about 17 percent of professional baseball players). Moreover, African Americans dominate the list of the highest moneymakers in sport (salaries, commercial sponsorships). These facts, while true, are illusory.

While African Americans dominate professional basketball, football, and to a lesser extent baseball, they are rarely found in certain sports such as hockey, automobile racing, tennis, golf, bowling, and skiing. Moreover, African Americans are severely under-represented in positions of authority in sport—as head coaches, referees, athletic directors, scouts, general managers, and owners. In the NFL in 1997, for example, where more than two-thirds of the players were African American, only three head coaches and five offensive or defensive coordinators were African American. In that year there were 11 head coaching vacancies filled none by African Americans. The reason for this racial imbalance in hiring, according to white sports columnist for the *Rocky Mountain News* Bob Kravitz is that: "something here stinks, and it stinks a lot like racism."

Second, while the odds of African American males making it as professional athletes are more favorable than is the case for whites (about 1 in 3,500 African American male high school athletes, compared to 1 in 10,000 white male high school athletes) these odds remain slim. Of the 40,000 or so African Americans boys who play high school basketball, only 35 will make the NBA and only 7 will be starters. Referring to the low odds for young African Americans, Harry Edwards, an African American sociologist specializing in the sociology of sport, said with a bit of hyperbole: "Statistically, you have a better chance of getting hit by a meteorite in the next ten years than getting work as an athlete."

Despite these discouraging facts, the myth is alive for poor youth. As noted earlier, two-thirds of African American boys believe they can be professional athletes. Their parents, too, accept this belief (African American parents are four times more likely than white parents to believe that their children will be professional athletes). The film *Hoop Dreams* and Darcey Frey's book *The Last Shot: City Street, Basketball Dreams* document the emphasis that young African American men place on sports as a way up and their ultimate disappointments from sport. For many of them, sport represents their only hope of escape from a life of crime, poverty, and despair. They latch on to the dream of athletic success partly because of the few opportunities for middle-class success. They spend many hours per day developing their speed, strength, jumping height, or "moves" to the virtual exclusion of those abilities that have a greater likelihood of paying off in upward mobility such as reading comprehension, mathematical reasoning, communication skills, and computer literacy.

Sociologist Jay Coakley puts it this way: "My best guess is that less than 3,500 African Americans . . . are making their livings as professional athletes. At the same time (in 1996), there are about 30,015 black physicians and about 30,800 black lawyers currently employed in the U.S. Therefore, there are 20 times more blacks working in these two professions than playing top level professional sports. And physicians and lawyers usually have lifetime earnings far in excess of the earnings of professional athletes, whose playing careers, on average, last less than five years."

Harry Edwards posits that by spending their energies and talents on athletic skills, young African Americans are not pursuing occupations that would help them meet their political and material needs. Thus, because of belief in the "sports as a way up" myth, they remain dependent on whites and white institutions. Salim Muwakkil, an African American political analyst, argues that "If African Americans are to exploit the socio-economic options opened by varied civil rights struggles more fully, blacks must reduce the disproportionate allure of sports in their communities. Black leadership must contextualize athletic success by promoting other avenues to social status, intensifying the struggle for access to those avenues and better educating youth about those pot-holes on the road to the stadium."

John Hoberman in his book *Darwin's Athletes* also challenges the assumption that sport has progressive consequences. The success of African Americans in the highly visible sports gives white Americans a false sense of black progress and interracial harmony. But the social progress of African Americans in general has little relationship to the apparent integration that they have achieved on the playing fields.

Hoberman also contends that the numerical superiority of African Americans in sport, coupled with their disproportionate under-representation in other professions, reinforces the racist ideology that African Americans, while physically superior to whites, are inferior to them intellectually.

I do not mean to say that African Americans should not seek a career in professional sport. What is harmful is that the odds of success are so slim, making the extraordinary efforts over many years futile and misguided for the vast majority.

MYTH: WOMEN HAVE SPORT AS A VEHICLE

Since the passage of Title IX in 1972 that required schools receiving federal funds to provide equal opportunities for women and men, sports participation by women in high school and college has increased dramatically. In 1973, for example, when 50,000 men received some form of college scholarship for their athletic abilities, women received only 50. Now, women receive about 35 percent of the money allotted for college athletic scholarships (while a dramatic improvement, this should not be equated with gender equality as many would have us believe). This allows many women athletes to attend college who otherwise could not afford it, thus receiving an indirect upward mobility boost.

Upward mobility as a result of being a professional athlete is another matter for women. Women have fewer opportunities than men in professional team sports. Beach volley-ball is a possibility for a few but the rewards are minimal. Two professional women's basketball leagues began in 1997, but the pay was very low compared to men and the leagues were on shaky financial ground (the average salary in the American Basketball League was $80,000). The other option for women is to play in professional leagues in Europe, Australia, and Asia but the pay is relatively low.

Women have more opportunities as professionals in individual sports such as tennis, golf, ice-skating, skiing, bowling, cycling, and track. Ironically, the sports with the greatest monetary rewards for women are those of the middle and upper classes (tennis, golf, and ice skating). These sports are expensive and require considerable individual coaching and access to private facilities.

Ironically, with the passage of Title IX, which increased the participation rates of women so dramatically, there has been a decline in the number and proportion of women as coaches and athletic administrators. In addition to the glaring pay gap between what the coaches of men's teams receive compared to the coaches of women's teams, men who coach women's teams tend to have higher salaries than women coaching women's teams. Women also have fewer opportunities than men as athletic trainers, officials, sports journalists, and other adjunct positions.

MYTH: SPORT PROVIDES LIFELONG SECURITY

Even when a professional sport career is attained, the probabilities of fame and fortune are limited. Of course, some athletes make incomes from salaries and endorsements that if invested wisely, provide financial security for life. Many professional athletes make relatively low salaries. During the 1996 season, for example, 17 percent of major league baseball players made the minimum salary of $247,500 for veterans and $220,000 for rookies. This is a lot of money, but for these marginal players their careers may not last very long. Indeed, the average length of a professional career in a team sport is about five years. A marginal athlete in individual sports such as golf, tennis, boxing, and bowling, struggle financially. They must cover their travel expenses, health insurance, equipment, and the like with no guaranteed paycheck. The brief career diverts them during their youth from developing other career skills and experiences that would benefit them.

Ex-professional athletes leave sport, on average, when they are in their late 20s or early 30s, at a time when their non-athletic peers have begun to establish themselves in occupations leading toward retirement in 40 years or so. What are the ex-professional athletes to do with their remaining productive years?

Exiting a sports career can be relatively smooth or difficult. Some athletes have planned ahead, preparing for other careers either in sport (coaching, scouting, administering) or some non-sport occupation. Others have not prepared for this abrupt change. They did not graduate from college. They did not spend the off seasons apprenticing non-sport jobs. Exiting the athlete role is difficult for many because they lose: (1) What has been the focus of their being for most of their lives; (2) the primary source of their identities; (3) their physical prowess; (4) the adulation bordering on worship from others; (5) the money and the perquisites of fame; (6) the camaraderie with teammates; (7) the intense "highs" of competition; and (8) for most ex-athletes retirement means a loss of status. As a result of these "losses," many ex-professional athletes have trouble adjusting to life after sport. A study by the NFL Players Association found, that emotional difficulties, divorce, and financial strain were common problems for ex-professional football players. A majority had "permanent injuries" from football.

The allure of sport, however, remains strong and this has at least two negative consequences. First, ghetto youngsters who devote their lives to the pursuit of athletic stardom are, except for the fortunate few, doomed to failure in sport and in the real world where sports skills are essentially irrelevant to occupational placement and advancement. The second negative consequence is more subtle but very important. Sport contributes to the ideology that legitimizes social inequalities and promotes the myth that all it takes is extraordinary effort to succeed. Sport sociologist George H. Sage makes this point forcefully: "Because sport is by nature meritocratic—that is, superior performance brings status and rewards—it provides convincing symbolic support for hegemonic [the dominant] ideology—that ambitious, dedicated, hard working individuals, regardless of social origin, can achieve success and ascend in the social hierarchy, obtaining high status and material rewards, while those who don't move upward simply didn't work hard enough. Because the rags-to-riches athletes are so visible, the social mobility theme is maintained. This reflects the opportunity structure of society in general—the success of a few reproduces the belief in social mobility among the many."

31

Uses of the Underclass in America

HERBERT J. GANS

This essay is vintage sociology, taking what everyone thinks they know and turning it on its head. Gans shows how the lives and work of the so-called "undeserving poor" benefit the nonpoor in ways most Americans seldom recognize. "Poverty is good for you," is another way to express Gans's message, "as long as you are not among the poor." This essay also shows how functional analysis, often accused of being conservative, can be a critical perspective.

I. INTRODUCTION

Poverty, like any other social phenomenon, can be analyzed in terms of the *causes* which initiate and perpetuate it, but once it exists, it can also be studied in terms of the consequences or *functions* which follow. These functions can be both *positive* and *negative*, adaptive and destructive, depending on their nature and the people and interests affected.

Poverty has many negative functions (or dysfunctions), most for the poor themselves, but also for the nonpoor. Among those of most concern to both populations, perhaps the major one is that a small but visible proportion of poor people is involved in activities which threaten their physical safety, for example street crime, or which deviate from important norms claimed to be "mainstream," such as failing to work, bearing children in adolescence and out of wedlock, and being "dependent" on welfare. In times of high unemployment, illegal and even legal immigrants are added to this list for endangering the job opportunities of native-born Americans.

Furthermore, many better-off Americans believe that the number of poor people who behave in these ways is far larger than it actually is. More important, many think that poor people act as they do because of moral shortcomings that express themselves in lawlessness or in the rejection of mainstream norms. Like many other sociologists, however, I argue that the behavior patterns which concern the more fortunate classes are *poverty-related*, because they are, and have historically been, associated with poverty. . . . They are in fact caused by poverty, although a variety of other causes must also be at work since most poor people are not involved in any of these activities.

* * *

Because their criminal or disapproved behavior is ascribed to moral short-comings, the poor people who resort to it are often classified as unworthy or *undeserving*. For example, even though the failure of poor young men (or women) to work may be the effect of a lack of jobs, they are frequently accused of laziness, and then judged undeserving. Likewise, even though poor young mothers may decide not to marry the fathers of their children, because they, being jobless, cannot support them, the women are still accused of violating conventional familial norms, and also judged undeserving. Moreover, once judged to be undeserving, poor people are then no longer thought to be deserving of public aid that is financially sufficient and secure enough to help them escape poverty.

Judgments of the poor as undeserving are not based on evidence, but derive from a stereotype, even if, like most others, it is a stereotype with a "kernel of truth" (e.g., the monopolization of street crime by the poor). Furthermore, it is a very old stereotype; Cicero already described the needy of Rome as criminals. By the middle of the sixteenth century, complicated laws to distinguish between the deserving and undeserving were in existence. However, the term undeserving poor was first used regularly in England in the 1830s, at the time of the institution of the Poor Law.[1]

In America, a series of other, more specific, terms were borrowed or invented, with new ones replacing old ones as conditions and fashions changed. Such terms have included *beggar, pauper,* the *dangerous class, rabble, vagabond* and *vagrant,* and so on, which the United States borrowed from Europe. America also invented its own terms, including *shiftless, tramp,* and *feeble-minded,* and in the late twentieth century, terms like *hard-core, drifter, culturally deprived*—and most recently, *underclass.*[2] Nonetheless, in terms of its popular uses and the people to whom it is applied, the term underclass differs little from its predecessors.[3]

---

1. However, the *Oxford English Dictionary*, compiled by J. A. Simpson and E. S. Weiner (New York: Oxford University Press, 1989), 19: 996, already has a 1647 reference to beggars as undeserving, and the adjective itself was earlier used to refer to nonpoor people, for example, by Shakespeare.

2. These terms were often, but not exclusively, applied to the poor "races" who arrived in the nineteenth and early twentieth century from Ireland, Germany, and later, Eastern and Southern Europe. They have also been applied, during and after slavery, to Blacks. Nonetheless, the functions to be discussed in this article are consequences of poverty, not of race, even though a disproportionate rate of those "selected" to be poor have always been darker-skinned than the more fortunate classes.

3. The popular definition of underclass must be distinguished from Gunnar Myrdal's initial scholarly one, which viewed the underclass as a stratum driven to the margins or out of the labor force by what are today called the postindustrial and global economies. Gunnar Myrdal, *Challenge to Affluence* (New York: Pantheon Books, 1963), 10 and passim. Myrdal's definition viewed the underclass as victims of economic change, and said nothing about its moral state.

It is not difficult to understand why people, poor and more fortunate, are fearful of street crime committed by poor people, and even why the jobless poor and welfare recipients, like paupers before them, may be perceived as economic threats for not working and drawing on public funds, at least in bad economic times. Also, one can understand why other forms of poverty-related behavior, such as the early sexual activity of poor youngsters and the dramatic number of poor single-parent families are viewed as moral threats, since they violate norms thought to uphold the two-parent nuclear family and related normative bases of the social order. However, there would seem to be no inherent reason for exaggerating these threats, for example, in the case of welfare recipients who obtain only a tiny proportion of governmental expenditures, or more generally, by stereotyping poor people as undeserving without evidence of what they have and have not done, and why.

One reason, if not the only one, for the exaggeration and the stereotyping, and for the continued attractiveness of the concept of the undeserving poor itself, is that undeservingness has a number of *positive* functions for the better-off population. Some of these functions, or uses, are positive for everyone who is not poor, but most are positive only for some people, interest groups, and institutions, ranging from moderate income to wealthy ones. Needless to say, that undeservingness has uses for some people does not justify it; the existence of functions just helps to explain why it persists.

My notion of function, or empirically observable adaptive consequence, is adapted from the classic conceptual scheme of Robert K. Merton. My analysis will concentrate on those positive functions which Merton conceptualized as *latent*, which are unrecognized and/or unintended, but with the proviso that the functions which are identified as latent would probably not be abolished once they were widely recognized. Positive functions are, after all, also benefits, and people are not necessarily ready to give up benefits, including unintended ones, even if they become aware of them.

* * *

II. FUNCTIONS OF THE UNDESERVING POOR[4]

I will discuss five sets of positive functions: microsocial, economic, normative-cultural, political, and macrosocial, which I divide into 13 specific functions, although the sets are arbitrarily chosen and interrelated, and I could add many more functions. The functions are not listed in order of importance, for such a listing is not possible without empirical research on the various beneficiaries of undeservingness.

---

4. For brevity's sake, I will hereafter refer to the undeserving poor instead of the poor-labeled undeserving, but I always mean the latter.

Two Microsocial Functions

1. *Risk reduction.* Perhaps the primary use of the idea of the undeserving poor, primary because it takes place at the microsocial scale of everyday life, is that it distances the labeled from those who label them. By stigmatizing people as undeserving, labelers protect themselves from the responsibility of having to associate with them, or even to treat them like moral equals, which reduces the risk of being hurt or angered by them. Risk reduction is a way of dealing with actual or imagined threats to physical safety, for example from people who might be muggers, or cultural threats attributed to poor youngsters or normative ones imagined to come from welfare recipients. All pejorative labels and stereotypes serve this function, which may help to explain why there are so many such labels.

2. *Scapegoating and displacement.* By being thought undeserving, the stigmatized poor can be blamed for virtually any shortcoming of everyday life which can be credibly ascribed to them—violations of the laws of logic or social causation notwithstanding. Faulting the undeserving poor can also support the desire for revenge and punishment. In a society in which punishment is reserved for legislative, judicial, and penal institutions, *feelings* of revenge and punitiveness toward the undeserving poor supply at least some emotional satisfaction.

Since labeling poor people undeserving opens the door for nearly unlimited scapegoating, the labeled are also available to serve what I call the displacement function. Being too weak to object, the stigmatized poor can be accused of having caused social problems which they did not actually cause and can serve as cathartic objects on which better-off people can unload their own problems, as well as those of the economy, the polity, or of any other institutions, for the shortcomings of which the poor can be blamed.

Whether societywide changes in the work ethic are displaced on to "shiftlessness," or economic stagnation on to "welfare dependency," the poor can be declared undeserving for what ails the more affluent. This may also help to explain why the national concern with poor Black unmarried mothers, although usually ascribed to the data presented in the 1965 Moynihan Report, did not gather steam until the beginning of the decline of the economy in the mid-1970s. Similarly, the furor about poor "babies having babies" waited for the awareness of rising adolescent sexual activity among the better-off classes in the 1980s—at which point rates of adolescent pregnancy among the poor had already declined. But when the country became ambivalent about the desirability of abortions, the issue was displaced on the poor by making it almost impossible for them to obtain abortions.

Many years ago, James Baldwin, writing in *The Fire Next Time*, illustrated the displacement function in racial terms, arguing that, as Andrew Hacker put it, Whites "need the 'nigger' because it is the 'nigger' within themselves that they cannot tolerate. Whatever it is that Whites feel 'nigger' signifies about Blacks—lust and laziness, stupidity or squalor, in fact exists within themselves.... By creating such a creature, Whites are able to say that because only members of the Black race can carry that taint, it follows that none of its attributes will be found in White people.[5]

Three Economic Functions

3. *Economic banishment and the reserve army of labor.* People who have successfully been labeled as undeserving can be banished from the formal labor market. If young people are designated "school dropouts," for example; they can also be thought to lack the needed work habits, such as proper adherence to the work ethic, and may not be offered jobs to begin with. Often, they are effectively banished from the labor market before entering it because employers imagine them to be poor workers simply because they are young, male, and Black. Many ex-convicts are declared unemployable in similar fashion, and some become recidivists because they have no other choice but to go back to their criminal occupations.

Banishing the undeserving also makes room for immigrant workers, who may work for lower wages, are more deferential, and are more easily exploitable by being threatened with deportation. In addition, banishment helps to reduce the official jobless rate, a sometimes useful political function, especially if the banished drop so completely out of the labor force that they are not even available to be counted as "discouraged workers."

The economic banishment function is in many ways a replacement for the old reserve army of labor function, which played itself out when the undeserving poor could be hired as strikebreakers, as defense workers in the case of sudden wartime economic mobilization, as "hypothetical workers," who by their very presence could be used to depress the wages of other workers, or to put pressure on the unions not to make wage and other demands. Today, however, with a plentiful supply of immigrants, as well as of a constantly growing number of banished workers who are becoming surplus labor, a reserve army is less rarely needed—and when needed, can be recruited from sources other than the undeserving poor.

* * *

4. *Supplying illegal goods.* The undeserving poor who are banished from other jobs remain eligible for work in the manufacture and sale of illegal goods, including drugs. Although it is estimated that 80 percent of all illegal drugs are sold to Whites who are not poor, the sellers are often people banished from the formal labor market. Other suppliers of illegal goods include the illegal immigrants, considered undeserving in many American communities, who work for garment industry sweatshops manufacturing clothing under illegal conditions.

---

5. Hacker is paraphrasing Baldwin. Andrew Hacker, *Two Nations: Black and White, Separate, Hostile, Unequal* (New York: Scribner, 1992), 61.

5. *Job creation.* Perhaps the most important economic function of the undeserving poor today is that their mere presence creates jobs for the better-off population, including professional ones. Since the undeserving poor are thought to be dangerous or improperly socialized, their behavior either has to be modified so that they act in socially approved ways, or they have to be isolated from the deserving sectors of society. The larger the number of people who are declared undeserving, the larger also the number of people needed to modify and isolate as well as control, guard, and care for them. Among these are the social workers, teachers, trainers, mentors, psychiatrists, doctors and their support staffs in juvenile training centers, "special" schools, drug treatment centers, and penal behavior modification institutions, as well as the police, prosecutors, defense attorneys, judges, court officers, probation personnel and others who constitute the criminal courts, and the guards and others who run the prisons.

Jobs created by the presence of undeserving poor also include the massive bureaucracy of professionals, investigators, and clerks who administer welfare. Other jobs go to the officials who seek out poor fathers for child support monies they may or may not have, as well as the welfare office personnel needed to take recipients in violation of welfare rules off the rolls, and those needed to put them back on the rolls when they reapply. In fact, one can argue that some of the rules for supervising, controlling, and punishing the undeserving poor are more effective at performing the latent function of creating clerical and professional jobs for the better-off population than the manifest function of achieving their official goals.

More jobs are created in the social sciences and in journalism for conducting research about the undeserving poor and producing popular books, articles, and TV documentaries for the more fortunate who want to learn about them. The "job chain" should also be extended to the teachers and others who train those who serve, control, and study the undeserving poor.

In addition, the undeserving poor make jobs for what I call the salvation industries, religious, civil, or medical, which also try to modify the behavior of those stigmatized as undeserving. Not all such jobs are paid, for the undeserving poor also provide occasional targets for charity and thus offer volunteer jobs for those providing it—and paid jobs for the professional fundraisers who obtain most of the charitable funds these days. Among the most visible volunteers are the members of "café" and "high" society who organize and contribute to these benefits.

Three Normative Functions

6. *Moral legitimation.* Undeservingness justifies the category of deservingness and thus supplies moral and political legitimacy, almost by definition, to the institutions and social structures that include the deserving and exclude the undeserving. Of these structures, the most important is undoubtedly the class hierarchy, for the existence of an undeserving class or stratum legitimates

the deserving classes, if not necessarily all of their class-related behavior. The alleged immorality of the undeserving also gives a moral flavor to, and justification for, the class hierarchy, which may help to explain why upward mobility itself is so praiseworthy.

7. *Norm reinforcement.* By violating, or being imagined as violating, a number of mainstream behavioral patterns and values, the undeserving poor help to reaffirm and reinforce the virtues of these patterns—and to do so visibly, since the violations by the undeserving are highly publicized. As Emile Durkheim pointed out nearly a century ago, norm violations and their punishments also provide an opportunity for preserving and reaffirming the norms. This is not insignificant, for norms sometimes disparaged as "motherhood" values gain new moral power when they are violated, and their violators are stigmatized.

If the undeserving poor can be imagined to be lazy, they help to reaffirm the Protestant work ethic; if poor single-parent families are publicly condemned, the two-parent family is once more legitimated as ideal. In the 1960s, middle-class morality was sometimes criticized as culturally parochial and therefore inappropriate for the poor, but since the 1980s, mainstream values have once more been regarded as vital sources of behavioral guidance for them.

Enforcing the norms also contributes further to preserving them in another way, for one of the standard punishments of the undeserving poor for misbehaving—as well as standard obligation in exchange for help—is practicing the mainstream norms, including those that the members of the mainstream may only be preaching, and that might die out if the poor were not required to incorporate them in their behavior. Old work rules that can no longer be enforced in the rest of the economy can be maintained in the regulations for workfare; old-fashioned austerity and thrift are built into the consumption patterns expected of welfare recipients. Economists like to argue that if the poor want to be deserving, they should take any kind of job, regardless of its low pay or demeaning character, reflecting a work ethic which economists themselves have never practiced.

Similarly, welfare recipients may be removed from the rolls if they are found to be living with a man—but the social worker who removes them has every right to cohabit and not lose his or her job. In most states, welfare recipients must observe rules of housecleaning and child care that middle-class people are free to ignore without being punished. While there are many norms and laws governing child care, only the poor are monitored to see if they obey these. Should they use more physical punishment on their children than social workers consider desirable, they can be charged with child neglect or abuse and can lose their children to foster care.[6]

---

6. Poor immigrants who still practice old-country discipline norms are particularly vulnerable to being accused of child abuse.

The fact is that the defenders of such widely preached norms as hard work, thrift, monogamy, and moderation need people who can be accused, accurately or not, of being lazy, spendthrift, promiscuous, and immoderate. One reason that welfare recipients are a ready target for punitive legislation is that politicians, and most likely some of their constituents, imagine them to be enjoying leisure and an active sex life at public expense. Whether or not very many poor people actually behave in the ways that are judged undeserving is irrelevant if they can be imagined as doing so. Once imagining and stereotyping are allowed to take over, then judgments of undeservingness can be made without much concern for empirical accuracy. For example, in the 1990s, the idea that young men from poor single-parent families were highly likely to commit street crimes became so universal that the news media no longer needed to quote experts to affirm the accuracy of the charge.

Actually, most of the time most of the poor are as law abiding and observant of mainstream norms as are other Americans. Sometimes they are even more observant; thus the proportion of welfare recipients who cheat is always far below the percentage of taxpayers who do so. Moreover, survey after survey has shown that the poor, including many street criminals and drug sellers, want to hold respectable jobs like everyone else, hope someday to live in the suburbs, and generally aspire to the same American dream as most moderate and middle-income Americans.[7]

8. *Supplying popular culture villains.* The undeserving poor have played a long-term role in supplying American popular culture with villains, allowing the producers of the culture both to reinforce further mainstream norms and to satisfy audience demands for revenge, notably by showing that crime and other norm violations do not pay. Street criminals are shown dead or alive in the hands of the police on local television news virtually every day, and more dramatically so in the crime and action movies and television series.

For many years before and after World War II, the criminal characters in Hollywood movies were often poor immigrants, frequently of Sicilian origin. Then they were complemented for some decades by communist spies and other Cold War enemies who were not poor, but even before the end of the Cold War, they were being replaced by Black and Hispanic drug dealers and gang leaders.

At the same time, however, the popular culture industry has also supplied music and other materials offering marketable cultural and political protest which does not reinforce mainstream norms, or at least not directly. Some of the creators and performers come from poor neighborhoods, however, and it may be that some rap music becomes commercially successful by displacing on ghetto musicians the cultural and political protest of record buyers from more affluent classes.

---

7. See Mark R. Rank, *Living on the Edge: The Realities of Welfare in America* (New York: Columbia University Press, 1994), 93.

Three Political Functions

9. *Institutional scapegoating.* The scapegoating of the undeserving poor mentioned in Function 2 above also extends to institutions which mistreat them. As a result, some of the responsibility for the existence of poverty, slum unemployment, poor schools, and the like is taken off the shoulders of elected and appointed officials who are supposed to deal with these problems. For example, to the extent that educational experts decide that the children of the poor are learning disabled or that they are culturally or genetically inferior in intelligence, attempts to improve the schools can be put off or watered down.

To put it another way, the availability of institutional scapegoats both personalizes and exonerates social systems. The alleged laziness of the jobless and the anger aimed at beggars take the heat off the failure of the economy and the imagined derelictions of slum dwellers and the homeless, off the housing industry. In effect, the undeserving poor are blamed both for their poverty and also for the absence of "political will" among the citizenry to do anything about it.

10. *Conservative power shifting.* Once poor people are declared undeserving they also lose their political legitimacy and whatever little political influence they had before they were stigmatized. Some cannot vote, and many do not choose to vote or mobilize because they know politicians do not listen to their demands. Elected officials might ignore them even if they voted or mobilized because these officials and the larger polity cannot easily satisfy their demands for economic and other kinds of justice.[8] As a result, the political system is able to pay additional attention to the demands of more affluent constituents. It can therefore shift to the "right."

The same shift to the right also takes place ideologically. Although injustices of poverty help justify the existence of liberals and the more radical left the undeserving poor themselves provide justification and opportunities for conservatives to attack their ideological enemies on their left. When liberals can be accused of favoring criminals over victims, their accusers can launch and legitimate incursions on the civil liberties and rights of the undeserving poor, and concurrently on the liberties and rights of defenders of the poor. Moreover, the undeservingness of the poor can be used to justify attacks on the welfare state. Charles Murray understood the essence of this ideological function when he argued that welfare and other welfare state legislation for the poor only increased the number of poor people.[9]

---

8. In addition, the undeserving poor make a dangerous constituency. Politicians who say kind words about them or who act to represent their interests are likely to be attacked for their words and actions. Jesse Jackson was hardly the first national politician to be criticized for being too favorable to the poor.

9. Charles Murray, *Losing Ground: American Social Policy, 1950–1980* (New York: Basic Books, 1984).

11. *Spatial purification.* Stigmatized populations are often used, deliberately or not, to stigmatize the areas in which they live, making such areas eligible for various kinds of purification. As a result, "underclass areas" can be torn down and their inhabitants moved to make room for more affluent residents or higher taxpayers.

However, such areas can also be used to isolate stigmatized poor people and facilities by selecting them as locations for homeless shelters, halfway houses for the mentally ill or for ex-convicts, drug treatment facilities, and even garbage dumps, which have been forced out of middle- and working-class areas following NIMBY (not in my backyard) protests. Drug dealers and other sellers of illegal goods also find a haven in areas stigmatized as underclass areas, partly because these supply some customers, but also because police protection in such areas is usually minimal enough to allow illegal activities without significant interference from the law. In fact, municipalities would face major economic and political obstacles to their operations without stigmatized areas in which stigmatized people and activities can be located.

Two Macrosocial Functions

12. *Reproduction of stigma and the stigmatized.* For centuries now, undeservingness has given rise to policies and agencies which are manifestly set up to help the poor economically and otherwise to become deserving, but which actually prevent the undeserving poor from being freed of their stigma, and which also manage, unwittingly, to see to it that their children face the same obstacles. In some instances, this process works so speedily that the children of the stigmatized face "anticipatory stigmatization," among them the children of welfare recipients who are frequently predicted to be unable to learn, to work, and to remain on the right side of the law even before they have been weaned.

If this outcome were planned deliberately, one could argue that politically and culturally dominant groups are reluctant to give up an easily accessible and always available scapegoat. In actuality, however, the reproduction function results unwittingly from other intended and seemingly popular practices. For example, the so-called War on Drugs, which has unsuccessfully sought to keep hard drugs out of the United States, but has meanwhile done little to provide drug treatment to addicts who want it, thereby aids the continuation of addiction, street crime, and a guaranteed prison population, not to mention the various disasters that visit the families of addicts and help to keep them poor.

The other major source of reproducing stigma and the stigmatized is the routine activities of the organizations which service welfare recipients, the homeless, and other stigmatized poor, and end up mistreating them. For one thing, such agencies, whether they exist to supply employment to the poor or to help the homeless, are almost certain to be underfunded because of the powerlessness of their clientele. No organization has ever had the funds or power to buy, build, or rehabilitate housing for the homeless in sufficient number. Typically, they have been able to fund or carry out small demonstration projects.

In addition, organizations which serve stigmatized people often attract less well-trained and qualified staff than those with high-status clients, and if the clients are deemed undeserving, competence may become even less important in choosing staff. Then too, helping organizations generally reflect the societal stratification hierarchy, which means that organizations with poor, low-status clients frequently treat them as undeserving. If they also fear some of their clients, they may not only withhold help, but attack the clients on a pre-emptive strike basis. Last but not least, the agencies that serve the undeserving poor are bureaucracies which operate by rules and regulations that routinize the work, encourage the stability and growth of the organizations, and serve the needs of their staffs before those of their clients.

When these factors are combined, as they often are, and become cumulative, as they often do, it should not be surprising that the organizations cut off escape routes from poverty not only for the clients, but in doing so, also make sure that some of their children remain poor as well.

13. *Extermination of the surplus.* In earlier times, when the living standards of all poor people were at or below subsistence, many died at an earlier age than the better off, thus performing the set of functions for the latter forever associated with Thomas Malthus. Standards of living, even for the very poor, have risen considerably in the last century, but even today, morbidity and mortality rates remain much higher among the poor than among moderate-income people. To put it another way, various social forces combine to do away with some of the people who have become surplus labor and are no longer needed by the economy.

Several of the killing illnesses and pathologies of the poor change over time; currently, they include AIDS, tuberculosis, hypertension, heart attacks, and cancer, as well as psychosis, substance abuse, street crime, injury and death during participation in the drug trade and other underworld activities, and intraclass homicide resulting from neighborhood conflicts over turf and "respect." Whether the poor people whose only problem is being unfairly stereotyped and stigmatized as undeserving die earlier than other poor people is not known.

Moreover, these rates can be expected to remain high or even to rise as rates of unemployment—and of banishment from the labor force—rise, especially for the least skilled. Even the better-off jobless created by the downsizing of the 1990s blame themselves for their unemployment if they cannot eventually find new jobs, become depressed, and in some instances begin the same process of being extruded permanently from the labor market experienced by the least skilled of the jobless.

* * *

The early departure of poor people from an economy and society which do not need them is useful for those who remain. Since the more fortunate classes have already developed a purposive blindness to the structural causes of unemployment and to the poverty-related causes of pathology and crime that

follow, those who benefit from the current job erosion and the possible extermination of the surplus labor may not admit it consciously either. Nonetheless, those left over to compete for scarce jobs and other resources will have a
somewhat easier time in the competition, thus assigning undeservingness a
final positive function for the more fortunate members of society.

III. CONCLUSION

I have described thirteen of the more important functions of the undeserving
poor, enough to support my argument that both the idea of the undeserving
poor and the stigmas with which some poor people are thus labeled may persist in part because they are useful in a variety of ways to the people who are
not poor.

This analysis does not imply that undeservingness will or should persist.
Whether it *will* persist is going to be determined by what happens to poverty
in America. If it declines, poverty-related crime should also decline, and then
fewer poor people will probably be described as undeserving. If poverty wors-
ens, so will poverty-related crime, as well as the stereotyping and stigmatization of the poor, and any worsening of the country's economy is likely to add
to the kinds and numbers of undeserving poor, if only because they make convenient and powerless scapegoats.

The functions that the undeserving poor play cannot, by themselves, perpetuate either poverty or undeservingness, for as I noted earlier, functions are
not causes. For example, if huge numbers of additional unskilled workers should
be needed, as they were for the World War II war effort, the undeserving poor
will be welcomed back into the labor force, at least temporarily. Of course, institutions often try to survive once they have lost both their reasons for existence
and their functions. Since the end of the Cold War, parts of the military-
industrial establishment both in the United States and Russia have been campaigning for the maintenance of some Cold War forces and weapons to
guarantee their own futures, but these establishments also supply jobs to their
national economies, and in the United States, for the constituents of elected
officials. Likewise, some of the institutions and interest groups that benefit from
the existence of undeservingness, or from controlling the undeserving poor,
may try to maintain undeservingness and its stigma. They may not even need
to, for if Émile Durkheim was right, the decline of undeservingness would lead
to the criminalization, or at least stigmatization, of new behavior patterns.

Whether applying the label of undeservingness to the poor *should* persist
is a normative question which ought to be answered in the negative. Although
people have a right to judge each other, that right does not extend to judging
large numbers of people as a single group, with one common moral fault, or to
stereotyping them without evidence either about their behavior or their values.
Even if a case could be made for judging large cohorts of people as undeserving,
these judgments should be distributed up and down the socioeconomic hierar-

chy, requiring Americans also to consider whether and how people in the working, middle, and upper classes are undeserving.

The same equality should extend to the punishment of crimes. Today, many Americans and courts still treat white-collar and upper-class criminals more leniently than poor ones. The public excuse given is that the street crime of the undeserving poor involves violence and thus injury or death, but as many students of white-collar and corporate crime have pointed out, these also hurt and kill people, and often in larger numbers, even if they do so less directly and perhaps less violently.

Changes also need to be made in the American conception of deviance, which like that of other countries, conflates people whose behavior is *different* with those whose behavior is socially *harmful*. Bearing children without marriage is a long-standing tradition among the poor. Born of necessity rather than preference, it is a poverty-related practice, but it is not, by itself, harmful, or at least not until it can be shown that either the children—or the moral sensibilities of the people who oppose illegitimacy—are significantly hurt. Poor single-parent families are hardly desirable, but as the lack of condemnation of more affluent single-parent families should suggest, the major problem of such families is not the number of parents, actual or surrogate, in the family, but its poverty.

Finally, because many of the poor are stereotyped unjustly as undeserving, scholars, writers, journalists, and others should launch a systematic and public effort to deconstruct and delegitimate the notion of the undeserving poor. This effort, which is necessary to help make effective antipoverty programs politically acceptable again, should place the following five ideas on the public agenda and encourage discussion as well as dissemination of available research.

The five ideas, all discussed earlier in this article, are that (1) the criminal and deviant behavior among the poor is largely poverty related rather than the product of free choice based on distinctive values; (2) the undeservingness of the poor is an ancient stereotype, and like all stereotypes, it vastly exaggerates the actual dangers that stem from the poor; (3) poverty-related deviance is not necessarily harmful just because it does not accord with mainstream norms; (4) the notion of undeservingness survives in part because of the positive functions it has for the better-off population; and (5) the only certain way to eliminate both this notion and the functions is to eliminate poverty.[10]

---

10. A fuller discussion of policy proposals . . . appear[s] in my . . . book, *Ending the War against the Poor.*

SOCIAL CONTROL AND ORGANIZATIONAL POWER

32

Panopticism

FROM *Discipline and Punish: The Birth of the Prison*

MICHEL FOUCAULT

Michel Foucault, a social historian and social theorist, is one of the most important sociologists of the last half century. As you read what appears to be a discussion of something long ago, you should realize he's also talking about society right now. Not only can we be watched wherever we are, but our comings and goings are now recorded with hidden cameras and microphones, iPhones, and webcams. Corporations are mining your every Internet search and web post. The National Security Agency (NSA) is collecting and storing every call you've made and every e-mail you've sent or received. This is the perfect panopticon, with an incredible capability to discipline and punish.

* * *

Bentham's* *Panopticon* is the architectural figure of this composition. We know the principle on which it was based: at the periphery, an annular building; at the centre, a tower; this tower is pierced with wide windows that open onto the inner side of the ring; the peripheric building is divided into cells, each of which extends the whole width of the building; they have two windows, one on the inside, corresponding to the windows of the tower; the other, on the outside, allows the light to cross the cell from one end to the other. All that is needed, then, is to place a supervisor in a central tower and to shut up in each cell a madman, a patient, a condemned man, a worker or a schoolboy. By the effect of backlighting, one can observe from the tower, standing out precisely against the light, the small captive shadows in the cells of the periphery. They are like so many cages, so many small theatres, in which each actor is alone, perfectly individualized and constantly visible. The panoptic mechanism arranges spatial unities that make it possible to see constantly and to recognize immediately. In short, it reverses the principle of the dungeon; or rather of its three functions—to enclose, to deprive of light and to hide—it preserves only the first and eliminates the other two. Full

---

*Jeremy Bentham (1748–1832), an English political theorist, was one of the founders of utilitarianism, an ethical philosophy that argued what is right and best is what provides the greatest happiness to the most people, identifying happiness with pleasure. [*Editors' note*]

lighting and the eye of a supervisor capture better than darkness, which ultimately protected. Visibility is a trap.

To begin with, this made it possible—as a negative effect—to avoid those compact, swarming, howling masses that were to be found in places of confinement, those painted by Goya or described by [the English prison reformer John] Howard. Each individual, in his place, is securely confined to a cell from which he is seen from the front by the supervisor; but the side walls prevent him from coming into contact with his companions. He is seen, but he does not see; he is the object of information, never a subject in communication. The arrangement of his room, opposite the central tower, imposes on him an axial visibility; but the divisions of the ring, those separated cells, imply a lateral invisibility. And this invisibility is a guarantee of order. If the inmates are convicts, there is no danger of a plot, an attempt at collective escape, the planning of new crimes for the future, bad reciprocal influences; if they are patients, there is no danger of contagion; if they are madmen there is no risk of their committing violence upon one another; if they are schoolchildren, there is no copying, no noise, no chatter, no waste of time; if they are workers, there are no disorders, no theft, no coalitions, none of those distractions that slow down the rate of work, make it less perfect or cause accidents. The crowd, a compact mass, a locus of multiple exchanges, individualities merging together, a collective effect, is abolished and replaced by a collection of separated individualities. From the point of view of the guardian, it is replaced by a multiplicity that can be numbered and supervised; from the point of view of the inmates, by a sequestered and observed solitude (Bentham, 60–64).

Hence the major effect of the Panopticon: to induce in the inmate a state of conscious and permanent visibility that assures the automatic functioning of power. So to arrange things that the surveillance is permanent in its effects, even if it is discontinuous in its action; that the perfection of power should tend to render its actual exercise unnecessary; that this architectural apparatus should be a machine for creating and sustaining a power relation independent of the person who exercises it; in short, that the inmates should be caught up in a power situation of which they are themselves the bearers. To achieve this, it is at once too much and too little that the prisoner should be constantly observed by an inspector: too little, for what matters is that he knows himself to be observed; too much, because he has no need in fact of being so. In view of this, Bentham laid down the principle that power should be visible and unverifiable. Visible: the inmate will constantly have before his eyes the tall outline of the central tower from which he is spied upon. Unverifiable: the inmate must never know whether he is being looked at at any one moment; but he must be sure that he may always be so.

* * *

A real subjection is born mechanically from a fictitious relation. So it is not necessary to use force to constrain the convict to good behaviour, the madman to calm, the worker to work, the schoolboy to application, the patient to the observation of the regulations. Bentham was surprised that panoptic institutions could be so light: there were no more bars, no more chains, no more heavy locks; all that was needed was that the separations should be clear and the openings well arranged. The heaviness of the old "houses of security," with their fortress-like architecture, could be replaced by the simple, economic geometry of a "house of certainty." The efficiency of power, its constraining force have, in a sense, passed over to the other side—to the side of its surface of application. He who is subjected to a field of visibility, and who knows it, assumes responsibility for the constraints of power; he makes them play spontaneously upon himself; he inscribes in himself the power relation in which he simultaneously plays both roles; he becomes the principle of his own subjection. By this very fact, the external power may throw off its physical weight; it tends to the non-corporal; and, the more it approaches this limit, the more constant, profound and permanent are its effects: it is a perpetual victory that avoids any physical confrontation and which is always decided in advance.

* * *

The Panopticon is a privileged place for experiments on men, and for analysing with complete certainty the transformations that may be obtained from them. The Panopticon may even provide an apparatus for supervising its own mechanisms. In this central tower, the director may spy on all the employees that he has under his orders: nurses, doctors, foremen, teachers, warders; he will be able to judge them continuously, alter their behaviour, impose upon them the methods he thinks best; and it will even be possible to observe the director himself. An inspector arriving unexpectedly at the centre of the Panopticon will be able to judge at a glance, without anything being concealed from him, how the entire establishment is functioning. And, in any case, enclosed as he is in the middle of this architectural mechanism, is not the director's own fate entirely bound up with it? The incompetent physician who has allowed contagion to spread, the incompetent prison governor or workshop manager will be the first victims of an epidemic or a revolt. "By every tie I could devise," said the master of the Panopticon, "my own fate had been bound up by me with theirs." The Panopticon functions as a kind of laboratory of power.

* * *

The celebrated, transparent, circular cage, with its high tower, powerful and knowing, may have been for Bentham a project of a perfect disciplinary institution; but he also set out to show how one may "unlock" the disciplines and get them to function in a diffused, multiple, polyvalent way throughout the whole social body. These disciplines, which the classical age had elaborated in specific, relatively enclosed places—barracks, schools, workshops—and whose total implementation had been imagined only at the limited and temporary scale of a plague-stricken town, Bentham dreamt of transforming into a network of mechanisms that would be everywhere and always alert, running through society without interruption in space or in time. The panoptic arrangement provides the formula for this generalization. It programmes, at the level of an elementary and easily transferable mechanism, the basic functioning of a society penetrated through and through with disciplinary mechanisms.

33

From the Panopticon* to Disney World:
The Development of Discipline

CLIFFORD D. SHEARING and PHILIP C. STENNING

To live in a modern society is to know and live within a vast array of invisible structures designed to ensure orderly behavior. Other structures are quite visible but not recognized: actual physical barriers, corridors, and messages directing us to come, go, turn, stop, be silent, not smoke, wear a shirt and shoes, and so forth. We conform to control systems with our own consent or what Shearing and Stenning call "structured compliance." Disney World is not the only place where this occurs, but it offers a good illustration for your own investigations.

One of the most distinctive features of that quintessentially American playground known as Disney World is the way it seeks to combine a sense of comfortable—even nostalgic—familiarity with an air of innovative technological advance. Mingled with the fantasies of one's childhood are the dreams of a better future. Next to the Magic Kingdom is the Epcot Center. As well as providing for a great escape, Disney World claims also to be a design for better living. And what impresses most about this place is that it seems to run like clockwork.

Yet the Disney order is no accidental by-product. Rather, it is a designed-in feature that provides—to the eye that is looking for it, but not to the casual visitor—an exemplar of modern private corporate policing. Along with the rest of the scenery of which it forms a discreet part, it too is recognizable as a design for the future.

We invite you to come with us on a guided tour of this modern police facility in which discipline and control are, like many of the characters one sees about, in costume.

The fun begins the moment the visitor enters Disney World. As one arrives by car one is greeted by a series of smiling young people who, with the aid of clearly visible road markings, direct one to one's parking spot, remind one to lock one's car and to remember its location and then direct one to await the rubber-wheeled train that will convey visitors away from the parking lot. At the boarding location one is directed to stand safely behind guard rails and to board the train in an orderly fashion. While climbing on board one is reminded

---

*Jeremy Bentham (1748–1832) coined this term to describe a perfect prison where nothing could be done outside the view of the custodial staff. [*Editors' note*]

to remember the name of the parking area and the row number in which one is parked (for instance, "Donald Duck, 1"). Once on the train one is encouraged to protect oneself from injury by keeping one's body within the bounds of the carriage and to do the same for children in one's care. Before disembarking one is told how to get from the train back to the monorail platform and where to wait for the train to the parking lot on one's return. At each transition from one stage of one's journey to the next, one is wished a happy day and a "good time" at Disney World (this begins as one drives in and is directed by road signs to tune one's car radio to the Disney radio network).

As one moves towards the monorail platform the directions one has just received are reinforced by physical barriers (that make it difficult to take a wrong turn), pavement markings, signs and more cheerful Disney employees who, like their counterparts in other locations, convey the message that Disney World is a "fun place" designed for one's comfort and pleasure. On approaching the monorail platform one is met by enthusiastic attendants who quickly and efficiently organize the mass of people moving onto it into corrals designed to accommodate enough people to fill one compartment on the monorail. In assigning people to these corrals the attendants ensure that groups visiting Disney World together remain together. Access to the edge of the platform is prevented by a gate which is opened once the monorail has arrived and disembarked the arriving passengers on the other side of the platform. If there is a delay of more than a minute or two in waiting for the next monorail one is kept informed of the reason for the delay and the progress the expected train is making towards the station.

Once aboard and the automatic doors of the monorail have closed, one is welcomed aboard, told to remain seated and "for one's own safety" to stay away from open windows. The monorail takes a circuitous route to one of the two Disney locations (the Epcot Center or the Magic Kingdom) during which time a friendly disembodied voice introduces one briefly to the pleasure of the world one is about to enter and the methods of transport available between its various locations. As the monorail slows towards its destination one is told how to disembark once the automatic doors open and how to move from the station to the entrance gates, and reminded to take one's possessions with one and to take care of oneself, and children in one's care, on disembarking. Once again these instructions are reinforced, in a variety of ways, as one moves towards the gates.

It will be apparent from the above that Disney Productions is able to handle large crowds of visitors in a most orderly fashion. Potential trouble is anticipated and prevented. Opportunities for disorder are minimized by constant instruction, by physical barriers which severely limit the choice of action available and by the surveillance of omnipresent employees who detect and rectify the slightest deviation.

The vehicles that carry people between locations are an important component of the system of physical barriers. Throughout Disney World vehicles are used as barriers. This is particularly apparent in the Epcot Center, . . . where many exhibits are accessible only via special vehicles which automatically secure one once they begin moving.

Control strategies are embedded in both environmental features and structural relations. In both cases control structures and activities have other functions which are highlighted so that the control function is overshadowed. Nonetheless, control is pervasive. For example, virtually every pool, fountain, and flower garden serves both as an aesthetic object and to direct visitors away from, or towards, particular locations. Similarly, every Disney Productions employee, while visibly and primarily engaged in other functions, is also engaged in the maintenance of order. This integration of functions is real and not simply an appearance: beauty *is* created, safety *is* protected, employees *are* helpful. The effect is, however, to embed the control function into the "woodwork" where its presence is unnoticed but its effects are ever present.

A critical consequence of this process of embedding control in other structures is that control becomes consensual. It is effected with the willing cooperation of those being controlled so that the controlled become, as Foucault (1977) has observed, the source of their own control. Thus, for example, the batching that keeps families together provides for family unity while at the same time ensuring that parents will be available to control their children. By seeking a definition of order within Disney World that can convincingly be presented as being in the interest of visitors, order maintenance is established as a voluntary activity which allows coercion to be reduced to a minimum. Thus, adult visitors willingly submit to a variety of devices that increase the flow of consumers through Disney World, such as being corralled on the monorail platform, so as to ensure the safety of their children. Furthermore, while doing so they gratefully acknowledge the concern Disney Productions has for their family, thereby legitimating its authority, not only in the particular situation in question, but in others as well. Thus, while profit ultimately underlies the order Disney Productions seeks to maintain, it is pursued in conjunction with other objectives that will encourage the willing compliance of visitors in maintaining Disney profits. This approach to profit making, which seeks a coincidence of corporate and individual interests (employee and consumer alike), extends beyond the control function and reflects a business philosophy to be applied to all corporate operations (Peters and Waterman, 1982).

The coercive edge of Disney's control system is seldom far from the surface, however, and becomes visible the moment the Disney-visitor consensus breaks down, that is, when a visitor attempts to exercise a choice that is incompatible with the Disney order. It is apparent in the physical barriers that forcefully prevent certain activities as well as in the action of employees who detect breaches of order. This can be illustrated by an incident that occurred during a visit to Disney World by Shearing and his daughter, during the course of which she developed a blister on her heel. To avoid further irritation she removed her shoes and proceeded to walk barefooted. They had not progressed ten yards before they were approached by a very personable security guard dressed as a Bahamian police officer, with white pith helmet and white gloves that perfectly suited the theme of the area they were moving through (so that he, at first, appeared more like a scenic prop than a security person), who informed them that walking barefoot was, "for the safety of visitors," not permitted. When informed that, given the blister, the safety of this visitor was likely to be better secured by remaining barefooted, at least on the walkways, they were informed that their safety and how best to protect it was a matter for Disney Productions to determine while they were on Disney property and that unless they complied he would be compelled to escort them out of Disney World. Shearing's daughter, on learning that failure to comply with the security guard's instruction would deprive her of the pleasures of Disney World, quickly decided that she would prefer to further injure her heel and remain on Disney property. As this example illustrates, the source of Disney Productions' power rests both in the physical coercion it can bring to bear and in its capacity to induce cooperation by depriving visitors of a resource that they value.

The effectiveness of the power that control of a "fun place" has is vividly illustrated by the incredible queues of visitors who patiently wait, sometimes for hours, for admission to exhibits. These queues not only call into question the common knowledge that queueing is a quintessentially English pastime (if Disney World is any indication Americans are at least as good, if not better, at it), but provide evidence of the considerable inconvenience that people can be persuaded to tolerate so long as they believe that their best interests require it. While the source of this perception is the image of Disney World that the visitor brings to it, it is, interestingly, reinforced through the queueing process itself. In many exhibits queues are structured so that one is brought close to the entrance at several points, thus periodically giving one a glimpse of the fun to come while at the same time encouraging one that the wait will soon be over.

Visitor participation in the production of order within Disney World goes beyond the more obvious control examples we have noted so far. An important aspect of the order Disney Productions attempts to maintain is a particular image of Disney World and the American industrialists who sponsor its exhibits (General Electric, Kodak, Kraft Foods, etc.). Considerable care is taken to ensure that every feature of Disney World reflects a positive view of the American Way, especially its use of, and reliance on, technology. Visitors are, for example, exposed to an almost constant stream of directions by employees, robots in human form and disembodied recorded voices (the use of recorded messages and robots permits precise control over the content and tone of the directions given) that convey the desired message. Disney World acts as a giant magnet attracting millions of Americans and visitors from other lands who pay to learn of the wonders of American capitalism.

Visitors are encouraged to participate in the production of the Disney image while they are in Disney World and to take it home with them so that they can reproduce it for their families and friends. One way this is done is through the "Picture Spots," marked with signposts, to be found throughout Disney World, that provide direction with respect to the images to capture on film (with cameras that one can borrow free of charge) for the slide shows and photo albums to be prepared "back home." Each spot provides views which exclude anything unsightly (such as garbage containers) so as to ensure that the visual images visitors take away of Disney World will properly capture Disney's order. A related technique is the Disney characters who wander through the complex to provide "photo opportunities" for young children. These characters apparently never talk to visitors, and the reason for this is presumably so that their media-based images will not be spoiled.

As we have hinted throughout this discussion, training is a pervasive feature of the control system of Disney Productions. It is not, however, the redemptive soul-training of the carceral project but an ever-present flow of directions for, and definitions of, order directed at every visitor. Unlike carceral training, these messages do not require detailed knowledge of the individual. They are, on the contrary, for anyone and everyone. Messages are, nonetheless, often conveyed to single individuals or small groups of friends and relatives. For example, in some of the newer exhibits, the vehicles that take one through swivel and turn so that one's gaze can be precisely directed. Similarly, each seat is fitted with individual sets of speakers that talk directly to one, thus permitting a seductive sense of intimacy while simultaneously imparting a uniform message.

In summary, within Disney World control is embedded, preventative, subtle, cooperative and apparently non-coercive and consensual. It focuses on categories, requires no knowledge of the individual and employs pervasive surveillance. Thus, although disciplinary, it is distinctively non-carceral. Its order is instrumental and determined by the interests of Disney Productions rather than moral and absolute. As anyone who has visited Disney World knows, it is extraordinarily effective.

While this new instrumental discipline is rapidly becoming a dominant force in social control it is as different from the Orwellian totalitarian nightmare as it is from the carceral regime. Surveillance is pervasive but it is the antithesis of the blatant control of the Orwellian State: its source is not government and its vehicle is not Big Brother. The order of instrumental discipline is not the unitary order of a central State but diffuse and separate orders defined by private authorities responsible for the feudal-like domains of Disney World, condominium estates, commercial complexes and the like. Within contemporary discipline, control is as fine-grained as Orwell imagined but its features are very different. It is thus, paradoxically, not to Orwell's socialist-inspired Utopia that we must look for a picture of contemporary control but to the capitalist-inspired disciplinary model conceived of by Huxley, who, in his *Brave New World*, painted a picture of consensually based control that bears a striking resemblance to the disciplinary control of Disney World and other corporate control systems. Within Huxley's imaginary world people are seduced into conformity by the pleasures offered by the drug "soma" rather than coerced into compliance by threat of Big Brother, just as people are today seduced to conform by the pleasures of consuming the goods that corporate power has to offer.

The contrasts between morally based justice and instrumental control, carceral punishment and corporate control, the Panopticon and Disney World and Orwell's and Huxley's visions is succinctly captured by the novelist Beryl Bainbridge's (1984) observations about a recent journey she made retracing J. B. Priestley's (1933) celebrated trip around Britain. She notes how during his travels in 1933 the center of the cities and towns he visited were defined by either a church or a center of government (depicting the coalition between Church and State in the production of order that characterizes morally based regimes).

During her more recent trip one of the changes that struck her most forcibly was the transformation that had taken place in the center of cities and towns. These were now identified not by churches or town halls, but by shopping centers, often vaulted glass-roofed structures that she found reminiscent of the cathedrals they had replaced both in their awe-inspiring architecture and in the hush that she found they sometimes created. What was worshipped in these contemporary cathedrals, she noted, was not an absolute moral order but something much more mundane: people were "worshipping shopping" and through it, we would add, the private authorities, the order and corporate power their worship makes possible.

REFERENCES

Bainbridge, B. 1984. Television interview with Robert Fulford on "Realities." Global Television, Toronto, October.

Foucault, M. 1977. *Discipline and Punish: The Birth of the Prison.* New York: Vintage.

Peters, T. J. and Waterman, R. H. 1982. *In Search of Excellence.* New York: Warner Books.

Priestley, J. B. 1934. *English Journey: Being a Rambling but Truthful Account of What One Man Saw and Heard and Felt and Thought during a Journey through England Autumn of the Year 1933.* London: Heinemann and Gollancz.

34

The Black Family in the Age of Mass Incarceration

TA-NEHISI COATES

Mass incarceration is defined by its sheer scope—a substantial deviation from historical and comparative norms—and the social concentration of its effects—on black men who are much more likely than others in the United States to be incarcerated. In this essay, Ta-Nehisi Coates explores the sociological, historical, and political roots of this phenomenon. He also describes how the effects of mass incarceration spiral out from the people who are incarcerated—to their families, communities, and society as a whole. He shows that rather than being a rational response to increasing crime, the "get tough" law enforcement policies that fueled the growth of mass incarceration in the late twentieth century—what Coates calls "the carceral state"—became a way to maintain the racial caste system that grew out of America's form of slavery and its Jim Crow era and has been threatened by the modern-day civil rights movement.

By his own lights, Daniel Patrick Moynihan, ambassador, senator, sociologist, and itinerant American intellectual, was the product of a broken home and a pathological family. He was born in 1927 in Tulsa, Oklahoma, but raised mostly in New York City. When Moynihan was 10 years old, his father, John, left the family, plunging it into poverty. Moynihan's mother, Margaret, remarried, had another child, divorced, moved to Indiana to stay with relatives, then returned to New York, where she worked as a nurse. Moynihan's childhood—a tangle of poverty, remarriage, relocation, and single motherhood—contrasted starkly with the idyllic American family life he would later extol. "My relations are obviously those of divided allegiance," Moynihan wrote in a diary he kept during the 1950s. "Apparently I loved the old man very much yet had to take sides . . . choosing mom in spite of loving pop." In the same journal, Moynihan, subjecting himself to the sort of analysis to which he would soon subject others, wrote, "Both my mother and father—They let me down badly . . . I find through the years this enormous emotional attachment to Father substitutes—of whom the least rejection was cause for untold agonies—the only answer is that I have repressed my feelings towards dad."

As a teenager, Moynihan divided his time between his studies and working at the docks in Manhattan to help out his family. In 1943, he tested into the City College of New York, walking into the examination room with a longshoreman's loading hook in his back pocket so that he would not "be mistaken for any sissy kid." After a year at CCNY, he enlisted in the Navy, which paid for him to go to Tufts University for a bachelor's degree. He stayed for a master's degree and then started a doctorate program, which took him to the London School of Economics, where he did research. In 1959, Moynihan began writing for Irving Kristol's magazine *The Reporter*, covering everything from organized crime to auto safety. The election of John F. Kennedy as president, in 1960, gave Moynihan a chance to put his broad curiosity to practical use; he was hired as an aide in the Department of Labor. Moynihan was, by then, an anticommunist liberal with a strong belief in the power of government to both study and solve social problems. He was also something of a scenester. His fear of being taken for a "sissy kid" had diminished. In London, he'd cultivated a love of wine, fine cheeses, tailored suits, and the mannerisms of an English aristocrat. He stood six feet five inches tall. A cultured civil servant not to the manor born, Moynihan—witty, colorful, loquacious—charmed the Washington elite, moving easily among congressional aides, politicians, and journalists. As the historian James Patterson writes in *Freedom Is Not Enough*, his book about Moynihan, he was possessed by "the optimism of youth." He believed in the marriage of government and social science to formulate policy. "All manner of later experiences in politics were to test this youthful faith."

Moynihan stayed on at the Labor Department during Lyndon B. Johnson's administration, but became increasingly disillusioned with Johnson's War on Poverty. He believed that the initiative should be run through an established societal institution: the patriarchal family. Fathers should be supported by public policy, in the form of jobs funded by the government. Moynihan believed that unemployment, specifically male unemployment, was the biggest impediment to the social mobility of the poor. He was, it might be said, a conservative radical who disdained service programs such as Head Start and traditional welfare programs such as Aid to Families With Dependent Children, and instead imagined a broad national program that subsidized families through jobs programs for men and a guaranteed minimum income for every family.

Influenced by the civil-rights movement, Moynihan focused on the black family. He believed that an undue optimism about the pending passage of civil-rights legislation was obscuring a pressing problem: a deficit of employed black men of strong character. He believed that this deficit went a long way toward explaining the African American community's relative poverty. Moynihan began searching for a way to press the point within the Johnson administration. "I felt I had to write a paper about the Negro family," Moynihan later recalled, "to explain to the fellows how there was a problem more difficult than they knew." In March of 1965, Moynihan printed up 100 copies of a report he and a small staff had labored over for only a few months.

The report was called "The Negro Family: The Case for National Action." Unsigned, it was meant to be an internal government document, with only one copy distributed at first and the other 99 kept locked in a vault. Running against the tide of optimism around civil rights, "The Negro Family" argued that the federal government was underestimating the damage done to black families by "three centuries of sometimes unimaginable mistreatment" as well as a "racist virus in the American blood stream," which would continue to plague blacks in the future:

> That the Negro American has survived at all is extraordinary—a lesser people might simply have died out, as indeed others have . . . But it may not be supposed that the Negro American community has not paid a fearful price for the incredible mistreatment to which it has been subjected over the past three centuries.

That price was clear to Moynihan. "The Negro family, battered and harassed by discrimination, injustice, and uprooting, is in the deepest trouble," he wrote. "While many young Negroes are moving ahead to unprecedented levels of achievement, many more are falling further and further behind." Out-of-wedlock births were on the rise, and with them, welfare dependency, while the unemployment rate among black men remained high. Moynihan believed that at the core of all these problems lay a black family structure mutated by white oppression:

> In essence, the Negro community has been forced into a matriarchal structure which, because it is so out of line with the rest of the American society, seriously retards the progress of the group as a whole, and imposes a crushing burden on the Negro male and, in consequence, on a great many Negro women as well.

Moynihan believed this matriarchal structure robbed black men of their birthright—"The very essence of the male animal, from the bantam rooster to the four-star general, is to strut," he wrote—and deformed the black family and, consequently, the black community. In what would become the most famous passage in the report, Moynihan equated the black community with a diseased patient:

> In a word, most Negro youth are in danger of being caught up in the tangle of pathology that affects their world, and probably a majority are so entrapped. Many of those who escape do so for one generation only: as things now are, their children may have to run the gauntlet all over again. That is not the least vicious aspect of the world that white America has made for the Negro.

Despite its alarming predictions, "The Negro Family" was a curious government report in that it advocated no specific policies to address the crisis it described. This was intentional. Moynihan had lots of ideas about what government could do—provide a guaranteed minimum income, establish a government jobs program, bring more black men into the military, enable better access to birth control, integrate the suburbs—but none of these ideas made it into the report. "A series of recommendations was at first included, then left out," Moynihan later recalled. "It would have got in the way of the attention-arousing argument that a crisis was coming and that family stability was the best measure of success or failure in dealing with it."

President Johnson offered the first public preview of the Moynihan Report in a speech written by Moynihan and the former Kennedy aide Richard Goodwin at Howard University in June of 1965, in which he highlighted "the breakdown of the Negro family structure." Johnson left no doubt about how this breakdown had come about. "For this, most of all, white America must accept responsibility," Johnson said. Family breakdown "flows from centuries of oppression and persecution of the Negro man. It flows from the long years of degradation and discrimination, which have attacked his dignity and assaulted his ability to produce for his family."

The press did not generally greet Johnson's speech as a claim of white responsibility, but rather as a condemnation of "the failure of Negro family life," as the journalist Mary McGrory put it. This interpretation was reinforced as second- and third-hand accounts of the Moynihan Report, which had not been made public, began making the rounds. On August 18, the widely syndicated [and conservative] newspaper columnists Rowland Evans and Robert Novak wrote that Moynihan's document had exposed "the breakdown of the Negro family," with its high rates of "broken homes, illegitimacy, and female-oriented homes." These dispatches fell on all-too-receptive ears. A week earlier, the drunk-driving arrest of Marquette Frye, an African American man in Los Angeles, had sparked six days of rioting in the city, which killed 34 people, injured 1,000 more, and caused tens of millions of dollars in property damage. Meanwhile, crime rates had begun to rise. People who read the newspapers but were not able to read the report could—and did—conclude that Johnson was conceding that no government effort could match the "tangle of pathology" that Moynihan had said beset the black family. Moynihan's aim in writing "The Negro Family" had been to muster support for an all-out government assault on the structural social problems that held black families down. ("Family as an issue raised the possibility of enlisting the support of conservative groups for quite radical social programs," he would later write.) Instead his report was portrayed as an argument for leaving the black family to fend for itself.

Moynihan himself was partly to blame for this. In its bombastic language, its omission of policy recommendations, its implication that black women were obstacles to black men's assuming their proper station, and its unnecessarily covert handling, the Moynihan Report militated against its author's aims. James Farmer, the civil-rights activist and a co-founder of the Congress of Racial Equality, attacked the report from the left as "a massive academic cop-out for the white conscience." William Ryan, the psychologist who first articulated the concept of "blaming the victim," accused Moynihan's report of doing just that. Moynihan had left the Johnson administration in the summer to run for president of the New York City Council. The bid failed, and liberal repudiations of the report kept raining down. "I am now known as a racist across the land," he wrote in a letter to the civil-rights leader Roy Wilkins.

In fact, the controversy transformed Moynihan into one of the most celebrated public intellectuals of his era. In the summer of 1966, Moynihan was featured in *The New York Times*. In the fall of 1967, after Detroit had exploded into riots, *Life* magazine dubbed him the "Idea Broker in the Race Crisis," declaring, "A troubled nation turns to Pat Moynihan." Between 1965 and 1979, *The New York Times Magazine* ran five features on Moynihan. His own writing was featured in *The Atlantic, The New Yorker, Commentary, The American Scholar, The Saturday Evening Post, The Public Interest*, and elsewhere. Yet despite the positive coverage, Moynihan remained "distressed not to have any influence on anybody" in Washington, as he put it in a 1968 letter to Harry McPherson, a Johnson aide.

Meanwhile, the civil-rights movement was fading and the radical New Left was rising. In September of 1967, worried about political instability in the country, Moynihan gave a speech calling for liberals and conservatives to unite "to preserve democratic institutions from the looming forces of the authoritarian left and right." Impressed by the speech, Richard Nixon offered Moynihan a post in the White House the following year. Moynihan was, by then, embittered by the attacks launched against him and, like Nixon, horrified by the late-'60s radical spirit.

But Moynihan still professed concern for the family, and for the black family in particular. He began pushing for a minimum income for all American families. Nixon promoted Moynihan's proposal—called the Family Assistance Plan—before the American public in a television address in August of 1969, and officially presented it to Congress in October. This was a personal victory for Moynihan—a triumph in an argument he had been waging since the War on Poverty began, over the need to help families, not individuals. "I felt I was finally *rid of a subject*. A subject that just . . . *spoiled* my life," Moynihan told *The New York Times* that November. "*Four—long—years* of being called awful things. The people you would most want to admire you detesting you. Being anathematized and stigmatized. And I said, 'Well, the President's *done* this, and now I'm rid of it.'"

But he was not rid of it. The Family Assistance Plan died in the Senate. In a 1972 essay in *The Public Interest*, Moynihan, who had by then left the White House and was a professor at Harvard, railed against "the poverty professionals" who had failed to support his efforts and the "upper-class" liars who had failed to see his perspective. He pointed out that his pessimistic predictions were now becoming reality. Crime was increasing. So were the number of children in poor, female-headed families. Moynihan issued a dire warning: "Lower-class behavior in our cities is shaking them apart."

From the mid-1970s to the mid-'80s, America's incarceration rate doubled, from about 150 people per 100,000 to about 300 per 100,000. From the mid-'80s to the mid-'90s, it doubled again. By 2007, it had reached a historic high of 767 people per 100,000, before registering a modest decline to 707 people per 100,000 in 2012. In absolute terms, America's prison and jail population from 1970 until today has increased sevenfold, from some 300,000 people to 2.2 million. The United States now accounts for less than 5 percent of the world's inhabitants—and about 25 percent of its incarcerated inhabitants. In 2000, one in 10 black males between the ages of 20 and 40 was incarcerated—10 times the rate of their white peers. In 2010, a third of all black male high-school dropouts between the ages of 20 and 39 were imprisoned, compared with only 13 percent of their white peers.

Our carceral state banishes American citizens to a gray wasteland far beyond the promises and protections the government grants its other citizens. Banishment continues long after one's actual time behind bars has ended, making housing and employment hard to secure. And banishment was not simply a well-intended response to rising crime. It was the method by which we chose to address the problems that preoccupied Moynihan, problems resulting from "three centuries of sometimes unimaginable mistreatment." At a cost of $80 billion a year, American correctional facilities are a social-service program—providing health care, meals, and shelter for a whole class of people.

As the civil-rights movement wound down, Moynihan looked out and saw a black population reeling under the effects of 350 years of bondage and plunder. He believed that these effects could be addressed through state action. They were—through the mass incarceration of millions of black people.

The Gray Wastes—our carceral state, a sprawling netherworld of prisons and jails—are a relatively recent invention. Through the middle of the 20th century, America's imprisonment rate hovered at about 110 people per 100,000. Presently, America's incarceration rate (which accounts for people in prisons *and* jails) is roughly 12 times the rate in Sweden, eight times the rate in Italy, seven times the rate in Canada, five times the rate in Australia, and four times the rate in Poland. America's closest to-scale competitor is Russia— and with an autocratic Vladimir Putin locking up about 450 people per 100,000, compared with our 700 or so, it isn't much of a competition. China has about four times America's population, but American jails and prisons hold half a million more people. "In short," an authoritative report issued last year by the National Research Council concluded, "the current U.S. rate of incarceration is unprecedented by both historical and comparative standards."

What caused this? Crime would seem the obvious culprit: Between 1963 and 1993, the murder rate doubled, the robbery rate quadrupled, and the aggravated-assault rate nearly quintupled. But the relationship between crime and incarceration is more discordant than it appears. Imprisonment rates actually fell from the 1960s through the early '70s, even as violent crime increased. From the mid-'70s to the late '80s, both imprisonment rates and violent-crime rates rose. Then, from the early '90s to the present, violent-crime rates fell while imprisonment rates increased [see Figure 34.1].

The incarceration rate rose independent of crime—but not of criminal-justice policy. Derek Neal, an economist at the University of Chicago, has found that by the early 2000s, a suite of tough-on-crime laws had made prison sentences much more likely than in the past. Examining a sample of states, Neal found that from 1985 to 2000, the likelihood of a long prison sentence nearly doubled for drug possession, tripled for drug trafficking, and quintupled for nonaggravated assault.

That explosion in rates and duration of imprisonment might be justified on grounds of cold pragmatism if a policy of mass incarceration actually caused crime to decline. Which is precisely what some politicians and policy makers of the tough-on-crime '90s were claiming. "Ask many politicians, newspaper editors, or criminal justice 'experts' about our prisons, and you will hear that our problem is that we put too many people in prison," a 1992 Justice Department report read. "The truth, however, is to the contrary; we are incarcerating too *few* criminals, and the public is suffering as a result."

History has not been kind to this conclusion. The rise and fall in crime in the late 20th century was an international phenomenon. Crime rates rose and fell in the United States and Canada at roughly the same clip—but in

Figure 34.1 Three Eras of the Violent Crime–Prison Nexus in the U.S. after 1960

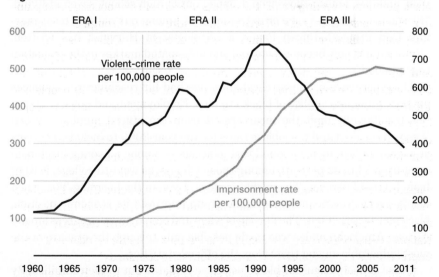

SOURCE: Robert Sampson. Data from Bureau of Justice Statistics; Sourcebook of Criminal Justice Statistics; Uniform Crime Reporting System.

Canada, imprisonment rates held steady. "If greatly increased severity of punishment and higher imprisonment rates caused American crime rates to fall after 1990," the researchers Michael Tonry and David P. Farrington have written, then "what caused the Canadian rates to fall?" The riddle is not particular to North America. In the latter half of the 20th century, crime rose and then fell in Nordic countries as well. During the period of rising crime, incarceration rates held steady in Denmark, Norway, and Sweden—but declined in Finland. "If punishment affects crime, Finland's crime rate should have shot up," Tonry and Farrington write, but it did not. After studying California's tough "Three Strikes and You're Out" law—which mandated at least a 25-year sentence for a third "strikeable offense," such as murder or robbery—researchers at UC Berkeley and the University of Sydney, in Australia, determined in 2001 that the law had reduced the rate of felony crime by no more than 2 percent. Bruce Western, a sociologist at Harvard and one of the leading academic experts on American incarceration, looked at the growth in state prisons in recent years and concluded that a 66 percent increase in the state prison population between 1993 and 2001 had reduced the rate of serious crime by a modest 2 to 5 percent—at a cost to taxpayers of $53 billion.

From the mid-1970s to the mid-'80s, America's incarceration rate doubled. From the mid-'80s to the mid-'90s, it doubled again. Then it went still higher.

This bloating of the prison population may not have reduced crime much, but it increased misery among the group that so concerned Moynihan. Among all black males born since the late 1970s, one in four went to prison by their mid-30s; among those who dropped out of high school, seven in 10 did. "Prison is no longer a rare or extreme event among our nation's most marginalized groups," Devah Pager, a sociologist at Harvard, has written. "Rather it has now become a normal and anticipated marker in the transition to adulthood."

The emergence of the carceral state has had far-reaching consequences for the economic viability of black families. Employment and poverty statistics traditionally omit the incarcerated from the official numbers. When Western recalculated the jobless rates for the year 2000 to include incarcerated young black men, he found that joblessness among all young black men went from 24 to 32 percent; among those who never went to college, it went from 30 to 42 percent. The upshot is stark. Even in the booming '90s, when nearly every American demographic group improved its economic position, black men were left out. The illusion of wage and employment progress among African American males was made possible only through the erasure of the most vulnerable among them from the official statistics.

These consequences for black men have radiated out to their families. By 2000, more than 1 million black children had a father in jail or prison—and roughly half of those fathers were living in the same household as their kids when they were locked up. Paternal incarceration is associated with behavior problems and delinquency, especially among boys.

"More than half of fathers in state prison report being the primary breadwinner in their family," the National Research Council report noted. Should the family attempt to stay together through incarceration, the loss of income only increases, as the mother must pay for phone time, travel costs for visits, and legal fees. The burden continues after the father returns home, because a criminal record tends to injure employment prospects. Through it all, the children suffer.

Many fathers simply fall through the cracks after they're released. It is estimated that between 30 and 50 percent of all parolees in Los Angeles and San Francisco are homeless. In that context—employment prospects diminished, cut off from one's children, nowhere to live—one can readily see the difficulty of eluding the ever-present grasp of incarceration, even once an individual is physically out of prison. Many do not elude its grasp. In 1984, 70 percent of all parolees successfully completed their term without arrest and were granted full freedom. In 1996, only 44 percent did. As of 2013, 33 percent do.*

The Gray Wastes differ in both size and mission from the penal systems of earlier eras. As African Americans began filling cells in the 1970s, rehabilitation was largely abandoned in favor of retribution—the idea that prison should not reform convicts but punish them. For instance, in the 1990s, South Carolina cut back on in-prison education, banned air conditioners, jettisoned televisions, and discontinued intramural sports. Over the next 10 years, Congress repeatedly attempted to pass a No Frills Prison Act, which would have granted extra funds to state correctional systems working to "prevent luxurious conditions in prisons." A goal of this "penal harm" movement, one criminal-justice researcher wrote at the time, was to find "creative strategies to make offenders suffer."

Last winter, I visited Detroit to take the measure of the Gray Wastes. Michigan, with an incarceration rate of 628 people per 100,000, is about average for an American state. I drove to the East Side to talk with a woman I'll call Tonya, who had done 18 years for murder and a gun charge and had been released five months earlier. She had an energetic smile and an edge to her voice that evidenced the time she'd spent locked up. Violence, for her, commenced not in the streets, but at home. "There was abuse in my grandmother's home, and I went to school and I told my teacher," she explained. "I had a spot on my nose because I had a lit cigarette stuck on my nose, and when I told her, they sent me to a temporary foster-care home . . . The foster parent was also abusive, so I just ran away from her and just stayed on the streets."

---

*John F. Pfaff's *Locked In: The True Causes of Mass Incarceration—and How to Achieve Real Reform* lays the blame, with excellent statistical analysis, on the decisions of zealous prosecutors. See Adam Gopnik, "Rattling the Cage," *The New Yorker*, April 10, 2017. [*Editors' note*]

Tonya began using crack. One night she gathered with some friends for a party. They smoked crack. They smoked marijuana. They drank. At some point, the woman hosting the party claimed that someone had stolen money from her home. Another woman accused Tonya of stealing it. A fight ensued. Tonya shot the woman who had accused her. She got 20 years for the murder and two for the gun. After the trial, the truth came out. The host had hidden the money, but was so high that she'd forgotten.

When the doors finally close and one finds oneself facing banishment to the carceral state—the years, the walls, the rules, the guards, the inmates— reactions vary. Some experience an intense sickening feeling. Others, a strong desire to sleep. Visions of suicide. A deep shame. A rage directed toward guards and other inmates. Utter disbelief. The incarcerated attempt to hold onto family and old social ties through phone calls and visitations. At first, friends and family do their best to keep up. But phone calls to prison are expensive, and many prisons are located far from one's hometown.

"First I would get one [visit] like every four months," Tonya explained to me. "And then I wouldn't get none for like maybe a year. You know, because it was too far away. And I started to have losses. I lost my mom, my brothers . . . So it was hard, you know, for me to get visits."

As the visits and phone calls diminish, the incarcerated begins to adjust to the fact that he or she is, indeed, a prisoner. New social ties are cultivated. New rules must be understood. A blizzard of acronyms, sayings, and jargon— PBF, CSC, ERD, "letters but no numbers"—must be comprehended. If the prisoner is lucky, someone—a cell mate, an older prisoner hailing from the same neighborhood—takes him under his wing. This can be the difference between survival and catastrophe. On Richard Braceful's first night in Carson City Correctional Facility, in central Michigan, where he had been sent away at age 29 for armed robbery, he decided to take a shower. It was 10 p.m. His cell mate stopped him. "Where are you going?" the cell mate asked. "I'm going to take a shower," Braceful responded. His cell mate, a 14-year veteran of the prison system, blocked his way and said, "You're not going to take a shower." Braceful, reading the signs, felt a fight was imminent. "Calm down," his cell mate told him. "You don't take a shower after 9 o'clock. People that are sexual predators, people that are rapists, they go in the showers right behind you." Braceful and the veteran sat down. The veteran looked at him. "It's your first time being locked up, ain't it?" he said. "Yeah, it is," Braceful responded. The veteran said to him, "Listen, this is what you have to do. For the next couple of weeks, just stay with me. I've been here for 14 years. I'll look out for you until you learn how to move around in here without getting yourself hurt."

* * *

The challenges of housing and employment bedevil many ex-offenders. "It's very common for them to go homeless," Linda VanderWaal, the associate director of prisoner reentry at a community-action agency in Michigan, told me. In the winter, VanderWaal says, she has a particularly hard time finding places to accommodate all the homeless ex-prisoners. Those who do find a place to live often find it difficult to pay their rent.

The carceral state has, in effect, become a credentialing institution as significant as the military, public schools, or universities—but the credentialing that prison or jail offers is negative. In her book, *Marked: Race, Crime, and Finding Work in an Era of Mass Incarceration*, Devah Pager, the Harvard sociologist, notes that most employers say that they would not hire a job applicant with a criminal record. "These employers appear less concerned about specific information conveyed by a criminal conviction and its bearing on a particular job," Pager writes, "but rather view this credential as an indicator of general employability or trustworthiness."

Ex-offenders are excluded from a wide variety of jobs, running the gamut from septic-tank cleaner to barber to real-estate agent, depending on the state. And in the limited job pool that ex-offenders can swim in, blacks and whites are not equal. For her research, Pager pulled together four testers to pose as men looking for low-wage work. One white man and one black man would pose as job seekers without a criminal record, and another black man and white man would pose as job seekers with a criminal record. The negative credential of prison impaired the employment efforts of both the black man and the white man, but it impaired those of the black man more. Startlingly, the effect was not limited to the black man with a criminal record. The black man *without* a criminal record fared worse than the white man *with* one. "High levels of incarceration cast a shadow of criminality over all black men, implicating even those (in the majority) who have remained crime free," Pager writes. Effectively, the job market in America regards black men who have never been criminals as though they were.[†]

* * *

The sociologist Bruce Western explains the current inevitability of prison for certain demographics of young black men. In America, the men and women who find themselves lost in the Gray Wastes are not picked at random. A series of risk factors—mental illness, illiteracy, drug addiction, poverty—increases one's chances of ending up in the ranks of the incarcerated. "Roughly half of today's prison inmates are functionally illiterate," Robert Perkinson, an associate professor of American studies at the University of Hawaii at Mānoa, has noted. "Four out of five criminal defendants qualify as indigent before the courts." Sixty-eight percent of jail inmates were struggling with substance dependence or abuse in 2002. One can imagine a separate world where the state would see these maladies through the lens of government education or public-health programs. Instead it has decided to see them through the lens of criminal justice. As the number of prison beds

---

[†]See essay 5, Devah Pager, "The Mark of a Criminal Record." [*Editors' note*]

has risen in this country, the number of public-psychiatric-hospital beds has fallen. The Gray Wastes draw from the most socioeconomically unfortunate among us, and thus take particular interest in those who are black.

* * *

Prosecutors were not alone in their quest to appear tough on crime. In the 1980s and '90s, legislators, focusing on the scourge of crack cocaine, vied with one another to appear toughest. There was no real doubt as to who would be the target of this newfound toughness. By then, Daniel Patrick Moynihan had gone from the White House to a U.S. Senate seat in New York. He was respected as a scholar and renowned for his intellect. But his preoccupations had not changed. "We cannot ignore the fact that when we talk about drug abuse in our country, in the main, we are talking about the consequence it has for young males in inner cities," he told the Senate in 1986. This might well have been true as a description of drug *enforcement policies*, but it was not true of actual drug abuse: Surveys have repeatedly shown that blacks and whites use drugs at remarkably comparable rates. Moynihan had by the late Reagan era evidently come to believe the worst distortions of his own 1965 report. Gone was any talk of root causes; in its place was something darker. The young inner-city males who had so concerned Moynihan led "wasted and ruined" lives and constituted a threat that could "bring about the destruction of whole communities and cities across this Nation."

* * *

Many African Americans concurred that crime was a problem. When Jesse Jackson confessed, in 1993, "There is nothing more painful to me at this stage in my life than to walk down the street and hear footsteps and start thinking about robbery, then look around and see somebody white and feel relieved," he was speaking to the very real fear of violent crime that dogs black communities. The argument that high crime is the predictable result of a series of oppressive racist policies does not render the victims of those policies bulletproof. Likewise, noting that fear of crime is well grounded does not make that fear a solid foundation for public policy.

The suite of drug laws adopted in the 1980s and '90s did little to reduce crime, but a lot to normalize prison in black communities. "No single offense type has more directly contributed to contemporary racial disparities in imprisonment than drug crimes," Devah Pager, the Harvard sociologist, has written.

Between 1983 and 1997, the number of African Americans admitted to prison for drug offenses increased more than twenty-six-fold, relative to a sevenfold increase for whites . . . By 2001, there were more than twice as many African Americans as whites in state prison for drug offenses.

In 2013, the ACLU published a report noting a 10-year uptick in marijuana arrests. The uptick was largely explained as "a result of the increase in the arrest rates of Blacks." To reiterate an important point: Surveys have concluded that blacks and whites use drugs at roughly the same rates. And yet by the close of the 20th century, prison was a more common experience for young black men than college graduation or military service.

* * *

On the evening of December 19, 1973, Odell Newton, who was then 16 years old, stepped into a cab in Baltimore with a friend, rode half a block, then shot and killed the driver, Edward Mintz. The State of Maryland charged Odell with crimes including murder in the first degree and sentenced him to life in prison. He has now spent 41 years behind bars, but by all accounts he is a man reformed. He has repeatedly expressed remorse for his crimes. He has not committed an infraction in 36 years.

The Maryland Parole Commission has recommended Odell for release three times since 1992. But in Maryland, all release recommendations for lifers are subject to the governor's approval. In the 1970s, when Odell committed his crime, this was largely a formality. But in our era of penal cruelty, Maryland has effectively abolished parole for lifers—even juvenile offenders such as Odell. In 2010, the U.S. Supreme Court ruled that life sentences without the possibility of parole for juveniles found guilty of crimes other than homicide were unconstitutional. Two years later, it held the same for mandatory life sentences without parole for juvenile homicide offenders. But the Court has yet to rule on whether that more recent decision was retroactive. Fifteen percent of Maryland's lifers committed their crimes as juveniles—the largest percentage in the nation, according to a 2015 report by the Maryland Restorative Justice Initiative and the state's ACLU affiliate. The vast majority of them—84 percent—are black.

This summer, I visited Odell's mother, Clara; his sister Jackie; and his brother Tim at Clara's home in a suburb of Baltimore. Clara had just driven seven hours round-trip to visit Odell at Eastern Correctional Institution, on the Eastern Shore of Maryland, and she was full of worry. He was being treated for hepatitis. He'd lost 50 pounds. He had sores around his eyes.

I asked Clara how they managed to visit Odell regularly. She explained that family members trade visits. "It takes a lot out of the family," she explained. "Then you come back home, [after] you've seen him up there like that, [and] you're crying. I got so bad one time, I was losing weight . . . Just thinking, *Was it gonna be all right? Was it gonna kill him? Was he gonna die?*"

Clara was born and raised in Westmoreland, Virginia. She had her first child, Jackie, when she was only 15. The next year she married Jackie's father, John Irvin Newton Sr. They moved to Baltimore so that John could pursue a job at a bakery. "We stuck it out and made things work," Clara told me. They were married for 53 years, until John passed away, in 2008.

Odell Newton was born in 1957. When he was 4 years old, he fell ill and almost died. The family took him to the hospital. Doctors put a hole in his throat to help him breathe. They transferred Odell to another hospital, where he was diagnosed with lead poisoning. It turned out that he had been putting his mouth on the windowsill. "We didn't sue nobody. We didn't know nothing about that," Clara told me. "And when we finally found out that you could sue, Odell was 15. And they said they couldn't do anything, because we waited too long."

In prison, Odell has repeatedly attempted to gain his GED, failing the test several times. "My previous grade school teacher noted that I should be placed in special education," Odell wrote in a 2014 letter to his lawyer. "It is unclear what roll childhood lead poisoning played in my analytical capabilities."

In June of 1964, the family moved into a nicer house, in Edmondson Village. Sometime around ninth grade, Clara began to suspect that Odell was lagging behind the other kids in his class. "We didn't find out that he was really delayed until he was almost ready to enter into high school," Jackie told me. "They just passed him on and passed him on." Around this time, Clara says, Odell got "mixed up with the wrong crowd." Not until he wrote his first letter home from prison did Clara understand the depth of his intellectual disability. The letter read as though it had been written by "a child just starting pre-K or kindergarten," Clara told me. "He couldn't really spell. And, I don't know, it just didn't look like a person of his age should be writing like that."

Odell Newton is now 57. He has spent the lion's share of his life doing time under state supervision. The time he's served has not affected him alone. If men and women like Odell are cast deep within the barrens of the Gray Wastes, their families are held in a kind of orbit, on the outskirts, by the relentless gravity of the carceral state. For starters, the family must contend with the financial expense of having a loved one incarcerated. Odell's parents took out a second mortgage to pay for their son's lawyers, and then a third. Beyond that, there's the expense of having to make long drives to prisons that are commonly built in rural white regions, far from the incarcerated's family. There's the expense of phone calls, and of constantly restocking an inmate's commissary. Taken together, these economic factors fray many a family's bonds.

* * *

Odell's brother Tim graduated from Salisbury State College with a degree in sociology in 1982. Two years later, he took a job with the State of Maryland as a corrections officer. For 20 years, while one son, Odell, served time under the state, another son, Tim, worked for it. This gave Tim a front-row seat for observing how Maryland's carceral system grew more punitive. Whereas inmates had once done their time and gone to pre-release facilities, now they were staying longer. Requirements for release became more onerous. Meanwhile, the prisons were filling to capacity and beyond. "They just kept overcrowding and overcrowding and not letting people go home," Tim told me. The prisons began holding two people in cells meant for one. "If you're in an 8-by-10 space that's only big enough for one person and now you got two people in there, it's just more aggravation," Tim said. "And then they cut out a lot of the college programs that they did have. They cut out the weights being in the yard."

* * *

For more than five years, from February 1988 to June 1993, Odell Newton worked in the community through work release; for part of that period, he was able to visit his relatives through the state's family-leave policy. Reports from Odell's former work-release employers are glowing. "His character is above reproach," one wrote in 1991. Another said: "I consider it a privilege to have Mr. Newton as an employee, and would rehire Odell at any time." With his family, he would often go out to eat, or have a cookout or a party. Family leave was supposed to be a bridge to Odell's eventual release. But the program was suspended for lifers in May of 1993, after a convicted murderer fled while visiting his son. The Stokes killing followed just weeks later. After that, parole was effectively taken off the table for all lifers, and Maryland ended work release for them as well. Believing for years that Odell was on his way to coming home, and then seeing the road to freedom snatched away, frustrated the family. "I could see you doing it to people that's starting out new, and this is a new law you're putting down," his sister Jackie told me. But this is "like me buying a house and I have it one price, then when you come in and sign the papers, they're going, 'Oh no, I changed my mind, I want $10,000 more for it.'"

I asked Odell's family how they coped with the experience. "You just have to pray and keep praying," his mother told me.

* * *

Born in the late 1950s, Odell Newton was part of the generation that so troubled Moynihan when he wrote his report on "The Negro Family." But Odell had the very bulwark that Moynihan treasured—a stable family—and it did not save him from incarceration. It would be wrong to conclude from this that family is irrelevant. But families don't exist independent of their environment. Odell was born in the midst of an era of government-backed housing discrimination. Indeed, Baltimore was a pioneer in this practice—in 1910, the city council had zoned the city by race. "Blacks should be quarantined in isolated slums," J. Barry Mahool, Baltimore's mayor, said. After the U.S. Supreme Court ruled such explicit racial-zoning schemes unconstitutional, in 1917, the city turned to other means—restrictive covenants, civic associations, and redlining—to keep blacks isolated.

These efforts curtailed the ability of black people to buy better housing, to move to better neighborhoods, and to build wealth. Also, by confining black people to the same neighborhoods, these efforts ensured that people who were discriminated against, and hence had little, tended to be neighbors only with others who also had little. Thus while an individual in that community might be high-achieving, even high-earning, his or her ability to increase that achievement and wealth and social capital, through friendship, marriage, or neighborhood organizations, would always be limited. Finally, racial zoning condemned black people to the oldest and worst housing in the city—the kind where one was more likely to be exposed, as Odell Newton was, to lead. A lawyer who handled more than 4,000 lead-poisoning cases across three decades recently described his client list to *The Washington Post*: "Nearly 99.9 percent of my clients were black." That families are better off the stronger and more stable they are is self-evidently important. But so is the notion that no family can ever be made impregnable, that families are social structures existing within larger social structures.

Robert Sampson, a sociologist at Harvard who focuses on crime and urban life, notes that in America's ghettos, "like things tend to go together." High rates of incarceration, single-parent households, dropping out of school, and poverty are not unrelated vectors. Instead, taken together, they constitute what Sampson calls "compounded deprivation"—entire families, entire neighborhoods, deprived in myriad ways, must navigate, all at once, a tangle of interrelated and reinforcing perils.

Black people face this tangle of perils at its densest. In a recent study, Sampson and a co-author looked at two types of deprivation—being individually poor, and living in a poor neighborhood. Unsurprisingly, they found that blacks tend to be individually poor and to live in poor neighborhoods. But even blacks who are not themselves individually poor are more likely to live in poor neighborhoods than whites and Latinos who are individually poor. For black people, escaping poverty does not mean escaping a poor neighborhood. And blacks are much more likely than all other groups to fall into compounded deprivation later in life, even if they managed to avoid it when they were young.

"It's not just being poor; it's discrimination in the housing market, it's subprime loans, it's drug addiction—and then all of that following you over time," Sampson told me recently. "We try to split things out and say, 'Well, you can be poor but still have these other characteristics and qualities.' It's the myth of the American Dream that with initiative and industriousness, an individual can always escape impoverished circumstances. But what the data show is that you have these multiple assaults on life chances that make transcending those circumstances difficult and at times nearly impossible."

* * *

The blacks incarcerated in this country are not like the majority of Americans. They do not merely hail from poor communities—they hail from communities that have been imperiled across both the deep and immediate past, and continue to be imperiled today. Peril is generational for black people in America—and incarceration is our current mechanism for ensuring that the peril continues. Incarceration pushes you out of the job market. Incarceration disqualifies you from feeding your family with food stamps. Incarceration allows for housing discrimination based on a criminal-background check. Incarceration increases your risk of homelessness. Incarceration increases your chances of being incarcerated again. "The prison boom helps us understand how racial inequality in America was sustained, despite great optimism for the social progress of African Americans," Bruce Western, the Harvard sociologist, writes. "The prison boom is not the main cause of inequality between blacks and whites in America, but it did foreclose upward mobility and deflate hopes for racial equality."

If generational peril is the pit in which all black people are born, incarceration is the trapdoor closing overhead. "African Americans in our data are distinct from both Latinos and whites," Robert Sampson told me. "Even when we control for marital status and family history of criminality, we still see these strong differences. The compounded deprivation that African Americans experience is a challenge even independent of all the characteristics we think are protective."

Characteristics such as the one Daniel Patrick Moynihan focused on—family.

* * *

A raft of sociological research has indeed borne out Moynihan's skepticism about black progress, as well as his warnings about the kind of concentrated poverty that flowed from segregation. Moynihan's observation about the insufficiency of civil-rights legislation has been proved largely correct. Moreover, Moynihan's concern about the declining rates of two-parent households would have struck the average black resident of Harlem in 1965 as well placed. Nationalist leaders like Malcolm X drew much of their appeal through their calls for shoring up the black family.

[THE OTHER HALF OF THE MOYNIHAN REPORT]

But if Moynihan's past critics exhibited an ignorance of his oeuvre and his intent, his current defenders exhibit a naïveté in defense of their hero. "The Negro Family" is a flawed work in part because it is a fundamentally sexist document that promotes the importance not just of family but of patriarchy, arguing that black men should be empowered at the expense of black women. "Men must have jobs," Moynihan wrote to President Johnson in 1965. "We must not rest until every able-bodied Negro male is working. Even if we have to displace some females." . . .

Moynihan's defenders also overlook his record after he entered the Nixon White House in 1969. Perhaps still smarting from his treatment in the Johnson administration, Moynihan fed Nixon's antipathies—against elites, college students, and blacks—and stoked the president's fears about crime. In a memo to Nixon, he asserted that "a great deal of the crime" in the black community was really a manifestation of anti-white racism: "Hatred—revenge—against whites is now an acceptable excuse for doing what might have been done anyway." Like his forebears who'd criminalized blacks, Moynihan claimed that education had done little to mollify the hatred. "It would be difficult to overestimate the degree to which young well educated blacks detest white America."

Whereas Johnson, guided by Moynihan, had declared that "white America must accept responsibility" for the problems of the black community, Moynihan wrote Nixon that "the Negro lower class would appear to be unusually self-damaging." . . . In casting African Americans as beyond the purview of polite and civilized society, in referring to them as a race of criminals, Moynihan joined the long tradition of black criminalization. In so doing, he undermined his own stated aims in writing "The Negro Family" in the first place. One does not build a safety net for a race of predators. One builds a cage.

* * *

In his inaugural year as the governor of Texas, 1995, George W. Bush presided over a government that opened a new prison nearly every week. Under Bush, the state's prison budget rose from $1.4 billion to $2.4 billion, and the total number of prison beds went from about 118,000 to more than 166,000. Almost a decade later Bush, by then the president of the United States, decided that he, and the rest of the country, had made a mistake. "This year, some 600,000 inmates will be released from prison back into society," Bush said during his 2004 State of the Union address. "We know from long experience that if they can't find work, or a home, or help, they are much more likely to commit crime and return to prison."

* * *

Decarceration raises a difficult question: What do we mean by violent crime, and how should it be punished? And what is the moral logic that allows forever banishing the Odell Newtons of America to the Gray Wastes? . . .

The Gray Wastes are a moral abomination for reasons beyond the sheer number of their tenants. In 1970 the national correctional system was much smaller than it is today, but even so, blacks were incarcerated at several times the rate of whites. There is no reason to assume that a smaller correctional system inevitably means a more equitable correctional system. Examining Minnesota's system, Richard S. Frase, a professor of criminal law at the University of Minnesota, found a state whose relatively sane justice policies give it one of the lowest incarceration rates in the country—and yet whose economic disparities give it one of the worst black-white incarceration ratios in the country. Changing criminal-justice policy did very little to change the fact that blacks committed crimes at a higher rate than whites in Minnesota. Why did blacks in Minnesota commit crimes at a higher rate than whites? Because the state's broad racial gulf in criminal offending mirrored another depressing gulf. "The black family poverty rate in Minnesota was over six times higher than the white poverty rate, whereas for the United States as a whole the black poverty rate was 3.4 times higher," Frase writes.

The lesson of Minnesota is that the chasm in incarceration rates is deeply tied to the socioeconomic chasm between black and white America. The two are self-reinforcing—impoverished black people are more likely to end up in prison, and that experience breeds impoverishment. An array of laws, differing across the country but all emanating from our tendency toward punitive criminal justice—limiting or banning food stamps for drug felons; prohibiting ex-offenders from obtaining public housing—ensure this. So does the rampant discrimination against ex-offenders and black men in general. This, too, is self-reinforcing. The American population most discriminated against is also its most incarcerated—and the incarceration of so many African Americans, the mark of criminality, justifies everything they endure after.

Mass incarceration is, ultimately, a problem of troublesome entanglements. To war seriously against the disparity in unfreedom requires a war against a disparity in resources. And to war against a disparity in resources is to confront a history in which both the plunder and the mass incarceration of blacks are accepted commonplaces. Our current debate over criminal-justice reform pretends that it is possible to disentangle ourselves without significantly disturbing the other aspects of our lives, that one can extract the thread of mass incarceration from the larger tapestry of racist American policy.

Daniel Patrick Moynihan knew better. His 1965 report on "The Negro Family" was explosive for what it claimed about black mothers and black fathers—but if it had contained all of Moynihan's thinking on the subject, including his policy recommendations, it likely would have been politically nuclear. "Now comes the proposition that the Negro is entitled to damages as to unequal favored treatment—in order to compensate for past unequal treatment of an opposite kind," Moynihan wrote in 1964. His point was simple if impolitic: blacks were suffering from the effects of centuries of ill treatment at the hands of white society. Ending that ill treatment would not be enough; the country would have to make amends for it. "It may be that without unequal treatment in the immediate future there is no way for [African Americans] to achieve anything like equal status in the long run," Moynihan wrote.

As we look ahead to what politicians are now saying will be the end of mass incarceration, we are confronted with the reality of what Moynihan observed in 1965, intensified and compounded by the past 50 years of the carceral state. What of the "damages" wrought by mass incarceration? What of the black men whose wages remained stagnant for decades largely due to our correctional policy? What of the 20th-century wars on drugs repeatedly pursued on racist grounds, and their devastating effects on black communities? The post-civil-rights consensus aims for the termination of injury. Remedy is beyond our field of vision. When old wounds fester, quackery is prescribed and hoary old fears and insidious old concepts burble to the surface— "matriarchy"; "super-predators"; "bio-underclass." This, too, was part of Moynihan, but it wasn't all of him.

A serious reformation of our carceral policy—one seeking a smaller prison population, and a prison population that looks more like America—cannot concern itself merely with sentencing reform, cannot pretend as though the past 50 years of criminal-justice policy did not do real damage. And so it is not possible to truly reform our justice system without reforming the institutional structures, the communities, and the politics that surround it. Robert Sampson argues for "affirmative action for neighborhoods"—reform that would target investment in both persistently poor neighborhoods and the poor individuals living in those neighborhoods. One class of people suffers deprivation at levels above and beyond the rest of the country—the same group that so disproportionately fills our jails and prisons. To pull too energetically on one thread is to tug at the entire tapestry.

Moynihan may have left any recommendations as to "favored treatment" for blacks out of his report. But the question has not disappeared. In fact, it is more urgent than ever. The economic and political marginalization of black people virtually ensured that they would be the ones who would bear the weight of what one of President Nixon's own aides called his "bullshit" crime policy, and thus be fed into the maw of the Gray Wastes. And should crime rates rise again, there is no reason to believe that black people, black communities, black families will not be fed into the great maw again. Indeed, the experience of mass incarceration, the warehousing and deprivation of whole swaths of our country, the transformation of that deprivation into wealth transmitted through government jobs and private investment, the pursuit of the War on Drugs on nakedly racist grounds, have only intensified the ancient American dilemma's white-hot core—the problem of "past unequal treatment," the difficulty of "damages," the question of reparations.

35

The End of Warrior Policing

FROM *Uneasy Peace: The Great Crime Decline, the Renewal of City Life, and the Next War on Violence*

PATRICK SHARKEY

During the past several decades, broken windows theory has been one of the most influential ways to explain (and reduce) violence and crime. It suggests that allowing minor offenses to go unchecked leads to situations where more serious crimes are likely to happen. In some cities, this has created a "warrior police" mentality where the police dominate public spaces and aggressively pursue even low-level offenses. However, these strategies have frayed relationships between police departments and communities in many places. More recently, based on sociological research, many police departments have reconsidered the broken windows approach to reducing crime. As sociologist Patrick Sharkey writes in this selection from his book Uneasy Peace, *police departments in cities such as New York and Los Angeles have adopted new strategies where police are seen as "guardians" rather than "warriors," and where stakeholders from throughout the community work together for safer communities. Sharkey warns that mending relationships between citizens and police will be slow, but that these new law enforcement strategies nonetheless offer new hope for creating communities that are both safe and just.*

The Jack Maple CompStat Center is something between a large conference room and a small auditorium. The room is on the eighth floor of the New York Police Department's headquarters at One Police Plaza, a huge building that is somehow tucked away behind an even larger municipal building next to lower Manhattan's City Hall Park. Outside the CompStat Center is a plaque honoring Jack Maple, the founder of CompStat. Maple was serving as deputy police commissioner at the time when he is said to have sketched out the four principles of CompStat on a napkin at Elaine's, the restaurant on the Upper East Side where New Yorkers like Woody Allen, Norman Mailer, and Police Commissioner William Bratton were regulars.*

He wrote just twelve words in total: (1) accurate and timely intelligence; (2) rapid deployment; (3) effective tactics; (4) relentless follow-up and assessment. These principles may seem basic in retrospect, but at the time they were revolutionary. Before the days of CompStat, police officers were dispatched

---

*References and footnotes can be found in Chapter 8 and pages 189–193 of the author's *Uneasy Peace: The Great Crime Decline, the Renewal of City Life, and the Next War on Violence* (W. W. Norton, 2018). [*Editors' note*]

across the city's streets without precise data on crime patterns to guide them, and they spent their time responding to crime rather than trying to prevent it. The department's resources were not tracked closely, and managers were not held accountable for outcomes in their precincts.

Maple's principles were the foundation of a management system that began with precise data on where and when serious crimes occurred, then quickly deployed police resources to shut down the criminal activity. And then in meetings that became legendary, officers responsible for each beat within New York City came together and answered pointed questions about where crimes were taking place, what was being done to respond, which tactics were working and which were not, and what would be done differently. The new management system, which has been replicated in police departments and public agencies across the country, was designed to focus the entire department on a tangible outcome and to hold every officer accountable, live and in person, when any hint of rising crime occurred on their beats.

And it all happened in the room that would be named in Jack Maple's honor. The CompStat Center has towering ceilings with large monitors attached to all four walls. At one end is a row of tables with microphones reserved for the leaders of the police department, allowing them to see the entire room. Facing them, about forty feet away, is a single podium where officers have stood for years, on their own, faced their superiors, and attempted to explain why crime was rising or falling in the section of the city under their watch.

I visited the CompStat Center on the morning of April 6, 2016, after waiting for fifteen minutes in a security line that formed well outside the visitor's entrance at One Police Plaza. The large group of community leaders, government officials, and residents waiting in line were not there for a traditional CompStat meeting held by the NYPD. We were there for the first meeting of NeighborhoodStat.

NeighborhoodStat was dreamed up by Elizabeth Glazer, the director of the Mayor's Office of Criminal Justice. She arrived in the de Blasio administration in the summer of 2014, the same summer that Eric Garner was killed by the NYPD, protests against police brutality took place across the city, and the police union feuded publicly with the mayor. Although the protests and political drama dominated the headlines that summer, the more troubling development was a sharp spike in shootings that had taken place in a small number of housing developments around the city, places that remained extremely violent even as most of the city had become historically safe.

To respond to the spike in violence, Glazer and Mayor de Blasio developed the Mayor's Action Plan for Neighborhood Safety, or MAP. The MAP initiative consisted of a set of investments targeting fifteen of the most violent housing developments in the city. Community centers stayed open later, lighting and security cameras were installed, the number of slots available for the youth summer employment program was increased, and meetings were planned to allow community residents the chance to develop and implement new ideas to keep their buildings safe.

But NeighborhoodStat was the piece of the MAP initiative that excited Glazer the most. Her vision built on the one sketched out by Jack Maple more than twenty years earlier, with one major difference. When Maple drew up CompStat, New York City was one of the most dangerous places in the country. When Glazer put together NeighborhoodStat, crime in New York was at a historic low point. Her vision was not focused entirely on crime, as Maple's was. Her vision was focused on building stronger neighborhoods.

Glazer envisioned a system that would enable an entire community to focus on the precise times and places where a broad range of community problems arose, including trash in public spaces, broken lights, truant kids, homeless people in need, and crews of drug dealers, as well as assaults, rapes, shootings, and other crimes. She envisioned a system that would change the way community resources were spent, one that would hold accountable public agencies like the department of sanitation and the New York City Housing Authority, as well as homelessness prevention agencies, tenants' associations, building managers, antiviolence organizations, police officers, and residents. The challenge addressed in NeighborhoodStat would be not only to deal with the problem of crime but also to find solutions to specific problems that weakened the entire community. And it would start by bringing every key actor within the community together in the room dedicated to Jack Maple.

On that morning in April 2016, Glazer's vision came to fruition. Roughly two hundred people packed into the CompStat Center for the first meeting of NeighborhoodStat, which focused on several housing developments in Brooklyn: Brownsville and Van Dyke, Red Hook, Boulevard, and Ingersoll Houses.

One by one the key representatives from each development came to the podium and answered questions about the state of the building and the neighborhood, while everyone in the room looked at maps showing statistics about each of the developments on the monitors overhead. A building manager was grilled about lobby doors that were frequently left open and unsecured, representatives from the sanitation department were asked about a pile of bulk trash that had grown outside one of the buildings, local service providers were asked what they were doing to understand the problem of domestic violence, and the president of a tenant association was asked why so few young people from her building had applied for summer jobs through the city.

There were uncomfortable moments when leaders of public agencies had no answers for the pointed questions directed at them. But if they didn't have an answer, they were given action steps to move toward a solution, and they were told to report back.

And in the midst of the discussions of sanitation, summer jobs, and lobby doors, a group of officers from the NYPD emerged as central figures in each community. The officers had been handpicked to become a new kind of cop, called neighborhood coordination officers (NCOs). The NCOs were part of the police department's ambitious plan—which, it should be said, was mandated by a court order—to end the aggressive policing that had targeted poor communities of color, and to create stronger ties between residents in disadvantaged neighborhoods and the police. The task of the NCOs was not to make arrests but to get to know every person within the neighborhood and to understand the problems of the community from the inside out. Officers for the program were selected carefully, and those who spoke at the NeighborhoodStat meetings were personable, funny, and exhibited a genuine concern for the neighborhood and its residents.

And they knew their neighborhoods intimately. When one of the NCOs in the Red Hook complex was asked about violence, he listed three "crews" of young men that had been actively involved in violent activity within the developments. These three crews had been responsible for much of the violence around Red Hook in previous years, but to that point in 2016 they had worked out a tenuous peace. As he finished his question and answer session, the officer stopped and said that if a new beef began, he would need everyone's help in the community to make sure it didn't erupt into violence. Those sitting in the section of the room reserved for the representatives of Red Hook, who had greeted the officer at the beginning of the meeting with hugs and handshakes and smiles, nodded in agreement.

The initial meeting of NeighborhoodStat was overcrowded and dragged beyond the allotted schedule. But as I left, I watched a resident seek out a public official from the department of sanitation to ask her what to do about an unkempt area around her complex. I saw a building manager assuring the leader of a tenant organization that he would find out why one of the doors on her building wasn't secured. And I saw the director of an antiviolence organization, a man who spoke up to express the anger felt by young men throughout the city, begin a conversation with an NCO from the same community.

Jack Maple's vision was still as powerful as it was when he first wrote it down on the famous napkin at Elaine's, but it had been revised. I walked out of the CompStat Center convinced that NeighborhoodStat should be the next model of policing in the United States.

The last model of policing in New York City began with an essay titled "Broken Windows," perhaps the most influential piece of writing on American law enforcement in the past century. The essay, which appeared in the *Atlantic Monthly* in 1982, was written by George Kelling and James Q. Wilson, both researchers who had spent a great deal of time studying and thinking about crime, policing, and how to make communities safer. Kelling in particular had taken part in several evaluations of policing tactics and strategies that were funded by the Police Foundation, which seeks to improve policing through experimentation and research. One of these evaluations was conducted in Newark, New Jersey.

The Newark "foot patrol" experiment was designed to assess whether taking officers out of patrol cars and asking them to patrol on foot would improve their capacity to control crime. Judging by the crime rate, the experiment didn't work. In the sections of the city where officers were switched to foot patrol, rates of criminal activity did not drop at all. What did change, however, were residents' perceptions of their neighborhoods. In the places where officers walked the streets, residents were less afraid of crime, felt better about the police, and thought their neighborhoods were getting safer even if the official crime rate suggested otherwise. Kelling walked alongside the officers on foot patrol to try to understand what officers were doing to make people feel more comfortable. "What foot-patrol officers did," he and Wilson concluded, "was to elevate, to the extent they could, the level of public order in these neighborhoods."

Kelling and Wilson argued that officers on foot patrol were able to get a feel for the informal rules that governed behavior in the community. Officers were able to understand who were the regulars and who were the strangers, what types of behaviors were tolerated and what types were discouraged, when was it necessary to let someone hang out and when was it necessary to move someone along. Maintaining order, according to the authors, had always been the most important function of the police. Sometime around the 1970s, however, the role of the police had become distorted, and this crucial element of policing was forgotten. Asking officers to patrol their beats by foot gave them the capacity to enforce a commonly understood set of norms, a local social order.

Kelling and Wilson then went further. Extending beyond the evidence from Newark, they put forth a theory of what happens when social order breaks down, and when signs of disorder begin to emerge. Their ideas came to be known as broken windows theory:

> A piece of property is abandoned, weeds grow up, a window is smashed. Adults stop scolding rowdy children; the children, emboldened, become more rowdy. Families move out, unattached adults move in. Teenagers gather in front of the corner store. The merchant asks them to move; they refuse. Fights occur. Litter accumulates. People start drinking in front of the grocery; in time, an inebriate slumps to the sidewalk and is allowed to sleep it off. Pedestrians are approached by panhandlers.
>
> At this point it is not inevitable that serious crime will flourish or violent attacks on strangers will occur. But many residents will think that crime, especially violent crime, is on the rise, and they will modify their behavior accordingly. They will use the streets less often, and when on the streets will stay apart from their fellows, moving with averted eyes, silent lips, and hurried steps. "Don't get involved." . . .
>
> Such an area is vulnerable to criminal invasion. Though it is not inevitable, it is more likely that here, rather than in places where people are confident they can regulate public behavior by informal controls, drugs will change hands, prostitutes will solicit, and cars will be stripped. That the drunks will be robbed

by boys who do it as a lark, and the prostitutes' customers will be robbed by men who do it purposefully and perhaps violently. That muggings will occur.

Their theory connecting small signs of disorder to violence and urban decline was anecdotal and speculative. Even so, it would change policing for the next several decades. One of the strongest advocates of broken windows theory was William Bratton, who in 1990 became chief of the New York City Transit Police and began to put Kelling and Wilson's ideas into action. Focusing on the process leading from small signs of disorder to major cycles of crime, he and his police force targeted even the most minor of violations. "Fare evasion and graffiti would no longer be considered too petty to address," Bratton wrote later. "In fact, we'd focus on them as vigorously as serious crimes like robberies, if not more so. Why? Because serious crime was more likely to occur in a lawless environment."

Over time, the subway cars became free of graffiti, panhandlers became less aggressive, and the transit system became cleaner and safer Bratton left the Transit Police for a brief stint in Boston, then was brought back as commissioner of the New York Police Department in 1994. Alongside Mayor Rudy Guiliani, Bratton took broken windows policing to a new level. Motivated by the idea of cracking down on the "small stuff," the NYPD arrested New Yorkers for minor crimes at an accelerating rate. Crime was declining, yet the number of arrests for misdemeanors (minor crimes like jumping a subway turnstile or carrying small amounts of marijuana) more than doubled in New York City from 1990 to 2010, rising from fewer than 120,000 arrests to roughly 250,000. In 1993, the year before Bratton took over the police department, there were fewer than 1,500 arrests across the city for marijuana possession. In 2000, the NYPD made more than 50,000 arrests for the same crime.

Lower-level criminal courts in New York City became flooded with minor offenders. The result, according to Yale Law professor Issa Kohler-Hausmann, was a fundamental shift in the function of the criminal justice system. Lower-level courts, instead of adjudicating guilt or punishment, were being used to "manage" minor offenders in the hope of keeping them under surveillance and occupied long enough to prevent more serious crimes. The logic of this approach was endorsed explicitly by Bratton himself: "A subway criminal arrested for a misdemeanor rather than a felony wouldn't be going to prison, but he wouldn't be victimizing anyone for a while, either."

In New York City, the idea of "fixing broken windows" evolved into the practice of arresting every potential troublemaker in sight. Hundreds of thousands of New Yorkers were arrested for minor offenses, and over time hundreds of thousands more were stopped and questioned on the street. The rise in "reasonable suspicion" stops of New York City residents represented an advanced stage in the NYPD's attempt to dominate public spaces. Under Mayor Michael Bloomberg and Police Commissioner Ray Kelly, the number of police stops rose from fewer than 100,000 to almost 700,000. And most of this activity was concentrated in the city's poorest, most segregated communities.

The model of policing developed in New York was replicated across the country. Since 1990, as crime declined nationally, the arrest rate for major crimes like burglary, motor vehicle theft, robbery, aggravated assault, and murder plummeted as well. Over the same period, the rate of arrests for possession of marijuana, a minor crime that is more closely tied to policing practices than to criminal activity, almost tripled. The rise of drug arrests is a hallmark of the dominant model of policing in use for the past twenty years. Under this model, police took over public spaces and became a constant, sometimes menacing presence in low-income communities of color. Arrests and stops were the metrics of police success, and incidents of police violence, excessive force, or brutality were the by-products.

This model of city policing has stood firm for most of the past two decades. But in the NYPD and many police departments elsewhere, there are strong signs that it is coming to an end. In 2013 a federal judge found the NYPD's racially imbalanced use of stop, question, and frisk to be unconstitutional. Mayor de Blasio campaigned on a platform to end the use of stop, question, and frisk as a central strategy of policing and brought William Bratton back to New York to implement a new model of policing for a safer time. The same police commissioner who had made broken windows policing famous used his final tour of duty to change the culture of the NYPD. Misdemeanor arrests declined during Bratton's second stint as commissioner, which ended in 2016, and the number of "reasonable suspicion" stops of citizens by police officers dropped by 93 percent from its peak of 685,000 stops in 2011 to just over 46,000 in 2014.

In his latest assignment in New York, Commissioner Bratton committed to a new version of broken windows policing that limits the need for aggressive enforcement. "We expect to see nearly a million fewer enforcement contacts like arrests, summonses, and reasonable-suspicion stops when compared to their respective historic highs," he wrote. "The diminished need to use enforcement tools for every problem is in keeping with one of the most salient observations that Kelling and Wilson made about Broken Windows: 'The essence of the police role in maintaining order is to reinforce the informal control mechanisms of the community itself.'"

These words are meaningful, even if they do not align with the vision of "broken windows" that Bratton himself put into place in New York City. His revised vision, however, may well be a guide to what policing can become after the era of violence.

How do we turn this vision into reality? The first step is to make sure that the efforts of police officers and their supervisors are aligned to achieve a goal that is broader than reducing crime. What made CompStat such a successful management tool was that the entire system was organized around a single outcome that was clear to everyone who entered the cavernous room named after Jack Maple: the crime rate. Incidents of major criminal activity were the sole focus of the tense forums that occurred every other week in the CompStat Center, and this focus led to undeniable improvements in the department's efficiency and effectiveness. But it is now clear that this singular focus on criminal incidents creates perverse incentives for police officers, encouraging them to take whatever steps necessary to show a drop in crime, while ignoring the perceptions of the community they were hired to serve.

Changing the behavior, tactics, and management of police officers requires changing the set of outcomes that police activity is organized to achieve. Police departments and the officers within them should be evaluated not only by the rate of crime or violence in a neighborhood or city but also through regularly collected surveys of residents' victimization, fear of crime, satisfaction with their community, and satisfaction with the police. An initial step in the effort to reform policing is to undertake a large-scale data collection project, one that moves beyond data on criminal complaints and arrests to include sensor data on shootings, administrative data on 911 calls and hospital admissions, and new data on community sentiment. If police officers are to play a new role in urban neighborhoods, they must have continuous data from every major city to assess how community conditions are changing. And that information must be used, in forums like NeighborhoodStat, to guide community-wide planning that includes the police.

A second, more challenging task is to reorient policing toward the goal of rebuilding trust between police and the communities they serve. In March 2015, President Obama's Task Force on 21st Century Policing put forth a document with compelling recommendations about how police departments can begin to rebuild trust and legitimacy. The task force recommended that police departments provide training to make officers aware of how implicit racial bias influences the perceptions and behaviors of everyone, including police officers, as they interact with people of color; that departments take conscious steps to continuously incorporate community discussion and input into their procedures on a regular basis; that they focus on transparency in responding to high-profile incidents involving potential misconduct of officers; and that they seek out opportunities for positive, nonenforcement interactions between officers and residents. The list, which reflects a thoughtful, smart vision of a new form of policing, goes well beyond these suggestions to include fifty-nine total recommendations.

The real challenge lies in executing these recommendations. For the past few decades, a very different vision of policing has been carried out in America's neighborhoods. Officers who have been taught to dominate public spaces are now being taught to take a different approach, and it is naïve to think that the adaptation will be simple or quick. Communities that have seen the police as a menacing, occupying force will not be convinced to accept the new role of the police without suspicion. And each video showing an officer abusing, humiliating, or killing a citizen on the streets of urban America makes it more difficult to imagine the police as a force for stability and peace within urban communities.

If police officers are to become a different kind of urban guardian, they will need assistance. Funding is necessary to implement new training and to allow departments to hire new officers whose role is not to enforce the law but rather to build relationships with community residents. Community policing is an old idea that has come to mean many different things to different people—but the neighborhood coordination officers in New York City, whose explicit job description is to build stronger relationships between officers and residents, provide a model for what the next stage of neighborhood policing should look like.

The last step is to acknowledge the role that police have played in reducing violence, and to double down on proven methods of controlling violent crime without targeting entire communities. One of the most consistent findings about crime and violence is that a large share of criminal activity happens in a small number of places. A study of the precise street segments and intersections where crime occurs in Boston found that about 8 percent of all such "micro-places" account for about two-thirds of all street robberies. Policing focused on "hot places" relies on close collaboration between community residents and police to identify the precise locations where, and times when, problems are likely to arise. Police resources and oversight are then directed toward those locations, and collaborative plans are made to address long-term problems like poor lighting, gang activity, graffiti, or vacant properties. This approach, which falls under the umbrella of problem-oriented policing, rests on some of the strongest empirical evidence of effectiveness that has ever been generated on police tactics and strategy.

Criminal activity is not only concentrated in a small number of hot spots, it is carried out by a tiny group of people who are linked together in a tight network of victims and offenders. The sociologists Andrew Papachristos, Chris Wildeman, and Elizabeth Roberto analyzed data on gun violence in Chicago and found that more than 70 percent of all nonfatal gunshot victims were part of a violent network of individuals that made up just 6 percent of the community population. Another study found that 40 percent of all firearm homicides occurred within a network containing just 4 percent of the population. Living within a high-crime neighborhood of Chicago does not automatically mean that young people are at high risk of becoming involved with violence. Being a part of the narrow network of young people who are linked together by criminal activity, however, raises the odds of becoming a gunshot victim exponentially.

Engaging the group of people within a community who are at greatest risk of victimization has become one of the most effective methods of interrupting exchanges of violent activity that account for a large share of gun violence. This engagement can happen by training "interrupters" to reach out to young people in the aftermath of violence, before they take action to reciprocate. It can happen by delivering a clear message to leaders of gangs or crews telling them that their entire network will be targeted if any member engages in gun violence. And it can happen through call-in meetings, where individuals who are enmeshed within the criminal justice system are given a warning and an offer. The warning is unflinching: *If you continue to engage in firearm violence, you will face serious, uncompromising prosecution.* But the offer must be equally sincere: *If you choose a different path, you will be supported with all resources and assistance that the community and the state can muster.*

Enforcement and outreach that are focused on hot spots and vulnerable people allow for a shift in the way the police interact with residents in high-crime neighborhoods. Instead of subjecting an entire community to intensive surveillance under a veil of suspicion, it is possible to target the very small number of places where an overwhelming share of violence occurs, and to focus resources on solving the problems in those places. It is possible to reach out to the people who are most likely to be victims and offer them resources that allow them to remain safe.

Police departments around the country have already implemented some of these ideas. The City of Fresno's police department implemented a survey to monitor residents' perceptions of, and attitudes toward, the police. Chicago created a task force calling for an overhaul of the police department's tactics and culture, and it undertook a massive effort to train its officers in the principles of procedural justice. The Washington State Criminal Justice Training Commission overhauled its law enforcement training curriculum: Officers who used to be required to stand silent and salute their instructors now have to initiate a conversation every time they cross paths, while addressing them with respect and a smile. In Los Angeles, officers have begun training on how to de-escalate conflict, how to talk to residents respectfully, and when it's appropriate to curse and when it's not. In a growing number of departments across the country, officers are being asked to change their role, to transform from warriors into guardians.

All the best evidence indicates that police will be essential to any effort to reduce violence. But even as we ask police departments to change the way they interact with communities, we must recognize the limits of any agenda for neighborhood change that relies primarily on reforms within police departments. For the past two decades, law enforcement has been asked to take over public spaces, to deal with the wide range of social problems that become visible on city streets, and to control crime. Now that police officers are being asked to step back from this role, it is imperative that others step up and play a larger role in overseeing urban communities. If there are no longer warriors on the street, there must be a larger supply of guardians.

36

The McDonald's System

FROM *The McDonaldization of Society*

GEORGE RITZER

McDonald's has become a buzzword not only for fast food but for a way of organizing activities, calculated to maximize efficiency by minimizing opportunities for error. For some this is wonderful, but for others this is lifeless and without joy, despite the images that appear in McDonald's commercials. Ultimately, it may not be as efficient as it seems.

THE DIMENSIONS OF MCDONALDIZATION: FROM DRIVE-THROUGHS TO UNCOMFORTABLE SEATS

Even if some domains are able to resist McDonaldization, this book intends to demonstrate that many other aspects of society are being, or will be, McDonaldized. This raises the issue of why the McDonald's model has proven so irresistible. Four basic and alluring dimensions lie at the heart of the success of the McDonald's model and, more generally, of the process of McDonaldization.

First, McDonald's offers *efficiency*. That is, the McDonald's system offers us the optimum method for getting from one point to another. Most generally, this means that McDonald's proffers the best available means of getting us from a state of being hungry to a state of being full. . . . Other institutions, fashioned on the McDonald's model, offer us similar efficiency in losing weight, lubricating our cars, filling eyeglass prescriptions, or completing income tax forms. In a fast-paced society in which both parents are likely to work, or where there may be only a single parent, efficiently satisfying the hunger and many other needs of people is very attractive. In a highly mobile society in which people are rushing, usually by car, from one spot to another, the efficiency of a fast-food meal, perhaps without leaving one's car while passing by the drive-through window, often proves impossible to resist. The fast-food model offers us, or at least appears to offer us, an efficient method for satisfying many of our needs.

Second, McDonald's offers us food and service that can be easily *quantified* and *calculated*. In effect, McDonald's seems to offer us "more bang for the buck." (One of its recent innovations, in response to the growth of other fast-food franchises, is to proffer "value meals" at discounted prices.) We often feel that we are getting a *lot* of food for a modest amount of money. Quantity has become equivalent to quality; a lot of something means it must be good. As two observers of contemporary American culture put it, "As a culture, we tend to believe—deeply—that in general 'bigger is better.'" Thus, we order the *Quarter Pounder*, the *Big* Mac, the *large* fries. We can quantify all of these things and feel that we are getting a lot of food, and, in return, we appear to be shelling out only a nominal sum of money. This calculus, of course, ignores an important point: the mushrooming of fast-food outlets, and the spread of the model to many other businesses, indicates that our calculation is illusory and it is the owners who are getting the best of the deal.

There is another kind of calculation involved in the success of McDonald's—a calculation involving time. People often, at least implicitly, calculate how much time it will take them to drive to McDonald's, eat their food, and return home and then compare that interval to the amount of time required to prepare the food at home. They often conclude, rightly or wrongly, that it will take less time to go and eat at the fast-food restaurant than to eat at home. This time calculation is a key factor in the success of Domino's and other home-delivery franchises, because to patronize them people do not even need to leave their homes. To take another notable example, Lens Crafters promises us "Glasses fast, glasses in one hour." Some McDonaldized institutions have come to combine the emphases on time and money. Domino's promises pizza delivery in one-half hour, *or* the pizza is free. Pizza Hut will serve us a personal pan pizza in five minutes, or it, too, will be free.

Third, McDonald's offers us *predictability*. We know that the Egg McMuffin we eat in New York will be, for all intents and purposes, identical to those we have eaten in Chicago and Los Angeles. We also know that the one we order next week or next year will be identical to the one we eat today. There is great comfort in knowing that McDonald's offers no surprises, that the food we eat at one time or in one place will be identical to the food we eat at another time or in another place. We know that the next Egg McMuffin we eat will not be awful, but we also know that it will not be exceptionally delicious. The success of the McDonald's model indicates that many people have come to prefer a world in which there are no surprises.

Fourth and finally, *control*, especially through the *substitution of non-human for human technology*, is exerted over the human beings who enter the world of McDonald's. The humans who work in fast-food restaurants are trained to do a very limited number of things in precisely the way they are told to do them. Managers and inspectors make sure that workers toe the line. The human beings who eat in fast-food restaurants are also controlled, albeit (usually) more subtly and indirectly. Lines, limited menus, few options, and uncomfortable seats all lead diners to do what the management wishes them to do—eat quickly and leave. Further, the drive-through (and in some cases walk-through) window leads diners to first leave and then eat rapidly. This attribute has most recently been extended by the Domino's model, according to which customers are expected to *never* come, yet still eat speedily.

McDonald's also controls people by using nonhuman technology to replace human workers. Human workers, no matter how well they are programmed and controlled, can foul up the operation of the system. A slow or indolent worker can make the preparation and delivery of a Big Mac inefficient. A worker who refuses to follow the rules can leave the pickles or special sauce off a hamburger, thereby making for unpredictability. And a distracted worker can put too few fries in the box, making an order of large fries seem awfully skimpy. For these and other reasons, McDonald's is compelled to steadily replace human beings with nonhuman technologies, such as the soft-drink dispenser that shuts itself off when the glass is full, the french-fry machine that rings when the fries are crisp, the preprogrammed cash register that eliminates the need for the cashier to calculate prices and amounts, and, perhaps at some future time, the robot capable of making hamburgers. (Experimental robots of this type already exist.) All of these technologies permit greater control over the human beings involved in the fast-food restaurant. The result is that McDonald's is able to reassure customers about the nature of the employee to be encountered and the nature of the service to be obtained.

In sum, McDonald's (and the McDonald's model) has succeeded because it offers the consumer efficiency and predictability, and because it seems to offer the diner a lot of food for little money and a slight expenditure of effort. It has also flourished because it has been able to exert greater control through non-human technologies over both employees and customers, leading them to behave the way the organization wishes them to. The substitution of non-human for human technologies has also allowed the fast-food restaurant to deliver its fare increasingly more efficiently and predictably. Thus, there are good, solid reasons why McDonald's has succeeded so phenomenally and why the process of McDonaldization continues unabated.

A CRITIQUE OF MCDONALDIZATION: THE IRRATIONALITY OF RATIONALITY

There is a downside to all of this. We can think of efficiency, predictability, calculability, and control through nonhuman technology as the basic components of a *rational* system. However, as we shall see in later chapters, rational systems often spawn irrationalities. The downside of McDonaldization will be dealt with most systematically under the heading of the *irrationality of rationality*. Another way of saying this is that rational systems serve to deny human reason; rational systems can be unreasonable.

For example, the fast-food restaurant is often a dehumanizing setting in which to eat or work. People lining up for a burger, or waiting in the drive-through line, often feel as if they are dining on an assembly line, and those who prepare the burgers often appear to be working on a burger assembly line. Assembly lines are hardly human settings in which to eat, and they have been shown to be inhuman settings in which to work. As we will see, dehumanization is only one of many ways in which the highly rationalized fast-food restaurant is extremely irrational.

Of course, the criticisms of the irrationality of the fast-food restaurant will be extended to all facets of our McDonaldizing world. This extension has recently been underscored and legitimated at the opening of Euro Disneyland outside Paris. A French socialist politician acknowledged the link between Disney and McDonald's as well as their common negative effects when he said that Euro Disney will "bombard France with uprooted creations that are to culture what fast food is to gastronomy."

Such critiques lead to a question: Is the headlong rush toward McDonaldization around the world advantageous or not? There are great gains to be made from McDonaldization, some of which will be discussed below. But there are also great costs and enormous risks, which this book will focus on. Ultimately, we must ask whether the creation of these rationalized systems creates an even greater number of irrationalities. At the minimum, we need to be aware of the costs associated with McDonaldization. McDonald's and other purveyors of the fast-food model spend billions of dollars each year outlining the benefits to be derived from their system. However, the critics of the system have few outlets for their ideas. There are no commercials on Saturday morning between cartoons warning children of the dangers associated with fast-food restaurants. Although few children are likely to read this book, it is aimed, at least in part, at their parents (or parents-to-be) in the hope that it will serve as a caution that might be passed on to their children.

A legitimate question may be raised about this analysis: Is this critique of McDonaldization animated by a romanticization of the past and an impossible desire to return to a world that no longer exists? For some critics, this is certainly the case. They remember the time when life was slower, less efficient, had more surprises, when people were freer, and when one was more likely to deal with a human being than a robot or a computer. Although they have a point, these critics have undoubtedly exaggerated the positive aspects of a world before McDonald's, and they have certainly tended to forget the liabilities associated with such a world. More importantly, they do not seem to realize that we are *not* returning to such a world. The increase in the number of people, the acceleration in technological change, the increasing pace of life—all this and more make it impossible to go back to a nonrationalized world, if it ever existed, of home-cooked meals, traditional restaurant dinners, high-quality foods, meals loaded with surprises, and restaurants populated only by workers free to fully express their creativity.

While one basis for a critique of McDonaldization is the past, another is the future. The future in this sense is what people have the potential to be if they are unfettered by the constraints of rational systems. This critique holds that people have the potential to be far more thoughtful, skillful, creative, and well-rounded than they now are, yet they are unable to express this potential because of the constraints of a rationalized world. If the world were less rationalized, or even derationalized, people would be better able to live up to their human potential. This critique is based not on what people were like in the past, but on what they could be like in the future, if only the constraints of McDonaldized systems were eliminated, or at least eased substantially. The criticisms to be put forth in this book are animated by the latter, future-oriented perspective rather than by a romanticization of the past and a desire to return to it.

THE ADVANTAGES OF MCDONALDIZATION: FROM THE CAJUN BAYOU TO SUBURBIA

Much of this book will focus on the negative side of McDonald's and McDonaldization. At this point it is important, however, to balance this view by mentioning some of the benefits of these systems and processes. The economic columnist, Robert Samuelson, for example, is a strong supporter of McDonald's and confesses to "openly worship McDonald's." He thinks of it as "the greatest restaurant chain in history." (However, Samuelson does recognize that there are those who "can't stand the food and regard McDonald's as the embodiment of all that is vulgar in American mass culture.")

Let me enumerate some of the advantages of the fast-food restaurant as well as other elements of our McDonaldized society:

- The fast-food restaurant has expanded the alternatives available to consumers. For example, more people now have ready access to Italian, Mexican, Chinese, and Cajun foods. A McDonaldized society is, in this sense, more egalitarian.
- The salad bar, which many fast-food restaurants and supermarkets now offer, enables people to make salads the way they want them.
- Microwave ovens and microwavable foods enable us to have dinner in minutes or even seconds.
- For those with a wide range of shopping needs, supermarkets and shopping malls are very efficient sites. Home shopping networks allow us to shop even more efficiently without ever leaving home.
- Today's high-tech, for-profit hospitals are likely to provide higher-quality medical care than their predecessors.
- We can receive almost instantaneous medical attention at our local, drive-in "McDoctors."
- Computerized phone systems (and "voice mail") allow people to do things that were impossible before, such as obtain a bank balance in the middle of the night or hear a report on what went on in their child's class during the day and what homework assignments were made. Similarly, automated bank teller machines allow people to obtain money any time of the day or night.
- Package tours permit large numbers of people to visit countries that they would otherwise not visit.

- Diet centers like Nutri/System allow people to lose weight in a carefully regulated and controlled system.
- The 24-second clock in professional basketball has enabled outstanding athletes such as Michael Jordan to more fully demonstrate their extraordinary talents.
- Recreational vehicles let the modern camper avoid excessive heat, rain, insects, and the like.
- Suburban tract houses have permitted large numbers of people to afford single-family homes.

CONCLUSION

The previous list gives the reader a sense not only of the advantages of McDonaldization but also of the range of phenomena that will be discussed under that heading throughout this book. In fact, such a wide range of phenomena will be discussed under the heading of McDonaldization that one is led to wonder: What isn't McDonaldized? Is McDonaldization the equivalent of modernity? Is everything contemporary McDonaldized?

While much of the world has been McDonaldized, it is possible to identify at least three aspects of contemporary society that have largely escaped McDonaldization. First, there are phenomena traceable to an earlier, "premodern" age that continue to exist within the modern world. A good example is the Mom and Pop grocery store. Second, there are recent creations that have come into existence, at least in part, as a reaction against McDonaldization. A good example is the boom in bed and breakfasts (B&Bs), which offer rooms in private homes with personalized attention and a homemade breakfast from the proprietor. People who are fed up with McDonaldized motel rooms in Holiday Inn or Motel 6 can instead stay in so-called B&Bs. Finally, some analysts believe that we have moved into a new, "postmodern" society and that aspects of that society are less rational than their predecessors. Thus, for example, in a postmodern society we witness the destruction of "modern" high-rise housing projects and their replacement with smaller, more livable communities. Thus, although it is ubiquitous, McDonaldization is *not* simply another term for contemporary society. There *is* more to the contemporary world than McDonaldization.

In discussing McDonaldization, we are *not* dealing with an all-or-nothing process. Things are not either McDonaldized or not McDonaldized. There are degrees of McDonaldization; it is a continuum. Some phenomena have been heavily McDonaldized, others moderately McDonaldized, and some only slightly McDonaldized. There are some phenomena that may have escaped McDonaldization completely. Fast-food restaurants, for example, have been heavily McDonaldized, universities moderately McDonaldized, and the Mom and Pop grocers mentioned earlier only slightly McDonaldized. It is difficult to think of social phenomena that have escaped McDonaldization totally, but I suppose there is local enterprise in Fiji that has been untouched by this process. In this context, McDonaldization thus represents a process—a process by which more and more social phenomena are being McDonaldized to an increasing degree.

Overall, the central thesis is that McDonald's represents a monumentally important development and the process that it has helped spawn, McDonaldization, is engulfing more and more sectors of society and areas of the world. It has yielded a number of benefits to society, but it also entails a considerable number of costs and risks.

Although the focus is on McDonald's and McDonaldization, it is important to realize that this system has important precursors in our recent history. . . . That is, McDonaldization is not something completely new, but rather its success has been based on its ability to bring together a series of earlier innovations. Among the most important precursors to McDonaldization are bureaucracy, scientific management, the assembly line, and the original McDonald brothers' hamburger stand.

37

The Social Organization of Toy Stores

FROM *Inside Toyland: Working, Shopping, and Social Inequality*

CHRISTINE L. WILLIAMS

Who would think a comparison of two toy stores could reveal so much about race, class, and gender? This piece by one of sociology's best organizational ethnographers is drawn from her book Inside Toyland, *in which she recounts her experiences working in an upscale store (Diamond Toys) and a low-brow store (Toy Warehouse)— stores that are not so different from ones where you may have worked. Gender segregation, racial stereotyping, social class, and "interpellation" (the integration of job expectations into one's identity) are only some of the sociological concepts that help make sense of working life in these businesses. Most important is how, in the face of organizational rules and practices that reflect and reinforce social inequality, people in the low-wage economy seek and find—often through resistance—dignity at work.*

Sociologists have not had much to say about the business of toy selling, or indeed about any kind of selling. For the most part, we have ceded the study of buying and selling to economists. In this book I make the case for a specifically sociological approach to shopping. Decisions regarding where to buy, how to buy, and what to buy are shaped by a complex of social, cultural, and psychological factors that sociologists are well equipped to analyze. Furthermore, I will argue that these consumer choices contribute to social inequality.

The connection between shopping and inequality begins with the decision of *where* to buy. Consumers make choices to enter one store and not another based in part on the images projected in advertisements. Corporate retail executives develop marketing plans, store designs, and labor policies to appeal to a certain kind of customer, or at least to a certain kind of customer desire, such as the desire for status or for low prices. Gender, race, and class distinctions all enter into the formation of this corporate image. Inside the store, corporate agendas are implemented in ways that favor certain groups over others. Workers are sorted into an organizational hierarchy and assigned specific duties according to their race, gender, and class. These internal practices shape *how* we buy: they determine with whom customers interact inside the store, which customers receive attentive service, and who ultimately benefits from the social norms that guide these interactions. The social inequalities of shopping are also taught to children, a practice especially apparent inside a toy store. Both in the style of interacting and in decisions about *what* to buy, adults instruct children on the values and meanings of consumerism, which contain lessons about race, class, and gender.

* * *

I chose to study toy stores because, although their merchandise is discretionary (unlike, say, that of grocery stores), they attract a wide range of customers. Interacting with customers is a central part of the retail worker's job, and I wanted the chance to observe the age, race, ethnicity, gender, and class differences among shoppers. Further, because children often accompany adults while shopping for toys, the toy store provides a window into the socialization of the next generation of consumers. Finally, toy stores are interesting to me because—as I was reminded in my job interview with Olive—toys can be a significant source of gender socialization for children.

One of the toy stores where I worked* I call the Toy Warehouse. It was located in the outskirts of an urban area in a redevelopment zone. It was what is sometimes called a big box store and was surrounded by several others, such as Home Depot, OfficeMax, and Petsmart. An enormous parking lot spread out like a lake between the stores. There were no sidewalks, no trees, no benches. Customers drove their cars to a specific store and then drove to another one if they wished to continue their shopping.

* * *

The other store where I worked, which I call Diamond Toys, was located in a upscale urban shopping district. Although it was a mere ten miles away from the Toy Warehouse, it was a world apart. Diamond Toys was a popular tourist destination, written up in guidebooks and often featured in the newspaper at Christmastime (during which I worked there). This high-priced store was also part of a national chain and also employed a staff of about seventy. But its racial composition was opposite to that of the Toy Warehouse: only three African Americans worked at the store (all women); the majority of the staff were white. Most of the customers were white too and were either middle or upper class.

The other major distinction between the two stores was that only one of them, Diamond Toys, was unionized. Union membership in the United States is at its lowest point in a hundred years, a reflection not only of the conservative political climate in America at the start of the twenty-first century but also of the interests of the big box retailers, who have unprecedented political and economic power, especially at the local level. Wal-Mart, for example, is notorious for its union-busting activities and violations of local labor laws and zoning ordinances.

* * *

*The author did three months of participant observation, working six weeks in each store. References and footnotes can be found in the original publication of her *Inside Toyland*, pages 213–224 (University of California Press, 2006). [*Editors' note*]

This [reading] explores the social construction of shopping and the implications of consumer choice for social inequality. I am especially interested in understanding how shopping in general and toy shopping in particular are implicated in reproducing gender, race, and class inequalities. The two stores I studied offer two different types of shopping experience: Diamond Toys cultivates its image as the purveyor of high-quality toys sold by a knowledgeable sales staff, while the Toy Warehouse's advertising strategy emphasizes its low prices on a vast array of popular toys.

The Toy Warehouse and Diamond Toys represented different moods that were intended to appeal to different desires, if not different sectors, of the toy-buying public. Both stores were parts of international chains of toy stores. The stores were governed by central corporate headquarters on the East Coast and regional offices located throughout the country. Corporate boards imagined what the store was supposed to look like, what kind of person shopped at the store, and how employees were supposed to behave. Advertising campaigns instructed consumers on this corporate culture. Employees learned about it in employee handbooks, videos, posters in the employee break room, and specific instructions handed down the chain of command from store director to manager to supervisor to salesclerk.

* * *

While the Toy Warehouse aspired to present an image as an exciting playground for kids and their families, Diamond Toys portrayed itself as a high-end specialty store oriented toward meeting the needs of discriminating adult shoppers. The store aimed to flatter the sophisticated tastes of the elite. The very setup of the store encouraged this aura. Diamond Toys looked like a fancy department store, not like a warehouse. A uniformed doorman out front greeted customers. Inside there were lavish displays of giant toys with mechanical moving parts. A theme song played in a continuous loop, making me at times feel trapped inside a ride at Disneyland.

* * *

Retail jobs, like other jobs in the service sector, have grown in number and changed dramatically over the past decades. Service jobs gradually have replaced manufacturing jobs as part of the general deindustrialization of the U.S. economy. This economic restructuring has resulted in boom times for wealthy American consumers as the prices for many commodities have dropped (a consequence of the movement of production overseas). It has also resulted in an erosion of working conditions for Americans in the bottom half of the economy, including service workers. Retail jobs have become increasingly "flexible," temporary, and part time. Over the past decades, workers in these jobs have experienced a loss of job security and benefits, a diminishment in the power of unions, and a lessening of the value of the minimum wage. Yet while most retail workers have lost ground, the giant corporations they work for have enjoyed unprecedented prosperity and political clout.

George Ritzer aptly uses the term *McJobs* to describe the working conditions found in a variety of service industries today. The word is a pun on McDonald's, the fast-food giant that introduced and popularized this labor system. McJobs are not careers; they are designed to discourage long-term commitment. They have short promotion ladders, they provide few opportunities for advancement or increased earnings, and the technical skills they require are not transferable outside the immediate work environment. They target sectors of the labor force that presumably don't "need" money to support themselves or their families: young people looking for "fun jobs" before college; mothers seeking part-time opportunities to fit around their family responsibilities; older, retired people looking for the chance to get out of the house and to socialize. However, this image does not resonate with the increasing numbers of workers in these jobs who are struggling to support themselves and their families. The marketing of McJobs on television commercials for Wal-Mart and fast-food restaurants obscures the harsh working conditions and low pay that contribute to the impoverished state of the working poor.

In addition to contributing to economic inequality, jobs in the retail industry are structured in ways that enhance inequality by gender and race. Although all retail workers are low paid, white men employed in this industry earn more money than any other group. Overall, about as many men as women work in retail trades, but they are concentrated in different kinds of stores. For example, men make up more than three quarters of workers in retail jobs selling motor vehicles, lumber, and home and auto supplies, while women predominate in apparel, gift, and needlework stores.

In both stores where I worked, the gender ratio was about 60:40, with women outnumbering men. I was surprised that so many men worked in these toy stores. In my admittedly limited experience, I associated women with the job of selling toys. But I learned that because of the way that jobs are divided and organized, customers usually don't see the substantial numbers of men who are working there too.

Retail work is also organized by race and ethnicity. Ten percent of all employees in the retail trade industry are African American, and 12 percent are of Hispanic origin, slightly less then their overall representation in the U.S. population. But again, whites, African Americans, and Latinas/os are likely to work in different types of stores. For example, African Americans are underrepresented (less than 5 percent) in stores that sell hardware, gardening equipment, and needlework supplies and overrepresented (more than 15 percent) in department stores, variety stores, and shoe stores. Similarly Latina/os are underrepresented (less than 6 percent) in bookstores and gas stations and overrepresented (more than 16 percent) in retail florists and household appliance stores.

The two stores where I worked had radically different racial compositions. Sixty percent of the workers at the Toy Warehouse were African American, and 60 percent of those at Diamond Toys were white. Only three African Americans, all women, worked at Diamond Toys. No black men worked at that store. In contrast, only four white women (including me) worked at the Toy Warehouse.

* * *

The hierarchy of jobs and power within the stores was marked by race and gender. In both stores the directors and assistant directors were white men. Immediately below them were managers, who were a more diverse group, including men and women, whites and Latinas/os, and, at the Toy Warehouse, an African American woman (Olive). There were far more managers at Diamond Toys than at the Toy Warehouse; I met at least ten managers during my time there, versus only two at the Toy Warehouse.

The next layer of the hierarchy under managers were supervisors, who were drawn from the ranks of associates. They were among those who had the most seniority and thus the most knowledge of store procedures, and they had limited authority to do things like void transactions at the registers. All of the supervisors at Diamond Toys were white and most were men, while at the Toy Warehouse supervisors were more racially diverse and most were women. It took me a long time to figure out who the supervisors were at the Toy Warehouse. Many of those I thought were supervisors turned out to be regular employees.

* * *

Associates were the largest group of workers at the stores (sometimes referred to as the staff). They included men and women of all races and ethnic groups and different ages, except at Diamond Toys, where I noted that there were no black men. Despite the apparent diversity among the staff, there was substantial segregation by race and gender in the tasks they were assigned. Employees of toy stores are divided between back- and front-of-house workers. The back-of-house employees and managers work in the storage areas, on the loading docks, and in the assembly rooms. In both stores where I worked, the back-of-house workers were virtually all men. The front-of-house workers, the ones who interacted with customers, included both men and women. But there, too, there was job segregation by gender and race, although, as I will discuss, it was harder to discern and on occasion it broke down.

There were two other jobs in the toy store: security guards and janitors, both of whom were subcontracted workers. Both the Toy Warehouse and Diamond Toys employed plainclothes security guards who watched surveillance monitors in their back offices and roamed the aisles looking for shoplifters. At the Toy Warehouse, the individuals who filled those jobs were mostly African American men and women, while only white men and women were hired for security at Diamond Toys. Finally, all of the cleaners at the two stores were Latinas. They were recent immigrants who didn't speak English.

What accounts for the race and gender segregation of jobs in the toy store? Conventional economic theory argues that job segregation is the product of differences in human capital attainment. According to this view, the marketplace sorts workers into jobs depending on their qualifications and preferences. Because men and women of different racial/ethnic groups possess different skills, aptitudes, and work experiences, they will be (and indeed should be) hired into different jobs. Economists generally see this process as benign, if not beneficial, in a society founded on meritocracy, individual liberty, and freedom of choice.

In contrast, when sociologists look at job segregation, they tend to see discrimination and structural inequality. Obtaining the right qualifications for a high-paying job is easier for some groups than others. Differential access to college education is an obvious example: society blocks opportunities for poor people to acquire this human capital asset while smoothing the path for the well-to-do. But the sociological critique of job segregation goes deeper than this. Sociologists argue that the definitions of who is qualified and what it means to be qualified for a job are linked to stereotypes about race and gender. Joan Acker argues that jobs are "gendered," meaning that qualities culturally associated with men (leadership, physical strength, aggression, goal orientation) are built into the job descriptions of the higher-status and higher-paid occupations in our economy. Qualities associated with women (dexterity, passivity, nurturing orientation) tend to be favored in low-paying jobs. In addition to being gendered, jobs are racialized. Black women have been subjected to a different set of gendered stereotypes than white women. Far from being seen as delicate and passive, they have been perceived as dominant, insubordinate, and aggressive. Those who make hiring decisions draw upon these kinds of racialized stereotypes of masculinity and femininity when appointing workers to specific jobs.

Leslie Salzinger has examined how this job placement works in manufacturing plants along the U.S.-Mexico border. She uses the concept of "interpellation" to describe how managers imagine a specific, embodied worker in each job and how workers come to see themselves in these imaginings. Workers, in other words, typically consent to and embrace the stereotypes, since their opportunities depend on their conformity to these managerial imaginings. She shows that to get a job on the assembly line, young women workers have to represent themselves as docile, dexterous, and unencumbered by family responsibilities. They really have no choice: to get a job they must become the embodiment of their bosses' stereotypes. Eventually, she argues, the line between the stereotype and the authentic self blurs.

* * *

Talwar notes in her study of fast-food restaurants that African American men are sometimes preferred as cashiers during the nighttime hours, especially in dangerous neighborhoods. This is presumed to offer some protection for the registers in case of attempted robbery. Here again we see how the image of "cashier" is linked to managers' race and gender stereotypes regarding the qualifications for the job. At the Toy Warehouse, African American men were not routinely assigned to the register at any time of day or night, but they were used to perform a security function in the evening. When the store closed at the end of the day, Olive would make an announcement over the public intercom instructing two black men to "clear the store" and "check the bathrooms." This was often said in a menacing way to scare the stragglers into leaving, especially if it had to be repeated more than once. This task assignment drew upon and bolstered stereotypes about the strength and inherent aggressiveness of African American men.

Cashiers did perform some security tasks at the Toy Warehouse. In addition to being responsible for requesting pulls, we were expected to check the customers' bags and receipts whenever the alarm sounded at the front door. The alarm was set off when people left the store with merchandise affixed with security tags that had not been properly deactivated. This happened approximately every ten minutes. Half of the people who set off the alarm turned around immediately to offer proof that they were not guilty of anything, and the other half just continued walking out the door. We tended to ignore both groups. We were usually too busy with other customers to stop and check the ones who came back into the store, so we just waved them out. We certainly were not going to run after customers who continued walking out. If they had indeed stolen any merchandise, we weren't about to expose ourselves to the potential danger of a physical confrontation. I thought that this should have been the job of a uniformed security force, but Olive told me that a uniformed guard would damage the store's image as a welcoming and happy place.

A few men were regularly assigned to work as cashiers at the Toy Warehouse, but this happened only in the electronics department. The electronics department was cordoned off from the rest of the store by a metal detector gate intended to curtail theft. All of the men with this regular assignment were Asian American. They had sought out this assignment because they were interested in computers and gaming equipment. Working a register in that section may have been more acceptable to them in part because the section was separated from the main registers and in part because Asian masculinity—as opposed to black or white masculinity—is often defined through technical expertise. My sense was that the stereotypical association of Asian American men with computers made these assignments desirable from management's perspective as well.

Occasionally men were assigned to work the registers outside the electronics department, but this happened only when there were staffing shortages or scheduling problems. Once I came to work to find Deshay, a twenty-five-year-old African American, and Shuresh, a twenty-one-year-old second-generation Indian American, both stationed at the main registers. I flew to the back of the store to clock in so I could take my station next to them, eager to observe them negotiating the demands of "women's work." But the minute I took my station they were relieved of cashiering and told to cash out their registers and return to their regular tasks. When a woman was available, the men didn't have to do the job.

On a previous occasion, I had observed Deshay skillfully evade the assignment to work register. Deshay normally worked as a merchandiser, and he also worked in the storeroom unloading boxes from the delivery trucks. I noticed when he was called to the register because I had never seen an African American man work there. Olive called Deshay to her office over the walkie-talkie (without telling him why—if he had known why, he later told me, he wouldn't have responded to the page). Next thing I saw him with a register drawer, and he was told to start counting it out in preparation for cashiering. He took the till over to the service desk, and I turned around for a moment and he was gone! Eventually I caught up with him in the break room and asked him what happened. I said, "That was some disappearing act!" He told me, with mounting exasperation and anger, that he did not want to work register, he was not hired to work register, he had too many other jobs to do, and if they forced him to work register he would file a lawsuit against them. He didn't say outright that cashiering was a lousy job, my guess is, because that was the job I was doing.

This is another example of interpellation. Deshay had come to see himself in managerial stereotypes about the appropriate roles for black men. But I think that another reason Deshay didn't want to cashier was that he felt his masculinity was at stake. For many men, work functions as outward proof of their masculine identity. Their poise, their sense of strength, and even their heterosexuality are challenged when they do "women's work." Even though there is nothing inherently feminine about working a cash register, management had defined the job as "women's work," and Deshay was eager to distance himself from any job considered "feminine." This psychological incentive fit in with managerial goals. In this way, workplaces draw on gender to "manufacture consent"—that is, to make workers complicit in the social organization that management prefers.

* * *

The stores exploited young men's insecurity in their masculinity by assigning them to jobs that required them to do a great deal of heavy lifting. They had to move freight and deliver large items (like baby car seats, play sets, and bikes) to the front of the store and occasionally out to the customer's car. Several men told me that the physical aspect of their work wore them out and meant that their jobs in retail could only be temporary. But at the same time they took a great deal of pride in these tasks. Because the tasks were defined as masculine, they seemed to experience a boost in self-esteem for accomplishing them.

Women also crossed over into the men's jobs, but this happened far less frequently. Management never assigned a woman to work in the back areas to make up for temporary staff shortfalls. At each store, only one woman worked in the back of the house, and both women were African American. At the Toy Warehouse, the only woman who worked in the back was Darlene, whom a coworker once described to me as "very masculine" (but also "really great"). Darlene, who worked in a contracting business on the side, took a lot of pride in her physical strength and stamina. She was also a lesbian, which made her the butt of mean-spirited joking (behind her back) but also probably made this assignment less dissonant in the eyes of management (women in nontraditional jobs are often stereotyped as lesbian). At Diamond Toys, the only woman in the back of the house was eighteen-year-old Chandrika. She started working in the back of the house but asked for and received a transfer to gift wrap. Chandrika, who was one of only three African Americans who worked at Diamond Toys, said she hated working in the storeroom because the men there were racist and "very misogynistic," telling sexist jokes and challenging her competence at the job.

Crossing over is a different experience for men and women. When a job is identified as masculine, men often will erect barriers to women, making them feel out of place and unwanted, which is what happened to Chandrika. In contrast, I never observed women trying to exclude men or marginalize men in "their" jobs. On the contrary, men tried to exclude themselves from "women's work." Job segregation by gender is in large part a product of men's efforts to establish all-male preserves, which help them to prove and to maintain their masculinity.

Management colludes in this insofar as they share similar stereotypes of appropriate task assignments for men and women or perceive the public to embrace such stereotypes. But they also insist on employee "flexibility," the widespread euphemism used to describe their fundamental right to hire, fire, and assign employees at will. At the Toy Warehouse, employees were often threatened that their hours would be cut if they were not "flexible" in terms of their available hours and willingness to perform any job. But in general managers shared men's preferences to avoid register duty unless no one else was available.

How and why a specific job comes to be "gendered" and "racialized," or considered appropriate only for women or for men, or for whites or non-whites, depends on the specific context (which in the case of these toy stores was shaped—but not determined—by their national marketing strategies. Thus, in contrast to the Toy Warehouse, Diamond Toys employed both men and women as cashiers, and only two of them were African American (both women). At the Toy Warehouse, most of the registers were lined up in the front of the store near the doors. Diamond Toys was more like a department store with cash registers scattered throughout the different sections. The preference for white workers seemed consistent with the marketing of the store's workers as "the ultimate toy experts." In retail service work, professional expertise is typically associated with whiteness, much as it is in domestic service.

Although both men and women worked the registers, there was gender segregation by the type of toy we sold. Only women were assigned to work in the doll and stuffed animal sections, for example, and only men worked in sporting goods and electronics. Also, only women worked in gift wrap. Some sections, like the book department, were gender neutral, but most were as gender marked as the toys we sold.

This gender segregation occasionally would break down at Diamond Toys, and men would be assigned to work in the women's sections when enough women weren't available. At Diamond Toys, Carl, a thirty-year-old white man, once had to work backup with me in dolls. He performed the role in a completely campy style, swishing around the floor and answering the phone with "Barbie speaking!" Carl, who normally didn't act this way, was parodying the assumed homosexuality of any man interested in dolls (and, indeed, many of the high-end Barbie customers were gay). Turning the role into a joke made his temporary assignment seem more palatable and less inconsistent with his masculinity.

* * *

HOURS, BENEFITS, AND PAY

When I started this project I thought I had the perfect career to combine with a part-time job in retail. As a college professor, I taught two courses per semester that met six hours per week. I thought I could pick a schedule for twenty hours a week that accommodated those teaching commitments. Wrong. To get a job in retail, workers must be willing to work weekends and to change their schedules from one week to another to meet the staffing needs of the store. This is the meaning of the word *flexible* in retail. It is exactly the kind of schedule that is incompatible with doing anything else.

Retail is often marketed as a great part-time work opportunity because of the "flexible" schedules. Mothers looking to combine work with their primary family responsibilities are drawn to these jobs. I met a mother of three preschool children at a job fair with this goal in mind. She and I met in a seminar room with four others who were applying for a job at a children's warehouse store.

Before the formal presentation started, we talked about why we were there. She told me that she preferred not to work, that she valued her role as full-time wife and mother, and that she would never put her kids in day care. But she had decided to get a job because of an argument she had had with her husband. She had recently asked him to buy her a cell phone. He had told her that if she really wanted a cell phone, she should get a job. So she had decided to look for a retail job for the hours 5:00 to 10:00 P.M. She had picked those hours because her husband would be home from work then and thus available to look after the children. He'd also have to feed them and put them to bed, she noted with a devious smile.

I didn't get that job, and I suspect that she didn't either. We wanted flexible jobs, but the store wanted flexible workers. I learned from my experience to never limit the hours I would work on job applications. Giant retailers do not cater to the needs of employees; their goal is to hire a constant stream of entry-level, malleable, and replaceable workers. This organizational preference for high turnover keeps labor costs down.

Workers with seniority can gain some control over their schedules, but it takes years of "flexibility" to attain . . . this status. Moreover, in my experience, this control was guaranteed only at Diamond Toys, thanks to the union. The senior associates who had worked there more than a year had the same schedule from week to week. This didn't apply to the supervisors, though. They had to be willing to fill in as needed, since there had to be a supervisor on the floor at all times. Occasionally they even had to forgo breaks.

* * *

Those who didn't live in the city faced long and often grueling commutes. When I first met Mario, a twenty-five-year-old Latino, he was trying to take a nap on one of the ratty couches in the break room. It was almost 9:00 A.M., the start of my shift, and I asked him when he was on. He told me that his shift didn't start until noon but that he had had to come in early to get a ride with his sister, Angie, who was working 9:00 to 5:00. They lived in a suburb about thirty-five miles away. He explained that it took about two and a half hours to get to work by public transportation, so he figured he came out ahead (and saved some money) by coming in three hours early. When he had first been hired at Diamond Toys he lived in the city, but he had moved out to the suburbs about a year ago and there were no jobs there as good as this one. He said he had just found out that he had to have work done on a tooth, probably a root canal, and that it was going to cost $2,000, but it was all going to be paid for, thanks to the union benefits. So the job—with the long commute—was worth it to him.

* * *

Interestingly, no one at Diamond Toys appeared to have any children. I asked Dennis about this, and he verified that no one had children that he could think of, a fact he attributed to their youth and their attendance at college. Several gay men worked at the store (at the managerial level), another possible reason behind the childlessness. I did meet one young associate who had a six-year-old daughter, but I later learned that the daughter lived with her father in another state. The complete absence of parents suggests a systematic bias in the hiring and/or retention of workers. Perhaps those with child care responsibilities were less able to conform to the "flexible" requirements of the job.

This was a huge contrast to my experience at the Toy Warehouse, where most of my women coworkers were single mothers. I met only three other women aside from myself who didn't have children. (Interestingly, those three others were full-time employees at the supervisory level.) Most of the men also had children. Here the systematic bias was in favor of hiring parents. This was in part a consequence of the fact that the Toy Warehouse participated in the "workfare" program, whereby businesses that hired welfare recipients could receive reimbursement for part of their wages. Since welfare was designed to provide aid to families with dependent children, all recipients had children. All new hires (including me) were given a form to certify their employment for the welfare office. These forms were also used by the store to obtain a federal reimbursement under the "work opportunity tax credit." This tax credit, part of the welfare reform of 1996, reimbursed businesses for 35 percent of wages for the first year and 50 percent the second, to a maximum of $8,500 per new hire (qualified wages were capped at $10,000 per year). Participating in the program helped the Toy Warehouse cut down significantly on its labor costs.

The unpredictability of scheduling presented a nightmare for many single mothers at the Toy Warehouse. Schedules were posted on Friday for the following week beginning on Sunday. The two-day notice of scheduling made it especially difficult to arrange child care. (In contrast, schedules came out on Tuesday for the following week at Diamond Toys, another benefit of the union.) Even worse, while I was working at the Toy Warehouse, management reduced everyone's hours, purportedly to make up for revenue shortfalls. We were all asked to fill in a form indicating our "availability" to work, from 6:00 A.M. until 10:00 P.M. This form, which was attached to our paychecks, warned that "associates with the flexible availability will get more hours than those who are limited." Part-timers who limited their availability were hit hard when schedules came out the following week, causing a great deal of anger and bad feelings. Angela, an experienced associate, was scheduled for only four hours, and she was so mad that no one could even talk to her. Some said that they were going to apply for unemployment. Deshay offered to get me the phone number for the county unemployment office because I was given only 13.5 hours, well below the 20 he told me was the maximum one could work in order to qualify for unemployment benefits.

One of the reasons management gave for cutting our hours was that the store had been experiencing major problems with "shrink," the retailer term for theft. It was insinuated that the workers were stealing, but I could never figure out how that could happen. In both stores, very elaborate surveillance systems were set up to monitor employees. Hidden cameras recorded activity throughout the store, including the areas around the emergency exits. Our bags, pockets, and purses were checked every time we left the store. Cashiers were monitored continuously via a backroom computer hooked up to every register. As I noted, the contents of the till had to match exactly with the register report. Being even slightly under was enough to cause a major panic.

* * *

But even at the Toy Warehouse, managers knew that service workers helped to produce happy and satisfied customers. They emphasized to us that repeat business depended on the customer's favorable experience with the workers, especially with the cashiers. Mark, the store director of the Toy Warehouse, kept urging us to smile at the customers, whom we were required to call "guests."

To reward us for good customer service, the Toy Warehouse management would occasionally give us "toy bucks," scriplike coupons redeemable for a Coke or an ice cream bar. The coupons were given for a variety of reasons, including "never letting a guest leave our store dissatisfied" and "thanking guests and inviting them to return." Once after an especially busy day, the entire closing staff got a toy buck, prompting one of my coworkers to remark cynically, "How many of these does it take to get a TV?"

Toy bucks were miserly rewards, but they did improve the morale of some workers, who, after all, were making very miserly incomes. The Toy Warehouse paid less than Diamond Toys. I earned $7.50 per hour, which I later found out was a relatively high starting salary. Pak Chew, who was hired at the same time I was, made only $7.10, but this was his first job ever. Later Pak Chew was offered a full-time job at UPS for $11 per hour, and to his and everyone's amazement, Mark offered him $9 to stay (he didn't).

There weren't rules against discussing wages at the Toy Warehouse, but most workers avoided the topic. It was an embarrassing subject, especially if it was revealed that some people (especially the new hires) earned more than the longer-term employees. I learned that some of my coworkers who had been at the store much longer made the same wage that I did. Vern, a fifty-year-old black man who had worked in bike assembly for two years, was distressed to learn that Paul, a new hire, was making as much as he was, even though Vern had just received a 25-cent raise. Paul, a twenty-two-year-old heavily tattooed white man, was hired for $8 per hour. Paul told me this when I first met him in the break room. He complained about his low wage and announced that in one month he would demand a raise to $9. He explained that his father was a good friend of Jack, the supervisor of the bike department. That was how he had gotten this job, along with the promise that he would be making more money.

Paul was one exception to the norm of not talking about wages, and it didn't make him any friends. Most thought he was a braggart and avoided him. Another exception was Michelle, a thirty-three-year-old African American woman. Michelle talked about wages and working conditions at every opportunity, but she was enormously popular and well liked. One day before my shift I was in the break room when Michelle arrived. She was furious because her paycheck didn't reflect the overtime she had been forced to work the previous Saturday when the staff had been required to come to an unscheduled meeting. (The issue of unpaid overtime is the subject of class action lawsuits brought against Wal-Mart.) Other employees said that they were going to make a point of noticing whether they were also shorted on their paychecks. Then Michelle started singing wonderful made-up rap songs about our lousy jobs and the whole break room erupted with laughter and shouting.

One of the issues that Michelle raised was that the new people (including me) were taking the established people's hours. None of the new workers were African American (we were white, Asian American, and Latina), and this formed an unspoken backdrop to her complaint. Michelle had tried to get a petition drive going to complain about the diminishing hours, but no one would sign her petition. She was very frustrated. People told her, "I don't want to lose my job; I need this job." Well, so did she, but who would fight for their rights, she wanted to know. She didn't involve the new people in the organizing, but she complained to me later that the others were not brave enough to fight for their rights. They talked a good deal in the break room, she said, but when push came to shove they were not there to support her and her campaign for better working conditions.

Michelle was one of several workers who had two jobs. Nationally, about 6 percent of all workers hold two jobs, but nearly every associate I met at the Toy Warehouse also worked someplace else to supplement his or her income. Michelle worked for the school district as a janitor, making about $11 per hour. She had started at the Toy Warehouse at Christmastime, when school was out, and Olive had asked her to stay on. She had explained about her other job, and Olive had promised to work around it, but as it turned out that didn't happen. She complained that sometimes she was asked to be at work at noon, but her other job required her to be there until 1:30, so how could she make it on time? Then she was written up for being late, which seemed totally unfair to her. She said she had two demerits against her which she had been called into the main office to sign, and she had said no, she didn't agree that she was in the wrong. She had been told that the demerits would go in her file anyway, and she had said, "Then what's the point of signing?"

Michelle was also upset because her perceived insubordination resulted in her being demoted to cashier. She had been working at the service desk, a position with more authority and more varied responsibilities but not more pay. The service desk worker could clear voided transactions and open registers to make change and pull out large amounts of cash to put into the safe. A person in this position wore register keys around her neck, a symbolic marker of her higher authority and status (only women were ever assigned this job). Michelle was furious to be assigned to a register, a situation made worse by the fact that the person assigned to the service desk was new at the job and had to ask Michelle how to perform most of her tasks.

Michelle was so frustrated that she eventually decided to resign. She composed her letter of resignation at the register next to mine, so we talked about it while she was working on it. The letter was addressed to Mark, the store director, who had replaced the former director in charge when Michelle was hired. She told me (in the break room with the others) that when she had been hired she had been promised $10 per hour, which she thought was OK combined with her other job at $11. But then she found out she would be getting only $9.25, which she thought was insulting, given her prior experience at Kmart. (One of the others backed her up and said that anything she was promised by the previous director was probably not honored, since he often lied to employees.) When she confronted the managers about this they said that this was standard but that after three months there would be a 25- to 50-cent raise. When her three months came up she was given 25 cents, which set her off. In fact, the very first time I met Michelle she was carrying on in the break room, shouting that she was going to tell the manager to shove that 25 cents up her ass.

CONCLUSION

Most sociological research on retail stores looks at them as sites of consumption. But stores are also workplaces. Retail work makes up an increasing proportion of the jobs in our economy. Yet these are "bad" jobs. A "good job" is one that pays enough to support a family and provides benefits, security, and autonomy. In contrast, most jobs in retail pay low wages, offer few benefits, have high turnover, and restrict workers' autonomy.

* * *

However, there is no reason why service sector jobs have to remain "bad" jobs. After all, manufacturing jobs did not start as "good" jobs. Anyone who has read Upton Sinclair, Charles Dickens, or the young Karl Marx is surely aware that factory labor was ill paid, dirty, and dangerous when it started. Factory jobs became good jobs only because, in the 1920s and 1930s, workers fought and bled for changes in policy and law. These jobs didn't become good jobs because of the magnanimity of factory owners. The motivations of the nineteenth-century robber barons were similar to those of the owners of Wal-Mart and other large retail outlets today: In the pursuit of profit, these owners of capital aimed to exploit labor to the extent permissible by law. Just as a great deal of organized effort was required to transform manufacturing jobs into good, sustainable jobs, the same is true of service jobs today.

38

The Rise and Fall of Mass Rail Transit

FROM *Building American Cities: The Urban Real Estate Game*

JOE R. FEAGIN and ROBERT PARKER

There are more automobiles than people in Los Angeles. Is this a consequence of the preferences and choices of individual consumers, a reflection of the so-called American love affair with the automobile, or is it the result of structured choices? The authors show that farsighted corporations found common cause in organizing transportation to suit their interests, and the romance of Americans and their cars began a new chapter.

Most U.S. cities have become *multinucleated*, with major commercial, industrial, and residential areas no longer closely linked to or dependent upon the downtown center. Decentralization has become characteristic of our cities from coast to coast. Essential to decentralization has been the development and regular extension of an automobile-dominated transportation system serving businesses and the general citizenry, but mostly paid for by rank-and-file taxpayers. With and without citizen consent, corporate capitalists, industrialists and developers, and allied political officials have made key decisions fundamentally shaping the type of transportation system upon which all Americans now depend.

THE AUTO-OIL-RUBBER INDUSTRIAL COMPLEX

The auto-oil-rubber industrial complex has long been central to both the general economy and the urban transportation system in the United States. Automobile and auto-related industries provide a large proportion, sometimes estimated at one-sixth, of all jobs, although this proportion may be decreasing with the decline and stagnation in the auto industry over the last two decades. An estimated one-quarter to one-half of the land in central cities is used for the movement, storage, selling, and parking of automobiles, trucks, and buses. The expanding production of automobiles and trucks has been coordinated with the expansion of highways and freeways and has facilitated the bulging suburbanization around today's cities.

Because of the dominance of autos and trucks in the U.S. transportation system, the traditional social scientists . . . have typically viewed that transportation system as preordained by the American "love" for the automobile. For example, in a recent book on Los Angeles, historian Scott Bottles argues that

"America's present urban transportation system largely reflects choices made by the public itself"; the public freely chose the automobile as a "liberating and democratic technology." Conventional explanations for auto-centered patterns focus on the response of a market system to these consumers. Auto-linked technologies are discussed as though they force human decisions: Thus "the city dweller, especially in recent times, has been a victim of the technological changes that have been wrought in transportation systems." . . . [T]raditional ecologists and other social scientists view the complexity and shape of cities as largely determined by technological developments in transportation—a reasonable view—but these technologies are not carefully examined in terms of their economic contexts, histories, and possible technological alternatives. For example, unlike the United States, numerous capitalist countries in Europe, including prosperous West Germany, have a mixed rail transit/automobile transport system. There interurban and intraurban rail transit remains very important. For this reason, the U.S. system cannot be assumed to be simply the result of "free" consumer choices in a market context. The capitalistic history and decision-making contexts that resulted in the positioning of automobiles at the heart of the U.S. transportation system must be examined.

EARLY MASS RAIL TRANSIT

Rural and urban Americans have not always been so dependent on automobiles for interurban and intraurban transport. In the years between the 1880s and the 1940s many cities had significant mass transit systems. By 1890 electric trolleys were in general use. Indeed, electric trolley routes, elevated railroads, and subways facilitated the first urban expansion and decentralization. Some investor-owned rail transit companies extended their trolley lines beyond existing urbanized areas out into the countryside in an attempt to profit from the land speculation along the rail lines. Glenn Yago has documented how transit owners and real estate speculators worked together to ensure the spatial and economic development of cities by private enterprise. Transit companies were a significant force in urban sprawl. The suburban spread of Los Angeles, for example, got its initial push from the expansion of trolley rail lines. Not initially laid out as an automobile city, this sprawling metropolis developed along streetcar tracks; only later was the streetcar network displaced by automobiles.

The reorganization and disruption of mass rail transit that took place in the early 1900s did not result just from the challenge of improved automobile technology. Rather, capitalist entrepreneurs and private corporations seeking profits reorganized and consolidated existing rail transit systems. Electrification of horse-drawn streetcars increased investment costs and stimulated concentration of ownership in larger "transit trusts" of landowning, finance, and utility entrepreneurs. Mergers of old transit firms and the assembly of new companies were commonplace, and there was much speculation in transit company stock. Yago has provided evidence on the corrupt accounting practices, over-extension of lines for real estate speculation, and overcapitalization which led to the bankruptcy of more than one-third of the private urban transit companies during the period 1916–1923. Sometimes the capitalists involved in the transit companies were too eager for profits. "These actions in turn," Charles Cheape notes, "drained funds, discouraged additional investment, and contributed significantly to the collapse and reorganization of many transit systems shortly after World War I and again in the 1930s."

Ironically, one consequence of the so-called "progressive" political reform movement in cities in the first decades of the twentieth century was that supervision of rail transit systems was often placed in the hands of business-dominated regulatory commissions, many of whose members were committed to the interests of corporate America (for example, transit stock manipulation for profit), rather than to the welfare of the general public. In numerous cases the extraordinary profits made by rail transit entrepreneurs, together with their ties to corrupt politicians, created a negative public image—which in turn made the public less enthusiastic about new tax-supported subsidies and fare hikes for the troubled rail transit systems. Moreover, as the profits of many of the private transit firms declined, public authorities in some cities, including Boston and New York, were forced to take over the transit lines from the poorly managed private companies in response to citizen pressure for mass transportation. This fact suggests that there has long been popular *demand* for publicly owned rail transit that is reliable, convenient, and inexpensive. Indeed, during the period 1910–1930 a *majority* of Americans either could not afford, because of modest incomes, or could not use, because of age or handicap, an automobile.

A CORPORATE PLAN TO KILL MASS TRANSIT?

By the late 1910s and 1920s the ascension of the U.S. auto-oil-rubber industrial complex brought new corporate strategies to expand automobile markets and secure government subsidies for road infrastructure. Mass rail transit hindered the profit-oriented interests of this car-centered industrial complex, whose executives became involved not only in pressuring governments to subsidize roads but also in the buying up of mass transit lines. For example, in the early 1920s, Los Angeles had the largest and most effective trolley car system in the United States. Utilizing more than a thousand miles of track, the system transported millions of people yearly. During World War II, the streetcars ran 2,800 scheduled runs a day. But by the end of that war, the trolleys were disappearing. And their demise had little to do with consumer choice. As news analyst Harry Reasoner has observed, it "was largely a result of a criminal conspiracy":

> The way it worked was that General Motors, Firestone Tire and Standard Oil of California and some other companies, depending on the location of the target, would arrange financing for an outfit called National City Lines, which cozied

up to city councils and county commissioners and bought up transit systems like
L.A.'s. Then they would junk or sell the electric cars and pry up the rails for scrap
and beautiful, modern buses would be substituted, buses made by General Motors
and running on Firestone Tires and burning Standard's gas.

Within a month after the trolley system in Los Angeles was purchased, 237
new buses arrived. It is important to realize that, for all the financial and management problems created by the private owners of the rail transit firms, the
old transit systems were still popular. In the year prior to the takeover, the
Los Angeles electric lines made $1.5 million in profits and carried more than
200 million passengers. The logic behind the corporate takeover plan was clear.
The auto-related firms acted because a trolley car can carry the passengers
of several dozen automobiles.

During the 1930s GM created a holding company through which it and other
auto-related companies channeled money to buy up electric transit systems
in 45 cities from New York to Los Angeles. As researcher Bradford Snell has
outlined it, the process had three stages. First, General Motors (GM) helped
the Greyhound corporation displace long-distance passenger transportation
from railroads to buses. Then GM and other auto-related companies bought
up and dismantled numerous local electric transit systems, replacing them with
the GM-built buses. Moreover, in the late 1940s, GM was convicted in a Chicago federal court of having conspired to destroy electric transit and to convert trolley systems to diesel buses, whose production GM monopolized. William
Dixon, the man who put together the criminal conspiracy case for the federal
government, argued that individual corporate executives should be sent to jail.
Instead, each received a trivial $1 fine. The corporations were assessed a mod-
est $5,000 penalty, the maximum under the law. In spite of this conviction, GM
continued to play a role in converting electric transit systems to diesel buses.
And these diesel buses provided more expensive mass transit: "The diesel bus,
as engineered by GM, has a shorter life expectancy, higher operating costs,
and lower overall productivity than electric buses. GM has thus made the bus
economically noncompetitive with the car also." One source of public discontent with mass transit was this inferiority of the new diesel buses compared
to the rail transit cars that had been displaced without any consultation with
consumers. Not surprisingly, between 1936 and 1955 the number of operating
trolley cars in the United States dropped from about 40,000 to 5,000.

In a lengthy report GM officials have argued that electric transit systems
were already in trouble when GM began intervening. As noted above, some
poorly managed transit systems were declining already, and some had begun
to convert partially to buses before GM's vigorous action. So from GM's view-
point, the corporations direct intervention only accelerated the process. This
point has been accented by Bottles, who shows that GM did not single-handedly
destroy the streetcar systems in Los Angeles. These privately controlled systems were providing a lesser quality of service before GM became involved.

The profit milking and corruption of the private streetcar firms in Los Angeles were not idiosyncratic but were common for privately owned mass transport in numerous cities.

Also important in destroying mass transit was the new and aggressive multimillion-dollar marketing of automobiles and trucks by General Motors and other automobile companies across the United States. And the automobile companies and their advertisers were not the only powerful actors involved in killing off numerous mass transit systems. Bankers and public officials also played a role. Yago notes that "after World War II, banks sold bankrupt and obsolete transit systems throughout the country at prices that bore no relation to the systems' real values." Often favoring the auto interests, local banks and other financial institutions tried to limit government bond issues that could be used to finance new equipment and refurbish the remaining rail transit systems.

Because of successful lobbying by executives from the auto-oil-rubber complex, and their own acceptance of a motorization perspective, most government officials increasingly backed street and highway construction. They cooperated with the auto industry in eliminating many mass transit systems. Increased governmental support for auto and truck transportation systems has meant systematic disinvestment in mass transit systems. Over the several decades since World War II, governmental mass transit subsidies have been small compared with highway subsidies. This decline has hurt low-and moderate-income people the most. Less public transit since World War II has meant increased commuting time in large cities where people are dependent on the automobile, which is especially troublesome for moderate-income workers who may not be able to afford a reliable car; less mass transit has also meant increased consumer expenditures for automobiles and gasoline. Auto expansion has frustrated the development of much mass transit because growing street congestion slows down buses and trolleys, further reducing their ridership. As a result, governmental funding for public rail transit has been cut, again chasing away riders who dislike poorly maintained equipment. And fares have been increased. Riders who can use automobiles do so. And the downward spiral has continued to the point of extinction of most public rail transit systems.

Mass transit was allowed to decline by the business-oriented government officials in most cities. Consumer desires were only partly responsible for this. Consumers did discover the freedom of movement of autos, and even in cities with excellent rail transit systems many prefer the auto for at least some types of travel. But consumers make their choices *from the alternatives available*. With no real rail transportation alternative to the automobile in most urban areas, consumers turned to it as a necessity. Ironically, as the auto and truck congestion of the cities has mounted between the 1950s and the 1980s, more and more citizens, and not a few business leaders, have called for new mass transit systems for their cities.

* * *

MASS TRANSIT IN OTHER CAPITALISTIC COUNTRIES

Comparative research on U.S. and German transportation systems by Yago has demonstrated the importance of looking at corporate power and economic structure. Mass rail transport developed in Germany before 1900. In the 1870s and 1880s the German national and local governments became interested in mass transit; at that time the coal, steel, iron, chemical, and electrical manufacturing companies were dominant in German capitalism. Interestingly, corporate executives in these industries supported the development of rail transportation; by 1900 the national and local governments had subsidized and institutionalized intraurban and interurban rail transport systems, which served the transport needs not only of the citizenry but also of the dominant coal, steel, chemical, and electrical industries. These industries also supplied equipment and supplies for the rail networks. In contrast, in the United States early transport companies were involved in manipulation and land speculation; transit service was rarely the central goal of the early rail transit firms. In contrast to Germany, dominance of U.S. industry by a major economic concentration did not come to the United States until after 1900, and when it did come, the auto-oil-rubber industrial complex was dominant. There was no other integrated industrial complex to contest this dominance of the auto-related firms, and governmental intervention was directed at support of motorization and the automobile. In Germany governmental intervention for mass rail transit had preceded this dominance of the motorization lobby. This suggests that the *timing* of the implementation of technological innovations in relation to corporate development is critical to their dominance, or lack of dominance, in cities and societies.

Interestingly, it was the Nazi interest in motorization and militarization in the 1930s that sharply increased the role of auto and truck transport in Germany. Adolf Hitler worked hard to motorize the military and the society. After World War II, the German auto lobby increased in power, and an auto transport system was placed alongside the rail transport system. However, the West German government and people have maintained a strong commitment to both systems; and the OPEC-generated oil crises of the 1970s brought an unparalleled revival of mass transit in Germany, whereas in the United States there was a more modest revival. The reason for the dramatic contrast between the two countries was that Germany had retained a rail passenger transport system, one that is still viable and energy conserving to the present day.

39

Scott's Law of Anarchist Calisthenics

FROM *Two Cheers for Anarchism: Six Easy Pieces on Autonomy, Dignity, and Meaningful Work and Play*

JAMES C. SCOTT

Sociologists are fascinated at the way people follow social norms, usually with little awareness of their conformity. Violating social norms can feel like a major undertaking; it can even be life changing. In what begins like a primer for any student who plans to study abroad, the author finds reason to challenge a practice of his host. It's not easy, but an awareness of the pressure to conform is the first step in sociological understanding. In the second part of the essay, the author offers an exciting possibility for changing many aspects of life to enhance "human agency" and the ability to work together.

I invented this law in Neubrandenburg, Germany, in the late summer of 1990.

In an effort to improve my barely existing German-language skills before spending a year in Berlin as a guest of the Wissenschaftskolleg, I hit on the idea of finding work on a farm rather than attending daily classes with pimply teenagers at a Goethe Institut center. Since the Wall had come down only a year earlier, I wondered whether I might be able to find a six-week summer job on a collective farm (landwirtschaftliche Produktionsgenossenschaft, or LPG), recently styled "cooperative," in eastern Germany. A friend at the Wissenschaftskolleg had, it turned out, a close relative whose brother-in-law was the head of a collective farm in the tiny village of Pletz. Though wary, the brother-in-law was willing to provide room and board in return for work and a handsome weekly rent.

As a plan for improving my German by the sink-or-swim method, it was perfect; as a plan for a pleasant and edifying farm visit, it was a nightmare. The villagers and, above all, my host were suspicious of my aims. Was I aiming to pore over the accounts of the collective farm and uncover "irregularities"? Was I an advance party for Dutch farmers, who were scouting the area for land to rent in the aftermath of the socialist bloc's collapse?

The collective farm at Pletz was a spectacular example of that collapse. Its specialization was growing "starch potatoes." They were no good for pommes frites, though pigs might eat them in a pinch; their intended use, when refined, was to provide the starch base for Eastern European cosmetics. Never had a market flatlined as quickly as the market for socialist bloc cosmetics the day after the Wall was breached. Mountain after mountain of starch potatoes lay rotting beside the rail sidings in the summer sun.

Besides wondering whether utter penury lay ahead for them and what role I might have in it, for my hosts there was the more immediate question of my frail comprehension of German and the danger it posed for their small farm. Would I let the pigs out the wrong gate and into a neighbor's field? Would I give the geese the feed intended for the bulls? Would I remember *always* to lock the door when I was working in the barn in case the Gypsies came? I had, it is true, given them more than ample cause for alarm in the first week, and they had taken to shouting at me in the vain hope we all seem to have that yelling will somehow overcome any language barrier. They managed to maintain a veneer of politeness, but the glances they exchanged at supper told me their patience was wearing thin. The aura of suspicion under which I labored, not to mention my manifest incompetence and incomprehension, was in turn getting on my nerves.

I decided, for my sanity as well as for theirs, to spend one day a week in the nearby town of Neubrandenburg. Getting there was not simple. The train didn't stop at Pletz unless you put up a flag along the tracks to indicate that a passenger was waiting and, on the way back, told the conductor that you wanted to get off at Pletz, in which case he would stop specially in the middle of the fields to let you out. Once in the town I wandered the streets, frequented cafes and bars, pretended to read German newspapers (surreptitiously consulting my little dictionary), and tried not to stick out.

The once-a-day train back from Neubrandenburg that could be made to stop at Pletz left at around ten at night. Lest I miss it and have to spend the night as a vagrant in this strange city, I made sure I was at the station at least half an hour early. Every week for six or seven weeks the same intriguing scene was played out in front of the railroad station, giving me ample time to ponder it both as observer and as participant. The idea of "anarchist calisthenics" was conceived in the course of what an anthropologist would call my participant observation.

Outside the station was a major, for Neubrandenburg at any rate, intersection. During the day there was a fairly brisk traffic of pedestrians, cars, and trucks, and a set of traffic lights to regulate it. Later in the evening, however, the vehicle traffic virtually ceased while the pedestrian traffic, if anything, swelled to take advantage of the cooler evening breeze. Regularly between 9:00 and 10:00 p.m. there would be fifty or sixty pedestrians, not a few of them tipsy, who would cross the intersection. The lights were timed, I suppose, for vehicle traffic at midday and not adjusted for the heavy evening foot traffic. Again and again, fifty or sixty people waited patiently at the corner for the light to change in their favor: four minutes, five minutes, perhaps longer. It seemed an eternity. The landscape of Neubrandenburg, on the Mecklenburg Plain, is flat as a pancake. Peering in each direction from the intersection, then, one could see a mile or so of roadway, with, typically, no traffic at all. Very occasionally a single, small Trabant made its slow, smoky way to the intersection.

Twice, perhaps, in the course of roughly five hours of my observing this scene did a pedestrian cross against the light, and then always to a chorus of scolding tongues and fingers wagging in disapproval. I too became part of the scene. If I had mangled my last exchange in German, sapping my confidence, I stood there with the rest for as long as it took for the light to change, afraid to brave the glares that awaited me if I crossed. If, more rarely, my last exchange in German had gone well and my confidence was high, I would cross against the light, thinking, to buck up my courage, that it was stupid to obey a minor law that, in this case, was so contrary to reason.

It surprised me how much I had to screw up my courage merely to cross a street against general disapproval. How little my rational convictions seemed to weigh against the pressure of their scolding. Striding out boldly into the intersection with apparent conviction made a more striking impression, perhaps, but it required more courage than I could normally muster.

As a way of justifying my conduct to myself, I began to rehearse a little discourse that I imagined delivering in perfect German. It went something like this. "You know, you and especially your grandparents could have used more of a spirit of lawbreaking. One day you will be called on to break a big law in the name of justice and rationality. Everything will depend on it. You have to be ready. How are you going to prepare for that day when it really matters? You have to stay 'in shape' so that when the big day comes you will be ready. What you need is 'anarchist calisthenics.' Every day or so break some trivial law that makes no sense, even if it's only jaywalking. Use your own head to judge whether a law is just or reasonable. That way, you'll keep trim; and when the big day comes, you'll be ready."

Judging when it makes sense to break a law requires careful thought, even in the relatively innocuous case of jaywalking. I was reminded of this when I visited a retired Dutch scholar whose work I had long admired. When I went to see him, he was an avowed Maoist and defender of the Cultural Revolution, and something of an incendiary in Dutch academic politics. He invited me to lunch at a Chinese restaurant near his apartment in the small town of Wageningen. We came to an intersection, and the light was against us. Now, Wageningen, like Neubrandenburg, is perfectly flat, and one can see for miles in all directions. There was absolutely nothing coming. Without thinking, I stepped into the street, and as I did so, Dr. Wertheim said, "James, you must wait." I protested weakly while regaining the curb, "But Dr. Wertheim, nothing is coming." "James," he replied instantly, "It would be a bad example for the children." I was both chastened and instructed. Here was a Maoist incendiary with, nevertheless, a fine-tuned, dare I say Dutch, sense of civic responsibility, while I was the Yankee cowboy heedless of the effects of my act on my fellow citizens. Now when I jaywalk I look around to see that there are no children who might be endangered by my bad example.

* * *

A MODEST, COUNTERINTUITIVE EXAMPLE:
RED LIGHT REMOVAL

The regulation of daily life is so ubiquitous and so embedded in our routines and expectations as to pass virtually unnoticed. Take the example of traffic lights at intersections. Invented in the United States after World War I, the traffic light substituted the judgment of the traffic engineer for the mutual give-and-take that had prevailed historically between pedestrians, carts, motor vehicles, and bicycles. Its purpose was to prevent accidents by imposing an engineered scheme of coordination. More than occasionally, the result has been the scene in Neubrandenburg with which I opened the book: scores of people waiting patiently for the light to change when it was perfectly apparent there was no traffic whatever. They were suspending their independent judgment out of habit, or perhaps out of a civic fear of the ultimate consequences of exercising it against the prevailing electronic legal order.

What would happen if there were no electronic order at the intersection, and motorists and pedestrians had to exercise their independent judgment? Since 1999, beginning in the city of Drachten, the Netherlands, this supposition has been put to the test with stunning results, leading to a wave of "red light removal" schemes across Europe and in the United States. Both the reasoning behind this small policy initiative and its results are, I believe, diagnostic for other, more far-reaching efforts to craft institutions that enlarge the scope for independent judgment and expand capacities.

Hans Moderman, the counterintuitive traffic engineer who first suggested the removal of a red light in Drachten in 2003, went on to promote the concept of "shared space," which took hold quickly in Europe. He began with the observation that, when an electrical failure incapacitated traffic lights, the result was improved flow rather than congestion. As an experiment, he replaced the busiest traffic-light intersection in Drachten, handling 22,000 cars a day, with a traffic circle, an extended cycle path, and a pedestrian area. In the two years following the removal of the traffic light, the number of accidents plummeted to only two, compared with thirty-six crashes in the four years prior. Traffic moves more briskly through the intersection when all drivers know they must be alert and use their common sense, while backups and the road rage associated with them have virtually disappeared. Monderman likened it to skaters in a crowded ice rink who manage successfully to tailor their movements to those of the other skaters. He also believed that an excess of signage led drivers to take their eyes off the road, and actually contributed to making junctions less safe.

Red light removal can, I believe, be seen as a modest training exercise in responsible driving and civic courtesy. Monderman was not against traffic lights in principle, he simply did not find any in Drachten that were truly useful in terms of safety, improving traffic flow, and lessening pollution. The traffic circle seems dangerous: and that is the point. He argued that when "motorists are made more wary about how they drive, they behave more carefully," and the statistics on "post–traffic light" accidents bear him out. Having to share the road with other users, and having no imperative coordination imposed by traffic lights, the context virtually requires alertness—an alertness abetted by the law, which, in the case of an accident where blame is hard to determine, presumptively blames the "strongest" (i.e., blames the car driver rather than the bicyclist, and the bicyclist rather than the pedestrian.)

The shared space concept of traffic management relies on the intelligence, good sense, and attentive observation of drivers, bicyclists, and pedestrians. At the same time, it arguably, in its small way, actually expands the skills and capacity of drivers, cyclists, and pedestrians to negotiate traffic without being treated like automata by thickets of imperative signs (Germany alone has 648 valid traffic symbols, which accumulate as one approaches a town) and signals. Monderman believed that the more numerous the prescriptions, the more it impelled drivers to seek the maximum advantage within the rules: speeding up between signals, beating the light, avoiding all unprescribed courtesies. Drivers had learned to run the maze of prescriptions to their maximum advantage. Without going overboard about its world-shaking significance, Moderman's innovation does make a palpable contribution to the gross human product.

The effect of what was a paradigm shift in traffic management was euphoria. Small towns in the Netherlands put up one sign boasting that they were "Free of Traffic Signs" (*Verkeersbordvrij*), and a conference discussing the new philosophy proclaimed "Unsafe is safe."

PART SEVEN

SOCIAL INSTITUTIONS: FAMILY AND RELIGION

40

The Radical Idea of Marrying for Love*

FROM *Marriage, a History*

STEPHANIE COONTZ

As Peter Berger discussed in Essay 1, what everyone knows is often not actually the case. Social historian Stephanie Coontz, in the best sociological fashion, explains with insight and humor how marital bonding and long-term partnerships have only recently been the responsibility of "so strong yet transient an emotion" as love. Author of the very popular The Way We Never Were *and other books, Coontz's historical and anthropological evidence provides some welcome understanding of marital patterns that may seem inappropriate, unnatural, or even immoral to those of us raised to believe there is one person with whom we can forever be happy. Record numbers of young people today are delaying marriage, and many who will never marry will be parents and have long-term monogamous relationships. Perhaps the Western version of love and marriage is changing, and those who embrace it can find guidance with Coontz's sociological insights.*

George Bernard Shaw described marriage as an institution that brings together two people "under the influence of the most violent, most insane, most delusive, and most transient of passions. They are required to swear that they will remain in that excited, abnormal, and exhausting condition continuously until death do them part."

Shaw's comment was amusing when he wrote it at the beginning of the twentieth century, and it still makes us smile today, because it pokes fun at the unrealistic expectations that spring from a dearly held cultural ideal—that marriage should be based on intense, profound love and a couple should maintain their ardor until death do them part. But for thousands of years the joke would have fallen flat.

For most of history it was inconceivable that people would choose their mates on the basis of something as fragile and irrational as love and then focus all their sexual, intimate, and altruistic desires on the resulting marriage. In fact, many historians, sociologists, and anthropologists used to think romantic love was a recent Western invention. This is not true. People have always fallen in love, and throughout the ages many couples have loved each other deeply.

---

*Footnotes and references can be found in the original publication of Stephanie Coontz's *Marriage, a History.* [*Editors' note*]

But only rarely in history has love been seen as the main reason for getting married. When someone did advocate such a strange belief, it was no laughing matter. Instead, it was considered a serious threat to social order.

In some cultures and times, true love was actually thought to be incompatible with marriage. Plato believed love was a wonderful emotion that led men to behave honorably. But the Greek philosopher was referring not to the love of women, "such as the meaner men feel," but to the love of one man for another.

Other societies considered it good if love developed after marriage or thought love should be factored in along with the more serious considerations involved in choosing a mate. But even when past societies did welcome or encourage married love, they kept it on a short leash. Couples were not to put their feelings for each other above more important commitments, such as their ties to parents, siblings, cousins, neighbors, or God.

In ancient India, falling in love before marriage was seen as a disruptive, almost antisocial act. The Greeks thought lovesickness was a type of insanity, a view that was adopted by medieval commentators in Europe. In the Middle Ages the French defined love as a "derangement of the mind" that could be cured by sexual intercourse, either with the loved one or with a different partner. This cure assumed, as Oscar Wilde once put it, that the quickest way to conquer yearning and temptation was to yield immediately and move on to more important matters.

In China, excessive love between husband and wife was seen as a threat to the solidarity of the extended family. Parents could force a son to divorce his wife if her behavior or work habits didn't please them, whether or not he loved her. They could also require him to take a concubine if his wife did not produce a son. If a son's romantic attachment to his wife rivaled his parents' claims on the couple's time and labor, the parents might even send her back to her parents. In the Chinese language the term *love* did not traditionally apply to feelings between husband and wife. It was used to describe an illicit, socially disapproved relationship. In the 1920s a group of intellectuals invented a new word for love between spouses because they thought such a radical new idea required its own special label.

In Europe, during the twelfth and thirteenth centuries, adultery became idealized as the highest form of love among the aristocracy. According to the Countess of Champagne, it was impossible for true love to "exert its powers between two people who are married to each other."

In twelfth-century France, Andreas Capellanus, chaplain to Countess Marie of Troyes, wrote a treatise on the principles of courtly love. The first rule was that "marriage is no real excuse for not loving." But he meant loving someone outside the marriage. As late as the eighteenth century the French essayist Montaigne wrote that any man who was in love with his wife was a man so dull that no one else could love him.

Courtly love probably loomed larger in literature than in real life. But for centuries, noblemen and kings fell in love with courtesans rather than the wives they married for political reasons. Queens and noblewomen had to be more discreet than their husbands, but they too looked beyond marriage for love and intimacy.

This sharp distinction between love and marriage was common among the lower and middle classes as well. Many of the songs and stories popular among peasants in medieval Europe mocked married love.

The most famous love affair of the Middle Ages was that of Peter Abelard, a well-known theologian in France, and Héloïse, the brilliant niece of a fellow churchman at Notre Dame. The two eloped without marrying, and she bore him a child. In an attempt to save his career but still placate Héloïse's furious uncle, Abelard proposed they marry in secret. This would mean that Héloïse would not be living in sin, while Abelard could still pursue his church ambitions. But Heloise resisted the idea, arguing that marriage would not only harm his career but also undermine their love.

LOVE, IN AND OUT OF MARRIAGE

"Nothing Is More Impure than to Love One's Wife as if She Were a Mistress"

Even in societies that esteemed married love, couples were expected to keep it under strict control. In many cultures, public displays of love between husband and wife were considered unseemly. A Roman was expelled from the Senate because he had kissed his wife in front of his daughter. Plutarch conceded that the punishment was somewhat extreme but pointed out that everyone knew that it was "disgraceful" to kiss one's wife in front of others.

Some Greek and Roman philosophers even said that a man who loved his wife with "excessive" ardor was "an adulterer." Many centuries later Catholic and Protestant theologians argued that husbands and wives who loved each other too much were committing the sin of idolatry. Theologians chided wives who used endearing nicknames for their husbands, because such familiarity on a wife's part undermined the husband's authority and the awe that his wife should feel for him. Although medieval Muslim thinkers were more approving of sexual passion between husband and wife than were Christian theologians, they also insisted that too much intimacy between husband and wife weakened a believer's devotion to God. And, like their European counterparts, secular writers in the Islamic world believed that love thrived best outside marriage.

Many cultures still frown on placing love at the center of marriage. In Africa, the Fulbe people of northern Cameroon do not see love as a legitimate emotion, especially within marriage. One observer reports that in conversations with their neighbors, Fulbe women "vehemently deny emotional attachment to a husband." In many peasant and working-class communities, too much love between husband and wife is seen as disruptive because it encourages the couple to withdraw from the wider web of dependence that makes the society work.

As a result, men and women often relate to each other in public, even after marriage, through the conventions of a war between the sexes, disguising the fondness they may really feel. They describe their marital behavior, no matter how exemplary it may actually be, in terms of convenience, compulsion, or self-interest rather than love or sentiment. In Cockney rhyming slang, the term for *wife* is *trouble and strife.*

Whether it is valued or not, love is rarely seen as the main ingredient for marital success. Among the Taita of Kenya, recognition and approval of married love are widespread. An eighty-year-old man recalled that his fourth wife "was the wife of my heart. . . . I could look at her and no words would pass, just a smile." In this society, where men often take several wives, women speak wistfully about how wonderful it is to be a "love wife." But only a small percentage of Taita women experience this luxury, because a Taita man normally marries a love wife only after he has accumulated a few more practical wives.

In many cultures, love has been seen as a desirable outcome of marriage but not as a good reason for getting married in the first place. The Hindu tradition celebrates love and sexuality in marriage, but love and sexual attraction are not considered valid reasons for marriage. "First we marry, then we'll fall in love" is the formula. As recently as 1975, a survey of college students in the Indian state of Karnataka found that only 18 percent "strongly" approved of marriages made on the basis of love, while 32 percent completely disapproved.

Similarly, in early modern Europe most people believed that love developed after marriage. Moralists of the sixteenth and seventeenth centuries argued that if a husband and wife each had a good character, they would probably come to love each other. But they insisted that youths be guided by their families in choosing spouses who were worth learning to love. It was up to parents and other relatives to make sure that the woman had a dowry or the man had a good yearly income. Such capital, it was thought, would certainly help love flower.

"[I]t Made Me Really Sick, Just as I Have Formerly Been When in Love with My Wife"

I don't believe that people of the past had more control over their hearts than we do today or that they were incapable of the deep love so many individuals now hope to achieve in marriage. But love in marriage was seen as a bonus, not as a necessity. The great Roman statesman Cicero exchanged many loving letters with his wife, Terentia, during their thirty-year marriage. But that didn't stop him from divorcing her when she was no longer able to support him in the style to which he had become accustomed.

Sometimes people didn't have to make such hard choices. In seventeenth-century America, Anne Bradstreet was the favorite child of an indulgent father who gave her the kind of education usually reserved for elite boys. He later arranged her marriage to a cherished childhood friend who eventually became the governor of Massachusetts. Combining love, duty, material security, and marriage was not the strain for her that it was for many men and women of that era. Anne wrote love poems to her husband that completely ignored the injunction of Puritan ministers not to place one's spouse too high in one's affections. "If ever two were one," she wrote him, "then surely we; if ever man were loved by wife, then thee. . . . I prize thy love more than whole mines of gold, or all the riches that the East doth hold; my love is such that rivers cannot quench, nor ought but love from thee, give recompense."

The famous seventeenth-century English diarist Samuel Pepys chose to marry for love rather than profit. But he was not as lucky as Anne. After hearing a particularly stirring piece of music, Pepys recorded that it "did wrap up my soul so that it made me really sick, just as I have formerly been when in love with my wife." Pepys would later disinherit a nephew for marrying under the influence of so strong yet transient an emotion.

There were always youngsters who resisted the pressures of parents, kin, and neighbors to marry for practical reasons rather than love, but most accepted or even welcomed the interference of parents and others in arranging their marriages. A common saying in early modern Europe was "He who marries for love has good nights and bad days." Nowadays a bitter wife or husband might ask, "Whatever possessed me to think I loved you enough to marry you?" Through most of the past, he or she was more likely to have asked, "Whatever possessed me to marry you just because I loved you?"

"Happily Ever After"

Through most of the past, individuals hoped to find love, or at least "tranquil affection," in marriage. But nowhere did they have the same recipe for marital happiness that prevails in most contemporary Western countries. Today there is general agreement on what it takes for a couple to live "happily ever after." First, they must love each other deeply and choose each other unswayed by outside pressure. From then on, each must make the partner the top priority in life, putting that relationship above any and all competing ties. A husband and wife, we believe, owe their highest obligations and deepest loyalties to each other and the children they raise. Parents and in-laws should not be allowed to interfere in the marriage. Married couples should be best friends, sharing their most intimate feelings and secrets. They should express affection openly but also talk candidly about problems. And of course they should be sexually faithful to each other.

This package of expectations about love, marriage, and sex, however, is extremely rare. When we look at the historical record around the world, the customs of modern America and Western Europe appear exotic and exceptional.

Leo Tolstoy once remarked that all happy families are alike, while every unhappy family is unhappy in its own way. But the more I study the history of marriage, the more I think the opposite is true. Most unhappy marriages in history share common patterns, leaving their tear-stained—and sometimes bloodstained—records across the ages. But each happy, successful marriage seems to be happy in its own way. And for most of human history, successful marriages have not been happy in *our* way.

A woman in ancient China might bring one or more of her sisters to her husband's home as backup wives. Eskimo couples often had cospousal arrangements, in which each partner had sexual relations with the other's spouse. In Tibet and parts of India, Kashmir, and Nepal, a woman may be married to two or more brothers, all of whom share sexual access to her.

In modern America, such practices are the stuff of trash TV: "I caught my sister in bed with my husband"; "My parents brought their lovers into our home"; "My wife slept with my brother"; "It broke my heart to share my husband with another woman." In other cultures, individuals often find such practices normal and comforting. The children of Eskimo cospouses felt that they shared a special bond, and society viewed them as siblings. Among Tibetan brothers who share the same wife, sexual jealousy is rare.

In some cultures, cowives see one another as allies rather than rivals. In Botswana women add an interesting wrinkle to the old European saying "Woman's work is never done." There they say: "Without cowives, a woman's work is never done." A researcher who worked with the Cheyenne Indians of the United States in the 1930s and 1940s told of a chief who tried to get rid of two of his three wives. All three women defied him, saying that if he sent two of them away, he would have to give away the third as well.

Even when societies celebrated the love between husband and wife as a pleasant by-product of marriage, people rarely had a high regard for marital intimacy. Chinese commentators on marriage discouraged a wife from confiding in her husband or telling him about her day. A good wife did not bother her husband with news of her own activities and feelings but treated him "like a guest," no matter how long they had been married. A husband who demonstrated open affection for his wife, even at home, was seen as having a weak character.

In the early eighteenth century, American lovers often said they looked for "candor" in each other. But they were not talking about the soul-baring intimacy idealized by modern Americans, and they certainly did not believe that couples should talk frankly about their grievances. Instead candor meant fairness, kindliness, and good temper. People wanted a spouse who did *not* pry too deeply. The ideal mate, wrote U.S. President John Adams in his diary, was willing "to palliate faults and Mistakes, to put the best Construction upon Words and Action, and to forgive Injuries."

Modern marital advice books invariably tell husbands and wives to put each other first. But in many societies, marriage ranks very low in the hierarchy of meaningful relationships. People's strongest loyalties and emotional connections may be reserved for members of their birth families. On the North American plains in the 1930s, a Kiowa Indian woman commented to a researcher that "a woman can always get another husband, but she has only one brother." In China it was said that "you have only one family, but you can always get another wife." In Christian texts prior to the seventeenth century, the word *love* usually referred to feelings toward God or neighbors rather than toward a spouse.

In Confucian philosophy, the two strongest relationships in family life are between father and son and between elder brother and younger brother, not between husband and wife. In thirteenth-century China the bond between father and son was so much stronger than the bond between husband and wife that legal commentators insisted a couple do nothing if the patriarch of the household raped his son's wife. In one case, although the judge was sure that a woman's rape accusation against her father-in-law was true, he ordered the young man to give up his sentimental desire "to grow old together" with his wife. Loyalty to parents was paramount, and therefore the son should send his wife back to her own father, who could then marry her to someone else. Sons were sometimes ordered beaten for siding with their wives against their father. No wonder that for 1,700 years women in one Chinese province guarded a secret language that they used to commiserate with each other about the griefs of marriage.

In many societies of the past, sexual loyalty was not a high priority. The expectation of mutual fidelity is a rather recent invention. Numerous cultures have allowed husbands to seek sexual gratification outside marriage. Less frequently, but often enough to challenge common preconceptions, wives have also been allowed to do this without threatening the marriage. In a study of 109 societies, anthropologists found that only 48 forbade extramarital sex to both husbands and wives.

When a woman has sex with someone other than her husband and he doesn't object, anthropologists have traditionally called it wife loaning. When a man does it, they call it male privilege. But in some societies the choice to switch partners rests with the woman. Among the Dogon of West Africa, young married women publicly pursued extramarital relationships with the encouragement of their mothers. Among the Rukuba of Nigeria, a wife can take a lover at the time of her first marriage. This relationship is so embedded in accepted custom that the lover has the right, later in life, to ask his former mistress to marry her daughter to his son.

Among the Eskimo of northern Alaska, as I noted earlier, husbands and wives, with mutual consent, established comarriages with other couples. Some anthropologists believe cospouse relationships were a more socially acceptable outlet for sexual attraction than was marriage itself. Expressing open jealousy about the sexual relationships involved was considered boorish.

Such different notions of marital rights and obligations made divorce and remarriage less emotionally volatile for the Eskimo than it is for most modern

Americans. In fact, the Eskimo believed that a remarried person's partner had an obligation to allow the former spouse, as well as any children of that union, the right to fish, hunt, and gather in the new spouse's territory.

Several small-scale societies in South America have sexual and marital norms that are especially startling for Europeans and North Americans. In these groups, people believe that any man who has sex with a woman during her pregnancy contributes part of his biological substance to the child. The husband is recognized as the primary father, but the woman's lover or lovers also have paternal responsibilities, including the obligation to share food with the woman and her child in the future. During the 1990s researchers taking life histories of elderly Bari women in Venezuela found that most had taken lovers during at least one of their pregnancies. Their husbands were usually aware and did not object. When a woman gave birth, she would name all the men she had slept with since learning she was pregnant, and a woman attending the birth would tell each of these men: "You have a child."

In Europe and the United States today such an arrangement would be a sure-fire recipe for jealousy, bitter breakups, and very mixed-up kids. But among the Bari people this practice was in the best interests of the child. The secondary fathers were expected to provide the child with fish and game, with the result that a child with a secondary father was twice as likely to live to the age of fifteen as a brother or sister without such a father.

Few other societies have incorporated extramarital relationships so successfully into marriage and child rearing. But all these examples of differing marital and sexual norms make it difficult to claim there is some universal model for the success or happiness of a marriage.

About two centuries ago Western Europe and North America developed a whole set of new values about the way to organize marriage and sexuality, and many of these values are now spreading across the globe. In this Western model, people expect marriage to satisfy more of their psychological and social needs than ever before. Marriage is supposed to be free of the coercion, violence, and gender inequalities that were tolerated in the past. Individuals want marriage to meet most of their needs for intimacy and affection and all their needs for sex.

Never before in history had societies thought that such a set of high expectations about marriage was either realistic or desirable. Although many Europeans and Americans found tremendous joy in building their relationships around these values, the adoption of these unprecedented goals for marriage had unanticipated and revolutionary consequences that have since come to threaten the stability of the entire institution.

41

Domestic Networks

FROM *All Our Kin: Strategies for Survival in a Black Community*

CAROL B. STACK

How far do family ties and responsibilities extend? For many African American families they extend beyond parents and children to cousins, aunts, uncles, and even fictive kin. Decades of discrimination and institutional racism have left many people with few resources of their own to draw on in times of need, and so helping relationships have remained a critical feature of the extended family. Linking ethnicity, class, and gender, Carol Stack reminds us of the strength and resilience of the human community.

In The Flats the responsibility for providing food, care, clothing, and shelter and for socializing children within domestic networks may be spread over several households. Which household a given individual belongs to is not a particularly meaningful question, as we have seen that daily domestic organization depends on several things: where people sleep, where they eat, and where they offer their time and money. Although those who eat together and contribute toward the rent are generally considered by Flats residents to form minimal domestic units, household changes rarely affect the exchanges and daily dependencies of those who take part in common activity.

The residence patterns and cooperative organization of people linked in domestic networks demonstrate the stability and collective power of family life in The Flats. Michael Lee grew up in The Flats and now has a job in Chicago. On a visit to The Flats, Michael described the residence and domestic organization of his kin. "Most of my kin in The Flats lived right here on Cricket Street, numbers sixteen, eighteen, and twenty-two, in these three apartment buildings joined together. My mama decided it would be best for me and my three brothers and sister to be on Cricket Street too. My daddy's mother had a small apartment in this building, her sister had one in the basement, and another brother and his family took a larger apartment upstairs. My uncle was really good to us. He got us things we wanted and he controlled us. All the women kept the younger kids together during the day. They cooked together too. It was good living."

Yvonne Diamond, a forty-year-old Chicago woman, moved to The Flats from Chicago with her four children. Soon afterwards they were evicted. "The landlord said he was going to build a parking lot there, but he never did. The old place is still standing and has folks in it today. My husband's mother and father

435

took me and the kids in and watched over them while I had my baby. We stayed on after my husband's mother died, and my husband joined us when he got a job in The Flats."

When families or individuals in The Flats are evicted, other kinsmen usually take them in. Households in The Flats expand or contract with the loss of a job, a death in the family, the beginning or end of a sexual partnership, or the end of a friendship. Welfare workers, researchers, and landlords have long known that the poor must move frequently. What is much less understood is the relationship between residence and domestic organization in the black community.

The spectrum of economic and legal pressures that act upon ghetto residents, requiring them to move—unemployment, welfare requirements, housing shortages, high rents, eviction—are clear-cut examples of external pressures affecting the daily lives of the poor. Flats residents are evicted from their dwellings by landlords who want to raise rents, tear the building down, or rid themselves of tenants who complain about rats, roaches, and the plumbing. Houses get condemned by the city on landlords' requests so that they can force tenants to move. After an eviction, a landlord can rent to a family in such great need of housing that they will not complain for a while.

Poor housing conditions and unenforced housing standards coupled with overcrowding, unemployment, and poverty produce hazardous living conditions and residence changes. "Our whole family had to move when the gas lines sprung a leak in our apartment and my son set the place on fire by accident," Sam Summer told me. "The place belonged to my sister-in-law's grandfather. We had been living there with my mother, my brother's eight children, and our eight children. My father lived in the basement apartment 'cause he and my mother were separated. After the fire burned the whole place down, we all moved to two places down the street near my cousin's house."

When people are unable to pay their rent because they have been temporarily "cut off aid," because the welfare office is suspicious of their eligibility, because they gave their rent money to a kinsman to help him through a crisis or illness, or because they were laid off from their job, they receive eviction notices almost immediately. Lydia Watson describes a chain of events starting with the welfare office stopping her sister's welfare checks, leading to an eviction, co-residence, overcrowding, and eventually murder. Lydia sadly related the story to me. "My oldest sister was cut off aid the day her husband got out of jail. She and her husband and their three children were evicted from their apartment and they came to live with us. We were in crowded conditions already. I had my son, my other sister was there with her two kids, and my mother was about going crazy. My mother put my sister's husband out 'cause she found out he was a dope addict. He came back one night soon after that and murdered my sister. After my sister's death my mother couldn't face living in Chicago any longer. One of my other sisters who had been adopted and raised by my mother's paternal grandmother visited us and persuaded us to move to The Flats, where she was staying. All of us moved there—my mother, my two sisters and their children, my two baby sisters, and my dead sister's children. My sister who had been staying in The Flats found us a house across the street from her own."

Overcrowded dwellings and the impossibility of finding adequate housing in The Flats have many long-term consequences regarding where and with whom children live. Terence Platt described where and with whom his kin lived when he was a child. "My brother stayed with my aunt, my mother's sister, and her husband until he was ten, 'cause he was the oldest in our family and we didn't have enough room—but he stayed with us most every weekend. Finally my aunt moved into the house behind ours with her husband, her brother, and my brother; my sisters and brothers and I lived up front with my mother and her old man."

KIN-STRUCTURED LOCAL NETWORKS

The material and cultural support needed to absorb, sustain, and socialize community members in The Flats is provided by networks of cooperating kinsmen. Local coalitions formed from these networks of kin and friends are mobilized within domestic networks; domestic organization is diffused over many kin-based households which themselves have elastic boundaries.

People in The Flats are immersed in a domestic web of a large number of kin and friends whom they can count on. From a social viewpoint, relationships within the community are "organized on the model of kin relationships." . . . Kin-constructs such as the perception of parenthood, the culturally determined criteria which affect the shape of personal kindreds, and the idiom of kinship, prescribe kin who can be recruited into domestic networks.

There are similarities in function between domestic networks and domestic groups which [one scholar] characterizes as "workshops of social reproduction." Both domains include three generations of members linked collaterally or otherwise. Kinship, jural and affectional bonds, and economic factors affect the composition of both domains and residential alignments within them. There are two striking differences between domestic networks and domestic groups. Domestic networks are not visible groups, because they do not have an obvious nucleus or defined boundary. But since a primary focus of domestic networks is child-care arrangements, the cooperation of a cluster of adult females is apparent. Participants in domestic networks are recruited from personal kindreds and friendships, but the personnel changes with fluctuating economic needs, changing life styles, and vacillating personal relationships.

In some loosely and complexly structured cognatic systems, kin-structured local networks (not groups) emerge. Localized coalitions of persons drawn from personal kindreds can be organized as networks of kinsmen. Good enough . . . correctly points out that anthropologists frequently describe "localized kin groups," but rarely describe kin-structured local groups. . . . The localized, kin-based, cooperative coalitions of people described in this chapter are organized as kin-structured domestic networks. For brevity, I refer to them as domestic networks.

* * *

GENEROSITY AND POVERTY

The combination of arbitrary and repressive economic forces and social behavior, modified by successive generations of poverty, make it almost impossible for people to break out of poverty. There is no way for those families poor enough to receive welfare to acquire any surplus cash which can be saved for emergencies or for acquiring adequate appliances or a home or a car. In contrast to the middle class, who are pressured to spend and save, the poor are not even permitted to establish an equity.

The following examples from Magnolia and Calvin Waters's life illustrates the ways in which the poor are prohibited from acquiring any surplus which might enable them to change their economic condition or life style.

In 1971 Magnolia's uncle died in Mississippi and left an unexpected inheritance of $1,500 to Magnolia and Calvin Waters. The cash came from a small run-down farm which Magnolia's uncle sold shortly before he died. It was the first time in their lives that Magnolia or Calvin ever had a cash reserve. Their first hope was to buy a home and use the money as a down payment.

Calvin had retired from his job as a seasonal laborer the year before and the family was on welfare. AFDC alloted the family $100 per month for rent. The housing that the family had been able to obtain over the years for their nine children at $100 or less was always small, roach infested, with poor plumbing and heating. The family was frequently evicted. Landlords complained about the noise and often observed an average of ten to fifteen children playing in the household. Magnolia and Calvin never even anticipated that they would be able to buy a home.

Three days after they received the check, news of its arrival spread throughout their domestic network. One niece borrowed $25 from Magnolia so that her phone would not be turned off. Within a week the welfare office knew about the money. Magnolia's children were immediately cut off welfare, including medical coverage and food stamps. Magnolia was told that she would not receive a welfare grant for her children until the money was used up, and she was given a minimum of four months in which to spend the money. The first surplus the family ever acquired was effectively taken from them.

During the weeks following the arrival of the money, Magnolia and Calvin's obligations to the needs of kin remained the same, but their ability to meet these needs had temporarily increased. When another uncle became very ill in the South, Magnolia and her older sister, Augusta, were called to sit by his side. Magnolia bought round-trip train tickets for both of them and for her three youngest children. When the uncle died, Magnolia bought round-trip train tickets so that she and Augusta could attend the funeral. Soon after his death, Augusta's first "old man" died in The Flats and he had no kin to pay for the burial. Augusta asked Magnolia to help pay for digging the grave. Magnolia was unable to refuse. Another sister's rent was two months overdue and Magnolia feared that she would get evicted. This sister was seriously ill and had no source of income. Magnolia paid her rent.

Winter was cold and Magnolia's children and grandchildren began staying home from school because they did not have warm winter coats and adequate shoes or boots. Magnolia and Calvin decided to buy coats, hats, and shoes for all of the children (at least fifteen). Magnolia also bought a winter coat for herself and Calvin bought himself a pair of sturdy shoes.

Within a month and a half, all of the money was gone. The money was channeled into the hands of the same individuals who ordinarily participate in daily domestic exchanges, but the premiums were temporarily higher. All of the money was quickly spent for necessary, compelling reasons.

Thus random fluctuations in the meager flow of available cash and goods tend to be of considerable importance to the poor. A late welfare check, sudden sickness, robbery, and other unexpected losses cannot be overcome with a cash reserve like more well-to-do families hold for emergencies. Increases in cash are either taken quickly from the poor by the welfare agencies or dissipated through the kin network.

Those living in poverty have little or no chance to escape from the economic situation into which they were born. Nor do they have the power to control the expansion or contraction of welfare benefits . . . or of employment opportunities, both of which have a momentous effect on their daily lives. In times of need, the only predictable resources that can be drawn upon are their own children and parents, and the fund of kin and friends obligated to them.

42

From *The Protestant Ethic and the Spirit of Capitalism*

MAX WEBER

Why did capitalism (and industrialization) emerge in Western Europe rather than in ancient China, Egypt, or India? All had sufficient knowledge and resources. What made the difference? In this classic study, Max Weber (1864–1920) presents his famous thesis about the connection between early Protestant beliefs and the emergence of industrial capitalism. His view of the fate of the Protestant ethic is, to many people, prophetic for the twentieth and twenty-first centuries. A contemporary of Émile Durkheim, Weber began writing soon after the death of Karl Marx. Weber is one of sociology's founders.

In the title of this study is used the somewhat pretentious phrase, the *spirit* of capitalism. What is to be understood by it? The attempt to give anything like a definition of it brings out certain difficulties which are in the very nature of this type of investigation.

If any object can be found to which this term can be applied with any understandable meaning, it can only be an historical individual, i.e., a complex of elements associated in historical reality which we unite into a conceptual whole from the standpoint of their cultural significance.*

* * *

"Remember, that *time* is money. He that can earn ten shillings a day by his labour, and goes abroad, or sits idle, one half of that day, though he spends but sixpence during his diversion or idleness, ought not to reckon *that* the only expense; he has really spent, or rather thrown away, five shillings besides.

* * *

"Remember, that money is of the prolific, generating nature. Money can beget money, and its offspring can beget more, and so on. Five shillings turned is six, turned again it is seven and threepence, and so on, till it becomes a hundred pounds. The more there is of it, the more it produces every turning, so that the profits rise quicker and quicker. He that kills a breeding sow, destroys

---

*This is what Weber calls an "ideal type" concept, which has become a commonly used feature of sociology. [*Editors' note*]

all her offspring to the thousandth generation. He that murders a crown, destroys all that it might have produced, even scores of pounds.

* * *

"For six pounds a year you may have the use of one hundred pounds, provided you are a man of known prudence and honesty.

"He that spends a groat a day idly, spends idly above six pounds a year, which is the price for the use of one hundred pounds.

"He that wastes idly a groat's worth of his time per day, one day with another, wastes the privilege of using one hundred pounds each day.

"He that idly loses five shillings' worth of time, loses five shillings, and might as prudently throw five shillings into the sea.

"He that loses five shillings, not only loses that sum, but all the advantage that might be made by turning it in dealing, which by the time that a young man becomes old, will amount to a considerable sum of money."

It is Benjamin Franklin who preaches to us in these [preceding paragraphs].

* * *

That it is the spirit of capitalism which here speaks in characteristic fashion, no one will doubt, however little we may wish to claim that everything which could be understood as pertaining to that spirit is contained in it. Let us pause a moment to consider this passage, the philosophy of which Kürnberger sums up in the words, "They make tallow out of cattle and money out of men." The peculiarity of this philosophy of avarice appears to be the ideal of the honest man of recognized credit, and above all the idea of a duty of the individual toward the increase of his capital, which is assumed as an end in itself. Truly what is here preached is not simply a means of making one's way in the world, but a peculiar ethic. The infraction of its rules is treated not as foolishness but as forgetfulness of duty. That is the essence of the matter. It is not mere business astuteness, that sort of thing is common enough, it is an ethos: *This* is the quality which interests us.

* * *

And in truth this peculiar idea, so familiar to us to-day, but in reality so little a matter of course, of one's duty in a calling, is what is most characteristic of the social ethic of capitalistic culture, and is in a sense the fundamental basis of it. It is an obligation which the individual is supposed to feel and does feel towards the content of his professional activity, no matter in what it consists, in particular no matter whether it appears on the surface as a utilization of his personal powers, or only of his material possessions (as capital).

* * *

Thus the capitalism of today, which has come to dominate economic life, educates and selects the economic subjects which it needs through a process of economic survival of the fittest. But here one can easily see the limits of the concept of selection as a means of historical explanation. In order that a manner of life so well adapted to the peculiarities of capitalism could be selected at all, i.e. should come to dominate others, it had to originate somewhere, and not in isolated individuals alone, but as a way of life common to whole groups of men. This origin is what really needs explanation. Concerning the doctrine of the more naïve historical materialism,† that such ideas originate as a reflection or superstructure of economic situations. . . . At this point it will suffice for our purpose to call attention to the fact that without doubt, in the country of Benjamin Franklin's birth (Massachusetts), the spirit of capitalism (in the sense we have attached to it) was present before the capitalistic order. There were complaints of a peculiarly calculating sort of profit-seeking in New England, as distinguished from other parts of America, as early as 1632. It is further undoubted that capitalism remained far less developed in some of the neighbouring colonies, the later Southern States of the United States of America, in spite of the fact that these latter were founded by large capitalists for business motives.

* * *

To be sure the capitalistic form of an enterprise and the spirit in which it is run generally stand in some sort of adequate relationship to each other, but not in one of necessary interdependence. Nevertheless, we provisionally use the expression spirit of (modern) capitalism to describe that attitude which seeks profit rationally and systematically in the manner which we have illustrated by the example of Benjamin Franklin. This, however, is justified by the historical fact that that attitude of mind has on the one hand found its most suitable expression in capitalistic enterprise, while on the other the enterprise has derived its most suitable motive force from the spirit of capitalism.

* * *

It will be our task to find out whose intellectual child the particular concrete form of rational thought was, from which the idea of a calling and the devotion to labour in the calling has grown, which is, as we have seen, so irrational from the standpoint of pure . . . self-interest, but which has been and still is one of the most characteristic elements of our capitalistic culture. We are here particularly interested in the origin of precisely the irrational element which lies in this, as in every conception of a calling.

---

†Weber is critiquing Marx's idea of historical materialism. [*Editors' note*]

LUTHER'S CONCEPTION OF THE CALLING

* * *

Now it is unmistakable that even in the German word *Beruf,* and perhaps still more clearly in the English *calling,* a religious conception, that of a task set by God, is at least suggested. . . . And if we trace the history of the word through the civilized languages, it appears that neither the predominantly Catholic peoples nor those of classical antiquity have possessed any expression of similar connotation for what we know as a calling (in the sense of a life-task, a definite field in which to work), while one has existed for all predominantly Protestant peoples.

* * *

Like the meaning of the word, the idea is new, a product of the Reformation. . . . It is true that certain suggestions of the positive valuation of routine activity in the world, which is contained in this conception of the calling, had already existed in the Middle Ages, and even in late Hellenistic antiquity. We shall speak of that later. But at least one thing was unquestionably new: the valuation of the fulfilment of duty in worldly affairs as the highest form which the moral activity of the individual could assume. This it was which inevitably gave every-day worldly activity a religious significance, and which first created the conception of a calling in this sense. The conception of the calling thus brings out that central dogma of all Protestant denominations. . . . The only way of living acceptably to God was not to surpass worldly morality in monastic asceticism, but solely through the fulfilment of the obligations imposed upon the individual by his position in the world. That was his calling.

Luther developed the conception in the course of the first decade of his activity as a reformer.

* * *

[L]abour in a calling appears to him as the outward expression of brotherly love. This he proves by the observation that the division of labour forces every individual to work for others. . . . [T]he fulfilment of worldly duties is under all circumstances the only way to live acceptably to God. It and it alone is the will of God, and hence every legitimate calling has exactly the same worth in the sight of God.

* * *

ASCETICISM AND THE SPIRIT OF CAPITALISM

[I]f that God, whose hand the Puritan sees in all the occurrences of life, shows one of His elect a chance of profit, he must do it with a purpose. Hence the faithful Christian must follow the call by taking advantage of the opportunity. "If God show you a way in which you may lawfully get more than in another way (without wrong to your soul or to any other), if you refuse this, and choose the less gainful way, you cross one of the ends of your calling, and you refuse to be God's steward, and to accept His gifts and use them for Him when He requireth it: you may labour to be rich for God, though not for the flesh and sin."‡

* * *

Wealth is thus bad ethically only in so far as it is a temptation to idleness and sinful enjoyment of life, and its acquisition is bad only when it is with the purpose of later living merrily and without care. But as a performance of duty in a calling it is not only morally permissible, but actually enjoined. The parable of the servant who was rejected because he did not increase the talent which was entrusted to him seemed to say so directly. To wish to be poor was, it was often argued, the same as wishing to be unhealthy; it is objectionable as a glorification of works and derogatory to the glory of God. Especially begging, on the part of one able to work, is not only the sin of slothfulness, but a violation of the duty of brotherly love according to the Apostle's own word.

The emphasis on the ascetic importance of a fixed calling provided an ethical justification of the modern specialized division of labour. In a similar way the providential interpretation of profit-making justified the activities of the business man. . . . But, on the other hand, it has the highest ethical appreciation of the sober, middle-class, self-made man. "God blesseth His trade" is a stock remark about those good men who had successfully followed the divine hints.

* * *

Let us now try to clarify the points in which the Puritan idea of the calling and the premium it placed upon ascetic conduct was bound directly to influence the development of a capitalistic way of life. As we have seen, this asceticism turned with all its force against one thing: the spontaneous enjoyment of life and all it had to offer.

* * *

As against this the Puritans upheld their decisive characteristic, the principle of ascetic conduct. For otherwise the Puritan aversion to sport, even for the Quakers, was by no means simply one of principle. Sport was accepted if it served a rational purpose, that of recreation necessary for physical efficiency. But as a means for the spontaneous expression of undisciplined impulses, it was under suspicion; and in so far as it became purely a means of enjoyment, or awakened pride, raw instincts or the irrational gambling instinct, it was of

---

‡Richard Baxter, Nonconformist (Puritan) scholar, 1615–1691. [Editors' note]

course strictly condemned. Impulsive enjoyment of life, which leads away both from work in a calling and from religion, was as such the enemy.

* * *

Man is only a trustee of the goods which have come to him through God's grace. He must, like the servant in the parable, give an account of every penny entrusted to him, and it is at least hazardous to spend any of it for a purpose which does not serve the glory of God but only one's own enjoyment. What person, who keeps his eyes open, has not met representatives of this view-point even in the present? The idea of a man's duty to his possessions, to which he subordinates himself as an obedient steward, or even as an acquisi-tive machine, bears with chilling weight on his life. The greater the posses-sions the heavier, if the ascetic attitude toward life stands the test, the feeling of responsibility for them, for holding them undiminished for the glory of God and increasing them by restless effort. The origin of this type of life also extends in certain roots, like so many aspects of the spirit of capitalism, back into the Middle Ages. But it was in the ethic of ascetic Protestantism that it first found a consistent ethical foundation. Its significance for the develop-ment of capitalism is obvious.

This worldly Protestant asceticism, as we may recapitulate up to this point, acted powerfully against the spontaneous enjoyment of possessions; it restricted consumption, especially of luxuries. On the other hand, it had the psychologi-cal effect of freeing the acquisition of goods from the inhibitions of tradition-alistic ethics. It broke the bonds of the impulse of acquisition in that it not only legalized it, but (in the sense discussed) looked upon it as directly willed by God. The campaign against the temptations of the flesh, and the dependence on external things, was, as besides the Puritans the great Quaker apologist Barclay expressly says, not a struggle against the rational acquisition, but against the irrational use of wealth.

* * *

On the side of the production of private wealth, asceticism condemned both dishonesty and impulsive avarice. What was condemned as covetous-ness, Mammonism, etc., was the pursuit of riches for their own sake. For wealth in itself was a temptation. But here asceticism was the power "which ever seeks the good but ever creates evil"; what was evil in its sense was possession and its temptations. For, in conformity with the Old Testament and in analogy to the ethical valuation of good works, asceticism looked upon the pursuit of wealth as an end in itself as highly reprehensible; but the attainment of it as a fruit of labour in a calling was a sign of God's blessing. And even more important: the religious valuation of restless, continuous, sys-tematic work in a worldly calling, as the highest means to asceticism, and at the same time the surest and most evident proof of rebirth and genuine faith, must have been the most powerful conceivable lever for the expansion of that attitude toward life which we have here called the spirit of capitalism.

When the limitation of consumption is combined with this release of acquisitive activity, the inevitable practical result is obvious: accumulation of capital through ascetic compulsion to save. The restraints which were imposed upon the consumption of wealth naturally served to increase it by making possible the productive investment of capital.

* * *

As far as the influence of the Puritan outlook extended, under all circumstances—and this is, of course, much more important than the mere encouragement of capital accumulation—it favoured the development of a rational bourgeois economic life; it was the most important, and above all the only consistent influence in the development of that life. It stood at the cradle of the modern economic man.

* * *

THE SPIRIT OF CAPITALISM TODAY

At present under our individualistic political, legal, and economic institutions, with the forms of organization and general structure which are peculiar to our economic order, this spirit of capitalism might be understandable, as has been said, purely as a result of adaptation. The capitalistic system so needs this devotion to the calling of making money, it is an attitude toward material goods which is so well suited to that system, so intimately bound up with the conditions of survival in the economic struggle for existence, that there can today no longer be any question of a necessary connection of that acquisitive manner of life with any single *Weltanschauung*. In fact, it no longer needs the support of any religious forces, and feels the attempts of religion to influence economic life, in so far as they can still be felt at all, to be as much an unjustified interference as its regulation by the State. In such circumstances men's commercial and social interests do tend to determine their opinions and attitudes. Whoever does not adapt his manner of life to the conditions of capitalistic success must go under, or at least cannot rise. But these are phenomena of a time in which modern capitalism has become dominant and has become emancipated from its old supports.

The Puritan wanted to work in a calling; we are forced to do so. For when asceticism was carried out of monastic cells into everyday life, and began to dominate worldly morality, it did its part in building the tremendous cosmos of the modern economic order. This order is now bound to the technical and economic conditions of machine production which to-day determine the lives of all the individuals who are born into this mechanism, not only those directly concerned with economic acquisition, with irresistible force. Perhaps it will so determine them until the last ton of fossilized coal is burnt. In Baxter's view the care for external goods should only lie on the shoulders of the "saint like a light cloak, which can be thrown aside at any moment." But fate decreed that the cloak should become an iron cage.

Since asceticism undertook to remodel the world and to work out its ideals in the world, material goods have gained an increasing and finally an inexorable power over the lives of men as at no previous period in history. To-day the spirit of religious asceticism—whether finally, who knows?—has escaped from the cage. But victorious capitalism, since it rests on mechanical foundations, needs its [asceticism's] support no longer. The rosy blush of its laughing heir, the Enlightenment, seems also to be irretrievably fading, and the idea of duty in one's calling prowls about in our lives like the ghost of dead religious beliefs. Where the fulfilment of the calling cannot directly be related to the highest spiritual and cultural values, or when, on the other hand, it need not be felt simply as economic compulsion, the individual generally abandons the attempt to justify it at all. In the field of its highest development, in the United States, the pursuit of wealth, stripped of its religious and ethical meaning, tends to become associated with purely mundane passions, which often actually give it the character of sport.

No one knows who will live in this cage in the future, or whether at the end of this tremendous development entirely new prophets will arise, or there will be a great rebirth of old ideas and ideals, or, if neither, mechanized petrification, embellished with a sort of convulsive self-importance. For of the last stage of this cultural development, it might well be truly said: "Specialists without spirit, sensualists without heart; this nullity imagines that it has attained a level of civilization never before achieved."

43

Politicized Evangelicalism and Secular Elites: Creating a Moral Other*

FROM *Evangelicals and Democracy in America; Volume II: Religion and Politics*

RHYS H. WILLIAMS

Among the most important ways social movements succeed is by creating effective "frames" that identify a problem and motivate movement participants to work toward a solution. Political sociology guides us through this process. Religious sentiments have, and continue to, inform and guide many successful social movements. In the United States today, none is more effective in pressing its political agenda than evangelical Christianity. Its bête noir *is secular humanism and non-believing "elites." Their demonization provides an effective framing device for adherents of a more religiously infused politics.*

In the discourse of much contemporary conservative Protestant evangelicalism, particularly that concerned with the place of religion in politics and the public sphere, one group stands out—portrayed as perhaps a singular threat to evangelical religion specifically, religion in general, and America's social and moral well-being. Under a variety of names, much of politicized evangelicalism has constructed "secular elites" as its primary political opponent, and even more expansively, as the primary threat to our societal health. This chapter examines the construction of secular elites as a moral "other," and the ways in which that construction works as a resource for political mobilization and resonates within evangelical culture. In particular, I argue that a construction labeled secular elites has become the primary foil and moral other for organized political evangelicalism.

* * *

POLITICAL CULTURE AND THE RHETORIC OF MOBILIZATION

A truism in sociology is that people's definition of a situation plays a large role in shaping social reality. A definition may begin as a subjective perception, but if it is acted upon, or is picked up and shared by others and regarded as an accurate understanding of the world, the consequences are decidedly

---

*References and footnotes can be found in the original publication of this article in Brint and Schroedel (eds.), *Evangelicals and Democracy in America; Volume II: Religion and Politics*. [*Editors' note*]

real—the definition of the situation moves from subjective understanding to objectively understood social reality. Shared definitions can in essence create their own reality.

The sociology of social movements has gained great understanding of collective action by studying how advocacy groups collectively define their situations, their opponents, and themselves. Social movements develop and promote *frames*—bundles of rhetorical claims and symbols that together represent a movement's attempt to communicate to its members and to others. Scholars have spent considerable energy examining the social movement frames that define issues, as well as studying framing processes through which collective actors develop these definitions. Effective movement frames are definitions of social situations and social identities that accomplish two tasks: they mobilize those who agree with the frames to take action—that is, they mobilize "internally" the movement's supporters; and they become generally and publicly accepted as the proper understandings of the issue among broader publics, such as news media or neutral bystanders—that is, they have "external" resonance in public discourse. Any given movement's frames are almost always countered by opponents who sponsor alternative frames. Thus, a significant aspect of public politics is the struggle over whose definition of the situation will dominate.

Effective social movement rhetoric, and the frames that comprise it, have several key components. First, movement frames must present a persuasive diagnosis of the social conditions the movement seeks to rectify—"here is the problem and here is why it is a problem." This diagnosis must identify the problem as an injustice, adding a moral valence to the situation, and assign responsibility for it—that is, who is to blame for the problem. Thus, movement frames are inherently moral claims—there is an injustice and a villain identified.

Second, effective frames must offer a prescription for solving the diagnosed problem. The seeds of the solution are often implied in the elements that go into the definition of the problem, but the diagnosis does not always determine the prescription. For example, Joseph Gusfield noted that solving the problem of alcohol-related traffic accidents could have resulted in a push for more mass transit; however, when the diagnostic frame became "drunk drivers," with an attendant moral condemnation, the prescription more easily became a legal crackdown and moral suasion aimed at individuals.

In addition to prescribing the solution, a movement's framing must be clear that a solution is possible—that is, provide activists a sense of agency by arguing that the problem is not so big as to be inevitable. This stands in a bit of tension with the diagnostic needs for emphasizing the seriousness and urgency of a problem. If a problem becomes constructed as too big, too entrenched, or inevitable, that framing undercuts the sense of agency that empowers people to feel that collective action can make a difference.

Finally, a good framing must motivate people to take action with regard to the cause. Partly this comes from a sense of agency—the conviction that things can change. But importantly, it makes those who are listening responsible for action and solving the problem. Just as responsibility for causing the problem is assigned, so must the responsibility for participating in the solution be accepted and borne willingly. One dimension of this motivation is constructing the basis for a collective identity, a sense of we that is connected to the issue at hand, and is clearly differentiated from those responsible for the problem. A collective identity is a distinction, and for movements it separates *them* as villains of the problem from *us* as the solution. A movement's collective identity can be an existing social category, but more often emerges during mobilization and is a cornerstone for the solidarity and commitment necessary for collective action.

Such definitional work is most effective when the boundaries between us and them are drawn clearly, but neither the we nor the they is defined too clearly. Specifying too clearly who constitutes the us may discourage some sympathetic constituents from joining, thinking they are not welcome, or else preclude forming alliances with other groups in the future. For example, one-time Christian Coalition director Ralph Reed consistently referred to the coalition's constituency as "people of faith." By not making explicit sectarian references, Reed implicitly expanded the forces of good to those with faith—without specifying which faith—while making those without faith the primary enemy. Similarly, one wants some flexibility in defining one's opponents in order to be able to adapt to circumstances.

Thus, social movement framings produce boundary-drawing distinctions between us and them. They are responsible for the problems identified, and those problems pose a threat and an injustice. But the problem can be solved and we are the ones with the moral responsibility for solving it. They are the problem, we are the solution, and there is a moral boundary dividing us. This distinction is seldom pregiven and unchanging; rather the differences emerge as a collective product of attempts at defining the situation.

One way of accomplishing this identity distinction is to create *demons*—identify another social group as the moral other against which one's own group stands as a bulwark. Thus political demonizing is a common outcome of the symbolic discourse of politics.

CREATING THE MORAL OTHER

The dynamic of creating an other is a broader phenomenon, however, and need not be confined to explicit attempts at a movement mobilization. One way to understand the discourse that shapes, and is shaped by, the evangelical worldview, as with any worldview, is to view it as a collection of symbolic boundaries that serve to distinguish those within the group or subculture from those outside it. Social groups create and maintain their collective identity at least in part by comparing and contrasting themselves to other groups. In that sense, collective identity is largely relational—its particular content may be centered in specific ideas, rituals, or ascribed characteristics, but those features are socially meaningful only because they serve comparatively to make one group distinct from others. As social creatures, we know who we are—in particular, who fits within the category of we—because we can determine who we are not based on certain socially significant features. Making these distinctions through comparison and contrast are key features of any group's ability to define itself. Thus it is not surprising that in political and social conflict, competing groups often mobilize themselves around a definition of their enemy—and rivals demonize each other with remarkably similar terms. Collective identity, particularly among people who do not share obvious social background characteristics, emerges and is defined in relation to others.

There is an important corollary to this relational logic when it concerns the world of politics. As Pierre Bourdieu persuasively argued, distinctions do not just order the social world horizontally—that is, by helping group members distinguish one group (us) from others (them), in the social landscape. Distinctions also have a vertical dimension in that this sorting has clear implications for social and institutional hierarchies. Bourdieu understood the cultural realm, the definition and enforcement of distinctions, as a key way in which inequalities are reinforced. Those with the ability to define standards apply them to others, leaving the others wanting, and in turn, reaffirming the worthiness of those in control. They create the "normal." Social movement culture similarly creates moral metrics that allocate worthiness and condemnation, and movements use these in the quest for change.

It seems as though it should be possible to make identity distinctions without implying normative differences between better and worse, privileged and despised. With some distinctions, that may be the case. However, when the markers of distinction—the things about which groups are judged differently—are loaded with normative meaning (such as who is moral, or who represents the one true religion, or who is responsible for a social threat), identity distinctions help create, reinforce, and challenge hierarchy and inequality. In the case I examine here, for reasons that I argue are integral to the American evangelical worldview, the distinctions being created—implicitly or explicitly—are marked as religious differences. These differences are theologized, and divide the social world not just into separate groups, but as well into the religious and the secular, the moral and the immoral—or in stark terms, good and evil. A binary classification scheme, which is commonly found in fundamentalist religious thought, though not only there, totalizes the world and infuses it with religious significance. The boundaries creating these distinctions pull together in powerful and easily comprehended terms the injustice frames needed for movement rhetoric, assign moral responsibility for public politics and social problems, and align moral identity with hierarchy and legitimacy

If boundaries become identified as sacred, their importance and need for protection is that much greater. Impermissible boundary crossing becomes a violation, and can be seen as pollution. For exclusivist religions—those that claim all divine truth for themselves—rival faiths can form just that sort of polluting menace. If one has the whole truth, other systems of belief can only be unwelcome and threatening. This often translates into a suspicion of religious pluralism in society, because most religious faiths have clear ideas about organizing human relationships and social institutions. Similarly, the secular world and its pleasures can also hold a polluting danger. And yet, in contemporary societies, religious people must live in that world and are often surrounded by other faiths, as well as those who are not religious. This condition helps explain the proliferation of what might be called "defensive fundamentalisms"—groups that are primarily interested in keeping the secular world out. For these groups, there is an easily identified and comprehended threat because secular modernity seems so ubiquitous. But whether the threats are rival religions or the secular world, totalizing groups must constantly be guarding their social boundaries and their worldviews.

However, many religions have as one of their missions changing this world to be in more accord with Divine Will, and they may have to interact with religious others or the secular to achieve that. This presents a paradox—the threat of pollution means that boundaries must be sharp and distinct, but many boundaries need to be potentially permeable to allow the faithful to reach out, organize, and convert the world. In practice, this dilemma can heighten, rather than lower, the need for clear marks of distinction.

This makes it clear why, for evangelical Protestants, the boundaries separating themselves from others are both important and potentially problematic. If one pursues an evangelical and universalistic faith, one is committed to the idea that others can be, potentially, converts. Christianity has an inherent universalism in its message, with the idea that the non-Christian can and should be brought into the fold. The conversion event is a key part of the evangelical identity. Further, there is a deep religious duty to help create a godly society, even if that goal is ultimately not achievable through human striving. But the risk of pollution is always present. Thus the boundaries between the godly and the secular are always tenuous and often fluid. The godly have certain responsibilities for reaching across boundaries to the other, but must be careful not to fall themselves. Given this ambiguity and the accompanying need for clear boundaries to mark the path of righteousness, it is small wonder that issues of subversion or infiltration are seen as such a threat. Those who might be a threat, but are disguised or hidden, make boundary issues all the more of a concern.

In sum, who gets constructed as other, especially religiously other in a deeply religious country whose moral tradition is constructed around differences between them and us, has implications for national identity, claims to public legitimacy, and political authority.

* * *

THE EMERGENCE OF A NEW OTHER: THE SECULAR ELITE

Anyone reading the books, advocacy literature, activist interviews, letters to the editor, or weblogs from contemporary evangelicals in the last decade or so cannot help but notice how seldom the descriptions of their current opponents, or the descriptions of those who threaten America's moral health, are named as Catholics, Jews, or communists. Certainly suspicion of religious others has not disappeared, but it is not difficult to claim that the demonizing of other religions within the Judeo-Christian tradition has diminished, particularly as a dimension of public political culture. Justin Watson summarized this transition in the primary other:

> [The Christian Coalition wants] a return to the de facto or quasi-establishment of evangelical Protestantism of the nineteenth century. The anti-Catholic nativism and anti-Semitism of that era would be dismissed by [Pat] Robertson and [Ralph] Reed because they define their enemies in terms of *hostility to religion* rather than by different religious beliefs. Catholics and Jews with a conservative or traditionalist orientation are seen as cobelligerents against secularism.

Rather than demonize rival faiths, much of the current rhetoric of outrage generated by politicized evangelicalism, the mobilizing frames calling American Christians to active political engagement, is directed at liberals, Hollywood, the media, the American Civil Liberties Union, and often, academics. These enemies are not associated with a competing religious faith or its people; instead, they are identified with secular professions or political ideologies that advocate secularizing public and political life. The opponents are said to be elites, and are regularly accused of being antireligious; sometimes they are called secularists. Thus, even though the term "secular elites" is only occasionally used as invective, I use it here because it encapsulates the fears of evangelical activists, and pulls together the two basic critiques of their opponents—that they are hostile to religion and they are antipopulist. Both qualities show them to be fundamentally un-American.

* * *

Tim LaHaye, whose 1980 book *The Battle for the Mind* is often credited with bringing the term *secular humanism* into the discourse of conservative Protestantism, is equally expansive. At some point in the book, humanism entails atheism, communism, liberalism, socialism, Freudianism, higher criticism, feminism, sexual liberation, art, self-determination, rock music, tolerance, evolution, rationalism, empiricism, situational ethics, and Unitarianism.

It is tempting to dismiss these loose and shotgun definitions, except that such ambiguity is neither trivial nor inconsequential. To the contrary, lack of precision is a strength of social movement rhetoric. There is an "artful ambiguity" that must be maintained for a mobilizing discourse to make the most of its potential audience. Too much specificity can open rhetorical claims up to debunking or ridicule. For example, Tim LaHaye once made the claim that just 275,000 dedicated humanists hold the media, the schools, and nearly the entire country under their control—a claim that could not possibly be substantiated and even supporters found exaggerated. Too much precision and specificity thus increases the potential for disconfirmation.

Those interested in mobilizing groups tend to avoid specificity and nuance in movement claims for two other reasons. First, well-defined frames may lead some sympathizers to conclude that they do not full agree with activists' calls to action. Leaving the framing symbols open enough for some individualized interpretation maximizes the number of potential supporters. Second, one power of symbols is to help produce unity; a symbol's emotive power can reach across cognitive differences in meanings and blur those differences until agreement seems to exist. In that way, an effective symbol can help create its own unity as it keeps people centered in a moral and affective core, rather than focusing on the cognitive differentiation that specificity entails. It is not in these activists' interest to generate tomes on exactly who forms their elite opposition— they want to generate activism and it is enough to know that they are secular and elites and we are Christians, believers, and Americans. It provides the necessary social and religious distinctions for collective identity and effective movement frames. And academic analysts who find it maddeningly vague simply demonstrate that their elite culture is out of touch with our emotive, populist sensibilities.

* * *

Academics and liberals in other culture industries have spearheaded or applauded many of the changes that de-Protestantized and secularized the public sphere. Groups such as the American Civil Liberties Union (ACLU), often representing secular plaintiffs, have challenged many dimensions of public religiosity since the 1960s. Evangelical Protestant values and attitudes have not disappeared, but there is more room for secular lifestyles and expressions in public and political culture. Further, as Robert Wuthnow and others have noted, the main political cleavages dividing American religion have shifted from denominational affiliations to ideological and cultural coalitions that cut across religious affiliation groups.

The expansion of higher education and the cultural conflicts of the 1960s divided liberal and conservatives within many religious groups.

Thus, politicized evangelicalism is not wholly inaccurate in identifying secular elites as their political rivals. Highly educated, upper-middle-class people with looser ties to religious communities, and with deep suspicions of conservative Protestantism, have worked to make the American public square more secular and more diverse. Whereas those who value public religious expressions now see the public square as "naked," more secular people find it more diverse, more accommodating, and less oppressive. There are different visions of the proper role of religion in American public life, and the visions of politicized evangelicals and politically progressive secular people conflict. The opponents are real, even if the rhetorical constructions of them as all-powerful and ubiquitous are exaggerated and fuzzily defined.

* * *

WHY OTHERING SECULAR ELITES WORKS

Constructing a secular elite as their primary political and cultural opponent has a number of advantages for politicized evangelicalism. As part of a social movement mobilizing frame, secular elites as other works just as sociologists argue such frames should. Christian Right advocacy groups find the nation beset by a number of social problems, many of them connected to changes in sex, gender, family relations, and raising children. They identify the retreat of evangelical Protestantism from the public square and a general secularization of society (in that major institutions such as schools do not reinforce what they consider a correct moral code) as the cause. That claim aligns convincingly with elements of evangelical culture, particularly the notion of a covenanted relationship between God and nation—if the nation neglects God's will, the Almighty removes his protection and the nation's favored status.

These diagnostic frames identify the social problems as well as those responsible for the situation. Demonizing secular elites—and naming the secular dimension as the salient qualifying adjective—clearly identifies that group, however vaguely defined, as responsible for these significant changes in American society, and thus the creators of the social problems that evangelical advocacy groups care about. Along with positing an identifiable agent responsible for causing the problem, the causal story about the secular elite establishes, through oppositional relation, evangelical Christians as responsible for the solution. Evangelicals become the hero of the frame in two ways—both as solving critical social problems caused by others, and, with their religious identity reaffirmed, proving their status as the quintessential American Christians.

* * *

Thus, the elitism charge, and the idea that the elites are conspiring against us in the hidden recesses of institutional power, resonates. Elite and conspiracy theories appeal because they assign blame to a definable group, cannot be falsified, and are parsimonious in that they explain many things with very few causal factors. But for evangelical Protestants, tales of conspiracies by elites align with many millennial religious accounts of evil being directed by a hidden, shadowy force, and the belief in an active evil in the world—as Satan disguises himself, often using ordinary people to infiltrate society and undermine God's kingdom.

Important to the resonance is the areas in which these elites are thought to operate. Three institutions in particular—Hollywood, the media, and higher educations—are major sites of knowledge and symbol production in our society. These institutions value education, cosmopolitan attitudes, and international perspectives, and the people in them are part of a new class that seems less connected to traditional communities. Further, they seem, to many evangelicals, to exude arrogance combined with a hedonistic disregard for the cultural proscriptions of Victorian bourgeois culture. This helps explain why the 1960s and their excesses remain so vivid to many on the Christian Right.

Moreover, Hollywood, the mainstream news media, and elite higher education are located on the coasts, the sources of liberalism and home to urbanism and immigrants, and are often portrayed as antithetical to the "real America" that exists in the Heartland (the historically Protestant-heavy Midwest and South).

* * *

CONCLUSION: EVANGELICAL PROTESTANTS AND SECULAR CULTURE

A number of indicators suggest that many evangelical Protestants find those with no religion particularly threatening. Secularism or secular humanism is often portrayed as a specific ideological threat that is oppressive to evangelicals and a threat to their children. Secular media and those that control cultural industries are often portrayed as enemies of American culture and a nefarious force in the nation's politics. It may be that evangelicals feel constrained to not level public attacks against members of rival religious groups: anti-Catholic and anti-Jewish prejudice is not as acceptable or normative in public discourse as it once was, and most evangelical political leaders avoid it. But such a taboo does not seem to apply to seculars, and for at least some sector of the evangelical population the appetite for books that criticize secularists as America's most dangerous enemy is seemingly insatiable. This suggests that evangelical culture finds its particular *bête noir* in the ranks of seculars, agnostics, and atheists. They have been constructed as political demons in ways that make that imagery a powerful mobilizing rhetoric and an idea that aligns closely with some long-standing elements of evangelical religious culture.

This rhetoric has potentially deleterious consequences for political life in a religiously pluralistic society, but the dynamics of the construction of this moral other has been a significant political resource for political mobilization, capturing attention in the public sphere and reaffirming evangelical identity.

PART EIGHT

SOCIAL CHANGE

44

Public Sociologies: Contradictions, Dilemmas, and Possibilities*

MICHAEL BURAWOY

Since the middle of the nineteenth century, social scientists have been asking about the influence of their work on society. Should it contribute to social order and stability? Should it address problems and seek to devise solutions? Or should it promote social change that could lead to a new and more progressive form of society? One view of science is that the best research is guided by idle curiosity, while another argues that necessity and crisis spur the greatest discoveries. Some scholars embrace their work with personal passion, while others believe scientific objectivity is compromised by too much emotional investment. Sociology is not immune to these debates. This article, a version of the presidential address to the American Sociological Association, again raises the question the great sociologist Howard Becker asked years ago, "Whose side are you on?"

In 2003 the members of the American Sociological Association (ASA) were asked to vote on a member resolution opposing the war in Iraq. The resolution included the following justification: "[F]oreign interventions that do not have the support of the world community create more problems than solutions . . . Instead of lessening the risk of terrorist attacks, this invasion could serve as the spark for multiple attacks in years to come." It passed by a two-thirds majority (with 22% of voting members abstaining) and became the association's official position. In an opinion poll on the same ballot, 75% of the members who expressed an opinion were opposed to the war. To assess the ethos of sociologists today, it is worthwhile comparing these results with those of 1968 when a similar double item was presented to the membership with respect to the Vietnam war. Then two-thirds of the votes cast *opposed* the ASA adopting a resolution against the war and only 54% were individually opposed to the war (Rhoades 1981:60).

It is complicated to interpret this apparent shift in political orientation, given the different national and military contexts within which the voting took place, given the different wording of the questions. Still two hypotheses present themselves. First, the membership of the ASA, always leaning toward the liberal end of the political spectrum, has moved much further to the left. In 1968 the

*"Public Sociologies: Contradiction, Dilemmas, and Possibilities," by Michael Burawoy. From *Social Forces*, 2004, Vol. 82, No. 4, pp. 1603–18.

opinion of sociologists was close to the rest of the population (54% of sociologists opposed the war as compared to between 46% and 54% of the general public), whereas in 2003 the two distributions were the inverse of each other—75% of voting sociologists opposed the war at the end of April, 2003, while at the same time 75% of the public supported the war. One might conjecture that in 1968 a very different generation dominated the profession—a postwar generation celebratory of the U.S. and its "victory over fascism," among them pioneers of professional sociology. Today's post-Vietnam generations are more accustomed to criticizing the U.S. government and in particular its foreign policy. They are also less concerned about the purity of sociology as science and more likely to assume that our accumulated knowledge should be put to public use, whether in the form of member resolutions or policy interventions.

Second, the world itself is different. In 1968 the world seemed ripe for change for the better. The civil rights movements, the women's movement, student movements around the world, antiwar marches and sit-ins captured the imagination of a new generation of sociologists who saw conventional sociology as lagging behind the most progressive movements; whereas today the world is lagging behind sociology, unapologetic about its drift into political and economic fundamentalism. Sociologists shift their critical eye ever more away from sociology toward the world it describes, a shift reflected in the insurgent interest in public sociology. In short, over the last 35 years there has been a scissors movement. The political context and the sociological conscience have moved in opposite directions, so that the world we inhabit is increasingly in conflict with the ethos and principles that animate sociologists—an ethos opposed to inequality, to the erosion of civil liberties, to the destruction of public life, and to discrimination and exclusion.

This shift in sociological ethos is not uncontroversial. It has, indeed, generated its own opposition. Dissatisfied with the political winds, 102 ASA members signed a petition, sent to the association's Committee on Professional Ethics, charging that the anti-Iraq-war resolution violated the ASA's code of conduct. Why? Because it did not rely on "scientifically and professionally derived knowledge." The complaint did not get far because, unlike other professional associations, there are no clear rules that limit the types of resolutions the ASA can endorse. Nonetheless, the 102 (and presumably many others) did take a principled position: scientific sociologists have no business making moral or political pronouncements. Taking a moral or political position is incompatible with scientific objectivity. Opposition to the resolution also took a more pragmatic form, fears that such a visible and public stance against the war (and I have not found another association to have taken such a stance) would undermine what legitimacy we have as sociologists, conceivably threaten research funding, and even prompt political reprisals. Alas, this is not so far fetched. . . .

The "pure science" position that research must be completely insulated from politics is untenable since antipolitics is no less political than *public engagement*.

The more usual "abstentionist" position limits politics to *professional self-defense*: that we should enter the political arena only to defend our immediate professional interests. Thus, we might mobilize resources to oppose the defunding of research into sexual behavior (as was attempted in Congress recently), or to protest the closure or dramatic cuts in a sociology department (as in Germany today), or to protect the human rights of an individual (e.g., Egyptian sociologist, Saad Eddin Ibrahim), or, most recently, to defend a journal's right to review and edit articles from "enemy" countries. In all these instances we enter the political arena, but solely to defend the integrity of our professional activities.

Between professional self-defense and public engagement there is a compromise position that moves from the defense of professional interests to *policy interventions*. Here the association takes a political position on the basis of an accumulated body of evidence whose validity is widely accepted and whose interpretation is unambiguous. One such example is the ASA's recent statement that summarized the sociological literature on race: race exists, it has social causes, and it has social consequences. An extension of this was the ASA's Amicus Curiae brief to the Supreme Court in the 2003 Michigan Law School affirmative action case, *Grutter v. Bollinger.* Again a body of sociological research was mobilized to show that racial discrimination exists and that efforts to diversify the student body would improve the educational experience of all.

So far, then, we have three possible political stances: "professional self-defense," "policy intervention" and "public engagement." There is, however, a fourth stance. The association is a political venue unto itself—a place to debate the stances we might adopt. We cannot advocate democracy for others if we are not internally democratic, if we do not attempt to arrive at public stances through maximal participation in collective deliberation. It is just such a critical debate that we are involved in today. The resolution against the Iraq War is but a dramatic instance of the broader issue we are discussing: what should be our involvement in the world beyond the academy? Recognizing we are part of the world we study, we must take some *stance* with respect to that world. To fail to do so is to take a stance by default.

We can problematize our place in society by asking two questions. The first was posed by Alfred McClung Lee in his 1976 Presidential Address to the American Sociological Association: "Knowledge for Whom?" As sociologists are we just talking to ourselves? Are we to remain locked up in the antechambers of society, never really entering its tumultuous currents, hiding behind the barricades of professional insularity? Or can we, ever cautious, ever vigilant, wade forth into society, armed with our sociological expertise? If we are going to talk to others, which others and how shall we do it? This leads directly to the second question, famously posed by Robert Lynd (1939): Knowledge for What? Do we take the values and goals of our research for granted, handed down to us by some external (funding or policy) agency? Should we only concentrate on providing solutions to predefined problems, focusing on the means to achieve predetermined ends, on what Weber called technical rationality and what I call *instrumental knowledge*? In other words, should we repress the question of ends and pretend that knowledge and laws spring spontaneously from the data, if only we can develop the right methods? Or should we be concerned explicitly with the goals for which our research may be mobilized, and with the values that underpin and guide our research? Going further afield, should sociologists be in the business of stimulating public discussions about the possible meanings of the "good society"? Like Weber, I believe that without value commitments there can be no sociology, no basis for the questions that guide our research programs. Without values social science is blind. . . . Thus, empirical science can only take us so far: it can help us understand the consequences of our value commitments and inform our value discussions, but it cannot determine those values. Determining values should take place through democratic and collective deliberation.

. . . Professional and policy sociology are forms of instrumental knowledge focusing respectively on academic and extra-academic audiences. Critical and public sociology are forms of reflexive knowledge focusing respectively on academic and extra-academic audiences. Let me consider each in turn.

Public sociology engages publics beyond the academy in dialogue about matters of political and moral concern. It has to be relevant to such publics without being faddish, that is subservient to publics. . . .

* * *

Public sociology should be distinguished from *policy sociology*. While public sociology generates conversation or debate between sociologist and public on a terrain of reciprocal engagement, policy sociology focuses on solutions to specific problems defined by clients. The relation between sociologist and client is often of a contractual character in which expertise is sold for a fee. The sociologist, thereby, cedes independence to the client. All manner of organizations may contract sociological expertise, from business to state, from multilateral organization to the small NGO [nongovernmental organization]. What makes the relation instrumental is that the research terrain is not defined by the sociologist. It is defined narrowly in the case of a "client" or broadly in the case of a "patron."

* * *

Public and policy sociologies could not exist without *professional sociology*, which provides legitimacy, expertise, distinctive problem definitions, relevant bodies of knowledge, and techniques for analyzing data. An effective public or policy sociology is not hostile to, but depends upon the professional sociology that lies at the core of our disciplinary field. Why do I call our disciplinary knowledge instrumental? As professional sociologists we are located in research traditions, sometimes going back to founding fathers (Weber, Durkheim, and Marx) and otherwise of a more recent pedigree (feminism, poststructuralism).

These research traditions may be elaborated into self-conscious research programs—structural functionalism, stratification theory, sex-gender systems, experimental social psychology—with their grounding assumptions, distinctive questions, exemplary models and appropriate techniques of research. Research programs (Lakatos 1978) advance by resolving internal contradictions and absorbing anomalies (discrepancies between theoretical expectation and empirical observations). They require a community of scientists committed to working on the important (collectively defined) *puzzles* that the research program generates. Flourishing public and policy sociologies increase the stakes of our knowledge and thus makes the vigilant pursuit of coherent research programs all the more important.

In the world of normal science we cannot push forward the frontiers of knowledge and at the same time question its foundations. The latter task is the province of *critical sociology*. In much the same way that public sociology interrogates the value assumptions of policy sociology, so in a similar and more direct way critical sociology is the conscience of professional sociology.

* * *

As sociology grew, its institutional base differentiated, so that today sociologists work both inside and outside academia. Those outside tend to occupy positions in government agencies, such as the census bureau or the department of corrections; in consulting companies for human resource management; or in international NGOs. Then, there are sociologists who are employed in professional schools—business schools, public administration, educational schools, agricultural extension, and so forth—where they may engage nonacademic audiences. Equally important is the complex hierarchy of the university system which ranges from elite private universities, to the different tiers of state university systems, liberal arts colleges, and two-year community colleges. The configuration of the division of sociological labor will vary with a department's location in this system. Thus, in state colleges where teaching takes up so much of one's time, research has a public or policy dimension, often driven by local issues. Based on my attendance at the meetings of state associations, such as the North Carolina Sociological Association, I have found public sociology to be both more widely practiced and more highly valued in state colleges than in most elite departments. I have found projects ranging from research on displaced workers, toxic waste, housing inequalities, and educational reform, to advocacy for public health campaigns around HIV-AIDS or needle exchange to training community organizers to deal with the media. Sadly, all too often, this public (and policy) sociology, widespread though it may be, remains invisible and unrecognized because its practitioners lack the time or incentive to write it up.

History and hierarchy give one sense of the possible variation in the configuration of the disciplinary field, international comparisons give another. When one travels the world talking about public sociology, one quickly learns just how distinctively American the concept is, marking the unique strength of professional sociology in the U.S. In many countries it is taken for granted that sociology has a public face. Why else be a sociologist? The career of sociology in many Third World countries reflects the succession of different political regimes. One of the first acts of the Pinochet regime in Chile was to abolish sociology. In South Africa sociology flourished in the late 1970s and 1980s as the anti-apartheid movement grew in strength, just as it has suffered amalgamation and budgetary cuts in the postapartheid period. Soviet sociology, nonexistent under Stalinism, reappeared in the 1950s as an ideological and surveillance arm of the party state. Sociological opinion research was deployed as a weapon of critique, revealing public discontent in order to justify swings in policy. This instrumental use of sociology comes home to roost in the post-Soviet period where, increasingly, it has become a form of market research. If it is not co-opted or repressed by authoritarian regimes, sociology's reflexive side may sustain critical opposition, as was often the case in Eastern Europe. In the social democratic countries of Scandinavia, by contrast, it is the policy dimension that often stands out. Although when conservative parties assume power, the sociological winds shift direction from policy to public.

Here then are just a few hints at national variation, underlining once again just how peculiar is U.S. sociology. It is not just peculiar, it is also very powerful, dominating the world scene. Accordingly in the international division of sociological labor, professional sociology is concentrated in the resource rich United States, and to a lesser extent in Western Europe, while public sociology has relatively greater strength in the poorer countries—a distribution that mirrors the hierarchy within the U.S.

* * *

Finally, we come to the critical question: what are the grounds for claiming sociology's affinity to the public? If political science's distinctive object of study is the state and its value the protection of political order, and if economics has as it distinctive object the economy and its value is the expansion of the market, then sociology's distinctive object is civil society and its value is the resilience and autonomy of the social. Sociology is born with civil society and dies with civil society. The classical sociology of Weber, Durkheim, Simmel, and Pareto arose with the expansion of trade unions, political parties, mass education, voluntary associations at the end of the nineteenth century, just as U.S. sociology was born amidst reform and religious organizations. Sociology disappears with the eclipse of civil society as in fascism, Stalinism or Pinochet's Chile, just as it quickly bubbles to the surface with the unfurling of perestroika in the Soviet Union or the civic and labor associations of South Africa's anti-apartheid movement.

* * *

The burgeoning interest in public sociology and the unanticipated vote against the war in Iraq suggest to me that the stakes are indeed becoming clearer. In a world tending toward market tyranny and state unilateralism, civil society is at once threatened with extinction and at the same time a major possible hold-out against deepening inequalities and multiplying threats to all manner of human rights. The interest of sociology in the very existence, let alone expansion, of civil society (even with all its warts) becomes the interest of humanity—locally, nationally and globally. If we can transcend our parochialism and recognize our distinctive relation to diverse publics within and across borders, sociologists could yet create the fulcrum around which a critical social science might evolve, one responsive to public issues while at the same time committed to professional excellence.

REFERENCES

Lakatos, Imre. 1978. *The Methodology of Scientific Research Programmes.* Cambridge University Press.

Lee, Alfred McClung. 1976. "Sociology for Whom?" *American Sociological Review* 44: 925–36.

Lynd, Robert. 1939. *Knowledge for What? The Place of Social Sciences in American Culture.* Princeton University Press.

Rhoades, Lawrence. 1981. *A History of the American Sociological Association, 1905–1980.* American Sociological Association, Washington D.C.

45

The Gender Revolution: Uneven and Stalled*

PAULA ENGLAND

Despite important gains made by women, progress toward gender equality in the United States has been uneven and even stalled in recent decades. Sociologist Paula England explains why by examining recent changes in women's and men's participation in school and the workplace. As she describes, widely shared cultural beliefs about gender and abilities—what sociologists call "gender essentialism"—are largely to blame. A consequence of these beliefs is that some kinds of work are "typed" as masculine while others are "typed" as feminine, making it very difficult to overcome differences in the kinds of careers women and men pursue.

We sometimes call the sweeping changes in the gender system since the 1960s a "revolution." Women's employment increased dramatically; birth control became widely available; women caught up with and surpassed men in rates of college graduation; undergraduate college majors desegregated substantially; more women than ever got doctorates as well as professional degrees in law, medicine, and business; many kinds of gender discrimination in employment and education became illegal; women entered many previously male-dominated occupations; and more women were elected to political office. As sweeping as these changes have been, change in the gender system has been uneven—affecting some groups more than others and some arenas of life more than others, and change has recently stalled. My goal in this article is not to argue over whether we should view the proverbial cup as half empty or half full (arguments I have always found uninteresting) but, rather, to stretch toward an understanding of why some things change so much more than others. To show the uneven nature of gender change, I will review trends on a number of indicators. While the shape of most of the trends is not in dispute among scholars, the explanations I offer for the uneven and halting nature of change have the status of hypotheses rather than well-documented conclusions.

I will argue that there has been little cultural or institutional change in the devaluation of traditionally female activities and jobs, and as a result, women have had more incentive than men to move into gender-nontraditional activities and positions. This led to asymmetric change; women's lives have

---

*References and endnotes can be found in the original publication of Paula England's 2010 article by the same name in *Gender & Society* 24(2/April): 149–166. [*Editors' note*]

changed much more than men's. Yet in some subgroups and arenas, there is less clear incentive for change even among women; examples are the relatively low employment rates of less educated women and the persistence of traditionally gendered patterns in heterosexual romantic, sexual, and marital relationships.

I also argue that the type of gender egalitarianism that did take hold was the type most compatible with American individualism and its cultural and institutional logics, which include rights of access to jobs and education and the desideratum of upward mobility and of expressing one's "true self." One form this gender egalitarianism has taken has been the reduction of discrimination in hiring. This has made much of the gender revolution that has occurred possible; women can now enter formerly "male" spheres. But co-occurring with this gender egalitarianism, and discouraging such integration is a strong (if often tacit) belief in gender essentialism—the notion that men and women are innately and fundamentally different in interests and skills. A result of these co-occurring logics is that women are most likely to challenge gender boundaries when there is no path of upward mobility without doing so, but otherwise gender blinders guide the paths of both men and women.

[DEVALUING "WOMEN'S" WORK] AND . . . INCENTIVES FOR WOMEN AND MEN TO CHANGE

Most of the changes in the gender system heralded as "revolutionary" involve women moving into positions and activities previously limited to men, with few changes in the opposite direction. The source of this asymmetry is an aspect of society's valuation and reward system that has not changed much—the tendency to devalue and badly reward activities and jobs traditionally done by women.

Women's Increased Employment

One form the devaluation of traditionally female activities takes is the failure to treat child rearing as a public good and support those who do it with state payments. In the United States, welfare reform took away much of what little such support had been present. Without this, women doing child rearing are reliant on the employment of male partners (if present) or their own employment. Thus, women have had a strong incentive to seek paid employment, and more so as wage levels rose across the decades. As Figure [45.1] shows, women's employment has increased dramatically. But change has not been continuous, as the trend line flattened after 1990 and turned down slightly after 2000 before turning up again. This turndown was hardly an "opt-out revolution," to use the popular-press term, as the decline was tiny relative to the dramatic increase across 40 years. But the stall after 1990 is clear, if unexplained.

Figure [45.1] also shows the asymmetry in change between men's and women's employment; women's employment has increased much more than

Figure 45.1 Percentage of U.S. Men and Women Employed, 1962–2007

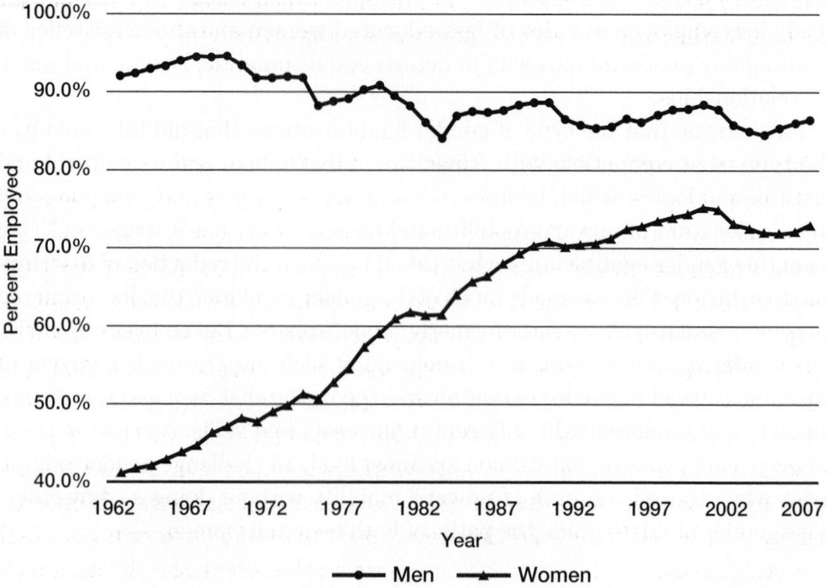

Persons are considered employed if they worked for pay anytime during the year. Refers to adults aged 25 to 54.

SOURCE: Cotter, David A., Joan M. Hermsen, and Reeve Vanneman. 2004. *Gender Inequality at Work.* New York: Russell Sage Foundation.

men's has declined. There was nowhere near one man leaving the labor force to become a full-time homemaker for every woman who entered, nor did men pick up household work to the extent women added hours of employment. Men had little incentive to leave employment.

Among women, incentives for employment vary. Class-based resources, such as education, affect these incentives. At first glance, we might expect less educated women to have higher employment rates than their better-educated peers because they are less likely to be married to a high-earning man. Most marriages are between two people at a similar education level, so the less educated woman, if she is married, typically has a husband earning less than the husband of the college graduate. Her family would seem to need the money from her employment more than the family headed by two college graduates. Let us call this the "need for income" effect. But the countervailing "opportunity cost" factor is that well-educated women have more economic incentive for employment because they can earn more. Put another way, the opportunity cost of staying at home is greater for the woman who can earn more. Indeed, the woman who did not graduate from high school may have potential earnings so low that she could not even cover child care costs with what she could earn. Thus, in typical cases, for the married college graduate, her own education encourages her employment, while her husband's high earnings discourage it. The less educated woman typically has a poor husband (if any), which encourages her employment, while her own low earning power discourages her employment.

* * *

Women Moving into "Male" Jobs and Fields of Study

The devaluation of and underpayment of predominantly female occupations is an important institutional reality that provides incentives for both men and women to choose "male" over "female" occupations and the fields of study that lead to them. Research has shown that predominantly female occupations pay less, on average, than jobs with a higher proportion of men. At least some of the gap is attributable to sex composition because it persists in statistical models controlling for occupations' educational requirements, amount of skill required, unionization, and so forth. I have argued that this is a form of gender discrimination—employers see the worth of predominantly female jobs through biased lenses and, as a result, set pay levels for both men and women in predominantly female jobs lower than they would be if the jobs had a more heavily male sex composition. While the overall sex gap in pay has diminished because more women have moved into "male" fields, there is no evidence that the devaluation of occupations because they are filled with women has diminished. Indeed, as U.S. courts have interpreted the law, this type of between-job discrimination is not even illegal, whereas it is illegal to pay women less than men in the same job, unless based on factors such as seniority, qualifications, or performance. Given this, both men and women continue to have a pecuniary incentive to choose male-dominated occupations. Thus, we should not be surprised that desegregation of occupations has largely taken the form of women moving into male-dominated fields, rather than men moving into female-dominated fields.

Consistent with the incentives embedded in the ongoing devaluation of female fields, desegregation of fields of college study came from more women going into fields that were predominantly male, not from more men entering "female" fields. Since 1970, women increasingly majored in previously male-dominated, business-related fields, such as business, marketing, and accounting; while fewer chose traditionally female majors like English, education, and sociology; and there was little increase of men's choice of these latter majors. Figure [45.2] shows the desegregation of fields of bachelor's degree receipt, using the index of dissimilarity (D), a scale on which complete segregation (all fields are all male or all female) is 100 and complete integration (all fields have the same proportion of women as women's proportion of all bachelor's degrees in the given year) is 0. It shows that segregation dropped significantly in the 1970s and early 1980s, but has been quite flat since the mid-1980s. Women's increased integration of business fields stopped then as well.

As women have increasingly trained for previously male-dominated fields, they have also integrated previously male-dominated occupations in

Figure 45.2 Sex Segregation of Fields of Study for U.S. Bachelor Degree Recipients, 1971–2006

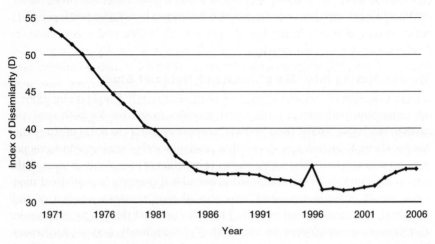

SOURCE: Author's calculations from the National Center for Education Statistics (NCES) 1971–2003 and NCES 2004–2007.

management and the professions in large numbers. Women may face discrimination and coworker resistance when they attempt to integrate these fields, but they have a strong pecuniary incentive to do so. Men lose money and suffer cultural disapproval when they choose traditionally female-dominated fields; they have little incentive to transgress gender boundaries. While some men have entered female-intensive retail service jobs after losing manufacturing jobs, there is little incentive for voluntary movement in this direction, making desegregation a largely one-way street.

* * *

The "Personal" Realm

"The personal is political" was a rallying cry of 1960s feminists, urging women to demand equality in private as well as public life. Yet conventions embodying male dominance have changed much less in "the personal" than in the job world. Where they have changed, the asymmetry described above for the job world prevails. For example, parents are more likely to give girls "boy" toys such as Legos than they are to give dolls to their sons. Girls have increased their participation in sports more than boys have taken up cheerleading or ballet. Women now commonly wear pants, while men wearing skirts remains rare. A few women started keeping their birth-given surname upon marriage, with little adoption by men of women's last names. Here, as with jobs, the asymmetry follows incentives, albeit nonmaterial ones. These social incentives themselves flow from a largely unchanged devaluation of things culturally defined as feminine. When boys and men take on "female" activities, they often suffer disrespect, but under some circumstances, girls and women gain respect for taking on "male" activities.

What is more striking than the asymmetry of gender change in the personal realm is how little gendering has changed at all in this realm, especially in dyadic heterosexual relationships. It is still men who usually ask women on dates, and sexual behavior is generally initiated by men. Sexual permissiveness has increased, making it more acceptable for both heterosexual men and women to have sex outside committed relationships. But the gendered part of this—the double standard—persists stubbornly; women are judged much more harshly than men for casual sex. The ubiquity of asking about height in Internet dating Web sites suggests that the convention that men should be taller than their female partner has not budged. The double standard of aging prevails, making women's chances of marriage decrease with age much more than men's. Men are still expected to propose marriage. Upon marriage, the vast majority of women take their husband's surname. The number of women keeping their own name increased in the 1970s and 1980s but little thereafter, never exceeding about 25 percent even for college graduates (who have higher rates than other women). Children are usually given their father's surname; a recent survey found that even in cases where the mother is not married to the father, 92 percent of babies are given the father's last name. While we do not have trend data on all these personal matters, my sense is that they have changed much less than gendered features of the world of paid work.

* * *

WOMEN'S RIGHTS TO UPWARD MOBILITY AND GENDER ESSENTIALISM

I have stressed that important change in the gender system has taken the form of women integrating traditionally male occupations and fields of study. But even here change is uneven. The main generalization is shown by Figure [45.3], which divides all occupations by a crude measure of class, calling professional, management, and nonretail sales occupations "middle class," and all others "working class" (including retail sales, assembly work in manufacturing, blue-collar trades, and other nonprofessional service work). Using the index of dissimilarity to measure segregation, Figure [45.3] shows that desegregation has proceeded much farther in middle-class than working-class jobs. Middle-class jobs showed dramatic desegregation, although the trend lessened its pace after 1990. By contrast, working-class jobs are almost as segregated as they were in 1950! Women have integrated the previously male strongholds of management, law, medicine, and academia in large numbers. But women have hardly gained a foothold in blue-collar, male-dominated jobs such as plumbing, construction, truck driving, welding, and assembly in durable manufacturing industries such as auto and steel. This is roughly the situation in other affluent nations as well.

Figure 45.3 Sex Segregation of Middle-Class and Working-Class Occupations in the United States, 1950–2000

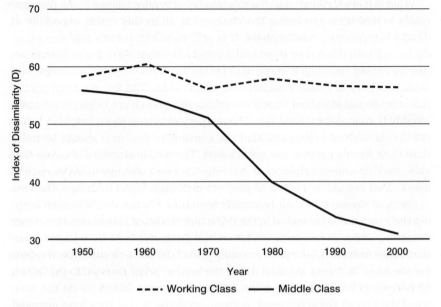

Middle-class occupations include professional, management, and nonretail sales. All others are classified as working-class occupations.

SOURCE: Cotter, David A., Joan M. Hermsen, and Reeve Vanneman. 2009. End of the gender revolution website, http://www.bsos.umd.edu/socy/vanneman/endofgr/default.html (accessed December 14, 2009).

This same class difference in trend can be seen if we compare the degree of segregation among those who have various levels of education; in the United States, sex segregation declined much more dramatically since 1970 for college graduates than any other group.

Why has desegregation been limited to high-level jobs? The question has two parts: why women did not integrate blue-collar male jobs in significant numbers, and why women did integrate professional and managerial jobs in droves. Why one and not the other?

* * *

I hypothesize that if women can move "up" in status or income relative to their reference group while still staying in a job typically filled by women, then because of gender beliefs and gendered identities, they are likely to do so. If they cannot move up without integrating a male field, and demand is present and discrimination not too strong, they are more likely to cross the gender boundary. Applying this hypothesis, why would women not enter male blue-collar fields? To be sure, many women without college degrees would earn much more in the skilled blue-collar crafts or unionized manufacturing jobs than in the service jobs typically filled by women at their education levels—jobs such as maid, child care worker, retail sales clerk, or assembler in the textile industry. So they have an economic incentive to enter these jobs. But such women could also move "up" to clerical work or teaching, higher status and better paying but still traditionally female jobs. Many take this path, often getting more education.

In contrast, consider women who assumed they would go to college and whose mothers were in female-dominated jobs requiring a college degree like teacher, nurse, librarian, or social worker. For these women, to move up in status or earnings from their reference group options requires them to enter traditionally male jobs; there are virtually no heavily female jobs with higher status than these female professions. These are just the women, usually of middle-class origins, who have been integrating management, law, medicine, and academia in recent decades. For them, upward mobility was not possible within traditional boundaries, so they were more likely to integrate male fields.

In sum, my argument is that one reason that women integrated male professions and management much more than blue-collar jobs is that the women for whom the blue-collar male jobs would have constituted "progress" also had the option to move up by entering higher-ranking female jobs via more education. They thus had options for upward mobility without transgressing gender boundaries not present for their middle-class sisters.

* * *

CONCLUSION

Change in the gender system has been uneven, changing the lives of some groups of people more than others and changing lives in some arenas more than others. Although many factors are at play, I have offered two broad explanations for the uneven nature of change.

First, I argued that, because of the cultural and institutional devaluation of characteristics and activities associated with women, men had little incentive to move into badly rewarded, traditionally female activities such as homemaking or female-dominated occupations. By contrast, women had powerful economic incentives to move into the traditionally male domains of paid employment and male-typical occupations; and when hiring discrimination declined, many did. . . .

Second, I explored the consequences of the co-occurrence of two Western cultural and institutional logics. Individualism, encompassing a belief in rights to equal opportunity in access to jobs and education in order to express one's "true self," promotes a certain kind of gender egalitarianism. It does not challenge the devaluation of traditionally female spheres, but it encourages the rights of women to upward mobility through equal access to education and jobs. To be sure, this ideal has been imperfectly realized, but this type of gender egalitarianism has taken hold strongly. But co-occurring with it, somewhat paradoxically, are strong (if tacit) beliefs in gender essentialism—that men and women are innately and fundamentally different in interests and skills. Almost no men and precious few women, even those who believe in "equal opportunity," have an explicit commitment to undoing gender differentiation for its own sake. Gender essentialism encourages traditional choices and leads women to see previous cohorts of women of their social class as the reference point from which they seek upward mobility. I concluded that the co-occurrence of these two logics—equal opportunity individualism and gender essentialism—make it most likely for women to move into nontraditional fields of study or work when there is no possible female field that constitutes upward mobility from the socially constructed reference point. This helps explain why women integrated male-dominated professional and managerial jobs more than blue-collar jobs. Women from working-class backgrounds, whose mother were maids or assemblers in nondurable manufacturing, could move up financially by entering blue-collar "male" trades but often decide instead to get more education and move up into a female job such as secretary or teacher. It is women with middle-class backgrounds, whose mothers were teachers or nurses, who cannot move up without entering a male-dominated career, and it is just such women who have integrated management, law, medicine, and academia. Yet even while integrating large fields such as academia, women often gravitate toward the more female-typical fields of study.

As sociologists, we emphasize links between parts of a social system. For example, we trace how gender inequality in jobs affects gender inequality in the family, and vice versa. Moreover, links between parts of the system are recognized in today's prevailing view in which gender is itself a multilevel system, with causal arrows going both ways from macro to micro. All these links undoubtedly exist, but the unevenness of gender-related change highlights how loosely coupled parts of the social system are and how much stronger some causal forces for change are than others. For example, because it resonated with liberal individualism well, the part of the feminist message that urged giving women equal access to jobs and education made considerable headway and led to much of what we call the gender revolution. But even as women integrated employment and "male" professional and managerial jobs, the part of feminism challenging the devaluation of traditionally female activities and jobs made little headway. The result is persistently low rewards for women who remain focused on mothering or in traditionally female jobs and little incentive for men to make the gender revolution a two-way street.

While discussing the uneven character of gender change, I also noted that the type of gender change with the most momentum—middle-class women entering traditionally male spheres—has recently stalled. Women's employment rates stabilized, desegregation of occupations slowed down, and desegregation of fields of college study stopped. Erosion of the sex gap in pay slowed as well. While the reason for the stalling is unclear, like the unevenness of change, the stalling of change reminds us how contingent and path-dependent gender egalitarian change is, with no inexorable equal endpoint.

46

The Ties That Bind Are Fraying

MILLER McPHERSON, LYNN SMITH-LOVIN, and MATTHEW BRASHEARS

As a student, you may have been lonely and recognized how frustrating, painful, and even debilitating loneliness can be. Human beings are social creatures. Our most important moments are spent with others. Our most significant life events involve ourselves with at least one other person. Conversely, the worst punishment we can inflict on another, short of torture or execution, is isolation. Why, then, are we, as Robert Putman asked, more likely to be "bowling alone" these days? Sociologists study social networks to understand political opinions, cultural ties, power and influence, and more recently health and well-being. In this essay, comparative data gathered from the General Social Survey of people in the United States reveal a decline in social networks, especially those outside one's immediate family. What is it about our jobs, neighborhoods, leisure, information technology, and friendships that could explain this?

Think back over the last six months and the people with whom you discussed the things most important to you. How many were there?

Sociologists asked that question in the 1985 General Social Survey (GSS), a national survey of nearly 1,500 adults, and created the first representative picture of Americans' networks of confidants. Answers to the same question in the 2004 GSS uncovered something remarkable: Americans had one-third fewer confidants than two decades earlier.

In 2004, many more people said they don't discuss matters of importance with anyone. And they've shifted away from ties formed in the community— at places like church choirs, neighborhood associations, social clubs, and sports teams—and toward conversations with family, especially spouses.

This question and its disturbing answer are significant because the closer and stronger the tie we have with someone, the more support they offer us. Close ties help us with routine things, like picking up a child at day care, and offer major aid in a crisis, like providing a place to live after a disaster. They influence us directly through our interactions and indirectly by shaping the people we become. Having at least one close connection can be vital for both physical and mental health.

Strong social ties can be important for society, too. Harvard political scientist Robert Putnam argues that neighborhood relationships and voluntary group membership are important for community well-being and democratic participation. He follows a rich tradition, dating back to Alexis de Tocqueville, suggesting that Americans' ties to other members of their communities enhance our democratic institutions.

MEASURES AND MISSES

When researchers study connections between people, a key issue is choosing which type of relationship to measure. In 1985 and 2004 the GSS focused on one type of relationship—who people use as their confidants. From earlier research we know these "discuss important matters" relationships are similar to questions asking about best friends and other very close emotional ties.

These aren't the kinds of friends we have on Internet sites like Facebook, MySpace, LinkedIn, or Friendster. While we may know more about people connected to us through those sites than people we talk to every day, what we know about these friends is equally available to hundreds of other people. These relationships are what sociologists call "weak ties"—friends of friends or acquaintances we know only through one type of connection. It may be interesting to collect hundreds of such contacts, but we aren't likely to call on them for help on a daily basis. When answering the GSS question, people tend to mention family members and friends who are as close as family—people they've known a long time and who they interact with several times a week.

The "important matters" question does not measure what people talk about in their relationships. Important matters vary dramatically from respondent to respondent, encompassing relevant personal matters like intimate relationships, finances, health, hobbies, and work problems, as well as more general topics like politics. For example, a 70-year-old man might talk about his health while a 21-year-old woman might talk about which job to accept after college.

We also tend to talk about different things with different people. Respondents talk about different things with their spouses (children, education, finances) than with their co-workers and neighbors (community, politics, work). In fact, one study found that some people interpreted the question in terms of the frequency or intimacy of relationships, rather than the specific discussion of an important matter during the last six months.

In other words, the GSS network question about discussing important matters leads people to tell us about a close set of confidants who make up an important interpersonal environment for the transmission of information, influence, and support. We would be unwise to interpret the answers to this question too literally. However, they do give us a window into an important set of close, routinely contacted people who make up our respondents' immediate, close social circle.

THE NUMBERS

Given the close, densely interconnected nature of the social ties measured by the GSS question, we didn't expect much change in the core confidants of the typical American between 1985 and 2004. We were clearly wrong.

Most notable was the large drop in the size of core discussion networks. The number of discussion partners decreased by nearly one person (from a mean of 2.9 to a mean of 2.1) in the past two decades. The most common answer to our question about confidants dropped from three to none. Almost half the population (43.6 percent) now reports they discuss important matters with only one other person or with no one at all—a level of connection Claude Fischer called "inadequate social support" in his classic book *To Dwell Among Friends.* Having only one close person was inadequate because it made one very vulnerable to losing that lone relationship, he argued. The change is especially dramatic among those who reported four or more discussion partners. These well-connected respondents have decreased from more than one-third of the population (38.4 percent) to only one-fifth (20.2 percent).

This large social change occurred in the context of both kin and non-kin discussion partners. The most common answer for each has dropped from one to zero. Because both types of discussion partners have declined in number, the proportion of family members among a person's network of discussion partners has increased only moderately across the 19-year span, from 53 percent to 60 percent. All the changes described in [Figures 46.1 through 46.5] are statistically significant—they are very unlikely to have been observed by chance.

Americans are also discussing important matters with family, especially spouses or partners, rather than friends or neighbors. Fully 38 percent of the

Figure 46.1 Number of Confidants

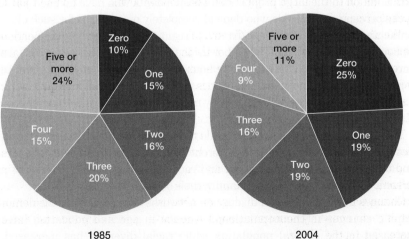

1985   2004

Figure 46.2 Types of Confidant Relationships

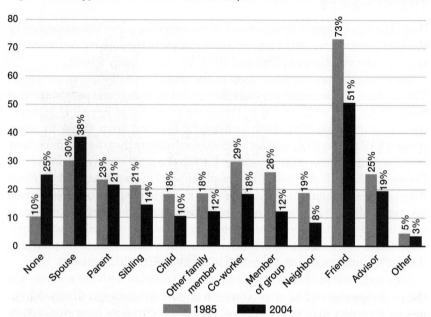

2004 discussion partners are spouses, as opposed to 30 percent in 1985. The proportion of respondents who mention at least one parent as a core confidant has decreased only slightly (from 24 percent to 21 percent). On the other hand, Americans are much less likely to discuss important matters with a neighbor or someone they know through community organizations. These are exactly the types of community ties that have been stressed by scholars like Putnam in the public policy debate over civic engagement.

In addition to the large proportion of respondents who have no one to talk to, the percentage of people who depend completely on a spouse for such close contact increased by 50 percent (from 6 percent to 9 percent). The proportion of people who talk to a family member aside from their spouses—kin who are more likely to reside outside the same household—has dropped (59 percent to 43 percent). But, the most striking drop is in the percentage of people who talk to at least one person who is not a family member, a decline from 80 percent to 57 percent.

This is significant because ties outside the family are the most likely to connect respondents to people from different parts of society. Family members tend to be similar in class, religion, and race. Therefore, if the majority of a person's connections are through family, their social world is limited.

Changes in the diversity of discussion networks seem to mirror the demographic changes in the population: Diversity in age and education have decreased in the general population while racial diversity has increased.

Figure 46.3 Types of Confidant Relationships

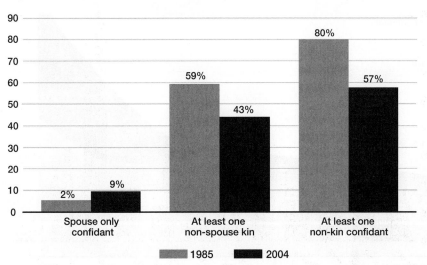

Also, compared to 1985 age has very little impact on contemporary confidant networks. In 1985, network size (especially non-family confidants) dropped off precipitously with increasing age. In contrast, age wasn't strongly related to the number of confidants or kinship composition in 2004.

Highly educated people have more confidants. In fact, education has a stronger effect on the number of family confidants than it did in 1985. Highly educated people have a smaller proportion of family in their networks than people with less education, which means highly educated people are more likely than others to be exposed to new perspectives by talking with their close friends.

Historically, women have had family-based networks while men had more ties outside the family, but in 2004 men and women didn't differ very much. Unfortunately, the equity is a product of men's shrinking connections with non-kin confidants rather than women's greater connections to the world outside the family. But, men's and women's lives are becoming more intertwined, as both are more likely to mention a spouse or partner as their closest confidant. As wives and husbands have become more similar—both are likely to work, and both contribute to household tasks and childcare—they have become more like friends or companions, at least for our purposes here. An earlier generation was more likely to have had a family where the husband and wife worked in different spheres. Now couples have more in common but are more dependent on each other for all kinds of support and emotional closeness.

Race continues to have a broad impact on networks in American society. Blacks and other non-white respondents have smaller networks of confidants than white Americans, and this pattern is most apparent in family networks, which are markedly smaller among non-whites.

Figure 46.4 Core Kin and Non-Kin Confidants

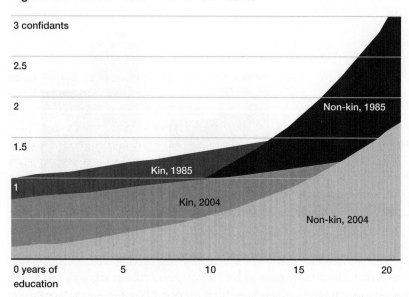

THE SHAPE OF SOCIAL ISOLATION

Given the close, interconnected nature of core discussion networks one might argue the crucial distinction isn't among different network sizes but between those who have *someone* to talk to and those who have *no one* with whom they can discuss important matters.

We know having at least one close tie is important to both physical and mental health. Socially isolated people who lack even one close confidant are missing both emotional support and concrete assistance in many areas of their lives. We found that younger, highly educated, married people are less likely to be socially isolated. Blacks are more likely than whites to be socially isolated, although other non-white people are not significantly different from whites. Men are not significantly more likely than women to be without a confidant. They have fewer discussion partners than women, controlling for other characteristics, but they are as likely as women to have at least one confidant (often a spouse). Education has the largest effect on social isolation, as it did in our analysis of network size.

To illustrate the effect of education, we can estimate the probability that a white, married, 25-year-old male high school graduate would have someone to talk to about important matters in 1985. He would be virtually assured of a discussion partner, since his probability of being isolated was only 0.07. The same type of person in 2004 would have a predicted probability of 0.24 of being isolated. If we "age" our 25-year-old to 44 in 2004 (as if we were tracking a real person through this time period), we find his probability of having no one to talk to about important matters would have more than tripled, rising from 0.07 to 0.28.

WHY SUCH BIG CHANGES?

Families, especially families with children, face time constraints that come from longer commutes and work hours. As more women have entered the labor force, family members spend more time outside the home. This increase has been most dramatic among well-educated, higher income, middle-aged parents. Such families can use new technologies, most notably cell phones and the Internet, to stay in touch with kin and friends. But while these technologies allow a network to spread out across geographic space and might even enhance contacts outside the home (for example, allowing them to arrange a meeting at a restaurant or bar), they seem to lower the probability of having face-to-face visits with family, neighbors, or friends in one's home.

Internet use may even interfere with communication in the home, creating a culture where family members spend time interacting with multiple computers rather than with each other. Some researchers suggest computer technology may foster a wider, less localized array of weak ties, replacing the strong, tightly interconnected ties to confidants that we measured here. This may not be all bad, of course. We know weak ties expose us to a wider range of information than strong, close (redundant) ties. But we also know strong ties offer a wider variety of support with everyday and emergency situations. Only geographically local ties can offer certain kinds of help and emotional support.

Whatever the reason, it appears Americans are far less tightly connected now than 19 years ago. Ties with local neighborhoods and groups have suffered at a higher rate than others. It's possible this is not so much a matter of increasing isolation but merely a shift in the form and type of connection. We know the nature of civic participation has been changing, as have modes of communication more generally. The evidence here may be telling us that structures of personal relationships are also shifting because of these developments.

WHAT WE'RE LOSING

If we assume that interpersonal environments are important—and most sociologists do—then obviously a large social change has taken place in the last two decades. The number of people with someone to talk to about important matters has declined dramatically. By Fischer's definition, now nearly half the entire American population has become isolated from social support. This result paints a picture of an already densely connected, close, homogeneous set of ties slowly closing in on itself, becoming smaller, more tightly interconnected, more focused on the very strong bonds of the nuclear family—our spouses, partners, and parents, but not our neighbors.

Figure 46.5 Increase in Social Isolation

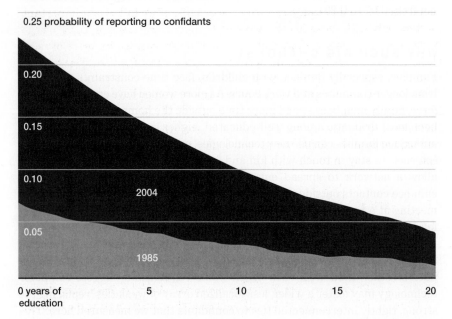

0.25 probability of reporting no confidants

0.20

0.15

0.10

2004

0.05

1985

0 years of education　　　　　5　　　　　10　　　　　15　　　　　20

Hard-pressed people need other people. Social science tells us that the tangible, material help we get from others leads to longer, healthier lives. People stranded on rooftops after Hurricane Katrina perhaps didn't know anyone with a car and didn't have a close friend they could stay with for a few days (or a few months). A harried mother who shows up 20 minutes late to day care is paying the price (usually by the minute) of not having a close friend she can ask to pick up her child when she's running late.

Unfortunately, our findings show that people who are disadvantaged in other ways—they're less educated or members of minority racial/ethnic groups—are likely to have smaller networks of close ties. These people lose out on the safety net that comes from community embeddedness, and they're more likely to experience emergencies and need help from social networks.

A study published soon after the 2004 GSS survey illustrated the sociobiological effects of greater stress. A psychologist and a molecular biologist studied people who scored highest in loneliness, people who said for four years straight that "there's really nobody that I feel close to." These lonely people had distinctive patterns of genetic activity, almost all of it involving the immune system. They showed higher levels of the chronic inflammation associated with heart and artery disease, arthritis, and Alzheimer's. As Robert Putnam's Bowling Alone website (www.bowlingalone.com) suggests, joining a social group or meeting a neighbor could be better for your health than regular exercise or an attempt to stop smoking.

But it isn't just individuals who may be hurt by shrinking numbers of close social ties. The community as a whole may suffer if we talk about important matters only with those in our own small family circles. While clubs, neighborhood associations, and workplaces are often segregated in terms of race, class, and gender, they are still more diverse than most families. Ties formed in such groups help hold communities together.

Without these bridges, we may be missing the chance to understand and interact with whole segments of our social world. We may cease to care about them because we have no strong bonds that span the social divides that separate us, because the social fabric that underlies our civil society continues to fray.

RECOMMENDED RESOURCES

Claude S. Fischer. *To Dwell among Friends: Personal Networks in Town and City* (University of Chicago Press, 1982). This California study is the classic reference on social networks and friendship.

Miller McPherson, Lynn Smith-Lovin, and Matthew E. Brashears. "Social isolation in America: Changes in core discussion networks," *American Sociological Review* (2006) 71: 353–375. This is the original research article reporting the findings described here.

Robert D. Putnam. *Bowling Alone: The Collapse and Revival of American Community* (Simon and Schuster, 2000). This book argues for the importance of social capital in creating community.

47

Work Freed Her, Then It Moved to Mexico

FARAH STOCKMAN

For decades, global capitalism has sent manufacturing jobs from wealthier to poorer countries where plants are being built and workers are finding jobs at low wages. Working conditions may be unsafe and unions may be outlawed, but the wages are higher than for most other jobs. Without a concerted commitment to job retraining and government action to staunch this decline in U.S. manufacturing, many parts of the country have become a "rust belt" of shuttered factories and shrinking communities. Union strength—anchored in manufacturing—has declined, and new technology such as robotics has replaced well-paid labor. The toll on workers, especially those with only a high school degree or none at all, has been severe. This essay chronicles one worker's plight in a system of global capitalism that takes no prisoners.

The man from Mexico followed a manager through the factory floor, past whirring exhaust fans, beeping forklifts, and drilling machines that whined against steel. Workers in safety glasses looked up and stared. Others looked away. Shannon Mulcahy felt her stomach lurch.

It was December 2016. The Rexnord Corporation's factory still churned out bearings as it always had. Trucks still dropped off steel pipes at the loading dock. Bill Stinnett, a die-hard Indiana Pacers fan, still cut them into pieces. The pieces still went to the "turning" department, where they were honed into rings as small as a bracelet or as big as a basketball. Then to "heat treat," where Shannon—who loves heavy metal music and abandoned dogs—hardened them with fire. Then to "grinding," where Shannon's cousin Lorry Mannix smoothed out any imperfections. And then to "assembly," where Mark Elliott, a former Marine, joined two rings together, one inside the other, with a wheel of spinning rollers in between. The whole contraption was encased in a cast-iron housing machined by John Feltner, a father of three who'd just recovered from bankruptcy.

The bearings they made—modern-day equivalents of a gadget designed by Leonardo da Vinci—were packed into crates like enormous Christmas ornaments and shipped around the world. To digging machines that claw the earth. To wheat combines that spin in the fields. To elevators and escalators in the cities.

Sometimes a bearing was rumored to have ended up in something notable—the retracting roof of the Dallas Cowboys football stadium or a nuclear submarine—giving the workers a feeling of greatness. But mostly, the bearings were unglamorous. Anonymous. Hidden from view. Like the workers themselves, they were rarely thought of beyond the factory walls.

That was fine with Shannon Mulcahy. When she first started working at the plant, at age 25, her only goal was to break free of a boyfriend who beat her. Back then, her frosted blond hair and hourglass figure turned heads on the factory floor. Now, at 43, men more often remarked on her broad shoulders, which can lift a 75-pound tray of steel. Or her hands, stained with oil. "My moneymakers," Shannon called them.

Being a female steelworker hadn't been easy. But she'd learned to hold her own. If a man spread a false rumor that he'd slept with her, she spread a false rumor right back that he'd been terrible in bed. If a woman wanted to fight, she learned to say "this is a place of business" instead of brawling then and there.

Shannon worked second shift—2 p.m. to 10 p.m.—which made it difficult for her to get custody of her daughter or keep her son in check during his teenage years. But the factory anchored her otherwise tumultuous life. Men had come and gone. Houses had been bought and lost. But the job had always been there. For 17 years. Until now.

Shannon and her co-workers had gotten the news back in October: The factory was closing. Ball bearings would move to a new plant in Monterrey, Mexico. Roller bearings would go to McAllen, Tex[as]. About 300 workers would lose their jobs. The bosses called it "a business decision." To Shannon, it felt like a backhand across the face.

Her boyfriend tried to console her. "We're survivors," he told her. "We'll get by." Shannon's daughter, Nicole Wynne, was not so sure. A high school senior, she had dreamed of being the first in her family to go to college. Figuring out how to pay for it kept her up at night. This news made her worry even more. And Shannon's 23-year-old son, Kent Roberts Jr.—known as Bub—depended on Shannon to help support his disabled 4-year-old daughter, who had just barely survived a litany of major surgeries.

"Oh my God, Mom," Nicole said. "What are you going to do?" Shannon had no idea. She wished the new factory in Mexico would burn to the ground. She cried that night. And the next night. And the next. Then, that Monday, Shannon did the only thing she knew how. She put on her electric-blue eyeliner and went back to work.

HALCYON DAYS AND STORMY MONTHS

For months, Shannon kept working as the factory shut down around her. She struggled with straightforward questions: Should she train workers from

Mexico for extra pay or refuse? Should she go back to school or find a new job, no matter what it paid?

And she was forced to confront a more sweeping question that nags at many of the 67 percent of adults in this country who do not have a four-year college degree: What does my future look like in the new American economy?

The 410,000-square-foot bearings plant, with its blue and gray tinted windows and flagpole out front, had been built by a company called Link-Belt in 1959, halcyon days for American manufacturing.

Link-Belt meant to bearings what Cadillac meant to cars. "Symbol of quality" was its motto. Even after a series of sales and mergers in the 1980s left the factory in the hands of Rexnord, a Milwaukee-based rival, the Link-Belt brand lived on, stamped into the housings of new bearings.

But over the years, cheaper bearings from overseas eroded profits. To stay profitable, the factory replaced some workers with machines and outsourced some components. Then Rexnord's chief executive announced the plan to send jobs to Mexico, which he said would reduce costs by $30 million and produce higher returns for investors.

Union representatives drew up a list of concessions in a bid to save the plant. But no concession could change the math. In Indiana, workers earned an average of $25 an hour, plus benefits. In Monterrey, they earned less than $6 an hour.

Moving the factory made sense to the people with college degrees. They expected that old workers could be swapped out for new ones, like interchangeable parts. That trainees could learn in a few weeks what Indianapolis workers had spent years mastering. That workers who had devoted their entire lives to building bearings they boasted were the best in the world would train their replacements and move on. But it didn't happen that way.

Rexnord had announced that the factory would close in six months. It took nearly a year. The company, which declined to comment for this article, struggled with setbacks, sabotage and bad publicity that turned the factory into a symbol of national angst at the loss of blue-collar jobs.

The factory's demise, which mirrored that of so many other American factories, had pierced the national consciousness because of a tweet. "Rexnord of Indianapolis is moving to Mexico and rather viciously firing all of its 300 workers," Donald J. Trump, then the president-elect, wrote in December. "No more!"

Two weeks later, a letter from Todd Adams, Rexnord's chief executive, appeared on the factory bulletin board. "Despite the political rhetoric," Mr. Adams wrote, "our US operations are home to approximately 4,000 associates—more than half of our global workforce." Rexnord's associates, he wrote, "are talented and valued." Someone drew a hand on the letter, middle finger pointing up.

Like many workers, Shannon held out hope that Mr. Trump would save the factory, especially after he had announced that he saved some jobs at Carrier, a plant a mile away. After Mr. Trump tweeted a threat to tax Rexnord "big" for moving across the border, Shannon tweeted back: "Go PRESIDENT TRUMP!"

Shannon didn't vote in the election. She considered politicians to be liars. But she found herself rooting for Mr. Trump. Democrats talked about social safety nets, but he talked about jobs.

"I don't look down on anybody who uses food stamps," she said. "But I want to work for a living."

She had always been proud of her job. When she ran into friends from high school, she told them she worked at Link-Belt, conscious of the envy it incited. Shannon was a legacy hire. Her uncle had worked at the factory since before she was born. Her sense of self-worth was tied to the brand. The bearings she built were top of the line.

She held onto that. "I still care," she said last March. "I don't know why. It becomes an identity. A part of you."

For workers like Shannon, the factory's final months were a time of reinvention and retribution. Of praying that Donald Trump would save them and arguing about why he didn't. Of squabbling over whether to train their Mexican replacements or shun them. Of vowing that one day, the corporate bosses would realize that making bearings isn't as easy as they thought.

"IT MAKES ME FEEL A LITTLE IMPORTANT"

The first day Shannon set foot in "heat treat" back in 2005, the guys working there instructed her to turn a valve and open a door on a furnace. Boom. A ball of fire leapt out. She screamed. They laughed.

"Heat treat is not for a woman," one declared.

Shannon thought about returning to her job on the factory's assembly line, where other women worked. But heat treat was practically a skilled trade. Opportunities like that were rare, especially for a single mother who had dropped out of high school.

Besides, Shannon hadn't been raised to pay much attention to rules about what a woman should or shouldn't do. Her own mother drank Wild Turkey and brawled with neighbors. Shannon's parents married when they were teenagers. Her father got a union job at Wonder Bread. He expected his uniform ironed and his eggs cooked over easy every morning. Shannon's mother, who kept breaking the yolks, once turned a plate over on his head.

Eventually, her parents divorced and her mother got a job cleaning hotel rooms. She made ends meet with food stamps, and drove a blue Ford Zephyr with no muffler or driver's side window. She thought she got lucky when she married a truck driver who lived in a trailer near theirs. He moved them to a real house in a quiet town where Shannon became a cheerleader and got interested in school.

But then the truck driver started sneaking into Shannon's bedroom at night. He went to prison. Without his paycheck, they lost the house.

"Don't ever depend on a man," her mother warned. Shannon never forgot that advice, but life had a way of intruding. Her mother died young from a heart problem, leaving 19-year-old Shannon to care for two little brothers and a baby boy of her own. She looked around for a savior. She thought she'd found one in Dan Wynne, who worked at a backhoe company and drove a nice truck, candy-apple red.

They'd met at a tattoo parlor when she was in her early 20s. He was the first man to take Shannon out to dinner. "I thought, 'O.K., what's it going to hurt?'" she recalled. But Dan was domineering and had a violent temper. Once, he grabbed her by the throat and banged her head against the floor, according to court records in a trial where he was found guilty of battery. Another time, he threw her car keys into a freezing ravine. After their daughter was born, Dan didn't want Shannon working, especially at a factory full of men.

The first night Shannon came home from work, Dan threw her belongings into the yard. For years, they had a tumultuous relationship, accusing each other of battery, according to court records.

Her job became her liberator. She worked her way up from a janitor to a heat treat operator, earning $25 an hour. With money like that, she wasn't going to let anybody drive her away from it.

She found a mentor in Stan Settles, who had worked at the factory for nearly half a century and knew everything about a forest-green heat-induction machine stamped with the word "DANGER" on its side. Its nickname was the "Tocco," after the Ohio Crankshaft Company that created it.

Stan showed Shannon how to bolt the right size coil to the Tocco's cabinet and make it heat up like a car cigarette lighter. He showed her how to make the machine spin the steel rings inside the hot coil for just the right amount of time and spit water onto them at the right moment, freezing a new molecular structure in place.

Shannon learned to look at a scrap of steel under a microscope in the factory's laboratory, to make sure the heat had done its work. Good steel looks like buckshot, Stan told her. That kind of steel could withstand the weight of a Ferris wheel or the openings and closings of a drawbridge. Bad steel looked like snowflakes. It could splinter inside a customer's machine.

Always check the sample under the microscope, Stan warned. It was a sacred rule passed down from the workers who had come before him, key to the quality of a Link-Belt bearing, upon which all else was built.

Over the years, Shannon got to know the furnaces as intimately as people. The auto-quench, with its yellow metal stairs, could be as high maintenance as an aging beauty queen. The batch furnace could belch fire out of its chimney, like an ill-tempered whiskey drinker. The Tocco, her favorite, broke down like a needy boyfriend whenever she left it alone too long.

Shannon had a reputation for taking too many smoke breaks and for putting on mascara in the lab. But she knew the furnaces better than almost anybody. She didn't mind getting calls from other workers asking her to troubleshoot problems. "It makes me feel a little important," she said.

Stan swore that he would never retire. A few years ago, Shannon found him behind the furnaces, straining to breathe. He begged her not to tell the factory's nurse, but she did. "I'll never forgive myself if you die here," she told him.

He died months later. Shannon became the veteran of the department, the one whom the bosses turned to when new operators needed to be trained. Still, she wasn't prepared for the latest request from Rexnord: Would she teach the workers from Mexico being hired to replace her?

DIVISIONS ON THE FACTORY FLOOR

Autumn faded into winter. Graffiti appeared in a men's bathroom at the factory: "Build the wall" and "Go back to Mexico!"

For years, Shannon had heard complaints that Mexicans were "taking our jobs" and that undocumented immigrants were driving down wages.

As more and more Indianapolis factories moved to Mexico, more and more Mexicans settled in Indianapolis. An estimated 30,000 people born in Mexico lived in Marion County, where Indianapolis is located, in 2015, more than twice as many as in 2000, according to the Migration Policy Institute.

Just blocks from the union hall of United Steelworkers Local 1999, a neighborhood once nicknamed "Hillbilly Heaven" was now known as "Little Mexico." Nearly every business along a busy stretch of road advertised in Spanish. Immigrants worked in lawn care, roofing, house painting—jobs that threw them into competition with unskilled American workers reeling from the loss of factory work.

Shannon once rented a house in Little Mexico, down the street from a place that sold $4 burritos as big as a forearm. She felt strange sitting among customers bantering in Spanish. But she was curious about the country. Her father's most recent wife had been born there.

"They are a lot better workers," Shannon said, "because they don't have that opportunity where they are from." At the Rexnord factory, the first trainees arrived around Christmastime.

John Feltner watched them from his machine. Everyone within earshot knew he'd refused to train them. "I won't sell my soul for an extra $4 an hour," he said. "That's less than a pack of cigarettes."

John, the unit vice president of the union, had come from a long line of union men. His grandfather was a Kentucky strip miner, his father a millwright at Wonder Bread. He had harsh words for those who volunteered to train: "It's no different than crossing the picket line."

Over in assembly, Mark Elliott welcomed the trainees with a booming voice. Mark's father, a machinist at Detroit Diesel-Allison, hadn't talked about the union. Mark volunteered to train the new hires as soon as Rexnord announced the move. Those who did the training in Mexico would get a

$5,000 bonus. "I'm going to get that money," he said. "I can't stop it from closing. All I can do is ride the wave on out."

At rallies, John urged his union brothers and sisters to unite against the company: "Come together and fight for your livelihood." But the crisis laid their differences bare.

At a factory where black and white workers bowled together on Tuesday nights, where at least two romances crossed racial lines, a subtle divide emerged: Many white men like John refused to train and shunned those who did; many black men like Mark openly volunteered. The white workers who did agree to train tended to do so quietly, and kept it a secret as long as they could, said Jim Swain, Shannon's supervisor.

Some white men complained that they'd watched their economic prospects decline for decades. They had shared their jobs with black men, then with women. Now that blacks and women were welcomed in every facet of factory life, the jobs were moving to Mexico. It seemed like proof that their best days were behind them.

One worker, Bill Jones, quit abruptly, walking away from more than $10,000 in severance because he could not stand seeing the Mexican trainees. "It's depressing," he said, "being reminded every day that you ain't got a future."

Many of the black workers talked about the factory's closing as an opportunity to go back to school or start a business. Their attitudes mirrored national polls that showed blacks to be more optimistic about the future. For them, the days ahead had little chance of being as bad as the past. Even those who declined to train refused to bad-mouth the Mexican workers. "It ain't their fault," Mark said.

Many of the women felt torn between the two viewpoints. Shannon, who is white, felt bitter about losing her job but needed the money. Groups of women—black and white—agreed to train together.

When the Mexican trainees arrived, Shannon stood near her red toolbox, which was decorated with photos of her granddaughter, Carmella. The girl had lain in a coma for months, after a string of complications from a rare chromosomal disorder. Shannon had taken off work to stay by her side. The little girl's fingers had turned black, like too-ripe bananas, from lack of circulation. Doctors snipped them off. Shannon cleaned and dressed the wounds.

Now Carmella slept in a little bed in Shannon's living room. Every night, when Shannon came home from the factory, Carmella flapped her arms, eager for a hug. Now that Shannon was losing her job, she needed that $5,000 bonus to keep a roof over the child's head. "I have to do it," she told her daughter, Nicole.

Once she made up her mind, she came up with reasons it was right to train them. It would help the Mexican people, who were poorer than her: "God would want you to share."

She wanted a passport and the chance to see Mexico on the company's dime: "I'd never get to do this otherwise." She wanted to make sure the Tocco's new operators cared for it properly: "It just gives me a little bit of closure with the Tocco. I know it sounds crazy. I feel like it's mine."

Shannon looked up Monterrey on the internet. She saw a big city, surrounded by mountains. It looked nothing like the dirt roads she'd imagined. She was surprised by how many of Rexnord's suppliers and competitors were already there.

"That's the future of manufacturing," she said. "Of everything, it seems like." She wanted to be a part of the future, if only for a few weeks. After word got out that she had decided to train, one co-worker refused to look at her. Shannon soldiered on, as though she didn't mind.

She worried more about Bob Osborne, a furnace maintenance man. Bob had been one of the few employees to visit Carmella in the hospital. He had collected more than $900 from co-workers to help her family. After Shannon agreed to train, Bob took her aside and told her that he didn't want any part of it. Nothing against the Mexicans, he said. He just didn't want to help Todd Adams carry out his plan.

"If you are working on that Tocco, training, and it goes down, I'm not going to come over and fix it," he warned.

But Bob didn't give Shannon the silent treatment. He still joked with her, and asked about Carmella. He criticized other trainers, but not her. "Your situation is different," he said.

The first day Shannon trained, someone turned a valve on the Tocco when she wasn't looking. Water overflowed everywhere. The second time, the Tocco's computerized brain stopped communicating with its mechanical parts. Even the electrician couldn't fix it. After the day had been wasted, Shannon noticed a wire had been disconnected.

A motherly anger welled up in her chest: Who would attack a defenseless machine? All around her, the factory beeped and whirred, as if life continued as normal. But nothing was normal. A lurking resentment had made itself known.

SIXTEEN RICARDOS FOR ONE SHANNON

Winter bloomed into spring. The plant was hollowed out, piece by piece. They took Lorry's grinder. Then Mark's assembly cell. Then John's machine. The emptiness in the factory grew. "Have you been down to see what it looks like?" Shannon's co-workers kept asking her. She hadn't, unable to bear the sight.

Shannon and her co-workers still talked about how to save the factory. Some blamed shareholders for its closing. Shannon thought that maybe if she wrote them a letter, she could change their minds. "It's not like they are losing money," she reasoned. "Why would you take jobs from your people? The American people?" One day, she searched the internet for shareholders' names.

Long ago, 40 percent of Link-Belt's stock was owned by its employees, according to a company document from 1925. Back then, business schools taught that a chief executive's role was to balance shareholders' interests with those of employees, customers and the government.

But today, most of Rexnord's shares are held by mutual funds managed on behalf of global investors. To many, Rexnord was nothing more than three letters on a page—RXN—with an arrow pointing up or down.

In today's model, chief executives like Mr. Adams get more compensation in stock, to align their interests with shareholders, who are now considered more important than other stakeholders. That's why Mr. Adams made more than $40 million over the last six years, as he cut the cost of labor. Shannon never found a list of Rexnord's shareholders. They remained a mystery, as anonymous as they were omnipotent.

Shannon still tended the furnaces each night, pretending that President Trump would still save their jobs. But reality became harder to ignore when two men from Mexico arrived to learn about the Tocco. Shannon knew she'd feel jealous of the men who would take it away. But she found them both likable. They showed her more respect than some Americans she had trained.

The younger one, a maintenance worker named Tadeo, exuded excitement that clashed with the sullen stares he got from American workers in the plant. The older one, a process engineer named Ricardo Valdez, was handsome, carried himself with confidence and liked to crack jokes. "You're strong!" he told Shannon, flexing his arms. (Ricardo did not return multiple calls and emails.)

One afternoon, she brought Ricardo into the lab and showed him their system for checking samples under the microscope. He glanced around, like a man searching for clues, Shannon recalled. "Why aren't you moving down with the factory?" he asked.

"They didn't offer for us to come down," she replied. Ricardo's eyes widened. Shannon got the impression that he had never been told that the Mexican workers were taking their American trainers' jobs. "So they are just leaving you?"

Shannon nodded. "How much are they paying you?" she asked him. "They pay me a lot." She pulled her pay stub up on the computer. "You're rich!" he told Shannon.

"I'm not rich, honey," she replied. "I've got bills to pay." Her mortgage: $1,300. Her car payment: $400. Diapers and medicine for Carmella. Taxes. Shannon's paychecks disappeared quickly.

She admits that she's no good at saving. She doles out money without hesitation to those in need. A dollar for the man by the side of the road. Nicole's car payment. A $1,200 surgery for a pit bull she'd adopted that had swallowed steel wool.

Ricardo pecked at a calculator. "Sixteen," he announced. Rexnord could pay 16 Ricardos for the cost of one Shannon.

"But you don't understand," Shannon said. "They have the money. They just don't want to give it to you."

Shannon felt closer to the younger trainee, Tadeo. (His last name has been withheld due to his concerns about future job prospects.) He was 23, the same age as her son. Shannon called him "Tad" or "Kid." He had a sparse goatee, and a habit of saying "yes, yes," even when Shannon wasn't sure he had understood.

He trailed behind her like a duckling when she went outside to smoke. "Want some chips?" she'd ask him. "What kind of music do you like?" He brought her cookies and showed her a video on his phone of his girlfriend receiving flowers he'd sent for her birthday.

Once, Shannon mentioned how long it took her to drive to work. "You own a car?" he asked. "You don't?" she replied.

Shannon could have given Tad the bare minimum of training, answering a few questions and collecting her pay. But just as Stan Settles had passed on his knowledge to Shannon, Shannon trained Tad as if he were one of her own.

She showed him how to bolt in the coil and to make sure the steel rings spun without touching the sides. Affix the wrong bullnose and the shaft could break. "O.K.," Shannon said. "It's your turn."

Tad worked on the Tocco all afternoon. Shannon noticed water leaking from the hoses. A loose hose could shoot water clear across the factory. "Tighten down your hoses," she said. He had also installed the copper piece backward. But that was no big deal. He had skillfully navigated the challenges of translating English to Spanish, inches to meters. She felt proud of Tad.

Before he returned to Mexico, Tad pulled Shannon aside. He put his hand over his heart. "My friend tells me that the reason a lot of people don't like us is because we're taking their jobs," he said, sounding distraught.

"I'm not mad at you," she said. "I'm happy that you get the opportunity to make some money. I was blessed for a while. I hate to see it go. Now it's your turn to be blessed."

* * *

NEW JOB, NO. OCTOPUS POOL, YES

Summer came. The hot sun turned into a coil, hardening the earth below. The factory's closing date got pushed from April to July because the plants in Monterrey, Mexico, and McAllen, Tex., were taking longer than expected to get up to speed.

Trainers returned with news about everything that was going wrong. Equipment was missing in Monterrey. A batch of bearings made in McAllen wouldn't spin. A joke went around the Indianapolis plant: "Rexnord has come out with a new line of bearings—the kind that doesn't move." The sheer variety of bearings, which numbered in the thousands, made it difficult for the trainees to learn them all. Instructions were in English. And not every step had been written down.

Over the years, workers had been forced to make adjustments. "That's in people's little notebooks, and in their heads," said Jim Swain, Shannon's former supervisor. The workers in Indianapolis were now needed more than ever, even as their layoffs loomed. They labored seven days a week, hating every minute of a job they didn't know what they were going to do without.

Shannon had been putting off looking for new employment. But finally, on a humid July day, she asked for permission to leave the factory early to attend a job fair.

Others had already moved on. Her cousin Lorry got a job at Allison Transmission. It paid about $15 an hour. John Feltner, who had refused to train the new hires, got a job repairing machines at Kroger for $22.51 an hour, then found a better position at a mechanical contractor. Mark, still training in Mexico and Texas, was getting tired of living out of a suitcase.

Those who had yet to find work wandered into the job fair and found one another, giving the room the feel of a reunion. Shannon ran into her friend Bill Jones, who'd quit abruptly. He was working as a trucker but wanted something better. They approached a table set by the Sheet Metal Workers Local 20. "If you are not afraid of hard work and you show up every day, the sky is the limit," a recruiter, Tim Choate, told them. Shannon's hand shot out for a brochure.

But the training period lasted five years. And pay started at $16.70 per hour. It would be years before she would make $33, journeyman's pay. "When is the next class?" Shannon asked.

"We'll need your high school diploma," Mr. Choate said. "A copy of your high school transcripts. Then we'll send you for your test. Once you pass the test, we will have you in for an interview." Shannon's brow furrowed. "But eventually you get in, right?" she asked. He smiled and admitted: "There's no guarantee."

Summer dragged on. The factory's closing date got pushed forward again, to September. The empty spaces there had grown so big that Shannon couldn't avoid them anymore. She rode a bicycle around the plant at night, pretending to be in "The Wizard of Oz."

She knew that she needed to put herself on a budget. But she couldn't. Shopping had become one of the few things she looked forward to.

As a kid, she'd hated buying groceries with her mother, ashamed of the food stamps they had used. In adulthood, Shannon liked the ritual of consumption.

She'd never felt much like the citizen of a democracy. "People like us," she said, "aren't heard." But her job had transformed her into a consumer of things—another respected role in American society. She had achieved a status: the kind of person who buys Heinz ketchup instead of the generic brand.

Several times a week, she pushed her cart through the 24-hour Meijer superstore by her house. She passed the clothing section, where dresses made in Indonesia sold for $19. She knew that other Americans lost their jobs because they couldn't make dresses that cheap. But she rarely thought of things in those terms, she said.

For champions of free trade, this is the true measure of prosperity. Jobs move overseas and wages stagnate, but Americans buy more stuff than ever.

Shannon knew she was in danger of losing her home. She pondered cashing in her 401(k) to pay the mortgage. Even so, she still filled the shopping cart with new toys for Carmella. That summer she bought a green octopus pool. A red plastic slide. A giant blowup bounce house, made in China.

"I see you here a lot," the cashier at Meijer told her one night. "Where do you work?" "Link-Belt," Shannon replied. "It's Rexnord now." The cashier's smile faded. "Isn't that the place that's closing?"

* * *

LOSING TWO BABIES IN A WEEK

The next day at the factory, Shannon watched yet another cord get cut. She walked in to find Bob on the scissor lift, looming above the Tocco, a giant puddle on the floor. "What's going on?" Shannon asked. But it was obvious. Bob was disconnecting the Tocco, days ahead of schedule.

Ricardo, the process engineer from Mexico, had arrived with his team to pack up the Tocco. Shannon had been looking forward to seeing Tad, the young trainee. She had a few more things to teach him. Time was running out. But Tad was nowhere to be found. He got another job, Ricardo told Shannon, one that paid more than Rexnord did.

Instead of Tad, Ricardo had come with a new guy who barely spoke English. This time, Shannon didn't bother to learn his name. But she tried to be nice. She brought the Mexican team outside to look at the solar eclipse. Shannon felt the eyes of her American co-workers on her.

No one harbored illusions anymore that President Trump would save the plant. Shannon didn't hold it against him. "Everybody's fighting him," she said. She did worry when she heard on the news that he was trying to roll back a federally funded health care program that Carmella relied on. Mr. Trump was turning into just another politician, the same way Link-Belt was turning into just another brand.

Shannon, who'd derived her self-worth from the quality of the bearings she made, felt unsure about who she'd become. In two weeks' time, her job would end. Her trip to Mexico would be canceled at the last minute, along with the $5,000 bonus she had been counting on. Training costs had gone over budget and needed to be reined in.

More than 17 years on the factory floor came down to this: the Tocco, disconnected from water and electricity, waiting to be cut into pieces. Ricardo stood at a table nearby, swaddling the last of its coils in Bubble Wrap. Shannon didn't offer to help. She walked outside to smoke. She didn't want Ricardo to see her cry.

Later that same day, a heat treat worker complained that when Ricardo had set up the Tocco to run one last batch of parts, the coil had gotten too hot. But Ricardo pressed on. Maybe he was confident in his work, Shannon thought, or maybe he was in a hurry to finish the order before the Tocco was hauled away. "I'd like to see the sample," Shannon said.

She slipped into the lab and found the scrap of steel archived in a drawer. She put it under the microscope. But then she thought about the dying factory. The turning department, with two lonely machines left. Grinding, nearly gone. The place where assembly once stood marked with tape on the floor, like a crime scene. Suddenly, she turned the microscope off.

"Forget it," she said. "It's not my problem anymore."

48

Undermined: A Local Activist Fights for the Future of Coal Country

ELIZA GRISWOLD

The 2016 U.S. presidential campaign spotlighted several issues around fossil fuels: their contribution to global warming; local environmental damage and regulations; black lung disease; and jobs in coal country. Whether in Wyoming or West Virginia, no one believes coal has a lock on the future, but how to move toward a future without fossil fuels is bitterly contended. Veronica Coptis grew up in coal country, but she is not content to let "the market" decide her future or the future of coal country. Rather, this woman of little means is challenging giant corporations by working with activist groups to save what is left of coal country and plan for a future beyond coal.

One Sunday morning, just after deer-hunting season ended, Veronica Coptis, a community organizer in rural Greene County, Pennsylvania, climbed onto her father's four-wheeler. She set off for a ridge a quarter of a mile from her parents' small farmhouse, where she was brought up with her brother and two sisters. "Those are coyote tracks," she called over the engine noise, pointing down at a set of fresh paw prints.

At the crest of the ridge, she stopped along a dirt track and scanned in both directions for security guards. Around her stretched a three-mile wasteland of valleys. Once an untouched landscape of white oak and shagbark hickory, it now belonged to Consol Energy and served as the refuse area for the Bailey Mine Complex, the largest underground coal mine in the United States.

Five hundred feet below the ridge-line lay a slate-colored expanse of sludge: 60 acres of coal waste, which filled the valley floor to a depth of more than 100 feet. Coptis stared; it was twice as deep as it had been when she'd visited a year before. "How can it be that after 200 years no one has come up with a better way of getting rid of coal waste?" she asked. A flock of geese cut a V through water puddled atop the sludge. Recently, activists in West Virginia had paddled an inflatable boat onto a similar pond to bring attention to the hazards of coal waste. Maybe the same tactic could work here, Coptis said. It was dangerous, though; the slurry was too thick to swim through, and at least one worker had fallen in and drowned.

Coptis directs the Center for Coal-field Justice, a regional organization that advocates for people living with the effects of resource extraction. Industrial mining, she believes, leaves places like Greene County environmentally ravaged and reliant on a single, dwindling resource. At 30, Coptis is an unlikely activist. She grew up among miners, and her father, a surveyor, sometimes works for the oil industry. She heard the word "environmentalist" for the first time in college, at West Virginia University. (Local hunters and fishermen, whom Coptis sees as some of her best potential allies, prefer to identify themselves as "conservationists.") After graduating, she moved back to Greene County and married Donald Fike, a former marine who worked in the mines. When Coptis brings in outside activists, she often warns them not to expect issues to break down along tidy ideological lines. "The assumption is that rural America is this monolithic community, and it's not," she told me. She also warns them to be prepared for shotguns leaning against kitchen walls. Like many locals, Coptis learned to shoot when she was a child. "I find firing handguns relaxing," she said. "Maybe because I'm so powerless over so much of my life."

Around Greene County, Coptis carries a Russian Makarov pistol, partly to reassure her father. Her fight against coal mining often puts her in opposition not only to energy companies but also to miners concerned about their jobs, and he fears that someone will run her Nissan Versa off a rural road one night. "The coal mines are multimillion-dollar projects," he told me. "Stopping them can be a nasty thing." Coal has dominated the area for more than a century, and mining companies own about 15 percent of the county's land. Above ground, their dominion is marked by yellow gates that block roads into valleys designated for waste; when Coptis was younger, a coal company that was expanding its waste area bought a neighboring village and razed it, leaving only a single mailbox. Below ground, the practice of "long-wall" mining, which removes an entire coal seam, can crack buildings' foundations and damage springs and wells, destroying water supplies.

In 2005, this process led to an environmental catastrophe in Ryerson Station State Park, a 1,200-acre preserve that contains some of the county's only pristine land. The center of the park was Duke Lake: a reservoir, created by damming a fork of Wheeling Creek, where people had gathered for decades to swim, paddle canoes, and fish. While Consol was mining nearby, the dam ruptured, and the water had to be drained away. The lake has not been restored; a survey commissioned by the state found that the ground was too unstable. But more than $15 million worth of coal remains under the park, and now Consol wants to return and mine it. Coptis's organization, along with the Sierra Club, has filed suit to block the mine from acquiring the necessary permits, arguing that the mining would destroy three endangered streams. According to Consol's own survey, the mining is predicted to crack the streambeds, draining the water and spoiling the last fishing in the park. "This is property owned by every resident in Pennsylvania," Coptis said. "They don't get to keep plowing through our communities as if we didn't matter."

Since the mid-eighteenth century, Appalachia has supplied coal to the rest of the country, in an arrangement that has brought employment but also pollution and disease. Coptis's opponents argue that the benefits outweigh the costs. Recently, on Twitter, an industry organization called Energy Jobs Matter taunted Coptis: "How much is the Sierra Club paying you to put these families on unemployment?" One of her neighbors warned that if she won her suit the Bailey mine would go bankrupt, devastating the local economy. There are 2,000 jobs underground in Greene County, and, according to state estimates, each one supports 3.7 others at the surface. Shutting the mine could eliminate more than 7,000 jobs, in a county of 37,000 people. "Greene County will become a ghost town," the neighbor wrote.

Coptis argues that the county is already dying. In the past eight years, as coal has ceased to be the dominant fuel used in power plants, production in the United States has dropped by 38 percent. Until recently, the Bailey mine had three competitors in Greene County; one has closed and another has gone through bankruptcy. Some 600 jobs have disappeared. In Coptis's old school district, enrollment has declined 24 percent. For Coptis, the changes are urgently personal—her husband was among the miners who lost jobs when the mines closed. "As a community, we need to start to talk about what happens when coal mining stops," she said. "In my lifetime, it's going to happen."

When Coptis goes out to canvass her neighbors, she has the advantage of familiarity. She is brown-eyed and sturdy, with deep dimples that make her look gentle and friendly, even when she is pressing a point, and she is skilled at breaking down the arcana of lawsuits and rights-of-way. "I come from the working class and struggled hard in college," she said. "I had to read aloud to understand things."

But some of her tendencies make her seem strikingly out of place; one local official referred to her, fondly, as a "radical." When Coptis drives to appointments, she often blasts the cast recording of "Hamilton." She teases her husband that she's going to put a sign in their yard bearing their nicknames, Roni and Donnie, so that passersby will think that their brick bungalow belongs to a same-sex couple. She has already planted one controversial sign, near their chicken coop. In black and red letters, it announces, "COAL ASH IS TOXIC."

* * *

Coptis's grandparents had retired to Greene County, near the West Virginia border, and Alice [her mother] found a two-bedroom farmhouse for sale there, across a dirt road from where they lived. The house was "undermined"—a mining company had bought rights to the land, then tunnelled underneath—and now a spring spurted from a wall in the basement. But there was space for the family, if the parents slept in an alcove off the living room, and it cost only $25,000. No bank would offer a mortgage on such a property, so Alice borrowed from her parents and paid for the house in cash.

Coptis's older siblings struggled to adjust to country life, but she loved it. She and her father spent hours in a canoe on Duke Lake, fishing for bluegill. With her grandfather, she hiked through the hills, learning to identify bullfrogs by their call and red-tailed hawks by their raked wing tips. Although the Bailey mine had begun operating a decade before, most of the surrounding valleys were still open land. Coptis grew up listening to the rumble of a conveyor belt, 31 miles long, that brought coal to market and carried away waste. As a child, she mistook its lights for those of a distant roller coaster.

Alice was determined that her daughters be given every opportunity that a boy would. She gave Veronica and her older sisters, Andrea and Becky, male nicknames—Roni, Andi, and B.J.—to ease their way in a male-dominated professional world. At West Greene High School, Veronica had a sympathetic English teacher, who helped her procure books—by Truman Capote, Jack Kerouac, and J. D. Salinger—that the school district had banned. Coptis was outraged that "In Cold Blood" had been disallowed because Capote was gay. "Catcher in the Rye" impressed her less. "Holden Caulfield was just some rich white kid," she said.

Despite her contrariness, Coptis was popular. "Roni was so cute—she fit in," Alice said. She ate lunch every day with Donald Fike, the class clown, and studied intently, especially science. Inspired by "CSI," she decided to become a forensic pathologist, and designed an audacious experiment for the state science fair: using the school's electron microscope, bought with a science grant for rural schools, she compared gun-shot residue from two of her father's pistols, to see if the higher-caliber one left a larger burn pattern.

During her high-school years, the Bailey mine grew into a catacomb the size of Manhattan, and the waste from it filled the valley, finally consuming more than 2,000 acres of woodlands. The mines shut down roads to move trucks more efficiently, adding 30 minutes to her father's commute, but her parents weren't concerned. "Pittsburgh back then was so polluted that we didn't think about it," Alice said. The mining companies helped quell dissent with gifts, paying for employees' Thanksgiving turkeys and funding Little League teams. In the nearby village of Graysville, the elementary school's marquee bore the logo of its corporate sponsor.

Yet the waste in the valley disturbed Coptis. Even if the company owned the land, what gave it the right to spoil the place where people lived? At school, other students told her that speaking out against coal could cost their parents jobs. Coptis, hoping that older people had answers, drove to Graysville, which consists of a single street, anchored by a Presbyterian church and the Creekside Kitchen diner. Outside the general store, she asked two elderly men about coal. They said that living alongside industry entailed "give and take." Cleaning up pollution was often left to the community, especially when companies went bankrupt, as many did. In Pennsylvania, the legacy cost of restoring mine land and streams has been estimated at $5 billion. But if the mines vanished how could people afford to live?

One afternoon, a few weeks after Coptis graduated from high school, she was driving by Duke Lake, on her way to her parents' house, when she caught the rank smell of rotting fish. Through the window, she saw that the water had drained from the lake, leaving a sprawling mud pit, glistening with bluegills' bodies. "Fish were left flopping in the muck, and people were scooping them up and trying to move them downstream," she said. The smell lingered for months, and Coptis drove another route to avoid it. Consol, whose mines lay near the lake, denied responsibility. But miners working below said that their digging had clearly breached the dam, according to Coptis: "One of my miner friends told me later that they were waist-deep in water."

That fall, Coptis was accepted to West Virginia University, and began pursuing every scholarship she could find for science students. Still, even with student loans, an additional loan from an aunt, and income from three part-time jobs, she could barely afford room and board on top of tuition. She applied for food stamps but didn't qualify. "They told me to have a kid," she said. Instead, she hunted deer for protein.

In school, Coptis became fascinated by Indiana bats—tiny, playful creatures that, she noted, are more closely related to humans than to mice. After graduating, in 2009, she wanted to work as a field biologist, so she trawled list boards and applied to field jobs. She heard nothing. Her personal life was stalled, too. During college, she'd got engaged, to a young man from a mining family, and they moved to an old coal-patch town called Nemacolin. Coptis, thrilled to be starting adult life, bought gifts for her fiancé on credit: a washer/dryer, a big-screen TV, a motorcycle. When she discovered, a few days before their wedding, that he'd left her for her best friend, she loaded everything she'd paid for into her father's truck and moved home. "I realized that I was making my decisions based on a man," she said. "I promised myself never to do that again."

Without any other job prospects, Coptis began waiting tables at the Creekside Kitchen, where her mother also worked. Greene County seemed diminished. As family farms and coal mines failed, the population was shrinking, on its way from a high of 45,394, in 1950, to about 37,000. At the restaurant, Coptis listened as laid-off miners and homeowners spoke about the loss of jobs and of drinking water. Some were distraught when undermining forced them out of their family homes. Others, eager to leave the county, were happy to be bought out, and thought of themselves as winners of the "long-wall lottery." But, when companies bought people's homes, they often instructed them not to discuss the deals. "Most are terrified that if they violate the terms, even in talking casually to a neighbor, the company will take the money back," she said.

Many customers had no Internet access, so Coptis brought her laptop to work for them to use. One morning, one of her regulars, a fisherman and conservationist, asked to look something up. Dunkard Creek, a stream that follows the Mason-Dixon Line, had recently suffered one of the worst fish die-offs in state history, and he wanted to know what had happened. As they were searching online, Coptis came upon the Web site for the Center for Coalfield Justice, founded in 1994 by activists from West Virginia, Ohio, and southwestern Pennsylvania to address the problems of long-wall mining. The site had a listing for a job: a yearlong position, funded by AmeriCorps. She applied and was hired. Later, she discovered that she was the only person to have inquired.

The CCJ office, in the Rust Belt town of Washington, Pennsylvania, occupied a brick storefront on Main Street, next door to a clinic for opioid addicts. When Coptis first arrived at the office, she was elated. "It was the first time I'd ever seen people other than me challenging coal," she said. CCJ was involved in a lawsuit, trying to force Consol to take responsibility for the draining of Duke Lake. Coptis, assigned to inform people about the case, organized an event called the Dryerson Festival. Standing at a table next to the dried lake bed, she discovered the first principle of organizing in poor communities: always offer food, and, when people who don't care about the cause come up for a second helping, smile and fill their plates. When she visited neighbors, trying to raise support, she learned not to lead with an argument. "I just listen," she said. "Sometimes I don't even mention what we're working on. Most people have never had the chance to tell their stories." The festival became an annual event, and the number of local attendees tripled, from 30 to 100—a small victory.

When the AmeriCorps position ended, Coptis moved to the Pittsburgh suburbs to organize against fracking, but it didn't engage her as coal had. "The reason that people pay more attention to fracking is that fracking threatens rich white suburbs," she said. In 2013, CCJ offered her a job as an organizer, and she moved back to Greene County. A few months later, the fight over Duke Lake came to an equivocal end: Consol paid the state a $36 million settlement, without admitting responsibility for the lost lake. In exchange, the company was granted rights to the coal and gas under the park.

In 2013, Coptis and Donald Fike were married in the park, on the ruins of an old church. A wedding photograph of Coptis—smiling, in sunglasses and a white satin dress, a beer can in hand—hangs in their living room, next to a Semper Fi plaque from Fike's days as a marine.

* * *

Fike's military record helped him get a job maintaining equipment at Emerald Mine. Most of the time, he sat in a shop at the surface, waiting for the phone to ring with orders for new shuttle-car tires, or for cutter shafts, which kept blades spinning to cut coal 24 hours a day. One afternoon, bored and lonely, he posted on Facebook that he wanted to go see "The Avengers." A friend told him that Veronica was single, so he called her.

Over dinner at TGI Friday's, Fike bristled when their conversation turned to politics. He was a miner, and Coptis was the enemy. But Fike thought of himself as "open-minded," and they agreed to go out again. After a few months of dating, he asked if she'd be his girlfriend. She said yes; the next day, she headed to an anti-fracking demonstration in Washington, D.C.

Not long afterward, as they drove to IKEA to buy a dresser, she risked a gentle lecture on the economic prospects of the white working class. "As a man from Appalachia, you have three choices," she told him. "The military, the mines, or prison." To Coptis, this wasn't abstract; her brother, Zach, had served tours in Afghanistan and Iraq. At first, Fike shrugged off her ideas. He felt proud of working at Emerald, where the camaraderie among miners helped him readjust to rural life. "Being a miner is a lot like being in the military," Fike said. During the two world wars, coal miners were often exempt from service, because their jobs were essential to the war effort, and miners retain the sense that they are risking danger to benefit their country. As Fike worked, accumulating underground hours to qualify as a "black hat"—a senior miner—he averted conflict by keeping Coptis's work a secret. "He could've been fired because of what I did," Coptis said. In one tense moment, Fike told her, "I love you, not your job." She replied, "But my job is a lot of who I am."

Still, her activism often riled her neighbors. When her father went out on surveying jobs, he would tell employers not to disclose his last name, for fear of being associated with his daughter. Coptis avoided situations in which talk of her work might lead to fights. "I don't go to high-school reunions," she said. Drinking in local bars, she told people that she handled bats at the zoo.

In 2013, as the EPA worked to tighten mercury regulations, two local power plants announced that they were shutting down. The closings were the result of corporate strategy as much as of regulations (the parent company had recently shut down a string of plants), but people in Greene County blamed CCJ. Soon after the announcement, a woman came into the office and said that her husband was losing his job at the plant. Distraught, she shouted at Coptis, "Are you going to pay our mortgage?" Coptis invited the woman to sit and talk, but she refused, and Coptis lost her temper. "We had nothing to do with closing those plants," she snapped. "That was the company's decision, not ours." When the woman stormed out, Coptis's boss, Patrick Grenter, admonished her: "Roni, you can't talk to people in the community like that." Later, he corrected himself—Coptis was part of the community.

* * *

One morning, Coptis sat at a table at the Creekside Kitchen, picking at an egg burrito. Before Duke Lake went dry, the Creekside Kitchen's owner ran an ice cream shop nearby, which attracted some 3,000 visitors each summer. After the lake vanished, she closed the shop and opened the diner, to serve miners. Now the seats were mostly filled with gas-well workers, who arrived in trucks with license plates from Texas, Arkansas, and North Dakota. They ate quietly, and were usually gone in a few weeks.

When Coptis wants to be left alone, she wears a T-shirt that says, "Beyond Coal." Very few people in Greene County want to contemplate a future without coal; most . . . hope that deregulation can preserve their way of life. But regulation isn't the essential problem. Since the 1930s, when the rise of unions drove up the price of labor, coal operators have increasingly turned to automation—a process that the unions supported, because it improved safety and efficiency. In the past three decades, employment in the industry has shrunk from 180,000 jobs to about 50,000.

More recently, the greatest factor in the demise of coal has been natural gas, which fracking has made abundant and cheap. Coal, which until not long ago generated half the country's electricity, now provides only a third. Consol has put the Bailey Mine Complex, its last coal asset, up for sale in favor of developing natural gas. Yet gas is not the only competition. "It's not just coal versus gas," Ed Morse, the global head of commodities research at Citigroup, said. "It's coal and gas versus renewables." Solar and wind power are already inexpensive enough to compete with fossil fuels, and, even if the Trump Administration withdraws subsidies for renewables, they are likely to remain economically viable. Trump complained, in his speech about the Paris accord, that under the agreement "China will be allowed to build hundreds of additional coal plants." But China, responding to dismal air quality, has promised to close a thousand coal mines and has increased its use of renewable fuels. "You've really got to overcome market forces, not just in the short term but systemically," Phil Smith, the communications director of the United Mine Workers Association, said. Opening a power plant is a fifty-year investment, and no investor is willing to gamble that coal will be the fuel of choice in 50 years. "Poor Mr. Trump will have a problem living up to his commitment to people whose future of employment is bleak," Morse said. "The age of coal is over."

* * *

According to county estimates, Greene County has 30 years left to mine at current rates of production. Now, Zimmerman said, he was facing the question "What can we do when coal leaves?" This conversation was already difficult under the Obama Administration, when federal money was beginning to flow into Appalachia. Now that money is almost sure to disappear. Trump hopes to defund hundreds of projects, such as the Appalachian Regional Commission, which helps retrain miners as coders and farmers. Greene County's power plants used to pay some $13 million a year in taxes; now they pay none. If not for environmental-impact fees coming from the natural-gas industry, Zimmerman said, his budget would collapse. He is struggling to find a way for the county to reshape itself, with almost no state or federal help. "This should've been looked at 50 years ago," he said.

He'd heard about a commissioner from Kentucky bidding for a zip line to attract tourists, which Zimmerman considered a well-meaning fantasy. "A zip line isn't going to replace 30 coal mines," he said. He hoped for a GM or a

Toyota factory, or, better yet, an Amazon distribution warehouse, which could supply as many as a thousand jobs. Coptis argues that managing environmental damage is essential to attracting new business. "No one's going to move here if we don't have parks or clean water," she said. She is placing her hope in the RECLAIM Act, now under consideration in a House committee, which would invest a billion dollars in cleaning up mines in ways that support new industries, including tourism and sustainable farming.

After breakfast, Coptis and Fike were going to Ryerson, bringing along Rory. Coptis strapped the baby into the back seat of her Nissan. Along the way, she pointed out the church ruins where she and Fike were married. Nearby, a creek flowed toward one of the endangered streams. Their future remained uncertain. The coal company was appealing the court's decision, and Coptis worried that the mood was against CCJ. Under Trump, the Environmental Protection Agency is being radically diminished, and the Administration's hostility toward regulation has emboldened local politicians who are sympathetic to coal. Last month, the Pennsylvania senate passed a bill to exempt underground mining from state clean-water regulations, which would eliminate the basis for the suit against Consol. Governor Tom Wolf, a Democrat, opposes the measure. But Coptis predicts more fights. "If Consol is allowed to destroy these streams, I'm not sure we can stay here," she said. "We've got nothing left to give." To her thinking, the county's residents had already sacrificed enough. "The coal companies took the valley by my parents' house," she said. "They depopulated the county. They took the lake. Why do I have to keep sacrificing?"

49

Change the World

GEORGE PACKER

Silicon Valley and the tech industry worldwide have brought forth the means to change the world, or at least how we communicate within the technological matrix of our work lives and leisure pursuits. To the millionaires and billionaires who have profited by our thirst for new information technologies and harvested our personal data for sale the way we now communicate and the social organizations that brought this about offer a model for solving many of today's social and economic problems. But can social change come, not—as Mao Zedong thought, "from the barrel of a gun"— but from the wallets of the fabulously rich and disruptive innovators?

In 1978, the year that I graduated from high school, in Palo Alto, the name Silicon Valley was not in use beyond a small group of tech *cognoscenti*. Apple Computer had incorporated the previous year, releasing the first popular personal computer, the Apple II. The major technology companies made electronics hardware, and on the way to school I rode my bike through the Stanford Industrial Park, past the offices of Hewlett-Packard, Varian, and Xerox PARC. The neighborhoods of the Santa Clara Valley were dotted with cheap, modern, one-story houses—called Eichlers, after the builder Joseph Eichler—with glass walls, open floor plans, and flat-roofed carports. (Steve Jobs grew up in an imitation Eichler, called a Likeler.) The average house in Palo Alto cost about a hundred and twenty-five thousand dollars. Along the main downtown street, University Avenue—the future address of PayPal, Facebook, and Google—were sports shops, discount variety stores, and several art-house cinemas, together with the shuttered, X-rated Paris Theatre. Across El Camino Real, the Stanford Shopping Center was anchored by Macy's and Woolworth's, with one boutique store—a Victoria's Secret had opened in 1977—and a parking lot full of Datsuns and Chevy Novas. High-end dining was virtually unknown in Palo Alto, as was the adjective "high-end." The public schools in the area were excellent and almost universally attended; the few kids I knew who went to private school had somehow messed up. The Valley was thoroughly middle class, egalitarian, pleasant, and a little boring.

Thirty-five years later, the average house in Palo Alto sells for more than two million dollars. The Stanford Shopping Center's parking lot is a sea of Lexuses and Audis, and their owners are shopping at Burberry and Louis Vuitton. There are fifty or so billionaires and tens of thousands of millionaires in

Silicon Valley; last year's Facebook public stock offering alone created half a dozen more of the former and more than a thousand of the latter. There are also record numbers of poor people, and the past two years have seen a twenty percent rise in homelessness, largely because of the soaring cost of housing. After decades in which the country has become less and less equal, Silicon Valley is one of the most unequal places in America.

Private-school attendance has surged, while public schools in poor communities—such as East Palo Alto, which is mostly cut off from the city by Highway 101—have fallen into disrepair and lack basic supplies. In wealthy districts, the public schools have essentially been privatized; they insulate themselves from shortfalls in state funding with money raised by foundations they have set up for themselves. In 1983, parents at Woodside Elementary School, which is surrounded by some of the Valley's wealthiest tech families, started a foundation in order to offset budget cuts resulting from the enactment of Proposition 13, in 1978, which drastically limited California property taxes. The Woodside School Foundation now brings in about two million dollars a year for a school with fewer than five hundred children, and every spring it hosts a gala with a live auction. I attended it two years ago, when the theme was Rock-Star, and one of Google's first employees sat at my table after performing in a pickup band called Parental Indiscretion. School benefactors, dressed up as Tina Turner or Jimmy Page, and consuming Jump'n Jack Flash hanger steaks, bid thirteen thousand dollars for Pimp My Hog! ("Ride through town in your very own customized 1996 Harley Davidson XLH1200C Sportster") and twenty thousand for a tour of the Japanese gardens on the estate of Larry Ellison, the founder of Oracle and the country's highest-paid chief executive. The climax arrived when a *Mad Men* Supper Club dinner for sixteen guests—which promised to transport couples back to a time when local residents lived in two-thousand-square-foot houses—sold for forty-three thousand dollars.

The technology industry's newest wealth is swallowing up the San Francisco Peninsula. If Silicon Valley remains the center of engineering breakthroughs, San Francisco has become a magnet for hundreds of software start-ups, many of them in the South of Market area, where Twitter has its headquarters. (Half the start-ups seem to have been founded by Facebook alumni.) A lot of younger employees of Silicon Valley companies live in the city and commute to work in white, Wi-Fi-equipped company buses, which collect passengers at fifteen or so stops around San Francisco. The buses—whose schedules are withheld from the public—have become a vivid emblem of the tech boom's stratifying effect in the Bay Area. Rebecca Solnit, who has lived in San Francisco for thirty years, recently wrote in *The London Review of Books*, "Sometimes the Google Bus just seems like one face of Janus-headed capitalism; it contains the people too valuable even to use public transport or drive themselves. Right by the Google bus stop on Cesar Chavez Street immigrant men from Latin America stand waiting for employers in the building trade to scoop them up, or to be arrested and deported by the government." Some of the city's hottest restaurants are popping up in the neighborhoods with shuttle stops. Rents there are rising even faster than elsewhere in San Francisco, and in some cases they have doubled in the past year.

The buses carry their wired cargo south to the "campuses" of Google, Facebook, Apple, and other companies, which are designed to be fully functioning communities, not just places for working. Google's grounds, in Mountain View—a working-class town when I was growing up—are modelled on the casual, Frisbee-throwing feel of Stanford University, the incubator of Silicon Valley, where the company's founders met, in grad school. A polychrome Google bike can be picked up anywhere on campus, and left anywhere, so that another employee can use it. Electric cars, kept at a charging station, allow employees to run errands. Facebook's buildings, in Menlo Park, between 101 and the salt marshes along the Bay, surround a simulated town square whose concrete surface is decorated with the word "HACK," in letters so large that they can be seen from the air.

At Facebook, employees can eat sushi or burritos, lift weights, get a haircut, have their clothes dry-cleaned, and see a dentist, all without leaving work. Apple, meanwhile, plans to spend nearly five billion dollars to build a giant, impenetrable ringed headquarters in the middle of a park that is technically part of Cupertino. These inward-looking places keep tech workers from having even accidental contact with the surrounding community. The design critic Alexandra Lange, in her recent e-book, *The Dot-Com City: Silicon Valley Urbanism*, writes, "The more Silicon Valley tech companies embrace an urban model, the harder it becomes for them to explain why they need to remain aloof. People who don't have badges aren't just a security risk."

The industry's splendid isolation inspires cognitive dissonance, for it's an article of faith in Silicon Valley that the technology industry represents something more utopian, and democratic, than mere special-interest groups. The information revolution (the phrase itself conveys a sense of business exceptionalism) emerged from the Bay Area counterculture of the sixties and seventies, influenced by the hobbyists who formed the Homebrew Computer Club and by idealistic engineers like Douglas Engelbart, who helped develop the concept of hypertext and argued that digital networks could boost our "collective I.Q." From the days of Apple's inception, the personal computer was seen as a tool for personal liberation; with the arrival of social media on the Internet, digital technology announced itself as a force for global betterment. The phrase "change the world" is tossed around Silicon Valley conversations and business plans as freely as talk of "early-stage investing" and "beta tests."

When financiers say that they're doing God's work by providing cheap credit, and oilmen claim to be patriots who are making the country energy-independent, no one takes them too seriously—it's a given that their motivation is profit. But when technology entrepreneurs describe their lofty goals there's no smirk or wink. "Many see their social responsibility fulfilled by their businesses, not by social or political action," one young entrepreneur said of his colleagues. "It's remarkably convenient that they can achieve all their goals just by doing their start-up." He added, "They actually think that Facebook is going to be the panacea for many of the world's problems. It isn't cynicism—it's arrogance and ignorance."

A few years ago, when Barack Obama visited one Silicon Valley campus, an employee of the company told a colleague that he wasn't going to take time from his work to go hear the president's remarks, explaining, "I'm making more of a difference than anybody in government could possibly make." In 2006, Google started its philanthropic arm, Google.org, but other tech giants did not follow its lead. At places like Facebook, it was felt that making the world a more open and connected place could do far more good than working on any charitable cause. Two of the key words in industry jargon are "impactful" and "scalable"—rapid growth and human progress are seen as virtually indistinguishable. One of the mottoes posted on the walls at Facebook is "Move fast and break things." Government is considered slow, staffed by mediocrities, ridden with obsolete rules and inefficiencies.

Reid Hoffman, the co-founder of the professional network LinkedIn and an investor in dozens of Silicon Valley firms, told me, "In investing, you want to have milestones that go between three and twelve months, to know you're making progress. The government *purchasing process* is a year plus!" Joshua Cohen, a Stanford political philosopher who also edits *Boston Review*, described a conversation he had with John Hennessy, the president of Stanford, who has extensive financial and professional ties to Silicon Valley. "He was talking about the incompetent people who are in government," Cohen recalled. "I said, 'If you think they're so incompetent, why don't you include in a speech you're making some urging of Stanford students to go into government?' He thought this was a ridiculous idea."

In a 2008 interview, Mark Zuckerberg recounted how young Lebanese Muslims who might have been tempted by extremism broadened their views after going on Facebook and friending people "who have gone to Europe." He suggested that the social network could help solve the problem of terrorism. "It's not out of a deep hatred of anyone," Zuckerberg offered. "It comes from a lack of connectedness, a lack of communication, a lack of empathy, and a lack of understanding." Successive U.S. Administrations had failed to resolve the Israeli-Palestinian conflict; perhaps the answer was to get as many people as possible on Facebook.

The conflicting pressures of Silicon Valley—its work ethic, status consciousness, idealism, and greed—were summed up in an ad for the University of San Francisco that I spotted on a public bus shelter south of Market Street: "Become wildly successful without becoming a jerk no one likes. Change the world from here."

The technology industry, by sequestering itself from the community it inhabits, has transformed the Bay Area without being changed by it—in a sense, without getting its hands dirty. Throughout most of Silicon Valley's history, its executives have displayed a libertarian instinct to stay as far from politics and government as possible. Reid Hoffman described the attitude this way: "Look what I can do as an individual myself—everyone else should be able to do that, too. I can make a multibillion-dollar company with a little bit of investment. Why can't the whole world do that?" But the imperative to change the world has recently led some Silicon Valley leaders to imagine that the values and concepts behind their success can be uploaded to the public sphere.

When Zuckerberg created Facebook, in 2004, he was a sophomore at Harvard. Most of his roommates joined the effort, but Joe Green did not. Zuckerberg and Green, who were members of Harvard's Jewish fraternity, had collaborated on Facemash, a site where Harvard students could rate the hotness of their classmates. This brought them both before the university's disciplinary board, and Green's father, a UCLA math professor, was not pleased. In any case, Green didn't really consider himself a tech persons—he was a political guy. At Santa Monica High School, he had won the student seat on the local school board and organized a living-wage campaign. At Harvard, he studied under Marshall Ganz, the theorist of community activism, and for his senior thesis he interviewed working-class men in Louisville about their ideas of economic opportunity and the American Dream. (In general, they believed that people were fundamentally equal and that income distribution should reflect that.) In the summer of 2003, between his sophomore and junior years, Green volunteered for John Kerry's Presidential campaign in New Hampshire, where he realized that the job of a political organizer would be much easier if everyone were on Friendster—an early, and doomed, social network that he had joined. He returned to Harvard, and urged Zuckerberg to use his programming talent to build a political social network. But Zuckerberg was more interested in starting a business. He had an idea for a college social network.

"No more Zuckerberg projects," Green's father warned him. And so Green chose not to drop out and move to Silicon Valley with Zuckerberg and the other roommates. That summer, while Facebook was being created, he went to work as a Kerry field organizer in Arizona and Nevada. For years afterward, Zuckerberg teased him: Instead of getting billions of dollars, he'd lost two states for Kerry.

In another era, Green might have gone on to an internship at *The Nation* or a job on Capitol Hill. Instead, he headed West after graduating and, with no programming skills, started two technology companies. In 2007, he and Sean Parker, the Silicon Valley entrepreneur, launched Causes, a Facebook application that helps grass-roots organizations and nonprofits raise money. . . . All the while, he continued to try to interest his ex-roommate in politics, but for a long time Zuckerberg was interested only in his own company.

"People in tech, when they talk about why they started their company, they tend to talk about changing the world," Green said. "I think it's actually genuine. On the other hand, people are just completely disconnected from politics. Partly because the operating principles of politics and the operating principles of tech are completely different." Whereas politics is transactional and opaque, based on hierarchies and handshakes, Green argued, technology is empirical and often transparent, driven by data.

In 2010, just ahead of the première of the film *The Social Network*, which portrayed the origins of Facebook in an unflattering light, Zuckerberg announced that he would pledge up to a hundred million dollars to the Newark public-school system—his first visible foray into philanthropy. The money was intended to encourage certain reforms in the education bureaucracy, including merit pay for teachers. Green pointed out that Zuckerberg was spending a lot of money just to change the rules in one mid-sized urban school district. He could spend that money in politics and potentially be more effective.

I recently met with Marc Andreessen, a general partner in one of Silicon Valley's most powerful venture-capital firms, Andreessen Horowitz. His office, in an idyllic ghetto of similar companies on Sand Hill Road, in Menlo Park, was clearly inspired by the décor of *Mad Men*: paintings by Robert Rauschenberg and other American artists of the sixties, a sideboard displaying bottles of expensive whiskey. On his desk sat the record player that adorned the office of Pete Campbell in the show's first three seasons. Andreessen is a big, bullet-headed man from Wisconsin, with a blunt, fast-talking manner. He supported Obama in 2008 but switched to Mitt Romney last year, because, he told me, Romney was a superb chief executive.

Andreessen described to me the stages of the industry's attitude toward political engagement. The first, prevailing in the seventies and eighties, was "Just leave us alone. Let us do our thing." T. J. Rodgers, the founder of Cypress Semiconductor, said that anyone who got involved in politics was making a big mistake, warning, "If you talk to these people, they'll just get in your ass." The Valley's libertarianism—which ignores the federal government's crucial role in providing research money—is less doctrinal than instinctive. Andreessen said, "It's very possible for somebody to show up here—a twenty-four-year-old engineer who's completely state of the art in building companies and products—and have had absolutely no exposure at all to politics, social issues, history. When the government shows up, it's bad news. They go, 'Oh, my God, government is evil, I didn't understand how bad it was. We must fight it.'"

Andreessen himself once fit this type. In 1993, when he was just twenty-one, he helped develop Mosaic, the first popular Web browser. After the company he co-founded, Netscape, launched its Navigator browser, the government insisted that its encryption—which was so strong that U.S. intelligence couldn't break it—be weakened for foreign sales, so that terrorists and other criminals couldn't use Netscape's cryptography. This demand required the company to create a different product for export. Ben Horowitz, Andreessen's partner, who ran Netscape's product division, said, "It's hard to describe what a royal pain in the ass this was. We were totally flabbergasted." Later, after other technology leaders were given classified briefings on how terrorists operated, he and Andreessen realized that the Feds had a point. "Maybe they didn't totally understand all the implications of everything," Horowitz said. "But we didn't understand their job, either." Eventually, industry arguments prevailed and the government, which didn't want foreign competitors to gain an advantage over U.S. businesses, withdrew its request.

Horowitz—who is the son of David Horowitz, the radical-turned-conservative polemicist—attributed Silicon Valley's strain of libertarianism to the mentality of engineers. "Libertarianism is, theoretically, a relatively elegant solution," he said. "People here have a great affinity for that kind of thing—they want elegance. Most people here are relatively apolitical and not that knowledgeable about how these large complicated systems of societies work. Libertarianism has got a lot of the false positives that Communism had, in that it's a very simple solution that solves everything." The intellectual model is not the dour Ayn Rand but Bay Area philosophers and gurus who imagine that limitless progress can be achieved through technology. Stewart Brand, now seventy-four, popularized the term "personal computer" and made "hacker" the tech equivalent of freedom fighter. His *Whole Earth Catalog*—a compendium of hippie products, generated by users, that is now considered an analog precursor of the Web—can still be found on desks at Facebook.

In the past fifteen years or so, Andreessen explained, Silicon Valley's hands-off attitude has changed, as the industry has grown larger and its activities keep colliding with regulations. Technology leaders began to realize that Washington could sometimes be useful to them. "A small number of very high-end Valley people have got involved in politics, but in a way that a lot of us think is relentlessly self-interested," Andreessen said. The issues that first animated these technology executives were stock options, subsidies, and tax breaks. "They started giving the Valley a bad name in Washington—that the Valley was just another special-interest group."

In early 2011, Zuckerberg, Steve Jobs, and other Silicon Valley moguls attended a dinner with President Obama in Woodside, at the home of John Doerr, a venture capitalist with ties to the Democratic Party. Instead of having a wide-ranging discussion, the tech leaders focussed narrowly on pet issues. John Chambers, of Cisco, kept pushing for a tax holiday on overseas profits that are reinvested in the United States. According to Walter Isaacson's biography of Jobs, while Chambers was lobbying Obama, over cod and lentil salad, Zuckerberg turned to Valerie Jarrett, the President's adviser, and whispered, "We should be talking about what's important to the country. Why is he just talking about what's good for him?" When it was Jobs's turn, he asked for more H-1B visas for foreign students who earn engineering degrees in the U.S.—a longtime Silicon Valley desire. Obama told him that the issue could be addressed only in the context of broader immigration reforms, such as allowing children who had arrived here illegally with their parents to gain legal status.

Zuckerberg came away from the gathering impressed with Obama but sorely disappointed in his own industry. The most dynamic sector of the American economy had no larger agenda.

Zuckerberg spoke about his concerns with Green, who said that the country's biggest challenge was to equip more Americans to benefit from the Information Age. With so many jobs lost to automation, and more wealth concentrated in fewer hands, that prospect was slipping farther away. Silicon Valley was racing into the future, but the kinds of people Green had interviewed in Louisville were becoming increasingly marginal. Fixing this dynamic would require the expertise, the time, and the money of technology leaders. "How do we move America into the knowledge economy?" Green asked me. "And how do we create a voice for the knowledge community that is about the future and not selfish? If we organize this community, it could be one of the most powerful voices in politics." He dropped the idea of selflessness. "I think our selfish interest actually aligns with the broader interest of creating jobs and growing the economy."*

Earlier this year, Zuckerberg began teaching a class on entrepreneurship, one afternoon a week, to middle-school students in a poor community near Facebook's headquarters. He decided to ask his students about their college plans. One young man said that he might not be able to attend college, because he and his parents had illegally entered the country, from Mexico, when he was a baby. The story stuck with Zuckerberg. After the Republican losses in the 2012 elections, comprehensive immigration reform—including more H-1B visas—suddenly seemed possible in Washington. It also looked like the most promising issue for technology leaders to organize around—a case of self-interest aligning with the broader interest.

Zuckerberg and Green began talking to Silicon Valley leaders about starting a political-advocacy group: Andreessen; Horowitz; Reid Hoffman; Marissa Mayer, of Yahoo; Eric Schmidt, of Google; and at least three dozen others. The interest was strong, as if they had all been waiting for something like this. Though Andreessen and Horowitz didn't join the project, Andreessen thought it represented "the maturation of the industry" and a greater level of engagement in politics—"deeper, longer-term, with, frankly, more money."

Hoffman, who believes that immigration reform would right a wrong and also create new jobs at every level, from software engineers to dry cleaners, told Zuckerberg, "The normal Silicon Valley thing is to focus on high-end visas and say, 'The rest of it's not my problem.'"

"Yes," Zuckerberg said. "But there's this huge moral component. We might as well go after all of it."

"O.K., good," Hoffman said. "I'm in."

Earlier this year, Green wrote up a fifteen-page plan—subsequently leaked to Politico—which had more to do with tapping Silicon Valley's potential as a political force than with the issue of immigration. One section of the text listed several reasons that "people in tech" could be organized into "one of the most

---

*What would Garrett Harden, author of "The Tragedy of the Commons" (essay 3), say about this? [*Editors' note*]

powerful political forces," including, "Our voice carries a lot of weight because we are broadly popular with Americans." This spring, the founders held a dinner, and pledged money from their personal fortunes; reportedly, the collective goal was fifty million dollars. A staff was hired in San Francisco, and political consultants from both parties were engaged in Washington. One afternoon last month, Green sat on the sunny rooftop terrace of a friend's town house in Pacific Heights, just south of the Presidio, with views of the Golden Gate Bridge and the Marin hills. He was barefoot, in jeans and a red T-shirt, with his left leg propped on a decorative rock bowl and immobilized in a brace. (He had broken it skiing.) A young assistant named Manny brought water and walnuts. Green's frizzy hair fluttered in the wind blowing off the ocean as he worked his phone and his MacBook Air, which was decorated with a sticker that said, "The Dream Is Now." An op-ed by Zuckerberg was going to run in the *Washington Post* the next morning, announcing the formation of a new group in Silicon Valley, called FWD.us. "I'm the president of the organization," Green said. "There will be an actual office." He was returning to his first passion, political organizing. His wide, stubbly face broke into a smile: he had spent ten years trying to convince Zuckerberg that politics matters, and he had finally done it.

* * *

Technology can be an answer to incompetence and inefficiency. But it has little to say about larger issues of justice and fairness, unless you think that political problems are bugs that can be fixed by engineering rather than fundamental conflicts of interest and value. Evgeny Morozov, in his new book *To Save Everything, Click Here,* calls this belief "solutionism." Morozov, who is twenty-nine and grew up in a mining town in Belarus, is the fiercest critic of technological optimism in America, tirelessly dismantling the language of its followers. "They want to be 'open,' they want to be 'disruptive,' they want to 'innovate,'" Morozov told me. "The open agenda is, in many ways, the opposite of equality and justice. They think anything that helps you to bypass institutions is, by default, empowering or liberating. You might not be able to pay for health care or your insurance, but if you have an app on your phone that alerts you to the fact that you need to exercise more, or you aren't eating healthily enough, they think they are solving the problem."

* * *

A favorite word in tech circles is "frictionless." It captures the pleasures of an app so beautifully designed that using it is intuitive, and it evokes a fantasy in which all inefficiencies, annoyances, and grievances have been smoothed out of existence—that is, an apolitical world. Dave Morin, who worked at Apple and Facebook, is the founder of a company called Path—a social network limited to one's fifty closest friends. In his office, which has a panoramic view of south San Francisco, he said that one of his company's goals is to make technology increasingly seamless with real life. He described San Francisco as a place where people already live in the future. They can hang out with their friends even when they're alone. They inhabit a "sharing economy": they can book a weeklong stay in a cool apartment through Airbnb, which has disrupted the hotel industry, or hire a luxury car anywhere in the city through the mobile app Uber, which has disrupted the taxi industry. "San Francisco is a place where we can go downstairs and get in an Uber and go to dinner at a place that I got a restaurant reservation for halfway there," Morin said. "And, if not, we could go to my place, and on the way there I could order takeout food from my favorite restaurant on Postmates, and a bike messenger will go and pick it up for me. We'll watch it happen on the phone. These things are crazy ideas."

It suddenly occurred to me that the hottest tech start-ups are solving all the problems of being twenty years old, with cash on hand, because that's who thinks them up.

In the real San Francisco, as elsewhere, Morin added, things don't always work very well: "There are all kinds of infrastructure problems that are, like, really, guys? This is San Francisco. The fact that some of the buses still run on diesel is crazy, or that the bus stop doesn't talk to your iPhone." [Former mayor of San Francisco Gavin] Newsom, in his book, describes an innovation in which hackers created an iPad app that allowed municipal transport workers to keep track of the status of trains and buses without standing on the street with clipboards and watching them go by. "What I'd like to see is 'Hackers 10,000, City 0,'" Newsom writes. "This is the perfect example of how the government can do best by simply getting out of the way." (Unfortunately, as Newsom notes, San Francisco's "budget crunch means the city hasn't yet bought the iPads needed to fully implement the app.") If innovation put the public-transportation system in San Francisco out of business, Newsom said, "I'm not inherently offended by that notion." Page and Brin, of Google, have led him to think that the company's emerging fleet of driverless cars might make long-term spending on high-speed rail in California irrelevant.

Near the Caltrain station south of Market Street, a twenty-nine-year-old entrepreneur named Logan Green is trying to realize something like this vision. Green grew up in Southern California and attended the University of California at Santa Barbara, where he decided to get by without a car, so that the inconvenience would force him to find creative solutions to transit and environmental problems. He joined the county transportation board, and found that the bus routes made no sense but couldn't be fixed, because of budget shortfalls and pressure from constituents.

"I learned that it's an incredibly broken and unscalable system," Green said. "I came out thinking, God, government's really not the right place to experiment with anything new. Government's really not the right place to look to solve these problems and to create innovative solutions and scalable solutions in transportation. This really belongs more in the private sector, where you're not burdened with all these impossible restrictions."

Last year, Green co-founded Lyft, a "rideshare" company with services in San Francisco and other cities. Its motto is "Your friend with a car." Through a mobile app, customers can call a car driven by an ordinary citizen who has been approved by Lyft, and who is available to give rides while going about his regular business. The cars have a telltale fuzzy pink mustache fastened to the front grille. "You get in the front seat, and the driver gives you a fist bump," Green explained. "It's a peer-to-peer relationship, not a service relationship." The customer pays a suggested donation, twenty per cent of which goes to Green's company. So far, Lyft has registered several hundred drivers, and Green hopes that a crowdsourced transportation system like Lyft will ultimately replace the existing public one, perhaps with a fleet of Google's driverless cars. That, however, would mean no fist bump.

San Francisco is becoming a city without a middle class. Pockets of intense poverty, in districts like the Fillmore and the Tenderloin, are increasingly isolated within the general rise of exorbitantly priced housing. The black population has dwindled from more than ten per cent of the electorate, in 1970, to less than four per cent today—that's not enough people to fill the forty thousand seats at A.T.&T. Park, where the Giants play. The number of Latinos is increasing much more slowly than elsewhere in California. Rent control and other features of the city's traditional liberalism still hold in check a mass exodus of all San Franciscans who don't work in tech, but it's common to hear stories of working families pushed south, into Bayview or Daly City, or across the bridge, into the East Bay.

Christina Olague, a former member of the city's Board of Supervisors, took me on a tour of several blocks in the Mission District, where she works at a nonprofit that prepares low-income people for whatever jobs might be available. The Mission, once a Latino neighborhood, has become extremely popular with technology workers. We met at a café on Valencia Street, called Four Barrel Coffee, which offers single-origin, hand-roasted craft coffee. Olague, who is in her fifties, is the daughter of Mexican farmworkers, and was once active in a local group called the Mission Anti-Displacement Coalition. "This is the kind of place I used to protest," she told me, looking around at the young Apple users. "And now here I am, hanging out, waiting for half an hour to get a cup of coffee." She was having trouble connecting with the newcomers. "People seem more self-absorbed, maybe more individualistic in a way, less empathetic," she went on. "They're really addicted to their iPads or phones. They communicate more, but there's less communication with the people they're actually around." Her larger complaint, though, was about the techies' indifference to the pain that their industry's triumph is inflicting on many people who have been a part of the fabric of San Francisco for decades. "Everyone's kind of wary, I think. A lot of people in the tech industry, sadly, feel judged—because they are."

Out on Valencia Street, Olague took me past an eyeglass boutique that had replaced a bookstore and, in the twin bays of a vanished auto-body shop, two artisanal establishments: one made pastries, the other chocolate. On the wall of the pastry shop, there were quotes that appealed to the customers' idea of their jobs as inspirational callings, including one from Saint-Exupéry: "If you want to build a ship don't gather people together to collect wood and don't assign them tasks and work but rather teach them to long for the endless immensity of the sea." In all the new restaurants, the menus highlighted locally sourced food. "But where are the local people?" Olague said. A few unmarked doors led up to S.R.O. hotels, protected by the city's affordable-housing ordinances, where immigrant families squeezed into one room. But no one on the sidewalk was speaking Spanish.

In the past few years, San Francisco's political leaders have grown close to the technology companies. Corey Cook, a political scientist at the University of San Francisco, who focuses on local politics, said, "The dominant narrative of the city is 'What's good for the tech industry is good for San Francisco.'" Historically, he said, what was good for General Motors wasn't always good for the country: there was conflict between business and labor, which was resolved by insuring that factories offered middle-class jobs. He added, "Now there's no conflict, but there are no middle-class jobs."

In 2011, Twitter, whose San Francisco headquarters employs a thousand people but draws tourists from around the world—the company turns them away—threatened to move out of the city. Liberal candidates in the mayoral election lined up to offer the company tax breaks, and called existing taxes "job killers." Cook said, sardonically, "It's Twitter! Twitter *has* to be in San Francisco." There was far less concern at City Hall when, in 2006, the 49ers announced their intention to move to Santa Clara.

* * *

Cook predicted that if, with the tech industry's money and competence, schools improved and buses ran on time then San Franciscans would put up with the soaring cost of living. He added, "But if that doesn't happen, and it's just seen as an agglomeration of wealth, then it won't be win-win-win, and there could be a backlash."

One question for technology boosters—maybe the crucial one—is why, during the decades of the personal computer and the Internet, the American economy has grown so slowly, average wages have stagnated, the middle class has been hollowed out, and inequality has surged. Why has a revolution that is supposed to be as historically important as the industrial revolution coincided with a period of broader economic decline? I posed the question in one form or another to everyone I talked to in the Bay Area. The answers became a measure of how people in the technology industry think about the world beyond it.

Few of them had given the topic much consideration. One young techie wondered if it was really true; another said that the problem was a shortage of trained software engineers; a third noted that the focus of the tech industry was shifting from engineering to design, and suggested that this would open up new job opportunities. Sam Lessin, who leads Facebook's "identity product group," which is in charge of the social network's Timeline feature, posited that traditional measures of wealth might not be applicable in the era of social media. He said, "I think as communication technology gets less expensive, and people can entertain each other and interact with each other and do things for each other much more efficiently, what's actually going to happen is that the percentage of the economy that's in cash is going to decline. Some people will choose to build social capital rather than financial capital. Given the opportunity to spend an extra hour or an extra dollar, they will choose to spend time with friends. It might be that the GDP, in the broader sense, is actually growing quite quickly—it's just that we're not measuring it properly."

We were talking in a Facebook conference room. Posters on nearby walls bore the messages "Keep Shipping" and "What Would You Do If You Weren't Afraid?" Lessin, wearing a green T-shirt and jeans, with a baseball cap that had "/lessin" on the front, spoke very quickly while drawing a graph—first on a napkin, then on a whiteboard—that plotted the vectors of technology, social capital, and cash, with tech rising fastest, social not far behind, and cash starting to lag. Lessin was a classmate of Zuckerberg's at Harvard. His late father was a prominent investment banker, and Lessin grew up in a New Jersey suburb where he understood the adult world through the filter of *Seinfeld*. This led him to formulate the Kramer Principle: nearly all the annoyances that gave the show its jokes—the time wasted trying to track down a friend, the inefficiencies that lead to ridiculous misunderstandings—had been "kind of erased." He said, "Most of those problems are now gone because of smartphones, GPS, traffic maps, texting, messaging. That's a huge deal. That's moving the ball forward—making people more efficient with their time and able to effectively live longer lives therefore, you know, and making them happier." Lessin found it impossible to believe that people's lives had not improved since the days of *Seinfeld*, because of technology.

Not everyone in Silicon Valley is so sanguine. Joshua Cohen, the Stanford political philosopher, founded Stanford's Program on Global Justice, where he has done research on how the supply chains of corporate products can be improved in the areas of fair compensation, working conditions, and the right of workers to organize. Since 2011, Cohen has also been a half-time professor at Apple University, down the street from Apple's headquarters, which offers courses to its executives on company culture and related topics. According to *Inside Apple*, by Adam Lashinsky, one course focused on "the fallen grocery store chain A&P as an example of what happened to a company that once dominated its field." The classrooms—sleek and white, like the company's devices, with huge black screens at the front—bear names that span the social sciences and the literature of hipness: "Margaret Mead," "Tocqueville," "Kerouac," "Pirsig."

In his office, Cohen freely criticized the tech industry for its casual optimism in assuming that its products can change the world. He said, "There is this complete horseshit attitude, this ridiculous attitude out here, that if it's new and different it must be really good, and there must be some new way of solving problems that avoids the old limitations, the roadblocks. And with a soupçon of 'We're smarter than everybody else.' It's total nonsense."

But, when it came to Apple, he insisted that anything he said about the company had to be off the record, including the titles and the content of the courses he teaches. When I asked how he viewed the relation between the information revolution and inequality, he hesitated. He started to answer, then hesitated again: "Um. I don't have any deep thoughts about it. I wish I did." This seemed surprising, since Cohen, an expert on democracy and justice, co-edited a book called *The New Inequality,* in the late nineties, before it was a hot topic, and has devoted many pages of *Boston Review* to the subject. I had imagined that his perch at Apple University would give him the perfect vantage point to think about just this problem. Later, I wondered if the question had put Cohen on the defensive. It was Steve Jobs, after all, who told President Obama that Apple's manufacturing jobs would not be coming back from China. Apple's position on issues like inequality was expressed last year by an executive who said, "We don't have an obligation to solve America's problems. Our only obligation is making the best product possible."

One obstacle in Silicon Valley to thinking about conditions in the rest of the country is the tech world's belief in itself as a meritocracy. "Not an aspirational meritocracy but an actual one," Mitch Kapor, who founded the software company Lotus, in the early eighties, told me. In this view, he explained, "it's the best and the brightest who have succeeded here." Kapor and his wife, Freada, now run a foundation, in Oakland, that seeks to make the benefits of technology more equally available. Kapor said that asking questions about the lack of racial and gender diversity in tech companies leaves people in Silicon Valley intensely uncomfortable. For example, only eight per cent of venture-backed tech start-ups are owned by women, and, in a region where Hispanics make up nearly a quarter of the working-age population, they constitute less than five per cent of employees in large tech companies; the representation of both Hispanics and blacks is actually declining. People in Silicon Valley may be the only Americans who don't like to advertise the fact if they come from humble backgrounds. According to Kapor, they would then have to admit that someone helped them along the way, which goes against the Valley's self-image.

The young start-up entrepreneur insisted that a person's race, gender, or class "just doesn't matter here. It's not a positive or a negative. What's cool here is having a lot of money—everybody knows you have a lot of money, but you don't show it off. Money is the metric by which people view and judge success, but, unlike in Hollywood or New York, you have to be very careful about how you spend that money." The way to convey status in Silicon Valley is by wearing jeans, driving a Tesla, and casually mentioning that you were hired at Facebook in 2005 and invested in Twitter in 2008. But, as the wealth reaches spectacular levels, these self-conscious restraints are breaking down amid displays of hedge fund–level decadence. Last June, David Sacks, a former PayPal executive who founded Yammer, a social network for businesses, threw himself a fortieth birthday party, in a Los Angeles château, that was rumored to have cost $1.4 million; the theme was "Let Him Eat Cake," with attendees dressed in Louis XVI costumes, and entertainment by Snoop Dogg. (Sacks, forgetting what kind of world he and his friends have created, ordered his several hundred guests not to share any of this on social media. The first picture from the party was tweeted by Snoop.) Soon after his birthday bash, Sacks sold Yammer to Microsoft, then bought a twenty-million-dollar fixer-upper in Pacific Heights. When I interviewed him, two years ago, Sacks said, "Part of believing in capitalism is you don't have to feel guilty about wanting to make money."

The ideal of a frictionless world, in which technology is a force for progress as well as a source of wealth, leaves out the fact that politics inevitably means clashing interests, with winners and losers. Silicon Valley tends to ignore even its own version of conflict: beneath its much popularized stories of aspiration and success is a netherworld of ruthless struggle that punishes more people than it rewards. "This is one of the things nobody talks about in the Valley," Andreessen told me. Trying to get a start-up off the ground is "absolutely terrifying. Everything is against you." Many young people wilt under the pressure. As a venture capitalist, he hears pitches from three thousand people a year and funds just twenty of them. "Our day job is saying no to entrepreneurs and crushing their dreams," he said. Meanwhile, "every entrepreneur has to pretend in every interaction that everything is going great. Every party you go to, every recruiter, every press interview—'Oh, everything's fantastic!'— and, inside, your soul is just being chewed apart, right? It's sort of like everybody's fake happy all the time."

One day, I dropped by the offices of a start-up company called Delphi, just down the road from Google, in Mountain View. Delphi makes software that allows cities to put large amounts of financial data online for public use. Two of its founders are Nate Levine, who is twenty-two, and Zac Bookman, who is thirty-three. They had just ordered pizza for lunch, and they seemed to be all but sleeping at the company. In a spare room, there was an austere metal bunk bed.

* * *

Young people drawn to Silicon Valley can be more insular than those in other industries—they tend to come from educated families and top universities, and achieve success at a very early age. "They're ignorant, because many of them don't feel the need to educate themselves outside their little world, and they're not rewarded for doing so," the young start-up entrepreneur said. "If you're an engineer in Silicon Valley, you have no incentive to read *The Economist.* It's not brought up at parties, your friends aren't going to talk about it, your employers don't care." He found that college friends who came out to the Valley to seek their fortune subsequently lost interest in the wider world. "People with whom I used to talk about politics or policy or the arts, they're just not as into it anymore. They don't read the *Wall Street Journal* or the *New York Times.* They read *TechCrunch* and *VentureBeat,* and maybe they happen to see something from the *Times* on somebody's Facebook news feed." He went on, "The divide among people in my generation is not as much between traditional liberals and libertarians. It's a divide between people who are inward-facing and outward-facing."

The more successful and wealthy entrepreneurs become, the more they can afford to face outward. Reid Hoffman, of LinkedIn, who published a book last year called *The Start-Up of You,* is regarded as one of the Valley's leading public voices, although, until recently, his political engagement had been limited to campaign contributions. Hoffman described Silicon Valley's intellectual culture as underdeveloped. Part of the problem, he said, is the competitiveness, which requires an unyielding focus on one's company, and "part of it is because of that libertarian strain—we're just all out building stuff, and everything else is kind of extraneous." Hoffman says that when he was a Stanford undergraduate, in the late eighties, his only concern was "how do I strengthen public intellectual culture in the U.S.: who are we as individuals and a society, and who should we be?" But he decided that the academic life would have too small a platform, and he became an Internet billionaire instead. When LinkedIn was in its early stages, a decade ago, Hoffman went a few years without reading a single book. Now in his mid-forties, he wants to make Silicon Valley a more reflective place, and increase its influence around the country and the world. He has started a monthly salon, flying in authors of new books on public affairs to talk with small groups of tech people, over dinner at a top-rated French restaurant in Palo Alto.

* * *

Mark Zuckerberg, in his op-ed announcing FWD.us, wrote, "In a knowledge economy, the most important resources are the talented people we educate and attract to our country. A knowledge economy can scale further, create better jobs, and provide a higher quality of living for everyone in our nation." Zuckerberg described himself as the great-grandson of immigrants, and the beneficiary of national policies that have created equal opportunity and upward mobility across generations.

"Everyone in FWD.us hopes it will go beyond immigration, over time," Reid Hoffman said. Other possible issues include education reform and spending on scientific research. "But, as with an entrepreneurial start-up, if we can't demonstrate that we can do something good about this problem, then what use are we to the other ones?"

Like industries that preceded it, Silicon Valley is not a philosophy, a revolution, or a cause. It's a group of powerful corporations and wealthy individuals with their own well-guarded interests. Sometimes those interests can be aligned with the public's, sometimes not. Though tech companies promote an open and connected world, they are extremely secretive, preventing outsiders from learning the most basic facts about their internal workings. Marc Andreessen predicted that conflicts over issues like privacy, intellectual property, and monopolies will bring a period of increased tension between the Valley and other sectors of society, along with new government intervention. Brian Goldsmith, who has known Green since college, and who now runs an online investment start-up called PubVest, said, "If this new generation of smart, wealthy, successful tech leaders want to make a difference in terms of policy, it's the right idea to leave their cool headquarters and gorgeous campuses and actually engage. They have a lot to bring to the table, and they may also learn the limits of their power and influence. I think it's healthy that they've decided to branch out and actually get involved in the political process the way that other industries and corporations do."

FWD.us has got off to a rough start—rougher than Facebook did. Rather than bringing fresh ideas to the project of organizing Americans and their elected leaders behind immigration reform, the group has hired veteran Washington operatives from both parties, who, following their standard practice, are spending Silicon Valley money on harsh and cynical political ads. The campaign attempts to bolster politicians who support immigration reform even though they represent states where the idea is unpopular. One ad, intended to cover Senator Lindsey Graham's right flank, in South Carolina, attacks Obama's health-care law; another, on behalf of Mark Begich, the Alaska senator, endorses oil drilling and a natural-gas pipeline there.

* * *

The South Carolina ad began airing in late April. It was made by a FWD.us shell organization called Americans for a Conservative Direction. Crude graphics are combined with footage of Graham attacking Obama. " 'Change you can believe in,' after this health-care-bill debacle, has now become an empty slogan," he says. "And it's really been replaced by seedy Chicago politics, when you think about it." The ad doesn't embody the spirit of "innovation" or of "disruption." But if Silicon Valley's idea of itself as a force for irresistible progress is running up against the unlovely reality of current American politics, that isn't necessarily a bad thing. It might mean that the industry is growing up.

CREDITS

Elijah Anderson: "The Code of the Streets," by Elijah Anderson. From *The Atlantic Monthly*, May 1994, pp. 81–94. Reprinted by permission of the author.

Peter L. Berger: Excerpt(s) from *Invitation to Sociology: A Humanistic Perspective* by Peter L. Berger, copyright © 1963 by Peter L. Berger. Copyright © renewed 1991 by Peter L. Berger. Used by permission of Doubleday, an imprint of the Knopf Doubleday Publishing Group, a division of Random House LLC. All rights reserved.

Joel Best: Excerpts from *Damned Lies and Statistics: Untangling Numbers from the Media, Politicians, and Activists,* by Joel Best. Copyright © 2001 by the Regents of the University of California. Reprinted by permission of the University of California Press.

Julie Bettie: From "Women Without Class: Chicas, Cholas, Trash, and the Presence/Absence of Class Identity," by Julie Bettie from *Signs: Journal of Women in Culture and Society*, Vol. 26, No. 1. © 2000 by The University of Chicago. All rights reserved. Reprinted by permission of The University of Chicago Press.

Eduardo Bonilla-Silva: From "The Strange Enigma of Race in Contemporary America," from *Racism Without Racists*, Fourth Edition. Copyright © 2014 Rowman & Littlefield Publishers, Inc. Reprinted by permission of the publisher.

Allan M. Brandt: "Racism and Research: The Case of the Tuskegee Syphilis Study" from *The Hastings Center Report*, December 1978, pp. 21–29. Reprinted by permission of the publisher.

Michael Burawoy: "Public Sociologies: Contradiction, Dilemmas and Possibilities," by Michael Burawoy. From *Social Forces*, Vol. 82, No. 4, pp. 1603–18. Copyright © 2004. Used by permission of Oxford Publishing, Ltd.

Ta-Nehisi Coates: Republished with permission of The Atlantic Monthly Co., from "The Black Family in the Age of Mass Incarceration," *The Atlantic*, October 2015; permission conveyed through Copyright Clearance Center, Inc.

Patricia Hill Collins: From *Black Feminist Thought: Knowledge, Consciousness, and the Politics of Empowerment*. Copyright © 2000 by Routledge. Reprinted by permission of Taylor & Francis.

Stephanie Coontz: "The Radical Idea of Marrying for Love," from *Marriage, A History: From Obedience to Intimacy, or How Love Conquered Marriage* by

Stephanie Coontz, copyright © 2005 by the S.J. Coontz Company. Used by permission of Viking Penguin, a division of Penguin Group (USA) LLC.

Lisa Dodson: Excerpt from *Moral Underground: How Ordinary Americans Subvert an Unfair Economy.* Copyright © 2009 by Lisa Dodson. Reprinted by permission of The New Press. www.thenewpress.com

D. Stanley Eitzen: "Upward Mobility through Sport?" from *Z Magazine,* March 1999, pp. 14–19. Reprinted by permission of the author.

Paula England: Excerpts from "The Gender Revolution: Uneven and Stalled," *Gender & Society,* Vol. 24, No. 2 (April 2010). Copyright © 2010 by SAGE Publications. Reprinted by permission of SAGE Publications.

Joe R. Feagin and Robert Parker: "The Rise and Fall of Mass Rail Transit" from *Building American Cities: The Urban Real Estate Game,* pp. 154–59. Reprinted by permission of the authors.

Michel Foucault: Excerpts from *Discipline and Punish* by Michel Foucault. English Translation copyright © 1977 by Alan Sheridan (New York: Pantheon). Originally published in French as *Surveiller et Punir.* Copyright © 1975 by Editions Gallimard. Reprinted by permission of Georges Borchardt, Inc., for Editions Gallimard.

Herbert J. Gans: "The Positive Functions of the Undeserving Poor" from *The American Journal of Sociology* Vol. 78, No. 2 (1972), pp. 275–88. Reprinted by permission of Herbert J. Gans.

Erving Goffman: "On Face-Work: An Analysis of Ritual Elements in Social Interaction" from *Psychiatry: Journal for the Study of Interpersonal Processes,* Vol. 18, No. 3, August 1955, pp. 213–31. Copyright © The Washington School of Psychiatry, www.wspdc.org, reprinted by permission of Taylor & Francis, Ltd., http://www.tandfonline.com on behalf of The Washington School of Psychiatry.

Eliza Griswold: From "Undermined: A Local Activist Fights for the Future of Coal Country," *The New Yorker,* July 3, 2017. Reprinted by permission of the author.

Garrett Hardin: Excerpts from "Tragedy of the Commons," by Garrett Hardin. *Science,* Vol. 162, No. 3859, pp. 1243–48. Copyright © 1968 by American Association for the Advancement of Science. Reprinted with permission from AAAS.

Arlie Russell Hochschild: "No Country for White Men" by Arlie Hochschild. Copyright © 2016 by Arlie Hochschild. Originally appeared in *Mother Jones* (September / October 2016). Reprinted by permission of Georges Borchardt, Inc. on behalf of the author.

John A. Hostetler: From *Amish Society.* Fourth Edition. pp. 3–12. © 1963, 1968, 1980, 1993 The Johns Hopkins University Press. Reprinted with permission of Johns Hopkins University Press.

Pico Iyer: "The Beauty of the Package," by Pico Iyer, *Granta* 127: Japan (Spring 2014). Reprinted by permission of *Granta* magazine.

Annette Lareau: *Unequal Childhoods: Class, Race, and Family Life*, by Annette Lareau, © 2011 by the Regents of the University of California. Published by the University of California Press.

Karl Marx and Friedrich Engels: From THE MARX-ENGELS READER, SECOND EDITON, edited by Robert C. Tucker. Copyright © 1978 W. W. Norton & Company. Used by permission of W. W. Norton & Company, Inc.

Miller McPherson, Lynn Smith-Lovin, and Matthew Brashears: Republished with permission of SAGE Publications, from "The Ties that Bind Are Fraying," *Contexts*, Vol. 7, No. 3, © 2008 American Sociological Association; permission conveyed through Copyright Clearance Center, Inc.

Michael Messner: "Boyhood, Organized Sports, and the Construction of Masculinities," by Michael Messner. *Journal of Contemporary Ethnography* Vol. 18, No. 4, pp. 416–44. Copyright © 1990 by SAGE Publications. Reprinted by permission of SAGE Publications.

C. Wright Mills: Excerpts from *The Sociological Imagination* by C. Wright Mills, pp. 3–8. Copyright © 1959, 2000 by Oxford University Press, Inc. Reprinted by permission of Oxford University Press, Inc.

George Packer: "Change the World," by George Packer. Copyright © George Packer, 2013, used by permission of The Wylie Agency LLC.

Devah Pager: "The Mark of a Criminal Record," *American Journal of Sociology*, Vol. 108, No. 5, pp. 937–75, 2003. © 2003 by The University of Chicago. All rights reserved. Reprinted by permission of The University of Chicago Press.

Greta Foff Paules: Material drawn from "'Getting' and 'Making' a Tip" from *Dishing It Out: Power and Resistance among Waitresses in a New Jersey Restaurant* by Greta Foff Paules. Used by permission of Temple University Press. © 1991 by Temple University. All Rights Reserved.

Michael Pollan: "America's National Eating Disorder," from *The Omnivore's Dilemma: A Natural History of Four Meals* by Michael Pollan, copyright © 2006 by Michael Pollan. Used by permission of The Penguin Press, a division of Penguin Group (USA) LLC.

George Ritzer: Republished with permission of SAGE Publications from *The McDonaldization of Society* by George Ritzer. Copyright © 1993 Pine Forge Press. Permission conveyed through Copyright Clearance Center, Inc.

James C. Scott: Republished with permission of Princeton University Press, from "Scott's Law of Anarchist Calisthenics," from *Two Cheers for Anarchism: Six Easy Pieces on Autonomy, Dignity, and Meaningful Work and Play*. Copyright © 2012 Princeton University Press; permission conveyed through Copyright Clearance Center, Inc.

Patrick Sharkey: From UNEASY PEACE: THE GREAT CRIME DECLINE, THE RENEWAL OF CITY LIFE, AND THE NEXT WAR ON VIOLENCE by Patrick Sharkey. Copyright © 2018 by Patrick Sharkey. Used by permission of W. W. Norton & Company, Inc.